T0127916

Get the eBooks FREE!
(PDF, ePub, Kindle, and liveBook all included)

We believe that once you buy a book from us, you should be able to read it in any format we have available. To get electronic versions of this book at no additional cost to you, purchase and then register this book at the Manning website.

Go to https://www.manning.com/freebook and follow the instructions to complete your pBook registration.

That's it!
Thanks from Manning!

Concurrency in .NET

Concurrency in .NET

Modern patterns of concurrent and parallel programming

RICCARDO TERRELL

MANNING

SHELTER ISLAND

Manning Publications Co.
20 Baldwin Road
PO Box 761
Shelter Island, NY 11964

Development editor:	Marina Michaels
Technical development editor:	Michael Lund
Technical proofreader:	Viorel Moisei
Review editor:	Aleksandar Dragosavljević
Project manager:	Tiffany Taylor
Copy editor:	Katie Petito
Proofreader:	Elizabeth Martin
Typesetter:	Happenstance Type-O-Rama
Cover designer:	Marija Tudor

ISBN 9781617292996
Printed in the United States of America

I dedicate this book to my wonderful and supportive wife, Bryony. Your support, love, care, and continued encouragement throughout my writing process are what allowed me to turn this project into a reality. I love you and admire you for your many efforts and patience while I was busy writing. Thank you for always believing in me.

I also dedicate this book to my loyal pugs, Bugghina and Stellina, who were always unconditionally and enthusiastically beside me while writing this book. You're man's best friends and this author's furriest fans.

brief contents

contents

14 Building a scalable mobile app with concurrent functional programming 449

preface

You're probably reading this book, *Concurrency in .NET,* because you want to build blazingly fast applications, or learn how to dramatically increase the performance of an existing one. You care about performance because you're dedicated to producing faster programs, and because you feel excited when a few changes in your code make your application faster and more responsive. Parallel programming provides endless possibilities for passionate developers who desire to exploit new technologies. When considering performance, the benefits of utilizing parallelism in your programming can't be overstated. But using imperative and object-oriented programming styles to write concurrent code can be convoluted and introduces complexities. For this reason, concurrent programming hasn't been embraced as common practice writ large, leading programmers to search for other options.

When I was in college, I took a class in functional programming. At the time, I was studying Haskell; and even though there was a steep learning curve, I enjoyed every lesson. I remember watching the first examples and being amazed by the elegance of the solutions as well as their simplicity. Fifteen years later, when I began searching for other options to enhance my programs utilizing concurrency, my thoughts returned to these lessons. This time, I was able to fully realize how powerful and useful functional programming would be in designing my daily programs. There are several benefits to using a functional approach in your programming style, and I discuss each of them in this book.

My academic adventures met my professional work when I was challenged to build a software system for the health care industry. This project involved making an application to analyze radiological medical images. The image processing required several steps such as image noise reduction, Gaussian algorithm, image interpolation, and image filtering to apply color to the gray image. The application was developed using Java and initially ran as anticipated. Eventually the department increased the demand, as often happens, and problems started to appear. The software didn't have any problems or bugs, but with the increasing number of images to analyze, it became slower.

Naturally, the first proposed solution to this problem was to buy a more powerful server. Although this was a valid solution at the time, today if you buy a new machine with the intention of gaining more CPU computation speed, you'll be disappointed. This is because the modern CPU has more than one core, but the speed of a single core isn't any faster than a single core purchased in 2007. The better and more enduring alternative to buying a new server/computer was to introduce parallelism to take advantage of multicore hardware and all of its resources, ultimately speeding up the image processing.

In theory, this was a simple task, but in practice it wasn't so trivial. I had to learn how to use threads and locking; and, unfortunately, I gained firsthand experience in what a deadlock is.

This deadlock spurred me to make massive changes to the code base of the application. There were so many changes that I introduced bugs not even related to the original purpose of my changes. I was frustrated, the code base was unmaintainable and fragile, and the overall process was prone to bugs. I had to step back from the original problem and look for a solution from a different perspective. There had to be a better way.

The tools we use have a profound (and devious!) influence on our thinking habits, and, therefore, on our thinking abilities.

—Edsger Dijkstra

After spending a few days looking for a possible solution to solve the multithreading madness, I realized the answer. Everything I researched and read was pointing toward the functional paradigm. The principles I had learned in that college class so many years ago became my mechanism for moving forward. I rewrote the core of the image processing application to run in parallel using a functional language. Initially, transitioning from an imperative to a functional style was a challenge. I had forgotten almost all that I learned in college, and I'm not proud to say that during this experience, I wrote code that looked very object-oriented in functional language; but it was a successful decision overall. The new program compiled and ran with a dramatic performance improvement, and the hardware resources were completely utilized and bug free. Above all, an unanticipated and fantastic surprise was that functional programming resulted in an impressive reduction in the number of lines of code: almost 50% fewer than the original implementation using object-oriented language.

This experience made me reconsider OOP as the answer for all my programming problems. I realized that this programming model and approach to problem solving had a limited perspective. My journey into functional programming began with a requirement for a good concurrent programming model.

Ever since, I've had a keen interest in functional programming applied to multi-threading and concurrency. Where others saw a complex problem and a source of issues, I saw a solution in functional programming as a powerful tool that could use the available hardware to run faster. I came to appreciate how the discipline leads to a coherent, composable, beautiful way of writing concurrent programs.

I first had the idea for this book in July 2010, after Microsoft introduced F# as part of Visual Studio 2010. It was already clear at that time that an increasing number of mainstream programming languages supported the functional paradigm, including C#, C++, Java, and Python. In 2007, C# 3.0 introduced first-class functions to the language, along with new constructs such as lambda expressions and type inference to allow programmers to introduce functional programming concepts. Soon to follow was Language Integrate Query (LINQ), permitting a declarative programming style.

In particular, the .NET platform has embraced the functional world. With the introduction of F#, Microsoft has full-featured languages that support both object-oriented and functional paradigms. Additionally, object-oriented languages like C# are becoming more hybrid and bridging the gap between different programming paradigms, allowing for both programming styles.

Furthermore, we're facing the multicore era, where the power of CPUs is measured by the number of cores available, instead of clock cycles per second. With this trend, single-threaded applications won't achieve improved speed on multicore systems unless the applications integrate parallelism and employ algorithms to spread the work across multiple cores.

It has become clear to me that multithreading is in demand, and it has ignited my passion to bring this programming approach to you. This book combines the power of concurrent programming and functional paradigm to write readable, more modular, maintainable code in both the C# and F# languages. Your code will benefit from these techniques to function at peak performance with fewer lines of code, resulting in increased productivity and resilient programs.

It's an exciting time to start developing multithreaded code. More than ever, software companies are making tools and capabilities available to choose the right programming style without compromise. The initial challenges of learning parallel programming will diminish quickly, and the reward for your perseverance is infinite. No matter what your field of expertise is, whether you're a backend developer or a frontend web developer, or if you build cloud-based applications or video games, the use of parallelism to obtain better performance and to build scalable applications is here to stay.

This book draws on my experience with functional programming for writing concurrent programs in .NET using both C# and F#. I believe that functional programming is becoming the de facto way to write concurrent code, to coordinate asynchronous and parallel programs in .NET, and that this book will give you everything you need to be ready and master this exciting world of multicore computers.

acknowledgments

Writing a book is a daunting feat for anyone. Doing so in your secondary language is infinitely more challenging and intimidating. For me, you don't dare entertain dreams such as this without being surrounded by a village of support. I would like to thank all of those who have supported me and participated in making this book a reality.

My adventure with F# started in 2013, when I attended a FastTrack to F# in NYC. I met Tomas Petricek, who inspired me to fall headfirst into the F# world. He welcomed me into the community and has been a mentor and confidant ever since.

I owe a huge debt of gratitude to the fantastic staff at Manning Publications. The heavy lifting for this book began 15 months ago with my development editor, Dan Maharry, and continued with Marina Michaels, both of whom have been patient and sage guides in this awesome task.

Thank you to the many technical reviewers, especially technical development editor Michael Lund and technical proofer Viorel Moisei. Your critical analysis was essential to ensuring that I communicated on paper all that is in my head, much of which was at risk of being "lost in translation." Thank you also to those who participated in Manning's MEAP program and provided support as peer reviewers: Andy Kirsch, Anton Herzog, Chris Bolyard, Craig Fullerton, Gareth van der Berg, Jeremy Lange, Jim Velch, Joel Kotarski, Kevin Orr, Luke Bearl, Pawel Klimczyk, Ricardo Peres, Rohit Sharma, Stefano Driussi, and Subhasis Ghosh.

I received endless support from the members of the F# community who have rallied behind me along the way, especially Sergey Tihon, who spent countless hours as my sounding board.

And thank you to my family and friends who have cheered me on and patiently waited for me to join the world again for social weekends, dinner outings, and the rest.

Above all, I would like to acknowledge my wife, who supports my every endeavor and has never allowed me to shy away from a challenge.

I must also recognize my dedicated and loyal pugs, Bugghina and Stellina, who were always at my side or on my lap while I was writing this book deep into the night. It was also during our long evening walks that I was able to clear my head and find the best ideas for this book.

about this book

Concurrency in .NET provides insights into the best practices necessary to build concurrent and scalable programs in .NET, illuminating the benefits of the functional paradigm to give you the right tools and principles for handling concurrency easily and correctly. Ultimately, armed with your newfound skills, you'll have the knowledge needed to become an expert at delivering successful high-performance solutions.

Who should read this book

If you're writing multithreaded code in .NET, this book can help. If you're interested in using the functional paradigm to ease the concurrent programming experience to maximize the performance of your applications, this book is an essential guide. This book will benefit any .NET developers who want to write concurrent, reactive, and asynchronous applications that scale and perform by self-adapting to the current hardware resources wherever the program runs.

This book is also suitable for developers who are curious about exploiting functional programming to implement concurrent techniques. Prior knowledge or experience with the functional paradigm isn't required, and the basic concepts are covered in appendix A.

The code examples use both the C# and F# languages. Readers familiar with C# will feel comfortable right away. Familiarity with the F# language isn't strictly required, and a basic overview is covered in appendix B. Functional programming experience and knowledge isn't required; the necessary concepts are included in the book.

A good working knowledge of .NET is assumed. You should have moderate experience in working with .NET collections and knowledge of the .NET Framework, with a minimum of .NET version 3.5 required (LINQ, Action<>, and Func<> delegates). Finally, this book is suitable for any platform supported by .NET (including .NET Core).

How this book is organized: a roadmap

The book's 14 chapters are divided into 3 parts. Part 1 introduces functional concurrent programming concepts and the skills you need in order to understand the functional aspects of writing multithreaded programs:

- Chapter 1 highlights the main foundations and purposes behind concurrent programming and the reasons for using functional programming to write multithreaded applications.
- Chapter 2 explores several functional programming techniques to improve the performance of a multithreaded application. The purpose of this chapter is to provide concepts used during the rest of the book, and to make you familiar with powerful ideas that have originated from the functional paradigm.
- Chapter 3 provides an overview of the functional concept of immutability. It explains how immutability is used to write predictable and correct concurrent programs, and how it's applied to implement and use functional data structures, which are intrinsically thread safe.

Part 2 dives into the different concurrent programming models of the functional paradigm. We'll explore subjects such as the Task Parallel Library (TPL), and implementing parallel patterns such as Fork/Join, Divide and Conquer, and MapReduce. Also discussed are declarative composition, high-level abstraction in asynchronous operations, the agent programming model, and the message-passing semantic:

- Chapter 4 covers the basics of processing a large amount of data in parallel, including patterns such as Fork/Join.
- Chapter 5 introduces more advanced techniques for parallel processing massive data, such as aggregating and reducing data in parallel and implementing a parallel MapReduce pattern.
- Chapter 6 provides details of the functional techniques to process real-time streams of events (data), using functional higher-order operators with .NET Reactive Extensions to compose asynchronous event combinators. The techniques learned are used to implement a concurrent friendly and reactive publisher-subscriber pattern.
- Chapter 7 explains the task-based programming model applied to functional programming to implement concurrent operations using the Monadic pattern based on a continuation-passing style. This technique is then used to build a concurrent- and functional-based pipeline.

- Chapter 8 concentrates on the C# asynchronous programming model to implement unbounded parallel computations. This chapter also examines error handling and compositional techniques for asynchronous operations.
- Chapter 9 focuses on the F# asynchronous workflow, explaining how the deferred and explicit evaluation of this model permits a higher compositional semantic. Then, we explore how to implement custom computation expressions to raise the level of abstraction, resulting in a declarative programming style.
- Chapter 10 wraps up the previous chapters and culminates in implementing combinators and patterns such as Functor, Monad, and Applicative to compose and run multiple asynchronous operations and handle errors, while avoiding side effects.
- Chapter 11 delves into reactive programming using the message-passing programming model. It covers the concept of natural isolation as a complementary technique with immutability for building concurrent programs. This chapter focuses on the F# `MailboxProcessor` for distributing parallel work using the agent model and the share-nothing approach.
- Chapter 12 explains the agent programming model using the .NET TPL Dataflow, with examples in C#. You'll implement both a stateless and stateful agent using C# and run multiple computations in parallel that communicate with each other using (passing) messages in a pipeline style

Part 3 puts into practice all the functional concurrent programming techniques learned in the previous chapters:

- Chapter 13 contains a set of reusable and useful recipes to solve complex concurrent issues based on real-world experiences. The recipes use the functional patterns you've seen throughout the book.
- Chapter 14 presents a full application designed and implemented using the functional concurrent patterns and techniques learned in the book. You'll build a highly scalable, responsive server application, and a reactive client-side program. Two versions are presented: one using Xamarin Visual Studio for an iOS (iPad)-based program, and one using WPF. The server-side application uses a combination of different programming models, such as asynchronous, agent-based, and reactive, to ensure maximum scalability.

The book also has three appendices:

- Appendix A summarizes the concepts of functional programming. This appendix provides basic theory about functional techniques used in the book.
- Appendix B covers the basic concepts of F#. It's a basic overview of F# to make you feel comfortable and help you gain familiarity with this programming language.
- Appendix C illustrates few techniques to ease the interoperability between the F# asynchronous workflow and the .NET task in C#.

About the code

This book contains many examples of source code, both in numbered listings and inline with normal text. In both cases, source code is formatted in a `fixed-width font` `like this` to separate it from ordinary text. Sometimes code is also **in bold** to highlight the topic under discussion.

In many cases, the original source code has been reformatted; we've added line breaks and reworked indentation to accommodate the available page space in the book. In some cases, even this was not enough, and listings include line-continuation markers (➥). Additionally, comments in the source code have often been removed from the listings when the code is described in the text. Code annotations accompany many of the listings, highlighting important concepts.

The source code for this book is available to download from the publisher's website (www.manning.com/books/concurrency-in-dot-net) and from GitHub (https://github.com/rikace/fConcBook). Most of the code is provided in both C# and F# versions. Instructions for using this code are provided in the README file included in the repository root.

Book forum

Purchase of *Concurrency in .NET* includes free access to a private web forum run by Manning Publications where you can make comments about the book, ask technical questions, and receive help from the author and from other users. To access the forum, go to https://forums.manning.com/forums/concurrency-in-dot-net. You can also learn more about Manning's forums and the rules of conduct at https://forums.manning.com/forums/about.

Manning's commitment to our readers is to provide a venue where a meaningful dialogue between individual readers and between readers and the author can take place. It is not a commitment to any specific amount of participation on the part of the author, whose contribution to the forum remains voluntary (and unpaid). We suggest you try asking the author some challenging questions, lest his interest stray! The forum and the archives of previous discussions will be accessible from the publisher's website as long as the book is in print.

about the author

RICCARDO TERRELL is a seasoned software engineer and Microsoft MVP who is passionate about functional programming. He has over 20 years' experience delivering cost-effective technology solutions in a competitive business environment.

In 1998, Riccardo started his own software business in Italy, where he specialized in providing customized medical software to his clients. In 2007, Riccardo moved to the United States and ever since has been working as a .NET senior software developer and senior software architect to deliver cost-effective technology solutions in the business environment. Riccardo is dedicated to integrating advanced technology tools to increase internal efficiency, enhance work productivity, and reduce operating costs.

He is well known and actively involved in the functional programming community, including .NET meetups and international conferences. Riccardo believes in multi-paradigm programming as a mechanism to maximize the power of code. You can keep up with Riccardo and his coding adventures on his blog, www.rickyterrell.com.

about the cover illustration

The figure on the cover of *Concurrency in .NET* is a man from a village in Abyssinia, today called Ethiopia. The illustration is taken from a Spanish compendium of regional dress customs first published in Madrid in 1799, engraved by Manuel Albuerne (1764-1815). The book's title page states

Coleccion general de los Trages que usan actualmente todas las Nacionas del Mundo desubierto, dibujados y grabados con la mayor exactitud por R.M.V.A.R. Obra muy util y en special para los que tienen la del viajero universal

which we translate, as literally as possible, thus:

General collection of costumes currently used in the nations of the known world, designed and printed with great exactitude by R.M.V.A.R. This work is very useful especially for those who hold themselves to be universal travelers

Although little is known of the engraver, designers, and workers who colored this illustration by hand, the exactitude of their execution is evident in this drawing. The Abyssinian is just one of many figures in this colorful collection. Their diversity speaks vividly of the uniqueness and individuality of the world's towns and regions just 200 years ago. This was a time when the dress codes of two regions separated by a few dozen miles identified people uniquely as belonging to one or the other. The collection brings to life a sense of isolation and distance of that period—and of every other historic period except our own hyperkinetic present.

Dress codes have changed since then, and the diversity by region, so rich at the time, has faded away. It's now often hard to tell the inhabitant of one continent from another. Perhaps, trying to view it optimistically, we have traded a cultural and visual diversity for a more varied personal life—or a more varied and interesting intellectual and technical life.

We at Manning celebrate the inventiveness, the initiative, and the fun of the computer business with book covers based on the rich diversity of regional life of two centuries ago, brought back to life by the pictures from this collection.

Part 1

Benefits of functional programming applicable to concurrent programs

Functional programming is a programming paradigm that focuses on abstraction and composition. In these first three chapters you'll learn how to treat computations as the evaluation of expressions to avoid the mutation of data. To enhance concurrent programming, the functional paradigm provides tools and techniques to write deterministic programs. Output only depends upon input and not on the state of the program at execution time. The functional paradigm also facilitates writing code with fewer bugs by emphasizing separation of concerns between purely functional aspects, isolating side effects, and controlling unwanted behaviors.

This part of the book introduces the main concepts and benefits of functional programming applicable to concurrent programs. Concepts discussed include programming with pure functions, immutability, laziness, and composition.

Functional concurrency foundations

This chapter covers

- Why you need concurrency
- Differences between concurrency, parallelism, and multithreading
- Avoiding common pitfalls when writing concurrent applications
- Sharing variables between threads
- Using the functional paradigm to develop concurrent programs

In the past, software developers were confident that, over time, their programs would run faster than ever. This proved true over the years due to improved hardware that enabled programs to increase speed with each new generation.

For the past 50 years, the hardware industry has experienced uninterrupted improvements. Prior to 2005, the processor evolution continuously delivered faster single-core CPUs, until finally reaching the limit of CPU speed predicted by Gordon Moore. Moore, a computer scientist, predicted in 1965 that the density and speed of transistors would double every 18 months before reaching a maximum speed beyond which technology couldn't advance. The original prediction for the increase of CPU speed presumed a speed-doubling trend for 10 years. Moore's prediction, known as Moore's Law, was correct—except that progress continued for almost 50 years (decades past his estimate).

Today, the single-processor CPU has nearly reached the speed of light, all the while generating an enormous amount of heat due to energy dissipation; this heat is the limiting factor to further improvements.

CPU has nearly reached the speed of light

The speed of light is the absolute physical limit for electric transmission, which is also the limit for electric signals in the CPU. No data propagation can be transmitted faster than the light medium. Consequentially, signals cannot propagate across the surface of the chip fast enough to allow higher speeds. Modern chips have a base cycle frequency of roughly 3.5 GHz, meaning 1 cycle every 1/3,500,000,000 seconds, or 2.85 nanoseconds. The speed of light is about 3e8 meters per second, which means that data can be propagated around 0.30 cm (about a foot) in a nanosecond. But the bigger the chip, the longer it takes for data to travel through it.

A fundamental relationship exists between circuit length (CPU physical size) and processing speed: the time required to perform an operation is a cycle of circuit length and the speed of light. Because the speed of light is constant, the only variable is the size of the CPU; that is, you need a small CPU to increase the speed, because shorter circuits require smaller and fewer switches. The smaller the CPU, the faster the transmission. In fact, creating a smaller chip was the primary approach to building faster CPUs with higher clock rates. This was done so effectively that we've nearly reached the physical limit for improving CPU speed.

For example, if the clock speed is increased to 100 GHz, a cycle will be 0.01 nanoseconds, and the signals will only propagate 3 mm in this time. Therefore, a CPU core ideally needs to be about 0.3 mm in size. This route leads to a physical size limitation. In addition, this high frequency rate in such a small CPU size introduces a thermal problem in the equation. Power in a switching transistor is roughly the frequency ^2, so in moving from 4 GHz to 6 GHz there is a 225% increase of energy (which translates to heat). The problem besides the size of the chip becomes its vulnerability to suffer thermal damage such as changes in crystal structure.

Moore's prediction about transistor speed has come to fruition (transistors cannot run any faster) but it isn't dead (modern transistors are increasing in density, providing opportunities for parallelism within the confines of that top speed). The combination of multicore architecture and parallel programming models is keeping Moore's Law alive! As CPU single-core performance improvement stagnates, developers adapt by segueing into multicore architecture and developing software that supports and integrates concurrency.

The processor revolution has begun. The new trend in multicore processor design has brought parallel programming into the mainstream. Multicore processor architecture offers the possibility of more efficient computing, but all this power requires additional work for developers. If programmers want more performance in their code, they must adapt to new design patterns to maximize hardware utilization, exploiting multiple cores through parallelism and concurrency.

In this chapter, we'll cover general information about concurrency by examining several of its benefits and the challenges of writing traditional concurrent programs. Next, we'll introduce functional paradigm concepts that make it possible to overcome traditional limitations by using simple and maintainable code. By the end of this chapter, you'll understand why concurrency is a valued programming model, and why the functional paradigm is the right tool for writing correct concurrent programs.

1.1 *What you'll learn from this book*

In this book I'll look at considerations and challenges for writing concurrent multi-threaded applications in a traditional programming paradigm. I'll explore how to successfully address these challenges and avoid concurrency pitfalls using the functional paradigm. Next, I'll introduce the benefits of using abstractions in functional programming to create declarative, simple-to-implement, and highly performant concurrent programs. Over the course of this book, we'll examine complex concurrent issues providing an insight into the best practices necessary to build concurrent and scalable programs in .NET using the functional paradigm. You'll become familiar with how functional programming helps developers support concurrency by encouraging immutable data structures that can be passed between threads without having to worry about a shared state, all while avoiding side effects. By the end of the book you'll master how to write more modular, readable, and maintainable code in both C# and F# languages. You'll be more productive and proficient while writing programs that function at peak performance with fewer lines of code. Ultimately, armed with your newfound skills, you'll have the knowledge needed to become an expert at delivering successful high-performance solutions.

Here's what you'll learn:

- How to combine asynchronous operations with the Task Parallel Library
- How to avoid common problems and troubleshoot your multithreaded and asynchronous applications
- Knowledge of concurrent programming models that adopt the functional paradigm (functional, asynchronous, event-driven, and message passing with agents and actors)
- How to build high-performance, concurrent systems using the functional paradigm
- How to express and compose asynchronous computations in a declarative style
- How to seamlessly accelerate sequential programs in a pure fashion by using data-parallel programming
- How to implement reactive and event-based programs declaratively with Rx-style event streams
- How to use functional concurrent collections for building lock-free multi-threaded programs

- How to write scalable, performant, and robust server-side applications
- How to solve problems using concurrent programming patterns such as the Fork/Join, parallel aggregation, and the Divide and Conquer technique
- How to process massive data sets with parallel streams and parallel Map/Reduce implementations

This book assumes you have knowledge of general programming, but not functional programming. To apply functional concurrency in your coding, you only need a subset of the concepts from functional programming, and I'll explain what you need to know along the way. In this fashion, you'll gain the many benefits of functional concurrency in a shorter learning curve, focused on what you can use right away in your day-to-day coding experiences.

1.2   *Let's start with terminology*

This section defines terms related to the topic of this book, so we start on common ground. In computer programming, some terms (such as *concurrency, parallelism,* and *multithreading*) are used in the same context, but have different meanings. Due to their similarities, the tendency to treat these terms as the same thing is common, but it is not correct. When it becomes important to reason about the behavior of a program, it's crucial to make a distinction between computer programming terms. For example, concurrency is, by definition, multithreading, but multithreading isn't necessarily concurrent. You can easily make a multicore CPU function like a single-core CPU, but not the other way around.

   This section aims to establish a common ground about the definitions and terminologies related to the topic of this book. By the end of this section, you'll learn the meaning of these terms:

- Sequential programming
- Concurrent programming
- Parallel programming
- Multitasking
- Multithreading

1.2.1   *Sequential programming performs one task at a time*

Sequential programming is the act of accomplishing things in steps. Let's consider a simple example, such as getting a cup of cappuccino at the local coffee shop. You first stand in line to place your order with the lone barista. The barista is responsible for taking the order and delivering the drink; moreover, they are able to make only one drink at a time so you must wait patiently—or not—in line before you order. Making a cappuccino involves grinding the coffee, brewing the coffee, steaming the milk, frothing the milk, and combining the coffee and milk, so more time passes before you get your cappuccino. Figure 1.1 shows this process.

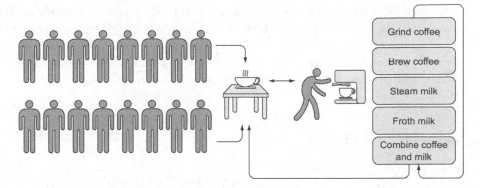

Figure 1.1 For each person in line, the barista is sequentially repeating the same set of instructions (grind coffee, brew coffee, steam milk, froth milk, and combine the coffee and the milk to make a cappuccino).

Figure 1.1 is an example of sequential work, where one task must be completed before the next. It is a convenient approach, with a clear set of systematic (step-by-step) instructions of what to do and when to do it. In this example, the barista will likely not get confused and make any mistakes while preparing the cappuccino because the steps are clear and ordered. The disadvantage of preparing a cappuccino step-by-step is that the barista must wait during parts of the process. While waiting for the coffee to be ground or the milk to be frothed, the barista is effectively inactive (blocked). The same concept applies to sequential and concurrent programming models. As shown in figure 1.2, sequential programming involves a consecutive, progressively ordered execution of processes, one instruction at a time in a linear fashion.

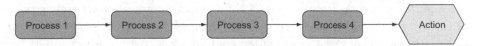

Figure 1.2 Typical sequential coding involving a consecutive, progressively ordered execution of processes

In imperative and object-oriented programming (OOP) we tend to write code that behaves sequentially, with all attention and resources focused on the task currently running. We model and execute the program by performing an ordered set of statements, one after another.

1.2.2 Concurrent programming runs multiple tasks at the same time

Suppose the barista prefers to initiate multiple steps and execute them concurrently? This moves the customer line along much faster (and, consequently, increases garnered tips). For example, once the coffee is ground, the barista can start brewing the espresso. During the brewing, the barista can take a new order or start the process of steaming and frothing the milk. In this instance, the barista gives the perception of doing multiple operations at the same time (multitasking), but this is only an illusion. More details on multitasking are covered in section 1.2.4. In fact, because the barista has only one espresso machine, they must stop one task to start or continue another, which means the barista executes only one task at a time, as shown in figure 1.3. In modern multicore computers, this is a waste of valuable resources.

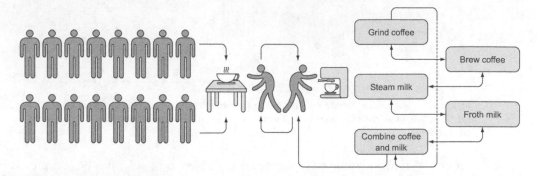

Figure 1.3   The barista switches between the operations (multitasking) of preparing the coffee (grind and brew) and preparing the milk (steam and froth). As a result, the barista executes segments of multiple tasks in an interleaved manner, giving the illusion of multitasking. But only one operation is executed at a time due to the sharing of common resources.

Concurrency describes the ability to run several programs or multiple parts of a program at the same time. In computer programming, using concurrency within an application provides actual multitasking, dividing the application into multiple and independent processes that run at the same time (concurrently) in different threads. This can happen either in a single CPU core or in parallel, if multiple CPU cores are available. The throughput (the rate at which the CPU processes a computation) and responsiveness of the program can be improved through the asynchronous or parallel execution of a task. An application that streams video content is concurrent, for example, because it simultaneously reads the digital data from the network, decompresses it, and updates its presentation onscreen.

Concurrency gives the impression that these threads are running in parallel and that different parts of the program can run simultaneously. But in a single-core environment, the execution of one thread is temporarily paused and switched to another thread, as is the case with the barista in figure 1.3. If the barista wishes to speed up production by simultaneously performing several tasks, then the available resources must be increased. In computer programming, this process is called parallelism.

1.2.3   *Parallel programming executes multiples tasks simultaneously*

From the developer's prospective, we think of parallelism when we consider the questions, "How can my program execute many things at once?" or "How can my program solve one problem faster?" *Parallelism* is the concept of executing multiple tasks at once concurrently, literally at the same time on different cores, to improve the speed of the application. Although all parallel programs are concurrent, we have seen that not all concurrency is parallel. That's because parallelism depends on the actual runtime environment, and it requires hardware support (multiple cores). Parallelism is achievable only in multicore devices (figure 1.4) and is the means to increasing performance and throughput of a program.

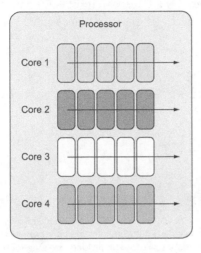

Figure 1.4 Only multicore machines allow parallelism for simultaneously executing different tasks. In this figure, each core is performing an independent task.

To return to the coffee shop example, imagine that you're the manager and wish to reduce the waiting time for customers by speeding up drink production. An intuitive solution is to hire a second barista and set up a second coffee station. With two baristas working simultaneously, the queues of customers can be processed independently and in parallel, and the preparation of cappuccinos (figure 1.5) speeds up.

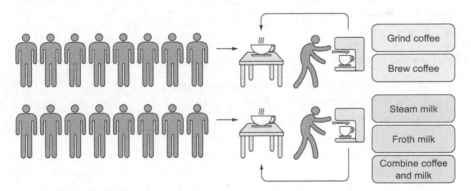

Figure 1.5 The production of cappuccinos is faster because two baristas can work in parallel with two coffee stations.

No break in production results in a benefit in performance. The goal of parallelism is to maximize the use of all available computational resources; in this case, the two baristas are working in parallel at separate stations (multicore processing).

Parallelism can be achieved when a single task is split into multiple independent subtasks, which are then run using all the available cores. In figure 1.5, a multicore machine (two coffee stations) allows parallelism for simultaneously executing different tasks (two busy baristas) without interruption.

The concept of timing is fundamental for simultaneously executing operations in parallel. In such a program, operations are *concurrent* if they can be executed in parallel, and these operations are *parallel* if the executions overlap in time (see figure 1.6).

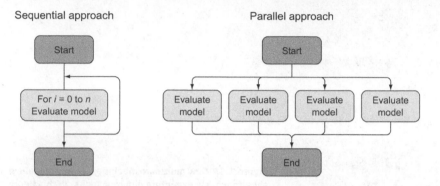

Figure 1.6   Parallel computing is a type of computation in which many calculations are carried out simultaneously, operating on the principle that large problems can often be divided into smaller ones, which are then solved at the same time.

Parallelism and concurrency are related programming models. A parallel program is also concurrent, but a concurrent program isn't always parallel, with parallel programming being a subset of concurrent programming. While concurrency refers to the design of the system, parallelism relates to the execution. Concurrent and parallel programming models are directly linked to the local hardware environment where they're performed.

1.2.4   *Multitasking performs multiple tasks concurrently over time*

Multitasking is the concept of performing multiple tasks over a period of time by executing them concurrently. We're familiar with this idea because we multitask all the time in our daily lives. For example, while waiting for the barista to prepare our cappuccino, we use our smartphone to check our emails or scan a news story. We're doing two things at one time: waiting and using a smartphone.

Computer multitasking was designed in the days when computers had a single CPU to concurrently perform many tasks while sharing the same computing resources. Initially, only one task could be executed at a time through time slicing of the CPU. (*Time slice* refers to a sophisticated scheduling logic that coordinates execution between multiple threads.) The amount of time the schedule allows a thread to run before scheduling a different thread is called *thread quantum*. The CPU is time sliced so that each thread gets to perform one operation before the execution context is switched to another thread. Context switching is a procedure handled by the operating system to multitask for optimized performance (figure 1.7). But in a single-core computer, it's possible that multitasking can slow down the performance of a program by introducing extra overhead for context switching between threads.

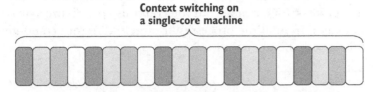

Figure 1.7 Each task has a different shade, indicating that the context switch in a single-core machine gives the illusion that multiple tasks run in parallel, but only one task is processed at a time.

There are two kinds of multitasking operating systems:

- *Cooperative multitasking systems*, where the scheduler lets each task run until it finishes or explicitly yields execution control back to the scheduler
- *Preemptive multitasking systems* (such as Microsoft Windows), where the scheduler prioritizes the execution of tasks, and the underlying system, considering the priority of the tasks, switches the execution sequence once the time allocation is completed by yielding control to other tasks

Most operating systems designed in the last decade have provided preemptive multitasking. Multitasking is useful for UI responsiveness to help avoid freezing the UI during long operations.

1.2.5 *Multithreading for performance improvement*

Multithreading is an extension of the concept of multitasking, aiming to improve the performance of a program by maximizing and optimizing computer resources. Multithreading is a form of concurrency that uses multiple threads of execution. Multithreading implies concurrency, but concurrency doesn't necessarily imply multithreading. Multithreading enables an application to explicitly subdivide specific tasks into individual threads that run in parallel within the same process.

> **NOTE** A *process* is an instance of a program running within a computer system. Each process has one or more threads of execution, and no thread can exist outside a process.

A *thread* is a unit of computation (an independent set of programming instructions designed to achieve a particular result), which the operating system scheduler independently executes and manages. Multithreading differs from multitasking: unlike multitasking, with multithreading the threads share resources. But this "sharing resources" design presents more programming challenges than multitasking does. We discuss the problem of sharing variables between threads later in this chapter in section 1.4.1.

The concepts of parallel and multithreading programming are closely related. But in contrast to parallelism, multithreading is hardware-agnostic, which means that it can be performed regardless of the number of cores. Parallel programming is a superset of multithreading. You could use multithreading to parallelize a program by sharing resources in the same process, for example, but you could also parallelize a program by executing the computation in multiple processes or even in different computers. Figure 1.8 shows the relationship between these terms.

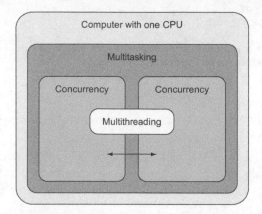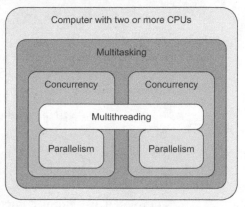

Figure 1.8   Relationship between concurrency, parallelism, multithreading, and multitasking in a single and a multicore device

To summarize:

- *Sequential programming* refers to a set of ordered instructions executed one at a time on one CPU.
- *Concurrent programming* handles several operations at one time and doesn't require hardware support (using either one or multiple cores).
- *Parallel programming* executes multiple operations at the same time on multiple CPUs. All parallel programs are concurrent, running simultaneously, but not all concurrency is parallel. The reason is that parallelism is achievable only on multi-core devices.
- *Multitasking* concurrently performs multiple threads from different processes. Multitasking doesn't necessarily mean parallel execution, which is achieved only when using multiple CPUs.
- *Multithreading* extends the idea of multitasking; it's a form of concurrency that uses multiple, independent threads of execution from the same process. Each thread can run concurrently or in parallel, depending on the hardware support.

1.3   *Why the need for concurrency?*

Concurrency is a natural part of life—as humans we're accustomed to multitasking. We can read an email while drinking a cup of coffee, or type while listening to our favorite song. The main reason to use concurrency in an application is to increase performance and responsiveness, and to achieve low latency. It's common sense that if one person does two tasks one after another it would take longer than if two people did those same two tasks simultaneously.

It's the same with applications. The problem is that most applications aren't written to evenly split the tasks required among the available CPUs. Computers are used in many different fields, such as analytics, finance, science, and health care. The amount of data analyzed is increasing year by year. Two good illustrations are Google and Pixar.

In 2012, Google received more than 2 million search queries per minute; in 2014, that number more than doubled. In 1995, Pixar produced the first completely computer-generated movie, *Toy Story*. In computer animation, myriad details and information must be rendered for each image, such as shading and lighting. All this information changes at the rate of 24 frames per second. In a 3D movie, an exponential increase in changing information is required.

The creators of *Toy Story* used 100 connected dual-processor machines to create their movie, and the use of parallel computation was indispensable. Pixar's tools evolved for *Toy Story 2*; the company used 1,400 computer processors for digital movie editing, thereby vastly improving digital quality and editing time. In the beginning of 2000, Pixar's computer power increased even more, to 3,500 processors. Sixteen years later, the computer power used to process a fully animated movie reached an absurd 24,000 cores. The need for parallel computing continues to increase exponentially.

Let's consider a processor with N (as any number) running cores. In a single-threaded application, only one core runs. The same application executing multiple threads will be faster, and as the demand for performance grows, so too will the demand for N to grow, making parallel programs the standard programming model choice for the future.

If you run an application in a multicore machine that wasn't designed with concurrency in mind, you're wasting computer productivity because the application as it sequences through the processes will only use a portion of the available computer power. In this case, if you open Task Manager, or any CPU performance counter, you'll notice only one core running high, possibly at 100%, while all the other cores are underused or idle. In a machine with eight cores, running non-concurrent programs means the overall use of the resources could be as low as 15% (figure 1.9).

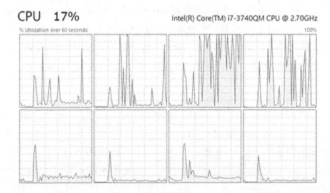

Figure 1.9 Windows Task Manager shows a program poorly utilizing CPU resources.

Such waste of computing power unequivocally illustrates that sequential code isn't the correct programming model for multicore processers. To maximize the use of the available computational resources, Microsoft's .NET platform provides parallel execution of code through multithreading. By using parallelism, a program can take full advantage of the resources available, as illustrated by the CPU performance counter in figure 1.10, where you'll notice that all the processor cores are running high, possibly at 100%. Current hardware trends predict more cores instead of faster clock speeds; therefore, developers have no choice but to embrace this evolution and become parallel programmers.

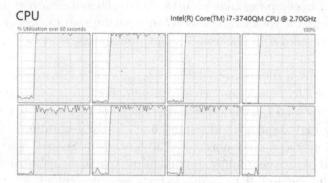

Figure 1.10   A program written with concurrency in mind can maximize CPU resources, possibly up to 100%.

1.3.1   *Present and future of concurrent programming*

Mastering concurrency to deliver scalable programs has become a required skill. Companies are interested in hiring and investing in engineers who have a deep knowledge of writing concurrent code. In fact, writing correct parallel computation can save time and money. It's cheaper to build scalable programs that use the computational resources available with fewer servers, than to keep buying and adding expensive hardware that is underused to reach the same level of performance. In addition, more hardware requires more maintenance and electric power to operate.

This is an exciting time to learn to write multithreaded code, and it's rewarding to improve the performance of your program with the functional programming (FP) approach. Functional programming is a programming style that treats computation as the evaluation of expressions and avoids changing-state and mutable data. Because immutability is the default, and with the addition of a fantastic composition and declarative programming style, FP makes it effortless to write concurrent programs. More details follow in section1.5.

While it's a bit unnerving to think in a new paradigm, the initial challenge of learning parallel programming diminishes quickly, and the reward for perseverance is infinite. You'll find something magical and spectacular about opening the Windows Task Manager and proudly noticing that the CPU usage spikes to 100% after your code changes. Once you become familiar and comfortable with writing highly scalable systems using the functional paradigm, it will be difficult to go back to the slow style of sequential code.

Concurrency is the next innovation that will dominate the computer industry, and it will transform how developers write software. The evolution of software requirements in the industry and the demand for high-performance software that delivers great user experience through non-blocking UIs will continue to spur the need for concurrency. In lockstep with the direction of hardware, it's evident that concurrency and parallelism are the future of programming.

1.4   *The pitfalls of concurrent programming*

Concurrent and parallel programming are without doubt beneficial for rapid responsiveness and speedy execution of a given computation. But this gain of performance and reactive experience comes with a price. Using sequential programs, the execution of the code takes the happy path of predictability and determinism. Conversely, multithreaded programming requires commitment and effort to achieve correctness. Furthermore, reasoning about multiple executions running simultaneously is difficult because we're used to thinking sequentially.

Determinism

Determinism is a fundamental requirement in building software as computer programs are often expected to return identical results from one run to the next. But this property becomes hard to resolve in a parallel execution. External circumstances, such as the operating system scheduler or cache coherence (covered in chapter 4), could influence the execution timing and, therefore, the order of access for two or more threads and modify the same memory location. This time variant could affect the outcome of the program.

The process of developing parallel programs involves more than creating and spawning multiple threads. Writing programs that execute in parallel is demanding and requires thoughtful design. You should design with the following questions in mind:

- How is it possible to use concurrency and parallelism to reach incredible computational performance and a highly responsive application?
- How can such programs take full advantage of the power provided by a multicore computer?
- How can communication with and access to the same memory location between threads be coordinated while ensuring thread safety? (A method is called *threadsafe* when the data and state don't get corrupted if two or more threads attempt to access and modify the data or state at the same time.)
- How can a program ensure deterministic execution?
- How can the execution of a program be parallelized without jeopardizing the quality of the final result?

These aren't easy questions to answer. But certain patterns and techniques can help. For example, in the presence of side effects,[1] the determinism of the computation is lost because the order in which concurrent tasks execute becomes variable. The

---

[1] A side effect arises when a method changes some state from outside its scope, or it communicates with the "outside world," such as calling a database or writing to the file system.

obvious solution is to avoid side effects in favor of pure functions. You'll learn these techniques and practices during the course of the book.

1.4.1 Concurrency hazards

Writing concurrent programs isn't easy, and many sophisticated elements must be considered during program design. Creating new threads or queuing multiple jobs on the thread pool is relatively simple, but how do you ensure correctness in the program? When many threads continually access shared data, you must consider how to safeguard the data structure to guarantee its integrity. A thread should write and modify a memory location atomically,[2] without interference by other threads. The reality is that programs written in imperative programming languages or in languages with variables whose values can change (mutable variables) will always be vulnerable to data races, regardless of the level of memory synchronization or concurrent libraries used.

> NOTE   A data race occurs when two or more threads in a single process access the same memory location concurrently, and at least one of the accesses updates the memory slot while other threads read the same value without using any exclusive locks to control their accesses to that memory.

Consider the case of two threads (Thread 1 and Thread 2) running in parallel, both trying to access and modify the shared value x as shown in figure 1.11. For Thread 1 to modify a variable requires more than one CPU instruction: the value must be read from memory, then modified and ultimately written back to memory. If Thread 2 tries to read from the same memory location while Thread 1 is writing back an updated value, the value of x changed. More precisely, it's possible that Thread 1 and Thread 2 read the value x simultaneously, then Thread 1 modifies the value x and writes it back to memory, while Thread 2 also modifies the value x. The result is data corruption. This phenomenon is called *race condition*.

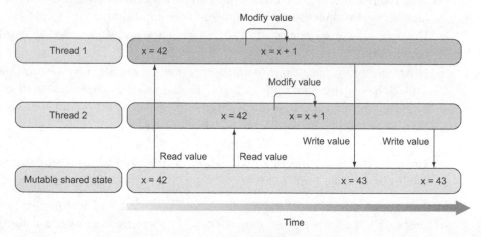

Figure 1.11   Two threads (Thread 1 and Thread 2) run in parallel, both trying to access and modify the shared value _x_. If Thread 2 tries to read from the same memory location while Thread 1 writes back an updated value, the value of _x_ changes. This result is data corruption or _race condition_.

---

[2]   An atomic operation accesses a shared memory and completes in a single step relative to other threads.

The combination of a mutable state and parallelism in a program is synonymous with problems. The solution from the imperative paradigm perspective is to protect the mutable state by locking access to more than one thread at a time. This technique is called *mutual exclusion* because the access of one thread to a given memory location prevents access of other threads at that time. The concept of timing is central as multiple threads must access the same data at the same time to benefit from this technique. The introduction of locks to synchronize access by multiple threads to shared resources solves the problem of data corruption, but introduces more complications that can lead to *deadlock*.

Consider the case in figure 1.12 where Thread 1 and Thread 2 are waiting for each other to complete work and are blocked indefinitely in that waiting. Thread 1 acquires Lock A, and, right after, Thread 2 acquires Lock B. At this point, both threads are waiting on a lock that will never be released. This is a case of deadlock.

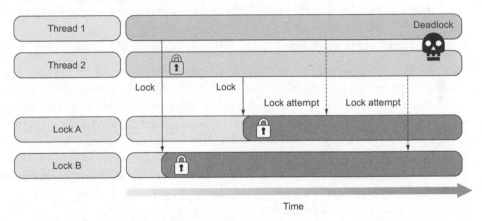

Figure 1.12. In this scenario, Thread 1 acquires Lock A, and Thread 2 acquires Lock B. Then, Thread 2 tries to acquire Lock A while Thread 1 tries to acquire Lock B that is already acquired by Thread 2, which is waiting to acquire Lock A before releasing Lock B. At this point, both threads are waiting at the lock that'll never be released. This is a case of deadlock.

Here is a list of concurrency hazards with a brief explanation. Later, you'll get more details on each, with a specific focus on how to avoid them:

- Race condition is a state that occurs when a shared mutable resource (a file, image, variable, or collection, for example) is accessed at the same time by multiple threads, leaving an inconsistent state. The consequent data corruption makes a program unreliable and unusable.

- Performance decline is a common problem when multiple threads share state contention that requires synchronization techniques. Mutual exclusion locks (or mutexes), as the name suggests, prevent the code from running in parallel by forcing multiple threads to stop work to communicate and synchronize memory access. The acquisition and release of locks comes with a performance penalty, slowing down all processes. As the number of cores gets larger, the cost of lock contention can potentially increase. As more tasks are introduced to share the same data, the overhead associated with locks can negatively impact the computation. Section 1.4.3 demonstrates the consequences and overhead costs due to introducing lock synchronization.

- Deadlock is a concurrency problem that originates from using locks. It occurs when a cycle of tasks exists in which each task is blocked while waiting for another to proceed. Because all tasks are waiting for another task to do something, they're blocked indefinitely. The more that resources are shared among threads, the more locks are needed to avoid race condition, and the higher the risk of deadlocks.

- Lack of composition is a design problem originating from the introduction of locks in the code. Locks don't compose. Composition encourages problem dismantling by breaking up a complex problem into smaller pieces that are easier to solve, then gluing them back together. Composition is a fundamental tenet in FP.

1.4.2 The sharing of state evolution

Real-world programs require interaction between tasks, such as exchanging information to coordinate work. This cannot be implemented without sharing data that's accessible to all the tasks. Dealing with this shared state is the root of most problems related to parallel programming, unless the shared data is immutable or each task has its own copy. The solution is to safeguard all the code from those concurrency problems. No compiler or tool can help you position these primitive synchronization locks in the correct location in your code. It all depends on your skill as a programmer.

Because of these potential problems, the programming community has cried out, and in response, libraries and frameworks have been written and introduced into mainstream object-oriented languages (such as C# and Java) to provide concurrency safeguards, which were not part of the original language design. This support is a design correction, illustrated with the presence of shared memory in imperative and object-oriented, general-purpose programming environments. Meanwhile, functional languages don't need safeguards because the concept of FP maps well onto concurrent programming models.

1.4.3 A simple real-world example: parallel quicksort

Sorting algorithms are used generally in technical computing and can be a bottleneck. Let's consider a Quicksort algorithm,[3] a CPU-bound computation amenable to parallelization that orders the elements of an array. This example aims to demonstrate the pitfalls of converting a sequential algorithm into a parallel version and points out that introducing

---

[3] Tony Hoare invented the Quicksort algorithm in 1960, and it remains one of the most acclaimed algorithms with great practical value.

parallelism in your code requires extra thinking before making any decisions. Otherwise, performance could potentially have an opposite outcome to that expected.

Quicksort is a Divide and Conquer algorithm; it first divides a large array into two smaller sub-arrays of low elements and high elements. Quicksort can then recursively sort the sub-arrays, and is amenable to parallelization. It can operate in place on an array, requiring small additional amounts of memory to perform the sorting. The algorithm consists of three simple steps, as shown in figure 1.13:

1 Select a pivot element.
2 Partition the sequence into subsequences according to their order relative to the pivot.
3 Quicksort the subsequences.

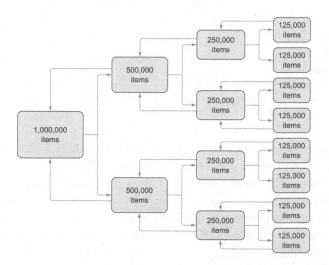

Figure 1.13. The recursive function divides and conquers. Each block is divided into equal halves, where the pivot element must be the median of the sequence, until each portion of code can be executed independently. When all the single blocks are completed, they send the result back to the previous caller to be aggregated. Quicksort is based on the idea of picking a pivot point and partitioning the sequence into sub-sequence elements smaller than the pivot and bigger than the pivot elements before recursively sorting the two smaller sequences.

Recursive algorithms, especially ones based on a form of Divide and Conquer, are a great candidate for parallelization and CPU-bound computations.

The Microsoft Task Parallel Library (TPL), introduced after the release of .NET 4.0, makes it easier to implement and exploit parallelism for this type of algorithm. Using the TPL, you can divide each step of the algorithm and perform each task in parallel, recursively. It's a straight and easy implementation, but you must be careful of the level of depth to which the threads are created to avoid adding more tasks than necessary.

To implement the Quicksort algorithm, you'll use the FP language F#. Due to its intrinsic recursive nature, however, the idea behind this implementation can also be applied to C#, which requires an imperative for loop approach with a mutable state. C# doesn't support optimized tail-recursive functions such as F#, so a hazard exists of raising a stack overflow exception when the call-stack pointer exceeds the stack constraint. In chapter 3, we'll go into detail on how to overcome this C# limitation.

Listing 1.1 shows a Quicksort function in F# that adopts the Divide and Conquer strategy. For each recursive iteration, you select a pivot point and use that to partition the total array. You partition the elements around the pivot point using the List.partition API, then recursively sort the lists on each side of the pivot. F# has great built-in support for data structure manipulation. In this case, you're using the List.partition API, which returns a tuple containing two lists: one that satisfies the predicate and another that doesn't.

Listing 1.1   Simple Quicksort algorithm

```
let rec quicksortSequential aList =
    match aList with
    | [] -> []
    | firstElement :: restOfList ->
        let smaller, larger =
            List.partition (fun number -> number < firstElement) restOfList
        quicksortSequential smaller @ (firstElement ::
➡ quicksortSequential larger)
```

Running this Quicksort algorithm against an array of 1 million random, unsorted integers on my system (eight logical cores; 2.2 GHz clock speed) takes an average of 6.5 seconds. But when you analyze this algorithm design, the opportunity to parallelize is evident. At the end of quicksortSequential, you recursively call into quicksortSequential with each partition of the array identified by the (fun number -> number < firstElement) restOfList. By spawning new tasks using the TPL, you can rewrite in parallel this portion of the code.

Listing 1.2   Parallel Quicksort algorithm using the TPL

```
let rec quicksortParallel aList =
    match aList with
    | [] -> []
    | firstElement :: restOfList ->
        let smaller, larger =
            List.partition (fun number -> number < firstElement) restOfList
        let left  = Task.Run(fun () -> quicksortParallel smaller)
        let right = Task.Run(fun () -> quicksortParallel larger)
        left.Result @ (firstElement :: right.Result)
```

Appends the result for each task into a sorted array

Task.Run executes the recursive calls in tasks that can run in parallel; for each recursive call, tasks are dynamically created.

The algorithm in listing 1.2 is running in parallel, which now is using more CPU resources by spreading the work across all available cores. But even with improved resource utilization, the overall performance result isn't meeting expectations.

Execution time dramatically increases instead of decreases. The parallelized Quicksort algorithm is passed from an average of 6.5 seconds per run to approximately 12 seconds. The overall processing time has slowed down. In this case, the problem is that the algorithm is *over-parallelized*. Each time the internal array is partitioned, two new tasks are spawned to parallelize this algorithm. This design is spawning too many tasks in relation to the cores available, which is inducing parallelization overhead. This is especially true in a Divide and Conquer algorithm that involves parallelizing a recursive function. It's important that you don't add more tasks than necessary. The disappointing result demonstrates an important characteristic of parallelism: inherent limitations exist on how much extra threading or extra processing will help a specific algorithmic implementation.

To achieve better optimization, you can refactor the previous `quicksortParallel` function by stopping the recursive parallelization after a certain point. In this way, the algorithm's first recursions will still be executed in parallel until the deepest recursion, which will revert to the serial approach. This design guarantees taking full advantage of cores. Plus, the overhead added by parallelizing is dramatically reduced.

Listing 1.3 shows this new design approach. It takes into account the level where the recursive function is running; if the level is below a predefined threshold, it stops parallelizing. The function `quicksortParallelWithDepth` has an extra argument, `depth`, whose purpose is to reduce and control the number of times a recursive function is parallelized. The `depth` argument is decremented on each recursive call, and new tasks are created until this argument value reaches zero. In this case, you're passing the value resulting from `Math.Log(float System.Enviroment.ProcessorCount, 2.) + 4.` for the `max depth`. This ensures that every level of the recursion will spawn two child tasks until all the available cores are enlisted.

Listing 1.3 A better parallel Quicksort algorithm using the TPL

```
let rec quicksortParallelWithDepth depth aList =        Tracks the function
  match aList with                                        recursion level with
  | [] -> []                                              the depth parameter
  | firstElement :: restOfList ->
     let smaller, larger =
        List.partition (fun number -> number < firstElement) restOfList
     if depth < 0 then
        let left  = quicksortParallelWithDepth depth smaller
        let right = quicksortParallelWithDepth depth larger
        left @ (firstElement :: right)
     else
        let left  = Task.Run(fun () ->               If the value of depth is
quicksortParallelWithDepth (depth - 1) smaller)      positive, allows the function
        let right = Task.Run(fun () ->               to be called recursively,
quicksortParallelWithDepth (depth - 1) larger)       spawning two new tasks
        left.Result @ (firstElement :: right.Result)
```

If the value of depth is negative, skips the parallelization

Sequentially executes the Quicksort using the current thread

One relevant factor in selecting the number of tasks is how similar the predicted run time of the tasks will be. In the case of `quicksortParallelWithDepth`, the duration of the tasks can vary substantially, because the pivot points depend on the unsorted data. They don't necessarily result in segments of equal size. To compensate for the uneven sizes of the tasks, the formula in this example calculates the `depth` argument to produce more tasks than cores. The formula limits the number of tasks to approximately 16 times the number of cores because the number of tasks can be no larger than 2 ^ `depth`. Our objective is to have a Quicksort workload that is balanced, and that doesn't start more tasks than required. Starting a `Task` during each iteration (recursion), when the depth level is reached, saturates the processors.

In most cases, the Quicksort generates an unbalanced workload because the fragments produced are not of equal size. The conceptual formula `log2(ProcessorCount) + 4` calculates the `depth` argument to limit and adapt the number of running tasks regardless of the cases.[4] If you substitute `depth = log2(ProcessorCount) + 4` and simplify the expression, you see that the number of tasks is 16 times `ProcessorCount`. Limiting the number of subtasks by measuring the recursion depth is an extremely important technique.[5]

For example, in the case of four-core machines, the depth is calculated as follows:

```
depth = log2(ProcessorCount) + 4
depth = log2(2) + 4
depth = 2 + 4
```

The result is a range between approximately 36 to 64 concurrent tasks, because during each iteration two tasks are started for each branch, which in turn double in each iteration. In this way, the overall work of partitioning among threads has a fair and suitable distribution for each core.

1.4.4 Benchmarking in F#

You executed the Quicksort sample using the F# REPL (Read-Evaluate-Print-Loop), which is a handy tool to run a targeted portion of code because it skips the compilation step of the program. The REPL fits quite well in prototyping and data-analysis development because it facilitates the programming process. Another benefit is the built-in `#time` functionality, which toggles the display of performance information. When it's enabled, F# `Interactive` measures real time, CPU time, and garbage collection information for each section of code that's interpreted and executed.

Table 1.1 sorts a 3 GB array, enabling the 64-bit environment flag to avoid size restriction. It's run on a computer with eight logical cores (four physical cores with hyper-threading). On an average of 10 runs, table 1.1 shows the execution times in seconds.

---

[4]   The function log2 is an abbreviation for *Log in base 2*. For example, log2(*x*) represents the logarithm of *x* to the base 2.

[5]   Recall that for any value *a*, 2 ^ (*a* + 4) is the same as 16×2^a; and that if $a = \log2(b)$, $2^a = b$.

Table 1.1 Benchmark of sorting with Quicksort

Serial	Parallel	Parallel 4 threads	Parallel 8 threads
6.52	12.41	4.76	3.50

It's important to mention that for a small array, fewer than 100 items, the parallel sort algorithms are slower than the serial version due to the overhead of creating and/or spawning new threads. Even if you correctly write a parallel program, the overhead introduced with concurrency constructors could overwhelm the program runtime, delivering the opposite expectation by decreasing performance. For this reason, it's important to benchmark the original sequential code as a baseline and then continue to measure each change to validate whether parallelism is beneficial. A complete strategy should consider this factor and approach parallelism only if the array size is greater than a threshold (recursive depth), which usually matches the number of cores, after which it defaults back to the serial behavior.

1.5 Why choose functional programming for concurrency?

The trouble is that essentially all the interesting applications of concurrency involve the deliberate and controlled mutation of shared state, such as screen real estate, the file system, or the internal data structures of the program. The right solution, therefore, is to provide mechanisms which allow the safe mutation of shared state section.

—*Peyton Jones, Andrew Gordon, and Sigbjorn Finne ("Concurrent Haskell,"*
Proceedings of the 23rd ACM Symposium on Principles of Programming
Languages, *St. Petersburg Beach, FL, January 1996)*

FP is about minimizing and controlling side effects, commonly referred to as *pure functional programming*. FP uses the concept of transformation, where a function creates a copy of a value *x* and then modifies the copy, leaving the original value *x* unchanged and free to be used by other parts of the program. It encourages considering whether mutability and side effects are necessary when designing the program. FP allows mutability and side effects, but in a strategic and explicit manner, isolating this area from the rest of the code by utilizing methods to encapsulate them.

The main reason for adopting functional paradigms is to solve the problems that exist in the multicore era. Highly concurrent applications, such as web servers and data-analysis databases, suffer from several architectural issues. These systems must be scalable to respond to a large number of concurrent requests, which leads to design challenges for handling maximum resource contention and high-scheduling frequency. Moreover, race conditions and deadlocks are common, which makes troubleshooting and debugging code difficult.

In this chapter, we discussed a number of common issues specific to developing concurrent applications in either imperative or OOP. In these programming paradigms, we're dealing with objects as a base construct. Conversely, in terms of concurrency, dealing with objects has caveats to consider when passing from a single-thread program to a massively parallelizing work, which is a challenging and entirely different scenario.

NOTE A *thread* is an operating system construct that functions like a virtual CPU. At any given moment, a thread is allowed to run on the physical CPU for a slice of time. When the time for a thread to run expires, it's swapped off the CPU for another thread. Therefore, if a single thread enters an infinite loop, it cannot monopolize all the CPU time on the system. At the end of its time slice, it will be switched out for another thread.

The traditional solution for these problems is to synchronize access to resources, avoiding contention between threads. But this same solution is a double-edged sword because using primitives for synchronization, such as `lock` for mutual exclusion, leads to possible deadlock or race conditions. In fact, the state of a variable (as the name *variable* implies) can mutate. In OOP, a variable usually represents an object that's liable to change over time. Because of this, you can never rely on its state and, consequentially, you must check its current value to avoid unwanted behaviors (figure 1.14).

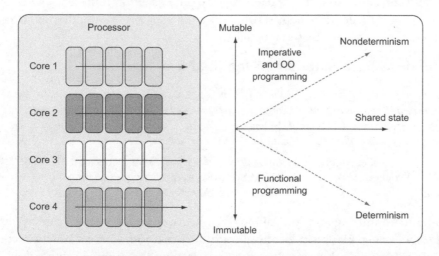

Figure 1.14   In the functional paradigm, due to immutability as a default construct, concurrent programming guarantees deterministic execution, even in the case of a shared state. Conversely, imperative and OOP use mutable states, which are hard to manage in a multithread environment, and this leads to nondeterministic programs.

It's important to consider that components of systems that embrace the FP concept can no longer interfere with each other, and they can be used in a multithreaded environment without using any locking strategies.

Development of safe parallel programs using a share of mutable variables and side-effect functions takes substantial effort from the programmer, who must make critical decisions, often leading to synchronization in the form of locking. By removing those fundamental problems through functional programming, you can also remove those concurrency-specific issues. This is why FP makes an excellent concurrent programming model. It is an exceptional fit for concurrent programmers to achieve correct high performance in highly multithreaded environments using simple code. At the heart of FP, neither variables nor state are mutable and cannot be shared, and functions may not have side effects.

FP is the most practical way to write concurrent programs. Trying to write them in imperative languages isn't only difficult, it also leads to bugs that are difficult to discover, reproduce, and fix.

How are you going to take advantage of every computer core available to you? The answer is simple: embrace the functional paradigm!

1.5.1 Benefits of functional programming

There are real advantages to learning FP, even if you have no plans to adopt this style in the immediate future. Still, it's hard to convince someone to spend their time on something new without showing immediate benefits. The benefits come in the form of idiomatic language features that can initially seem overwhelming. FP, however, is a paradigm that will give you great coding power and positive impact in your programs after a short learning curve. Within a few weeks of using FP techniques, you'll improve the readability and correctness of your applications.

The benefits of FP (with focus on concurrency) include the following:

- *Immutability*—A property that prevents modification of an object state after creation. In FP, variable assignment is not a concept. Once a value has been associated with an identifier, it cannot change. Functional code is immutable by definition. Immutable objects can be safely transferred between threads, leading to great optimization opportunities. Immutability removes the problems of memory corruption (race condition) and deadlocks because of the absence of mutual exclusion.
- *Pure function*—This has no side effects, which means that functions don't change any input or data of any type outside the function body. Functions are said to be pure if they're transparent to the user, and their return value depends only on the input arguments. By passing the same arguments into a pure function, the result won't change, and each process will return the same value, producing consistent and expected behavior.
- *Referential transparency*—The idea of a function whose output depends on and maps only to its input. In other words, each time a function receives the same arguments, the result is the same. This concept is valuable in concurrent programming because the definition of the expression can be replaced with its value and will have the same meaning. Referential transparency guarantees that a set of functions can be evaluated in any order and in parallel, without changing the application's behavior.
- *Lazy evaluation*—Used in FP to retrieve the result of a function on demand or to defer the analysis of a big data stream until needed.
- *Composability*—Used to compose functions and create higher-level abstractions out of simple functions. Composability is the most powerful tool to defeat complexity, letting you define and build solutions for complex problems.

Learning to program functionally allows you to write more modular, expression-oriented, and conceptually simple code. The combinations of these FP assets will let you understand what your code is doing, regardless of how many threads the code is executing.

Later in this book, you'll learn techniques to apply parallelism and bypass issues associated with mutable states and side effects. The functional paradigm approach to these concepts aims to simplify and maximize efficiency in coding with a declarative programming style.

1.6 *Embracing the functional paradigm*

Sometimes, change is difficult. Often, developers who are comfortable in their domain knowledge lack the motivation to look at programming problems from a different perspective. Learning any new program paradigm is hard and requires time to transition to developing in a different style. Changing your programming perspective requires a switch in your thinking and approach, not solely learning new code syntax for a new programming language.

Going from a language such as Java to C# isn't difficult; in terms of concepts, they're the same. Going from an imperative paradigm to a functional paradigm is a far more difficult challenge. Core concepts are replaced. You have no more state. You have no more variables. You have no more side effects.

But the effort you make to change paradigms will pay large dividends. Most developers will agree that learning a new language makes you a better developer, and liken that to a patient whose doctor prescribes 30 minutes of exercise per day to be healthy. The patient knows the real benefits in exercise, but is also aware that daily exercise implies commitment and sacrifice.

Similarly, learning a new paradigm isn't hard, but does require dedication, engagement, and time. I encourage everyone who wants to be a better programmer to consider learning the FP paradigm. Learning FP is like riding a roller coaster: during the process there will be times when you feel excited and levitated, followed by times when you believe that you understand a principle only to descend steeply—screaming—but the ride is worth it. Think of learning FP as a journey, an investment in your personal and professional career with guaranteed return. Keep in mind that part of the learning is to make mistakes and develop skills to avoid those in the future.

Throughout this process, you should identify the concepts that are difficult to understand and try to overcome those difficulties. Think about how to use these abstractions in practice, solving simple problems to begin with. My experience shows that you can break through a mental roadblock by finding out what the intent of a concept is by using a real example. This book will walk you through the benefits of FP applied to concurrency and a distributed system. It's a narrow path, but on the other side, you'll emerge with several great foundational concepts to use in your everyday programming. I am confident you'll gain new insights into how to solve complex problems and become a superior software engineer using the immense power of FP.

1.7 Why use F# and C# for functional concurrent programming?

The focus of this book is to develop and design highly scalable and performant systems, adopting the functional paradigm to write correct concurrent code. This doesn't mean you must learn a new language; you can apply the functional paradigm by using tools that you're already familiar with, such as the multipurpose languages C# and F#. Over the years several functional features have been added to those languages, making it easier for you to shift to incorporating this new paradigm.

The intrinsically different approach to solving problems is the reason these languages were chosen. Both programming languages can be used to solve the same problem in very different ways, which makes a case for choosing the best tool for the job. With a well-rounded toolset, you can design a better and easier solution. In fact, as software engineers, you *should* think of programming languages as tools.

Ideally, a solution should be a combination of C# and F# projects that work together cohesively. Both languages cover a different programming model, but the option to choose which tool to use for the job provides an enormous benefit in terms of productivity and efficiency. Another aspect to selecting these languages is their different concurrent programming model support, which can be mixed. For instance:

- F# offers a much simpler model than C# for asynchronous computation, called *asynchronous workflows*.
- Both C# and F# are strongly typed, multipurpose programming languages with support for multiple paradigms that encompass functional, imperative, and OOP techniques.
- Both languages are part of the .NET ecosystem and derive a rich set of libraries that can be used equally by both languages.
- F# is a functional-first programming language that provides an enormous productivity boost. In fact, programs written in F# tend to be more succinct and lead to less code to maintain.
- F# combines the benefits of a functional declarative programming style with support from the imperative object-oriented style. This lets you develop applications using your existing object-oriented and imperative programming skills.
- F# has a set of built-in lock-free data structures, due to default immutable constructors. An example is the discriminated union and the record types. These types have structural equality and don't allow `null`s that lead to "trusting" the integrity of the data and easier comparisons.
- F#, different from C#, strongly discourages the use of `null` values, also known as the billion-dollar mistake, and, instead, encourages the use of immutable data structures. This lack of null reference helps to minimize the number of bugs in programming.

The null reference origin

Tony Hoare introduced the null reference in 1965, while he was designing the ALGOL object-oriented language. Some 44 years later, he apologized for inventing it by calling it the billion-dollar mistake. He also said this:

". . . I couldn't resist the temptation to put in a null reference, simply because it was so easy to implement. This has led to innumerable errors, vulnerabilities, and system crashes . . .." [6]

- F# is naturally parallelizable because it uses immutably as a default type constructor, and because of its .NET foundation, it integrates with the C# language with state-of-the-art capability at the implementation level.

- C# design tends toward an imperative language, first with full support for OOP. (I like to define this as imperative OO.) The functional paradigm, during the past years and since the release of .NET 3.5, has influenced the C# language with the addition of features like lambda expressions and LINQ for list comprehension.

- C# also has great concurrency tools that let you easily write parallel programs and readily solve tough real-world problems. Indeed, exceptional multicore development support within the C# language is versatile, and capable of rapid development and prototyping of highly parallel symmetric multiprocessing (SMP) applications. These programming languages are great tools for writing concurrent software, and the power and options for workable solutions aggregate when used in coexistence. SMP is the processing of programs by multiple processors that share a common operating system and memory.

- F# and C# can interoperate. In fact, an F# function can call a method in a C# library, and vice versa.

In the coming chapters, we'll discuss alternative concurrent approaches, such as data parallelism, asynchronous, and the message-passing programming model. We'll build libraries using the best tools that each of these programming languages can offer and compare those with other languages. We'll also examine tools and libraries like the TPL and Reactive Extensions (Rx) that have been successfully designed, inspired, and implemented by adopting the functional paradigm to obtain composable abstraction.

It's obvious that the industry is looking for a reliable and simple concurrent programming model, shown by the fact that software companies are investing in libraries that remove the level of abstraction from the traditional and complex memory-synchronization models. Examples of these higher-level libraries are Intel's Threading Building Blocks (TBB) and Microsoft's TPL.

There are also interesting open source projects, such as OpenMP (which provides pragmas [compiler-specific definitions that you can use to create new preprocessor

---

[6]   From a speech at QCon London in 2009: http://mng.bz/u74T.

functionality or to send implementation-defined information to the compiler] that you can insert into a program to make parts of it parallel) and OpenCL (a low-level language to communicate with Graphic Processing Units [GPUs]). GPU programming has traction and has been sanctioned by Microsoft with C++ AMP extensions and Accelerator .NET.

Summary

- No silver bullet exists for the challenges and complexities of concurrent and parallel programming. As a professional engineer, you need different types of ammunition, and you need to know how and when to use them to hit the target.
- Programs must be designed with concurrency in mind; programmers cannot continue writing sequential code, turning a blind eye to the benefits of parallel programming.
- Moore's Law isn't incorrect. Instead, it has changed direction toward an increased number of cores per processor rather than increased speed for a single CPU.
- While writing concurrent code, you must keep in mind the distinction between concurrency, multithreading, multitasking, and parallelism.
- The share of mutable states and side effects are the primary concerns to avoid in a concurrent environment because they lead to unwanted program behaviors and bugs.
- To avoid the pitfalls of writing concurrent applications, you should use programming models and tools that raise the level of abstraction.
- The functional paradigm gives you the right tools and principles to handle concurrency easily and correctly in your code.
- Functional programming excels in parallel computation because immutability is the default, making it simpler to reason about the share of data.

Functional programming techniques for concurrency

This chapter covers

- Solving complex problems by composing simple solutions
- Simplifying functional programming with closures
- Improving program performance with functional techniques
- Using lazy evaluation

Writing code in functional programming can make you feel like the driver of fast car, speeding along without the need to know how the underlying mechanics work. In chapter 1, you learned that taking an FP approach to writing concurrent applications better answers the challenges in writing those applications than, for example, an object-oriented approach does. Key concepts, such as immutable variables and purity, in any FP language mean that while writing concurrent applications remains far from easy, developers can be confident that they won't face several of the traditional pitfalls of parallel programming. The design of FP means issues such as race conditions and deadlocks can't happen.

In this chapter we'll look in more detail at the main FP principles that help in our quest to write high-quality concurrent applications. You'll learn what the principles are, how they work in both C# (as far as possible) and in F#, and how they fit into the patterns for parallel programming.

In this chapter, I assume that you have a familiarity with the basic principles of FP. If you don't, see appendix A for the detailed information you need to continue. By the end of this chapter, you'll know how to use functional techniques to compose simple functions to solve complex problems and to cache and precompute data safely in a multithreaded environment to speed up your program execution.

2.1 Using function composition to solve complex problems

Function composition is the combining of functions in a manner where the output from one function becomes the input for the next function, leading to the creation of a new function. This process can continue endlessly, chaining functions together to create powerful new functions to solve complex problems. Through composition, you can achieve modularization to simplify the structure of your program.

The *functional paradigm* leads to simple program design. The main motivation behind function composition is to provide a simple mechanism for building easy-to-understand, maintainable, reusable, and succinct code. In addition, the composition of functions with no side effects keeps the code pure, which preserves the logic of parallelism. Basically, concurrent programs that are based on function composition are easier to design and less convoluted than programs that aren't.

Function composition makes it possible to construct and glue together a series of simple functions into a single massive and more complex function. Why is it important to glue code together? Imagine solving a problem in a top-down way. You start with the big problem and then deconstruct it into smaller problems, until eventually it's small enough that you can directly solve the problem. The outcome is a set of small solutions that you can then glue back together to solve the original larger problem. Composition is the glue to piece together big solutions.

Think of function composition as pipelining in the sense that the resulting value of one function supplies the first parameter to the subsequent function. There are differences:

- Pipelining executes a sequence of operations, where the input of each function is the output of the previous function.
- Function composition returns a new function that's the combination of two or more functions and isn't immediately invoked (input -> function -> output).

2.1.1 Function composition in C#

The C# language doesn't support function composition natively, which creates semantic challenges. But it's possible to introduce the functionality in a straightforward manner. Consider a simple case in C# (shown in listing 2.1) using a lambda expression to define two functions.

Listing 2.1   HOFs `grindCoffee` and `brewCoffee` to `Espresso` in C#

A higher-order function, grindCoffee, returns a Func delegate that takes CoffeeBeans as an argument and then returns CoffeeGround.

```
Func<CoffeeBeans, CoffeeGround> grindCoffee = coffeeBeans
                    => new CoffeeGround(coffeeBeans);
Func<CoffeeGround, Espresso> brewCoffee = coffeeGround
                    => new Espresso(coffeeGround);
```

A higher-order function brewCoffee returns an Espresso and takes a coffeeGround object as a parameter.

The first function, `grindCoffee`, accepts an object `coffeeBeans` as a parameter and returns an instance of a new `CoffeeGround`. The second function, `brewCoffee`, takes as a parameter a `coffeeGround` object and returns an instance of a new `Espresso`. The intent of these functions is to make an `Espresso` by combining the ingredients resulting from their evaluation. How can you combine these functions? In C#, you have the option of executing the functions consecutively, passing the result of the first function into the second one as a chain.

Listing 2.2   Composition function in C# (bad)

```
CoffeeGround coffeeGround = grindCoffee(coffeeBeans);
Espresso espresso = brewCoffee(coffeeGround);

Espresso espresso = brewCoffee(grindCoffee(coffeeBeans));
```

Shows the bad function composition that reads inside out

First, execute the function `grindCoffee`, passing the parameter `coffeeBeans`, then pass the result `coffeeGround` into the function `brewCoffee`. A second and equivalent option is to concatenate the execution of both `grindCoffee` and `brewCoffee`, which implements the basic idea of function composition. But this is a bad pattern in terms of readability because it forces you to read the code from right to left, which isn't the natural way to read English. It would be nice to read the code logically from left to right.

A better solution is to create a generic, specialized extension method that can be used to compose any two functions with one or more generic input arguments. The following listing defines a `Compose` function and refactors the previous example. (The generic arguments are in bold.)

Listing 2.3   `Compose` function in C#

```
static Func<A, C> Compose<A, B, C>(this Func<A, B> f, Func<B, C> g)
                    => (n) => g(f(n));

Func<CoffeeBeans, Espresso> makeEspresso =
    grindCoffee.Compose(brewCoffee);
Espresso espresso = makeEspresso(coffeeBeans);
```

Creates a generic extension method for any generic delegate Func<A,B>, which takes as an input argument a generic delegate Func<B,C> and returns a combined function Func<A,C>

The F# compiler has deduced that the function must use the same type for both input and output.

As shown in figure 2.1, the higher-order function `Compose` chains the functions `grind-Coffee` and `brewCoffee`, creating a new function `makeEspresso` that accepts an argument `coffeeBeans` and executes `brewCoffee (grindCoffee(coffeeBeans)`.

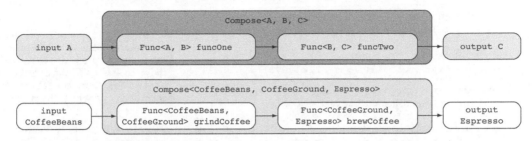

Figure 2.1   Function composition from function `Func<CoffeeBeans, CoffeeGround>` `grindCoffee` to function `Func<CoffeeGround, Espresso> brewCoffee`. Because the output of function `grindCoffee` matches the input of function `brewCoffee`, the functions can be composed in a new function that maps from input `CoffeeBeans` to output `Espresso`.

In the function body, you can easily see the line that looks precisely like the lambda expression `makeEspresso`. This extension method encapsulates the notion of composing functions. The idea is to create a function that returns the result of applying the inner function `grindCoffee` and then applying the outer function `brewCoffee` to the result. This is a common pattern in mathematics, and it would be represented by the notation `brewCoffee` of `grindCoffee`, meaning `grindCoffee` applied to `brewCoffee`. It's easy to create higher-order functions (HOFs)[1] using extension methods to raise the level of abstraction defining reusable and modular functions.

Having a compositional semantic built into the language, such as in F#, helps structure the code in a declarative nature. It's unfortunate that there's no similarly sophisticated solution in C#. In the source code for this book, you'll find a library with several overloads of the `Compose` extension methods that can provide similar useful and reusable solutions.

2.1.2   *Function composition in F#*

Function composition is natively supported in F#. In fact, the definition of the `compose` function is built into the language with the `>>` infix operator. Using this operator in F#, you can combine existing functions to build new ones.

Let's consider a simple scenario where you want to increase by 4 and multiply by 3 each element in a list. The following listing shows how to construct this function with and without the help of function composition so you can compare the two approaches.

Listing 2.4   F# support for function composition

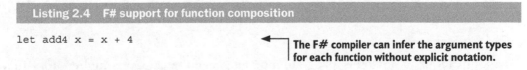

```
let add4 x = x + 4
```

The F# compiler can infer the argument types for each function without explicit notation.

---

[1]   A higher-order function (HOF) takes one or more functions as input and returns a function as its result.

```
let multiplyBy3 x = x * 3
```
◄──── The F# compiler has deduced that the function must use the same type for both input and output.

```
let list = [0..10]
```
◄──── Defines a range of numbers from 0 to 10. In F#, you can define a collection using a range indicated by integers separated by the range operator.

```
let newList = List.map(fun x ->
    multiplyBy3(add4(x))) list
```

```
let newList = list |>
    List.map(add4 >> multiplyBy3)
```
──► Applies HOF operations combining the function add4 and multiplyBy3 using function composition

◄──── In F#, you can apply HOF operations using list comprehension. The HOF map applies the same function projection to each element of the given list. In F#, the collection modules, like List, Seq, Array, and Set, take the collection argument as the last position.

The example code applies the function add4 and multiplyBy3 to each element of the list using the map, part of the List module in F#. List.map is equivalent to the Select static method in LINQ. The combination of the two functions is accomplished using a sequential semantic approach that forces the code to read unnaturally from inside out: multiplyBy3(add4(x)). The function composition style, which uses a more idiomatic F# with the >> infix operator, allows the code to read from left to right as in a textbook, and the result is much more refined, succinct, and easier to understand.

Another way to achieve function composition with simple and modular code semantics is by using a technique called closures.

2.2   *Closures to simplify functional thinking*

A *closure* aims to simplify functional thinking, and it allows the runtime to manage state, releasing extra complexity for the developer. A closure is a first-class function with free variables that are bound in the lexical environment. Behind these buzzwords hides a simple concept: closures are a more convenient way to give functions access to local state and to pass data into background operations. They are special functions that carry an implicit binding to all the nonlocal variables (also called *free variables* or *up-values*) referenced. Moreover, a closure allows a function to access one or more nonlocal variables even when invoked outside its immediate lexical scope, and the body of this special function can transport these *free variables* as a single entity, defined in its enclosing scope. More importantly, a closure encapsulates behavior and passes it around like any other object, granting access to the context in which the closure was created, reading, and updating these values.

> ### Free variables and closures
>
> The notion of a *free variable* refers to a variable referenced in a function that has neither the local variables nor the parameters of that function. The purpose of closures is to make these variables available when the function is executed, even if the original variables have gone out of scope.

In FP or in any other programming language that supports higher-order functions, without the support of closures the scope of the data could create problems and disadvantages. In the case of C# and F#, however, the compiler uses closures to increase and expand the scope of variables. Consequently, the data is accessible and visible in the current context, as shown in figure 2.2.

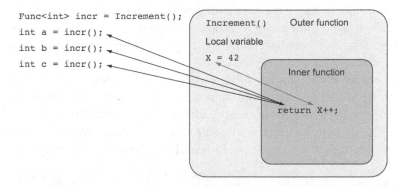

```
Func<int> incr = Increment();
int a = incr();
int b = incr();
int c = incr();
```

Figure 2.2. In this example using a closure, the local variable X, in the body of the outer function Increment, is exposed in the form of a function (Func<int>) generated by the inner function. The important thing is the return type of the function Increment, which is a function capturing the enclosed variable X, not the variable itself. Each time the function reference incr runs, the value of the captured variable X increases.

In C#, closures have been available since .NET 2.0; but the use and definition of closures is easier since the introduction of lambda expressions and the anonymous method in .NET, which make for a harmonious mixture.

This section uses C# for the code samples, though the same concepts and techniques apply to F#. This listing defines a closure using an anonymous method.

Listing 2.5   Closure defined in C# using an anonymous method

Indicates the free variable

```
string freeVariable = "I am a free variable";
Func<string, string> lambda = value => freeVariable + " " + value;
```

Shows the anonymous function referencing a free variable

In this example, the anonymous function `lambda` references a free variable `freeVariable` that's in its enclosing scope. The closure gives the function access to its surrounding state (in this case, `freeVariable`), providing clearer and more readable code. Replicating the same functionality without a closure probably means creating a class that you want the function to use (and that knows about the local variable), and passing that class as an argument. Here, the closure helps the runtime to manage state, avoiding the extra and unnecessary boilerplate of creating fields to manage state. This is one of the benefits of a closure: it can be used as a portable execution mechanism for passing extra context into HOFs. Not surprisingly, closures are often used in combination with LINQ. You should consider closures as a positive side effect of lambda expressions and a great programming trick for your toolbox.

2.2.1 *Captured variables in closures with lambda expressions*

The power of closures emerges when the same variable can be used even when it would have gone out of scope. Because the variable has been captured, it isn't garbage collected. The advantage of using closures is that you can have a method-level variable, which is generally used to implement techniques for memory caching to improve computational performance. These functional techniques of *memoization* and *functional precomputation* are discussed later in this chapter.

Listing 2.6 uses an event programming model (EPM) to download an image that asynchronously illustrates how captured variables work with closures. When the download completes, the process continues updating a client application UI. The implementation uses an asynchronous semantic API call. When the request completes, the registered event `DownloadDataCompleted` fires and executes the remaining logic.

> **Listing 2.6   Event register with a lambda expression capturing a local variable**

```
void UpdateImage(string url)
{                                                        Captures an instance of the
    System.Windows.Controls.Image image = img;           local image control into
                                                         the variable image

    var client = new WebClient();                        Registers the event
    client.DownloadDataCompleted += (o, e) =>            DownloadDataCompleted using
    {                                                    an inline lambda expression
        if (image != null)
            using (var ms = new MemoryStream(e.Result))
            {
                var imageConverter = new ImageSourceConverter();
                image.Source = (ImageSource)
                imageConverter.ConvertFrom(ms);
            }
    };                                                   Starts DownloadDataAsync
    client.DownloadDataAsync(new Uri(url));              asynchronously
}
```

First, you get a reference of the image control named `img`. Then you use a lambda expression to register the handler callback for the event `DownloadDataCompleted` to process when `DownloadDataAsync` completes. Inside the lambda block, the code can access the state from out of scope directly due to closures. This access allows you to check the state of the image pointer, and, if it isn't `null`, update the UI.

This is a fairly straightforward process, but the timeline flow adds interesting behavior. The method is asynchronous, so by the time data has returned from the service and the callback updates the `image`, the method is already complete.

If the method completes, should the local variable `image` be out of scope? How is the image updated then? The answer is called a *captured variable*. The lambda expression captures the local variable `image`, which consequently stays in scope even though normally it would be released. From this example, you should consider captured variables as a snapshot of the values of the variables at the time the closure was created. If you built the same process without this captured variable, you'd need a class-level variable to hold the image value.

NOTE The variable captured by the lambda expression contains the value at the time of evaluation, not the time of capture. Instance and static variables may be used and changed without restriction in the body of a lambda.

To prove this, let's analyze what happens if we add a line of code at the end of listing 2.6, changing the image reference to a `null` pointer (in bold).

Listing 2.7 Proving the time of captured variable evaluation

```
void UpdateImage(string url)
{
    System.Windows.Controls.Image image = img;

    var client = new WebClient();
    client.DownloadDataCompleted += (o, e) =>
    {
        if (image != null) {
            using (var ms = new MemoryStream(e.Result))
            {
                var imageConverter = new ImageSourceConverter();
                image.Source = (ImageSource)
                    imageConverter.ConvertFrom(ms);
            }
        }
    };
    client.DownloadDataAsync(new Uri(url));

    image = null;
}
```

> **Variable image is nulled; consequently, it will be disposed when out of scope. This method completes before the callback executes because the asynchronous function DownloadDataAsync doesn't block, provoking unwanted behavior.**

By running the program with the applied changes, the image in the UI won't update because the pointer is set to `null` before executing the lambda expression body. Even though the image had a value at the time it was captured, it's null at the time the code is executed. The lifetime of captured variables is extended until all the closures referencing the variables become eligible for garbage collection.

In F#, the concept of `null` objects doesn't exist, so it isn't possible to run such undesirable scenarios.

2.2.2 Closures in a multithreading environment

Let's analyze a use case scenario where you use closures to provide data to a task that often runs in a different thread than the main one. In FP, closures are commonly used to manage mutable state to limit and isolate the scope of mutable structures, allowing thread-safe access. This fits well in a multithreading environment.

In listing 2.8, a lambda expression invokes the method `Console.WriteLine` from a new `Task` of the TPL (`System.Threading.Tasks.Task`). When this task starts, the lambda expression constructs a closure that encloses the local variable `iteration`, which is passed as an argument to the method that runs in another thread. In this case, the compiler is automatically generating an anonymous class with this variable as an exposed property.

Listing 2.8   Closure capturing variables in a multithreaded environment

```
for (int iteration = 1; iteration < 10; iteration++)
{
    Task.Factory.StartNew(() => Console.WriteLine("{0} - {1}",
➡ Thread.CurrentThread.ManagedThreadId, iteration));
}
```

Closures can lead to strange behaviors. In theory, this program should work: you expect the program to print the numbers 1 to 10. But in practice, this isn't the case; the program will print the number 10 ten times, because you're using the same variable in several lambda expressions, and these anonymous functions share the variable value.

Let's analyze another example. In this listing, you pass data into two different threads using lambda expressions.

Listing 2.9   Strange behavior using closures in multithreaded code

```
Action<int> displayNumber = n => Console.WriteLine(n);
int i = 5;
Task taskOne =  Task.Factory.StartNew(() => displayNumber(i));
i = 7;
Task taskTwo =  Task.Factory.StartNew(() => displayNumber(i));

Task.WaitAll(taskOne, taskTwo);
```

Even if the first lambda expression captures the variable i before its value changes, both threads will print the number 7 because the variable i is changed before both threads start. The reason for this subtle problem is the mutable nature of C#. When a closure captures a mutable variable by a lambda expression, the lambda captures the reference of the variable instead of the current value of that variable. Consequently, if a task runs after the referenced value of the variable is changed, the value will be the latest in memory rather than the one at the time the variable was captured.

This is a reason to adopt other solutions instead of manually coding the parallel loop. `Parallel.For` from the TPL solves this bug. One possible solution in C# is to create and capture a new temporary variable for each `Task`. That way, the declaration of the new variable is allocated in a new heap location, conserving the original value. This same sophisticated and ingenious behavior doesn't apply in functional languages. Let's look at a similar scenario using F#.

Listing 2.10   Closures capturing variables in a multithreaded environment in F#

```
let tasks = Array.zeroCreate<Task> 10

for index = 1 to 10 do
    tasks.[index - 1] <- Task.Factory.StartNew(fun () ->
➡ Console.WriteLine index)
```

Running this version of the code, the result is as expected: the program prints the numbers 1 to 10. The explanation is that F# handles its procedural for loop differently than does C#. Instead of using a mutable variable and updating its value during each iteration, the F# compiler creates a new immutable value for every iteration with a different location in memory. The outcome of this functional behavior of preferring immutable types is that the lambda captures a reference to an immutable value that never changes.

Multithreading environments commonly use closures because of the simplicity of capturing and passing variables in different contexts that require extra thinking. The following listing illustrates how the .NET TPL library can use closures to execute multiple threads using the `Parallel.Invoke` API.

Listing 2.11   Closures capturing variables in a multithreaded environment

```
public void ProcessImage(Bitmap image) {
    byte[] array = image.ToByteArray(ImageFormat.Bmp);      Shows the functions
    Parallel.Invoke(                                        that convert an image
        () => ProcessArray(array, 0, array.Length / 2),     to byte array format
        () => ProcessArray(array, array.Length / 2, array.Length));
}
                                               Shows the functions to process in
                                               parallel the byte array split in half
```

In the example, `Parallel.Invoke` spawns two independent tasks, each running the `ProcessArray` method against a portion of the `array` whose variable is captured and enclosed by the lambda expressions.

> **TIP** Keep in mind that the compiler handles closures by allocating an object underneath that encapsulates the function and its environment. Therefore, closures are heavier in terms of memory allocations than regular functions, and invoking them is slower.

In the context of task parallelism, be aware of variables captured in closures: because closures capture the reference of a variable, not its actual value, you can end up sharing what isn't obvious. Closures are a powerful technique that you can use to implement patterns to increase the performance of your program.

2.3   *Memoization-caching technique for program speedup*

Memoization, also known as *tabling*, is an FP technique that aims to increase the performance of an application. The program speedup is achieved by caching the results of a function, and avoiding unnecessary extra computational overhead that originates from repeating the same computations. This is possible because memoization bypasses the execution of expensive function calls by storing the result of prior computations with the identical arguments (as shown in figure 2.3) for retrieval when the arguments are presented again. A memoized function keeps in memory the result of a computation so it can be returned immediately in future calls.

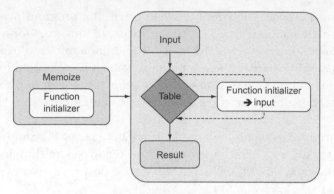

Figure 2.3   Memoization is a technique to cache values for a function, ensuring a run of only one evaluation. When an input value is passed into a memoized function, the internal table storage verifies if an associated result exists for this input to return immediately. Otherwise, the function initializer runs the computation, and then it updates the internal table storage and returns the result. The next time the same input value is passed into the memoized function, the table storage contains the associated result and the computation is skipped.

This concept may sound complex at first, but it's a simple technique once applied. Memoization uses closures to facilitate the conversion of a function into a data structure that facilitates access to a local variable. A closure is used as a wrapper for each call to a memoized function. The purpose of this local variable, usually a lookup table, is to store the results of the internal function as a value and to use the arguments passed into this function as a key reference.

The memoization technique fits well in a multithreaded environment, providing an enormous performance boost. The main benefit arises when a function is repeatedly applied to the same arguments; but, running the function is more expensive in terms of CPU computation than accessing the corresponding data structure. To apply a color filter to an image, for example, it's a good idea to run multiple threads in parallel. Each thread accesses a portion of the image and modifies the pixels in context. But it's possible that the filter color is applied to a set of pixels having identical values. In this case, if the computation will get the same result, why should it be re-evaluated? Instead, the result can be cached using memoization, and the threads can skip unnecessary work and finish the image processing more quickly.

> **Cache**
>
> A *cache* is a component that stores data so future requests for that data can be served faster; the data stored in a cache might be the result of an earlier computation or a duplicate of data stored elsewhere.

The following listing shows a basic implementation of a memoized function in C#.

Listing 2.12   Simple example that clarifies how memoization works

Lists an instance of a mutable collection dictionary to store and look up values

```
static Func<T, R> Memoize<T, R>(Func<T, R> func)
where T : IComparable
{
    Dictionary<T, R> cache = new Dictionary<T, R>();

    return arg => {

        if (cache.ContainsKey(arg))

            return cache[arg];

        return (cache[arg] = func(arg));
            };
}
```

Shows the generic Memoize function, which requires the generic type of T to be comparable because this value is used for lookups

Uses a lambda expression that captures the local table with a closure

Verifies that the value arg has been computed and stored in the cache

If the key passed as an argument exists in the table, then the value associated is returned as the result.

If the key doesn't exist, then the value is computed, stored in the table, and returned as the result.

First, you define the `Memoize` function, which internally uses the generic collection `Dictionary` as a table variable for caching. A closure captures the local variable so it can be accessed from both the delegate pointing to the closure and the outer function. When the HOF is called, it first tries to match the input to the function to validate whether the parameter has already been cached. If the parameter key exists, the cache table returns the result. If the parameter key doesn't exist, the first step is to evaluate the function with the parameter, add the parameter and the relative result to the cache table, and ultimately return the result. It's important to mention that memoization is an HOF because it takes a function as input and returns a function as output.

> **TIP** Dictionary lookups occur in constant time, but the hash function used by the dictionary can be slow to execute in certain circumstances. This is the case with strings, where the time it takes to hash a string is proportional to its length. Unmemoized functions perform better than the memoized ones in certain scenarios. I recommend profiling the code to decide if the optimization is needed and whether memoization improves performance.

This is the equivalent `memoize` function implemented in F#.

Listing 2.13   `memoize` function in F#

```
let memoize func =
    let table = Dictionary<_,_>()
    fun x ->   if table.ContainsKey(x) then table.[x]
            else
                let result = func x
                table.[x] <- result
                result
```

This is a simple example using the previously defined `memoize` function. In listing 2.14, the `Greeting` function returns a string with a welcoming message for the name passed as an argument. The message also includes the time when the function is called, which is used to keep track of time when the function runs. The code applies a two-second delay between each call for demonstration purposes.

Listing 2.14   Greeting example in C#

```
public static string Greeting(string name)
{
     return $"Warm greetings {name}, the time is
➡ {DateTime.Now.ToString("hh:mm:ss")}";
}

Console.WriteLine(Greeting ("Richard"));
System.Threading.Thread.Sleep(2000);
Console.WriteLine(Greeting ("Paul"));
System.Threading.Thread.Sleep(2000);
Console.WriteLine(Greeting ("Richard"));

// output
Warm greetings Richard, the time is 10:55:34
Warm greetings Paul, the time is 10:55:36
Warm greetings Richard, the time is 10:55:38
```

Next, the code re-executes the same messages but uses a memoized version of the function `Greeting`.

Listing 2.15   Greeting example using a memoized function

```
var greetingMemoize = Memoize<string, string>(Greeting);

Console.WriteLine(greetingMemoize ("Richard"));
System.Threading.Thread.Sleep(2000);
Console.WriteLine(greetingMemoize ("Paul"));
System.Threading.Thread.Sleep(2000);
Console.WriteLine(greetingMemoize("Richard"));

// output
Warm greetings Richard, the time is 10:57:21
Warm greetings Paul, the time is 10:57:23
Warm greetings Richard, the time is 10:57:21
```

Memoize is an HOF, so you pass a function as an argument that constrains the signature of the former function. In this way, the memoized function can replace the original one, injecting caching functionality.

The time of the Greeting function is the same because the computation happens only once and then the result is memoized.

The output indicates that the first two calls happened at different times as anticipated. But what happens in a third call? Why does the third function call return the message with the exact same time as the first one? The answer is memoization.

The first and third function `greetingMemoize("Richard")` calls have the same arguments, and their results have been cached only once during the initial call by the function `greetingMemoize`. The result from the third function call isn't the effect of its execution, but is the stored result of the function with the same argument, and consequently the time matches.

This is how memoization works. The memoized function's job is to look up the argument passed in an internal table. If it finds the input value, it returns the previously computed result. Otherwise, the function stores the result in the table.

2.4 Memoize in action for a fast web crawler

Now, you'll implement a more interesting example using what you learned in the previous section. For this example, you'll build a web crawler that extracts and prints into the console the page title of each website visited. Listing 2.16 runs the code without memoization. Then you'll re-execute the same program using the memoization technique and compare the outcome. Ultimately, you'll download multiple websites' contents, combining parallel execution and memoization.

Listing 2.16   Web crawler in C#

```
public static IEnumerable<string> WebCrawler(string url) {       Shows the function that
        string content = GetWebContent(url);                     recursively fetches and
        yield return content;                                    analyzes the content of a
                                                                 website and sub-websites
        foreach (string item in AnalyzeHtmlContent(content))
        yield return GetWebContent(item);
}
                                                            Downloads the content of
                                                            a website in string format
static string GetWebContent(string url) {
        using (var wc = new WebClient())
            return wc.DownloadString(new Uri(url));
}
                                                          Extracts sub-links from
                                                          the content of a website
static readonly Regex regexLink =
        new Regex(@"(?<=href=('|""))https?://.*?(?=\1)");

static IEnumerable<string> AnalyzeHtmlContent(string text) {
        foreach (var url in regexLink.Matches(text))
                yield return url.ToString();
}

static readonly Regex regexTitle =
        new Regex("<title>(?<title>.*?)<\\/title>", RegexOptions.Compiled);

static string ExtractWebPageTitle(string textPage) {     Extracts the page title of a website
        if (regexTitle.IsMatch(textPage))
                return regexTitle.Match(textPage).Groups["title"].Value;
        return "No Page Title Found!";
}
```

The `WebCrawler` function downloads the content of the web page URL passed as an argument by calling the method `GetWebContent`. Next, it analyzes the content downloaded and extracts the hyperlinks contained in the web page, which are sent back to the initial function to be processed, repeating the operations for each of the hyperlinks. Here is the web crawler in action.

Listing 2.17   Web crawler execution

```
List<string> urls = new List<string> {       Initializes a website list to analyze
    @"http://www.google.com",
    @"http://www.microsoft.com",
```

```
            @"http://www.bing.com",
            @"http://www.google.com"
};
```

> Uses a LINQ expression to analyze the websites from the URL collection

```
var webPageTitles = from url in urls
                    from pageContent in WebCrawler(url)
                    select ExtractWebPageTitle(pageContent);

foreach (var webPageTitle in webPageTitles)
    Console.WriteLine(webPageTitle);

// OUTPUT
Starting Web Crawler for http://www.google.com...
Google
Google Images
  ...
Web Crawler completed for http://www.google.com in 5759ms
Starting Web Crawler for http://www.microsoft.com...
Microsoft Corporation
Microsoft - Official Home Page
Web Crawler completed for http://www.microsoft.com in 412ms
Starting Web Crawler for http://www.bing.com...
Bing
Msn
...
Web Crawler completed for http://www.bing.com in 6203ms
Starting Web Crawler for http://www.google.com...
Google
Google Images
...
Web Crawler completed for http://www.google.com in 5814ms
```

You're using LINQ (Language Integrated Query) to run the web crawler against a collection of given URLs. When the query expression is materialized during the foreach loop, the function ExtractWebPageTitle extracts the page title from each page's content and prints it to the console. Because of the cross-network nature of the operation, the function GetWebContent requires time to complete the download. One problem with the previous code implementation is the existence of duplicate hyperlinks. It's common that web pages have duplicate hyperlinks, which in this example cause redundant and unnecessary downloads. A better solution is to memoize the function WebCrawler.

> Listing 2.18 **Web crawler execution using memoization**

> Memoized version of the function WebCrawler

```
static Func<string, IEnumerable<string>> WebCrawlerMemoized =
➥Memoize<string, IEnumerable<string>>(WebCrawler);

var webPageTitles = from url in urls
                    from pageContent in WebCrawlerMemoized(url)
                    select ExtractWebPageTitle(pageContent);
```

> Uses a LINQ expression in combination with the memoize function to analyze the websites

```
foreach (var webPageTitle in webPageTitles)
            Console.WriteLine(webPageTitle);

// OUTPUT
Starting Web Crawler for http://www.google.com...
Google
Google Images
 ...
Web Crawler completed for http://www.google.com in 5801ms
Starting Web Crawler for http://www.microsoft.com...
Microsoft Corporation
Microsoft - Official Home Page
Web Crawler completed for http://www.microsoft.com in 4398ms
Starting Web Crawler for http://www.bing.com...
Bing
Msn
...
Web Crawler completed for http://www.bing.com in 6171ms
Starting Web Crawler for http://www.google.com...
Google
Google Images
...
Web Crawler completed for http://www.google.com in 02ms
```

In this example, you implemented the HOF `WebCrawlerMemoized`, which is the memoized version of the function `WebCrawler`. The output confirms that the memoized version of the code runs faster. In fact, to extract the content a second time from the web page www.google.com took only 2 ms, as opposed to more than 5 seconds without memoization.

A further improvement should involve downloading the web pages in parallel. Fortunately, because you used LINQ to process the query, only a marginal code change is required to use multiple threads. Since the advent of the .NET 4.0 framework, LINQ has an extension method `AsParallel()` to enable a parallel version of LINQ (or PLINQ). The nature of PLINQ is to deal with data parallelism; both topics will be covered in chapter 4.

LINQ and PLINQ are technologies designed and implemented using functional programming concepts, with special attention to emphasizing a declarative programming style. This is achievable because the functional paradigm tends to raise the level of abstraction in comparison with other program paradigms. Abstraction consents to write code without the need to know the implementation details of the underlying library, as shown here.

Listing 2.19   Web crawler query using PLINQ

```
var webPageTitles = from url in urls.AsParallel()
            from pageContent in WebCrawlerMemoized(url)
            select ExtractWebPageTitle(pageContent);
```

◄── **Implements an extension method that enables LINQ to use multiple threads to process the query**

PLINQ is easy to use and can give you substantial performance benefits. Although we only showed one method, the AsParallel extension method, there's more to it than that.

Before running the program, you have one more refactoring to apply—caches. Because they must be accessible by all threads, caches tend to be static. With the introduction of parallelism, it's possible for multiple threads to simultaneously access the memoize function, causing a race-condition problem due to the underlying mutable data structure exposed. The race-condition problem is discussed in the previous chapter. Fortunately, this is an easy fix, as shown in this listing.

Listing 2.20   Thread-safe memoization function

```
public Func<T, R> MemoizeThreadSafe<T, R>(Func<T, R> func)
                                          where T : IComparable
{
  ConcurrentDictionary<T, R> cache = new ConcurrentDictionary<T, R>();     ◄─┐
  return arg => cache.GetOrAdd(arg, a => func(a));
}
```

> Shows thread-safe memoization using the
> Concurrent collection ConcurrentDictionary

```
public Func<string, IEnumerable<string>> WebCrawlerMemoizedThreadSafe =
           MemoizeThreadSafe<string, IEnumerable<string>>(WebCrawler);

var webPageTitles =
           from url in urls.AsParallel()
           from pageContent in WebCrawlerMemoizedThreadSafe(url)
           select ExtractWebPageTitle(pageContent);
```

Uses a PLINQ expression to analyze the websites in parallel

The quick answer is to replace the current Dictionary collection with the equivalent thread-safe version ConcurrentDictionary. This refactoring interestingly requires less code. Next, you implement a thread-safe memoized version of the function GetWeb-Content, which is used for the LINQ expression. Now you can run the web crawler in parallel. To process the pages from the example, a dual-core machine can complete the analysis in less than 7 seconds, compared to the 18 seconds of the initial implementation. The upgraded code, besides running faster, also reduces the network I/O operations.

2.5   *Lazy memoization for better performance*

In the previous example, the web crawler allows multiple concurrent threads to access the memoized function with minimum overhead. But it doesn't enforce the function initializer func(a) from being executed multiple times for the same value, while evaluating the expression. This might appear to be a small issue, but in highly concurrent applications, the occurrences multiply (in particular, if the object initialization is expensive). The solution is to add an object to the cache that isn't initialized, but rather a function that initializes the item on demand. You can wrap the result value from the function initializer into a Lazy type (as highlighted with bold in listing 2.21). The listing shows the memoization solution, which represents a perfect design in terms of thread safety and performance, while avoiding duplicate cache item initialization.

Listing 2.21 Thread-safe memoization function with safe lazy evaluation

```
static Func<T, R> MemoizeLazyThreadSafe<T, R>(Func<T, R> func)
where T : IComparable
{
    ConcurrentDictionary<T, Lazy<R>> cache =
 ➡ new ConcurrentDictionary<T, Lazy<R>>();
    return arg => cache.GetOrAdd(arg, a =>
 ➡ new Lazy<R>(() => func(a))).Value;
}
```

> Uses thread-safe and lazy-evaluated memoization

According to the Microsoft documentation, the method GetOrAdd doesn't prevent the function func from being called more than once for the same given argument, but it does guarantee that the result of only one "evaluation of the function" is added to the collection. There could be multiple threads checking the cache concurrently before the cached value is added, for example. Also, there's no way to enforce the function func(a) to be thread safe. Without this guarantee, it's possible that in a multithreaded environment, multiple threads could access the same function simultaneously—meaning func(a) should also be thread safe itself. The solution proposed, avoiding primitive locks, is to use the Lazy<T> construct in .NET 4.0. This solution gives you the guarantee of full thread safety, regardless of the implementation of the function func, and ensures a single evaluation of the function.

2.5.1 Gotchas for function memoization

The implementations of memoization introduced in the previous code examples are a somewhat naive approach. The solution of storing data in a simple dictionary works, but it isn't a long-term solution. A dictionary is unbounded; consequently, the items are never removed from memory but only added, which can, at some point, lead to memory leak issues. Solutions exist to all these problems. One option is to implement a memoize function that uses a WeakReference type to store the result values, which permits the results to be collected when the garbage collector (GC) runs. Since the introduction of the collection ConditionalWeakDictionary with the .NET 4.0 framework, this implementation is simple: a dictionary takes as a key a type instance that's held as a *weak reference*. The associated values are kept as long as the key lives. When the key is reclaimed by the GC to be collocated, the reference to the data is removed, making it available for collection.

Weak references are a valuable mechanism for handling references to managed objects. The typical object reference (also known as a strong reference) has a deterministic behavior, where as long as you have a reference to the object, the GC won't collect the object that consequently stays alive. But in certain scenarios, you want to keep an invisible string attached to an object without interfering with the GC's ability to reclaim that object's memory. If the GC reclaimed the memory, your string becomes unattached and you can detect this. If the GC hasn't touched the object yet, you can pull the string and retrieve a strong reference to the object to use it again. This facility is useful for automatically managing a cache that can keep weak references to the least recently used objects without preventing them from being collected and inevitably optimizing the memory resources.

An alternative option is to use a cache-expiration policy by storing a timestamp with each result, indicating the time when the item is persisted. In this case, you have to define a constant time to invalidate the items. When the time expires, the item is removed from the collection. The downloadable source code for this book holds both of these implementations.

> **TIP** It's good practice to consider memoization only when the cost to evaluate a result is higher than the cost to store all the results computed during runtime. Before making the final decision, benchmark your code with and without memoization, using a varying range of values.

2.6 *Effective concurrent speculation to amortize the cost of expensive computations*

Speculative Processing (precomputation) is a good reason to exploit concurrency. Speculative Processing is an FP pattern in which computations are performed before the actual algorithm runs, and as soon as all the inputs of the function are available. The idea behind concurrent speculation is to amortize the cost of expensive computation and improve the performance and responsiveness of a program. This technique is easily applicable in parallel computing, where multicore hardware can be used to precompute multiple operations spawning a concurrently running task and have the data ready to read without delay.

Let's say you're given a long list of input words, and you want to compute a function that finds the best fuzzy match[2] of a word in the list. For the fuzzy-match algorithm, you're going to apply the *Jaro-Winkler distance*, which measures the similarity between two strings. We're not going to cover the implementation of this algorithm here. You can find the complete implementation in the online source code.

Jaro-Winkler algorithm

The *Jaro-Winkler distance* is a measure of similarity between two strings. The higher the Jaro-Winkler distance, the more similar the strings. The metric is best suited for short strings, such as proper names. The score is normalized so that 0 equates to no similarity and 1 is an exact match.

This listing shows the implementation of the fuzzy-match function using the Jaro-Winkler algorithm (highlighted in bold).

Listing 2.22   Implementing a fuzzy match in C#

```
public static string FuzzyMatch(List<string> words, string word)
{
```

---

[2]   Fuzzy matching is a technique of finding segments of text and corresponding matches that may be less than 100% perfect.

```
        var wordSet = new HashSet<string>(words);

        string bestMatch =
            (from w in wordSet.AsParallel()
                select JaroWinklerModule.Match(w, word))
                .OrderByDescending(w => w.Distance)
                .Select(w => w.Word)
                .FirstOrDefault();
        return bestMatch;
    }
```

◄─── **Uses PLINQ to run in parallel the best match algorithm**

◄─── **Returns the best match**

Removes possible word duplicates by creating a HashSet collection from the word list. HashSet is an efficient data structure for lookups.

The function `FuzzyMatch` uses PLINQ to compute in parallel the fuzzy match for the word passed as an argument against another array of strings. The result is a `HashSet` collection of matches, which is then ordered by best match to return the first value from the list. `HashSet` is an efficient data structure for lookups.

The logic is similar to a lookup. Because `List<string>` words could contain duplicates, the function first instantiates a data structure that's more efficient. Then the function utilizes this data structure to run the actual fuzzy match. This implementation isn't efficient, as the design issue is evident: `FuzzyMatch` is applied each time it's called to both of its arguments. The internal table structure is rebuilt every time `FuzzyMatch` is executed, wasting any positive effect.

How can you improve this efficiency? By applying a combination of a partial function application or a partial application and the memoization technique from FP, you can achieve precomputation. For more details about partial application, see appendix A. The concept of precomputation is closely related to memoization, which in this case uses a table containing pre-calculated values. The next listing shows the implementation of a faster fuzzy-match function (as highlighted in bold).

> **Listing 2.23   Fast fuzzy match using precomputation**

A partial applied function takes only one parameter and returns a new function that performs a clever lookup.

```
static Func<string, string> PartialFuzzyMatch(List<string> words)
{
    var wordSet = new HashSet<string>(words);

    return word =>
        (from w in wordSet.AsParallel()
            select JaroWinklerModule.Match(w, word))
            .OrderByDescending(w => w.Distance)
            .Select(w => w.Word)
            .FirstOrDefault();
}

Func<string, string> fastFuzzyMatch =
    PartialFuzzyMatch(words);

string magicFuzzyMatch = fastFuzzyMatch("magic");
string lightFuzzyMatch = fastFuzzyMatch("light");
```

◄─── **Efficient lookup data structure is kept in a closure after instantiation and is used by the lambda expression.**

◄─── **New function that uses the same lookup data for each call, reducing repetitive computation**

◄─── **Shows the function that precomputes the List<string> words passed and returns a function that takes the word argument**

Uses the fastFuzzyMatch function

First, you create a partial applied version of the function `PartialFuzzyMatch`. This new function takes as an argument only `List<string>` words and returns a new function that handles the second argument. This is a clever strategy because it consumes the first argument as soon as it's passed, by precomputing the efficient lookup structure.

Interestingly, the compiler uses a closure to store the data structure, which is accessible through the lambda expression returned from the function. A lambda expression is an especially handy way to provide a function with a precomputed state. Then, you can define the `fastFuzzyMatch` function by supplying the argument `List<string>` words, which is used to prepare an underlying lookup table, resulting in faster computation. After supplying `List<string>` words, `fastFuzzyMatch` returns a function that takes the string `word` argument, but immediately computes the `HashSet` for the lookup.

> **NOTE** The function `fuzzyMatch` in listing 2.22 is compiled as a static function that constructs a set of strings on every call. Instead, `fastFuzzyMatch` in listing 2.23 is compiled as a static read-only property, where the value is initialized in a static constructor. This is a fine difference, but it has a massive effect on code performance.

With these changes, the processing time is reduced by half when performing the fuzzy match against the strings *magic* and *light*, compared to the one that calculates these values as needed.

2.6.1 Precomputation with natural functional support

Now let's look at the same fuzzy-match implementation using the functional language F#. Listing 2.24 shows a slightly different implementation due to the intrinsic functional semantic of F# (the `AsParallel` method is highlighted in bold).

Listing 2.24   Implementing a fast fuzzy match in F#

Creates an efficient lookup data structure
HashSet that also removes duplicate words

In F#, all the functions are curried as a default: the signature of the FuzzyMatch function is (string set -> string -> string), which implies that it can be directly partially applied. In this case, by supplying only the first argument, wordSet, you create the partial applied function partialFuzzyMatch.

```
let fuzzyMatch (words:string list) =
    let wordSet = new HashSet<string>(words)
    let partialFuzzyMatch word =
        query { for w in wordSet.AsParallel() do
                    select (JaroWinkler.getMatch w word) }
        |> Seq.sortBy(fun x -> -x.Distance)
        |> Seq.head

    fun word -> partialFuzzyMatch word

let fastFuzzyMatch = fuzzyMatch words

let magicFuzzyMatch = fastFuzzyMatch "magic"
let lightFuzzyMatch = fastFuzzyMatch "light""
```

Returns a function that uses a lambda expression to "closure over" and exposes the internal HashSet

Uses the fastFuzzyMatch function

Applies the precomputation technique by supplying the first argument to the function fuzzyMatch, which immediately computes the HashSet with the values passed

The implementation of `fuzzyMatch` forces the F# runtime to generate the internal set of strings on each call. In opposition, the partial applied function `fastFuzzyMatch` initializes the internal set only once and reuses it for all the subsequent calls. Precomputation is a caching technique that performs an initial computation to create, in this case, a `HashSet<string>` ready to be accessed.

The F# implementation uses a query expression to query and transform the data. This approach lets you use PLINQ as in the equivalent C# in listing 2.23. But in F# there's a more functional style to parallelize operations on sequences—adopting the parallel sequence (`PSeq`). Using this module, the function `fuzzyMatch` can be rewritten in a compositional form:

```
let fuzzyMatch (words:string list) =
    let wordSet = new HashSet<string>(words)
    fun word ->
        wordSet
        |> PSeq.map(fun w -> JaroWinkler.getMatch w word)
        |> PSeq.sortBy(fun x -> -x.Distance)
        |> Seq.head
```

The code implementations of `fuzzyMatch` in C# and F# are equivalent, but the former functional language is curried as a default. This makes it easier to refactor using partial application. The F# parallel sequence `PSeq` used in the previous code snippet is covered in chapter 5.

It's clearer by looking at the `fuzzyMatch` signature type:

```
string set -> (string -> string)
```

The signature reads as a function that takes a string set as an argument, returns a function that takes a string as an argument, and then returns a string as a return type. This chain of functions lets you utilize the partial application strategy without thinking about it.

2.6.2 Let the best computation win

Another example of speculative evaluation is inspired by the unambiguous choice operator,[3] created by Conal Elliott (http://conal.net) for his functional reactive programming (FRP) implementation (http://conal.net/papers/push-pull-frp). The idea behind this operator is simple: it's a function that takes two arguments and concurrently evaluates them, returning the first result available.

This concept can be extended to more than two parallel functions. Imagine that you're using multiple weather services to check the temperature in a city. You can simultaneously spawn separate tasks to query each service, and after the fastest task returns, you don't need to wait for the other to complete. The function waits for the fastest task to come back and cancels the remaining tasks. The following listing shows a simple implementation without support for error handling.

---

[3] Conal Elliott, "Functional Concurrency with Unambiguous Choice," November 21, 2008, http://mng.bz/4mKK.

Listing 2.25   Implementing the fastest weather task

```
public Temperature SpeculativeTempCityQuery(string city,
    params Uri[] weatherServices)
{
    var cts = new CancellationTokenSource();
    var tasks =
    (from uri in weatherServices
        select Task.Factory.StartNew<Temperature>(() =>
            queryService(uri, city), cts.Token)).ToArray();

    int taskIndex = Task.WaitAny(tasks);
    Temperature tempCity = tasks[taskIndex].Result;
    cts.Cancel();
    return tempCity;
}
```

Uses a cancellation token to cancel a task when the fastest completes

Waits for the fastest task to come back

Cancels remaining slower tasks

Uses LINQ to spawn in parallel one task for each weather service

Precomputation is a crucial technique for implementing any kind of function and service, from simple to complex and more advanced computation engines. Speculative evaluation aims to consume CPU resources that would otherwise sit idle. This is a convenient technique in any program, and it can be implemented in any language that supports closure to capture and expose these partial values.

2.7   *Being lazy is a good thing*

A common problem in concurrency is having the ability to correctly initialize a shared object in a thread-safe manner. To improve the startup time of an application when the object has an expensive and time-consuming construct, this need is even more accentuated.

Lazy evaluation is a programming technique used to defer the evaluation of an expression until the last possible moment, when it's accessed. Believe it or not, laziness can lead to success—and in this case, it's an essential tool for your tool belt. Somewhat counterintuitive, the power of lazy evaluation makes a program run faster because it only provides what's required for the query result, preventing excessive computations. Imagine writing a program that executes different long-running operations, possibly analyzing large amounts of data to produce various reports. If these operations are evaluated simultaneously, the system can run into performance issues and hang. Plus, it's possible that not all of these long-running operations are immediately necessary, which provokes a waste of resources and time if they begin right away.

A better strategy is to perform long-running operations on demand and only as needed, which also reduces memory pressure in the system. In effect, lazy evaluation also leads to efficient memory management, improving performance due to lower memory consumption. Being lazy in this case is more efficient. Reducing unnecessary and expensive garbage collection cleanups in managed programming languages—such as C#, Java, and F#—makes the programs run faster.

2.7.1 Strict languages for understanding concurrent behaviors

The opposite of lazy evaluation is *eager evaluation*, also known as *strict evaluation*, which means that the expression is evaluated immediately. C# and F#, as well as the majority of other mainstream programming languages, are strict languages.

Imperative programming languages don't have an internal model for containing and controlling side effects, so it's reasonable that they're eagerly evaluated. To understand how a program executes, a language that's strictly evaluated must know the order in which side effects (such as I/O) run, making it easy to understand how the program executes. In fact, a strict language can analyze the computation and have an idea of the work that must be done.

Because both C# and F# aren't purely FP languages, there's no guarantee that every value is referentially transparent; consequently, they cannot be lazily evaluated programming languages.

In general, lazy evaluation can be difficult to mix with imperative features, which sometimes introduce side effects, such as exception and I/O operation, because the order of operations becomes non-deterministic. For more information, I recommend "Why Functional Programming Matters," by John Hughes (http://mng.bz/qp3B).

In FP, lazy evaluation and side effects cannot coexist. Despite the possibility of adding the notion of lazy evaluation in an imperative language, the combination with side effects makes the program complex. In fact, lazy evaluation forces the developer to remove the order of execution constraints and dependencies according to which parts of the program are evaluated. Writing a program with side effects can become difficult because it requires the notion of function order of execution, which reduces the opportunity for code modularity and compositionality. Functional programming aims to be explicit about side effects, to be aware of them, and to provide tools to isolate and control them. For instance, Haskell uses the functional programming language convention of identifying a function with side effects with the IO type. This Haskell function definition reads a file, causing side effects:

```
readFile :: IO ()
```

This explicit definition notifies the compiler of the presence of side effects, and the compiler then applies optimization and validation as needed.

Lazy evaluation becomes an important technique with multicore and multithreading programs. To support this technique, Microsoft introduced (with Framework 4.0) a generic type constructor called Lazy<T>, which simplifies the initialization of objects with deferred creation in a thread-safe fashion. Here's the definition of a lazy object Person.

Listing 2.26 Lazy initialization of the Person object

```
class Person    {            ←  Defines the Person class
    public readonly string FullName;        ←  Shows the read-only field for
    public Person(string firstName, string lastName)    the full name of the person
    {                                                    assigned in the constructor
        FullName = firstName + " " + lastName;
```

```
            Console.WriteLine(FullName);
    }
}
```

Initializes the lazy object Person; the return value is **Lazy<Person>**, which isn't evaluated until it's forced

```
Lazy<Person> fredFlintstone = new Lazy<Person>(() =>
    new Person("Fred", "Flintstone"), true);
```

```
Person[] freds = new Person[5];       ◄── Shows the array of five people
for(int i = 0;i < freds.Length;i++)
        freds[i] = fredFlintstone.Value;
```

The instance of the underlying lazy object is available via the **Value** property.

```
// output
Fred Flintstone
```

In the example, you define a simple `Person` class with a read-only field, which also causes `FullName` to print on the console. Then, you create a lazy initializer for this object by supplying a factory delegate into `Lazy<Person>`, which is responsible for the object instantiation. In this case, a lambda expression is convenient to use in place of the factory delegate. Figure 2.4 illustrates this.

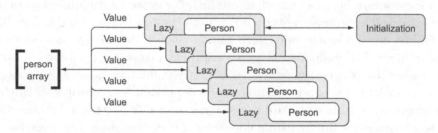

Figure 2.4. The value of the `Person` object is initialized only once, when the `Value` property is accessed the first time. Successive calls return the same cached value. If you have an array of Lazy<Person> objects, when the items of the array are accessed, only the first one is initialized. The others will reuse the cache result.

When the actual evaluation of the expression is required to use the underlying object `Person`, you access the `Value` property on the identifier, which forces the factory delegate of the `Lazy` object to be performed only one time if the value isn't materialized yet. No matter how many consecutive calls or how many threads simultaneously access the lazy initializer, they all wait for the same instance. To prove it, the listing creates an array of five `Persons`, which is initialized in the `for` loop. During each iteration, the `Person` object is retrieved by calling the identifier property `Value`, but even if it's called five times, the output (`Fred Flintstone`) is called only once.

2.7.2   *Lazy caching technique and thread-safe Singleton pattern*

Lazy evaluation in .NET is considered a caching technique because it remembers the result of the operation that has been performed, and the program can run more efficiently by avoiding repetitive and duplicate operations.

Because the execution operations are done on demand and, more importantly, only once, the `Lazy<T>` construct is the recommended mechanism to implement a Singleton pattern. The Singleton pattern creates a single instance of a given resource, which is shared within the multiple parts of your code. This resource needs to be initialized only once, the first time it's accessed, which is precisely the behavior of Lazy<T>.

You have different ways of implementing the Singleton pattern in .NET, but certain of these techniques have limitations, such as unguaranteed thread safety or lost lazy instantiation.[4] The Lazy<T> construct provides a better and simpler singleton design, which ensures true laziness and thread safety, as shown next.

Listing 2.27 A Singleton pattern using Lazy<T>

```
public sealed class Singleton
{
    private static readonly Lazy<Singleton> lazy =          Calls the Singleton
        new Lazy<Singleton>(() => new Singleton(), true);   constructor delegate

    public static Singleton Instance => lazy.Value;

    private Singleton()
    { }
}
```

The Lazy<T> primitive also takes a Boolean flag, passed after the lambda expression, as an optional argument to enable thread-safe behavior. This implements a sophisticated and light version of the Double-Check Locking pattern.

> **NOTE** In software engineering, *Double-Checked Locking* (also known as double-checked locking optimization) is a software design pattern used to reduce the overhead of acquiring a lock by first testing the locking criterion (the "lock hint") without acquiring the lock.

This property guarantees that the initialization of the object is thread safe. When the flag is enabled, which is the default mode, no matter how many threads call the Singleton LazyInitializer, all the threads receive the same instance, which is cached after the first call. This is a great advantage, without which you'd be forced to manually guard and ensure the thread safety for the shared field.

It's important to emphasize that if the lazy-evaluated object implementation is thread-safe, that doesn't automatically mean that all its properties are thread safe as well.

LazyInitializer

In .NET, LazyInitializer is an alternative static class that works like Lazy<T>, but with optimized initialization performance and more convenient access. In fact, there's no need for the new object initialization to create a Lazy type due to the exposure of its functionality through a static method. Here's a simple example showing how to lazily initialize a big image using LazyInitializer:

```
private BigImage bigImage;
public BigImage BigImage =>
    LazyInitializer.EnsureInitialized(ref bigImage, () => new
BigImage());
```

---

[4] See "Implementing Singleton in C#," MSDN, http://mng.bz/pLf4.

2.7.3   *Lazy support in F#*

F# supports the same Lazy<T> type with the addition of lazy computation, which is of type Lazy<T>, where the actual generic type that is used for T is determined from the result of the expression. The F# standard library automatically enforces mutual exclusion, so that pure function code is thread safe when simultaneously forcing the same lazy value from separate threads. The F# use of the Lazy type is a little different from C#, where you wrap the function around a Lazy data type. This code example shows the F# Lazy computation of a Person object:

```
let barneyRubble = lazy( Person("barney", "rubble") )
printfn "%s" (barneyRubble.Force().FullName)
```

The function barneyRubble creates an instance of Lazy<Person>, for which the value isn't yet materialized. Then, to force the computation, you call the method Force that retrieves the value on demand.

2.7.4   *Lazy and Task, a powerful combination*

For performance and scalability reasons, in a concurrent application it's useful to combine a lazy evaluation that can be executed on demand using an independent thread. The Lazy initializer Lazy<T> can be utilized to implement a useful pattern to instantiate objects that require asynchronous operations. Let's consider the class Person that was used in the previous section. If the first and second name fields are loaded from a database, you can apply a type Lazy<Task<Person>> to defer the I/O computation. It's interesting that between Task<T> and Lazy<T> there's a commonality: both evaluate a given expression exactly once.

> **Listing 2.29   Lazy asynchronous operation to initialize the `Person` object**

```
Lazy<Task<Person>> person =                          ◄── Shows the asynchronous lambda
    new Lazy<Task<Person>>(async () =>                     constructor for the Lazy type
    {
        using (var cmd = new SqlCommand(cmdText, conn))
        using (var reader = await cmd.ExecuteReaderAsync())
        {
            if (await reader.ReadAsync())
            {
                string firstName = reader["first_name"].ToString();
                string lastName = reader["last_name"].ToString();
                return new Person(firstName, lastName);
            }
        }
        throw new Exception("Failed to fetch Person");
    });

async Task<Person> FetchPerson()
{                                         ◄── Materialized asynchronously
    return await person.Value;                 the Lazy type
}
```

In this example, the delegate returns a `Task<Person>`, which asynchronously determines the value once and returns the value to all callers. These are the kind of designs that ultimately improve the scalability of your program. In the example, this feature implements asynchronous operations using the `async-await` keywords (introduced in C# 5.0). Chapter 8 covers in detail the topics of asynchronicity and scalability.

This is a useful design that can improve scalability and parallelism in your program. But there's a subtle risk. Because the lambda expression is asynchronous, it can be executed on any thread that calls `Value`, and the expression will run within the context. A better solution is to wrap the expression in an underlying `Task`, which will force the asynchronous execution on a thread-pool thread. This listing shows the preferred pattern.

Listing 2.30 Better pattern

```
Lazy<Task<Person>> person =
    new Lazy<Task<Person>>(() => Task.Run(
        async () =>
        {
            using (var cmd = new SqlCommand(cmdText, conn))
            using (var reader = await cmd.ExecuteReaderAsync())
            {
                if(await reader.ReadAsync())
                {
                    string firstName = reader["first_name"].ToString();
                    string lastName = reader["last_name"].ToString();
                    return new Person(firstName, lastName);
                } else throw new Exception("No record available");
            }
        }
    ));
```

Summary

- Function composition applies the result of one function to the input of another, creating a new function. You can use it in FP to solve complex problems by decomposing them into smaller and simpler problems that are easier to solve and then ultimately piece together these sets of solutions.
- Closure is an in-line delegate/anonymous method attached to its parent method, where the variables defined in the parent's method body can be referenced from within the anonymous method. Closure provides a convenient way to give a function access to local state (which is enclosed in the function), even if it's out of scope. It's the foundation to designing functional programming code segments that include memoization, lazy initialization, and precomputation to increase computation speed.
- Memoization is a functional programming technique that maintains the results of intermediate computations instead of recomputing them. It's considered a form of caching.

- Precomputation is a technique to perform an initial computation that generates a series of results, usually in the form of a lookup table. These precomputed values can be used directly from an algorithm to avoid needless, repetitive, and expensive computations each time your code is executed. Generally, precomputation replaces memoization and is used in combination with partial applied functions.
- Lazy initialization is another variation of caching. Specifically, this technique defers the computation of a factory function for the instantiation of an object until needed, creating the object only once. The main purpose of lazy initialization is to improve performance by reducing memory consumption and avoiding unnecessary computation.

Functional data structures and immutability

This chapter covers

- Building parallel applications with functional data structures
- Using immutability for high-performant, lock-free code
- Implementing parallel patterns with functional recursion
- Implementing immutable objects in C# and F#
- Working with tree data structures

Data comes in a multitude of forms. Consequently, it's not surprising that many computer programs are organized around two primary constraints: data and data manipulation. Functional programming fits well into this world because, to a large extent, this programming paradigm is about data transformation. Functional transformations allow you to alter a set of structured data from its original form into another form without having to worry about side effects or state. For example, you can transform a collection of countries into a collection of cities using a map function and keep the initial data unchanged. Side effects are a key challenge for concurrent programming because the effects raised in one thread can influence the behavior of another thread.

Over the past few years, mainstream programming languages have added new features to make multithreaded applications easier to develop. Microsoft, for example, has added the TPL and the `async`/`await` keywords to the .NET framework to reduce programmers' apprehension when implementing concurrent code. But there are still challenges with keeping a mutable state protected from corruption when multiple threads are involved. The good news is that FP lets you write code that transforms immutable data without side effects.

In this chapter, you'll learn to write concurrent code using a functional data structure and using immutable states, adopting the right data structure in a concurrent environment to improve performance effortlessly. *Functional data structures* boost performance by sharing data structures between threads and running in parallel without synchronization.

As a first step in this chapter, you'll develop a functional list in both C# and F#. These are great exercises for understanding how immutable functional data structures work. Next, we'll cover immutable tree data structures, and you'll learn how to use recursion in FP to build a binary tree structure in parallel. Parallel recursion is used in an example to simultaneously download multiple images from the web.

By the end of the chapter, you'll exploit immutability and functional data structures to run a program faster in parallel, avoiding the pitfalls, such as race conditions, of shared mutable of state. In other words, if you want concurrency and a strong guarantee of correctness, you must give up mutation.

3.1   *Real-world example: hunting the thread-unsafe object*

Building software in a controlled environment usually doesn't lead to unwelcome surprises. Unfortunately, if a program that you write on your local machine is deployed to a server that isn't under your control, this might introduce different variables. In the production environment, programs can run into unanticipated problems and unpredictable heavy loads. I'm sure that more than once in your career, you've heard, "It works on my machine."

When software goes live, multiple factors can go wrong, causing the programs to behave unreliably. A while ago, my boss called me to analyze a production issue. The application was a simple chat system used for customer support. The program was using web sockets to communicate from the frontend directly with the Windows server hub written in C#. The underlying technology to establish the bidirectional communication between client and server was Microsoft SignalR (http://mng.bz/Fal1). See figure 3.1.

> ### SignalR from MSDN documentation
> ASP.NET SignalR is a library for ASP.NET developers that simplifies the process of adding real-time web functionality to applications. Real-time web functionality has server code

push content to connected clients instantly as it becomes available, rather than having the server wait for a client to request new data. SignalR can be used to add any sort of real-time web functionality to your ASP.NET application. While chat is often used as an example, you can do much more. Any time a user refreshes a web page to see new data, or the page implements long pooling to retrieve new data, it's a candidate for using SignalR. Examples include dashboards and monitoring applications, collaborative applications (such as simultaneous editing of documents), job progress updates, and real-time forms.

Before being deployed in production, the program had passed all the tests. Once deployed, however, the server's resources were stressed. The CPU usage was continually between 85% to 95% of capacity, negatively affecting overall performance by preventing the system from being responsive to incoming requests. The result was unacceptable, and the problem needed a quick resolution.

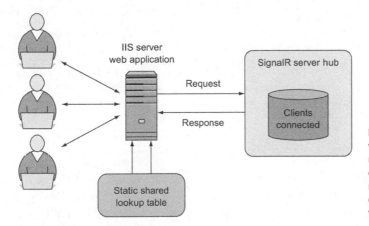

Figure 3.1 Architecture of a web server chat application using a SignalR hub. The clients connected are registered in a local static dictionary (lookup table) whose instance is shared.

As Sherlock Holmes said, "When you have eliminated the impossible, whatever remains, however improbable, must be the truth." I put on my super-sleuth hat and then, using a valued lens, I began to look at the code. After debugging and investigation, I detected the portion of code that caused the bottleneck.

I used a profiling tool to analyze the application's performance. Sampling and profiling the application is a good place to start looking for bottlenecks in the application. The profiling tool samples the program when it runs, examining the execution times to inspect as conventional data. The data collected is a statistical profiling representation of the individual methods that are doing the most work in the application. The final report shows these methods, which can be inspected by looking for the hot path (http://mng.bz/agzj) where most of the work in the application is executed.

The high CPU-core utilization problem originated in the OnConnected and OnDisconnected methods due to the contention of a shared state. In this case, the shared state was a generic Dictionary type, used to keep the connected users in memory. A *Thread contention* is a condition where one thread is waiting for an object, being held by another thread, to be released. The waiting thread cannot continue until the other thread releases the object (it's locked). This listing shows the problematic server code.

> **Listing 3.1   SignalR hub in C# that registers connections in context**

Checks if the current user is already connected and stored in the dictionary

```
static Dictionary<Guid, string> onlineUsers =
    new Dictionary<Guid, string>();

public override Task OnConnected() {
    Guid connectionId = new Guid (Context.ConnectionId);
    System.Security.Principal.IPrincipal user = Context.User;
    string userName;
    if (!onlineUsers.TryGetValue(connectionId, out userName)){
        RegisterUserConnection (connectionId, user.Identity.Name);
        onlineUsers.Add(connectionId, user.Identity.Name);
    }
    return base.OnConnected();
}
public override Task OnDisconnected() {
    Guid connectionId = new Guid (Context.ConnectionId);
    string userName;
    if (onlineUsers.TryGetValue(connectionId, out userName)){
        DeregisterUserConnection(connectionId, userName);
        onlineUsers.Remove(connectionId);
    }
    return base.OnDisconnected();
}
```

Shares an instance of a static dictionary to handle the state of online users

Each connection is associated with a unique identifier Guid.

Both operations of adding and removing a user are performed after checking the state of the dictionary.

The operations `OnConnected` and `OnDisconnected` rely on a shared global dictionary, communally used in these types of programs to maintain a local state. Notice that each time one of these methods is executed, the underlying collection is called twice. The program logic checks whether the `User Connection Id` exists and applies some behavior accordingly:

```
string userName;
if (!onlineUsers.TryGetValue(connectionId, out userName)){
```

Can you see the issue? For each new client request, a new connection is established, and a new instance of the hub is created. The local state is maintained by a static variable, which keeps track of the current user connection and is shared by all instances of the hub. According to the Microsoft documentation, "A static constructor is only called one time, and a static class remains in memory for the lifetime of the application domain in which your program resides."[1]

Here's the collection used for user-connection tracking:

```
static Dictionary<Guid, string> onlineUsers =
    new Dictionary<Guid, string>();
```

---

[1] For more information on static classes and static class members, see http://mng.bz/agzj.

`Guid` is the unique connection identifier created by SignalR when the connection between client and server is established. The string represents the name of the user defined during login. In this case, the program clearly runs in a multithreaded environment. Every incoming request is a new thread; consequently, there will be several requests simultaneously accessing the shared state, which eventually leads to multithreading problems.

The MSDN documentation is clear in this regard. It says that a `Dictionary` collection can support multiple readers concurrently, as long as the collection isn't modified.[2] Enumerating through the collection is intrinsically not thread safe because a thread could update the dictionary while another thread is changing the state of the collection.

Several possible solutions exist to avoid this limitation. The first approach is to make the collection thread safe and accessible by multiple threads for both `read` and `write` operations using `lock` primitive. This solution is correct but downgrades performance.

The preferred alternative is to achieve the same level of thread safety without synchronization; for example, using immutable collections.

3.1.1   *.NET immutable collections: a safe solution*

Microsoft introduced immutable collections, found in the namespace `System.Collections.Immutable`, with .NET Framework 4.5. This is part of the evolution of threading tools after TPL in .NET 4.0 and the `async` and `await` keywords after .NET 4.5.

The immutable collections follow the functional paradigm concepts covered in this chapter, and provide implicit thread safety in multithreaded applications to overcome the challenge to maintain and control mutable state. Similar to concurrent collections, they're also thread safe, but the underlying implementation is different. Any operations that change the data structures don't modify the original instance. Instead, they return a changed copy and leave the original instance unchanged. The immutable collections have been heavily tuned for maximum performance and use the *Structural Sharing*[3] pattern to minimize garbage collector (GC) demands. As an example, this code snippet creates an immutable collection from a generic mutable one (the immutable command is in bold). Then, by updating the collections with a new item, a new collection is created, leaving the original unaffected:

```
var original = new Dictionary<int, int>().ToImmutableDictionary();
var modifiedCollection = original.Add(key, value);
```

Any changes to the collection in one thread aren't visible to the other threads, because they still reference the original unmodified collection, which is the reason why immutable collections are inherently thread safe.

Table 3.1 shows an implementation of an immutable collection for each of the related mutable generic collections.

---

[2]   For more information on thread safety, see http://mng.bz/k8Gg.

[3]   "Persistent Data Structure," https://en.wikipedia.org/wiki/Persistent_data_structure.

Table 3.1   Immutable collections for .NET Framework 4.5

Immutable collection	Mutable collection
`ImmutableList<T>`	`List<T>`
`ImmutableDictionary<TKey, TValue>`	`Dictionary<TKey, TValue>`
`ImmutableHashSet<T>`	`HashSet<T>`
`ImmutableStack<T>`	`Stack<T>`
`ImmutableQueue<T>`	`Queue<T>`

NOTE The previous version of .NET attempted to provide collections with immutable capabilities using the generic `ReadOnlyCollection` and the extension method `AsReadOnly`, which transforms a given mutable collection into a read-only one. But this collection is a wrapper that prevents modifying the underlying collection. Therefore, in a multithreaded program, if a thread changes the wrapped collection, the read-only collection reflects those changes. Immutable collections resolve this issue.

Here are two ways to create an immutable list.

Listing 3.2   Constructing .NET immutable collections

```
var list = ImmutableList.Create<int>();         ◄─────── Creates an empty immutable list
list = list.Add(1);   ◄─
list = list.Add(2);       Adds a new item to the list
list = list.Add(3);       and returns a new list
                                                 Creates a list builder to construct
                                                 a list definition, with mutable
var builder = ImmutableList.CreateBuilder<int>();  ◄───  semantics, then freezes the collection
builder.Add(1);   ◄─
builder.Add(2);       Adds a new item to the list builder,
builder.Add(3);       which mutates the collection in place    Closes the list builder to
list = builder.ToImmutable();                            ◄──── create the immutable list
```

The second approach simplifies the construction of the list by creating a temporary list builder, which is used to add an element to the list and then seals (freezes) the elements into an immutable structure.

In reference to the data corruption (race condition) problem in the original chat program, immutable collections can be used in a Windows server hub to maintain the state of the open SignalR connections. This is safely accomplished with multithread access. Luckily, the `System.Collections.Immutable` namespace contains the equivalent version of `Dictionary` for lookups: `ImmutableDictionary`.

You may ask, "But if the collection is immutable, how it can be updated while preserving thread safety?" You can use lock statements around operations that involve reading or writing the collection. Building a thread-safe collection using locks is straightforward; but it is a more expensive approach than required. A better option is to protect the writes with a single compare-and-swap (CAS) operation, which removes the need for locks and leaves the read operation unguarded. This lock-free technique is more scalable and performs better than the counterpart (one that uses a synchronization primitive).

CAS OPERATIONS

CAS is a special instruction used in multithreaded programming as a form of synchronization that atomically performs an operation on memory locations. An atomic operation either succeeds or fails as a unit.

Atomicity refers to operations that alter a state in a single step in such a way that the outcome is autonomous, observed as either done or not done, with no in-between state. Other parallel threads can only see the old or the new state. When an atomic operation is performed on a shared variable, threads cannot observe its modification until it completes. In fact, an atomic operation reads a value as it appears at a single moment in time. Primitive atomic operations are machine instructions and can be exposed by .NET in the `System.Threading.Interlocked` class, such as the `Interlocked.Compare-Exchange` and the `Interlocked.Increment` methods.

The CAS instruction modifies shared data without the need to acquire and release a lock and allows extreme levels of parallelism. This is where immutable data structures really shine because they minimize the chances of incurring ABA problems (https://en.wikipedia.org/wiki/ABA_problem).

The ABA problem

The ABA problem occurs when executing an atomic CAS operation: one thread is suspended before executing the CAS, and a second thread modifies the target of the CAS instruction from its initial value. When the first thread resumes, the CAS succeeds, despite the changes to the target value.

The idea is to keep the state that has to change contained into a single and, most importantly, isolated immutable object (in this case, the `ImmutableDictionary`). Because the object is isolated, there's no sharing of state; therefore, there's nothing to synchronize.

The following listing shows the implementation of a helper object called `Atom`. The name is inspired by the Clojure atom (https://clojure.org/reference/atoms), which internally uses the `Interlocked.CompareExchange` operator to perform atomic CAS operations.

Listing 3.3 `Atom` **object to perform CAS instructions**

```
public sealed class Atom<T> where T : class          ◄─── Creates a helper object for
{                                                         atomic CAS instructions
    public Atom(T value)
    {
        this.value = value;
    }
```

```
    private volatile T value;                    Gets the current
    public T Value => value;                      value of this instance

    public T Swap(Func<T, T> factory)            Computes a new value based on
    {                                             the current value of the instance
        T original, temp;
        do {
            original = value;
            temp = factory (original);
        }
        while (Interlocked.CompareExchange(ref value, temp, original)
!= original);                         Repeats the CAS instruction
        return original;                  until it succeeds
    }
}
```

The Atom class encapsulates a reference object of type T marked volatile,[4] which must be immutable to achieve the correct behavior of value swapping. The property Value is used to read the current state of a wrapped object. The purpose of the Swap function is to execute the CAS instruction to pass to the caller of this function a new value based on the previous value using the factory delegate. The CAS operation takes an old and a new value, and it atomically sets the Atom to the new value only if the current value equals the passed-in old value. If the Swap function can't set the new value using Interlocked.CompareExchange, it continues to retry until it's successful.

Listing 3.4 shows how to use the Atom class with the ImmutableDictionary object in the context of a SignalR server hub. The code implements only the OnConnected method. The same concept applies to the OnDisconnected function.

Listing 3.4   Thread-safe ImmutableDictionary using an Atom object

```
                                             Passes an empty ImmutableDictionary
                                             as the argument to the Atom object to
Atom<ImmutableDictionary<Guid, string>> onlineUsers =   initialize the first state
    new Atom<ImmutableDictionary<Guid, string>>
        (ImmutableDictionary<Guid, string>.Empty);

public override Task OnConnected() {
    Grid connectionId = new Guid (Context.ConnectionId);
    System.Security.Principal.IPrincipal user = Context.User;

    var temp = onlineUsers.Value;            Creates a temporary copy of the original
    if(onlineUsers.Swap(d => {               ImmutableDictionary and calls the Value property
                    if (d.ContainsKey(connectionId)) return d;
                    return d.Add(connectionId, user.Identity.Name);
                    }) != temp) {
        RegisterUserConnection (connectionId, user.Identity.Name);
    }                                        Registers the new user connection, if the
    return base.OnConnected();               original ImmutableDictionary and the collection
}                                            returned from the Swap function are different
                                             and an update has been performed
Updates atomically the underlying
immutable collection with the swap
operation if the key connectionId isn't found
```

---

[4] For more information on the volatile keyword, see https://msdn.microsoft.com/en-us/library/x13ttww7.aspx.

The `Atom Swap` method wraps the call to update the underlying `Immutable-Dictionary`. The `Atom Value` property can be accessed at any time to check the current open SignalR connections. This operation is thread safe because it's read-only. The `Atom` class is generic, and it can be used to update atomically any type. But immutable collections have a specialized helper class (described next).

THE IMMUTABLEINTERLOCKED CLASS

Because you need to update the immutable collections in a thread-safe manner, Microsoft introduced the `ImmutableInterlocked` class, which can be found in the `System.Collections.Immutable` namespace. This class provides a set of functions that handles updating immutable collections using the CAS mechanism previously mentioned. It exposes the same functionality of the `Atom` object. In this listing, `Immutable-Dictionary` replaces `Dictionary`.

> **Listing 3.5 Hub maintaining open connections using `ImmutableDictionary`**

```
static ImmutableDictionary<Guid, string> onlineUsers =
    ImmutableDictionary<Guid, string>.Empty;
```
Shows an instance of an empty ImmutableDictionary

```
public override Task OnConnected() {
    Grid connectionId = new Guid (Context.ConnectionId);
    System.Security.Principal.IPrincipal user = Context.User;
```
ImmutableInterlocked tries to add a new item to the immutable collections in a thread-safe manner.

```
    if(ImmutableInterlocked.TryAdd (ref onlineUsers,
 connectionId, user.Identity.Name)) {
        RegisterUserConnection (connectionId, user.Identity.Name);
    }
    return base.OnConnected();
}
```
ImmutableInterlocked removes an item. If the item exists, the function returns true.

```
public override Task OnDisconnected() {
    Grid connectionId = new Guid (Context.ConnectionId);
    string userName;
    if(ImmutableInterlocked.TryRemove (ref onlineUsers,
 connectionId, out userName)) {
        DeregisterUserConnection(connectionId, userName);
    }
    return base.OnDisconnected();
}
```

Updating an `ImmutableDictionary` is performed atomically, which means in this case that a user connection is added only if it doesn't exist. With this change, the SignalR hub works correctly and is lock free, and the server didn't spike high percentages of CPU utilization. But there's a cost to using immutable collections for frequent updates. For example, the time required to add 1 million users to the `ImmutableDictionary` using `ImmutableInterlocked` is 2.518 seconds. This value is probably acceptable in most cases, but if you're aiming to produce a highly performant system, it's important to do the research and employ the right tool for the job.

In general, the use of immutable collections fits perfectly for shared state among different threads, when the number of updates is low. Their value (state) is guaranteed to be thread safe; it can be safely passed among additional threads. If you need a collection that has to handle many updates concurrently, a better solution is to exploit a .NET concurrent collection.

3.1.2 .NET concurrent collections: a faster solution

In the .NET framework, the `System.Collections.Concurrent` namespace provides a set of thread-safe collections designed to simplify thread-safe access to shared data. Concurrent collections are mutable collection instances that aim to increase the performance and scalability of multithreaded applications. Because they can be safely accessed and updated by multiple threads at the same time, they're recommended for multithreaded programs instead of the analogous collections in `System.Collections.Generic`. Table 3.2 shows the concurrent collections available in .NET.

Table 3.2   Concurrent collection details

Concurrent collection	Implementation details	Synchronization techniques
`ConcurrentBag<T>`	Works like a generic list	If multiple threads are detected, a primitive monitor coordinates their access; otherwise, the synchronization is avoided.
`ConcurrentStack<T>`	Generic stack implemented using a singly linked list	Lock free using a CAS technique.
`ConcurrentQueue<T>`	Generic queue implemented using a linked list of array segments	Lock free using CAS technique.
`ConcurrentDictionary<K, V>`	Generic dictionary implemented using a hash table	Lock free for read operations; lock synchronization for updates.

Back to the SignalR hub example of "Hunt the thread-unsafe object," `Concurrent-Dictionary` is a better option than the not-thread-safe `Dictionary`, and due to the frequent and wide number of updates, it's also a better option than `ImmutableDictionary`. In fact, `System.Collections.Concurrent` has been designed for high performance using a mix of fine-grained[5] and lock-free patterns. These techniques ensure that threads accessing the concurrent collection are blocked for a minimum amount of time or, in certain cases, completely avoid the blocking.

`ConcurrentDictionary` can ensure scalability while handling several requests per second. It's possible to assign and retrieve values using square-bracket indexing like the conventional generic `Dictionary`, but `ConcurrentDictionary` also offers a number of methods that are concurrency friendly such as `AddOrUpdate` or `GetOrAdd`. The `AddOrUpdate` method takes a key and a value parameter, and another parameter that is a

---

[5] For more information on parallel computing, see https://en.wikipedia.org/wiki/Parallel_computing.

delegate. If the key isn't in the dictionary, it's inserted using the value parameter. If the key is in the dictionary, the delegate is called and the dictionary is updated with the resulting value. Providing what you do in the delegate is also thread safe, this removes the danger of another thread coming in and changing the dictionary between you reading a value out of it and writing another back.

> **NOTE** Be aware that regardless of whether the methods exposed by `Concurrent-Dictionary` are atomic and thread safe, the class has no control over the delegates called by `AddOrUpdate` and `GetOrAdd`, which could be implemented without a thread-safety guard.

In the following listing, the `ConcurrentDictionary` keeps the state of open connections in the SignalR hub.

Listing 3.6 Hub maintaining open connections using `ConcurrentDictionary`

```
static ConcurrentDictionary<Guid, string> onlineUsers =
    new ConcurrentDictionary<Guid, string>();          ◄─── Shows the instance of an
                                                            empty ConcurrentDictionary
public override Task OnConnected() {
    Grid connectionId = new Guid (Context.ConnectionId);
    System.Security.Principal.IPrincipal user = Context.User;

    if(onlineUsers.TryAdd(connectionId, user.Identity.Name)) {    ◄───
        RegisterUserConnection (connectionId, user.Identity.Name);
    }
    return base.OnConnected();        The onlineUsers ConcurrentDictionary
}                                     tries to add a new item; if the item doesn't
                                      exist, it's added and the user is registered.

public override Task OnDisconnected() {
    Grid connectionId = new Guid (Context.ConnectionId);
    string userName;
    if(onlineUsers.TryRemove (connectionId, out userName)) {    ◄───
        DeregisterUserConnection(connectionId, userName);
    }
    return base.OnDisconnected();        The onlineUsers ConcurrentDictionary
}                                        removes the connectionId if it exists.
```

The code looks similar to the code listing using the `ImmutableDictionary`, (listing 3.5), but the performance of adding and removing many connections (`connection`) is faster. For example, the time required to add 1 million users to the `ConcurrentDictionarry` is only 52 ms, in comparison to the 2.518 s of the `ImmutableDictionary`. This value is probably fine in many cases, but if you want to produce a highly performant system, it's important to research and employ the right tool.

You need to understand how these collections work. Initially, it seems the collections are used without any FP style, due to their mutable characteristics. But the collections create an internal snapshot that mimics a temporary immutability to preserve thread safety during their iteration, allowing the snapshot to be enumerated safely.

Concurrent collections work well with algorithms that consider the producer/consumer[6] implementation. A *Producer/Consumer pattern* aims to partition and balance the workload between one or more producers and one or more consumers. A *producer* generates data in an independent thread and inserts it into a queue. A *consumer* runs a separate thread concurrently, which consumes the data from the queue. For example, a producer could download images and store them in a queue that's accessed by a consumer that performs image processing. These two entities work independently, and if the workload from the producer increases, you can spawn a new consumer to balance the workload. The Producer/Consumer pattern is one of the most widely used parallel programming patterns, and it will be discussed and implemented in chapter 7.

3.1.3 *The agent message-passing pattern: a faster, better solution*

The final solution for "Hunt the thread-unsafe object" was the introduction of a local agent into the SignalR hub, which provides asynchronous access to maintain high scalability during high-volume access. An agent is a unit of computation that handles one message at a time, and the message is sent asynchronously, which means the sender doesn't have to wait for the answer, so there's no blocking. In this case, the dictionary is isolated and can be accessed only by the agent, which updates the collection in a single-thread fashion, eliminating the hazard of data corruption and the need for locks. This fix is scalable because the agent's asynchronous semantic operation can process 3 million messages per second, and the code runs faster because it removes the extra overhead from using synchronizations.

Programming with agents and message passing is discussed in chapter 11. Don't worry if you don't completely understand the code; it will become clear during this journey, and you can always reference appendix B. This approach requires fewer changes in the code compared to the previous solutions, but application performance isn't jeopardized. This listing shows the implementation of the agent in F#.

Listing 3.7   F# agent that ensures thread-safe access to mutable states

Uses a discriminated union that represents the type of messages for the agent

```
type AgentMessage =
    | AddIfNoExists of id:Guid * userName:string
    | RemoveIfNoExists of id:Guid

type AgentOnlineUsers() =
    let agent = MailboxProcessor<AgentMessage>.Start(fun inbox ->
        let onlineUsers = Dictionary<Guid, string>()
        let rec loop() = async {
            let! msg = inbox.Receive()
            match msg with
            | AddIfNoExists(id, userName) ->
                let exists, _ = onlineUsers.TryGetValue(id)
```

Inside the body of the agent, even a mutable collection is thread safe because it's isolated.

The message received is pattern-matched to branch out to the corresponding functionality.

The lookup operation is thread safe because it's executed by the single-thread agent.

---

[6]   For more information on the producer-consumer problem, also known as the bounded-buffer problem, see https://en.wikipedia.org/wiki/Producer–consumer_problem.

<table>
<tr><td>

The message received is
pattern-matched to branch
out to the corresponding
functionality.

The lookup operation is
thread safe because it's
executed by the
single-thread agent.
</td><td>

```
        if not exists = true then
            onlineUsers.Add(id, userName)
            RegisterUserConnection (id, userName)
    | RemoveIfNoExists(id) ->
        let exists, userName = onlineUsers.TryGetValue(id)
        if exists = true then
            onlineUsers.Remove(id) |> ignore
            DeregisterUserConnection(id, userName)
    return! loop() }
loop() )
```
</td></tr>
</table>

In the following listing, the refactored C# code uses the final solution. Because of the interoperability between .NET programming languages, it's possible to develop a library using one language that's accessed by the other. In this case, C# is accessing the F# library with the `MailboxProcessor (Agent)` code.

Listing 3.8   SignalR hub in C# using an F# agent

```
static AgentOnlineUsers onlineUsers = new AgentOnlineUsers()
```
Uses a static instance of the F# agent from the referenced library

```
public override Task OnConnected() {
    Guid connectionId = new Guid (Context.ConnectionId);
    System.Security.Principal.IPrincipal user = Context.User;

    onlineUsers.AddIfNoExists(connectionId, user.Identity.Name);
    return base.OnConnected();
}
public override Task OnDisconnected() {
    Guid connectionId = new Guid (Context.ConnectionId);

    onlineUsers.RemoveIfNoExists(connectionId);
    return base.OnDisconnected();
}
```
Methods that asynchronously, with no blocking, send a message to the agent to perform thread-safe update operations

In summary, the final solution solved the problem by dramatically reducing the CPU consumption to almost zero (figure 3.2).

The takeaway from this experience is that sharing a mutable state in the multithreading environment isn't a good idea. Originally, the `Dictionary` collection had to maintain the user connections currently online; mutability was almost a necessity. You could use a functional approach with an immutable structure, but instead create a new collection for each update, which is probably overkill. A better solution is to use an agent to isolate mutability and make the agent accessible from the caller methods. This is a functional approach that uses the natural thread safety of agents.

The result of this approach is an increase of scalability because access is asynchronous without blocking, and it allows you to easily add logic in the agent body, such as logging and error handling.

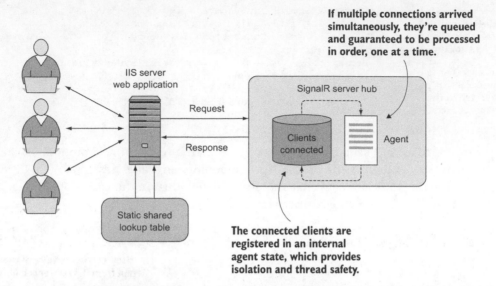

If multiple connections arrived simultaneously, they're queued and guaranteed to be processed in order, one at a time.

The connected clients are registered in an internal agent state, which provides isolation and thread safety.

Figure 3.2   Architecture of a web server for a chat application using a SignalR hub. This solution, compared to figure 3.1, removes the mutable dictionary that was shared between multiple threads to handle the incoming requests. To replace the dictionary, there is a local agent that guarantees high scalability and thread safety in this multithreaded scenario.

3.2   Safely sharing functional data structures among threads

A *persistent data structure* (also known as a *functional data structure*) is a data structure in which no operations result in permanent changes to the underlying structure. *Persistent* means that all versions of the structure that are modified endure over time. In other words, such a data structure is immutable because update operations don't modify the data structure but return a new one with the updated values.

Persistent, in terms of data, is commonly misconstrued as storing data in a physical entity, such as a database or filesystem. In FP, a functional data structure is long lasting. Most traditional imperative data structures (such as those from System.Collections .Generic: Dictionary, List, Queue, Stack, and so forth) are ephemeral because their state exists only for a short time between updates. Updates are destructive, as shown in figure 3.3.

A functional data structure guarantees consistent behavior regardless of whether the structure is accessed by different threads of execution or even by a different process, with no concern for potential changes to the data. Persistent data structures don't support destructive updates, but instead keep the old versions of a data structure.

Understandably, when compared to traditional imperative data structures, purely functional data structures are notoriously memory allocation intensive, which leads to substantial performance degradation. Fortunately, persistent data structures are designed with efficiency in mind, by carefully reusing a common state between versions of a data structure. This is possible by using the immutable nature of the functional data structures: Because they can never be changed, reusing different versions is effortless. You can compose a new data structure from parts of an old one by referring to the existing data rather than copying it. This technique is called *structural sharing* (see section 3.3.5). This implementation is more streamlined than creating a new copy of data every time an update is performed, leading to improved performance.

A new list is created with the value 5 replacing the value 3. The original list isn't mutated.

Updating the value 3 with number 5, mutating the list in place

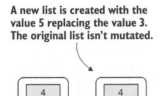

Figure 3.3   Destructive update vs. a persistent update of a list. The list at right is updating in place to mutate the value 3 with the value 5, without preserving the original list. This process is also known as destructive. At left, the functional list doesn't mutate its values, but creates a new list with the updated value.

3.3   Immutability for a change

In *Working Effectively with Legacy Code*, author Michael Feathers compares OOP and FP as follows:

> *Object-oriented programming makes code understandable by encapsulating moving parts. Functional programming makes code understandable by minimizing moving parts.*
>
> — *Michael Feathers, Working Effectively with Legacy Code (Prentice Hall, 2004)*

What this means is that immutability minimizes the parts of code that change, making it easier to reason about how those parts behave. *Immutability* makes the functional code free of side effects. A shared variable, which is an example of a side effect, is a serious obstacle for creating parallel code and results in non-deterministic execution. By removing the side effect, you can have a good coding approach.

In .NET, for example, the framework designers decided to construct `strings` as immutable objects, using a functional approach, to make it easier to write better code. As you recall, an immutable object is one whose state cannot be modified after it's created. The adoption of immutability in your coding style and the learning curve required by this necessitates extra attention; but the resulting cleaner code syntax and devolution (reducing unnecessary boilerplate code) will be well worth the effort. Moreover, the outcome of adopting this transformation of data versus the mutation of data significantly reduces the likelihood of bugs in your code, and the interactions and dependencies between different parts of your code base become easier to manage.

The use of immutable objects as part of your programming model forces each thread to process against its own copy of data, which facilitates writing correct, concurrent code. In addition, it is safe to have multiple threads simultaneously accessing shared data if that access is read-only. In fact, because you do not need locks or synchronization techniques, the hazards of possible deadlocks and race conditions will never occur (figure 3.4). We discussed these techniques in chapter 1.

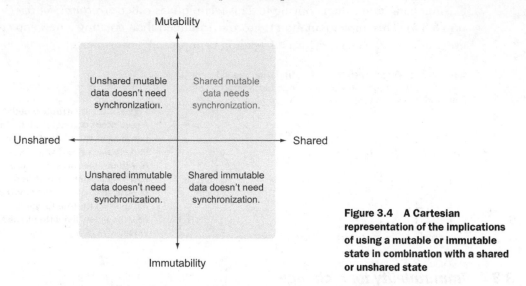

Figure 3.4   A Cartesian representation of the implications of using a mutable or immutable state in combination with a shared or unshared state

Functional languages, such as F#, are immutable by default, which makes them perfect for concurrency. Immutability won't instantaneously cause your code to run faster or make your program massively scalable, but it does prepare your code to be parallelized with small changes in the code base.

In object-oriented languages, such as C# and Java, writing concurrent applications can be difficult because mutability is the default behavior, and there's no tool to help prevent or offset it. In imperative programming languages, mutable data structures are considered perfectly normal and, although global state isn't recommended, mutable state is commonly shared across areas of a program. This is a recipe for disaster in parallel programming. Fortunately, as mentioned earlier, C# and F# when compiled share the same intermediate language, which makes it easy to share functionality. You can define the domain and objects of your program in F# to take advantage of its types and conciseness (most importantly, its types are immutable by default), for example. Then, develop your program in C# to consume the F# library, which guarantees immutable behavior without extra work.

Immutability is an important tool for building concurrent applications, but using immutable types doesn't make the program run faster. But it does make the code ready for parallelism; immutability facilitates increased degrees of concurrency, which in a multicore computer translates into better performance and speed. Immutable objects can be shared safely among multiple threads, avoiding the need of lock synchronization, which can keep programs from running in parallel.

The .NET framework provides several immutable types—some are functional, some can be used in multithreaded programs, and some both. Table 3.3 lists the characteristics of these types, which will be covered later in this chapter.

Table 3.3 Characteristics of .NET framework immutable types

Type	.NET lang.	Is it functional?	Characteristics	Thread safe?	Utilization
F# list	F#	Yes	Immutable linked list with fast append insertion	Yes	Used in combination with recursion to build and traverse *n*-element lists
Array	C# and F#	No	Zero-indexed mutable array type stored in a continuous memory location	Yes with partition[a]	Efficient data storage for fast access
Concurrent collections	C# and F#	No	Set of collections optimized for multithreaded read/ write access	Yes	Shared data in multithreaded program; perfect fit for the Producer/Consumer pattern
Immutable collections	C# and F#	Yes	Set of collections that make it easier to work with a parallel computing environment; their value can be passed freely between different threads without generating data corruption	Yes	Keeping state under control when multiple threads are involved
Discriminated union (DU)	F#	Yes	Represents a data type that stores one of several possible options	Yes	Commonly used to model domains and to represent hierarchical structures like an abstract syntax tree
Tuple	C# and F#	Yes	Type that groups two or more values of any (possibly different) type	No	Used to return multiple values from functions
F# tuple	F#	Yes		Yes	
Record type	F#	Yes	Represents aggregates of named value properties; can be viewed as a tuple with named members that can be accessed using dot notation	Yes	Used in place of conventional classes providing immutable semantics; fits well in domain design like DU and can be used in C#

[a] Each thread works on a separate part of the array.

3.3.1 *Functional data structure for data parallelism*

Immutable data structures are a perfect fit for data parallelism because they facilitate sharing data among otherwise isolated tasks in an efficient zero-copy manner. In fact, when multiple threads access partitionable data in parallel, the role of immutability is fundamental to safely processing chunks of data that belong to the same structure but that appear isolated. It's possible to achieve the same grade of correct data parallelism by adopting functional purity, which means instead of immutability using a function that avoids side effects.

The underlying functionality of PLINQ, for instance, promotes *purity*. A function is pure when it has no side effects and its return value is only determined by its input values.

PLINQ is a higher-level abstraction language that lies on top of multithreading components, abstracting the lower-level details while still exposing a simplified LINQ semantic. PLINQ aims to reduce the time of execution and increase the overall performance of the query, using all available computer resources. (PLINQ is covered in chapter 5.)

3.3.2 *Performance implications of using immutability*

Certain coders assume that programming with immutable objects is inefficient and has severe performance implications. For example, the pure functional way to append something to a list is to return a new copy of the list with the new element added, leaving the original list unchanged. This can involve increased memory pressure for the GC. Because every modification returns a new value, the GC must deal with a large number of short-lived variables. But, because the compiler knows that existing data is immutable, and because the data will not change, the compiler can optimize memory allocation by reusing the collection partially or as a whole. Consequently, the performance impact of using immutable objects is minimum, almost irrelevant, because a typical copy of an object, in place of a traditional mutation, creates a shallow copy. In this way, the objects referenced by the original object are not copied; only the reference is copied, which is a small bitwise replica of the original.

> ### GC's origin in functional programming
>
> In 1959, in response to memory issues found in Lisp, John McCarthy invented the GC. The GC attempts to reclaim garbage (memory) occupied by objects that are no longer useful to the program. It's a form of automatic memory management. Forty years later, mainstream languages such as Java and C# adopted the GC. The GC provides enhancements in terms of shared data structures, which can be difficult to accomplish correctly in unmanaged programming languages like C and C++, because certain pieces of code must be responsible for deallocation. Because the elements are shared, it isn't obvious which code should be responsible for deallocation. In memory-managed programming languages such as C# and F#, the garbage collector automates this process.

With the speed of CPUs today, this is almost an irrelevant price to pay in comparison to the benefits achieved as a thread-safety guarantee. A mitigating factor to consider is that, currently, performance translates into parallel programming, which requires more copying of objects and more memory pressure.

3.3.3 Immutability in C#

In C#, immutability isn't a supported construct. But it isn't difficult to create immutable objects in C#; the problem is that the compiler doesn't enforce this style and the programmer must do so with code. Adopting immutability in C# requires additional effort and extra diligence. In C#, an immutable object can be created by using the keyword `const` or `readonly`.

Any field can be decorated with the `const` keyword; the only precondition is that the assignment and declaration are a single-line statement. Once declared and assigned, the `const` value cannot be changed, and it belongs at the class level, accessing it directly and not by an instance.

The other option, decorating a value with the `readonly` keyword, can be done inline or through the constructor when the class is instantiated. After the initialization of a field marked `readonly`, the field value cannot be changed, and its value is accessible through the instance of the class. More important, to maintain the object as immutable when there are required changes to properties or state, you should create a new instance of the original object with the updated state. Keep in mind that `readonly` objects in C# are first-level immutable and shallow immutable only. In C#, an object is shallow immutable when the immutability isn't guaranteed to all its fields and properties, but only to the object itself. If an object `Person` has a read-only property `Address`, which is a complex object exposing properties such as street, city, and ZIP code, then these properties don't inherit the immutability behavior if not marked as read-only. Conversely, an immutable object with all the fields and properties marked as read-only is deeply immutable.

This listing shows immutable class `Person` in C#.

> ### Listing 3.9 Shallow immutable class `Person` in C#

```
class Address{
    public Address(string street, string city, string zipcode){
        Street = street;
        City = city;
        ZipCode = zipcode;
    }
    public string Street;          │  Fields of the Address object
    public string City;            │  that aren't marked read-only
    public string ZipCode;
}
class Person {
    public Person(string firstName, string lastName, int age,
➥ Address address){
        FirstName = firstName;
        LastName = lastName;
        Age = age;
        Address = address;
    }
```

```
    public readonly string FirstName;
    public readonly string LastName;
    public readonly int Age;
    public readonly Address Address;
}
```

Fields of the Person object that are marked read-only

In this code, the Person object is shallow immutable because, despite the field Address being immune to modification (it's marked read-only), its underlying fields can be changed. In fact, you can create an instance of the object Person and Address as

```
Address address = new Address("Brown st.", "Springfield", "55555");
Person person = new Person("John", "Doe", 42, address);
```

Now, if you try to modify the field Address, the compiler throws an exception (in bold), but you can still change the fields of the object address.ZipCode:

```
person.Address = // Error
person.Address.ZipCode = "77777";
```

This is an example of a shallow immutable object. Microsoft realized the importance of programming with immutability in a modern context and introduced a feature to easily create an immutable class with C# 6.0. This feature, called *getter-only auto-properties*, lets you declare auto-properties without a setter method, which implicitly creates a readonly backing field. This, unfortunately, implements the shallow immutable behavior.

Listing 3.10   Immutable class in C# with getter-only auto-properties

```
class Person {
    public Person(string firstName, string lastName, int age,
    Address address){
        FirstName = firstName;
        LastName = lastName;
        Age = age;
        Address = address;
    }

    public string FirstName {get;}
    public string LastName {get;}
    public int Age {get;}
    public Address Address {get;}

    public Person ChangeFirstName(string firstName) {
        return new Person(firstName, this.LastName, this.Age, this.Address);
    }
    public Person ChangeLstName(string lastName) {
        return new Person(this.FirstName, lastName, this.Age, this.Address);
    }
    public Person ChangeAge(int age) {
        return new Person(this.FirstName, this.LastName, age, this.Address);
    }
    public Person ChangeAddress(Address address) {
        return new Person(this.firstName, this.LastName, this.Age, address);
    }
}
```

The getter-only property is assigned directly to the underlying field from the constructor.

Shows the functions to update the fields of a Person object by creating a new instance without changing the original

In this immutable version of the class Person, it's important to notice that the methods responsible for updating the FirstName, LastName, Age, and Address don't mutate any state; instead, they create a new instance of Person. In OOP, objects are instantiated by invoking the constructor, then setting the state of the object by updating properties and calling methods. This approach results in an inconvenient and verbose construction syntax. This is where the functions added to Change the properties of the Person object come into play. Using these functions, it's possible to adopt a chain pattern, which is known as *fluent interface*. Here's an example of such a pattern by creating an instance of a class Person and changing the age and address:

```
Address newAddress = new Address("Red st.", "Gotham", "123459");
Person john = new Person("John", "Doe", 42, address);
Person olderJohn = john.ChangeAge(43).ChangeAddress(newAddress);
```

In summary, to make a class immutable in C#, you must:

- Always design a class with a constructor that takes the argument that's used to set the state of the object.
- Define the fields as read-only and utilize properties without a public setter; the values will be assigned in the constructor.
- Avoid any method designed to mutate the internal state of the class.

3.3.4 Immutability in F#

As mentioned, the programming language F# is immutable by default. Therefore, the concept of a variable doesn't exist because, by definition, if a variable is immutable, then it isn't a variable. F# replaces a variable with an identifier, which associates (binds) with a value using the keyword let. After this association, the value cannot change. Besides a full set of immutable collections, F# has a built-in series of helpful immutable constructs, designed for pure functional programming, as shown in listing 3.11. These built-in types are tuple and record, and they have a number of advantages over the CLI types:

- They are immutable.
- They cannot be null.
- They have built-in structural equality and comparison.

This listing shows use of an immutable type in F#.

Listing 3.11 F# immutable types

Uses a tuple that defines two values

It's possible to deconstruct the tuple and access its values.

Uses a record type to define a person type

Shows an instance of a person using a record type

```
let point = (31, 57)
let (x,y) = point

type Person= { First : string; Last: string; Age:int}
let person = { First="John"; Last="Doe"; Age=42}
```

The type tuple is a set of unnamed ordered values, which can be of different heterogeneous (https://en.wikipedia.org/wiki/Homogeneity_and_heterogeneity) types.

`Tuple` has the advantage of being usable on the fly, and is perfect for defining temporary and lightweight structures containing an arbitrary number of elements. For example, (true, "Hello", 2, 3.14) is a four tuple.

The type `record` is similar to `tuple`, where each element is labeled, giving a name to each of the values. The advantage of `record` over `tuple` is that the labels help to distinguish and to document what each element is for. Moreover, the properties of a record are automatically created for the fields defined, which is convenient because it saves keystrokes. A record in F# can be considered as a C# class with all properties read-only. Most valuable is the ability to correctly and quickly implement immutable classes in C# by using this type. In fact, it's possible to create an F# library in your solution by creating your domain model using the `record` type and then reference this library into your C# project. Here's how C# code looks when it references the F# library with the record type:

```
Person person = new Person("John", "Doe", 42)
```

This is a simple and effective way to create an immutable object. Additionally, the F# implementation requires only one line of code, compared to the equivalent in C# (11 lines of code using read-only fields).

3.3.5 *Functional lists: linking cells in a chain*

The most common and generally adopted functional data structure is the list, which is a series of homogeneous types used to store an arbitrary number of items. In FP, lists are recursive data structures composed by two linked elements: `Head` or `Cons` and `Tail`. The purpose of `Cons` is to provide a mechanism to contain a value and a connection to other `Cons` elements via an object reference pointer. This pointer reference is known as the `Next` pointer.

Lists also have a special state called `nil` to represent a list with no items, which is the last link connected to anything. The `nil`, or empty, case is convenient during a recursive traverse of a list to determine its end. Figure 3.5 shows a constructed list of four `Cons` cells and an empty list. Each cell (`Head`) contains a number and a reference to the remaining list (`Tail`), until the last `Cons` cell, which defines an empty list. This data structure is similar to a singly linked list (https://en.wikipedia.org/wiki/Linked_list), where each node in the chain has a single link to another node, representing a series of nodes linked together into a chain.

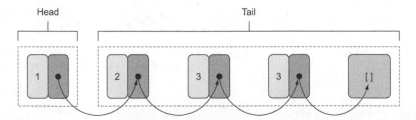

Figure 3.5   Functional list of integers composed by four numbers and an empty list (the last box [ ] on the right). Each item has a reference, the black arrow, linked to the rest of the list. The first item on the left is the head of the list, which is linked to the rest of the list, the tail.

In functional lists, the operations to add new elements or remove existing elements don't modify the current structure but return a new one with the updated values. Under the hood, immutable collections can safely share common structures, which limits memory consumption. This technique is called *structural sharing*. Figure 3.6 shows how structural sharing minimizes memory consumption to generate and update functional lists.

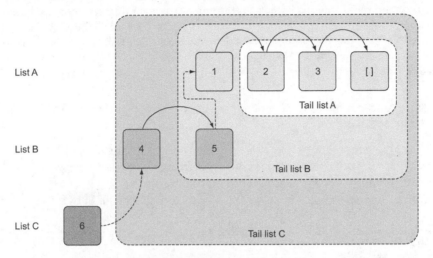

Figure 3.6   The structural sharing technique to create new lists optimizing memory space. In summary, List A has three items plus an empty cell, List B has five, and List C six. Each item is linked to the rest of the list. For example, the head item of List B is the number 4, which is linked to the tail (the numbers 5,1, 2, 3, and [ ]).

In figure 3.6, List A is composed of three numbers and an empty list. By adding two new items to List A, the structural sharing technique gives the impression that a new List B is created, but in reality it links a pointer from the two items to the previous and unmodified List A. The same scenario repeats for List C. At this point, all three lists (A, B, and C) are accessible, each with its own elements.

Clearly, functional lists are designed to provide better performance by adding or removing items from the head. In fact, lists work well for linear traversal, and appending performs in constant time $O(1)$ because the new item is added to the head of the previous list. But it isn't efficient for random access because the list must be traversed from the left for each lookup, which has $O(n)$ time, where n is the number of elements in the collection.

Big O notation

Big O notation, also known as *asymptotic notation*, is a way of summarizing the performance of algorithms based on problem size. A*symptotic* describes the behavior of a function as its input size approaches infinity. If you have a list of 100 elements, appending a new item to the front of the list has constant time of $O(1)$ because the operation involves a single step, regardless of the size of the list. Conversely, if you're searching for an item, then the cost of the operation is $O(100)$ because the worst-case scenario requires 100

(continued)

iterations through the list to find the element. The problem size is usually designated as *n*, and the measure is generalized as O(*n*).

What about the complexity of parallel programs?

Big O notation measures the complexity of running an algorithm sequentially, but in the case of a parallel program, this measure doesn't apply. It's possible, though, to express complexity of a parallel algorithm by introducing a parameter *P* that represents the number of cores on a machine. For example, the cost complexity of a parallel search is O(*n*/*P*) because you can break the list into a segment for each core to simultaneously execute the search.

This list represents the most common types of complexity, which are in order, starting with the least expensive:

- *O(1) constant*—The time is always 1, regardless of the size of the input.
- *O(log* n) *logarithmic*—Time increases as a fraction of the input size.
- *O(n) linear*—Time increases linearly with input size.
- *O(n log n)* log linear—Time increases by multiplying the input by a fraction of its size.
- *O(n²) quadratic*—Time increases with the square of the input size.

A new list is created by prepending a new element to an existing list by taking an empty list as initial value, and then linking the new element to the existing list structure. This operation to Cons onto the head of the list is repeated for all items, and consequently, every list terminates with an empty state.

One of the biggest attractions of functional lists is the ease with which they can be used to write thread-safe code. In fact, functional data structures can be passed by reference to a callee with no risk of it being corrupted, as shown in figure 3.7.

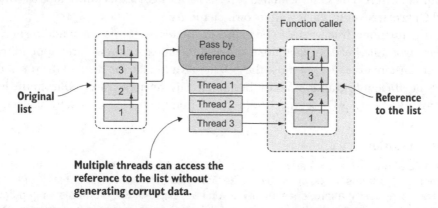

Figure 3.7   The list is passed by reference to the function caller (callee). Because the list is immutable, multiple threads can access the reference without generating any data corruption.

By definition, to be thread safe, an object must preserve a consistent state every time it's observed. You shouldn't observe a data structure collection removing an item from it while in the middle of a resize, for example. In a multithreaded program, applying the execution against an isolated portion of a functional data structure is an excellent and safe way to avoid sharing data.

FUNCTIONAL LISTS IN F#

F# has a built-in implementation of an immutable list structure, which is represented as a *linked list* (a linear data structure that consists of a set of items linked together in a chain). Every programmer has written a linked list at one point. In the case of functional lists, however, the implementation requires a little more effort to guarantee the immutable behavior that the list never changes once created. Fortunately, the representation of a list in F# is simple, taking advantage of the support for algebraic data types (ADT) (https://en.wikipedia.org/wiki/Algebraic_data_type) that let you define a generic recursive List type.

An ADT is a composite type, which means that its structure is the result of combining other types. In F#, ADTs are called *discriminated unions* (DU), and they're a precise modeling tool to represent well-defined sets of data shapes under the same type. These different shapes are called *cases* of a DU.

Think about a representation of the motor vehicle domain, where the types Car and Truck belong to the same base type Vehicle. DUs fit well for building complicated data structures (like linked lists and a wide range of trees) because they're a simpler alternative to a small-object hierarchy. For example, this is a DU definition for the domain Vehicle:

```
type Vehicle=
    | Motorcycle of int
    | Car of int
    | Truck of int
```

You can think of DUs as a mechanism to provide additional semantic meaning over a type. For example, the previous DU can be read as "A Vehicle type that can be a Car, a Motorcycle, or a Truck."

The same representation in C# should use a Vehicle base class with derived types for Car, Truck, and Motorcycle. The real power of a DU is when it's combined with pattern matching to branch to the appropriate computation, depending on the discriminated case passed. The following F# function prints the number of wheels for the vehicle passed:

```
let printWheels vehicle =
    match vehicle with
    | Car(n) -> Console.WriteLine("Car has {0} wheels", n)
    | Motorcycle(n) -> Console.WriteLine("Motorcycle has {0} wheels", n)
    | Truck(n) -> Console.WriteLine("Truck has {0} wheels", n)
```

This listing represents a recursive list, using the F# DU that satisfies the definition given in the previous section. A list can either be empty or is formed by an element and an existing list.

Listing 3.13   Representation of a list in F# using discriminated unions

```
type FList<'a> =
    | Empty
    | Cons of head:'a * tail:FList<'a>
```
Empty case
Cons case has the head element and the tail

```
let rec map f (list:FList<'a>) =
    match list with
    | Empty -> Empty
    | Cons(hd,tl) -> Cons(f hd, map f tl)
```
Recursive function that traverses a list using pattern matching to deconstruct and performs a transformation on each item

```
let rec filter p (list:FList<'a>) =
    match list with
    | Empty -> Empty
    | Cons(hd,tl) when p hd = true -> Cons(hd, filter p tl)
    | Cons(hd,tl) -> filter p tl
```

You can now create a new list of integers as follows:

```
let list = Cons (1, Cons (2, Cons(3, Empty)))
```

F# already has a built-in generic `List` type that lets you rewrite the previous implemented `FList` using the following two (equivalent) options:

```
let list = 1 :: 2 :: 3 :: []
let list = [1; 2; 3]
```

The F# list is implemented as a singly linked list, which provides instant access to the head of the list O(1) and linear time O(n) for element access, where (n) is the index of the item.

FUNCTIONAL LISTS IN C#

You have several ways to represent a functional list in OOP. The solution adopted in C# is a generic class `FList<T>`, so it can store values of any type. This class exposes read-only auto-getter properties for defining the head element of the list and the `FList<T>` tail linked list. The `IsEmpty` property indicates if the current instance contains at least a value. The following listing shows the full implementation.

Listing 3.14   Functional list in C#

```
public sealed class FList<T>
{
    private FList(T head, FList<T> tail)
    {
        Head = head;
        Tail = tail.IsEmpty
                ? FList<T>.Empty : tail;
        IsEmpty = false;
    }
    private FList()
    {
        IsEmpty = true;
    }
    public T Head { get; }
    public FList<T> Tail { get; }
```
Creates a list with a value and a reference to tail

Creates a new list that's empty

The Head property returns the first element from the list.

The Tail property returns the rest of the linked list.

```
public bool IsEmpty { get; }                      ◄——— This property indicates the state of the list.
public static FList<T> Cons(T head, FList<T> tail)  ◄
{
    return tail.IsEmpty                              A static method provides a
        ? new FList<T>(head, Empty)                  nicer syntax for creating lists.
        : new FList<T>(head, tail);
}                                                    This Cons function provides a fluent
public FList<T> Cons(T element)                 ◄    semantic to chain an item to a given list.
{
    return FList<T>.Cons(element, this);             This static constructor
}                                                    instantiates an empty list.
public static readonly FList<T> Empty = new FList<T>();  ◄
}
```

The FList<T> class has a private constructor to enforce its instantiation using either
the static helper method Cons or the static field Empty. This last option returns an
empty instance of the FList<T> object, which can be used to append new elements
with the instance method Cons. Using the FList<T> data structure, it's possible to create functional lists in C# as follows:

```
FList<int> list1 = FList<int>.Empty;
FList<int> list2 = list1.Cons(1).Cons(2).Cons(3);
FList<int> list3 = FList<int>.Cons(1, FList<int>.Empty);
FList<int> list4 = list2.Cons(2).Cons(3);
```

The code sample shows a few important properties for building an FList of integers.
The first list1 is created from an initial state of empty list using the field Empty
FList<int>.Empty, which is a common pattern used in immutable data structures.
Then, with this initial state, you can use the fluent semantic approach to chain a series
of Cons to build the collection as shown with list2 in the code example.

LAZINESS VALUES IN FUNCTIONAL LISTS

In chapter 2, you saw how lazy evaluation is an excellent solution to avoid excessive
duplicate operations by remembering operation results. Moreover, lazily evaluated
code benefits from a thread-safe implementation. This technique can be useful in the
context of functional lists by deferring computations and consequently gaining in performance. In F#, lazy *thunks* (computations that have been deferred) are created using
the lazy keyword:

```
let thunkFunction = lazy(21 * 2)
```

This listing defines a generic lazy list implementation.

Listing 3.15 Lazy list implementation using F#

```
type LazyList<'a> =                                  Uses a DU to define a list
    | Cons of head:'a * tail:Lazy<'a LazyList>  ◄    with a lazy evaluated tail
    | Empty
let empty = lazy(Empty)                         ◄    Uses a helper function to
                                                     represent an empty list
let rec append items list =                     ◄    Shows the function that appends
    match items with                                 an item at the top of a given list
```

```
        | Cons(head, Lazy(tail)) ->
            Cons(head, lazy(append tail list))
        | Empty -> list

let list1 = Cons(42, lazy(Cons(21, empty)))
// val list1: LazyList<int> = Cons (42,Value is not created.)

let list = append (Cons(3, empty)) list1
// val list : LazyList<int> = Cons (3,Value is not created.)

let rec iter action list =
    match list with
    | Cons(head, Lazy(tail)) ->
        action(head)
        iter action tail
    | Empty -> ()

list |> iter (printf "%d .. ")
// 3 .. 42 .. 21 ..
```

Creates a list with two elements: 42 and 21

Appends the value 3 to list1 previously created

Uses a function to iterate recursively through a list

Prints the values of the list using the iter function

The append function reclusively adds an item to a list; it can be used to append two lists.

To be more efficient in handling empty states, the lazy list implementation shifts the laziness into the tail of the Cons constructor, improving performance for the successive data structures. For example, the append operation is delayed until the head is retrieved from the list.

3.3.6 *Building a persistent data structure: an immutable binary tree*

In this section, you'll learn how to build a binary tree (B-tree) in F#, using recursion and multithreaded processes. A *tree structure* is, in layman's terms, a collection of nodes that are connected in such a way that no cycles are allowed. A tree tends to be used where performance matters. (It's odd that the .NET Framework never shipped with a tree in its collection namespaces.) Trees are the most common and useful data structures in computer programming and are a core concept in functional programming languages.

A tree is a polymorphic recursive data structure containing an arbitrary number of trees—trees within a tree. This data structure is primarily used to organize data based on keys, which makes it an efficient tool for searches. Due to its recursive definition, trees are best used to represent hierarchical structures, such as a filesystem or a database. Moreover, trees are considered advanced data structures, which are generally used in subjects such as machine learning and compiler design. FP provides recursion as a primary constructor to iterate data structures, making it complementary for this purpose.

Tree structures allow representing hierarchies and composing complex structures out of simple relationships and are used to design and implement a variety of efficient algorithms. Common uses of trees in XML/Markup are parsing, searching, compressing, sorting, image processing, social networking, machine learning, and decision trees. This last example is widely used in domains such as forecasting, finance, and gaming.

The ability to express a tree in which each node may have an arbitrary number of branches, like *n*-ary and B-tree, turns out to be an impediment rather than a benefit.

This section covers the B-tree, which is a self-balancing tree where every node has between zero to two child nodes at most, and the difference in depth (called height) of the tree between any leaves is at most one. *Depth of a node* is defined as the number of edges from the node to the root node. In the B-tree, each node points to two other nodes, called the left and right child nodes.

A better tree definition is provided by figure 3.8, which shows key properties of the data structure.

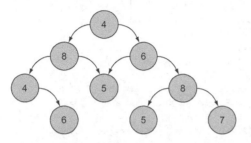

Figure 3.8 Binary tree representation where every node has between zero and two child nodes. In this figure, node 4 is the root from which two branches start, nodes 8 and 6. The left branch is a link to the left subtree and the right branch is a link to the right subtree. The nodes without child nodes, 6, 5, 5, and 7, are called *leaves*.

A tree has a special node call *root*, which has no parent (node 4 in figure 3.8), and may be either a leaf or a node with two or more children. A parent node has at least one child, and each child has one parent. Nodes with no children are treated as leaves (nodes 6, 5, 5, 7 in the figure), and children of the same parent are known as *siblings*.

B-TREES IN FUNCTIONAL F#

With F#, it's easy to represent a tree structure because of the support of ADTs and discriminated unions. In this case, DU provides an idiomatic functional way to represent a tree. This listing shows a generic DU-based binary tree definition with a special case for empty branches.

Listing 3.16 Immutable B-tree representation in F#

```
type Tree<'a> =
    | Empty                                         ◁──┐ Uses a DU that defines the generic tree
    | Node of leaf:'a * left:Tree<'a> * right:Tree<'a>  ◁──

let tree =                ◁── Shows an instance of a tree of integers
    Node (20,
        Node (9, Node (4, Node (2, Empty, Empty), Empty),
                Node (10, Empty, Empty)),
        Empty)
```

Uses a node case that defines a generic value leaf, and recursively branches out to left and right sub-trees

Shows an empty case

The elements in a B-tree are stored using the `Node` type constructor, and the `Empty` case identifier represents an empty node that doesn't specify any type information. The `Empty` case serves as a placeholder identifier. With this B-tree definition, you can create helper functions to insert or to verify an item in the tree. These functions are implemented in idiomatic F#, using recursion and pattern matching.

Listing 3.17   B-tree helper recursive functions

```
let rec contains item tree =
    match tree with
    | Empty -> false
    | Node(leaf, left, right) ->
        if leaf = item then true
        elif item < leaf then contains item left
        else contains item right

let rec insert item tree =
    match tree with
    | Empty -> Node(item, Empty, Empty)
    | Node(leaf, left, right) as node ->
        if leaf = item then node
        elif item < leaf then Node(leaf, insert item left, right)
        else Node(leaf, left, insert item right)

let ``exist 9`` = tree |> contains 9
let ``tree 21`` = tree |> insert 21
let ``exist 21`` = ``tree 21`` |> contains 21
```

> Uses recursion to define functions that walk through a tree structure

Because the tree is immutable, the function insert returns a new tree, with the copy of only the nodes that are in the path of the node being inserted. Traversing a DU tree in functional programming to look at all the nodes involves a recursive function. Three main approaches exist to traversing a tree: in-order, post-order, and pre-order traversal (https://en.wikipedia.org/wiki/Tree_traversal). For example, in the in-order tree navigation, the nodes on the left side of the root are processed first, then the root, and ultimately the nodes on its right as shown here.

Listing 3.18   In-order navigation function

```
let rec inorder action tree =
    seq {
        match tree with
        | Node(leaf, left, right) ->
            yield! inorder action left
            yield action leaf
            yield! inorder action right
        | Empty -> ()
    }

tree |> inorder (printfn "%d") |> ignore
```

> Uses a function that traverses the tree structure from the root to the left sub-nodes and then moving to the right sub-nodes

> Uses the inorder function to print all node values in the tree

The function inorder takes as an argument a function to apply to each value of the tree. In the example, this function is an anonymous lambda that prints the integer stored in the tree.

3.4   *Recursive functions: a natural way to iterate*

Recursion is calling a function on itself, a deceptively simple programming concept. Have you ever stood in between two mirrors? The reflections seem to carry on forever—this is recursion. Functional recursion is the natural way to iterate in FP because it avoids mutation of state. During each iteration, a new value is passed into the loop constructor instead to be updated (mutated). In addition, a recursive function can be composed, making your program more modular, as well as introducing opportunities to exploit parallelization.

Recursive functions are expressive and provide an effective strategy to solve complex problems by breaking them into smaller, although identical, subtasks. (Think in terms of Russian nesting dolls, with each doll being identical to the one before, only smaller.) While the whole task may seem daunting to solve, the smaller tasks are easier to solve directly by applying the same function to each of them. The ability to split the task into smaller tasks that can be performed separately makes recursive algorithms candidates for parallelization. This pattern, also called Divide and Conquer,[8] leads to dynamic task parallelism, in which tasks are added to the computation as the iteration advances. For more information, reference the example in section 1.4.3. Problems with recursive data structures naturally use the Divide and Conquer strategy due to its inherent potential for concurrency.

When considering recursion, many developers fear performance penalties for the execution time of a large number of iterations, as well as receiving a `Stackoverflow` exception. The correct way to write recursive functions is using the techniques of tail recursion and CPS. Both strategies are good ways to minimize stack consumption and increase speed, as you'll see in the examples to come.

3.4.1 *The tail of a correct recursive function: tail-call optimization*

A *tail call*, also known as tail-call optimization (TCO), is a subroutine call performed as the final action of a procedure. If a tail call might lead to the same subroutine being called again in the call chain, then the subroutine is said to be *tail recursive*, a special case of recursion. *Tail-call recursion* is a technique that converts a regular recursive function into an optimized version that can handle large inputs without any risks and side effects.

> **NOTE** The primary reason for a tail call as an optimization is to improve data locality, memory usage, and cache usage. By doing a tail call, the callee uses the same stack space as the caller. This reduces memory pressure. It marginally improves the cache because the same memory is reused for subsequent callers and can stay in the cache, rather than evicting an older cache line to make room for a new cache line.

With tail-call recursion, there are no outstanding operations to perform within the function it returns, and the last call of the function is a call to itself. You'll refactor the implementation of a factorial number function into a tail-call optimized function. The following listing shows the tail-call optimized recursive function implementation.

---

[8] The Divide and Conquer pattern solves a problem by recursively dividing it into subproblems, solving each one independently, and then recombining the sub-solutions into a solution to the original problem.

Listing 3.19   Tail-call recursive implementation of a factorial in F#

```
let rec factorialTCO (n:int) (acc:int) =
    if n <= 1 then acc
    else factorialTCO (n-1) (acc * n)

let factorial n = factorialTCO n 1
```

> The last operation of the function recursively calls itself without computing any other operations.

In this implementation of the recursive function, the parameter acc acts as an accumulator. By using an accumulator and ensuring that the recursive call is the last operation in the function, the compiler optimizes the execution to reuse a single-stack frame, instead of storing each intermediate result of the recursion onto different stack frames as shown in figure 3.9.

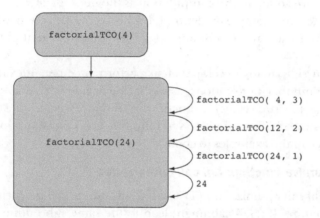

Figure 3.9   **Tail-recursive definition of a factorial, which can reuse a single stack frame**

The figure illustrates the tail-recursive definitions of factorials. Although F# supports tail-call recursive functions, unfortunately, the C# compiler isn't designed to optimize tail-call recursive functions.

3.4.2   *Continuation passing style to optimize recursive function*

Sometimes, optimized tail-call recursive functions aren't the right solution or can be difficult to implement. In this case, one possible alternative approach is CPS, a technique to pass the result of a function into a continuation. CPS is used to optimize recursive functions because it avoids stack allocation. Moreover, CPS is used in the Microsoft TPL, in async/await in C#, and in async-workflow in F#.

CPS plays an important role in concurrent programming. This following code example shows how the CPS pattern is used in a function GetMaxCPS:

```
static void GetMaxCPS(int x, int y, Action<int> action)
                                => action(x > y ? x : y);

GetMaxCPS (5, 7, n => Console.WriteLine(n));
```

The argument for the continuation passing is defined as a delegate Action<int>, which can be used conveniently to pass a lambda expression. The interesting part is that the function with this design never returns a result directly; instead, it supplies the result to the continuation procedure. CPS can also be used to implement recursive functions using tail calls.

RECURSIVE FUNCTIONS WITH CPS

At this point, with basic knowledge about CPS, you'll refactor the factorial example from listing 3.19 to use the CPS approach in F#. (You can find the C# implementation in the downloadable source code for this book.)

Listing 3.20   Recursive implementation of factorials using CPS in F#

```
let rec factorialCPS x continuation =
    if x <= 1 then continuation()
    else factorialCPS (x - 1) (fun () -> x * continuation())

let result = factorialCPS 4 (fun () -> 1)        ◄─── The value of result is 24.
```

This function is similar to the previous implementation with the accumulator; the difference is that the function is passed instead of the accumulator variable. In this case, the action of the function `factorialCPS` applies the `continuation` function to its result.

B-TREE STRUCTURE WALKED IN PARALLEL RECURSIVELY

Listing 3.21 shows an example that iterates recursively through a tree structure to perform an action against each element. The function `WebCrawler`, from chapter 2, builds a hierarchy representation of web links from a given website. Then it scans the HTML content from each web page, looking for image links that download in parallel. The code examples from chapter 2 (listings 2.16, 2.17, 2.18, and 2.19) were intended to be an introduction to a parallel technique rather than a typical task-based parallelism procedure. Downloading any sort of data from the internet is an I/O operation; you'll learn in chapter 8 that it's best practice to perform I/O operations asynchronously.

Listing 3.21   Parallel recursive divide-and-conquer function

```
let maxDepth = int(Math.Log(float System.Environment.ProcessorCount,
⇒ 2.)+4.)                          ◄──────       Uses a threshold to avoid the creation of too many
                                                 tasks in comparison with the number of cores

let webSites : Tree<string> =
    WebCrawlerExample.WebCrawler("http://www.foxnews.com")
    |> Seq.fold(fun tree site -> insert site tree ) Empty        ◄───

                                                 Uses a fold constructor to create
                                                 the tree structure representing
                                                 the website hierarchy

let downloadImage (url:string) =
    use client = new System.Net.WebClient()
    let fileName = Path.GetFileName(url)
    client.DownloadFile(url, @"c:\Images\" + fileName)        ◄───
                                                 Downloads the image
                                                 into a local file

let rec parallelDownloadImages tree depth =        ◄───
    match tree with
    | _ when depth = maxDepth ->                     Shows the recursive function that walks
        tree |> inorder downloadImage |> ignore      the tree structure in parallel to download
    | Node(leaf, left, right) ->                     simultaneously multiple images
        let taskLeft  = Task.Run(fun() ->
            parallelDownloadImages left (depth + 1))
        let taskRight = Task.Run(fun() ->
            parallelDownloadImages right (depth + 1))
```

```
        let taskLeaf  = Task.Run(fun() -> downloadImage leaf)
        Task.WaitAll([|taskLeft;taskRight;taskLeaf|])
    | Empty -> ()
```
← **Waits for the tasks to complete**

The `Task.Run` constructor is used to create and spawn the tasks. The parallel recursive function `parallelDownloadImages` takes the argument depth, which is used to limit the number of tasks created to optimize resource consumption.

In every recursive call, the depth value increases by one, and when it exceeds the threshold `maxDepth`, the rest of the tree is processed sequentially. If a separate task is created for every tree node, then the overhead of creating new tasks would exceed the benefit gained from running the computations in parallel. If you have a computer with eight processors, then spawning 50 tasks will impact the performance tremendously because of the contention generated from the tasks sharing the same processors. The TPL scheduler is designed to handle large numbers of concurrent tasks, but its behavior isn't appropriate for every case of dynamic task parallelism (http://mng.bz/ww1i), and in some circumstances, as in the previous parallel recursive function, a manual tune-up is preferred.

Ultimately, the `Task.WaitAll` construct is used to wait for the tasks to complete. Figure 3.10 shows the hierarchy representation of the spawned tasks running in parallel.

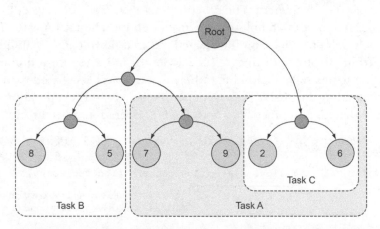

Figure 3.10   From the root node, Task C is created to process the right side of the subtree. This process is repeated for the subtree running Task A. When it completes, the left side of the subtree is processed by Task B. This operation is repeated for all the subtrees, and for each iteration, a new task is created.

The execution time to complete the recursive parallel operation `parallelDownload-Images` has been measured against a sequential version. The benchmark is the average of downloading 50 images three times (table 3.4).

Table 3.4   Benchmark of downloading 50 images using parallel recursion

Serial	Parallel
19.71	4.12

PARALLEL CALCULATOR

Another interesting way to use a tree structure is building a parallel calculator. After what you've learned, the implementation of such a program isn't trivial. You can use ADTs in the form of F# DUs to define the type of operations to perform:

```
type Operation = Add | Sub | Mul | Div | Pow
```

Then, the calculator can be represented as a tree structure, where each operation is a node with the details to perform a calculation:

```
type Calculator =
    | Value of double
    | Expr of Operation * Calculator * Calculator
```

Clearly, from this code, you can see the resemblance to the tree structure previously used:

```
type Tree<'a> =
    | Empty
    | Node of leaf:'a * left:Tree<'a> * right:Tree<'a>
```

The only difference is that the Empty case in the tree structure is replaced with the value case in the calculator. To perform any mathematical operation you need a value. The leaf of the tree becomes the Operation type, and the left and right branches recursively reference the calculator type itself, exactly as the tree did.

Next, you can implement a recursive function that iterates through the calculator tree and performs the operations in parallel. This listing shows the implementation of the eval function and its use.

Listing 3.23   Parallel calculator

```
let spawn (op:unit->double) = Task.Run(op)        ◄──┐ Uses a helper function to spawn a
                                                     │ Task to run an operation

let rec eval expr =                    │ Pattern-matches against the calculator DU to branch the evolution
    match expr with        ◄───────────┘
                                       │ If the expr case is a Value, extracts the value and returns it
    | Value(value) -> value    ◄───────┘

    | Expr(op, lExpr, rExpr) ->                          If the expr case is an Expr, extracts the
                                       ◄──────────────── operation and recursively reevaluates
                                                         the branches to extract the values

        let op1 = spawn(fun () -> eval lExpr)    ┐ Spawns a task for each reevaluation, which
        let op2 = spawn(fun () -> eval rExpr)    ┘ could be another operation to compute

        let apply = Task.WhenAll([op1;op2])                          ◄──┐ Waits for the
        let lRes, rRes = apply.Result.[0], apply.Result.[1]            │ operations to
        match op with        ◄─────────────────────┐                  ┘ complete
        | Add -> lRes + rRes                        │ After having evaluated the
        | Sub -> lRes - rRes                        │ values, which could be the
        | Mul -> lRes * rRes                        │ result from other operations,
        | Div -> lRes / rRes                        │ performs the current operation
        | Pow -> System.Math.Pow(lRes, rRes)        ┘
```

The function eval recursively evaluates in parallel a set of operations defined as a tree structure. During each iteration, the expression passed is pattern matched to extract the value if the case is a Value type, or to compute the operation if the case is an Expr type. Interestingly, the recursive re-evolution for each branch of the node case `Expr` is made in parallel. Each branch `Expr` returns a `value` type, which is calculated in each child (sub-nodes) operation. Then, these values are used for the last operation, which is the root of the operation tree passed as argument for the final result. Here is a simple set of operations in the shape of a calculator tree, which compute the operations $2^{\wedge}10 / 2^{\wedge}9 + 2 * 2$:

```
let operations =
  Expr(Add,
    Expr(Div,
      Expr(Pow, Value(2.0), Value(10.0)),
      Expr(Pow, Value(2.0), Value(9.0))),
    Expr(Mul, Value(2.0), Value(2.0)))

let value = eval operations
```

In this section, the code for defining a tree data structure and performing a recursive task-based function is shown in F#; but the implementation is feasible in C# as well. Rather than showing all the code here, you can download the full code from the book's website.

Summary

- Immutable data structures use intelligent approaches, such as structural sharing, to minimize the copy-shared elements to minimize GC pressure.

- It's important to dedicate some time to profiling application performance to avoid bottlenecks and bad surprises when the program runs in production and under heavy payloads.

- Lazy evaluation can be used to guarantee thread safety during the instantiation of an object and to gain performance in functional data structures by deferring computation to the last moment.

- Functional recursion is the natural way to iterate in functional programming because it avoids mutation of state. In addition, a recursive function can be composed, making your program more modular.

- Tail-call recursion is a technique that converts a regular recursive function into an optimized version that can handle large inputs without any risks or side effects.

- Continuation passing style (CPS) is a technique to pass the result of a function into a continuation. This technique is used to optimize recursive functions because it avoids stack allocation. Moreover, CPS is used in the Task Parallel Library in .NET 4.0, in `async`/`await` in C#, and in `async-workflow` in F#.

- Recursive functions are great candidates to implement a Divide and Conquer technique, which leads to dynamic task parallelism.

Part 2

How to approach the different parts of a concurrent program

This part of the book dives into functional programming concepts and applicability. We'll explore various concurrent programming models, with an emphasis on the benefits and advantages of this paradigm. Topics will include the Task Parallel Library along with parallel patterns such as Fork/Join, Divide and Conquer, and MapReduce. We'll also discuss declarative composition, high-level abstraction in asynchronous operations, the agent programming model, and the message-passing semantic. You'll see firsthand how functional programming allows you to compose program elements without evaluating them. These techniques parallelize work and make programs easier to reason about and more efficient to run due to optimal memory consumption.

The basics of
processing big data:
data parallelism, part 1

This chapter covers

- The importance of data parallelism in a world of big data
- Applying the Fork/Join pattern
- Writing declarative parallel programs
- Understanding the limitation of a parallel `for` loop
- Increasing performance with data parallelism

Imagine you're cooking a spaghetti for dinner for four, and let's say it takes 10 minutes to prepare and serve the pasta. You begin the preparation by filling a medium-sized pot with water to boil. Then, two more friends show up at your house for dinner. Clearly, you need to make more pasta. You can switch to a bigger pot of water with more spaghetti, which will take longer to cook, or you can use a second pot in tandem with the first, so that both pots of pasta will finish cooking at the same time. Data parallelism works in much the same way. Massive amounts of data can be processed if "cooked" in parallel.

In the last decade, the amount of data being generated has increased exponentially. In 2017 it was estimated that every minute there were 4,750,000 "likes" on

Facebook, almost 400,000 tweets, more than 2.5 million posts on Instagram, and more than 4 million Google searches. These numbers continue to increase at the rate of 15% every year. This acceleration impacts businesses that now must quickly analyze multitudes of big data (https://en.wikipedia.org/wiki/Big_data). How is it possible to analyze this massive amount of data while maintaining quick responses? The answer comes from a new breed of technologies designed with data parallelism in mind, specifically, with a focus on the ability to maintain performance in the event of continually increasing data.

In this chapter, you'll learn concepts, design patterns, and techniques to rapidly process tons of data. You'll analyze the problems originating from parallel loop constructs and learn about solutions. You'll also learn that by using functional programming in combination with data parallelism it's possible to achieve impressive performance improvements in your algorithms with minimal code changes.

4.1   What is data parallelism?

Data parallelism is a programming model that performs the same set of operations on a large quantity of data in parallel. This programming model is gaining traction because it quickly processes massive volumes of data in the face of a variety of big data problems. Parallelism can compute an algorithm without requiring reorganization of its structure, thereby progressively increasing scalability.

The two models of data parallelism are single instruction single data and single instruction multiple data:

- *Single instruction single data (SISD)* is used to define a single-core architecture. A single-core processor system executes one task per any CPU clock cycle; therefore, the execution is sequential and deterministic. It receives one instruction (single instruction), performs the work required for a single piece of data, and returns the results of the computation. This processor architecture will not be covered in this book.
- *Single instruction multiple data (SIMD)* is a form of parallelism achieved by distributing the data among the available multiple cores and applies the same operations at any given CPU clock cycle. This type of parallel, multicore CPU architecture is commonly used to exploit data parallelism.

To achieve data parallelism, the data is split into chunks, and each chunk is subject to intensive computations and processed independently, either to produce new data to aggregate or to reduce to a scalar value. If you aren't familiar with these terms, they should be clear by the end of the chapter.

The ability to compute chunks of data independently is the key to achieving significant performance increase, because removing dependencies between blocks of data eliminates the need for synchronization to access data and any concerns about race conditions, as shown in figure 4.1.

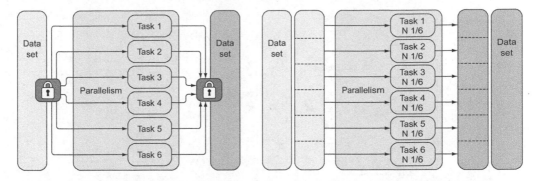

Figure 4.1 Data parallelism is achieved by splitting the data set into chunks and independently processing each partition in parallel, assigning each chunk to a separate task. When the tasks complete, the data set is reassembled. In this figure, the data set on the left is processed by multiple tasks using a lock to synchronize their access to the data as a whole. In this case, the synchronization is a source of contention between threads and creates performance overhead. The data set on the right is split into six parts, and each task performs against one-sixth of the total size *N* of the data set. This design removes the necessity of using locks to synchronize.

Data parallelism can be achieved in a distributed system, by dividing the work among multiple nodes; or in a single computer; or by partitioning the work into separated threads. This chapter focuses on implanting and using multicore hardware to perform data parallelism.

4.1.1 Data and task parallelism

The goal of data parallelism is decomposing a given data set and generating a sufficient number of tasks to maximize the use of CPU resources. In addition, each task should be scheduled to compute enough operations to guarantee a faster execution time. This is in contrast to context switching, which could introduce negative overhead.

Data parallelism comes in two flavors:

- *Task parallelism* targets the execution of computer programs across multiple processors, where each thread is responsible for performing a different operation at the same time. It is the simultaneous execution of many different functions across the same or different data sets on multiple cores.
- *Data parallelism* targets the distribution of a given data set into smaller partitions across multiple tasks, where each task performs the same instruction in parallel. For example, data parallelism could refer to an image-processing algorithm, where each image or pixel is updated in parallel by independent tasks. Conversely, task parallelism would compute in parallel a set of images, applying a different operation for each image. See figure 4.2.

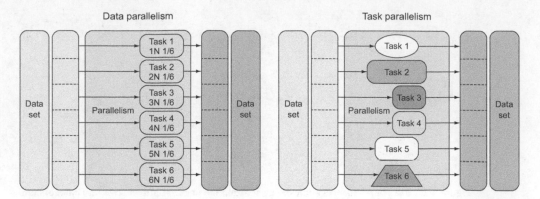

Figure 4.2   Data parallelism is the simultaneous execution of the same function across the elements of a data set. Task parallelism is the simultaneous execution of multiple different functions across the same or different data sets.

Is summary, task parallelism focuses on executing multiple functions (tasks), and aims to reduce the overall time of computation by running these tasks simultaneously. Data parallelism reduces the time it takes to process a data set by splitting the same algorithm computation among multiple CPUs to be performed in parallel.

4.1.2   *The "embarrassingly parallel" concept*

In data parallelism, the algorithms applied to process the data are sometimes referred to as "embarrassingly parallel" and have the special property of natural scalability.[1] This property influences the amount of parallelism in the algorithm as the number of available hardware threads increases. The algorithm will run faster in a more powerful computer. In data parallelism, the algorithms should be designed to run each operation independently in a separate task associated with a hardware core. This structure has the advantage of automatically adapting the workload at runtime and adjusting the data partitioning based on the current computer. This behavior guarantees running the program on all available cores.

Consider summing a large array of numbers. Any part of this array may be summed up independently from any other part. The partial sums can then be summed together themselves and achieve the same result as if the array had been summed in series. Whether or not the partial sums are computed on the same processor or at the same time doesn't matter. Algorithms like this one with a high degree of independence are known as embarrassingly parallel problems: the more processors that you throw at them, the faster they will run. In chapter 3 you saw the Divide and Conquer pattern that provides natural parallelism. It distributes work to numerous tasks and then combines (reduces) the results again. Other embarrassingly parallel designs don't require a complex coordination mechanism to provide natural auto-scalability. Examples of

---

[1] For more information on embarrassingly parallel, also known as pleasing parallel, see https://en .wikipedia.org/wiki/Embarrassingly_parallel.

design patterns that use this approach are Fork/Join, Parallel Aggregation (reduce), and MapReduce. We'll discuss these designs later in this chapter.

4.1.3 *Data parallelism support in .NET*

Identifying code in your programs that can be parallelized isn't a trivial task, but common rules and practices can help. The first thing to do is profiling the application. This analysis of the program identifies where the code spends its time, which is your clue for where you should start deeper investigations to improve performance and to detect opportunities for parallelism. As a guide, an opportunity for parallelism is when two or more portions of source code can be executed deterministically in parallel, without changing the output of the program. Alternatively, if the introduction of parallelism would change the output of the program, the program isn't deterministic and could become unreliable; therefore, parallelism is unusable.

To ensure deterministic results in a parallel program, the blocks of source code that run simultaneously should have no dependencies between them. In fact, a program can be parallelized easily when there are no dependencies or when existing dependencies can be eliminated. For example, in the Divide and Conquer pattern, there are no dependencies among the recursive executions of the functions so that parallelism can be accomplished.

A prime candidate for parallelism is a large data set where a CPU-intensive operation can be performed independently on each element. In general, loops in any form (for loop, while loop, and for-each loop) are great candidates to exploit parallelism. Using Microsoft's TPL, reshaping a sequential loop into a parallel one is an easy task. This library provides a layer of abstraction that simplifies the implementation over common parallelizable patterns that are involved in data parallelism. These patterns can be materialized using the parallel constructs Parallel.For and Parallel.ForEach offered by the TPL Parallel class.

Here are a few patterns found in programs that provide an opportunity for parallelism:

- Sequential loops, where there are no dependencies between the iteration steps.
- Reduction and/or aggregation operations, where the results of the computation between steps are partially merged. This model can be expressed using a MapReduce pattern.
- Unit of computation, where explicit dependencies can be converted into a Fork/Join pattern to run each step in parallel.
- Recursive type of algorithms using a Divide and Conquer approach, where each iteration can be executed independently in a different thread in parallel.

In the .NET framework, data parallelism is also supported through PLINQ, which I recommend. The query language offers a more declarative model for data parallelism, compared to the Parallel class, and is used for parallel evaluation of arbitrary queries against a data source. Declarative implies what you want to be done with data rather than how you want that to be done. Internally, the TPL uses sophisticated scheduling algorithms to distribute parallelized computations efficiently between the available processing cores. Both C# and F# take advantage of these technologies in a similar way. In the next section, you'll see these technologies in both programming languages, which can be mixed and complement each other nicely.

4.2   *The Fork/Join pattern: parallel Mandelbrot*

The best way to understand how to convert a sequential program into a parallel one is with an example. In this section, we'll transform a program using the Fork/Join pattern to exploit parallel computation and to achieve faster performance.

In the Fork/Join pattern, a single thread forks and coordinates with multiple independent parallel workers and then merges the individual results when complete. Fork/Join parallelism manifests in two primary steps:

1   Split a given task into a set of subtasks scheduled to run independently in parallel.

2   Wait for the forked parallel operations to complete, and then successively join the subtask results into the original work.

Regarding data parallelism, figure 4.3 shows a close resemblance to figure 4.1. The difference is in the last step, where the Fork/Join pattern merges the results back into one.

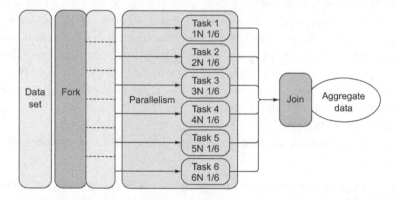

Figure 4.3   The Fork/Join pattern splits a task into subtasks that can be executed independently in parallel. When the operations complete, the subtasks are joined again. It isn't a coincidence that this pattern is often used to achieve data parallelism. There are clearly similarities.

As you can see, this pattern fits well in data parallelism. The Fork/Join pattern speeds up the execution of a program by partitioning the work into chunks (fork) and running each chunk individually in parallel. After each parallel operation completes, the chunks are merged back again (join). In general, Fork/Join is a great pattern for encoding structured parallelism because the fork and join happen at once (synchronously with respect to the caller), but in parallel (from the perspective of performance and speed). The Fork/Join abstraction can be accomplished easily using the

`Parallel.For` loop from the .NET `Parallel` class. This static method transparently deals with the partition of data and execution of tasks.

Let's analyze the `Parallel.For` loop construct with an example. First, you implement a sequential `for` loop to draw a Mandelbrot image (see figure 4.4), and then the code will be refactored to run faster. We'll evaluate the pros and cons of the approach.

> **Mandelbrot**
>
> A Mandelbrot set of images is made by sampling complex numbers and, for each, determining whether the result tends toward infinity when a particular mathematical operation is iterated on it. A *complex number* is a combination of a real number and an imaginary number, where any number you can think of is a real number, and an imaginary number is when a squared value gives a negative result. Treating the real and imaginary parts of each number as image coordinates, pixels are colored according to how rapidly the sequence diverges, if at all. Images of the Mandelbrot set display an elaborate boundary that reveals progressively ever-finer recursive detail at increasing magnifications. It's one of the best-known examples of mathematical visualization.

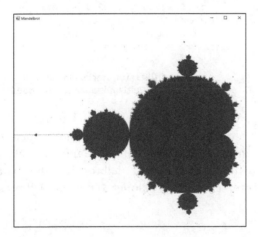

Figure 4.4   The Mandelbrot drawing resulting from running the code in this section

For this example, the details of implementing the algorithm aren't important. What's important is that for each pixel in the picture (image), a computation runs for each assigned color. This computation is independent because each pixel color doesn't depend on other pixel colors, and the assignment can be done in parallel. In fact, each pixel can have a different color assigned regardless of the color of the other pixels in the image. The absence of dependencies affects the execution strategy; each computation can run in parallel.

In this context, the Mandelbrot algorithm is used to draw an image representing the magnitude value of the complex number. The natural representation of this program uses a `for` loop to iterate through each value of the Cartesian plane to assign the corresponding color for each point. The Mandelbrot algorithm decides the color. Before delving into the core implementation, you need an object for the complex number. The following listing shows a simple implementation of a complex number used to make operations over other imaginary complex numbers.

Listing 4.1   Complex number object

```
class Complex
{
    public Complex(float real, float imaginary)
    {
        Real = real;
        Imaginary = imaginary;
    }

    public float Imaginary { get; }
    public float Real { get; }

    public float Magnitude
      => (float)Math.Sqrt(Real * Real + Imaginary * Imaginary);

    public static Complex operator +(Complex c1, Complex c2)
      => new Complex(c1.Real + c2.Real, c1.Imaginary + c2.Imaginary);
    public static Complex operator *(Complex c1, Complex c2)
      => new Complex(c1.Real * c2.Real - c1.Imaginary * c2.Imaginary,
                      c1.Real * c2.Imaginary + c1.Imaginary * c2.Real);
}
```

Uses the auto-getter property that enforces immutability

The Magnitude property determines the relative size of the complex number.

Operator overloading performs addition and multiplication on complex types.

The `Complex` class contains a definition for the `Magnitude` property. The interesting part of this code is the two overloaded operators for the `Complex` object. These operators are used to add and multiply a complex number, which is used in the Mandelbrot algorithm. The following listing shows the two core functions of the Mandelbrot algorithm. The function `isMandelbrot` determines if the complex number belongs to the Mandelbrot set.

Listing 4.2   Sequential Mandelbrot

```
Func<Complex, int, bool> isMandelbrot = (complex, iterations) =>
{
    var z = new Complex(0.0f, 0.0f);
    int acc = 0;
    while (acc < iterations && z.Magnitude < 2.0)
    {
        z = z * z + complex;
        acc += 1;
    }
    return acc == iterations;
};

for (int col = 0; col < Cols; col++) {
    for (int row = 0; row < Rows; row++) {
        var x = ComputeRow(row);
        var y = ComputeColumn(col);
        var c = new Complex(x, y);
```

Uses the function to determine if a complex number is part of the Mandelbrot set

Uses outer and inner loops over the columns and rows of the image

Shows the operations to convert the current pixel points into values to construct a complex number

```
                        var color = isMandelbrot(c, 100) ? Color.Black : Color.White;
                        var offset = (col * bitmapData.Stride) + (3 * row);
                        pixels[offset + 0] = color.B; // Blue component
                        pixels[offset + 1] = color.G; // Green component
                        pixels[offset + 2] = color.R; // Red component
                    }
                }
```

Uses this code to assign color attributes to the image pixel

Uses a function to determine the color of a pixel

The code omits details regarding the bitmap generation, which isn't relevant for the purpose of the example. You can find the full solution in the downloadable source code online.

In this example, there are two loops: the outer loop iterates over the columns of the picture box, and the inner loop iterates over its rows. Each iteration uses the functions ComputeColumn and ComputeRow, respectively, to convert the current pixel coordinates into the real and imaginary parts of a complex number. Then, the function isMandelbrot evaluates if the complex number belongs to the Mandelbrot set. This function takes as arguments a complex number and a number of iterations, and it returns a Boolean if—or not—the complex number is a member of the Mandelbrot set. The function body contains a loop that accumulates a value and decrements a count. The value returned is a Boolean that's true if the accumulator acc equals the iterations count.

In the code implementation, the program requires 3.666 seconds to evaluate the function isMandelbrot 1 million times, which is the number of pixels composing the Mandelbrot image. A faster solution is to run the loop in the Mandelbrot algorithm in parallel. As mentioned earlier, the TPL provides constructs that can be used to blindly parallelize programs, which results in incredible performance improvements. In this example, the higher-order Parallel.For function is used as a drop-in replacement for the sequential loop. This listing shows the parallel transformation with minimal changes, keeping the sequential structure of the code.

Listing 4.3   Parallel Mandelbrot

```
Func<Complex, int, bool> isMandelbrot = (complex, iterations) =>
{
    var z = new Complex(0.0f, 0.0f);
    int acc = 0;
    while (acc < iterations && z.Magnitude < 2.0)
    {
        z = z * z + complex;
        acc += 1;
    }
    return acc == iterations;
};

System.Threading.Tasks.Parallel.For(0, Cols - 1, col => {
    for (int row = 0; row < Rows; row++) {
        var x = ComputeRow(row);
        var y = ComputeColumn(col);
```

The parallel for-loop construct is applied only to the outer loop to prevent oversaturation of CPU resources.

```
        var c = new Complex(x, y);
        var color = isMandelbrot(c, 100) ? Color.DarkBlue : Color.White;
        var offset = (col * bitmapData.Stride) + (3 * row);
        pixels[offset + 0] = color.B; // Blue component
        pixels[offset + 1] = color.G; // Green component
        pixels[offset + 2] = color.R; // Red component
    }
});
```

Note that only the outer loop is paralleled to prevent oversaturation of the cores with work items. With a simple change, the execution time decreased to 0.699 seconds in a quad-core machine.

Oversaturation is a form of extra overhead, originating in parallel programming, when the number of threads created and managed by the scheduler to perform a computation grossly exceeds the available hardware cores. In this case, parallelism could make the application slower than the sequential implementation.

As a rule of thumb, I recommend that you parallelize expensive operations at the highest level. For example, figure 4.5 shows nested `for` loops; I suggest you apply parallelism only to the outer loop.

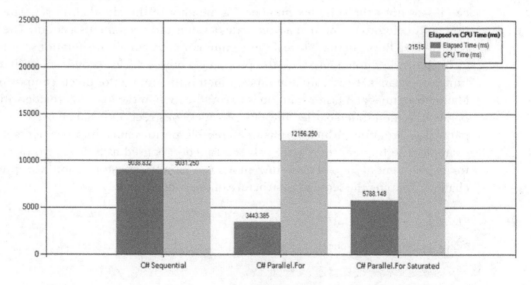

Figure 4.5   Using a `Parallel.For` construct, this benchmark compares the execution time of the sequential loop, which runs in 9.038 seconds, against the parallel, which runs in 3.443 seconds. The `Parallel.For` loop is about three times faster than the sequential code. Moreover, the last column on the right is the execution time of the over-saturated parallel loop, where both outer and inner loops are using the `Parallel.For` construct. The over-saturated parallel loop runs in 5.788 seconds, which is 50% slower than the non-saturated version.

Elapsed time vs. CPU time

From the chart in figure 4.5, the CPU time is the time for which the CPU was executing a given task. The elapsed time is the total clock time that the operation took to complete regardless of resource delays or parallel execution. In general, the elapsed time is higher than CPU time; but this value changes in a multicore machine.

When a concurrent program runs in a multicore machine, you achieve true parallelism. In this case, CPU time becomes the sum of all the execution times for each thread running in a different CPU at same given time. In a quad-core computer, for example, when you run a single-threaded (sequential) program, the elapsed time is almost equal to CPU time because there's only one core working. When running the same program in parallel using all four cores, the elapsed time becomes lower, because the program runs faster, but the CPU time increases because it's calculated by the sum of the execution time of all four parallel threads. When a program uses more than one CPU to complete the task, the CPU time may be more than the elapsed time.

In summary, the elapsed time refers to how much time the program takes with all the parallelism going on, while the CPU time measures how much time all the threads are taking, ignoring the fact that the threads overlap when running in parallel.

In general, the optimal number of worker threads for a parallel task should be equal to the number of available hardware cores divided by the average fraction of core utilization per task. For example, in a quad-core computer with 50% average core utilization per task, the perfect number of worker threads for maximum throughput is eight: (4 cores × (100% max CPU utilization / 50% average core utilization per task)). Any number of worker threads above this value could introduce extra overhead due to additional context switching, which would downgrade the performance and processor utilization.

4.2.1 *When the GC is the bottleneck: structs vs. class objects*

The goal of the Mandelbrot example is to transform a sequential algorithm into a faster one. No doubt you've achieved a speed improvement; 9.038 to 3.443 seconds is a little more than three times faster on a quad-core machine. Is it possible to further optimize performance? The TPL scheduler is partitioning the image and assigning the work to different tasks automatically, so how can you improve the speed? In this case, the optimization involves reducing memory consumption, specifically by minimizing memory allocation to optimize garbage collection. When the GC runs, the execution of the program stops until the garbage collection operation completes.

In the Mandelbrot example, a new `Complex` object is created in each iteration to decide if the pixel coordinate belongs to the Mandelbrot set. The `Complex` object is a reference type, which means that new instances of this object are allocated on the heap. This piling of objects onto the heap results in memory overhead, which forces the GC to intervene to free space.

A reference object, as compared to a value type, has extra memory overhead due to the pointer size required to access the memory location of the object allocated in the heap. Instances of a class are always allocated on the heap and accessed via a pointer dereference. Therefore, passing reference objects around, because they're a copy of the pointer, is cheap in terms of memory allocation: around 4 or 8 bytes, according the hardware architecture. Additionally, it's important to keep in mind that an object also has a fixed overhead of 8 bytes for 32-bit processes and 16 bytes for 64-bit processes. In comparison, a value type isn't allocated in the heap but rather in the stack, which removes any overhead memory allocation and garbage collection.

Keep in mind, if a value type (struct) is declared as a local variable in a method, it's allocated on the stack. Instead, if the value type is declared as part of a reference type (class), then the struct allocation becomes part of that object memory layout and exists on the heap.

The Mandelbrot algorithm creates and destroys 1 million Complex objects in the for loop; this high rate of allocation creates significant work for the GC. By replacing the Complex object from reference to value type, the speed of execution should increase because allocating a struct to the stack will never cause the GC to perform cleanup operations and won't result in a program pause. In fact, when passing a value type to a method, it's copied byte for byte, therefore allocating a struct that will never cause garbage collection because it isn't on the heap.

> **NOTE** In many cases, the use of a reference type versus a value type can result in huge differences in performance. As an example, let's compare an array of objects with an array of struct types in a 32-bit machine. Given an array of 1 million items, with each item represented by an object that contains 24 bytes of data, with reference types, the total size of the array is 72 MB (8 bytes array overhead + (4 bytes for the pointer × 1,000,000) + (8 bytes object overhead + 24 bytes data) × 1,000,000) = 72 MB). For the same array using a struct type, the size is different; it's only 24 MB (8 bytes overhead for the array) + (24 bytes data) × 1,000,000) = 24 MB). Interestingly, in a 64-bit machine, the size of the array using value types doesn't change; but for the array using reference types, the size increases to more than 40 MB for the extra pointer byte overhead.

The optimization of converting the Complex object from reference to value type is simple, requiring only that you change the keyword class to struct as shown next. (The full implementation of the Complex object is intentionally omitted.) The struct keyword converts a reference type (class) to a value type:

```
class Complex {                      struct Complex {
public Complex(float real,           public Complex(float real,
       float imaginary)                     float imaginary)
{                                    {
    this.Real = real;                    this.Real = real;
    this.Imaginary =                     this.Imaginary =
    imaginary;                           imaginary;
}                                    }
```

After this simple code change, the execution time to draw the Mandelbrot algorithm has increased the speed approximately 20%, as shown in figure 4.6.

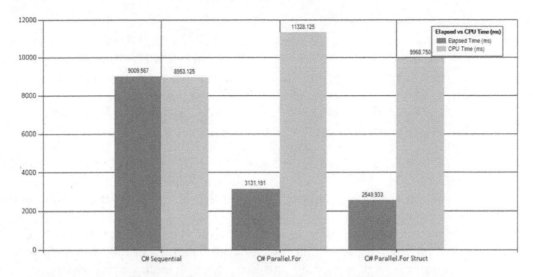

Figure 4.6 The `Parallel.For` construct benchmark comparison of the Mandelbrot algorithm computed in a quad-core machine with 8 GB of RAM. The sequential code runs in 9.009 seconds, compared to the parallel version, which runs in 3.131 seconds—almost three times faster. In the right column, the better performance is achieved by the parallel version of the code that uses the value type as a complex number in place of the reference type. This code runs in 2.548 seconds, 20% faster than the original parallel code, because there are no GC generations involved during its execution to slow the process.

The real improvement is the number of GC generations to free memory, which is reduced to zero using the struct type instead of the class reference type.[2] Table 4.1 shows GC generation comparison between a `Parallel.For` loop using many reference types (class) and a `Parallel.For` loop using many value types (struct).

Table 4.1   GC generations comparison

Operation	GC gen0	GC gen1	GC gen2
Parallel.For	1390	1	1
Parallel.For with struct value type	0	0	0

The version of the code that runs using the `Complex` object as a reference type makes many short-lived allocations to the heap: more than 4 million.[3] A short-lived object is stored in the first GC generation, and it's scheduled to be removed from the memory sooner than generations 1 and 2. This high rate of allocation forces the GC to run, which involves stopping all the threads that are running, except the threads needed for the GC. The interrupted tasks resume only after the GC operation completes. Clearly, the smaller the number of the GC generations, the faster the application performs.

---

[2]   "Fundamentals of Garbage Collection," http://mng.bz/v998.

[3]   "Dynamic Memory Allocation," http://mng.bz/w8kA.

4.2.2 The downside of parallel loops

In the previous section, you ran both the sequential and parallel versions of the Mandelbrot algorithm to compare performance. The parallel code was implemented using the TPL `Parallel` class and a `Parallel.For` construct, which can provide significant performance improvements over ordinary sequential loops.

In general, the parallel `for` loop pattern is useful to perform an operation that can be executed independently for each element of a collection (where the elements don't rely on each other). For example, mutable arrays fit perfectly in parallel loops because every element is located in a different location in memory, and the update can be effected in place without race conditions. The work of parallelizing the loop introduces complexity that can lead to problems that aren't common or even encountered in sequential code. For example, in sequential code, it's common to have a variable that plays the role of accumulator to read from or write to. If you try to parallelize a loop that uses an accumulator, you have a high probability of encountering a race condition problem because multiple threads are concurrently accessing the variables.

In a parallel `for` loop, by default, the degree of parallelism depends on the number of available cores. The *degree of parallelism* refers to the number of iterations that can be run at the same time in a computer. In general, the higher the number of available cores, the faster the parallel `for` loop executes. This is true until the point of diminishing return that Amdahl's Law (the speed of a parallel loop depends on the kind of work it does) predicts is reached.

4.3 Measuring performance speed

Achieving an increase in performance is without a doubt the main reason for writing parallel code. *Speedup* refers to the performance gained from executing a program in parallel on a multicore computer as compared to a single-core computer.

A few different aspects should be considered when evaluating speedup. The common way to gain speedup is by dividing the work between the available cores. In this way, when running one task per processor with n cores, the expectation is to run the program n times faster than the original program. This result is called *linear speedup*, which in the real world is improbable to reach due to overhead introduced by thread creation and coordination. This overhead is amplified in the case of parallelism, which involves the creation and partition of multiple threads. To measure the speedup of an application, the single-core benchmark is considered the baseline.

The formula to calculate the linear speedup of a sequential program ported into a parallel version is *speedup = sequential time / parallel time*. For example, assuming the execution time of an application running in a single-core machine is 60 minutes, when the application runs on a two-core computer, the time decreases to 40 minutes. In this case, the speedup is 1.5 (60 / 40).

Why didn't the execution time drop to 30 minutes? Because parallelizing the application involves the introduction of some overhead, which prevents the linear speedup according to the number of cores. This overhead is due to the creation of new threads, which implicate contention, context switching, and thread scheduling.

Measuring performance and anticipating speedup is fundamental for the benchmarking, designing, and implementing of parallel programs. For that reason, parallelism execution is an expensive luxury—it isn't free but instead requires an investment of time in planning. Inherent overhead costs are related to the creation and coordination of threads. Sometimes, if the amount of work is too small, the overhead brought in parallelism can exceed the benefit and, therefore, overshadow the performance gain. Frequently, the scope and volume of a problem affect the code design and the time required to execute it. Sometimes, better performance is achievable by approaching the same problem with a different, more scalable solution.

Another tool to calculate whether the investment is worth the return is Amdahl's Law, a popular formula for calculating the speedup of a parallel program.

4.3.1 Amdahl's Law defines the limit of performance improvement

At this point, it's clear that to increase the performance of your program and reduce the overall execution time of your code, it's necessary to take advantage of parallel programming and the multicore resources available. Almost every program has a portion of the code that must run sequentially to coordinate parallel execution. As in the Mandelbrot example, rendering the image is a sequential process. Another common example is the Fork/Join pattern, which starts the execution of multiple threads in parallel and then waits for them to complete before continuing the flow.

In 1965, Gene Amdahl concluded that the presence of sequential code in a program jeopardizes overall performance improvement. This concept counters the idea of linear speedup. A linear speedup means that the time T (units of time) it takes to execute a problem with p processors is T/p (the time it takes to execute a problem with one processor). This can be explained by the fact that programs cannot run entirely in parallel; therefore, the increase of performance expected isn't linear and is limited by the sequential (serial) code constraint.

Amdahl's Law says that, given a fixed data-set size, the maximum performance increase of a program implemented using parallelism is limited by the time needed for the sequential portion of the program. According to Amdahl's Law, no matter how many cores are involved in the parallel computation, the maximum speedup the program can achieve depends on the percent of time spent in sequential processing.

Amdahl's Law determines the speedup of a parallel program by using three variables:

- Baseline duration of the program executed in a single-core computer
- The number of available cores
- The percentage of parallel code

Here's the formula to calculate the speedup according with Amdahl's Law:

   Speedup $= 1 / (1 - P + (P / N))$

The numerator of the equation is always 1 because it represents the base duration. In the denominator, the variable *N* is the number of available cores, and *P* represents the percentage of parallel code.

For example, if the parallelizable code is 70% in a quad-core machine, the maximum expected speedup is 2.13:

   Speedup $= 1 / (1 - .70 + (.70 / 4)) = 1 / (.30 + .17) = 1 / 0.47 = 2.13$ times

A few conditions may discredit the result of this formula. For the one related to data parallelism, with the onset of big data, the portion of the code that runs in parallel for processing data analysis has more effect on performance as a whole. A more precise formula to calculate performance improvement due to parallelism is Gustafson's Law.

4.3.2   *Gustafson's Law: a step further to measure performance improvement*

Gustafson's Law is considered the evolution of Amdahl's Law and examines the speedup gain by a different and more contemporary perspective—considering the increased number of cores available and the increasing volume of data to process.

Gustafson's Law considers the variables that are missing in Amdahl's Law for the performance improvement calculation, making this formula more realistic for modern scenarios, such as the increase of parallel processing due to multicore hardware.

The amount of data to process is growing exponentially each year, thereby influencing software development toward parallelism, distributed systems, and cloud computing. Today, this is an important factor that invalidates Amdahl's Law and legitimizes Gustafson's Law.

Here's the formula for calculating the speedup according to Gustafson's Law:

   Speedup $= S + (N \times P)$

S represents the sequential units of work, *P* defines the number of units of work that can be executed in parallel, and *N* is the number of available cores.

A final explanation: Amdahl's Law predicts the speedup achievable by parallelizing sequential code, but Gustafson's Law calculates the speedup reachable from an existing parallel program.

4.3.3   *The limitations of parallel loops: the sum of prime numbers*

This section covers some of the limitations resulting from the sequential semantics of the parallel loop and techniques to overcome these disadvantages. Let's first consider a simple example that parallelizes the sum of the prime numbers in a collection. Listing 4.4 calculates the sum of the prime numbers of a collection with 1 million items. This calculation is a perfect candidate for parallelism because each iteration performs the same operation exactly. The implementation of the code skips the sequential version, whose execution time to perform the calculation runs in 6.551 seconds. This value will be used as a baseline to compare the speed with the parallel version of the code.

Listing 4.4 Parallel sum of prime numbers using a `Parallel.For` loop construct

```
int len = 10000000;
long total = 0;                    The total variable is used
                                   as the accumulator.

Func<int, bool> isPrime = n => {         The function isPrime determines
    if (n == 1) return false;            if a number is a prime.
    if (n == 2) return true;
    var boundary = (int)Math.Floor(Math.Sqrt(n));
    for (int i = 2; i <= boundary; ++i)
            if (n % i == 0) return false;
    return true;
};                                       The Parallel.For loop construct uses an
                                         anonymous lambda to access the current counter.

Parallel.For(0, len, i => {
                if (isPrime(i))          If the counter i is a prime number,
                    total += i;          it's added to the accumulator total.
});
```

The function `isPrime` is a simple implementation used to verify whether a given number is prime. The `for` loop uses the `total` variable as the accumulator to sum all the prime numbers in the collection. The execution time to run the code is 1.049 seconds in a quad-core computer. The speed of the parallel code is six times faster as compared with the sequential code. Perfect! But, not so fast.

If you run the code again, you'll get a different value for the `total` accumulator. The code isn't deterministic, so every time the code runs, the output will be different, because the accumulator variable `total` is shared among different threads.

One easy solution is to use a lock to synchronize the access of the threads to the `total` variable, but the cost of synchronization in this solution hurts performance. A better solution is to use a `ThreadLocal<T>` variable to store the thread's local state during loop execution. Fortunately, `Parallel.For` offers an overload that provides a built-in construct for instantiating a thread-local object. Each thread has its own instance of `ThreadLocal`, removing any opportunity for negative sharing of state. The `ThreadLocal<T>` type is part of the `System.Threading` namespace as shown in bold here.

Listing 4.5 Using `Parallel.For` with `ThreadLocal` variables

```
Parallel.For(0, len,      The total variable is used          The function isPrime determines
                          as an accumulator.                  if a number is a prime.
    () => 0,
    (int i, ParallelLoopState loopState, long tlsValue) => {
            return isPrime(i) ? tlsValue += i : tlsValue;
    },
    value => Interlocked.Add(ref total, value));
```

Seed initialization functions to create a defensive copy of the tlsValue variable by each thread; each thread will access its own copy using a ThreadLocal variable.

The code still uses a global mutual variable `total`, but in a different way. In this version of the code, the third parameter of the `Parallel.For` loop initializes a local state whose lifetime corresponds to the first iteration on the current thread through the last one. In this way, each thread uses a thread-local variable to operate against an isolated copy of state, which can be stored and retrieved separately in a thread-safe manner.

When a piece of data is stored in a managed *thread-local storage* (TLS), as in the example, it's unique to a thread. In this case, the thread is called the *owner* of the data. The purpose of using thread-local data storage is to avoid the overhead due to lock synchronizations accessing a shared state. In the example, a copy of the local variable `tlsValue` is assigned and used by each thread to calculate the sum of a given range of the collection that has been partitioned by the parallel partitioner algorithm. The parallel partitioner uses a sophisticated algorithm to decide the best approach to divide and distribute the chunks of the collection between threads.

After a thread completes all of the iterations, the last parameter in the `Parallel.For` loop that defines the `join` operation is called. Then, during the `join` operation, the results from each thread are aggregated. This step uses the `Interlocked` class for high performance and thread-safe operation of addition operations. This class was introduced in chapter 3 to perform CAS operations to safely mutate (actually swap) the value of an object in multithreaded environments. The `Interlock` class provides other useful operations, such as increment, decrement, and exchange of variables.

This section has mentioned an important term in data parallelism: aggregate. The aggregate concept will be covered in chapter 5.

Listing 4.5, the final version of the code, produces a deterministic result with a speed of execution of *1.178 seconds*: almost equivalent to the previous one. You pay a little extra overhead in exchange for correctness. When using shared state in a parallel loop, scalability is often lost because of synchronization on the shared state access.

4.3.4   *What can possibly go wrong with a simple loop?*

Now we consider a simple code block that sums the integers from a given array. Using any OOP language, you could write something like this.

Listing 4.6   Common `for` loop

```
int sum = 0;
for (int i = 0; i < data.Length; i++)
{
    sum += data[i];          ◄——— The sum variable is used as an accumulator
}                                 whose value updates each iteration.
```

You've written something similar in your career as a programmer; likely, a few years ago, when programs were executed single-threaded. Back then this code was fine, but these days, you're dealing with different scenarios and with complex systems and programs that simultaneously perform multiple tasks. With these challenges, the previous code can have a subtle bug, in the `sum` line of code:

```
sum += data[i];
```

What happens if the values of the array are mutated while it's traversed? In a multi-threaded program, this code presents the issue of mutability, and it cannot guarantee consistency.

Note that not all state mutation is equally evil, if the mutation of state that's only visible within the scope of a function is inelegant, but harmless. For example, suppose the previous sum in a for loop is isolated in a function as follows:

```
int Sum(int[] data)
{
    int sum = 0;
    for (int i = 0; i < data.Length; i++)
    {
        sum += data[i];
    }
}
```

Despite updating the sum value, its mutation isn't visible from outside the scope of the function. As a result, this implementation of sum can be considered a pure function.

To reduce complexity and errors in your program, you must raise the level of abstraction in the code. For example, to compute a sum of numeric values, express your intention in "what you want," without repeating "how to do." Common functionality should be part of the language, so you can express your intentions as

```
int sum = data.Sum();
```

Indeed, the Sum extension method (http://mng.bz/f3nF) is part of the System .Linq namespace in .NET. In this namespace, many methods, such as List and Array, extend the functionality for any IEnumerable object (http://mng.bz/2bBv). It's not a coincidence that the ideas behind LINQ originate from functional concepts. The LINQ namespace promotes immutability, and it operates on the concept of transformation instead of mutation, where a LINQ query (and lambda) let you transform a set of structured data from its original form into another form, without worrying about side effects or state.

4.3.5 *The declarative parallel programming model*

In the sum of prime numbers example in listing 4.5, the Parallel.For loop constructor definitely fits the purpose of speedup compared to the sequential code and does it efficiently, although the implementation is a bit more difficult to understand and maintain compared to the sequential version. The final code isn't immediately clear to a developer looking at it for the first time. Ultimately, the intent of the code is to sum the prime numbers of a collection. It would be nice to have the ability to express the intentions of the program, defining step by step how to implement the algorithm.

This is where PLINQ comes into play. The following listing is the equivalent of the parallel Sum using PLINQ (in bold) in place of the Parallel.For loop.

Listing 4.7 Parallel sum of a collection using declarative PLINQ

```
long total = 0;
Parallel.For(0, len,   ◀——— Parallel sum using the Parallel.For construct
```

```
        () => 0,
        (int i, ParallelLoopState loopState, long tlsValue) => {
            return isPrime(i) ? tlsValue += i : tlsValue;
},
value => Interlocked.Add(ref total, value));
```

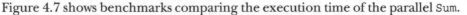

```
        long total = Enumerable.Range(0, len).AsParallel()
                            .Where(isPrime).Sum(x => (long)x);
```

Parallel sum using PLINQ

Sum of the values, casting the results into a long type to avoid overflow exception

The functional declarative approach is only one line of code. Clearly, when compared to the for loop implementation, it's simple to understand, succinct, maintainable, and without any mutation of state. The PLINQ construct represents the code as a chain of functions, each one providing a small piece of functionality to accomplish the task. The solution adopts the higher-order-function aggregate part of the LINQ/PLINQ API, which in this case is the function Sum(). The aggregate applies a function to each successive element of a collection, providing the aggregated result of all previous elements. Other common aggregate functions are Average(), Max(), Min(), and Count().

Figure 4.7 shows benchmarks comparing the execution time of the parallel Sum.

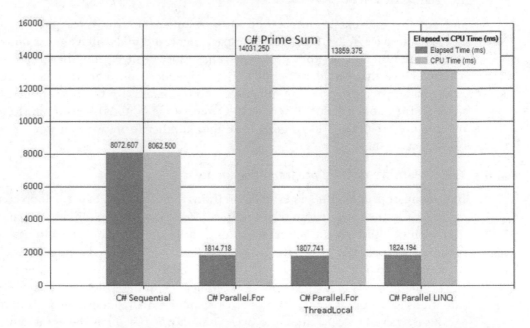

Figure 4.7   Benchmarking comparison of the sum of prime numbers. The benchmark runs in an eight-core machine with 8 GB of RAM. The sequential version runs in 8.072 seconds. This value is used as a base for the other versions of the code. The Parallel.For version took 1.814 seconds, which is approximately 4.5 times faster than the sequential code. The Parallel.For ThreadLocal version is a little faster than the parallel Loop. Ultimately, the PLINQ program is slowest among the parallel versions; it took 1.824 seconds to run.

Aggregating values to avoid an arithmetic overflow exception

The previous PLINQ query isn't optimized. Shortly, you'll learn techniques to make this code more performant. Moreover, the size of the sequence to sum was reduced to 10,000 instead of the 1 million used earlier, because the `Sum()` function in PLINQ is compiled to execute in a checked block, which throws an arithmetic overflow exception. The solution is to convert the base number from an `integer-32` to `integer-64` (`long`), or to use the `Aggregate` function instead, in this form:

```
Enumerable.Range(0, len).AsParallel()
        .Aggregate((acc,i) => isPrime(i) ? acc += i : acc);
```

The function `Aggregate` will be covered in detail in chapter 5.

Summary

- Data parallelism aims to process massive amounts of data by partitioning and performing each chunk separately, then regrouping the results when completed. This lets you analyze the chunks in parallel, gaining speed and performance.
- Mental models used in this chapter, which apply to data parallelism, are Fork/Join, Parallel Data Reduction, and Parallel Aggregation. These design patterns share a common approach that separates the data and runs the same task in parallel on each divided portion.
- Utilizing functional programming constructs, it's possible to write sophisticated code to process and analyze data in a declarative and simple manner. This paradigm lets you achieve parallelism with little change in your code.
- Profiling the program is a way to understand and ensure that the changes you make to adopt parallelism in your code are beneficial. To do that, measure the speed of the program running sequentially, then use a benchmark as a baseline to compare the code changes.

PLINQ and MapReduce: data parallelism, part 2

This chapter covers

- Using declarative programming semantics

- Isolating and controlling side effects

- Implementing and using a parallel `Reduce` function

- Maximizing hardware resource utilization

- Implementing a reusable parallel MapReduce pattern

This chapter presents MapReduce, one of the most widely used functional programming patterns in software engineering. Before delving into MapReduce, we'll analyze the declarative programming style that the functional paradigm emphasizes and enforces, using PLINQ and the idiomatic F#, PSeq. Both technologies analyze a query statement at runtime and make the best strategy decision concerning how to execute the query in accordance with available system resources. Consequently, the more CPU power added to the computer, the faster your code will run. Using these strategies, you can develop code ready for next-generation computers. Next, you'll learn how to implement a parallel `Reduce` function in .NET, which you can reuse in your daily work to increase the speed of execution of aggregates functions.

Using FP, you can engage data parallelism in your programs without introducing complexity, compared to conventional programming. FP prefers declarative over procedural semantics to express the intent of a program instead of describing the steps to achieve the task. This declarative programming style simplifies the adoption of parallelism in your code.

5.1 A short introduction to PLINQ

Before we delve into PLINQ, we'll define its sequential double, LINQ, an extension to the .NET Framework that provides a declarative programming style by raising the level of abstraction and simplifying the application into a rich set of operations to transform any object that implements the `IEnumerable` interface. The most common operations are mapping, sorting, and filtering. LINQ operators accept behavior as the parameter that usually can be passed in the form of lambda expressions. In this case, the lambda expression provided will be applied to each single item of the sequence. With the introduction of LINQ and lambda expressions, FP becomes a reality in .NET.

You can make queries run in parallel using all the cores of the development system to convert LINQ to PLINQ by adding the extension `.AsParallel()` to the query. PLINQ can be defined as a concurrency engine for executing LINQ queries. The objective of parallel programming is to maximize processor utilization with increased throughput in a multicore architecture. For a multicore computer, your application should recognize and scale performance to the number of available processor cores.

The best way to write parallel applications isn't to think about parallelism, and PLINQ fits this abstraction perfectly because it takes care of all the underlying requirements, such as partitioning the sequences into smaller chunks to run individually and applying the logic to each item of each subsequence. Does that sound familiar? That's because PLINQ implements the Fork/Join model underneath, as shown in figure 5.1.

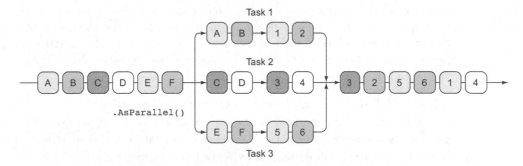

Figure 5.1 A PLINQ execution model. Converting a LINQ query to PLINQ is as simple as applying the `AsParallel()` extension method, which runs in parallel the execution using a Fork/Join pattern. In this figure, the input characters are transformed in parallel into numbers. Notice that the order of the input elements isn't preserved.

As a rule of thumb, every time there is a `for` or `for-each` loop in your code that does something with a collection, without performing a side effect outside the loop, consider transforming the loop into a LINQ. Then benchmark the execution and evaluate whether the query could be a fit to run in parallel using PLINQ.

> **NOTE**   This is a book about concurrency, so from now on it will mention only PLINQ, but for the majority of the cases, the same constructs, principles, and higher-order functions used to define a query also apply to LINQ.

The advantage of using PLINQ, compared to a parallel `for` loop, is its capability of handling automatically aggregation of temporary processing results within each running thread that executes the query.

5.1.1   How is PLINQ more functional?

PLINQ is considered an ideal functional library, but why? Why consider the PLINQ version of code more functional than the original `Parallel.For` loop?

With `Parallel.For`, you're telling the computer what to do:

- Loop through the collection.
- Verify if the number is prime.
- If the number is prime, add it to a local accumulator.
- When all iterations are done, add the accumulator to a shared value.

By using LINQ/PLINQ, you can tell the computer what you want in the form of a sentence: "Given a range from 0 to 1,000,000, where the number is prime, sum them all."

FP emphasizes writing declarative code over imperative code. Declarative code focuses on what you want to achieve rather than how to achieve it. PLINQ tends to emphasize the intent of the code rather than the mechanism and is, therefore, much more functional.

> **NOTE**   In section 13.9, you'll use a `Parallel.ForEach` loop to build a high-performance and reusable operator that combines the functions `filter` and `map`. In this case, because the implementation details of the function are abstracted away and hidden from the eyes of the developer, the function parallel `FilterMap` becomes a higher-order operator that satisfies the declarative programming concept.

In addition, FP favors the use of functions to raise the level of abstraction, which aims to hide complexity. In this regard, PLINQ raises the concurrency programming model abstraction by handling the query expression and analyzing the structure to decide how to run in parallel, which maximizes performance speed.

FP also encourages combining small and simple functions to solve complex problems. The PLINQ pipeline fully satisfies this tenet with the approach of chaining pieces of extension methods together.

Another functional aspect of PLINQ is the absence of mutation. The PLINQ operators don't mutate the original sequence, but instead return a new sequence as a result of the transformation. Consequently, the PLINQ functional implementation gives you predictable results, even when the tasks are executed in parallel.

5.1.2 PLINQ and pure functions: the parallel word counter

Now let's consider an example where a program loads a series of text files from a given folder and then parses each document to provide the list of the 10 most frequently used words. The process flow is the following (shown in figure 5.2):

1 Collect the files from a given folder path.
2 Iterate the files.
3 For each text file, read the content.
4 For each line, break it down into words.
5 Transform each word into uppercase, which is useful for comparison.
6 Group the collection by word.
7 Order by higher count.
8 Take the first 10 results.
9 Project the result into tabular format (a dictionary).

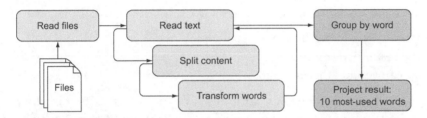

Figure 5.2 Representation of the flow process to count the times each word has been mentioned. First, the files are read from a given folder, then each text file is read, and the content is split in lines and single words to be grouped by.

The following listing defines this functionality in the WordsCounter method, which takes as input the path of a folder and then calculates how many times each word has been used in all files. This listing shows the AsParallel command in bold.

Listing 5.1 Parallel word-counting program with side effects

```
public static Dictionary<string, int> WordsCounter(string source)
{
    var wordsCount =
            (from filePath in
                Directory.GetFiles(source, "*.txt")          ◄── The side effect of reading
                            .AsParallel()                          from the filesystem
                from line in File.ReadLines(filePath)        ◄── Parallelizes the
                from word in line.Split(' ')                     sequence of files
                select word.ToUpper())
        .GroupBy(w => w)
```

```
        .OrderByDescending(v => v.Count()).Take(10);
    return wordsCount.ToDictionary(k => k.Key, v => v.Count());
}
```

Orders the words mentioned by count and takes the first 10 values

The logic of the program follows the previously defined flow step by step. It's declarative, readable, and runs in parallel, but there's a hidden problem. It has a side effect. The method reads files from the filesystem, generating an I/O side effect. As mentioned previously, a function or expression is said to have a side effect if it modifies a state outside its scope or if its output doesn't depend solely on its input. In this case, passing the same input to a function with side effects doesn't guarantee to always produce the same output. These types of functions are problematic in concurrent code because a side effect implies a form of mutation. Examples of impure functions are getting a random number, getting the current system time, reading data from a file or a network, printing something to a console, and so forth. To understand better why reading data from a file is a side effect, consider that the content of the file could change any time, and whenever the content of the file changes, it can return something different. Furthermore, reading a file could also yield an error if in the meantime it was deleted. The point is to expect that the function can return something different every time it's called.

Due to the presence of side effects, there are complexities to consider:

- Is it really safe to run this code in parallel?
- Is the result deterministic?
- How can you test this method?

A function that takes a filesystem path may throw an error if the directory doesn't exist or if the running program doesn't have the required permissions to read from the directory. Another point to consider is that with a function run in parallel using PLINQ, the query execution is deferred until its materialization. *Materialization* is the term used to specify when a query is executed and produces a result. For this reason, successive materialization of a PLINQ query that contains side effects might generate different results due to the underlying data that might have changed. The result isn't deterministic. This could happen if a file is deleted from the directory between different calls, and then throws an exception.

Moreover, functions with side effects (also called *impure*) are hard to test. One possible solution is to create a testing directory with a few text files that cannot change. This approach requires that you know how many words are in these files, and how many times they have been used to verify the correctness of the function. Another solution is to mock the directory and the data contained, which can be even more complex than the previous solution. A better approach exists: remove the side effects and raise the level of abstraction, simplifying the code while decoupling it from external dependencies.

But what are side effects? What's a pure function, and why should you care?

5.1.3 Avoiding side effects with pure functions

One principle of functional programming is purity. *Pure functions* are those without side effects, where the result is independent of state, which can change with time. That is, pure functions always return the same value when given the same inputs. This listing shows pure pure functions in C#.

Listing 5.2 Pure functions in C#

```
public static string AreaCircle(int radius) =>
                Math.Pow(radius, 2) * Math.PI;          The output never changes because
                                                        the functions have no side effects.
public static int Add(int x, int y) => x + y;
```

The listing is an example of side effects that are functions that mutate state, setting values of global variables. Because variables live in the block where they're declared, a variable that's defined globally introduces possible collision and affects the readability and maintainability of the program. This requires extra checking of the current value of the variable at any point and each time it's called. The main problem of dealing with side effects is that they make your program unpredictable and problematic in concurrent code, because a side effect implies a form of mutation.

Imagine passing the same argument to a function and each time obtaining a different outcome. A function is said to have side effects if it does any of the following:

- Performs any I/O operation (this includes reading/writing to the filesystem, to a database, or to the console)
- Mutates global state and any state outside of the function's scope
- Throws exceptions

At first, removing side effects from a program can seem extremely limiting, but there are numerous benefits to writing code in this style:

- Easy to reason about the correctness of your program.
- Easy to compose functions for creating new behavior.
- Easy to isolate and, therefore, easy to test, and less bug-prone.
- Easy to execute in parallel. Because pure functions don't have external dependencies, their order of execution (evaluation) doesn't matter.

As you can see, introducing pure functions as part of your toolset immediately benefits your code. Moreover, the result of pure functions depends precisely on their input, which introduces the property of *referential transparency*.

Referential transparency

Referential transparency has a fundamental implication for side-effect-free functions; therefore, it's a desirable property because it represents the capability to replace a function call for a defined set of parameters with the value it returns without changing the meaning of the program. Using referential transparency, you can exchange the

(continued)

expression for its value, and nothing changes. The concept is about representing the result of any pure function directly with the result of the evaluation. The order of evaluation isn't important, and evaluating a function multiple times always leads to the same result—execution can be easily parallelized.

Mathematics is always referentially transparent. Given a function and an input value, the function maps always have the same output with the same input. For example, any function $f(x) = y$ is a pure function if for the same value x you end up getting the same result y without any internal or external state change.

A program inevitably needs side effects to do something useful, of course, and functional programming doesn't prohibit side effects, but rather encourages minimizing and isolating them.

5.1.4   Isolate and control side effects: refactoring the parallel word counter

Let's re-evaluate listing 5.1, the `WordsCounter` example. How can you isolate and control side effects in this code?

```
static Dictionary<string, int> WordsCounter(string source) {
        var wordsCount = (from filePath in
                    Directory.GetFiles(source, "*.txt")
                        .AsParallel()
            from linein File.ReadLines(filePath)
                from word in line.Split(' ')
                select word.ToUpper())
            .GroupBy(w => w)
            .OrderByDescending(v => v.Count()).Take(10);

        return wordsCount.ToDictionary(k => k.Key, v => v.Count());
}
```

The bold code shows the side effect of reading from the filesystem.

The function can be split into a pure function at the core and a pair of functions with side effects. The I/O side effect cannot be avoided, but it can be separated from the pure logic. In this listing, the logic to count each word mentioned per file is extracted, and the side effects are isolated.

Listing 5.3   Decoupling and isolating side effects

The pure function without side effects; in this case, the I/O operation is removed.

```
static Dictionary<string, int> PureWordsPartitioner
                        (IEnumerable<IEnumerable<string>> content) =>
    (from lines in content.AsParallel()
        from line in lines
        from word in line.Split(' ')
        select word.ToUpper())
        .GroupBy(w => w)
```

The result from the side-effect-free function can be parallelized without issues.

```
        .OrderByDescending(v => v.Count()).Take(10)
        .ToDictionary(k => k.Key, v => v.Count());

static Dictionary<string, int> WordsPartitioner(string source)
{
    var contentFiles =
        (from filePath in Directory.GetFiles(source, "*.txt")
            let lines = File.ReadLines(filePath)
            select lines);

    return PureWordsPartitioner(contentFiles);
}
```

Calls the side-effect-free function from an impure function

The code to merge the results into one dictionary, avoiding duplicates

The new function `PureWordsPartitioner` is pure, where the result depends only on the input argument. This function is side effect free and easy to prove correct. Conversely, the method `WordsPartitioner` is responsible for reading a text file from the filesystem, which is a side effect operation, and then aggregating the results from the analysis.

As you can see from the example, separating the pure from the impure parts of your code not only facilitates testing and optimization of the pure parts, but will also make you more aware of the side effects of your program and help you avoid making the impure parts bigger than they need to be. Designing with pure functions and decoupling side effects from pure logic are the two basic tenets that functional thinking brings to the forefront.

5.2 *Aggregating and reducing data in parallel*

In FP, a *fold,* also known as *reduce and accumulate,* is a higher-order function that reduces a given data structure, typically a sequence of elements, into a single value. Reduction, for example, could return an average value for a series of numbers, calculating a summation, maximum value, or minimum value.

The `fold` function takes an initial value, commonly called the *accumulator,* which is used as a container for intermediate results. As a second argument it takes a binary expression that acts as a *reduction* function to apply against each element in the sequence to return the new value for the accumulator. In general, in reduction you take a binary operator—that is, a function with two arguments—and compute it over a vector or set of elements of size n, usually from left to right. Sometimes, a special seed value is used for the first operation with the first element, because there's no previous value to use. During each step of the iteration, the binary expression takes the current element from the sequence and the accumulator value as inputs, and returns a value that overwrites the accumulator. The final result is the value of the last accumulator, as shown in figure 5.3.

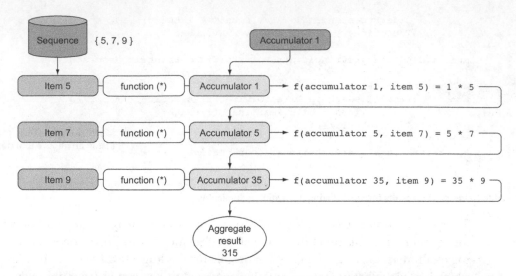

Figure 5.3   The `fold` **function reduces a sequence to a single value. The function** `(f)`**, in this case, is multiplication and takes an initial accumulator with a value of 1. For each iteration in the sequence (5, 7, 9), the function applies the calculation to the current item and accumulator. The result is then used to update the accumulator with the new value.**

The `fold` function has two forms, right-fold and left-fold, depending on where the first item of the sequence to process is located. The right-fold starts from the first item in the list and iterates forward; the left-fold starts from the last item in the list and iterates backward. This section covers the right-fold because it's most often used. For the remainder of the section, the term *fold* will be used in place of *right-fold*.

> **NOTE** Consider several performance implications when choosing between the right-fold and left-fold functions. In the case of folding over a list, the right-fold occurs in $O(1)$ because it adds an item to the front of a list that is constant time. The left-fold requires $O(n)$, because it has to run through the whole list to add an item. The left-fold cannot be used to handle or generate infinite lists, because the size of the list should be known to start folding backward from the last item.

The `fold` function is particularly useful and interesting: it's possible to express a variety of operations in terms of aggregation, such as `filter`, `map`, and `sum`. The `fold` function is probably the most difficult to learn among the other functions in list comprehension, but one of the most powerful.

If you haven't read it yet, I recommend "Why Functional Programming Matters," by John Hughes (www.cs.kent.ac.uk/people/staff/dat/miranda/whyfp90.pdf). This paper goes into detail about the high applicability and importance of the `fold` function in FP. This listing uses F# and `fold` to demonstrate the implementation of a few useful functions.

Listing 5.4   Implementing `max` **and** `map` **using the F#** `fold` **function**

```
let map (projection:'a -> 'b) (sequence:seq<'a>) =
    sequence |> Seq.fold(fun acc item -> (projection item)::acc) []
```

The map function using fold in F#

```
let max (sequence:seq<int>) =
    sequence |> Seq.fold(fun acc item -> max item acc) 0
```

← The max function using fold in F#

```
let filter (predicate:'a -> bool) (sequence:seq<'a>) =
    sequence |> Seq.fold(fun acc item ->
        if predicate item = true then item::acc else acc) []
```

← The filter function using fold in F#

```
let length (sequence:seq<'a>) =
    sequence |> Seq.fold(fun acc item -> acc + 1) 0
```

The length function to calculate the length of a collection using fold in F#

The equivalent of `fold` in LINQ in C# is `Aggregate`. This listing uses the C# `Aggregate` function to implement other useful functions.

Listing 5.5 Implementing `Filter` and `Length` using LINQ `Aggregate` in C#

```
IEnumerable<T> Map<T, R>(IEnumerable<T> sequence, Func<T, R> projection){
    return sequence.Aggregate(new List<R>(), (acc, item) => {
                acc.Add(projection(item));
                return acc;
    });
}
```

The Map function using LINQ Aggregate in C#

```
int Max(IEnumerable<int> sequence) {
    return sequence.Aggregate(0, (acc, item) => Math.Max(item, acc));
}
```

← The Max function using LINQ Aggregate in C#

```
IEnumerable<T> Filter<T>(IEnumerable<T> sequence, Func<T, bool> predicate){
    return sequence.Aggregate(new List<T>(), (acc, item) => {
            if (predicate(item))
                acc.Add(item);
            return acc;
    });
}
```

The Filter function using LINQ Aggregate in C#

```
int Length<T>(IEnumerable<T> sequence) {
    return sequence.Aggregate(0, (acc, _) => acc + 1);
}
```

← The Length function using LINQ Aggregate in C#

Because of the inclusion of .NET list-comprehension support for parallelism, including the LINQ `Aggregate` and `Seq.fold` operators, the implementation of these functions in C# and F# can be easily converted to run concurrently. More details about this conversion are discussed in the next sections.

5.2.1 Deforesting: one of many advantages to folding

Reusability and maintainability are a few advantages that the `fold` function provides. But one special feature that this function permits is worth special mention. The `fold` function can be used to increase the performance of a list-comprehension query. *List comprehension* is a construct, similar to LINQ/PLINQ in C#, to facilitate list-based queries on existing lists (https://en.wikipedia.org/wiki/List_comprehension).

How can the `fold` function increase the performance speed of a list query regardless of parallelism? To answer, let's analyze a simple PLINQ query. You saw that the use of functional constructs, like LINQ/PLINQ in .NET, transforms the original sequence avoiding mutation, which in strict-evaluated programming languages such as F# and C# often leads to the generation of intermediate data structures that are unnecessary. This listing shows a PLINQ query that filters and then transforms a sequence of numbers to calculate the sum of the even values times two (doubled). The parallel execution is in bold.

Listing 5.6   PLINQ query to sum the double of even numbers in parallel

```
var data = new int[100000];
for(int i = 0; i < data.Length; i++)
    data[i]=i;

long total =
    data.AsParallel()
        .Where(n => n % 2 == 0)
        .Select(n => n + n)
        .Sum(x => (long)x);
```

> Due to parallelism, the order in which the values are processed isn't guaranteed; but the result is deterministic because the Sum operation is commutative.

> The value is cast to long number Sum(x => (long)x) to avoid an overflow exception.

In these few lines of code, for each `Where` and `Select` of the PLINQ query, there's a generation of intermediate sequences that unnecessarily increase memory allocation. In the case of large sequences to transform, the penalty paid to the GC to free memory becomes increasingly higher, with negative consequences for performance. The allocation of objects in memory is expensive; consequently, optimization that avoids extra allocation is valuable for making functional programs run faster. Fortunately, the creation of these unnecessary data structures can often be avoided. The elimination of intermediate data structures to reduce the size of temporary memory allocation is referred to as *deforesting*. This technique is easily exploitable with the higher-order function `fold`, which takes the name `Aggregate` in LINQ. This function is capable of eliminating intermediate data-structure allocations by combining multiple operations, such as `filter` and `map`, in a single step, which would otherwise have an allocation for each operation. This code example shows a PLINQ query to sum the double of even numbers in parallel using the `Aggregate` operator:

```
long total = data.AsParallel().Aggregate(0L, (acc, n) =>
                      n % 2 == 0 ? acc + (n + n) : acc);
```

The PLINQ function `Aggregate` has several overloads; in this case, the first argument `0` is the initial value of the accumulator `acc`, which is passed and updated each iteration. The second argument is the function that performs an operation against the item from the sequence, and updates the value of the accumulator `acc`. The body of this function merges the behaviors of the previously defined `Where`, `Select`, and `Sum` PLINQ extensions, producing the same result. The only difference is the execution time. The original code ran in 13 ms; the updated version of the code, deforesting the function, ran in 8 ms.

Deforesting is a productive optimization tool when used with eager data structures, such as lists and arrays; but lazy collections behave a little differently. Instead of generating intermediate data structures, lazy sequences store the function to be mapped and the original data structure. But you'll still have better performance speed improvement compared to a function that isn't deforested.

5.2.2 Fold in PLINQ: Aggregate functions

The same concepts you learned about the `fold` function can be applied to PLINQ in both F# and C#. As mentioned earlier, PLINQ has the equivalent of the `fold` function called `Aggregate`. The PLINQ `Aggregate` is a right-fold. Here's one of its overloaded signatures:

```
public static TAccumulate Aggregate<TSource, TAccumulate>(
    this IEnumerable<TSource> source,
    TAccumulate seed,
    Func<TAccumulate, TSource, TAccumulate> func);
```

The function takes three arguments that map to the sequence source: the sequence source to process, the initial accumulator seed, and the function `func`, which updates the accumulator for each element.

The best way to understand how `Aggregate` works is with an example. In the example in the sidebar, you'll parallelize the k-means clustering algorithm using PLINQ and the `Aggregate` function. The example shows how remarkably simple and performant a program becomes by using this construct.

---

k-means clustering

k-means, also called Lloyd's algorithm, is an unsupervised machine-learning algorithm that categorizes a set of data points into clusters, each centered on its own centroid. A *centroid* of a cluster is the sum of points in it divided by the number of total points. It represents the center of the mass of a geometric shape having uniform density.

The k-means clustering algorithm takes an input data and a value *k* that indicates the number of clusters to set, and then places the centroids randomly in these clusters. This algorithm takes as a parameter the number of clusters to find and makes an initial guess at the center of each cluster. The idea is to generate a number of centroids that produce the centers of the clusters. Each point in the data is linked with its nearest centroid. The distance is calculated using a simple Euclidean distance function (https://en.wikipedia.org/wiki/Euclidean_distance). Each centroid is then moved to the average of the positions of the points that are associated with it. A centroid is computed by taking the sum of its points and then dividing the result by the size of the cluster. The iteration involves these steps:

1. Sum, or `reduction`, computes the sum of the points in each cluster.
2. Divide each cluster sum by the number of points in that cluster.
3. Reassign, or map, the points of each cluster to the closest centroid.

(continued)

   4 Repeat the steps until the cluster locations stabilize. You cut off processing after an arbitrarily chosen number of iterations, because sometimes the algorithm does not converge.

The process is iterative, meaning that it repeats until the algorithm reaches a final result or exceeds the maximum number of steps. When the algorithm runs, it corrects continuously and updates the centroids in each iteration to better cluster the input data.

For the data source used as input in the k-means clustering algorithm, you'll use the "white wine quality" public records (figure 5.4), available for download at http://mng.bz/9mdt.

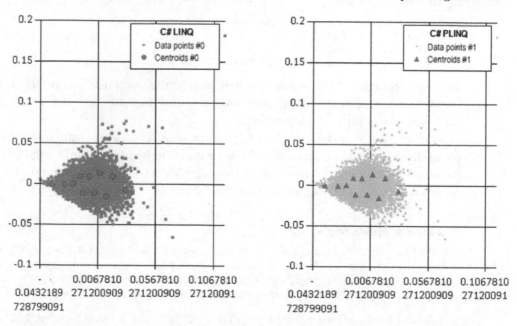

Figure 5.4   The result of running the k-means algorithms using C# LINQ for the serial version of code and C# PLINQ for the parallelized version. The centroids are the large points in both clusters. Each image represents one iteration of the k-means algorithm, with 11 centroids in the cluster. Each iteration of the algorithm computes the centroid of each cluster and then assigns each point to the cluster with the closest centroid.

The full implementation of the k-means program is omitted because of the length of the code; only the relevant excerpt of the code is shown in listings 5.7 and 5.8. But the full code implementation, in both F# and C#, is available and downloadable in the source code for this book.

    Let's review two core functions: `GetNearestCentroid` and `UpdateCentroids`. `GetNearestCentroid` is used to update the clusters, as shown in listing 5.7. For every data input, this function finds the closest centroid assigned to the cluster to which the input belongs (in bold).

Listing 5.7 Finding the closest centroid (updating the clusters)

```
double[] GetNearestCentroid(double[][] centroids, double[] center){
        return centroids.Aggregate((centroid1, centroid2) =>
            Dist(center, centroid2) < Dist(center, centroid1)
            ? centroid2
            : centroid1);
    }
```

Uses the Aggregate LINQ function to find the closest centroid

The `GetNearestCentroid` implementation uses the `Aggregate` function to compare the distances between the centroids to find the nearest one. During this step, if the inputs in any of the clusters aren't updated because a closer centroid is not found, then the algorithm is complete and returns the result.

The next step, shown in listing 5.8, after the clusters are updated, is to update the centroid locations. `UpdateCentroids` calculates the center for each cluster and shifts the centroids to that point. Then, with the updated centroid values, the algorithm repeats the previous step, running `GetNearestCentroid` until it finds the closest result. These operations continue running until a convergence condition is met, and the positions of the cluster centers become stable. The bold code highlights commands discussed in more depth following the listing.

The following implementation of the k-means clustering algorithm uses FP, sequence expressions with PLINQ, and several of the many built-in functions for manipulating data.

Listing 5.8 Updating the location of the centroids

```
double[][] UpdateCentroids(double[][] centroids)
{
    var partitioner = Partitioner.Create(data, true);
    var result = partitioner.AsParallel()
        .WithExecutionMode(ParallelExecutionMode.ForceParallelism)
        .GroupBy(u => GetNearestCentroid(centroids, u))
        .Select(points =>
            points
            .Aggregate(
                seed: new double[N],
                func: (acc, item) =>
                    acc.Zip(item, (a, b) => a + b).ToArray())
            .Select(items => items / points.Count())
            .ToArray());
    return result.ToArray();
}
```

Uses a tailored partitioner for maximizing the performance

Runs the query in parallel from the partitioner

Uses the Aggregate function to find the center of the centroids in the cluster; the seed initial value is a double array with size N (the dimensionality of data).

Uses the Zip function to thread the centroid-locations and accumulator sequences

Forces parallelism regardless of the shape of the query, bypassing the default PLINQ analysis that could decide to run part of the operation sequentially

With the `UpdateCentroids` function, there's a great deal of processing to compute, so the use of PLINQ can effectively parallelize the code, thereby increasing the speed.

NOTE Even if centroids don't move on the plane, they may change their indexes in the resulting array due to the nature of `GroupBy` and `AsParallel`.

The PLINQ query in the body of UpdateCentroids performs aggregation in two steps. The first uses the GroupBy function, which takes as an argument a function that provides the key used for the aggregation. In this case, the key is computed by the previous function GetNearestCentroid. The second step, mapping, which runs the Select function, calculates the centers of new clusters for each given point. This calculation is performed by the Aggregate function, which takes the list of points as inputs (the location coordinates of each centroid) and calculates their centers mapped to the same cluster using the local accumulator acc as shown in listing 5.8.

The accumulator is an array of doubles with size N, which is the *dimensionality* (the number of characteristics/measurements) of the data to process. The value N is defined as a constant in the parent class because it never changes and can be safely shared. The Zip function threads together the nearest centroids (points) and the accumulator sequences. Then, the center of that cluster is recomputed by averaging the position of the points in the cluster.

The implementation details of the algorithm aren't crucial; the key point is that the description of the algorithm is translated precisely and directly into PLINQ using Aggregate. If you try to re-implement the same functionality without the Aggregate function, the program runs in ugly and hard-to-understand loops with mutable shared variables.

The following listing shows the equivalent of the UpdateCentroids function without the help of the Aggregate function. The bold code is discussed further following the listing.

Listing 5.9   UpdateCentroids function implemented without Aggregate

```
double[][] UpdateCentroidsWithMutableState(double[][] centroids)
{
    var result = data.AsParallel()
        .GroupBy(u => GetNearestCentroid(centroids, u))
        .Select(points => {
            var res = new double[N];        ◄─── Uses an imperative loop to calculate the
            foreach (var x in points)            center of the centroids in the cluster
                for (var i = 0; i < N; i++)
                    res[i] += x[i];        ◄───
            var count = points.Count();
            for (var i = 0; i < N; i++)         Uses the mutable state
                res[i] /= count;        ◄───
            return res;
        });
    return result.ToArray();
}
```

Figure 5.5 shows benchmark results of running the k-means clustering algorithm. The benchmark was executed in a quad-core machine with 8 GB of RAM. The algorithms tested are the sequential LINQ, the parallel PLINQ, and the parallel PLINQ using a custom partitioner.

NOTE When multiple threads are used on a multiprocessor, more than one CPU may be used to complete a task. In this case, the CPU time may be more than the elapsed time.

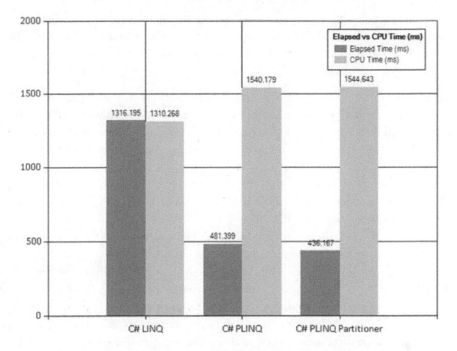

Figure 5.5 Benchmark running the k-means algorithm using a quad-core machine with 8 GB of RAM. The algorithms tested are the sequential LINQ and the parallel PLINQ with a variant of a tailored partitioner. The parallel PLINQ runs in 0.481 seconds, which is three times faster than the sequential LINQ version, which runs in 1.316 seconds. A slight improvement is the PLINQ with tailored partitioner that runs in 0.436 sec, which is 11% faster than the original PLINQ version.

The benchmark results are impressive. The parallel version of the k-means algorithm using PLINQ runs three times faster than the sequential version in a quad-core machine. The PLINQ partitioner version, shown in listing 5.8, is 11% faster than the PLINQ version. An interesting PLINQ extension is used in the function `UpdateCentroids`. The `WithExecutionMode(ParallelExecution Mode.ForceParallelism)` extension is used to notify the TPL scheduler that the query must be performed concurrently.

The two options to configure `ParallelExecutionMode` are `ForceParallelism` and `Default`. The `ForceParallelism` enumeration forces parallel execution. The `Default` value defers to the PLINQ query for the appropriate decision on execution.

In general, a PLINQ query isn't absolutely guaranteed to run in parallel. The TPL scheduler doesn't automatically parallelize every query, but it can decide to run the entire query, or only a part, sequentially, based upon factors such as the size and complexity of the operations and the current state of the available computer resources. The overhead involved in enabling parallelizing execution is more expensive than the speedup that's obtained. But cases exist when you want to force the parallelism because you may know more about the query execution than PLINQ can determine from its analysis. You may be aware that a delegate is expensive, and consequently the query will absolutely benefit from parallelization, for example.

The other interesting extension used in the `UpdateCentroids` function is the custom partitioner. When parallelizing k-means, you divided the input data into chunks to avoid creating parallelism with excessively fine granularity:

```
var partitioner = Partitioner.Create(data, true)
```

The `Partitioner<T>` class is an abstract class that allows for static and dynamic partitioning. The default TPL `Partitioner` has built-in strategies that automatically handle the partitioning, offering good performance for a wide range of data sources. The goal of the TPL `Partitioner` is to find the balance between having too many partitions (which introduces overhead) and having too few partitions (which underutilizes the available resources). But situations exist where the default partitioning may not be appropriate, and you can gain better performance from a PLINQ query by using a tailored partitioning strategy.

In the code snippet, the custom partitioner is created using an overloaded version of the `Partitioner.Create` method, which takes as an argument the data source and a flag indicating which strategy to use, either dynamic or static. When the flag is true, the partitioner strategy is dynamic, and static otherwise. Static partitioning often provides speedup on a multicore computer with a small number of cores (two or four). Dynamic partitioning aims to load balance the work between tasks by assigning an arbitrary size of chunks and then incrementally expanding the length after each iteration. It's possible to build sophisticated partitioners (http://mng.bz/48UP) with complex strategies.

Understanding how partitioning works

In PLINQ, there are four kinds of partitioning algorithms:

- *Range partitioning* works with a data source with a defined size. Arrays are part of this category:

  ```
  int[] data = Enumerable.Range(0, 1000).ToArray();
  data.AsParallel().Select(n => Compute(n));
  ```

- *Stripped partitioning* is the opposite of `Range`. The data source size isn't predefined, so the PLINQ query fetches one item at a time and assigns it to a task until the data source becomes empty. The main benefit of this strategy is that the load can be balanced between tasks:

  ```
  IEnumerable<int> data = Enumerable.Range(0, 1000);
  data.AsParallel().Select(n => Compute(n));
  ```

- *Hash partitioning* uses the value's hash code to assign elements with the same hash code to the same task (for example, when a PLINQ query performs a `GroupBy`).

- *Chunk partitioning* works with incremental chunk size, where each task fetches from the data source a chunk of items, whose length expands with the number of iterations. With each iteration, larger chunks keep the task busy as much as possible.

5.2.3 *Implementing a parallel Reduce function for PLINQ*

Now you've learned about the power of aggregate operations, which are particularly suited to scalable parallelization on multicore hardware due to low memory consumption and deforesting optimization. The low memory bandwidth occurs because aggregate functions produce less data than they ingest. For example, other aggregate functions such as Sum() and Average() reduce a collection of items to a single value. That's the concept of reduction: it takes a function to reduce a sequence of elements to a single value. The PLINQ list extensions don't have a specific function Reduce, as in F# list comprehension or other functional programming languages such as Scala and Elixir. But after having gained familiarity with the Aggregate function, the implementation of a reusable Reduce function is an easy job. This listing shows the implementation of a Reduce function in two variants. The bold highlights annotated code.

> **Listing 5.10 Parallel Reduce function implementation using Aggregate**

For each iteration, the function func is applied to the current item, and the previous value is used as an accumulator.

Uses a function to determinate if a number is prime

```
static TSource Reduce<TSource>(this ParallelQuery<TSource> source,
                               Func<TSource, TSource, TSource> reduce) =>
    ParallelEnumerable.Aggregate(source,
                               (item1, item2) => reduce(item1, item2));

static TValue Reduce<TValue>(this IEnumerable<TValue> source, TValue seed,
    Func<TValue, TValue, TValue> reduce) =>
    source.AsParallel()
    .Aggregate(
        seed: seed,
        updateAccumulatorFunc: (local, value) => reduce(local, value),
        combineAccumulatorsFunc: (overall, local) =>
                                            reduce(overall, local),
        resultSelector: overall => overall);

int[] source = Enumerable.Range(0, 100000).ToArray();
int result = source.AsParallel()
        .Reduce((value1, value2) => value1 + value2);
```

Combines intermediates results from each thread (partition result)

Returns the final result; in this place you could have a transformation against the output.

Uses the Reduce function, passing an anonymous lambda to apply as a reducing function

The first Reduce function takes two arguments: the sequence to reduce and a delegate (function) to apply for the reduction. The delegate has two parameters: the partial result and the next element of the collection. The underlying implementation uses Aggregate to treat the first item from the source sequence as an accumulator.

The second variant of the Reduce function takes an extra parameter seed, which is used as the initial value to start the reduction with the first value of the sequence to aggregate. This version of the function merges the results from multiple threads. This action creates a potential dependency on both the source collection and the result. For this reason, each thread uses thread-local storage, which is non-shared memory, to cache partial results. When each operation has completed, the separate partial results are combined into a final result.

`updateAccumulatorFunc` calculates the partial result for a thread. The `combine-AccumulatorsFunc` function merges the partial results into a final result. The last parameter is `resultSelector`, which is used to perform a user-defined operation on the final results. In this case, it returns the original value. The remainder of the code is an example to apply the `Reduce` function to calculate the sum of a given sequence in parallel.

ASSOCIATIVITY AND COMMUTATIVITY FOR DETERMINISTIC AGGREGATION

The order of computation of an aggregation that runs in parallel using PLINQ (or PSeq) applies the `Reduce` function differently than the sequential version. In listing 5.8, the sequential result was computed in a different order than the parallel result, but the two outputs are guaranteed to be equal because the operator + (plus) used to update the centroid distances has the special properties of associativity and commutativity. This is the line of code used to find the nearest centroid:

```
Dist(center, centroid2) < Dist(center, centroid1)
```

This is the line of code used to find updates to the centroids:

```
points
    .Aggregate(
        seed: new double[N],
        func: (acc, item) => acc.Zip(item, (a, b) => a + b).ToArray())
    .Select(items => items / points.Count())
```

In FP, the mathematical operators are functions. The + (plus) is a binary operator, so it performs on two values and manipulates them to return a result.

A function is *associative* when the order in which it's applied doesn't change the result. This property is important for *reduction operations*. The + (plus) operator and the * (multiply) operator are associative because:

$$(a + b) + c = a + (b + c)$$
$$(a * b) * c = a * (b * c)$$

A function is *commutative* when the order of the operands doesn't change its output, so long as each operand is accounted for. This property is important for *combiner operations*. The + (plus) operator and the * (multiply) operator are commutative because:

$$a + b + c = b + c + a$$
$$a * b * c = b * c * a$$

WHY DOES THIS MATTER?

Using these properties, it's possible to partition the data and have multiple threads operating independently on their own chunks, achieving parallelism, and still return the correct result at the end. The combination of these properties permits the implementation of a parallel pattern such as Divide and Conquer, Fork/Join, or MapReduce.

For a parallel aggregation in PLINQ PSeq to work correctly, the applied operation must be both associative and commutative. The good news is that many of the most popular kinds of reduction functions are both.

5.2.4 Parallel list comprehension in F#: PSeq

At this point, you understand that declarative programming lends itself to data parallelization, and PLINQ makes this particularly easy. PLINQ provides extension methods and higher-order functions that can be used from both C# and F#. But a wrapper module around the functionality provided in PLINQ for F# makes the code more idiomatic than working with PLINQ directly. This module is called PSeq, and it provides the parallel equivalent of the functions part of the Seq computation expression module. In F#, the Seq module is a thin wrapper over the .NET IEnumerable<T> class to mimic similar functionality. In F#, all the built-in sequential containers, such as arrays, lists, and sets are subtypes of the Seq type.

In summary, if parallel LINQ is the right tool to use in your code, then the PSeq module is the best way to use it in F#. This listing shows the implementation of the update-Centroids function using PSeq in idiomatic F# (in bold).

Listing 5.11 Idiomatic F# using PSeq to implement updateCentroids

```
let updateCentroids centroids =
        data
        |> PSeq.groupBy (nearestCentroid centroids)
        |> PSeq.map (fun (_,points) ->
           Array.init N (fun i ->
                points |> PSeq.averageBy (fun x -> x.[i])))
        |> PSeq.sort
        |> PSeq.toArray
```

The code uses the F# pipe operator |> for construct pipeline semantics to compute a series of operations as a chain of expressions. The applied higher-order operations with the PSeq.groupBy and PSeq.map functions follow the same pattern as the original updateCentroids function. The map function is the equivalent of Select in PLINQ. The Aggregate function PSeq.averageBy is useful because it replaces boilerplate code (necessary in PLINQ) that doesn't have such functionality built in.

5.2.5 Parallel arrays in F#

Although the PSeq module provides many familiar and useful functional constructs, such as map and reduce, these functions are inherently limited by the fact that they must act upon sequences and not divisible ranges. Consequently, the functions provided by the Array.Parallel module from the F# standard library typically scale much more efficiently when you increase the number of cores in the machine.

Listing 5.12 Parallel sum of prime numbers using F# Array.Parallel

```
let len = 10000000                          Uses a function to determinate
                                            if a number is prime
let isPrime n =
    if n = 1 then false
    elif n = 2 then true
    else
```

```
            let boundary = int (Math.Floor(Math.Sqrt(float(n))))
            [2..boundary - 1]
            |> Seq.forall(fun i -> n % i <> 0)

let primeSum =
    [|0.. len|]
    |> Array.Parallel.filter (fun x-> isPrime x)
    |> Array.sum
```

> Uses a built-in parallel array module in F#; the function filter is developed using the Array.Parallel.choose function. See the book's source code.

The `Array.Parallel` module provides versions of many ordinary higher-order array functions that were parallelized using the TPL `Parallel` class. These functions are generally much more efficient than their `PSeq` equivalents because they operate on contiguous ranges of arrays that are divisible in chunks rather than linear sequences. The `Array.Parallel` module provided by the F# standard library includes parallelized versions of several useful aggregate operators, most notably `map`. The function filter is developed using the `Array.Parallel.choose` function. See the the book's source code.

DIFFERENT STRATEGIES IN DATA PARALLELISM: VECTOR CHECK

We've covered fundamental programming design patterns that originated with functional programming and are used to process data in parallel quickly. As a refresher, these patterns are shown in table 5.1.

Table 5.1   Parallel data patterns analyzed so far

Pattern	Definition	Pros and cons
Divide and Conquer	Recursively breaks down a problem into smaller problems until these become small enough to be solved directly. For each recursive call, an independent task is created to perform a sub-problem in parallel. The most popular example of the Divide and Conquer algorithm is Quicksort.	With many recursive calls, this pattern could create extra overhead associated with parallel processing that saturates the processors.
Fork/Join	This pattern aims to split, or fork, a given data set into chunks of work so that each individual chunk is executed in parallel. After each parallel portion of work is completed, the parallel chunks are then merged, or joined, together. The parallel section forks could be implemented using recursion, similar to Divide and Conquer, until a certain task's granularity is reached.	This provides efficient load balancing.
Aggregate/Reduce	This pattern aims to combine in parallel all the elements of a given data set into a single value, by evaluating tasks on independent processing elements. This is the first level of optimization to consider when parallelizing loops with shared state.	The elements of a data set to be reduced in parallel should satisfy the associative property. Using an associative operator, any two elements of the data set can be combined into one.

The parallel programming abstractions in table 5.1 can be quickly implemented using the multicore development features available in .NET. Other patterns will be analyzed in the rest of the book. In the next section, we'll examine the parallel MapReduce pattern.

5.3 *Parallel MapReduce pattern*

MapReduce is a pattern introduced in 2004 in the paper "MapReduce: Simplified Data Processing on Large Clusters," by Jeffrey Dean and Sanjay Ghemawat (https://research.google.com/archive/mapreduce-osdi04.pdf).

MapReduce provides particularly interesting solutions for big data analysis and to crunch massive amounts of data using parallel processing. It's extremely scalable and is used in some of the largest distributed applications in the world. Additionally, it's designed for processing and generating large data sets to be distributed across multiple machines. Google's implementation runs on a large cluster of machines and can process terabytes of data at a time. The design and principles are applicable for both a single machine (single-core) on a smaller scale, and in powerful multicore machines.

This chapter focuses on applying data parallelism in a single multicore computer, but the same concepts can be applied for partitioning the work among multiple computers in the network. In chapters 11 and 12, we'll cover the agent (and actor) programming model, which can be used to achieve such network distribution of tasks.

The idea for the MapReduce model (as shown in figure 5.6) is derived from the functional paradigm, and its name originates from concepts known as map and reduce combinators. Programs written using this more functional style can be parallelized over a large cluster of machines without requiring knowledge of concurrent programming. The actual runtime can then partition the data, schedule, and handle any potential failure.

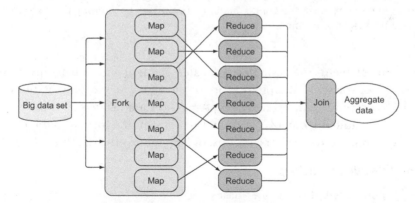

Figure 5.6   A schematic illustration of the phases of a MapReduce computation. The MapReduce pattern is composed primarily of two steps: map and reduce. The Map function is applied to all items and produces intermediate results, which are merged using the Reduce function. This pattern is similar to the Fork/Join pattern because after splitting the data in chunks, it applies in parallel the tasks map and reduce independently. In the image, a given data set is partitioned into chunks that can be performed independently because of the absence of dependencies. Then, each chunk is transformed into a different shape using the Map function. Each Map execution runs simultaneously. As each map chunk operation completes, the result is passed to the next step to be aggregated using the Reduce function. (The aggregation can be compared to the join step in the Fork/Join pattern.)

The MapReduce model is useful in domains where there's a need to execute a massive number of operations in parallel. Machine learning, image processing, data mining, and distributed sort are a few examples of domains where MapReduce is widely used.

In general, the programming model is based upon five simple concepts. The order isn't a rule and can be changed based on your needs:

1 Iteration over input
2 Computation of key/value pairs from each input
3 Grouping of all intermediate values by key
4 Iteration over the resulting groups
5 Reduction of each group

The overall idea of MapReduce is to use a combination of maps and reductions to query a stream of data. To do so, you can map the available data to a different format, producing a new data item in a different format for each original datum. During a `Map` operation you can also reorder the items, either before or after you map them. Operations that preserve the number of elements are `Map` operations. If you have many elements you may want to reduce the number of them to answer a question. You can filter the input stream by throwing away elements you don't care about.

> **MapReduce pattern and GroupBy**
>
> The `Reduce` function reduces an input stream to a single value. Sometimes instead of a single value you'll need to reduce a large number of input elements by grouping them according to a condition. This doesn't actually reduce the number of elements, it only groups them, but you can then reduce each group by aggregating the group to a single value. You could, for example, calculate the sum of values in each group if the group contains values that can be summed.

You can combine elements into a single aggregated element and return only those that provide the answer you seek. Mapping before reducing is one way to do it, but you can also `Reduce` before you `Map` or even `Reduce`, `Map`, and then `Reduce` even more, and so on. In summary, MapReduce maps (translates data from one format to the other and orders the data) and reduces (filters, groups, or aggregates) the data.

5.3.1 *The Map and Reduce functions*

MapReduce is composed of two main phases:

- `Map` receives the input and performs a `map` function to produce an output of intermediate key/value pairs. The values with the same key are then joined and passed to the second phase.
- `Reduce` aggregates the results from `Map` by applying a function to the values associated with the same intermediate key to produce a possibly smaller set of values.

The important aspect of MapReduce is that the output of the Map phase is compatible with the input of the Reduce phase. This characteristic leads to functional compositionality.

5.3.2 Using MapReduce with the NuGet package gallery

In this section, you'll learn how to implement and apply the MapReduce pattern using a program to download and analyze NuGet packages from the online gallery. NuGet is a package manager for the Microsoft development platform including .NET, and the NuGet gallery is the central package repository used by all package developers. At the time of writing, there were over 800,000 NuGet packages. The purpose of the program is to rank and determine the five most important NuGet packages, calculating the importance of each by adding its score rate with the score values of all its dependencies.

Because of the intrinsic relation between MapReduce and FP, listing 5.13 will be implemented using F# and PSeq to support data parallelism. The C# version of the code can be found in the downloadable source code.

It's possible to use the same basic idea to find other information, such as the dependencies for a package that you are using, what the dependencies of dependencies are, and so on.

> **NOTE** Downloading all the information about the versions of all NuGet packages takes some time. In the solution, there's a zipped file (nuget-latest-versions.model) in the subfolder Models in the downloadable source code. If you want to update the most current values, delete this file, run the application, and be patient. The new updated file will be zipped and saved for the next time.

Listing 5.13 defines both the Map and Reduce functions. The Map function transforms a NuGet package input into a key/value pair data structure, where the key is the name of the package and the value is the rank value (float). This data structure is defined as a sequence of key/value types because each package could have dependencies, which will be evaluated as part of the total score. The Reduce function takes as an argument the name of the package with the sequence of associated score/values. This input matches the output of the previous Map function.

Listing 5.13 PageRank object encapsulating the Map and Reduce functions

```
type PageRank (ranks:seq<string*float>) =
    let mapCache = Map.ofSeq ranks                         ◀── Uses an internal table to keep in
                                                                memory the NuGet collection of
                                                                name and score value pair

    let getRank (package:string) =
        match mapCache.TryFind package with
        | Some(rank) -> rank                               ◀── If the NuGet package isn't
        | None -> 1.0                                          found, a default score of 1.0 is
                                                                used as the default rank.

    member this.Map (package:NuGet.NuGetPackageCache) =
```

```
let score =
    (getRank package.PackageName)
    /float(package.Dependencies.Length)

package.Dependencies
|> Seq.map (fun (Domain.PackageName(name,_),_,_) -> (name, score))

member this.Reduce (name:string) (values:seq<float>) =
    (name, Seq.sum values)
```

Uses a function to calculate the average score of the NuGet dependencies

Uses a function to reduce to a single value all the scores related to one package

The `PageRank` object encapsulates the `Map` and `Reduce` functions, providing easy access to the same underlying data structure ranks. Next, you need to build the core of the program, MapReduce. Using FP style, you can model a reusable MapReduce function, passing the functions as input for both `Map` and `Reduce` phases. Here is the implementation of `mapF`.

Listing 5.14   `mapF` function for the first phase of the MapReduce pattern

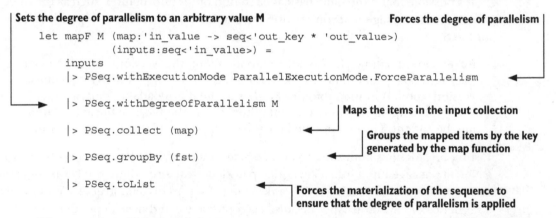

Sets the degree of parallelism to an arbitrary value M

Forces the degree of parallelism

```
let mapF M (map:'in_value -> seq<'out_key * 'out_value>)
           (inputs:seq<'in_value>) =
    inputs
    |> PSeq.withExecutionMode ParallelExecutionMode.ForceParallelism

    |> PSeq.withDegreeOfParallelism M

    |> PSeq.collect (map)

    |> PSeq.groupBy (fst)

    |> PSeq.toList
```

Maps the items in the input collection

Groups the mapped items by the key generated by the map function

Forces the materialization of the sequence to ensure that the degree of parallelism is applied

The `mapF` function takes as its first parameter an integer value `M`, which determines the level of parallelism to apply. This argument is intentionally positioned first because it makes it easier to partially apply the function to reuse with the same value. Inside the body of `mapF` the degree of parallelism is set using `PSeq.withDegreeOfParallelism M`. This extension method is also used in PLINQ. The purpose of the configuration is to restrict the number of threads that could run in parallel, and it isn't a coincidence that the query is eagerly materialized exercising the last function `PSeq.toList`. If you omit `PSeq.with-DegreeOfParallelism`, then the degree of parallelism isn't guaranteed to be enforced.

In the case of a multicore single machine, it's sometimes useful to limit the number of running threads per function. In the parallel MapReduce pattern, because `Map` and `Reduce` are executed simultaneously, you might find it beneficial to constrain the resources dedicated for each step. For example, the value `maxThreads` defined as

```
let maxThreads = max (Environment.ProcessorCount / 2, 1)
```

could be used to restrict each of the two MapReduce phases to half of the system threads.

The second argument of `mapF` is the core `map` function, which operates on each input value and returns the output sequence key/value pairs. The type of the output sequence can be different from the type of the inputs. The last argument is the sequence of input values to operate against.

After the `map` function, you implement the `reduce` aggregation. This listing shows the implementation of the aggregation function `reduceF` to run the second and final result.

Listing 5.15   `reduceF` function for the second phase of MapReduce

```
let reduceF R (reduce:'key -> seq<'value> -> 'reducedValues)
              (inputs:('key * seq<'key * 'value>) seq) =
    inputs
    |> PSeq.withExecutionMode ParallelExecutionMode.ForceParallelism

    |> PSeq.withDegreeOfParallelism R

    |> PSeq.map (fun (key, items) ->
        items
        |> Seq.map (snd)
        |> reduce key)
    |> PSeq.toList
```

Forces the degree of parallelism

Sets the degree of parallelism to an arbitrary value R

Maps the items in the input collection in the form of a key/value pair

Extracts the values from the input sequence to apply the reduce function

The first argument `R` of the `reduceF` function has the same purpose of setting the degree of parallelism as the argument `M` in the previous `mapF` function. The second argument is the `reduce` function that operates on each key/values pair of the input parameter. In the case of the NuGet package example, the key is a string for the name of the package, and the sequence of values is the list of ranks associated with the package. Ultimately, the input argument is the sequence of key/value pairs, which matches the output of the `mapF` function. The `reduceF` function generates the final output.

After having defined the functions `map` and `reduce`, the last step is the easy one: putting everything together (in bold).

Listing 5.16   `mapReduce` composed of the `mapF` and `reduceF` functions

```
let mapReduce
        (inputs:seq<'in_value>)
        (map:'in_value -> seq<'out_key * 'out_value>)
        (reduce:'out_key -> seq<'out_value> -> 'reducedValues)
        M R =

    inputs |> (mapF M map >> reduceF R reduce)
```

The functions map and reduce are composed using the F# forward-composition >> operator.

Because the output of the `map` function matches the input of the `reduce` function, you can easily compose them together. The listing shows this functional approach in the implementation of the `mapReduce` function. The `mapReduce` function arguments feed the underlying `mapF` and `reduceF` functions. The same explanation applies. The important part of this code is the last line. Using the F# built-in pipe operator (`|>`) and forward composition operator (`>>`), you can put everything together.

This code shows how you can now utilize the function `mapReduce` from listing 5.16 to calculate the NuGet package ranking:

```
let executeMapReduce (ranks:(string*float)seq) =
let M,R = 10,5
let data = Data.loadPackages()
let pg = MapReduce.Task.PageRank(ranks)
mapReduce data (pg.Map) (pg.Reduce) M R
```

The class `pg` (PageRank) is defined in listing 5.13 to provide the implementation of both the `map` and `reduce` functions. The arbitrary values `M` and `R` set how many workers to create for each step of the MapReduce. After the implementation of the `mapF` and `reduceF` functions, you compose them to implement a `mapReduce` function that can be conveniently utilized as a new function.

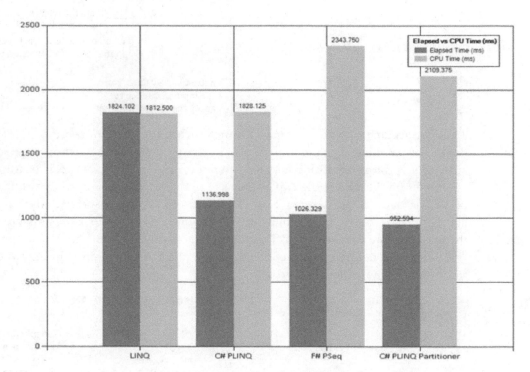

Figure 5.7   Benchmark running the MapReduce algorithm using a quad-core machine with 8 GB of RAM. The algorithms tested are sequential LINQ, parallel F# PSeq, and PLINQ with a variant of tailored partitioner. The parallel version of MapReduce that uses PLINQ runs in 1.136 seconds, which is 38% faster than the sequential version using regular LINQ in C#. The F# PSeq performance is almost equivalent to PLINQ, as expected, because they share the same technology underneath. The parallel C# PLINQ with tailored partitioner is the fastest solution, running in 0.952 sec, about 18% faster than ordinary PLINQ, and twice as fast as the baseline (the sequential version).

As expected, the serial implementation in figure 5.7 is the slowest one. Because the parallel versions F# `PSeq` and C# PLINQ use the same underlying library, the speed values are almost equivalent. The F# `PSeq` version is a little slower with a higher CPU time because of the extra overhead induced by the wrapper. The fastest MapReduce is the PLINQ parallel version with tailored partitioner, which can be found in the source code for this book.

This is the result of the five most important NuGet packages:

```
Microsoft.NETCore.Platforms :    6033.799540
Microsoft.NETCore.Targets :      5887.339802
System.Runtime :                 5661.039574
Newtonsoft.Json :                4009.295644
NETStandard.Library :            1876.720832
```

In MapReduce, any form of reduction performed in parallel can offer different results than a serial one if the operation isn't associative.

MAPREDUCE AND A LITTLE MATH

The associative and commutative properties introduced earlier in this chapter prove the correctness and deterministic behavior of aggregative functions. In parallel and functional programming, the adoption of mathematical patterns is common to guarantee accuracy in the implementation of a program. But a deep knowledge of mathematics isn't necessary.

Can you determine the values of x in the following equations?

$$9 + x = 12$$

$$2 < x < 4$$

If you answered 3 for both functions, good news, you already know all the math that it takes to write deterministic concurrent programs in functional style using techniques from linear algebra (https://en.wikipedia.org/wiki/Linear_algebra).

WHAT MATH CAN DO TO SIMPLIFY PARALLELISM: MONOIDS

The property of association leads to a common technique known as a monoid (https://wiki.haskell.org/Monoid), which works with many different types of values in a simple way. The term *monoid* (not to be confused with monad: https://wiki.haskell.org/Monad) comes from mathematics, but the concept is applicable to computer programming without any math knowledge. Essentially, monoids are operations whose output type is the same as the input, and which must satisfy some rules: associativity, identity, and closure.

You read about associativity in the previous section. The *identity* property says that a computation can be executed multiple times without affecting the result. For example, an aggregation that is associative and commutative can be applied to one or more reduction steps of the final result without affecting the output type. The *closure* rule enforces that the input(s) and output(s) types of a given function must be the same. For example, addition takes two numbers as parameters and returns a third number as a result. This rule can be expressed in .NET with a function signature `Func<T, T, T>` that ensures that all arguments belong to the same type, in opposition to a function signature such as `Func<T1, T2, R>`.

In the k-means example, the function `UpdateCentroids` satisfies these laws because the operations used in the algorithm are monoidal—a scary word that hides a simple concept. This operation is addition (for reduce).

The addition function takes two numbers and produces output of the same type. In this case, the identity element is 0 (zero) because a value 0 can be added to the result of the operation without changing it. Multiplication is also a monoid, with the identity element 1. The value of a number multiplied by 1 does not change.

Why is it important that an operation returns a result of the same type as the input(s)? Because it lets you chain and compose multiple objects using the monoidal operation, making it simple to introduce parallelism for these operations.

The fact that an operation is associative, for example, means you can fold a data structure to reduce a list sequentially. But if you have a monoid, you can reduce a list using a `fold` (`Aggregate`), which can be more efficient for certain operations and also allows for parallelism.

To calculate the factorial of the number 8, the multiplication operations running in parallel on a two-core CPU should look something like table 5.2.

Table 5.2   Parallel calculation of the factorial product of the number 8

	Core 1	Core 2
Step 1	M1 = 1 * 2	M2 = 3 * 4
Step 2	M3 = M2 * 5	M4 = 6 * M1
Step 3	M5 = M4 * 7	M6= 8 * M3
Step 4	idle	M7= M6 * M5
Result	40320	

The same result can be achieved using parallel aggregation in either F# or C# to reduce the list of numbers 1 to 8 into a single value:

```
[1..8] |> PSeq.reduce (*)
Enumerable.Range(1,8).AsParallel().Reduce((a,b)=> a * b);
```

Because multiplication is a monoidal operation for the type `integer`, you can be sure that the result of running the operation in parallel is deterministic.

NOTE Many factors are involved when exploiting parallelism, so it's important to continually benchmark and measure the speedup of an algorithm using the sequential version as baseline. In fact, in certain cases, a parallel loop might run slower than its sequential equivalent. If the sequence is too small to run in parallel, then the extra overhead introduced for the task coordination can produce negative effects. In this case, the sequential loop fits the scenario better.

Summary

- Parallel LINQ and F# `PSeq` both originate from the functional paradigm and are designed for data parallelism, simple code, and high performance. By default, these technologies take the logical processor count as the degree of parallelism.

These technologies handle the underlying processes regarding the partitioning of sequences in smaller chunks, set the degree of parallelism counting the logical machine cores, and run individually to process each subsequence.

- PLINQ and F# `PSeq` are higher-level abstraction technologies that lie on top of multithreading components. These technologies aim to reduce the time of query execution, engaging the available computer resources.

- The .NET Framework allows tailored techniques to maximize performance in data analysis. Consider value types over reference types to reduce memory problems, which otherwise could provoke a bottleneck due to the generation of too many GCs.

- Writing pure functions, or functions without side effects, makes it easier to reason about the correctness of your program. Furthermore, because pure functions are deterministic, when passing the same input, the output doesn't change. The order of execution doesn't matter, so functions without side effects can easily be executed in parallel.

- Designing with pure functions and decoupling side effects from pure logic are the two basic tenets that functional thinking brings to the forefront.

- Deforestation is the technique to eliminate the generation of intermediate data structures to reduce the size of temporary memory allocation, which benefits the performance of the application. This technique is easily exploitable with the higher-order function `Aggregate` in LINQ. It combines multiple operations in a single step, such as `filter` and `map`, which would have otherwise had an allocation for each operation.

- Writing functions that are associative and commutative permits the implementation of a parallel pattern like Divide and Conquer, Fork/Join, or MapReduce.

- The MapReduce pattern is composed primarily of two steps: map and reduce. The `Map` function is applied to all items and produces intermediate results, which are merged using the `Reduce` function. This pattern is similar to Fork/Join because after splitting the data into chunks, it applies in parallel the tasks `Map` and `Reduce` independently.

Real-time event streams: functional reactive programming

This chapter covers

- Understanding queryable event streams
- Working with Reactive Extensions (Rx)
- Combining F# and C# to make events first-class values
- Processing high-rate data streams
- Implementing a Publisher-Subscriber pattern

We're used to responding to events in our lives daily. If it starts to rain, we get an umbrella. If the daylight in a room begins to dim, we flip the switch to turn on the electric light. The same is true in our applications, where a program must react to (or handle) events caused by something else happening in the application or a user interacting with it. Almost every program must handle events, whether they're the receipt of an HTTP request for a web page on a server, a notification from your favorite social media platform, a change in your filesystem, or a simple click of a button.

Today's challenge for applications isn't reacting to one event, but reacting to a constant high volume of events in (near) real time. Consider the humble smartphone. We depend on these devices to be constantly connected to the internet and continuously sending and receiving data. These multidevice interconnections can be compared to billions of sensors that are acquiring and sharing information, with the need for real-time analysis. In addition, this unstoppable massive stream of notifications continues to flow from the internet fire hose, requiring that the system be designed to handle back-pressure (https://en.wikipedia.org/wiki/Back_pressure) and notifications in parallel.

Back-pressure refers to a situation where the event-fetching producer is getting too far ahead of the event-processing consumer. This could generate potential spikes in memory consumption and possibly reserve more system resources for the consumer until the consumer is caught up. More details regarding back-pressure are covered later in the chapter.

It's predicted that by 2020 more than 50 billion devices will be connected to the internet. Even more stunning is that this expansion of digital information shows no signs of slowing any time soon! For this reason, the ability to manipulate and analyze high-speed data streams in real time will continue to dominate the field of data (big data) analysis and digital information.

Numerous challenges exist to using a traditional programming paradigm for the implementation of these kinds of real-time processing systems. What kinds of technologies and tools can you use to simplify the event programming model? How can you concurrently handle multiple events without thinking concurrently? The answers lie with reactive programming.

> *In computing, reactive programming is a programming paradigm that maintains a continuous interaction with their environment, but at a speed which is determined by the environment, not the program itself.*
>
> —*Gèrard Berry ("Real Time Programming: Special Purpose or General Purpose Languages," Inria (1989), http://mng.bz/br08)*

Reactive programming is programming with everlasting asynchronous streams of events made simple. On top of that, it combines the benefits of functional programming for concurrency, which you've seen in earlier chapters, with the reactive programming toolkit to make event-driven programming highly beneficial, approachable, and safe. Furthermore, by applying various high-order operators on streams, you can easily achieve different computational goals.

By the end of this chapter, you'll know how reactive programming avoids the problems that occur when using imperative techniques to build reactive systems. You'll design and implement event-driven applications, coupled with support for asynchronicity, that are responsive, scalable, and loose.

6.1 Reactive programming: big event processing

Reactive programming, not to be confused with functional reactive programming, refers to a programming paradigm that focuses on listening and processing events asynchronously as a data stream, where the availability of new information drives the logic forward rather than having the control flow driven by a thread of execution.

A common example of reactive programming is a spreadsheet, where cells contain literal values or formulas such as *C1 = A1 + B1* or, in Excel lingo, `C1 = Sum(A1:B1)`. In this case, the value in the cell C1 is evaluated based on the values in other cells. When the value of one of the other cells B1 or A1 changes, the value of the formula automatically recalculates to update the value of C1, as seen in figure 6.1.

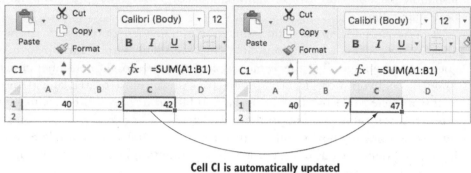

Cell CI is automatically updated
when cell AI or BI changes.

Figure 6.1   This Excel spreadsheet is reactive, meaning that cell C1 reacts to a change of value in either cell A1 or B1 through the formula Sum(A1:B1).

The same principle is applicable for processing data to notify the system when a change of state occurs. Analyzing data collections is a common requirement in software development. In many circumstances, your code could benefit from using a reactive event handler. The reactive event handler allows a compositional reactive semantic to express operations, such as Filter and Map, against events elegantly and succinctly, rather than a regular event handler, which is designed to handle simple scenarios with limited flexibility.

The reactive programming approach to event handling is different from the traditional approach because events are treated as streams. This provides the ability to manipulate effortless events with different features, such as the ability to filter, map, and merge, in a declarative and expressive way. For example, you might design a web service that filters the event stream to a subset of events based on specified rules. The resulting solution uses reactive programming to capture the intended behaviors by describing the operations in a declarative manner, which is one of the tenets of FP. This is one reason why it's commonly called functional reactive programming; but this term requires further explanation.

What is *functional reactive programming* (FRP)? Technically, FRP is a programming paradigm based on *values that change over time,* using a set of simple compositional Reactive operators (behavior and event) that, in turn, are used to build more complex operators. This programming paradigm is commonly used for developing UIs, robotics, and games, and for solving distributed and networked system challenges. Due to the powerful and simplified compositional aspect of FRP, several modern technologies use FRP principles to develop sophisticated systems. For example, the programming languages Elm (http://elm-lang.org) and Yampa (https://wiki.haskell.org/Yampa) are based on FRP.

From the industry standpoint, FRP is a set of different but related functional programming technologies combined under the umbrella of event handling. The confusion is derived from similarity and misrepresentation—using the same words in different combinations:

- *Functional programming* is a paradigm that treats computation as the evaluation of an expression and avoids changing state and mutable data.
- *Reactive programming* is a paradigm that implements any application where there's a real-time component.

Reactive programming is becoming increasingly more important in the context of real-time stream processing for big data analytics. The benefits of reactive programming are increased use of computing resources on multicore and multi-CPU hardware by providing a straightforward and maintainable approach for dealing with asynchronous and no-blocking computation and IO. Similarly, FRP offers the right abstraction to make event-driven programming highly beneficial, approachable, safe, and composable. These aspects let you build real-time, reactive programs with clean and readable code that's easy to maintain and expand, all without sacrificing performance.

The reactive programming concept is non-blocking asynchronous based, reverting control from "asking" to "waiting" for events, as shown in figure 6.2. This principle is called *inversion of control* (http://martinfowler.com/bliki/InversionOfControl.html), also referred to as the Hollywood Principle (don't call me, I'll call you).

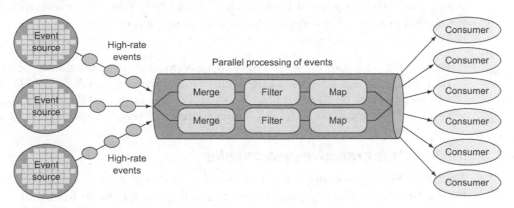

Figure 6.2 **Real-time reactive programming promotes non-blocking (asynchronous) operations that are designed to deal with high-volume, high-velocity event sequences over time by handling multiple events simultaneously, possibly in parallel.**

Reactive programming aims to operate on a high-rate sequence of events over time, simplifying the concurrent aspect of handling multiple events simultaneously (in parallel).

Writing applications that are capable of reacting to events at a high rate is becoming increasingly important. Figure 6.3 shows a system that's processing a massive number of tweets per minute. These messages are sent by literally millions of devices, representing the event sources, into the system that analyzes, transforms, and then dispatches the tweets to those registered to read them. It's common to annotate a tweet message with a hashtag to create a dedicated channel and group of interests. The system uses a hashtag to filter and partition the notifications by topic.

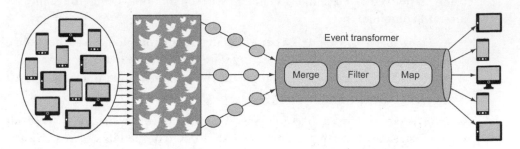

Figure 6.3   Millions of devices represent a rich source of events, capable of sending a massive number of tweets per minute. A real-time reactive system can handle the massive quantities of tweets as an event stream by applying non-blocking (asynchronous) operations (`merge`, `filter`, and `map`) and then dispatching the tweets to the listeners (consumers).

Every day, millions of devices send and receive notifications that could overflow and potentially crash the system if it isn't designed to handle such a large number of sustained events. How would you write such a system?

A close relationship exists between FP and reactive programming. Reactive programming uses functional constructors to achieve composable event abstraction. As previously mentioned, it's possible to exploit higher-order operations on events such as `map`, `filter`, and `reduce`. The term FRP is commonly used to refer to reactive programming, but this isn't completely correct.

> **NOTE**   FRP is a comprehensive topic; but only the basic principles are covered in this chapter. For a deeper explanation of FRP, I recommend *Functional Reactive Programming* by Stephen Blackheath and Anthony Jones (Manning Publications, 2016, www.manning.com/books/functional-reactive-programming).

6.2   *.NET tools for reactive programming*

The .NET Framework supports events based on a delegate model. An event handler for a subscriber registers a chain of events and triggers the events when called. Using an imperative programming paradigm, the event handlers need a mutable state to keep track of the subscriptions to register a callback, which wraps the behavior inside a function to limit composability.

Here's a typical example of a button-click event registration that uses an event handler and anonymous lambda:

```
public MainWindow()
{
    myButton.Click += new System.EventHandler(myButton_Click);

    myButton.Click += (sender, args) => MessageBox.Show("Bye!");
}
```

```
void myButton_Click(object sender, RoutedEventArgs e)
{
    MessageBox.Show("Hello!");
}
```

This pattern is the primary reason that .NET events are difficult to compose, almost impossible to transform, and, ultimately, the reason for accidental memory leaks. In general, using the imperative programming model requires a shared mutable state for communication between events, which could potentially hide undesirable side effects. When implementing complex event combinations, the imperative programming approach tends to be convoluted. Additionally, providing an explicit callback function limits your options to express code functionality in a declarative style. The result is a program that's hard to understand and, over time, becomes impossible to expand and to debug. Furthermore, .NET events don't provide support for concurrent programs to raise an event on a separate thread, making them a poor fit for today's reactive and scalable applications.

> **NOTE** Event streams are unbounded flows of data processing, originating from a multitude of sources, which are analyzed and transformed asynchronously through a pipeline of composed operations.

Events in .NET are the first step toward reactive programming. Events have been part of the .NET Framework since the beginning. In the early days of the .NET Framework, events were primarily used when working with graphical user interfaces (GUIs). Today, their potential is being explored more fully. With the .NET Framework, Microsoft introduced a way to reason and treat events as first-class values by using the F# `Event` (and `Observable`) module and .NET Reactive Extensions (Rx). Rx lets you compose events easily and declaratively in a powerful way. Additionally, you can handle events as a data stream capable of encapsulating logic and state, ensuring that your code is without side effects and mutable variables. Now your code can fully embrace the functional paradigm, which focuses on listening and processing events asynchronously.

6.2.1 Event combinators—a better solution

Currently, most systems get a callback and process these events when and as they happen. But if you consider events as a stream, similar to lists or other collections, then you can use techniques for working with collections or processing events, which eliminates the need for callbacks. The F# list comprehension, introduced in chapter 5, provides a set of higher-order functions, such as `filter` and `map`, for working with lists in a declarative style:

```
let squareOfDigits (chars:char list)
    |> List.filter (fun c -> Char.IsDigit c && int c % 2 = 0)
    |> List.map (fun n -> int n * int n)
```

In this code, the function `squareOfDigits` takes a list of characters and returns the square of the digits in the list. The first function `filter` returns a list with elements for which a given predicate is true; in this case, the characters are even digits. The second function, `map`, transforms each element n passed into an integer and calculates its square value n * n. The pipeline operator (|>) sequences the operations as a chain of evaluations. In other words, the result of the operation on the left side of the equation will be used as an argument for the next operation in the pipeline.

The same code can be translated into LINQ to be more C# friendly:

```
List<int> SquareOfDigits(List<char> chars) =>
    chars.Where(c => char.IsDigit(c) && char.GetNumericValue(c) % 2 == 0)
        .Select(c => (int)c * (int)c).ToList();
```

This expressive programming style is a perfect fit for working with events. Different than C#, F# has the advantage of treating events intrinsically (natively) as first-class values, which means you can pass them around like data. Additionally, you can write a function that takes an event as an argument to generate a new event. Consequently, an event can be passed into functions with the pipe operator (|>) like any other value. This design and method of using events in F# is based on combinators, which look like programming using list comprehension against sequences. The event combinators are exposed in the F# module `Event` that can be used to compose events:

```
textBox.KeyPress
|> Event.filter (fun c -> Char.IsDigit c.KeyChar && int c.KeyChar % 2 = 0)
|> Event.map (fun n -> int n.KeyChar * n.KeyChar)
```

In this code, the `KeyPress` keyboard event is treated as a stream, which is filtered to ignore events that aren't interesting, so that the final computation occurs only when the keys pressed are digits. The biggest benefit of using higher-order functions is a cleaner *separation of concerns*.[1] C# can reach the same level of expressiveness and compositionality using .NET Rx, as briefly described later in this chapter.

6.2.2   *.NET interoperability with F# combinators*

Using F# event combinators, you can write code using an algebra of events that aims to separate complex events from simple ones. Is it possible to take advantage of the F# event combinators module to write more declarative C# code? Yes.

Both .NET programming languages F# and C# use the same *common language runtime* (CLR), and both are compiled into an intermediate language (IL) that conforms to the *Common Language Infrastructure* (CLI) specification. This makes it possible to share the same code.

In general, events are understood by all .NET languages, but F# events are used as first-class values and, consequently, require only a small amount of extra attention. To ensure that the F# events can be used by other .NET languages, the compiler must be notified by decorating the event with the `[<CLIEvent>]` attribute. It's convenient and efficient to use the intrinsic compositional aspect of F# event combinators to build sophisticated event handlers that can be consumed in C# code.

Let's see an example to better understand how F# event combinators work and how they can easily be consumed by other .NET programming languages. Listing 6.1 shows how to implement a simple game to guess a secret word using F# event combinators.

---

[1] The design principle separates a computer program into sections so each addresses a particular concern. The value is simplifying development and maintenance of computer programs (https://en.wikipedia.org/wiki/Separation_of_concerns).

The code registers two events: the KeyPress event from the WinForms control passed into the construct of KeyPressedEventCombinators, and the Elapsed time event from System.Timers.Timer. The user enters text—in this case, only letters are allowed (no digits)—until either the secret word is guessed or the timer (the given time interval) has elapsed. When the user presses a key, the filter and event combinators transform the event source into a new event through a *chain of expressions*. If the time expires before the secret word is guessed, a notification triggers a "Game Over" message; otherwise, it triggers the "You Won!" message when the secret word matches the input.

> **Listing 6.1   F# Event combinator to manage key-down events**

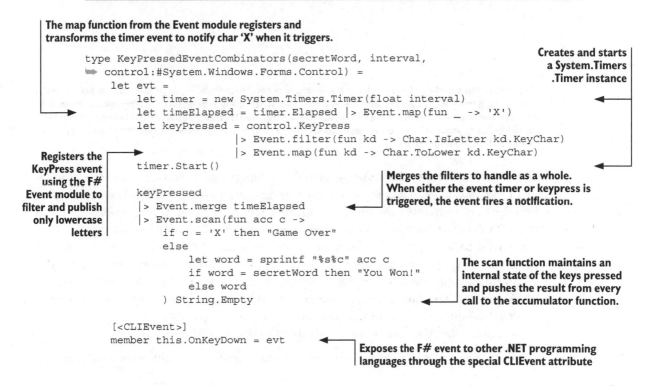

The map function from the Event module registers and transforms the timer event to notify char 'X' when it triggers.

Creates and starts a System.Timers .Timer instance

Registers the KeyPress event using the F# Event module to filter and publish only lowercase letters

```
type KeyPressedEventCombinators(secretWord, interval,
    control:#System.Windows.Forms.Control) =
    let evt =
        let timer = new System.Timers.Timer(float interval)
        let timeElapsed = timer.Elapsed |> Event.map(fun _ -> 'X')
        let keyPressed = control.KeyPress
                    |> Event.filter(fun kd -> Char.IsLetter kd.KeyChar)
                    |> Event.map(fun kd -> Char.ToLower kd.KeyChar)
        timer.Start()

        keyPressed
        |> Event.merge timeElapsed
        |> Event.scan(fun acc c ->
            if c = 'X' then "Game Over"
            else
                let word = sprintf "%s%c" acc c
                if word = secretWord then "You Won!"
                else word
        ) String.Empty

    [<CLIEvent>]
    member this.OnKeyDown = evt
```

Merges the filters to handle as a whole. When either the event timer or keypress is triggered, the event fires a notIfIcation.

The scan function maintains an internal state of the keys pressed and pushes the result from every call to the accumulator function.

Exposes the F# event to other .NET programming languages through the special CLIEvent attribute

The type KeyPressedEventCombinators has a constrvuctor parameter control, which refers to any object that derives from System.Windows.Forms.Control. The # annotation in F# is called a flexible type, which indicates that a parameter is compatible with a specified base type (http://mng.bz/FSp2).

The KeyPress event is linked to the System.Windows.Forms.Control base control passed into the type constructor, and its event stream flows into the F# event-combinators pipeline for further manipulation. The OnKeyDown event is decorated with the attribute [<CLIEvent>] to be exposed (published) and visible to other .NET languages. In this way, the event can be subscribed to and consumed from C# code, obtaining reactive programmability by referencing the F# library project. Figure 6.4 presents the F# event-combinators pipeline, where the KeyPress event stream runs through the series of functions linked as a chain.

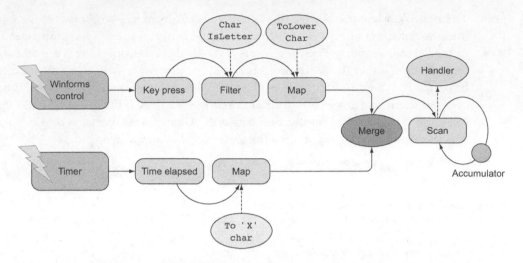

Figure 6.4 An event-combinator pipeline showing how two event flows manage their own set of events before being merged and passed into the accumulator. When a key is pressed on a WinForms control, the `filter` event checks whether the key pressed is a letter, and then `map` retrieves the lowercase version of that letter to scan. When the time elapses on the timer, the `map` operator passes an "X" as in "no value" to the `scan` function.

The event-combinator chain in figure 6.4 is complex, but it demonstrates the simplicity of expressing such a convoluted code design using events as first-class values. The F# event combinators raise the level of abstraction to facilitate higher-order operations for events, which makes the code more readable and easier to understand when compared to an equivalent program written in imperative style. Implementing the program using the typical imperative style requires creating two different events that communicate the state of the timer and maintain the state of the text with a shared mutable state. The functional approach with event combinators removes the need for a shared immutable state; and, moreover, events are composable.

To summarize, the main benefits of using F# event combinators are:

- *Composability*—You can define events that capture complex logic from simpler events.
- *Declarative*—The code written using F# event combinators is based on functional principles; therefore, event combinators express what to accomplish, rather than how to accomplish a task.
- *Interoperability*—F# event combinators can be shared across .NET languages so the complexity can be hidden in a library.

6.3   *Reactive programming in .NET: Reactive Extensions (Rx)*

The .NET Rx library facilitates the composition of asynchronous event-based programs using observable sequences. Rx combines the simplicity of LINQ-style semantics for manipulating collections and the power of asynchronous programming models to use the clean async/await patterns from .NET 4.5. This powerful combination enables a toolset that lets you treat event streams using the same simple, composable, and declarative style used for data collections (`List` and `Array`, for example). Rx provides a domain-specific language (DSL) that provides a significantly simpler and more fluent API for handling complex, asynchronous event-based logic. Rx can be used to either develop a responsive UI or increase scalability in a server-side application.

In the nutshell, Rx is a set of extensions built for the `IObservable<T>` and `IObserver<T>` interfaces that provide a generalized mechanism for push-based notifications based on the Observer pattern from the Gang of Four (GoF) book.

The Observer design pattern is based on events, and it's one of the most common patterns in OOP. This pattern publishes changes made to an object's state (the observable) to other objects (the observers) that subscribe to notifications describing any changes to that object (shown in figure 6.5).

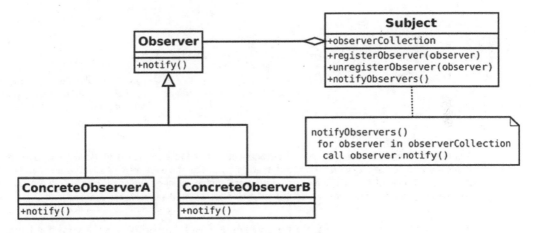

Figure 6.5 The original Observer pattern from the GoF book

Using GoF terminology, the `IObservable` interfaces are *subjects*, and the `IObserver` interfaces are *observers*. These interfaces, introduced in .NET 4.0 as part of the `System` namespace, are an important component in the reactive programming model.

> ### The Gang of Four book
>
> This software engineering book by Martin Fowler et al. describes software design patterns in OOP. The title, *Design Patterns: Elements of Reusable Object-Oriented Software,* is far too long, especially in an email, so the nickname "book by the Gang of Four" became the common way to refer to it. The authors are often referred to as the Gang of Four (GoF).

Here's the definition for both `IObserver` and `IObservable` interface signatures in C#:

```
public interface IObserver<T>
{
    void OnCompleted();
    void OnError(Exception exception);
    void OnNext(T value);
}
```

```
public interface IObservable<T>
{
    IDisposable Subscribe(IObserver<T> observer);
}
```

These interfaces implement the Observer pattern, which allows Rx to create an observable from existing .NET CLR events. Figure 6.6 attempts to clarify the original Unified Modeling Language (UML) for the Observer pattern from the GoF book.

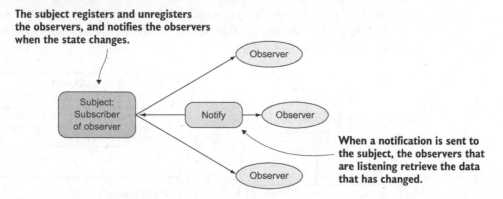

The subject registers and unregisters the observers, and notifies the observers when the state changes.

When a notification is sent to the subject, the observers that are listening retrieve the data that has changed.

Figure 6.6   The Observer pattern is based on an object called `Subject`**, which maintains a list of dependencies (called observers) and automatically notifies the observers of any change of state to** `Subject`**. This pattern defines a one-to-many relationship between the observer subscribers, so that when an object changes state, all its dependencies are notified and updated automatically.**

The `IObservable<T>` functional interface (www.lambdafaq.org/what-is-a-functional-interface) only implements the method `Subscribe`. When this method is called by an observer, a notification is triggered to publish the new item through the `IObserver<T>.OnNext` method. The `IObservable` interface, as the name implies, can be considered a source of data that's constantly observed, which automatically notifies all registered observers of any state changes. Similarly, notifications for errors and completion are published through the `IObserver<T>.OnError` and `IObserver<T>.OnCompleted` methods, respectively. The `Subscribe` method returns an `IDisposable` object, which acts as a handle for the subscribed observer. When the `Dispose` method is called, the corresponding observer is detached from the `Observable`, and it stops receiving notifications. In summary:

- `IObserver<T>.OnNext` supplies the observer with new data or state information.
- `IObserver<T>.OnError` indicates that the provider has experienced an error condition.
- `IObserver<T>.OnCompleted` indicates that the observer finished sending notifications to observers.

The same interfaces are used as a base definition for the F# IEvent<'a> type, which is the interface used to implement the F# event combinators previously discussed. As you can see, the same principles are applied with a slightly different approach to achieve the same design. The ability to code multiple asynchronous event sources is the main advantage of Rx.

> **NOTE** .NET Rx can be downloaded using the Install-Package System.Reactive command and referenced in your project through the NuGet package manager.

6.3.1 From LINQ/PLINQ to Rx

The .NET LINQ/PLINQ query providers, as discussed in chapter 5, operate as a mechanism against an in-memory sequence. Conceptually, this mechanism is based on a pull model, which means that the items of the collections are pulled from the query during its evaluation. This behavior is represented by the iterator pattern of IEnumerable<T> - IEnumerator<T>, which can cause a block while it's waiting for data to iterate. In opposition, Rx treats events as a data stream by defining the query to react over time as events arrive. This is a push model, where the events arrive and autonomously travel through the query. Figure 6.7 shows both models.

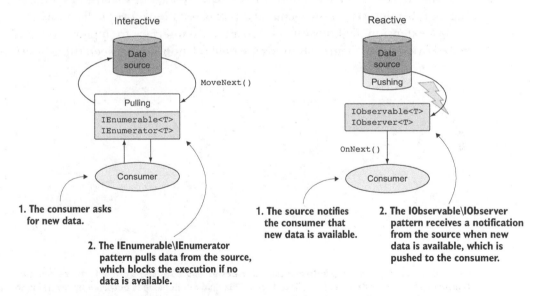

Figure 6.7   Push vs. pull model. The IEnumerable/IEnumerator pattern is based on the pull model, which asks for new data from the source. Alternatively, the IObservable/IObserver pattern is based on the push model, which receives a notification when new data is available to send to the consumer.

In the reactive case, the application is passive and causes no blocking in the data-retrieval process.

> ## F#: the inspiration for Rx
>
> During an interview on Microsoft's Channel 9 (http://bit.ly/2v8exjV), Erik Meijer, the mind behind Rx, mentioned that F# was an inspiration for the creation of Reactive Extensions. One of the inspiring ideas behind the Reactive framework, composable events, does in fact come from F#.

6.3.2   *IObservable: the dual IEnumerable*

The Rx push-based event model is abstracted by the `IObservable<T>` interface, which is the dual of the `IEnumerable<T>` interface.[2] While the term *duality* can sound daunting, it's a simple and powerful concept. You can compare duality to the two sides of a coin, where the opposite side can be inferred from the one exposed.

In the context of computer science, this concept has been exploited by De Morgan's Law,[3] which achieves the duality between conjunction `&&` (AND) and disjunction `||` (OR) to prove that negation distributes over both conjunction and disjunction:

```
!(a || b) == !a && !b
!(a && b) == !a || !b
```

Like the inverse of LINQ, where LINQ exposes a set of extension methods for the `IEnumerable` interface to implement a pull-based model over collections, Rx exposes a set of extension methods for the `IObservable` interface to implement a push-based model over events. Figure 6.8 shows the dual relationship between these interfaces.

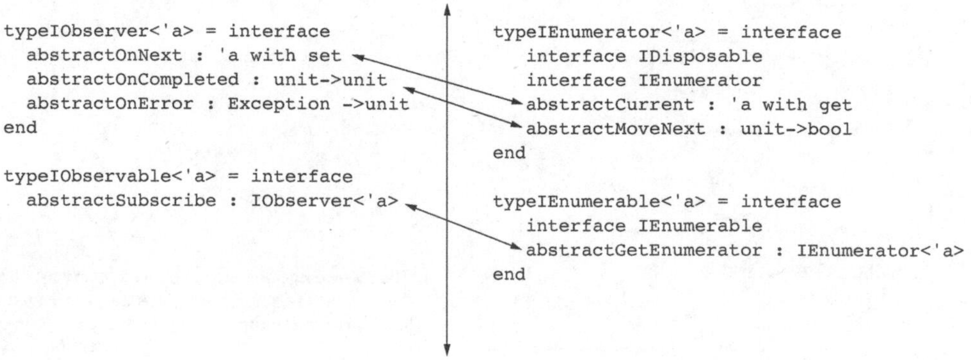

```
typeIObserver<'a> = interface            typeIEnumerator<'a> = interface
  abstractOnNext : 'a with set             interface IDisposable
  abstractOnCompleted : unit->unit         interface IEnumerator
  abstractOnError : Exception ->unit       abstractCurrent : 'a with get
end                                        abstractMoveNext : unit->bool
                                         end
typeIObservable<'a> = interface
  abstractSubscribe : IObserver<'a>      typeIEnumerable<'a> = interface
                                           interface IEnumerable
                                           abstractGetEnumerator : IEnumerator<'a>
                                         end
```

Figure 6.8   Dual relationship between the `IObserver` and `IEnumerator` interfaces, and the `IObservable` and `IEnumerable` interfaces. This dual relationship is obtained by reversing the arrow in the functions, which means swapping the input and output.

As figure 6.8 shows, the `IObservable` and `IObserver` interfaces are obtained by reversing the arrow of the corresponding `IEnumerable` and `IEnumerator` interfaces.

---

[2] The term comes from *duality*. For further explanation, see https://en.wikipedia.org/wiki/Dual_ (category_theory).

[3] For more information, see https://en.wikipedia.org/wiki/De_Morgan%27s_laws.

Reversing the arrow means swapping the input and output of a method. For example, the current property of the `IEnumerator` interface has this signature:

```
Unit (or void in C#) -> get 'a
```

Reversing the arrow of this property, you can obtain its dual: `Unit <- set 'a`. This signature in the reciprocal `IObserver` interface matches the `OnNext` method, which has the following signature:

```
set 'a -> Unit (or void in C#)
```

The `GetEnumerator` function takes no arguments and returns `IEnumerator<T>`, which returns the next item in the list through the `MoveNext` and `Current` functions. The reverse `IEnumerable` method can be used to traverse the `IObservable`, which pushes data into the subscribed `IObserver` by invoking its methods.

6.3.3 *Reactive Extensions in action*

Combining existing events is an essential characteristic of Rx, which permits a level of abstraction and compositionality that's otherwise impossible to achieve. In .NET, events are one form of an asynchronous data source that can be consumed by Rx. To convert existing events into observables, Rx takes an event and returns an `Event-Pattern` object, which contains the sender and event arguments. For example, a key-pressed event is converted into a reactive observable (in bold):

```
Observable.FromEventPattern<KeyPressedEventArgs>(this.textBox,
                                    nameof(this.textBox.KeyPress));
```

As you can see, Rx lets you handle events in a rich and reusable form.

Let's put the Rx framework into action by implementing the C# equivalent of the secret word game previously defined using the F# event combinators `KeyPressed-EventCombinators`. This listing shows the implementation using this pattern and the corresponding reactive framework.

Listing 6.2   Rx `KeyPressedEventCombinators` in C#

> The LINQ-like semantic functions Select and Where register, compose, and transform events to notify subscribers.

```
var timer = new System.Timers.Timer(timerInterval);
var timerElapsed = Observable.FromEventPattern<ElapsedEventArgs>
                (timer, "Elapsed").Select(_ => 'X');
var keyPressed = Observable.FromEventPattern<KeyPressEventArgs>
                (this.textBox, nameof(this.textBox.KeyPress));
                .Select(kd => Char.ToLower(kd.EventArgs.KeyChar))
                .Where(c => Char.IsLetter(c));
timer.Start();

timerElapsed
    .Merge(keyPressed)
    .Scan(String.Empty, (acc, c) =>
    {
```

> The filters are merged to be handled as a whole. When either event is triggered, this event fires a notification.

> The Scan function maintains the internal state of the keys pressed and pushes the result from every call to the accumulator function.

> The Rx method FromEventPattern converts a .NET event into an observable.

```
            if (c == 'X') return "Game Over";
            else
            {
                var word = acc + c;
                if (word == secretWord) return "You Won!";
                else return word;
            }
        }).
        .Subscribe(value =>
            this.label.BeginInvoke(
                (Action)(() => this.label.Text = value)));
```

The `Observable.FromEventPattern` method creates a link between the .NET event and the Rx `IObservable`, which wraps both `Sender` and `EventArgs`. In the listing, the imperative C# events for handling the key pressed (`KeyPressEventArgs`) and the elapsed timer (`ElapsedEventArgs`) are transformed into observables and then merged to be treated as a whole stream of events. Now it's possible to construct all of the event handling as a single and concise chain of expressions.

Reactive Extensions are functional

The Rx framework provides a functional approach to handling events asynchronously as a stream. The functional aspect refers to a declarative programming style that uses fewer variables to maintain state and to avoid mutations, so you can compose events as a chain of expressions.

6.3.4 *Real-time streaming with RX*

An *event stream* is a channel on which a sequence of ongoing events, by order of time, arrives as values. Streams of events come from diverse sources, such as social media, the stock market, smartphones, or a computer mouse. Real-time stream processing aims to consume a live data stream that can be shaped into other forms. Consuming this data, which in many cases is delivered at a high rate, can be overwhelming, like drinking directly from a fire hose. Take, for example, the analysis of stock prices that continually change and then dispatching the result to multiple consumers, as shown in figure 6.9.

The Rx framework fits well in this scenario because it handles multiple asynchronous data sources while delivering high-performance operations to combine, transform, and filter any of those data streams. At its core, Rx uses the `IObservable<T>` interface to maintain a list of dependent `IObserver<T>` interfaces that are notified automatically of any event or data change.

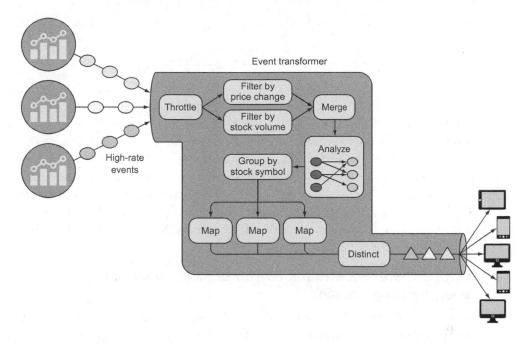

Figure 6.9 Event streams from different sources push data to an event transformer, which applies higher-order operations and then notifies the subscribed observers.

6.3.5   *From events to F# observables*

As you may recall, F# uses events for configurable callback constructs. In addition, it supports an alternative and more advanced mechanism for configurable callbacks that are more compositional than events. The F# language treats .NET events as values of type IEvent<'T>, which inherits from the interface IObservable<'T>, the same type used by Rx. For this reason, the main F# assembly, FSharp.Core, already provides an Observable module that exposes a set of useful functions over the values of the IObservable interface. This is considered a subset of Rx.

For example, in the following code snippet, the F# observables (in bold) are used to handle keypress and timer events from the KeyPressedEventCombinators example (listing 6.2):

```
let timeElapsed = timer.Elapsed |> Observable.map(fun _ -> 'X')
let keyPressed = control.KeyPress
                        |> Observable.filter(fun c -> Char.IsLetter c)
                        |> Observable.map(fun kd -> Char.ToLower kd.KeyChar)

let disposable =
keyPressed
|> Observable.merge timeElapsed
|> Observable.scan(fun acc c ->
```

```
            if c = 'X' then "Game Over"
            else
                let word = sprintf "%s%c" acc c
                if word = secretWord then "You Won!"
                else word
) String.Empty
|> Observable.subscribe(fun text -> printfn "%s" text)
```

It's possible to choose (and use) either `Observable` or `Event` when using F# to build reactive systems; but to avoid memory leaks, the preferred choice is `Observable`. When using the F# `Event` module, composed events are attached to the original event, and they don't have an unsubscribe mechanism that can lead to memory leaks. Instead, the `Observable` module provides the `subscribe` operator to register a callback function. This operator returns an `IDisposable` object that can be used to stop event-stream processing and to de-register all subscribed observable (or event) handlers in the pipeline with one call of the `Dispose` method.

6.4   *Taming the event stream: Twitter emotion analysis using Rx programming*

In this age of digital information where billions of devices are connected to the internet, programs must correlate, merge, filter, and run real-time analytics. The speed of processing data has moved into the realm of real-time analytics, reducing latency to virtually zero when accessing information. Reactive programming is a superb approach for handling high-performance requirements because it's concurrency friendly and scalable, and it provides a composable asynchronous data-processing semantic.

It's estimated that in the United States there is an average of 24 million tweets per hour, amounting to almost 7,000 messages per second. This is a massive quantity of data to evaluate, and presents a serious challenge for consuming such a high-traffic stream. Consequently, a system should be designed to tame the occurrence of backpressure. This backpressure, for example, in the case of Twitter could be generated by a consumer of the live stream of data that can't cope with the rate at which the producers emit events.

Backpressure

Backpressure occurs when a computer system can't process the incoming data fast enough, so it starts to buffer the arriving data until the space to buffer it is reduced to the point of deteriorating the responsiveness of the system or, worse, raising an "Out Of Memory" exception. In the case of iterating over the items in an `IEnumerable`, the consumer of the items is "pulling"; the items are processed at a controlled pace. With `IObservable`, the items are "pushed" to the consumer. In this case, `IObservable` could potentially produce values more rapidly than the subscribed observers can handle. This scenario generates excessive backpressure, causing strain on the system. To ease backpressure, Rx provides operators such as `Throttle` and `Buffer`.

The F# example in figure 6.10 illustrates a real-time analysis stream for determining the current feeling (emotion) of tweets published in the United States.

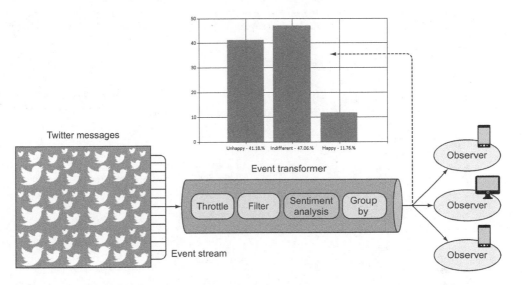

Figure 6.10 **The Twitter messages push a high-rate event stream to the consumer, so it's important to have tools like Rx to tame the continuous burst of notifications. First, the stream is throttled, then the messages are filtered, analyzed, and grouped by emotions. The result is a data stream from the incoming tweets that represents the latest status of emotions, whose values constantly update a chart and notify the subscribed observers.**

This example uses F# to demonstrate the existing built-in support for observables, which is missing in C#. But the same functionality can be reproduced in C#, either using .NET Rx or by referencing and consuming an F# library, where the code exposes the implemented observable.

The analysis of the stream of tweets is performed by consuming and extracting the information from each message. Emotional analysis is performed using the Stanford CoreNLP library. The result of this analysis is sent to a live animated chart that takes `IObservable` as input and automatically updates the graph as the data changes.

Stanford CoreNLP

The Stanford CoreNLP (http://nlp.stanford.edu) is a natural-language analysis library written in Java, but it can be integrated in .NET using the IKVM bridge (www.ikvm.net). This library has several tools, including emotion analysis tools that predict the emotion of a sentence. You can install the Stanford CoreNLP library using the NuGet package Install-Package Stanford.NLP.CoreNLP (www.nuget.org/packages/Stanford.NLP.CoreNLP), which also configures the IKVM bridge. For more details regarding how the CoreNLP library works, I recommend the online material.

The following listing shows the emotion analysis function and the settings to enable the Stanford CoreNLP library.

Listing 6.3   Evaluating a sentence's emotion using the CoreNLP library

```
let properties = Properties()
properties.setProperty("annotators", "tokenize,ssplit,pos,parse,emotion")
⇒ |> ignore

IO.Directory.SetCurrentDirectory(jarDirectory)        ← Sets the properties and creates an
let stanfordNLP = StanfordCoreNLP(properties)            instance of StanfordCoreNLP

type Emotion =
    | Unhappy                                         A discriminated union categorizes
    | Indifferent                                     emotions for each text message.
    | Happy

let getEmotionMeaning value =
    match value with
    | 0 | 1 -> Unhappy
    | 2 -> Indifferent                                Gives a value from 0 to 4 to
    | 3 | 4 -> Happy                                  determine the emotion

let evaluateEmotion (text:string) =
    let annotation = Annotation(text)
    stanfordNLP.annotate(annotation)

    let emotions =
        let emotionAnnotationClassName =
                SentimentCoreAnnotations.SentimentAnnotatedTree().getClass()
        let sentences = annotation.get(CoreAnnotations.SentencesAnnotation().
    getClass())
⇒ :?> java.util.ArrayList                             Analyzes a text message, providing
            [ for s in sentences ->                          the associated emotion
                let sentence = s :?> Annotation
                let sentenceTree = sentence.get(emotionAnnotationClassName)
⇒ :?> Tree
                let emotion = NNCoreAnnotations.getPredictedClass(sentenceTree)
                getEmotionMeaning emotion]
    (emotions.[0])
```

In the code, the F# DU defines different emotion levels (case values): Unhappy, Indifferent, and Happy. These case values compute the distribution percentage among the tweets. The function evaluateEmotion combines the text analysis from the Stanford library and returns the resulting case value (emotion).

To retrieve the stream of tweets, I used the Tweetinvi library (https://github.com/linvi/tweetinvi). It provides a well-documented API and, more importantly, it's designed to run streams concurrently while managing multithreaded scenarios. You can download and install this library from the NuGet package TweetinviAPI.

NOTE Twitter provides great support to developers who build applications using its API. All that's required is a Twitter account and an Application

Management (https://apps.twitter.com) account to obtain the key and secret access. With this information, it's possible to send and receive tweets and interact with the Twitter API.

This listing shows how to create an instance for the Tweetinvi library and how to access the settings to enable interaction with Twitter.

Listing 6.4   Settings to enable the Twitterinvi library

```
let consumerKey = "<your Key>"
let consumerSecretKey = "<your secret key>"
let accessToken = "<your access token>"
let accessTokenSecret = "<your secret access token>"

let cred = new TwitterCredentials(consumerKey, consumerSecretKey,
➡ accessToken, accessTokenSecret)
let stream = Stream.CreateSampleStream(cred)
stream.FilterLevel <- StreamFilterLevel.Low
```

This straightforward code creates an instance of the Twitter stream. The core of the Rx programming is in the following listing (highlighted in bold), where Rx and the F# `Observable` module are used in combination to handle and analyze the event stream.

Listing 6.5   Observable pipeline to analyze tweets

```
let emotionMap =
    [(Unhappy, 0)                         Generates the event stream
     (Indifferent, 0)                     from the Twitter API
     (Happy, 0)] |> Map.ofSeq
                                          Controls the rate of events to avoid
                                          overwhelming the consumer
let observableTweets =
    stream.TweetReceived
    |> Observable.throttle(TimeSpan.FromMilliseconds(100.))
    |> Observable.filter(fun args ->                        Filters the incoming messages
        args.Tweet.Language = Language.English)             to target only those in English
    |> Observable.groupBy(fun args ->                       Partitions the message
        evaluateEmotion args.Tweet.FullText)                by emotion analysis
    |> Observable.selectMany(fun args ->
        args |> Observable.map(fun i ->                     Flattens messages into one
            (args.Key, (max 1 i.Tweet.FavoriteCount))))     sequence of emotions with
    |> Observable.scan(fun sm (key,count) ->                the count of favorites
        match sm |> Map.tryFind key with
        | Some(v) -> sm |> Map.add key (v + count)          Maintains the state of the total
        | None    -> sm ) emotionMap                        partition of messages by emotion
    |> Observable.map(fun sm ->
        let total = sm |> Seq.sumBy(fun v -> v.Value)
        sm |> Seq.map(fun k ->
            let percentageEmotion = ((float k.Value) * 100.)
➡ / (float total)
            let labelText = sprintf "%A - %.2f.%%" (k.Key)
➡ percentageEmotion
            (labelText, percentageEmotion)
        ))
```

Calculates the total percentage of emotions and
returns an observable to live update a chart

The result of the `observableTweets` pipeline is an `IDisposable`, which is used to stop listening to the tweets and remove the subscription from the subscribed observable. Tweetinvi exposes the event handler `TweetReceived`, which notifies the subscribers when a new tweet has arrived. The observables are combined as a chain to form the `observableTweets` pipeline. Each step returns a new observable that listens to the original observable and then triggers the resulting event from the given function.

The first step in the observable channel is managing the backpressure, which is a result of the high rate of arriving events. When writing Rx code, be aware that it's possible for the process to be overwhelmed when the event stream comes in too quickly.

In figure 6.11, the system on the left has no problem processing the incoming event streams because the frequency of notifications over time has a sustainable throughput (desired flow). The system on the right struggles to keep up with a huge number of notifications (backpressure) that it receives over time, which could potentially collapse the system. In this case, the system responds by throttling the event streams to avoid failure. The result is a different rate of notifications between the observable and an observer.

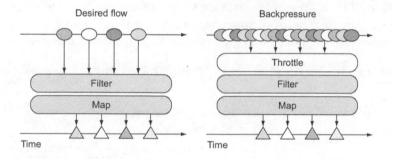

Figure 6.11   Backpressure could negatively affect the responsiveness of a system, but it's possible to reduce the rate of the incoming events and keep the system healthy by using the `throttle` function to manage the different rates between an observable and an observer.

To avoid the problem of backpressure, the `throttle` function provides a layer of protection that controls the rate of messages, preventing them from flowing too quickly:

```
stream.TweetReceived
    |> Observable.throttle(TimeSpan.FromMilliseconds(50.))
```

The `throttle` function reduces a rapid fire of data down to a subset, corresponding to a specific cadence (rhythm) as shown in figures 6.9 and 6.10. `Throttle` extracts the last value from a burst of data in an observable sequence by ignoring any value that's followed by another value in less than a time period specified. In listing 6.5, the frequency of event propagation was throttled to no more than once every 50 ms.

> ### Throttle and buffer Rx operators for taming large volumes of events
>
> Be aware that the `throttle` function can have destructive effects, which means the signals that arrive with a higher rate than the given frequency are lost, not buffered. This happens because the `throttle` function discharges the signals from an observable sequence that's followed by another signal before the given time expires. The `throttle` operator is also called *debounce*, which stops messages from flowing in at a higher rate by setting an interval between messages.
>
> The `buffer` function is useful in cases where it's too expensive to process one signal at a time, and consequently it's preferred for processing the signals in batches, at the cost of accepting a delay. There's an issue to consider when using `buffer` with large-volume events. In large-volume events, the signals are stored in memory for a period of time and the system could run into memory overflow problems. The purpose of the `buffer` operator is to stash away a specified series of signals and then republish them once either the given time has expired or the buffer is full.
>
> Here, for example, the code in C# gets all the events that happened either every second or every 50 signals depending on which rule is satisfied first.
>
> ```
> Observable.Buffer(TimeSpan.FromSeconds(1), 50)
> ```
>
> In the example of the tweet emotion analysis, the `Buffer` extension method can be applied as follows:
>
> ```
> stream.TweetReceived.Buffer(TimeSpan.FromSeconds(1), 50)
> ```

The next step in the pipeline is filtering events that aren't relevant (the command is in bold):

```
|> Observable.filter(fun args -> args.Tweet.Language = Language.English)
```

This `filter` function ensures that only the tweets that originate using the English language are processed. The `Tweet` object, from the tweet message, has a series of properties, including the sender of the message, the hashtag, and the coordinates (*location*) that can be accessed.

Next, the Rx `groupBy` operator provides the ability to partition the sequence into a series of observable groups related to a selector function. Each of these sub-observables corresponds to a unique key value, containing all the elements that share that same key value the way it does in LINQ and in SQL:

```
|> Observable.groupBy(fun args -> evaluateEmotion args.Tweet.FullText)
|> Observable.selectMany(fun args -> args |> Observable.map(fun i ->
   (args.Key, i.Tweet.FavoriteCount)))
```

In this case, the key-value emotion partitions the event stream. The function `evaluate-Emotion`, which behaves as a group selector, computes and classifies the emotion for each incoming message. Each nested observable can have its own unique operation; the `selectMany` operator is used to further subscribe these groups of observables by flattening them into one. Then, using the `map` function, the sequence is transformed into a new sequence of pairs (tuple) consisting of the `Tweet-Emotion` value and the count of how many times the tweet has been liked (or favored).

After having been partitioned and analyzed, the data must be aggregated into a meaningful format. The observable `scan` function does this by pushing the result of each call to the `accumulator` function. The returned observable will trigger notifications for each computed state value, as shown in figure 6.12.

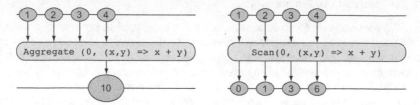

Figure 6.12   The `aggregate` function returns a single value that is the accumulation of each value from running the given function (`x,y`) against the initial accumulator `0`. The `scan` function returns a value for each item in the collection, which is the result of performing the given function against the accumulator in the current iteration.

The `scan` function is like `fold`, or the LINQ `Aggregate`, but instead of returning a single value, it returns the intermediate evaluations resulting from each iteration (as shown in bold in the following code snippet). Moreover, it satisfies the functional paradigm, maintaining state in an immutable fashion. The aggregate functions (such as `scan` and `fold`) are described as the generic concept of *catamorphism* (https://wiki.haskell.org/Catamorphisms) in FP:

```
< code here that passes an Observable of tweets with emotions analysis >
|> Observable.scan(fun sm (key,count) ->
          match sm |> Map.tryFind key with
          | Some(v) -> sm |> Map.add key (v + count)
          | None -> sm) emotionMap
```

This function `scan` takes three arguments: an observable that's passed conceptually in the form of stream tweets with emotion analysis, an anonymous function to apply the underlying values of the observable to the accumulator, and an accumulator `emotion-Map`. The result of the `scan` function is an updated accumulator that's injected into the following iteration. The initial accumulator state in the previous code is used by the `scan` function in an empty F# `Map`, which is equivalent to an immutable .NET generic `Dictionary` (`System.Collections.Generic.Dictionary<K,V>`), where the key is one of the emotions and the value is the count of its related tweets. The accumulator function `scan` updates the entries of the collection with the new evaluated types and returns the updated collection as new accumulator.

The last operation in the pipeline is to run the `map` function used to transform the observables of the source into the representation of the total percentage of tweets analyzed by emotions:

```
|> Observable.map(fun sm ->
     let total = sm |> Seq.sumBy(fun v -> v.Value)
     sm |> Seq.map(fun k ->
```

```
    let percentageEmotion = ((float k.Value) * 100.) / (float total)
    let labelText = sprintf "%A - %.2f.%%" (k.Key) percentageEmotion
    (labelText, percentageEmotion)
))
```

The transformation function is executed once for each subscribed observer. The `map` function calculates the total number of tweets from the observable passed, which contains the value of the accumulator from the previous `scan` function:

```
sm |> Seq.sumBy(fun v -> v.Value)
```

The result is returned in a format that represents the percentage of each emotion from the map table received so far. The final observable is passed into a `LiveChart`, which renders the real-time updates. Now that the code is developed, you can use the `Start-StreamAsync()` function to start the process of listening and receiving the tweets and have the observable notify subscribers:

```
LiveChart.Column(observableTweets,Name= sprintf "Tweet Emotions").ShowChart()
do stream.StartStreamAsync()
```

> ### Cold and hot observables
>
> Observables come in two flavors: hot and cold. A *hot* observable represents a stream of data that pushes notifications regardless of whether there are any subscribers. For example, the stream of tweets is a hot stream of data because the data will keep flowing regardless of the status of subscribers. A *cold* observable is a stream of events that will always push notifications from the beginning of the stream, regardless of whether the subscribers start listening after the event is pushed.

Much like the `Event` module in F#, the `Observable` module defines a set of combinators for using the `IObservable<T>` interface. The F# `Observable` module includes `add`, `filter`, `map`, `partition`, `merge`, `choose`, and `scan`. For more details, see appendix B.

In the previous example, the observable functions `groupBy` and `selectMany` are part of the Rx framework. This illustrates the utility that F# provides, providing the developer options to mix and match tools to customize the best fit for the task.

6.4.1 SelectMany: the monadic bind operator

`SelectMany` is a powerful operator that corresponds to the `bind` (or `flatMap`) operator in other programming languages. This operator constructs one monadic value from another and has the generic monadic binding signature

```
M a -> (a -> M b) -> M b
```

where `M` represents any elevated type that behaves as a container. In the case of observables, it has this signature:

```
IObservable<'T> -> ('T -> IObservable<'R>) -> IObservable<'R>
```

In .NET, there are several types that match this signature, such as IObservable, IEnumerable, and Task. Monads (http://bit.ly/2vDusZa), despite their reputation for complexity, can be thought of in simple terms: they are containers that encapsulate and abstract a given functionality with the objective of promoting composition between elevated types and avoiding side effects. Basically, when working with monads, you can think of working with boxes (containers) that are unpacked at the last moment—when they're needed.

The main purpose of monadic computation is to make composition possible where it couldn't be achieved otherwise. For example, by using monads in C#, it's possible to directly sum an integer and a Task type from the System.Threading.Tasks namespace of integer (Task<int>) (highlighted in bold):

```
Task<int> result = from task in Task.Run<int>(() => 40)
                   select task + 2;
```

The bind, or SelectMany, operation takes an elevated type and applies a function to its underlying value, returning another elevated type. An *elevated type* is a wrapper around another type, like IEnumerable<int>, Nullable<bool>, or IObservable<Tweets>. The meaning of bind depends on the monad type. For IObservable, each event in the observables input is evaluated to create a new observable. The resulting observables are then flattened to produce the output observable, as shown in figure 6.13.

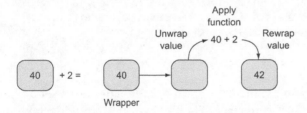

Figure 6.13   An elevated type can be considered a special container where it's possible to apply a function directly to the underlying type (in this case, 40). The elevated type works like a wrapper that contains a value, which can be extracted to apply a given function, after which the result is put back into the container.

The SelectMany binder not only *flattens* data values but, as an operator, it also transforms and then flattens the nested monadic values. The underlying theory of monads is used by LINQ, which is used by the .NET compiler to interpret the SelectMany pattern to apply the monadic behavior. For example, by implementing the SelectMany extension method over the Task type (as highlighted in bold in the following code snippet), the compiler recognizes the pattern and interprets it as the monadic binding, allowing the special composition:

```
Task<R> SelectMany<T, R>(this Task<T> source, Func<T, Task<R>> selector) =>
        source.ContinueWith(t => selector(t.Result)).Unwrap();
```

With this method in place, the previous LINQ-based code will compile and evaluate to a `Task<int>` that returns 42. Monads play an import role in functional concurrency and are covered more thoroughly in chapter 7.

6.5 *An Rx publisher-subscriber*

The Publish/Subscribe pattern allows any number of publishers to communicate with any number of subscribers asynchronously via an event channel. In general, to accomplish this communication, an intermediary hub is employed to receive the notifications, which are then forwarded to subscribers. Using Rx, it becomes possible to effectively define a Publish/Subscribe pattern by using the built-in tools and concurrency model.

The `Subject` type is a perfect candidate for this implementation. It implements the `ISubject` interface, which is the combination of `IObservable` and `IObserver`. This makes the `Subject` behave as both an observer and an observable, which allows it to operate like a broker to intercept notifications as an observer and to broadcast these notifications to all its observers. Think of the `IObserver` and the `IObservable` as consumer and publisher interfaces, respectively, as shown in figure 6.14.

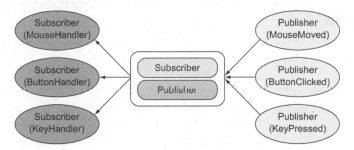

Figure 6.14 The publisher-subscriber hub manages the communication between any number of subscribers (observers) with any number of publishers (observables). The hub, also known as a broker, receives the notifications from the publishers, which are then forwarded to the subscribers.

Using the `Subject` type from Rx to represent a Publish/Subscribe pattern has the advantage of giving you the control to inject extra logic, such as `merge` and `filter`, into the notification before it's published.

6.5.1 *Using the Subject type for a powerful publisher-subscriber hub*

`Subjects` are the components of Rx, and their intention is to synchronize the values produced by an observable and the observers that consume them. `Subjects` don't completely embrace the functional paradigm because they maintain or manage states that could potentially mutate. Despite this fact, however, they're useful for creating an event-like observable as a field, which is a perfect fit for a Publish/Subscribe pattern implementation.

The Subject type implements the ISubject interface (highlighted in bold in the following code snippet), which resides in the System.Reactive.Subjects namespace

```
interface ISubject<T, R> : IObserver<T>, IObservable<R> { }
```

or ISubject<T>, if the source and result are of the same type.

Because a Subject<T> and, consequently, ISubject<T> are observers, they expose the OnNext, OnCompleted, and OnError methods. Therefore, when they're called, the same methods are called on all the subscribed observers.

Rx out of the box has different implementations of the Subject class, each with a diverse behavior. In addition, if the existing Subjects don't satisfy your needs, then you can implement your own. The only requirement to implementing a custom subject class is satisfying the ISubject interface implementation.

Here are the other Subject variants:

- ReplaySubject behaves like a normal Subject, but it stores all the messages received, providing the ability to make the messages available for current and future subscribers.
- BehaviorSubject always saves the latest available value, which makes it available for future subscribers.
- AsyncSubject represents an asynchronous operation that routes only the last notification received while waiting for the OnComplete message.

NOTE The Subject type is hot, which makes it vulnerable to losing notification messages pushed from the source observable when there are no listening observers. To offset this, carefully consider the type of Subject to use, specifically if all the messages prior to the subscription are required. An example of a hot observable is a mouse movement, where movements still happen and notifications are emitted regardless of whether there are listening observers.

6.5.2   *Rx in relation to concurrency*

The Rx framework is based on a push model with support for multithreading. But it's important to remember that Rx is single-threaded by default, and the parallel constructs that let you combine asynchronous sources must be enabled using Rx schedulers.

One of the main reasons to introduce concurrency in Rx programming is to facilitate and manage offloading the payload for an event stream. This allows a set of concurrent tasks to be performed, such as maintaining a responsive UI, to free the current thread.

NOTE Reactive Extensions allow you to combine asynchronous sources using parallel computations. These asynchronous sources could be potentially generated independently from parallel computations. Rx handles the complexity involved in compositing these sources and lets you focus on their composition aspect in a declarative style.

Moreover, Rx lets you control the flow of incoming messages as specific threads to achieve high-concurrency computation. Rx is a system for querying event streams asynchronously, which requires a level of concurrency control.

When multithreading is enabled, Rx programming increases the use of computing resources on multicore hardware, which improves the performance of computations. In this case, it's possible for different messages to arrive from different execution contexts simultaneously. In fact, several asynchronous sources could be the output from separate and parallel computations, merging into the same `Observable` pipeline. In other words, observables and observers deal with asynchronous operations against a sequence of values in a push model. Ultimately, Rx handles all the complexity involved in managing access to these notifications and avoiding common concurrency problems as if they were running in a single thread.

Using a `Subject` type (or any other observables from Rx), the code isn't converted automatically to run faster or concurrently. As a default, the operation to push the messages to multiple subscribers by a `Subject` is executed in the same thread. Moreover, the notification messages are sent to all subscribers sequentially following their subscription order and possibly blocking the operation until it completes.

The Rx framework solves this limitation by exposing the `ObserveOn` and `SubscribeOn` methods, which lets you register a `Scheduler` to handle concurrency. Rx schedulers are designed to generate and process events concurrently, increasing responsiveness and scalability while reducing complexity. They provide an abstraction over the concurrency model, which lets you perform operations against a stream of data moving without the need to be exposed directly to the underlying concurrent implementation. Moreover, Rx schedulers integrate support for task cancellation, error handling, and passing of state. All Rx schedulers implement the `IScheduler` interface, which can be found in the `System.Reactive.Concurrency` namespace.

NOTE The recommended built-in schedulers for .NET Frameworks after .NET 4.0 are either `TaskPoolScheduler` or `ThreadPoolScheduler`.

The `SubscribeOn` method determines which `Scheduler` to enable to queue messages that run on a different thread. The `ObserveOn` method determines which thread the callback function will be run in. This method targets the `Scheduler` that handles output messages and UI programming (for example, to update a WPF interface). `ObserveOn` is primarily used for UI programming and `Synchronization-Context` (http://bit.ly/2wiVBxu) interaction.

In the case of UI programming, both the `SubscribeOn` and `ObserveOn` operators can be combined to better control which thread will run in each step of your observable pipeline.

6.5.3   *Implementing a reusable Rx publisher-subscriber*

Armed with the knowledge of Rx and the `Subject` classes, it's much easier to define a reusable generic `Pub-Sub` object that combines publication and subscription into the same source. In this section, you'll first build a concurrent publisher-subscriber hub using the Subject type in Rx. Then you'll refactor the previous Twitter emotion analyzer code example to exploit the new and simpler functionality provided by the Rx-based publisher-subscriber hub.

The implementation of the reactive publisher-subscriber hub uses a Subject to subscribe and then route values to the observers, allowing multicasting notifications emitted by the sources to the observers. This listing shows the implementation of the RxPubSub class, which uses Rx to build the generic Pub-Sub object.

Listing 6.6   Reactive publisher-subscriber in C#

Shows the internal state of observers

```csharp
public class RxPubSub<T> : IDisposable
{
    private ISubject<T> subject;
    private List<IObserver<T>> observers = new List<IObserver<T>>();
    private List<IDisposable> observables = new List<IDisposable>();

    public RxPubSub(ISubject<T> subject)
    {
        this.subject = subject;
    }
    public RxPubSub() : this(new Subject<T>()) { }

    public IDisposable Subscribe(IObserver<T> observer)
    {
        observers.Add(observer);
        subject.Subscribe(observer);
        return new Subscription<T>(observer, observers);
    }

    public IDisposable AddPublisher(IObservable<T> observable) =>
        observable.SubscribeOn(TaskPoolScheduler.Default).Subscribe(subject);

    public IObservable<T> AsObservable() => subject.AsObservable();
    public void Dispose()
    {
        observers.ForEach(x => x.OnCompleted());
        observers.Clear();
    }
}

class ObserverHandler<T> : IDisposable
{
    private IObserver<T> observer;
    private List<IObserver<T>> observers;

    public ObserverHandler(IObserver<T> observer,
    List<IObserver<T>> observers)
    {
```

The private subject notifies all registered observers when a change of the observables' state is published.

Shows the internal state of observables

The constructor creates an instance of the internal subject.

The Subscribe method registers the observer to be notified and returns an IDisposable to remove the observer.

AddPublisher subscribes the observable using the default TaskPoolScheduler to handle concurrent notifications.

Exposes IObservable<T> from the internal ISubject to apply higher-order operations against event notifications

Removes all subscribers when the object is disposed

The internal class ObserverHandler wraps an IObserver to produce an IDisposable object used to stop the notification flow and to remove it from the observers collection.

```
        this.observer = observer;
        this.observers = observers;
    }

    public void Dispose()
    {
        observer.OnCompleted();
        observers.Remove(observer);
    }
}
```

An instance of the RxPubSub class can be defined either by a constructor that specifies a Subject version or by the primary constructor that instantiated and passed the default Subject from the primary constructor. In addition to the private Subject field, there are two private collection fields: the observers collection and the subscribed observables.

First, the observers collection maintains the state of the observers subscribed to the Subject through a new instance of the class Subscription. This class provides the unsubscribe method Dispose through the interface IDisposable, which then removes the specific observer when called.

The second private collection is observables. Observables maintain a list of IDisposable interfaces, which originated from the registration of each observable by the AddPublisher method. Each observable can then be unregistered using the exposed Dispose method.

In this implementation, the Subject is subscribed to the TaskPoolScheduler scheduler:

```
observable.SubscribeOn(TaskPoolScheduler.Default)
```

TaskPoolScheduler schedules the units of work for each observer to run in a different thread using the current provided TaskFactory (http://bit.ly/2vaemTA). You can easily modify the code to accept any arbitrary scheduler.

The subscribed observables from the internal Subject are exposed through the IObservable interface, obtained by calling the method AsObservable. This property is used to apply high-order operations against event notifications:

```
public IObservable<T> AsObservable() => subject.AsObservable();
```

The reason to expose the IObservable interface on the Subject is to guarantee that no one can perform an upper cast back to an ISubject and mess things up. Subjects are stateful components, so it's good practice to isolate access to them through encapsulation; otherwise, Subjects could be reinitialized or updated directly.

6.5.4 *Analyzing tweet emotions using an Rx Pub-Sub class*

In listing 6.7, you'll use the C# Reactive Pub-Sub class (RxPubSub) to handle a stream of tweet emotions. The listing is another example of how simple it is to make the two programming languages C# and F# interoperable and allow them to coexist in the same solution. From the F# library implemented in section 6.4, the observable that pushes a stream of tweet emotions is exposed so it's easily subscribed to by external observers. (The observable commands are in bold.)

Listing 6.7   Implementing observable tweet emotions

```fsharp
let tweetEmotionObservable(throttle:TimeSpan) =

    Observable.Create(fun (observer:IObserver<_>) ->
        let cred = new TwitterCredentials(consumerKey, consumerSecretKey,
    accessToken, accessTokenSecret)
        let stream = Stream.CreateSampleStream(cred)
        stream.FilterLevel <- StreamFilterLevel.Low
        stream.StartStreamAsync() |> ignore

        stream.TweetReceived
        |> Observable.throttle(throttle)
        |> Observable.filter(fun args ->
            args.Tweet.Language = Language.English)
        |> Observable.groupBy(fun args ->
            evaluateEmotion args.Tweet.FullText)
        |> Observable.selectMany(fun args ->
            args |> Observable.map(fun tw ->
                            TweetEmotion.Create tw.Tweet args.Key))
        |> Observable.subscribe(observer.OnNext)
    )
```

> **Observable.Create creates an observable by a given function that takes an observer as a parameter, which is subscribed to the returned observable.**

> **The observable subscribes to the OnNext method in the observer to push the changes.**

The listing shows the implementation of tweetEmotionObservable using the observable Create factory operator. This operator accepts a function with an observer as its parameter, where the function behaves as an observable by calling its methods.

The Observable.Create operator registers the observer passed into the function and starts to push notifications as they arrive. The observable is defined from the subscribe method, which pushes the notifications to the observer calling the method OnNext. The following listing shows the equivalent C# implementation of tweetEmotion-Observable (in bold).

Listing 6.8   Implementing tweetEmotionObservable in C#

```csharp
var tweetObservable = Observable.FromEventPattern<TweetEventArgs>(stream,
    "TweetReceived");

Observable.Create<TweetEmotion>(observer =>
{
    var cred = new TwitterCredentials(
        consumerKey, consumerSecretKey, accessToken, accessTokenSecret);
    var stream = Stream.CreateSampleStream(cred);
    stream.FilterLevel = StreamFilterLevel.Low;
    stream.StartStreamAsync();

    return Observable.FromEventPattern<TweetReceivedEventArgs>(stream,
    "TweetReceived")
        .Throttle(throttle)
        .Select(args => args.EventArgs)
        .Where(args => args.Tweet.Language == Language.English)
        .GroupBy(args =>
                    evaluateEmotion(args.Tweet.FullText))
```

```
            .SelectMany(args =>
                    args.Select(tw => TweetEmotion.Create(tw.Tweet, args.Key)))
            .Subscribe(o=>observer.OnNext(o));
});
```

The `FromEventPattern` method converts a .NET CLR event into an observable. In this case, it transforms the `TweetReceived` events into an `IObservable`.

One difference between the C# and F# implementation is that the F# code doesn't require creating an `Observable tweetObservable` using `FromEventPattern`. In fact, the event handler `TweetReceived` automatically becomes an observable in F# when passed into the pipeline `stream.TweetReceived |> Observable`. `TweetEmotion` is a value type (structure) that carries the information of the tweet emotion (in bold).

Listing 6.9 `TweetEmotion` **struct to maintain tweet details**

```
[<Struct>]
type TweetEmotion(tweet:ITweet, emotion:Emotion) =
        member this.Tweet with get() = tweet
        member this.Emotion  with get() = emotion

        static member Create tweet emotion =
                        TweetEmotion(tweet, emotion)
```

This next listing shows the implementation of `RxTweetEmotion`, which inherits from the `RxPubSub` class and subscribes an `IObservable` to manage the tweet emotion notifications (in bold).

Listing 6.10   Implementing `RxPubSub TweetEmotion`

Inherits RxTweetEmotion from RxPubSub

Passes the throttle value into the constructor, then into the tweetEmotionObservable definition

```
class RxTweetEmotion : RxPubSub<TweetEmotion>
{
    public RxTweetEmotion(TimeSpan throttle)
    {
        var obs = TweetsAnalysis.tweetEmotionObservable(throttle)
                    .SubscribeOn(TaskPoolScheduler.Default);
                base.AddPublisher(obs);
    }
}
```

Concurrently runs the Tweet-Emotions notifications using TaskPoolScheduler. This is useful when handling concurrent messages and multiple observers.

The class `RxTweetEmotion` creates and registers the `tweetEmotionObservable` observable to the base class using the `AddPublisher` method through the `obs` observable, which elevates the notification bubble from the internal `TweetReceived`. The next step, to accomplish something useful, is to register the observers.

6.5.5   *Observers in action*

The implementation of the `RxTweetEmotion` class is completed. But without subscribing any observers, there's no way to notify or react to an event when it occurs. To create an implementation of the `IObserver` interface, you could create a class that inherits and implements each of its methods. Fortunately, Rx has a set of helper functions to make this job easier. The method `Observer.Create()` can define new observers:

```
IObserver<T> Create<T>(Action<T> onNext,
                       Action<Exception> onError,
                       Action onCompleted)
```

This method has a series of overloads, passing an arbitrary implementation of the `OnNext`, `OnError`, and `OnCompleted` methods and returning an `IObserver<T>` object that calls the provided functions.

These Rx helper functions minimize the number of types created in a program as well as unnecessary proliferation of classes. Here's an example of an `IObserver` that prints only positive tweets to the console:

```
var tweetPositiveObserver = Observer.Create<TweetEmotion>(tweet => {
    if (tweet.Emotion.IsHappy)
        Console.WriteLine(tweet.Tweet.Text);
});
```

After creating the `tweetPositiveObserver` observer, its instance is registered to an instance of the previous implemented `RxTweetEmotion` class, which notifies each subscribed observer if a tweet with positive emotion is received:

```
var rxTweetEmotion = new RxTweetEmotion(TimeSpan.FromMilliseconds(150));
IDisposable posTweets = rxTweetEmotion.Subscribe(tweetPositiveObserver);
```

An instance of the `IDisposable` interface is returned for each observer subscribed. This interface can be used to stop the observer from receiving the notifications and to unregister (remove) the observer from the publisher by calling the `Dispose` method.

6.5.6   *The convenient F# object expression*

The F# object expression is a convenient way to implement on the fly any instance of an anonymous object that's based on a known existing interface (or interfaces). Object expressions in F# work similarly to the `Observer.Create()` method but can be applied to any given interface. Additionally, the instance created by an object expression in F# can also feed other .NET programming languages due to the supported interoperability.

The following code shows how to use an object expression in F# to create an instance of `IObserver<TweetEmotion>` to display only unhappy emotions to the console:

```
let printUnhappyTweets() =
    { new IObserver<TweetEmotion> with
        member this.OnNext(tweet) =
            if tweet.Emotion = Unhappy then
                Console.WriteLine(tweet.Tweet.text)

        member this.OnCompleted() = ()
        member this.OnError(exn) = () }
```

The aim of object expressions is to avoid the extra code required to define and create new named types. The instance resulting from the previous object expression can be used in the C# project by referencing the F# library and importing the correlated namespace. Here's how you can use the F# object expression in the C# code:

```
IObserver<TweetEmotion> unhappyTweetObserver = printUnhappyTweets();

IDisposable disposable = rxTweetEmotion.Subscribe(unhappyTweetObserver);
```

An instance of the `unhappyTweetObserver` observer is defined using the F# object expression and is then subscribed to by `rxTweetEmotion`, which is now ready to receive notifications.

Summary

- The reactive programming paradigm employs non-blocking asynchronous operations with a high rate of event sequences over time. This programming paradigm focuses on listening and treating a series of events asynchronously as an event stream.
- Rx treats an event stream as a sequence of events. Rx lets you exercise the same expressive programming semantic as LINQ and apply higher-order operations such as `filter`, `map`, and `reduce` against events.
- Rx for .NET provides full support for multithreaded programming. In fact, Rx is capable of handling multiple events simultaneously, possibly in parallel. Moreover, it integrates with client programming, allowing GUI updates directly.
- The Rx schedulers are designed to generate and process events concurrently, increasing responsiveness and scalability, while also reducing complexity. The Rx schedulers provide an abstraction over the concurrency model, which let you perform operations against moving data streams without the need to be exposed directly to the underlying concurrent implementation.
- The programming language F# treats events as first-class values, which means you can pass them around as data. This approach is the root that influences event combinators that let you program against events as a regular sequence.
- The special event combinators in F# can be exposed and consumed by other .NET programming languages, using this powerful programming style to simplify the traditional event-based programming model.
- Reactive programming excels at taking full advantage of asynchronous execution in the creation of components and composition of workflows. Furthermore, the inclusion of Rx capabilities to tame backpressure is crucial to avoid overuse or unbounded consumption of resources.
- Rx tames backpressure for continuous bursts of notifications, permitting you to control a high-rate stream of events that could potentially overwhelm consumers.
- Rx provides a set of tools for implementing useful reactive patterns, such as Publish/Subscribe.

Task-based functional parallelism

7

This chapter covers

- Task parallelism and declarative programming semantics

- Composing parallel operations with functional combinators

- Maximizing resource utilization with the Task Parallel Library

- Implementing a parallel functional pipeline pattern

The task parallelism paradigm splits program execution and runs each part in parallel by reducing the total runtime. This paradigm targets the distribution of tasks across different processors to maximize processor utilization and improve performance. Traditionally, to run a program in parallel, code is separated into distinct areas of functionality and then computed by different threads. In these scenarios, primitive locks are used to synchronize the access to shared resources in the presence of multiple threads. The purpose of locks is to avoid race conditions and memory corruption by ensuring concurrent mutual exclusion. The main reason locks are used is due to the design legacy of waiting for the current thread to complete before a resource is available to continue running the thread.

A newer and better mechanism is to pass the rest of the computation to a callback function (which runs after the thread completes execution) to continue the work. This technique in FP is called *continuation-passing style (CPS)*. In this chapter, you'll learn how to adopt this mechanism to run multiple tasks in parallel without blocking program execution. With this technique, you'll also learn how to implement task-based parallel programs by isolating side effects and mastering function composition, which simplifies the achievement of task parallelism in your code. Because compositionality is one of the most important features in FP, it eases the adoption of a declarative programming style. Code that's easy to understand is also simple to maintain. Using FP, you'll engage task parallelism in your programs without introducing complexity, as compared to conventional programming.

7.1   A short introduction to task parallelism

Task parallelism refers to the process of running a set of independent tasks in parallel across several processors. This paradigm partitions a computation into a set of smaller tasks and executes those smaller tasks on multiple threads. The execution time is reduced by simultaneously processing multiple functions.

In general, parallel jobs begin from the same point, with the same data, and can either terminate in a fire-and-forget fashion or complete altogether in a task-group continuation. Any time a computer program simultaneously evaluates different and autonomous expressions using the same starting data, you have task parallelism. The core of this concept is based on small units of computations called *futures*. Figure 7.1 shows the comparison between data parallelism and task parallelism.

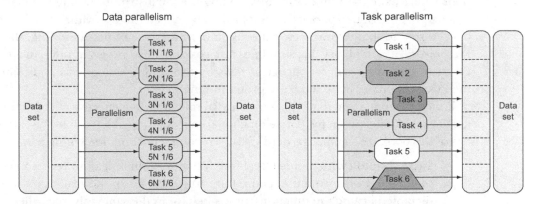

Figure 7.1　Data parallelism is the simultaneous execution of the same function across the elements of a data set. Task parallelism is the simultaneous execution of multiple and different functions across the same or different data sets.

Task parallelism isn't data parallelism

Chapter 4 explains the differences between task parallelism and data parallelism. To refresh your memory, these paradigms are at two ends of the spectrum. *Data parallelism* occurs when a single operation is applied to many inputs. *Task parallelism* occurs when multiple diverse operations perform against their own input. It is used to query and call multiple Web APIs at one time, or to store data against different database servers. In short, task parallelism parallelizes functions; data parallelism parallelizes data.

Task parallelism achieves its best performance by adjusting the number of running tasks, depending on the amount of parallelism available on your system, which corresponds to the number of available cores and, possibly, their current loads.

7.1.1   *Why task parallelism and functional programming?*

In the previous chapters, you've seen code examples that deal with data parallelism and task composition. Those data-parallel patterns, such as Divide and Conquer, Fork/ Join, and MapReduce, aim to solve the computational problem of splitting and computing in parallel smaller, independent jobs. Ultimately, when the jobs are terminated, their outputs are combined into the final result.

In real-world parallel programming, however, you commonly deal with different and more complex structures that aren't so easily split and reduced. For example, the computations of a task that processes input data could rely on the result of other tasks. In this case, the design and approach to coordinating the work among multiple tasks is different than for the data parallelism model and can sometimes be challenging. This challenge is due to task dependencies, which can reach convoluted connections where execution times can vary, making the job distribution tough to manage.

The purpose of task parallelism is to tackle these scenarios, providing you, the developer, with a toolkit of practices, patterns, and, in the case of programming, the .NET Framework, a rich library that simplifies task-based parallel programming. In addition, FP eases the compositional aspect of tasks by controlling side effects and managing their dependencies in a declarative programming style.

Functional paradigm tenets play an essential role in writing effective and deterministic task-based parallel programs. These functional concepts were discussed in the early chapters of this book. To summarize, here's a list of recommendations for writing parallel code:

- Tasks should evaluate side-effect-free functions, which lead to referential transparency and deterministic code. Pure functions make the program more predictable because the functions always behave in the same way, regardless of the external state.
- Remember that pure functions can run in parallel because the order of execution is irrelevant.

- If side effects are required, control them locally by performing the computation in a function with run-in isolation.
- Avoid sharing data between tasks by applying a defensive copy approach.
- Use immutable structures when data sharing between tasks cannot be avoided.

NOTE A *defensive copy* is a mechanism that reduces (or eliminates) the negative side effects of modifying a shared mutable object. The idea is to create a copy of the original object that can be safely shared; its modification won't affect the original object.

7.1.2 Task parallelism support in .NET

Since its first release, the .NET Framework has supported the parallel execution of code through multithreading. Multithreaded programs are based on an independent execution unit called a *thread*, which is a lightweight process responsible for multitasking within a single application. (The Thread class can be found in the Base Class Library (BCL) System.Threading namespace.) Threads are handled by the CLR. The creation of new threads is expensive in terms of overhead and memory. For example, the memory stack size associated with the creation of a thread is about 1 MB in an x86 architecture-based processor because it involves the stack, thread local storage, and context switches.

Fortunately, the .NET Framework provides a class ThreadPool that helps to overcome these performance problems. In fact, it's capable of optimizing the costs associated with complex operations, such as creating, starting, and destroying threads. Furthermore, the .NET ThreadPool is designed to reuse existing threads as much as possible to minimize the costs associated with the instantiation of new ones. Figure 7.2 compares the two processes.

The ThreadPool class

The .NET Framework provides a ThreadPool static class that loads a set of threads during the initialization of a multithreaded application and then reuses those threads, instead of creating new threads, to run new tasks as required. In this way, the ThreadPool class limits the number of threads that are running at any given point, avoiding the overhead of creating and destroying application threads. In the case of parallel computation, Thread-Pool optimizes the performance and improves the application's responsiveness by avoiding context switches.

The ThreadPool class exposes the static method QueueUserWorkItem, which accepts a function (delegate) that represents an asynchronous operation.

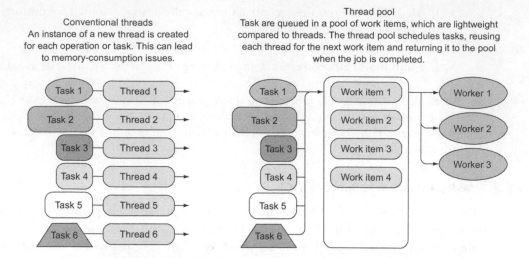

Figure 7.2   If using conventional threads, you must create an instance of a new thread for each operation or task. This can create memory consumption issues. By contrast, if using a thread pool, you queue a task in a pool of work items, which are lightweight compared to threads. The thread pool then schedules these tasks, reusing the thread for the next work item and returning it back to the pool when the job is completed.

The following listing compares starting a thread in a traditional way versus starting a thread using the `ThreadPool.QueueUserWorkItem` static method.

Listing 7.1   Spawning threads and `ThreadPool.QueueUserWorkItem`

```
Action<string> downloadSite = url => {              ◄──────────────
    var content = new WebClient().DownloadString(url);
    Console.WriteLine($"The size of the web site {url} is
➥ {content.Length}");
                                                    Uses a function to download
};                                                           a given website

var threadA = new Thread(() => downloadSite("http://www.nasdaq.com"));
var threadB = new Thread(() => downloadSite("http://www.bbc.com"));

threadA.Start();
threadB.Start();        ◄──── Threads must start explicitly, providing
threadA.Join();              the option to wait (join) for completion.
threadB.Join();

ThreadPool.QueueUserWorkItem(o => downloadSite("http://www.nasdaq.com"));
ThreadPool.QueueUserWorkItem(o => downloadSite("http://www.bbc.com"));  ◄──

                        The ThreadPool.QueueUserWorkItem immediately
                           starts an operation considered "fire and forget,"
                         which means the work item needs to produce side
                            effects in order for the calculation to be visible.
```

A thread starts explicitly, but the `Thread` class provides an option using the instance method `Join` to wait for the thread. Each thread then creates an additional memory load, which is harmful to the runtime environment. Initiating an asynchronous computation using `ThreadPool`'s `QueueUserWorkItem` is simple, but there are a few restraints when using this technique that introduce serious complications in developing a task-based parallel system:

- No built-in notification mechanism when an asynchronous operation completes
- No easy way to get back a result from a `ThreadPool` worker
- No built-in mechanism to propagate exceptions to the original thread
- No easy way to coordinate dependent asynchronous operations

To overcome these limitations, Microsoft introduced the notion of tasks with the TPL, accessible through the `System.Threading.Tasks` namespace. The tasks concept is the recommended approach for building task-based parallel systems in .NET.

7.2 *The .NET Task Parallel Library*

The .NET TPL implements a number of extra optimizations on top of `ThreadPool`, including a sophisticated `TaskScheduler` work-stealing algorithm (http://mng.bz/j4Kl) to scale dynamically the degree of concurrency, as shown in figure 7.3. This algorithm guarantees an effective use of the available system processor resources to maximize the overall performance of the concurrent code.

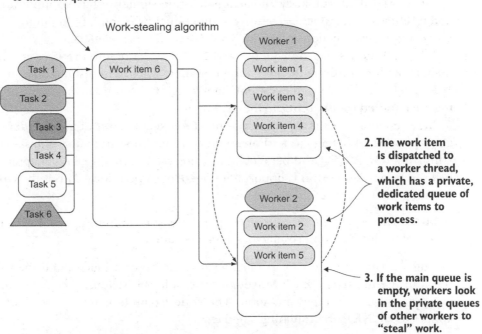

Figure 7.3 The TPL uses the work-stealing algorithm to optimize the scheduler. Initially, the TPL sends jobs to the main queue (step 1). Then it dispatches the work items to one of the worker threads, which has a private and dedicated queue of work items to process (step 2). If the main queue is empty, the workers look in the private queues of the other workers to "steal" work (step 3).

With the introduction of the task concept in place of the traditional and limited thread model, the Microsoft TPL eases the process of adding concurrency and parallelism to a program with a set of new types. Furthermore, the TPL provides support through the Task object to cancel and manage state, to handle and propagate exceptions, and to control the execution of working threads. The TPL abstracts away the implementation details from the developer, offering control over executing the code in parallel.

When using a task-based programming model, it becomes almost effortless to introduce parallelism in a program and concurrently execute parts of the code by converting those parts into tasks.

> **NOTE** The TPL provides the necessary infrastructure to achieve optimal utilization of CPU resources, regardless of whether you're running a parallel program on a single or multicore computer.

You have several ways to invoke parallel tasks. This chapter reviews the relevant techniques to implement task parallelism.

7.2.1 *Running operations in parallel with TPL Parallel.Invoke*

Using the .NET TPL, you can schedule a task in several ways, the Parallel.Invoke method being the simplest. This method accepts an arbitrary number of actions (delegates) as an argument in the form ParamArray and creates a task for each of the delegates passed. Unfortunately, the action-delegate signature has no input arguments, and it returns void, which is contrary to functional principles. In imperative programming languages, functions returning void are used for side effects.

When all the tasks terminate, the Parallel.Invoke method returns control to the main thread to continue the execution flow. One important distinction of the Parallel.Invoke method is that exception handling, synchronous invocation, and scheduling are handled transparently to the developer.

Let's imagine a scenario where you need to execute a set of independent, heterogeneous tasks in parallel as a whole, then continue the work after all tasks complete. Unfortunately, PLINQ and parallel loops (discussed in the previous chapters) cannot be used because they don't support heterogeneous operations. This is the typical case for using the Parallel.Invoke method.

> **NOTE** *Heterogeneous tasks* are a set of operations that compute as a whole regardless of having different result types or diverse outcomes.

Listing 7.2 runs functions in parallel against three given images and then saves the result in the filesystem. Each function creates a locally defensive copy of the original image to avoid unwanted mutation. The code example is in F#; the same concept applies to all .NET programming languages.

Listing 7.2 `Parallel.Invoke` executing multiple heterogeneous tasks

Creates an image with a 3D effect from a given image

```
let convertImageTo3D (sourceImage:string) (destinationImage:string) =
    let bitmap = Bitmap.FromFile(sourceImage) :?> Bitmap        ◄──── Creates a copy of
    let w,h = bitmap.Width, bitmap.Height                                an image from a
    for x in 20 .. (w-1) do                                              given file path
        for y in 0 .. (h-1) do           ◄──────────────────── A nested for loop accesses
            let c1 = bitmap.GetPixel(x,y)                       the pixels of the image.
            let c2 = bitmap.GetPixel(x - 20,y)
            let color3D = Color.FromArgb(int c1.R, int c2.G, int c2.B)
            bitmap.SetPixel(x - 20 ,y,color3D)
    bitmap.Save(destinationImage, ImageFormat.Jpeg)       ◄──── Saves the newly created
                                                                image in the filesystem
```

Creates an image, transforming the colors to shades of gray

```
let setGrayscale (sourceImage:string) (destinationImage:string) =
    let bitmap = Bitmap.FromFile(sourceImage) :?> Bitmap ◄─────────────┐
    let w,h = bitmap.Width, bitmap.Height                              │
    for x = 0 to (w-1) do                 A nested for loop accesses   │
        for y = 0 to  (h-1) do   ◄─────── the pixels of the image.     │
            let c = bitmap.GetPixel(x,y)                               │
            let gray = int(0.299 * float c.R + 0.587 * float c.G + 0.114 * │
➥ float c.B)                                                         │
            bitmap.SetPixel(x,y, Color.FromArgb(gray, gray, gray))     │
    bitmap.Save(destinationImage, ImageFormat.Jpeg)                    │
                                                                       │
                          Creates an image by applying the Red color filter │
                                                                       │
let setRedscale (sourceImage:string) (destinationImage:string) = ◄─────┘
    let bitmap = Bitmap.FromFile(sourceImage) :?> Bitmap ◄─────────────
    let w,h = bitmap.Width, bitmap.Height
    for x = 0 to (w-1) do
        for y = 0 to  (h-1) do   ◄──────────────────── A nested for loop
            let c = bitmap.GetPixel(x,y)               accesses the pixels
            bitmap.SetPixel(x,y, Color.FromArgb(int c.R, of the image.
➥ abs(int c.G - 255), abs(int c.B - 255)))
    bitmap.Save(destinationImage, ImageFormat.Jpeg)

System.Threading.Tasks.Parallel.Invoke(
    Action(fun ()-> convertImageTo3D "MonaLisa.jpg" "MonaLisa3D.jpg"),
    Action(fun ()-> setGrayscale "LadyErmine.jpg" "LadyErmineRed.jpg"),
    Action(fun ()-> setRedscale "GinevraBenci.jpg" "GinevraBenciGray.jpg"))
```

Saves the newly created image in the filesystem

In the code, `Parallel.Invoke` creates and starts the three tasks independently, one for each function, and blocks the execution flow of the main thread until all tasks complete. Due to the parallelism achieved, the total execution time coincides with the time to compute the slower method.

NOTE The source code intentionally uses the methods `GetPixel` and `SetPixel` to modify a `Bitmap`. These methods (especially `GetPixel`) are notoriously slow; but for the sake of the example we want to test the parallelism creating little extra overhead to induce extra CPU stress. In production code, if you need to iterate throughout an entire image, you're better off marshaling the entire image into a byte array and iterating through that.

It's interesting to notice that the `Parallel.Invoke` method could be used to implement a Fork/Join pattern, where multiple operations run in parallel and then join when they're all completed. Figure 7.4 shows the images before and after the image processing.

Ginevra de' Benci   *Ginevra de' Benci,* red filter

Mona Lisa   *Mona Lisa,* 3D

Lady with an Ermine   *Lady with an Ermine,* shades of gray

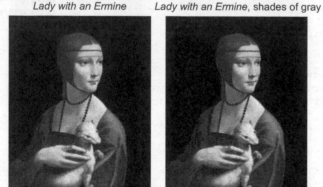

Figure 7.4   The resulting images from running the code in listing 7.2. You can find the full implementation in the downloadable source code.

Despite the convenience of executing multiple tasks in parallel, `Parallel.Invoke` limits the control of the parallel operation because of the `void` signature type. This method doesn't expose any resources to provide details regarding the status and outcome, either succeed or fail, of each individual task. `Parallel.Invoke` can either complete successfully or throw an exception in the form of an `AggregateException` instance. In the latter case, any exception that occurs during the execution is postponed and rethrown when all tasks have completed. In FP, exceptions are side effects that should be avoided. Therefore, FP provides a better mechanism to handle errors, a subject which will be covered in chapter 11.

Ultimately, there are two important limitations to consider when using the `Parallel.Invoke` method:

- The signature of the method returns `void`, which prevents compositionality.
- The order of task execution isn't guaranteed, which constrains the design of computations that have dependencies.

7.3 The problem of void in C#

It's common, in imperative programming languages such as C#, to define methods and delegates that don't return values (`void`), such as the `Parallel.Invoke` method. This method's signature prevents compositionality. Two functions can compose when the output of a function matches the input of the other function.

In function-first programming languages such as F#, every function has a return value, including the case of the `unit` type, which is comparable to a `void` but is treated as a value, conceptually not much different from a Boolean or integer.

`unit` is the type of any expression that lacks any other specific value. Think of functions used for printing to the screen. There's nothing specific that needs to be returned, and therefore functions may return `unit` so that the code is still valid. This is the F# equivalent of C#'s `void`. The reason F# doesn't use `void` is that every valid piece of code has a return type, whereas `void` is the absence of a return. Rather than the concept of `void`, a functional programmer thinks of `unit`. In F#, the `unit` type is written as `()`. This design enables function composition.

In principle, it isn't required for a programming language to support methods with return values. But a method without a defined output (`void`) suggests that the function performs some side effect, which makes it difficult to run tasks in parallel.

7.3.1 The solution for void in C#: the unit type

In functional programming, a function defines a relationship between its input and output values. This is similar to the way mathematical theorems are written. For example, in the case of a pure function, the return value is only determined by its input values.

In mathematics, every function returns a value. In FP, a function is a mapping, and a mapping has to have a value to map. This concept is missing in mainstream imperative programming languages such as C#, C++, and Java, which treat `void`s as methods that don't return anything, instead of as functions that can return something meaningful.

In C#, you can implement a Unit type as a struct with a single value that can be used as a return type in place of a void-returning method. Alternatively, the Rx, discussed in chapter 6, provides a unit type as part of its library. This listing shows the implementation of the Unit type in C#, which was borrowed from the Microsoft Rx (http://bit.ly/2vEzMeM).

Listing 7.3   Unit type implementation in C#

```
public struct Unit : IEquatable<Unit>    ◄─── The unit struct that implements the IEquatable
{                                              interface to force the definition of a type-
                                               specific method for determining equality
```

Uses a helper static method to retrieve   Overrides the base methods to
the instance of the Unit type   force equality between Unit types

```
        public static readonly Unit Default = new Unit();
        public override int GetHashCode() => 0;
        public override bool Equals(object obj) => obj is Unit;
        public override string ToString() => "()";

        public bool Equals(Unit other) => true;
        public static bool operator ==(Unit lhs, Unit rhs) => true;
        public static bool operator !=(Unit lhs, Unit rhs) => false;
}
```

Equality between unit types is always true.

The Unit struct implements the IEquatable interface in such a way that forces all values of the Unit type to be equal. But what's the real benefit of having the Unit type as a value in a language type system? What is its practical use?

Here are two main answers:

- The type Unit can be used to publish an acknowledgment that a function is completed.
- Having a Unit type is useful for writing generic code, including where a generic first-class function is required, which reduces code duplication.

Using the Unit type, for example, you could avoid repeating code to implement Action<T> or Func<T, R>, or functions that return a Task or a Task<T>. Let's consider a function that runs a Task<TInput> and transforms the result of the computation into a TResult type:

```
TResult Compute<TInput, TResult>(Task<TInput> task,
            Func<TInput, TResult> projection) => projection(task.Result);

Task<int> task = Task.Run<int>(() => 42);
bool isTheAnswerOfLife = Compute(task, n => n == 42);
```

This function has two arguments. The first is a Task<TInput> that evaluates to an expression. The result is passed into the second argument, a Func<TInput, TResult> delegate, to apply a transformation and then return the final value.

NOTE This code implementation is for demo purposes only. It isn't recommended to block the evaluation of the task to retrieve the result as the `Compute` function does in the previous code snippet. Section 7.4 covers the right approach.

How would you convert the `Compute` function into a function that prints the result? You're forced to write a new function to replace the `Func<T>` delegate projection into an `Action` delegate type. The new method has this signature:

```
void Compute<TInput>(Task<TInput> task, Action<TInput> action) =>
                    action(task.Result);

Task<int> task = Task.Run<int>(() => 42);
Compute(task, n => Console.WriteLine($"Is {n} the answer of life?
  {n == 42}"));
```

It's also important to point out that the `Action` delegate type is performing a side effect: in this case, printing the result on the console, which is a function conceptually similar to the previous one.

It would be ideal to reuse the same function instead of having to duplicate code for the function with the `Action` delegate type as an argument. To do so, you'll need to pass a void into the `Func` delegate, which isn't possible in C#. This is the case where the `Unit` type removes code repetition. By using the `struct` `Unit` type definition, you can use the same function that takes a `Func` delegate to also produce the same behavior as the function with the `Action` delegate type:

```
Task<int> task = Task.Run<int>(() => 42);

Unit unit = Compute(task, n => {
    Console.WriteLine($"Is {n} the answer of life? {n == 42}");
    return Unit.Default;});
```

In that way, introducing the `Unit` type in the C# language, you can write one `Compute` function to handle both cases of returning a value or computing a side effect. Ultimately, a function returning a `Unit` type indicates the presence of side effects, which is meaningful information for writing concurrent code. Moreover, there are FP languages, such as Haskell, where the `Unit` type notifies the compiler, which then distinguishes between pure and impure functions to apply more granular optimization.

7.4 *Continuation-passing style: a functional control flow*

Task continuation is based on the functional idea of the CPS paradigm, discussed in chapter 3. This approach gives you execution control, in the form of continuation, by passing the result of the current function to the next one. Essentially, function continuation is a delegate that represents "what happens next." CPS is an alternative for the conventional control flow in imperative programming style, where each command is executed one after another. Instead, using CPS, a function is passed as an argument into a method, explicitly defining the next operation to execute after its own computation is completed. This lets you design your own flow-of-control commands.

7.4.1   Why exploit CPS?

The main benefit of applying CPS in a concurrent environment is avoiding inconvenient thread blocking that negatively impacts the performance of the program. For example, it's inefficient for a method to wait for one or more tasks to complete, blocking the main execution thread until its child tasks complete. Often the parent task, which in this case is the main thread, can continue, but cannot proceed immediately because its thread is still executing one of the other tasks. The solution: CPS, which allows the thread to return to the caller immediately, without waiting on its children. This ensures that the continuation will be invoked when it completes.

One downside of using explicit CPS is that code complexity can escalate quickly because CPS makes programs longer and less readable. You'll see later in this chapter how to combat this issue by combining TPL and functional paradigms to abstract the complexity behind the code, making it flexible and simple to use. CPS enables several helpful task advantages:

- Function continuations can be composed as a chain of operations.
- A continuation can specify the conditions under which the function is called.
- A continuation function can invoke a set of other continuations.
- A continuation function can be canceled easily at any time during computation or even before it starts.

In the .NET Framework, a task is an abstraction of the classic (traditional) .NET thread (http://mng.bz/DK6K), representing an independent asynchronous unit of work. The Task object is part of the System.Threading.Tasks namespace. The higher level of abstraction provided by the Task type aims to simplify the implementation of concurrent code and facilitate the control of the life cycle for each task operation. It's possible, for example, to verify the status of the computation and confirm whether the operation is terminated, failed, or canceled. Moreover, tasks are composable in a chain of operations by using continuations, which permit a declarative and fluent programming style.

The following listing shows how to create and run operations using the Task type. The code uses the functions from listing 7.2.

Listing 7.4   Creating and starting tasks

```
Task monaLisaTask = Task.Factory.StartNew(() =>
    convertImageTo3D("MonaLisa.jpg", "MonaLisa3D.jpg"));

Task ladyErmineTask = new Task(() =>
    setGrayscale("LadyErmine.jpg", "LadyErmine3D.jpg"));
ladyErmineTask.Start();

Task ginevraBenciTask = Task.Run(() =>
    setRedscale("GinevraBenci.jpg", "GinevraBenci3D.jpg"));
```

Runs the method convertImageTo3D using the StartNew Task static helper method

Runs the method setGrayscale by creating a new Task instance, and then calls the Start() Task instance method

Runs the method setRedscale using the simplified static method Run(), which runs a task with the default common properties

The code shows three different ways to create and execute a task:

- The first technique creates and immediately starts a new task using the built-in `Task.Factory.StartNew` method constructor.
- The second technique creates a new instance of a task, which needs a function as a constructor parameter to serve as the body of the task. Then, calling the `Start` instance method, the `Task` begins the computation. This technique provides the flexibility to delay task execution until the `Start` function is called; in this way, the `Task` object can be passed into another method that decides when to schedule the task for execution.
- The third approach creates the `Task` object and then immediately calls the `Run` method to schedule the task. This is a convenient way to create and work with tasks using the default constructor that applies the standard option values.

The first two options are a better choice if you need a particular option to instantiate a task, such as setting the `LongRunning` option. In general, tasks promote a natural way to isolate data that depends on functions to communicate with their related input and output values, as shown in the conceptual example in figure 7.5.

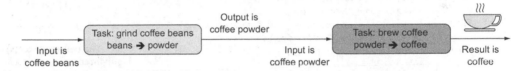

Figure 7.5 When two tasks are composed together, the output of the first task becomes the input for the second. This is the same as function composition.

> **NOTE** The `Task` object can be instantiated with different options to control and customize its behavior. The `TaskCreationOptions.LongRunning` option notifies the underlying scheduler that the task will be a long-running one, for example. In this case, the task scheduler might be bypassed to create an additional and dedicated thread whose work won't be impacted by thread-pool scheduling. For more information regarding `TaskCreationOptions`, see the Microsoft MSDN documentation online (http://bit.ly/2uxg1R6).

7.4.2 *Waiting for a task to complete: the continuation model*

You've seen how to use tasks to parallelize independent units of work. But in common cases the structure of the code is more complex than launching operations in a fire-and-forget manner. The majority of task-based parallel computations require a more sophisticated level of coordination between concurrent operations, where order of execution can be influenced by the underlying algorithms and control flow of the program. Fortunately, the .NET TPL library provides mechanisms for coordinating tasks.

Let's start with an example of multiple operations running sequentially, and incrementally redesign and refactor the program to improve the code compositionality and performance. You'll start with the sequential implementation, and then you'll apply different techniques incrementally to improve and maximize the overall computational performance.

Listing 7.5 implements a face-detection program that can detect specific faces in a given image. For this example, you'll use the images of the presidents of the United States on $20, $50, and $100 bills, using the side on which the president's image is printed. The program will detect the face of the president in each image and return a new image with a square box surrounding the detected face. In this example, focus on the important code without being distracted by the details of the UI implementation. The full source code is downloadable from the book's website.

Listing 7.5   Face-detection function in C#

```
Bitmap DetectFaces(string fileName) {
    var imageFrame = new Image<Bgr, byte>(fileName);
    var cascadeClassifier = new CascadeClassifier();
    var grayframe = imageFrame.Convert<Gray, byte>();
    var faces = cascadeClassifier.DetectMultiScale(
        grayframe, 1.1, 3, System.Drawing.Size.Empty);
    foreach (var face in faces)
        imageFrame.Draw(face,
                new Bgr(System.Drawing.Color.BurlyWood), 3);
    return imageFrame.ToBitmap();
}

void StartFaceDetection(string imagesFolder) {
    var filePaths = Directory.GetFiles(imagesFolder);
        foreach (string filePath in filePaths) {
            var bitmap = DetectFaces(filePath);
            var bitmapImage = bitmap.ToBitmapImage();
            Images.Add(bitmapImage);
        }
}
```

Uses a classifier to detect face features in an image

Instance of an Emgu.CV image to interop with the OpenCV library

Face-detection process

The detected face(s) is highlighted here, using a box that's drawn around it.

The processed image is added to the Images observable collection to update the UI.

The function `DetectFaces` loads an image from the filesystem using the given filename path and then detects the presence of any faces. The library `Emgu.CV` is responsible for performing the face detection. The `Emgu.CV` library is a .NET wrapper that permits interoperability with programming languages such as C# and F#, both of which can interact and call the functions of the underlying Intel OpenCV image-processing library.[1] The function `StartFaceDetection` initiates the execution, getting the filesystem path of the images to evaluate, and then sequentially processes the face detection in a `for-each` loop by calling the function `DetectFaces`. The result is a new `BitmapImage` type, which is added to the observable collection `Images` to update the UI. Figure 7.6 shows the expected result—the detected faces are highlighted in a box.

---

[1]   OpenCV (Open Source Computer Vision Library) is a high-performance image processing library by Intel (https://opencv.org).

Figure 7.6 Result of the face-detection process. The right side has the images with the detected face surrounded by a box frame.

The first step in improving the performance of the program is to run the face-detection function in parallel, creating a new task for each image to evaluate.

Listing 7.6 Parallel-task implementation of the face-detection program

```
void StartFaceDetection(string imagesFolder)
{
    var filePaths = Directory.GetFiles(imagesFolder);

    var bitmaps = from filePath in filePaths
                select Task.Run<Bitmap>(() => DetectFaces(filePath));

    foreach (var bitmap in bitmaps) {
        var bitmapImage = bitmap.Result;
            Images.Add(bitmapImage.ToBitmapImage());
    }
}
```

> Starts a task sequentially from the TPL for each image to process

In this code, a LINQ expression creates an `IEnumerable` of `Task<Bitmap>`, which is constructed with the convenient `Task.Run` method. With a collection of tasks in place, the code starts an independent computation in the for-each loop; but the performance of the program isn't improved. The problem is that the tasks still run sequentially, one by one. The loop processes one task at a time, awaiting its completion before continuing to the next task. The code isn't running in parallel.

You could argue that choosing a different approach, such as using `Parallel.ForEach` or `Parallel.Invoke` to compute the `DetectFaces` function, could avoid the problem and guarantee parallelism. But you'll see why this isn't a good idea.

Let's adjust the design to fix the problem by analyzing what the foundational issue is. The `IEnumerable` of `Task<Bitmap>` generated by the LINQ expression is materialized during the execution of the for-each loop. During each iteration, a `Task<Bitmap>` is retrieved, but at this point, the task isn't competed; in fact, it's not even started. The reason lies in the fact that the `IEnumerable` collection is lazily evaluated, so the underlying task starts the computation at the last possible moment during its materialization. Consequently, when the result of the task bitmap inside the loop is accessed through the `Task<Bitmap>.Result` property, the task will block the joining thread until the task is done. The execution will resume after the task terminates the computation and returns the result.

To write scalable software, you can't have any blocked threads. In the previous code, when the task's `Result` property is accessed because the task hasn't yet finished running, the thread pool will most likely create a new thread. This increases resource consumption and hurts performance.

After this analysis, it appears that there are two issues to be corrected to ensure parallelism (figure 7.7):

- Ensure that the tasks run in parallel.
- Avoid blocking the main working thread and waiting for each task to complete.

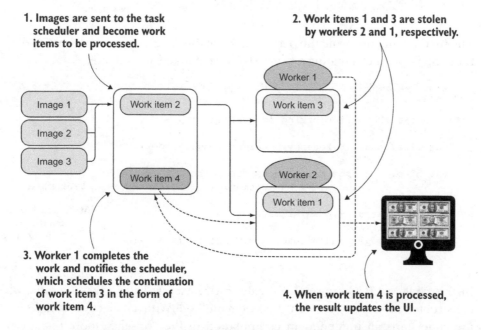

1. Images are sent to the task scheduler and become work items to be processed.

2. Work items 1 and 3 are stolen by workers 2 and 1, respectively.

3. Worker 1 completes the work and notifies the scheduler, which schedules the continuation of work item 3 in the form of work item 4.

4. When work item 4 is processed, the result updates the UI.

Figure 7.7　The images are sent to the task scheduler, becoming work items to be processed (step 1). Work item 3 and work item 1 are then "stolen" by worker 1 and worker 2, respectively (step 2). Worker 1 completes the work and notifies the task scheduler, which schedules the rest of the work for continuation in the form of the new work item 4, which is the continuation of work item 3 (step 3). When work item 4 is processed, the result updates the UI (step 4).

Here is how to fix issues to ensure the code runs in parallel and reduces memory consumption.

Listing 7.7　Correct parallel-task implementation of the `DetectFaces` function

```
ThreadLocal<CascadeClassifier> CascadeClassifierThreadLocal =
    new ThreadLocal<CascadeClassifier>(() => new CascadeClassifier());

Bitmap DetectFaces(string fileName) {
```

Uses a ThreadLocal instance to ensure a defensive copy of CascadeClassifier for each working task

```
    var imageFrame = new Image<Bgr, byte>(fileName);
    var cascadeClassifier = CascadeClassifierThreadLocal.Value;
    var grayframe = imageFrame.Convert<Gray, byte>();
    var faces = cascadeClassifier.DetectMultiScale(grayframe, 1.1, 3,
        System.Drawing.Size.Empty);

    foreach (var face in faces)
        imageFrame.Draw(face, new Bgr(System.Drawing.Color.BurlyWood), 3);
    return imageFrame.ToBitmap();
}

void StartFaceDetection(string imagesFolder) {
    var filePaths = Directory.GetFiles(imagesFolder);
    var bitmapTasks =
     (from filePath in filePaths
     select Task.Run<Bitmap>(() => DetectFaces(filePath))).ToList();

    foreach (var bitmapTask in bitmapTasks)
            bitmapTask.ContinueWith(bitmap => {
                var bitmapImage = bitmap.Result;
                Images.Add(bitmapImage.ToBitmapImage());
            }, TaskScheduler.FromCurrentSynchronizationContext());
}
```

Uses a LINQ expression on the file paths that starts image processing in parallel

TaskScheduler FromCurrentSynchronizationContext chooses the appropriate context to schedule work on the relevant UI.

Task continuation ensures no blocking; the operation passes the continuation of the work when it completes.

In the example, to keep the code structure simple, there's the assumption that each computation completes successfully. A few code changes exist, but the good news is that true parallel computation is achieved without blocking any threads (by continuing the task operation when it completes). The main function `StartFaceDetection` guarantees executing the tasks in parallel by materializing the LINQ expression immediately with a call to `ToList()` on the `IEnumerable` of `Task<Bitmap>`.

> **NOTE** When you write a computation that creates a load of tasks, fire a LINQ query and make sure to materialize the query first. Otherwise, there's no benefit, because parallelism will be lost and the task will be computed sequentially in the for-each loop.

Next, a `ThreadLocal` object is used to create a defensive copy of `CascadeClassifier` for each thread accessing the function `DetectFaces`. `CascadeClassifier` loads into memory a local resource, which isn't thread safe. To solve this problem of thread unsafety, a local variable `CascadeClassifier` is instantiated for each thread that runs the function. This is the purpose of the `ThreadLocal` object (discussed in detail in chapter 4).

Then, in the function `StartFaceDetection`, the for-each loop iterates through the list of `Task<Bitmap>`, creating a continuation for each task instead of blocking the execution if the task is not completed. Because `bitmapTask` is an asynchronous operation, there's no guarantee that the task has completed executing before the `Result` property is accessed. It's good practice to use task continuation with the function `ContinueWith` to access the result as part of a continuation. Defining a task continuation is similar to creating a regular task, but the function passed with the `ContinueWith` method takes as an argument a type of `Task<Bitmap>`. This argument represents the antecedent task, which can be used to inspect the status of the computation and branch accordingly.

When the antecedent task completes, the function `ContinueWith` starts execution as a new task. Task continuation runs in the captured current synchronization context, `TaskScheduler.FromCurrentSynchronizationContext`, which automatically chooses the appropriate context to schedule work on the relevant UI thread.

> **NOTE**   When the `ContinueWith` function is called, it's possible to initiate starting the new task only if the first task terminates with certain conditions, such as if the task is canceled, by specifying the `TaskContinuationOptions.OnlyOnCanceled` flag, or if an exception is thrown, by using the `TaskContinuationOptions` `.OnlyOnFaulted` flag.

As previously mentioned, you could have used `Parallel.ForEach`, but the problem is that this approach waits until all the operations have finished before continuing, blocking the main thread. Moreover, it makes it more complex to update the UI directly because the operations run in different threads.

7.5   *Strategies for composing task operations*

Continuations are the real power of the TPL. It's possible, for example, to execute multiple continuations for a single task and to create a chain of task continuations that maintains dependencies with each other. Moreover, using task continuation, the underlying scheduler can take full advantage of the work-stealing mechanism and optimize the scheduling mechanisms based on the available resources at runtime.

Let's use task continuation in the face-detection example. The final code runs in parallel, providing a boost in performance. But the program can be further optimized in terms of scalability. The function `DetectFaces` sequentially performs the series of operations as a chain of computations. To improve resource use and overall performance, a better design is to split the tasks and subsequent task continuations for each `DetectFaces` operation run in a different thread.

Using task continuation, this change is simple. The following listing shows a new `DetectFaces` function, with each step of the face-detection algorithm running in a dedicated and independent task.

Listing 7.8   `DetectFaces` function using task continuation

```
Task<Bitmap> DetectFaces(string fileName)
{
    var imageTask = Task.Run<Image<Bgr, byte>>(
        () => new Image<Bgr, byte>(fileName)
    );
    var imageFrameTask = imageTask.ContinueWith(
        image => image.Result.Convert<Gray, byte>()
    );
```

Uses task continuation to pass the result of the work into the attached function without blocking

```
        var grayframeTask = imageFrameTask.ContinueWith(
            imageFrame => imageFrame.Result.Convert<Gray, byte>()
    );


    var facesTask = grayframeTask.ContinueWith(grayFrame =>
        {
            var cascadeClassifier = CascadeClassifierThreadLocal.Value;
            return cascadeClassifier.DetectMultiScale(
                grayFrame.Result, 1.1, 3, System.Drawing.Size.Empty);
        }
    );


    var bitmapTask = facesTask.ContinueWith(faces =>
        {
            foreach (var face in faces.Result)
                imageTask.Result.Draw(
                face, new Bgr(System.Drawing.Color.BurlyWood), 3);
            return imageTask.Result.ToBitmap();
        }
    );
    return bitmapTask;
}
```

Uses task continuation to pass the result of the work into the attached function without blocking

The code works as expected; the execution time isn't enhanced, although the program can potentially handle a larger number of images to process while still maintaining lower resource consumption. This is due to the smart `TaskScheduler` optimization. Because of this, the code has become cumbersome and hard to change. For example, if you add error handling or cancellation support, the code becomes a pile of spaghetti code—hard to understand and to maintain. It can be better. Composition is the key to controlling complexity in software.

The objective is to be able to apply a LINQ-style semantic to compose the functions that run the face-detection program, as shown here (the command and module names to note are in bold):

```
from image in Task.Run<Emgu.CV.Image<Bgr, byte>()
from imageFrame in Task.Run<Emgu.CV.Image<Gray, byte>>()
from faces in Task.Run<System.Drawing.Rectangle[]>()
select faces;
```

This is an example of how mathematical patterns can help to exploit declarative compositional semantics.

7.5.1 *Using mathematical patterns for better composition*

Task continuation provides support to enable task composition. How do you combine tasks? In general, function composition takes two functions and injects the result from the first function into the input of the second function, thereby forming one function. In chapter 2, you implemented this `Compose` function in C# (in bold):

```
Func<A, C> Compose<A, B, C>(this Func<A, B> f, Func<B, C> g) =>
                                        (n) => g(f(n));
```

Can you use this function to combine two tasks? Not directly, no. First, the return type of the compositional function should be exposing the task's elevated type as follows (noted in bold):

```
Func<A, Task<C>> Compose<A, B, C>(this Func<A, Task<B>> f,
                                  Func<B, Task<C>> g) => (n) => g(f(n));
```

But there's a problem: the code doesn't compile. The return type from the function f doesn't match the input of the function g: the function f(n) returns a type Task<B>, which isn't compatible with the type B in function g.

The solution is to implement a function that accesses the underlying value of the elevated type (in this case, the task) and then passes the value into the next function. This is a common pattern, called Monad, in FP; the Monad pattern is another design pattern, like the Decorator and Adapter patterns. This concept was introduced in section 6.4.1, but let's analyze this idea further so you can apply the concept to improve the face-detection code.

Monads are mathematical patterns that control the execution of side effects by encapsulating program logic, maintaining functional purity, and providing a powerful compositional tool to combine computations that work with elevated types. According to the monad definition, to define a monadic constructor, there are two functions, Bind and Return, to implement.

THE MONADIC OPERATORS, BIND AND RETURN

Bind takes an instance of an elevated type, unwraps the underlying value, and then invokes the function over the extracted value, returning a new elevated type. This function is performed in the future when it's needed. Here the Bind signature uses the Task object as an elevated type:

```
Task<R> Bind<T, R>(this Task<T> m, Func<T, Task<R>> k)
```

The Return value is an operator that wraps any type T into an instance of the elevated type. Following the example of the Task type, here's the signature:

```
Task<T> Return(T value)
```

> **NOTE** The same applies to other elevated types: for example, replacing the Task type with another elevated type such as the Lazy and Observable types.

THE MONAD LAWS

Ultimately, to define a correct monad, the Bind and Return operations need to satisfy the monad laws:

1 *Left identity*—Applying the Bind operation to a value wrapped by the Return operation and then passed into a function is the same as passing the value straight into the function:

```
Bind(Return value, function) = function(value)
```

2 *Right identity*—Returning a bind-wrapped value is equal to the wrapped value directly:

```
Bind(elevated-value, Return) = elevated-value
```

3 *Associative*—Passing a value into a function f whose result is passed into a second function g is the same as composing the two functions f and g and then passing the initial value:

```
Bind(elevated-value, f(Bind(g(elevated-value)) =
            Bind(elevated-value, Bind(f.Compose(g), elevated-value))
```

Now, using these monadic operations, you can fix the error in the previous `Compose` function to combine the `Task` elevated types as shown here:

```
Func<A, Task<C>> Compose<A, B, C>(this Func<A, Task<B>> f,
                        Func<B, Task<C>> g) => (n) => Bind(f(n), g);
```

Monads are powerful because they can represent any arbitrary operations against elevated types. In the case of the `Task` elevated type, monads let you implement function combinators to compose asynchronous operations in many ways, as shown in figure 7.8.

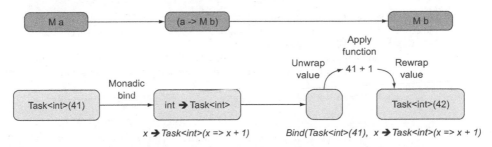

Figure 7.8   The monadic `Bind` operator takes the elevated value `Task` that acts as a container (wrapper) for the value 42, and then it applies the function x ➜ Task<int>(x => x + 1), where x is the number 41 unwrapped. Basically, the `Bind` operator unwraps an elevated value (Task<int>(41)) and then applies a function (x + 1) to return a new elevated value (Task<int>(42).

Surprisingly, these monadic operators are already built into the .NET Framework in the form of LINQ operators. The LINQ `SelectMany` definition corresponds directly to the monadic `Bind` function. Listing 7.9 shows both the `Bind` and `Return` operators applied to the `Task` type. The functions are then used to implement a LINQ-style semantic to compose asynchronous operations in a monadic fashion. The code is in F# and then consumed in C# to keep proving the easy interoperability between these programming languages (the code to note is in bold).

> **Listing 7.9   Task extension in F# to enable LINQ-style operators for tasks**

```
[<Sealed; Extension; CompiledName("Task")>]
type TaskExtensions =
  // 'T -> M<'T>
  static member Return value : Task<'T> = Task.FromResult<'T> (value)
```

The Return monadic operator takes any type T and returns a Task<T>.

```
// M<'T> * ('T -> M<'U>) -> M<'U>
```

The Bind operator takes a Task object as an elevated type, applies a function to the underlying type, and returns a new elevated type Task<U>

```
static member Bind (input : Task<'T>, binder : 'T -> Task<'U>) =
    let tcs = new TaskCompletionSource<'U>()
    input.ContinueWith(fun (task:Task<'T>) ->
        if (task.IsFaulted) then
            tcs.SetException(task.Exception.InnerExceptions)
        elif (task.IsCanceled) then
            tcs.SetCanceled()
        else
            try
```

The Bind operator unwraps the result from the Task elevated type and passes the result into the continuation that executes the monadic function binder.

```
                (binder(task.Result)).ContinueWith(fun
    (nextTask:Task<'U>) -> tcs.SetResult(nextTask.Result)) |> ignore
            with
            | ex -> tcs.SetException(ex)) |> ignore
    tcs.Task

static member Select (task : Task<'T>, selector : 'T -> 'U) : Task<'U> =
    task.ContinueWith(fun (t:Task<'T>) -> selector(t.Result))

static member SelectMany(input:Task<'T>, binder:'T -> Task<'I>,
    projection:'T -> 'I -> 'R): Task<'R> =
    TaskExtensions.Bind(input,
        fun outer -> TaskExtensions.Bind(binder(outer), fun inner ->
        TaskExtensions.Return(projection outer inner)))

static member SelectMany(input:Task<'T>, binder:'T -> Task<'R>) : Task<'R>
    =
    TaskExtensions.Bind(input,
        fun outer -> TaskExtensions.Bind(binder(outer), fun inner ->
        TaskExtensions.Return(inner)))
```

TaskCompletionSource initializes a behavior in the form of Task, so it can be treated like one.

The LINQ SelectMany operator acts as the Bind monadic operator.

The implementation of the Return operation is straightforward, but the Bind operation is a little more complex. The Bind definition can be reused to create other LINQ-style combinators for tasks, such as the Select and two variants of the SelectMany operators. In the body of the function Bind, the function ContinueWith, from the underlying task instance, is used to extract the result from the computation of the input task. Then to continue the work, it applies the binder function to the result of the input task. Ultimately, the output of the nextTask continuation is set as the result of the tcs TaskCompletionSource. The returning task is an instance of the underlying TaskCompletionSource, which is introduced to initialize a task from any operation that starts and finishes in the future. The idea of the TaskCompletionSource is to create a task that can be governed and updated manually to indicate when and how a given operation completes. The power of the TaskCompletionSource type is in the capability of creating tasks that don't tie up threads.

> ## TaskCompletionSource
>
> The purpose of the `TaskCompletionSource<T>` object is to provide control and refer to an arbitrary asynchronous operation as a `Task<T>`. When a `TaskCompletionSource` (http://bit.ly/2vDOmSN) is created, the underlying task properties are accessible through a set of methods to manage the lifetime and completion of the task. This includes `SetResult`, `SetException`, and `SetCanceled`.

APPLYING THE MONAD PATTERN TO TASK OPERATIONS

With the LINQ operations `SelectMany` on tasks in place, you can rewrite the `DetectFaces` function using an expressive and comprehension query (the code to note is in bold).

Listing 7.10 `DetectFaces` using task continuation based on a LINQ expression

```
Task<Bitmap> DetectFaces(string fileName)  {
    Func<System.Drawing.Rectangle[],Image<Bgr, byte>, Bitmap>
 drawBoundries =
        (faces, image) => {
                faces.ForAll(face => image.Draw(face, new
 Bgr(System.Drawing.Color.BurlyWood), 3));
                return image.ToBitmap();
        };

        return from image in Task.Run(() => new Image<Bgr, byte>(fileName))
                from imageFrame in Task.Run(() => image.Convert<Gray,
    byte>())
                from bitmap in Task.Run(() =>
            CascadeClassifierThreadLocal.Value.DetectMultiScale(imageFrame,
 1.1, 3, System.Drawing.Size.Empty)).Select(faces =>
                                            drawBoundries(faces, image))
                select bitmap;
}
```

The detected face(s) are highlighted using a box that's drawn around them.

Task composition using the LINQ-like Task operators defined with the Task monadic operators

This code shows the power of the monadic pattern, providing composition semantics over elevated types such as tasks. Moreover, the code of the monadic operations is concentrated into the two operators `Bind` and `Return`, making the code maintainable and easy to debug. To add logging functionality or special error handling, for example, you only need to change one place in code, which is convenient.

In listing 7.10, the `Return` and `Bind` operators were exposed in F# and consumed in C#, as a demonstration of the simple interoperability between the two programming languages. The source code for this book contains the implementation in C#. A beautiful composition of elevated types requires monads; the *continuation monad* shows how monads can readily express complex computations.

USING THE HIDDEN FMAP FUNCTOR PATTERN TO APPLY TRANSFORMATION

One important function in FP is `Map`, which transforms one input type into a different one. The signature of the `Map` function is

```
Map :  (T -> R) -> [T] -> [R]
```

An example in C# is the LINQ `Select` operator, which is a map function for `IEnumerable` types:

```
IEnumerable<R>  Select<T,R>(IEnumerable<T> en, Func<T, R> projection)
```

In FP, this similar concept is called a *functor*, and the map function is defined as `fmap`. Functors are basically types that can be mapped over. In F#, there are many:

```
Seq.map : ('a -> 'b) -> 'a seq -> 'b seq
List.map : ('a -> 'b) -> 'a list -> 'b list
Array.map : ('a -> 'b) -> 'a [] -> 'b []
Option.map : ('a -> 'b) -> 'a Option -> 'b Option
```

This mapping idea seems simple, but the complexity starts when you have to map elevated types. This is when the functor pattern becomes useful.

Think about a functor as a container that wraps an elevated type and offers a way to transform a normal function into one that operates on the contained values. In the case of the `Task` type, this is the signature:

```
fmap : ('T -> 'R) -> Task<'T> -> Task<'R>
```

This function has been previously implemented for the `Task` type in the form of the `Select` operator as part of the LINQ-style operators set for tasks built in F#. In the last LINQ expression computation of the function `DetectFaces`, the `Select` operator projects (map) the input `Task<Rectangle[]>` into a `Task<Bitmap>`:

```
from image in Task.Run(() => new Image<Bgr, byte>(fileName))
from imageFrame in Task.Run(() => image.Convert<Gray, byte>())
from bitmap in Task.Run(() =>
            CascadeClassifierThreadLocal.Value.DetectMultiScale
                        (imageFrame, 1.1, 3, System.Drawing.Size.Empty))
    .select(faces => drawBoundries(faces, image))
select bitmap;
```

The concept of functors becomes useful when working with another functional pattern, applicative functors, which will be covered in chapter 10.

> **NOTE** The concepts of functors and monads come from the branch of mathematics called *category theory*,[2] but it isn't necessary to have any category theory background to follow and use these patterns.

THE ABILITIES BEHIND MONADS

Monads provide an elegant solution to composing elevated types. Monads aim to control functions with side effects, such as those that perform I/O operations, providing a mechanism to perform operations directly on the result of the I/O without having a value from impure functions floating around the rest of your pure program. For this reason, monads are useful in designing and implementing concurrent applications.

---

[2] For more information, see https://wiki.haskell.org/Category_theory.

7.5.2 *Guidelines for using tasks*

Here are several guidelines for using tasks:

- It's good practice to use immutable types for return values. This makes it easier to ensure that your code is correct.
- It's good practice to avoid tasks that produce side effects; instead, tasks should communicate with the rest of the program only with their returned values.
- It's recommended that you use the task continuation model to continue with the computation, which avoids unnecessary blocking.

7.6 *The parallel functional Pipeline pattern*

In this section, you're going to implement one of the most common coordination techniques—the Pipeline pattern. In general, a pipeline is composed of a series of computational steps, composed as a chain of stages, where each stage depends on the output of its predecessor and usually performs a transformation on the input data. You can think of the Pipeline pattern as an assembly line in a factory, where each item is constructed in stages. The evolution of an entire chain is expressed as a function, and it uses a message queue to execute the function each time new input is received. The message queue is non-blocking because it runs in a separate thread, so even if the stages of the pipeline take a while to execute, it won't block the sender of the input from pushing more data to the chain.

This pattern is similar to the Producer/Consumer pattern, where a producer manages one or more worker threads to generate data. There can be one or more consumers that consume the data being created by the producer. Pipelines allow these series to run in parallel. The implementation of the pipeline in this section follows a slightly different design as compared to the traditional one seen in figure 7.9.

The traditional Pipeline pattern with serial stages has a speedup, measured in throughput, which is limited to the throughput of the slowest stage. Every item pushed into the pipeline must pass through that stage. The traditional Pipeline pattern cannot scale automatically with the number of cores, but is limited to the number of stages. Only a linear pipeline, where the number of stages matches the number of available logical cores, can take full advantage of the computer power. In a computer with eight cores, a pipeline composed of four stages can use only half of the resources, leaving 50% of the cores idle.

FP promotes composition, which is the concept the Pipeline pattern is based on. In listing 7.11, the pipeline embraces this tenet by composing each step into a single function and then distributing the work in parallel, fully using the available resources. In an abstract way, each function acts as the continuation of the previous one, behaving as a continuation-passing style. The code listing implementing the pipeline is in F#, then consumed in C#. But in the downloadable source code, you can find the full implementation in both programming languages. Here the `IPipeline` interface defines the functionality of the pipeline.

Traditional parallel pipeline
The pipeline creates a buffer between each stage that works as a parallel Producer/Consumer pattern. There
are almost as many buffers as there are stages. Each work item is sent to stage 1; the result is passed
into the first buffer, which coordinates the work in parallel to push it into stage 2. This process
continues until the end of the pipeline, when all the stages are computed.

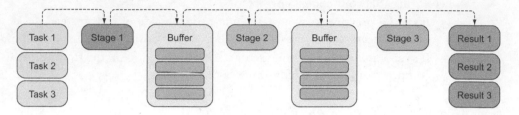

Functional parallel pipeline
The pipeline combines all the stages into one, as if composing multiple functions.
Each work item is pushed into the combined steps to be processed
in parallel, using the TPL and the optimized scheduler.

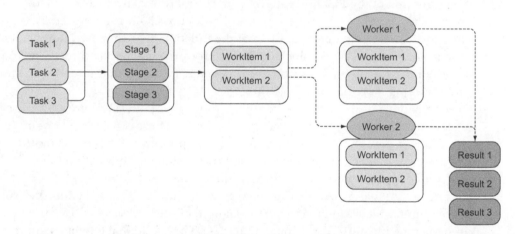

Figure 7.9   The traditional pipeline creates a buffer between each stage that works as a parallel Producer/ Consumer pattern. There are almost as many buffers as there are number of stages. With this design, each work item to process is sent to the initial stage, then the result is passed into the first buffer, which coordinates the work in parallel to push it into the second stage. This process continues until the end of the pipeline when all the stages are computed. By contrast, the functional parallel pipeline combines all the stages into one, as if composing multiple functions. Then, using a `Task` object, each work item is pushed into the combined steps to be processed in parallel and uses the TPL and the optimized scheduler.

Listing 7.11   `IPipeline` interface

```
[<Interface>]
type IPipeline<'a,'b> =          ◄─── Interface that defines the pipeline contract
    abstract member Then : Func<'b, 'c> -> IPipeline<'a,'c>

    abstract member Enqueue : 'a * Func<('a * 'b), unit)> -> unit
```

Uses a function to expose a fluent API approach

Uses a function to push new input to process into the pipeline

```
abstract member Execute : (int * CancellationToken) -> IDisposable   ◄──┐
abstract member Stop : unit -> unit   ◄──────┐                           │
```
                                                                    Starts the pipeline
The pipeline can be stopped at any time; this   **execution**
function triggers the underlying cancellation token.

The function `Then` is the core of the pipeline, where the input function is composed of
the previous one, applying a transformation. This function returns a new instance of
the pipeline, providing a convenient and fluent API to build the process.

The `Enqueue` function is responsible for pushing work items into the pipeline for
processing. It takes a `Callback` as an argument, which is applied at the end of the pipeline to further process the final result. This design gives flexibility to apply any arbitrary
function for each item pushed.

The `Execute` function starts the computation. Its input arguments set the size of the
internal buffer and a cancellation token to stop the pipeline on demand. This function
returns an `IDisposable` type, which can be used to trigger the cancellation token to
stop the pipeline. Here is the full implementation of the pipeline (the code to note is
in bold).

Listing 7.12 Parallel functional pipeline pattern

```
[<Struct>]
type Continuation<'a, 'b>(input:'a, callback:Func<('a * 'b), unit) =
    member this.Input with get() = input
    member this.Callback with get() = callback   ◄──┐
```

The Continuation struct encapsulates the
input value for each task with the callback
to run when the computation completes.

Initializes the
BlockingCollection
that buffers the work

```
type Pipeline<'a, 'b> private (func:Func<'a, 'b>) as this =
    let continuations = Array.init 3 (fun _ -> new
                BlockingCollection<Continuation<'a,'b>>(100))   ◄──┘

    let then' (nextFunction:Func<'b,'c>) =
        Pipeline(func.Compose(nextFunction)) :> IPipeline<_,_>   ◄──┐
```

Uses function composition to combine the
current function of the pipeline with the new
one passed and returns a new pipeline. The
compose function was introduced in chapter 2.

```
    let enqueue (input:'a) (callback:Func<('a * 'b), unit>) =
        BlockingCollection<Continuation<_,_>>.AddToAny(continuations,
➡  Continuation(input, callback))   ◄──────┐
```

The Enqueue function pushes the
work into the buffer.

```
    let stop() = for continuation in continuations do continuation.
        CompleteAdding()   ◄──────┐
```

The BlockingCollection is notified to complete,
which stops the pipeline.

```
        let execute blockingCollectionPoolSize
            (cancellationToken:CancellationToken) =
```
> **Registers the cancellation token to run the stop function when it's triggered**

```
        cancellationToken.Register(Action(stop)) |> ignore ◄
```

> **Starts the tasks to compute in parallel**

```
        for i = 0 to blockingCollectionPoolSize - 1 do
            Task.Factory.StartNew(fun ( )->
                while (not <| continuations.All(fun bc -> bc.IsCompleted))
                    && (not <| cancellationToken.IsCancellationRequested) do
                    let continuation = ref
    Unchecked.defaultof<Continuation<_,_>>
                        BlockingCollection.TakeFromAny(continuations,
    continuation)
                    let continuation = continuation.Value
                    continuation.Callback.Invoke(continuation.Input,
    func.Invoke(continuation.Input)),
                cancellationToken, TaskCreationOptions.LongRunning,
    TaskScheduler.Default) |> ignore
```

```
        static member Create(func:Func<'a, 'b>) =
            Pipeline(func) :> IPipeline<_,_> ◄
```
> **The static method creates a new instance of the pipeline.**

```
    interface IPipeline<'a, 'b> with
        member this.Then(nextFunction) = then' nextFunction
        member this.Enqueue(input, callback) = enqueue input callback
        member this.Stop() = stop()
        member this.Execute (blockingCollectionPoolSize,cancellationToken) =
            execute blockingCollectionPoolSize cancellationToken
            { new IDisposable with member self.Dispose() = stop() }
```

The Continuation structure is used internally to pass through the pipeline functions to compute the items. The implementation of the pipeline uses an internal buffer composed by an array of the concurrent collection BlockingCollection<Collection>, which ensures thread safety during parallel computation of the items. The argument to this collection constructor specifies the maximum number of items to buffer at any given time. In this case, the value is 100 for each buffer.

Each item pushed into the pipeline is added to the collection, which in the future will be processed in parallel. The Then function is composing the function argument nextFunction with the function func, which is passed into the pipeline constructor. Note that you use the Compose function defined in chapter 2 in listing 2.3 to combine the functions func and nextFunction:

```
Func<A, C> Compose<A, B, C>(this Func<A, B> f, Func<B, C> g) =>
(n) => g(f(n));
```

When the pipeline starts the process, it applies the final composed function to each input value. The parallelism in the pipeline is achieved in the Execute function, which spawns one task for each BlockingCollection instantiated. This guarantees a buffer for running the thread. The tasks are created with the LongRunning option to schedule a dedicated thread. The BlockingCollection concurrent collection allows thread-safe access to the items stored using the static methods TakeFromAny and AddToAny, which internally distribute the items and balance the workload among the running threads. This collation is used to manage the connection between the input and output of the pipeline, which behave as producer/consumer threads.

> **NOTE** Using `BlockingCollection`, remember to call `GetConsumingEnumerable` because the `BlockingCollection` class implements `IEnumerable<T>`. Enumerating over the blocking collection instance won't consume values.

The pipeline constructor is set as `private` to avoid direct instantiation. Instead, the static method `Create` initializes a new instance of the pipeline. This facilitates a fluent API approach to manipulate the pipeline.

This pipeline design ultimately resembles a parallel Produce/Consumer pattern capable of managing the concurrent communication between many-producers to many-consumers.

The following listing uses the implemented pipeline to refactor the `DetectFaces` program from the previous section. In C#, a fluent API approach is a convenient way to express and compose the steps of the pipeline.

Listing 7.13 Refactored `DetectFaces` code using the parallel pipeline

```
var files = Directory.GetFiles(ImagesFolder);

var imagePipe = Pipeline<string, Image<Bgr, byte>>
    .Create(filePath => new Image<Bgr, byte>(filePath))
    .Then(image => Tuple.Create(image, image.Convert<Gray, byte>()))
    .Then(frames => Tuple.Create(frames.Item1,
    CascadeClassifierThreadLocal.Value.DetectMultiScale(frames.Item2, 1.1,
        3, System.Drawing.Size.Empty)))
    .Then(faces =>{                                    Constructs the pipeline
        foreach (var face in faces.Item2)             using fluent API.
            faces.Item1.Draw(face,
 ➡ new Bgr(System.Drawing.Color.BurlyWood), 3);
        return faces.Item1.ToBitmap();                Starts the execution of the pipeline.
    });                                               The cancellation token stops the
                                                      pipeline at any given time.

imagePipe.Execute(cancellationToken);
                                                      The iteration pushes (enqueues) the
foreach (string fileName in files)                    file paths into the pipeline queue,
    imagePipe.Enqueue(file, (_, bitmapImage)          whose operation is non-blocking.
                        => Images.Add(bitmapImage));
```

By exploiting the pipeline you developed, the code structure is changed considerably.

> **NOTE** The F# pipeline implementation, in the previous section, uses the `Func` delegate to be consumed effortlessly by C# code. In the source code of the book you can find the implementation of the same pipeline that uses F# functions in place of the .NET `Func` delegate, which makes it a better fit for projects completely built in F#. In the case of consuming native F# functions from C#, the helper extension method `ToFunc` provides support for interoperability. The `ToFunc` extension method can be found in the source code.

The pipeline definition is elegant, and it can be used to construct the process to detect the faces in the images using a nice, fluent API. Each function is composed step by step, and then the Execute function is called to start the pipeline. Because the underlying pipeline processing is already running in parallel, the loop to push the file path of the images is sequential. The Enqueue function of the pipeline is non-blocking, so there are no performance penalties involved. Later, when an image is returned from the computation, the Callback passed into the Enqueue function will update the result to update the UI. Table 7.1 shows the benchmark to compare the different approaches implemented.

Table 7.1 Benchmark processing of 100 images using four logical core computers with 16 GB RAM. The results, expressed in seconds, represent the average from running each design three times.

Serial loop	Parallel	Parallel continuation	Parallel LINQ combination	Parallel pipeline
68.57	22.89	19.73	20.43	17.59

The benchmark shows that, over the average of downloading 100 images for three times, the pipeline parallel design is the fastest. It's also the most expressive and concise pattern.

Summary

- Task-based parallel programs are designed with the functional paradigm in mind to guarantee more reliable and less vulnerable (or corrupt) code from functional properties such as immutability, isolation of side effects, and defensive copy. This makes it easier to ensure that your code is correct.
- The Microsoft TPL embraces functional paradigms in the form of using a continuation-passing style. This allows for a convenient way to chain a series of non-blocking operations.
- A method that returns void in C# code is a string signal that can produce side effects. A method with void as output doesn't permit composition in tasks using continuation.
- FP unmasks mathematical patterns to ease parallel task composition in a declarative and fluent programming style. (The monad and functor patterns are hidden in LINQ.) The same patterns can be used to reveal monadic operations with tasks, exposing a LINQ-semantic style.
- A functional parallel pipeline is a pattern designed to compose a series of operations into one function, which is then applied concurrently to a sequence of input values queued to be processed. Pipelines are often useful when the data elements are received from a real-time event stream.
- Task dependency is the Achilles heel of parallelism. Parallelism is restricted when two or more operations cannot run until other operations have completed. It's essential to use tools and patterns to maximize parallelism as much as possible. A functional pipeline, CPS, and mathematical patterns like monad are the keys.

8

Task asynchronicity
for the win

This chapter covers

- Understanding the Task-based Asynchronous Programming model (TAP)

- Performing numerous asynchronous operations in parallel

- Customizing asynchronous execution flow

Asynchronous programming has become a major topic of interest over the last several years. In the beginning, asynchronous programming was used primarily on the client side to deliver a responsive GUI and to convey a high-quality user experience for customers. To maintain a responsive GUI, asynchronous programming must have consistent communication with the backend, and vice versa, or delays may be introduced into the response time. An example of this communication issue is when an application window appears to hang for a few seconds while background processing catches up with your commands.

Companies must address increasing client demands and requests while analyzing data quickly. Using asynchronous programming on the application's server side is the solution to allowing the system to remain responsive, regardless of the number of requests. Moreover, from a business point of view, an Asynchronous Programming

213

Model (APM) is beneficial. Companies have begun to realize that it's less expensive to develop software designed with this model because the number of servers required to satisfy requests is considerably reduced by using a non-blocking (asynchronous) I/O system compared to a system with blocking (synchronous) I/O operations. Keep in mind that scalability and asynchronicity are terms unrelated to speed or velocity. Don't worry if these terms are unfamiliar; they're covered in the following sections.

Asynchronous programming is an essential addition to your skill set as a developer because programming robust, responsive, and scalable programs is, and will continue to be, in high demand. This chapter will help you understand the performance semantics related to APM and how to write scalable applications. By the end of this chapter, you'll know how to use asynchronicity to process multiple I/O operations in parallel regardless of the hardware resources available.

8.1   *The Asynchronous Programming Model (APM)*

The word *asynchronous* derives from the combination of the Greek words *asyn* (meaning "not with") and *chronos* (meaning "time"), which describe actions that aren't occurring at the same time. In the context of running a program asynchronously, *asynchronous* refers to an operation that begins with a specific request, which may or may not succeed, and that completes at a point in the future. In general, asynchronous operations are executed independently from other processes without waiting for the result, whereas synchronous operations wait to finish before moving on to another task.

Imagine yourself in a restaurant with only one server. The server comes to your table to take the order, goes to the kitchen to place the order, and then stays in the kitchen, waiting for the meal to be cooked and ready to serve! If the restaurant had only one table, this process would be fine, but what if there are numerous tables? In this case, the process would be slow, and you wouldn't receive good service. A solution is to hire more waiters, maybe one per table, which would increase the restaurant's overhead due to increased salaries and would be wildly inefficient. A more efficient and effective solution is to have the server deliver the order to the chef in the kitchen and then continue to serve other tables. When the chef has finished preparing the meal, the waiter receives a notification from the kitchen to pick up the food and deliver it to your table. In this way, the waiter can serve multiple tables in a timely fashion.

In computer programming, the same concept applies. Several operations are performed asynchronously, from starting execution of an operation to continuing to process other work while waiting for that operation to complete, then resuming execution once the data has been received.

> **NOTE** The term *continuing* refers to continuation-passing style (CPS), which is a form of programming where a function determines what to do next and can decide to continue the operation or to do something completely different. As you'll see shortly, the APM is based on CPS (discussed in chapter 3).

Asynchronous programs don't sit idly waiting for any one operation, such as requesting data from a web service or querying a database, to complete.

8.1.1 *The value of asynchronous programming*

Asynchronous programming is an excellent model to exploit every time you build a program that involves blocking I/O operations. In synchronous programming, when a method is called, the caller is blocked until the method completes its current execution. With I/O operations, the time that the caller must wait before a return of control to continue with the rest of code varies depending on the current operation in process.

Often applications use a large number of external services, which perform operations that take a user noticeable time to execute. For this reason, it's vital to program in an asynchronous way. In general, developers feel comfortable when thinking sequentially: send a request or execute a method, wait for the response, and then process it. But a performant and scalable application cannot afford to wait synchronously for an action to complete. Furthermore, if an application joins the results of multiple operations, it's necessary to perform all of these operations simultaneously for good performance.

What happens if control never comes back to the caller because something went wrong during the I/O operation? If the caller never receives a return of control, then the program could hang.

Let's consider a server-side, multiuser application. For example, a regular e-commerce website application exists where, for each incoming request, the program has to make a database call. If the program is designed to run synchronously (figure 8.1), then only one dedicated thread is committed for each incoming request. In this case, each additional database call blocks the current thread that owns the incoming request, while waiting for the database to respond with the result. During this time, the thread pool must create a new thread to satisfy each incoming request, which will also block program execution while waiting for the database response.

If the application receives a high volume of requests (hundreds or perhaps thousands) simultaneously, the system will become unresponsive while trying to create the many threads needed to handle the requests. It will continue in this way until reaching the thread-pool limit, now with the risk of running out of resources. These circumstances can lead to large memory consumption or worse, failure of the system.

When the thread-pool resources are exhausted, successive incoming requests are queued and waiting to be processed, which results in an unreactive system. More importantly, when the database responses come back, the blocked threads are freed to continue to process the requests, which can provoke a high frequency of context switches, negatively impacting performance. Consequently, the client requests to the website slow down, the UI turns unresponsive, and ultimately your company loses potential customers and revenue.

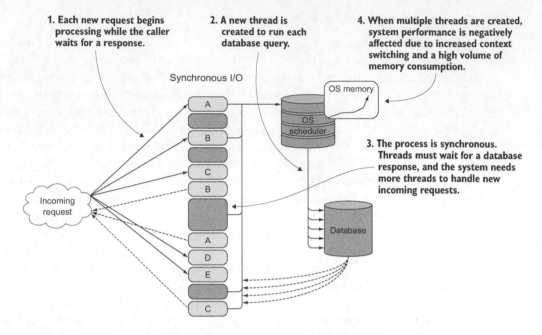

Figure 8.1   Servers that handle incoming requests synchronously aren't scalable.

Clearly, efficiency is a major reason to asynchronously model operations so that threads don't need to wait for I/O operations to complete, allowing them to be reused by the scheduler to serve other incoming requests. When a thread that has been deployed for an asynchronous I/O operation is idle, perhaps waiting for a database response as in figure 8.1, the scheduler can send the thread back to the thread pool to engage in further work. When the database completes, the scheduler notifies the thread pool to wake an available thread and send it on to continue the operation with the database result.

In server-side programs, asynchronous programming lets you deal effectively with massive concurrent I/O operations by intelligently recycling resources during their idle time and by avoiding the creation of new resources (figure 8.2). This optimizes memory consumption and enhances performance.

Users ask much from the modern applications they must interact with. Modern applications must communicate with external resources, such as databases and web services, and work with disks or REST-based APIs to meet user demands. Also, today's applications must retrieve and transform massive amounts of data, cooperate in cloud computations, and respond to notifications from parallel processes. To accommodate these complex interactions, the APM provides the ability to express computations without blocking executing threads, which improves availability (a reliable system) and throughput. The result is notably improved performance and scalability.

This is particularly relevant on servers where there can be a large amount of concurrent I/O-bound activity. In this case the APM can handle many concurrent operations with low memory consumption due to the small number of threads involved. Even in the case where there aren't many (thousands) concurrent operations, the synchronous approach is advantageous because it keeps the I/O-bound operations performing out of the .NET thread pool.

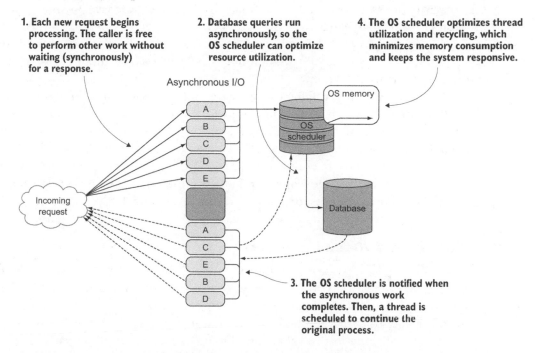

1. Each new request begins processing. The caller is free to perform other work without waiting (synchronously) for a response.

2. Database queries run asynchronously, so the OS scheduler can optimize resource utilization.

4. The OS scheduler optimizes thread utilization and recycling, which minimizes memory consumption and keeps the system responsive.

Asynchronous I/O

OS memory

A
B
C
D
E

OS scheduler

Incoming request

A
C
E
B
D

Database

3. The OS scheduler is notified when the asynchronous work completes. Then, a thread is scheduled to continue the original process.

Figure 8.2 Asynchronous I/O operations can start several operations in parallel without constraints that will return to the caller when complete, which keeps the system scalable.

By enabling asynchronous programming in your application, your code derives several benefits:

- Decoupled operations do a minimum amount of work in performance-critical paths.
- Increased thread resource availability allows the system to reuse the same resources without the need to create new ones.
- Better employment of the thread-pool scheduler enables scalability in server-based programs.

8.1.2   Scalability and asynchronous programming

Scalability refers to a system with the ability to respond to an increased number of requests through the addition of resources, which affects a commensurate boost in parallel speedup. A system designed with this ability aims to continue performing well under the circumstance of a sustained, large number of incoming requests that can strain the application's resources. Incremental scalability is achieved by different components—memory and CPU bandwidth, workload distribution, and quality of code, for example. If you design your application with the APM, it's most likely scalable.

Keep in mind that scalability isn't about speed. In general, a scalable system doesn't necessarily run faster than a non-scalable system. In fact, an asynchronous operation doesn't perform any faster than the equivalent synchronous operation. The true benefit is in minimizing performance bottlenecks in the application and optimizing the consumption of resources that allow other asynchronous operations to run in parallel, ultimately performing faster.

Scalability is vital in satisfying today's increasing demands for instantaneous responsiveness. For example, in high-volume web applications, such as stock trading or social media, it's essential that applications be both responsive and capable of concurrently managing a massive number of requests. Humans naturally think sequentially, evaluating one action at a time in consecutive order. For the sake of simplicity, programs have been written in this manner, one step following the other, which is clumsy and time-consuming. The need exists for a new model, the APM, that lets you write non-blocking applications that can run out of sequence, as required, with unbounded power.

8.1.3   *CPU-bound and I/O-bound operations*

In CPU-bound computations, methods require CPU cycles where there's one thread running on each CPU to do the work. In contrast, asynchronous I/O-bound computations are unrelated to the number of CPU cores. Figure 8.3 shows the comparison. As previously mentioned, when an asynchronous method is called, the execution thread returns immediately to the caller and continues execution of the current method, while the previously called function runs in the background, thereby preventing *blocking*. The terms *non-blocking* and *asynchronous* are commonly used interchangeably because both define similar concepts.

CPU-bound computations receive input from the keyboard to do some work, and then print the result to the screen. In a single-core machine, each computation must be completed before proceeding to the next one.

I/O-bound computations are executed independently from the CPU, and the operation is done elsewhere. In this case several asynchronous database calls are executing simultaneously. Later, a notification will inform the caller when the operation is complete (a callback).

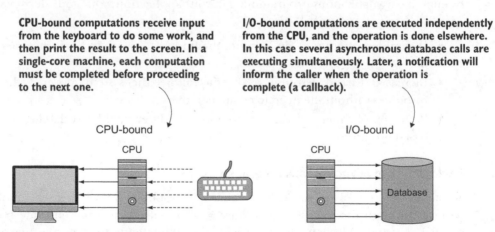

Figure 8.3   Comparison between CPU-bound and I/O-bound operations

CPU-bound computations are operations that spend time performing CPU-intensive work, using hardware resources to run all the operations. Therefore, as a ratio, it's appropriate to have one thread for each CPU, where execution time is determined by the speed of each CPU. Conversely, with *I/O-bound computations*, the number of threads running is unrelated to the number of CPUs available, and execution time depends on the period spent waiting for the I/O operations to complete, bound only by the I/O drivers.

8.2 Unbounded parallelism with asynchronous programming

Asynchronous programming provides an effortless way to execute multiple tasks independently and, therefore, in parallel. You may be thinking about CPU-bound computations that can be parallelized using a task-based programming model (chapter 7). But what makes an APM special, as compared to CPU-bound computation, is its I/O-bound computation nature, which overcomes the hardware constraint of one working thread for each CPU core.

Asynchronous, non-CPU-bound computations can benefit from having a larger number of threads running on one CPU. It's possible to perform hundreds or even thousands of I/O operations on a single-core machine because it's the nature of asynchronous programming to take advantage of parallelism to run I/O operations that can outnumber the available cores in a computer by an order of magnitude. You can do this because the asynchronous I/O operations push the work to a different location without impacting local CPU resources, which are kept free, providing the opportunity to execute additional work on local threads. To demonstrate this unbounded power, listing 8.1 is an example of running 20 asynchronous operations (in bold). These operations can run in parallel, regardless of the number of available cores.

Listing 8.1 Parallel asynchronous computations

```
let httpAsync (url : string) = async {            Reads asynchronously
    let req = WebRequest.Create(url)              content of a given website
    let! resp = req.AsyncGetResponse()
    use stream = resp.GetResponseStream()
    use reader = new StreamReader(stream)
    let! text = reader.ReadToEndAsync()
    return text }
                                                  Lists arbitrary websites to download
let sites =
    [ "http://www.live.com";"      "http://www.fsharp.org";
      "http://news.live.com";       "http://www.digg.com";
      "http://www.yahoo.com";       "http://www.amazon.com"
      "http://news.yahoo.com";      "http://www.microsoft.com";
      "http://www.google.com";      "http://www.netflix.com";
      "http://news.google.com";     "http://www.maps.google.com";
      "http://www.bing.com";        "http://www.microsoft.com";
      "http://www.facebook.com";    "http://www.docs.google.com";
      "http://www.youtube.com";     "http://www.gmail.com";
      "http://www.reddit.com";      "http://www.twitter.com"; ]
```

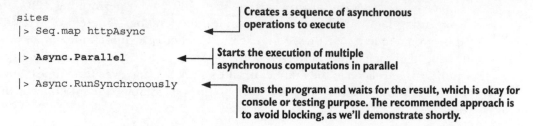

```
sites
|> Seq.map httpAsync
```
Creates a sequence of asynchronous operations to execute

```
|> Async.Parallel
```
Starts the execution of multiple asynchronous computations in parallel

```
|> Async.RunSynchronously
```
Runs the program and waits for the result, which is okay for console or testing purpose. The recommended approach is to avoid blocking, as we'll demonstrate shortly.

In this full asynchronous implementation example, the execution time is 1.546 seconds on a four-core machine. The same synchronous implementation runs in 11.230 seconds (the synchronous code is omitted, but you can find it in the source code companion of this book). Although the time varies according to network speed and bandwidth, the asynchronous code is about 7× faster than the synchronous code.

In a CPU-bound operation running on a single-core device, there's no performance improvement in simultaneously running two or more threads. This can reduce or decrease performance due to the extra overhead. This also applies to multicore processors, where the number of threads running far exceeds the number of cores. Asynchronicity doesn't increase CPU parallelism, but it does increment performance and reduce the number of threads needed. Despite many attempts to make operating system threads cheap (low memory consumption and overhead for their instantiation), their allocation produces a large memory stack, becoming an unrealistic solution for problems that require numerous outstanding asynchronous operations. This was discussed in section 7.1.2.

> ### Asynchrony vs. parallelism
>
> Parallelism is primarily about application performance, and it also facilitates CPU-intensive work on multiple threads, taking advantage of modern multicore computer architectures. Asynchrony is a superset of concurrency, focusing on I/O-bound rather than CPU-bound operations. Asynchronous programming addresses the issue of latency (anything that takes a long time to run).

8.3   *Asynchronous support in .NET*

The APM has been a part of the Microsoft .NET Framework since the beginning (v1.1). It offloads the work from the main execution thread to other working threads with the purpose of delivering better responsiveness and of gaining scalability.

The original asynchronous programming pattern consists of splitting a long-running function into two parts. One part is responsible for starting the asynchronous operation (Begin), and the other part is invoked when the operation completes (End).

This code shows a synchronous (blocking) operation that reads from a file stream and then processes the generated byte array (the code to note is in bold):

```
void ReadFileBlocking(string filePath, Action<byte[]> process)
{
    using (var fileStream = new FileStream(filePath, FileMode.Open,
                                    FileAccess.Read, FileShare.Read))
```

```
    {
            byte[] buffer = new byte[fileStream.Length];
            int bytesRead = fileStream.Read(buffer, 0, buffer.Length);
            process(buffer);
    }
}
```

Transforming this code into an equivalent asynchronous (*non-blocking*) operation requires a notification in the form of a *callback* to continue the original call-site (where the function is called) upon completion of the asynchronous I/O operation. In this case, the callback keeps the opportune state from the Begin function, as shown in the following listing (the code to note is highlighted in bold). The state is then rehydrated (restored to its original representation) when the callback resumes.

Listing 8.2   Reading from the filesystem asynchronously

Creates a FileStream instance using the option Asynchronous. Note the stream isn't disposed here to avoid the error of accessing a disposed object later when the Async computation completes.

Passes the state into the callback payload. The function process is passed as part of the tuple.

```
IAsyncResult ReadFileNoBlocking(string filePath, Action<byte[]> process)
{
        var fileStream = new FileStream(filePath, FileMode.Open,
                            FileAccess.Read, FileShare.Read, 0x1000,
                            FileOptions.Asynchronous)
        byte[] buffer = new byte[fileStream.Length];
        var state = Tuple.Create(buffer, fileStream, process);
        return fileStream.BeginRead(buffer, 0, buffer.Length,
                                        EndReadCallback, state);
}
void EndReadCallback(IAsyncResult ar)
{
        var state = ar.AsyncState;
                    as (Tuple<byte[], FileStream, Action<byte[]>>)
        using (state.Item2) state.Item2.EndRead(ar);
        state.Item3(state.Item1);
}
```

The BeginRead function starts, and EndReadCallback is passed as a callback to notify when the operations completes.

The FileStream is disposed and the data is processed.

The callback rehydrates the state in the original form to access the underlying values.

Why is the asynchronous version of the operation that's using the Begin/End pattern not blocking? Because when the I/O operation starts, the thread in context is sent back to the thread pool to perform other useful work if needed. In .NET, the thread-pool scheduler is responsible for scheduling work to be executed on a pool of threads, managed by the CLR.

TIP   The flag FileOptions.Asynchronous is passed as an argument in the constructor FileStream, which guarantees a true asynchronous I/O operation at the operating system level. It notifies the thread pool to avoid blocking. In the previous example, the FileStream isn't disposed, in the BeginRead call, to avoid the error of accessing a disposed object later when the Async computation completes.

Writing APM programs is considered more difficult than writing the sequential version. An APM program requires more code, which is more complex and harder to read and write. The code can be even more convoluted if a series of asynchronous operations is chained together. In the next example, a series of asynchronous operations require a notification to proceed with the work assigned. The notification is achieved through a callback.

Callbacks

A *callback* is a function used to speed up the program. Asynchronous programming, using a callback, creates new threads to run methods independently. While running asynchronously, a program notifies the calling thread of any update, which includes failure, cancellation, progress, and completion, by a reentrant function used to register the continuation of another function. This process takes some time to produce a result.

This chain of asynchronous operations in the code produces a series of nested callbacks, also known as "callback hell" (http://callbackhell.com). Callback-based code is problematic because it forces the programmer to cede control, restricting expressiveness and, more importantly, eliminating the compositionality semantic aspect.

This is an example of code (conceptual) to read from a file stream, then compress and send the data to the network (the code to note is in bold):

```
IAsyncResult ReadFileNoBlocking(string filePath)
{
    // keep context and BeginRead
}
void EndReadCallback(IAsyncResult ar)
{
    // get Read and rehydrate state, then BeginWrite (compress)
}
void EndCompressCallback(IAsyncResult ar)
{
    // get Write and rehydrate state, then BeginWrite (send to the network)
}
void EndWriteCallback(IAsyncResult ar)
{
    // get Write and rehydrate state, completed process
}
```

How would you introduce more functionality to this process? The code isn't easy to maintain! How can you compose this series of asynchronous operations to avoid the callback hell? And where and how would you manage error handling and release resources? The solutions are complex!

In general, the asynchronous Begin/End pattern is somewhat workable for a single call, but it fails miserably when composing a series of asynchronous operations. Later in this chapter I'll show how to conquer exceptions and cancellations such as these.

8.3.1 Asynchronous programming breaks the code structure

As you can see from the previous code, an issue originating from traditional APM is the decoupled execution time between the start (`Begin`) of the operation and its callback notification (`End`). This broken-code design divides the operation in two, violating the imperative sequential structure of the program. Consequently, the operation continues and completes in a different scope and possibly in a different thread, making it hard to debug, difficult to handle exceptions, and impossible to manage transaction scopes.

In general, with the APM pattern, it's a challenge to maintain state between each asynchronous call. You're forced to pass a state into each continuation through the callback to continue the work. This requires a tailored state machine to handle the passing of state between each stage of the asynchronous pipeline.

In the previous example, to maintain the state between the `fileStream.BeginRead` and its callback `EndReadCallback`, a tailored `state` object was created to access the stream, the byte array buffer, and the function process:

```
var state = Tuple.Create(buffer, fileStream, process);
```

This `state` object was rehydrated when the operation completed to access the underlying objects to continue further work.

8.3.2 Event-based Asynchronous Programming

Microsoft recognized the intrinsic problems of APM and consequently introduced (with .NET 2.0) an alternate pattern called Event-based Asynchronous Programming (EAP).[1] The EAP model was the first attempt to address issues with APM. The idea behind EAP is to set up an event handler for an event to notify the asynchronous operation when a task completes. This event replaces the callback notification semantic. Because the event is raised on the correct thread and provides direct support access to UI elements, EAP has several advantages. Additionally, it's built with support for progress reporting, canceling, and error handling—all occurring transparently for the developer.

EAP provides a simpler model for asynchronous programming than APM, and it's based on the standard event mechanism in .NET, rather than on requiring a custom class and callbacks. But it's still not ideal because it continues to separate your code into method calls and event handlers, increasing the complexity of your program's logic.

8.4 C# Task-based Asynchronous Programming

Compared to its predecessor, .NET APM, Task-based Asynchronous Programming (TAP) aims to simplify the implementation of asynchronous programs and ease composition of concurrent operation sequences. The TAP model deprecates both APM and EAP, so if you're writing asynchronous code in C#, TAP is the recommended model. TAP presents a clean and declarative style for writing asynchronous code that

---

[1] For more information, see http://mng.bz/2287.

looks similar to the F# asynchronous workflow by which it was inspired. The F# asynchronous workflow will be covered in detail in the next chapter.

In C# (since version 5.0), the objects `Task` and `Task<T>`, with the support of the keywords `async` and `await`, have become the main components to model asynchronous operations. The TAP model solves the callback problem by focusing purely on the syntactic aspect, while bypassing the difficulties that arise in reasoning about the sequence of events expressed in the code. Asynchronous functions in C# 5.0 address the issue of latency, which refers to anything that takes time to run.

The idea is to compute an asynchronous method, returning a task (also called a *future*) that isolates and encapsulates a long-running operation that will complete at a point in the future, as shown in figure 8.4.

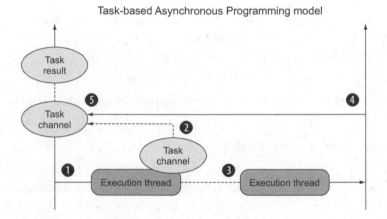

Figure 8.4   The task acts as a channel for the execution thread, which can continue working while the caller of the operation receives the handle to the task. When the operation completes, the task is notified and the underlying result can be accessed.

Here's the task flow from figure 8.4:

1 The I/O operation starts asynchronously in a separate execution thread. A new task instance is created to handle the operation.
2 The task created is returned to the caller. The task contains a callback, which acts as a channel between the caller and the asynchronous operation. This channel communicates when the operation completes.
3 The execution thread continues the operation while the main thread from the operation caller is available to process other work.
4 The operation completes asynchronously.
5 The task is notified, and the result is accessible by the caller of the operation.

The `Task` object returned from the `async`/`await` expression provides the details of the encapsulated computation and a reference to its result that will become available when the operation itself is completed. These details include the status of the task, the result, if completed, and exception information, if any.

The .NET `Task` and `Task<T>` constructs were introduced in the previous chapter, specifically for CPU-bound computations. The same model in combination with the `async`/`await` keywords can be used for I/O-bound operations.

NOTE The thread pool has two groups of threads: worker and I/O threads. A worker thread targets a job that's CPU-bound. An I/O thread is more efficient for I/O-bound operations. The thread pool keeps a cache of worker threads because threads are expensive to create. The CLR thread pool keeps separate pools of each to avoid a situation where high demand on worker threads exhausts all the threads available to dispatch native I/O callbacks, potentially leading to deadlock. Imagine an application using a large number of worker threads, where each one is waiting for an I/O to complete.

In a nutshell, TAP consists of the following:

- The `Task` and `Task<T>` constructs to represent asynchronous operations
- The `await` keyword to wait for the task operation to complete asynchronously, while the current thread isn't blocked from performing other work

For example, given an operation to execute in a separate thread, you must wrap it into a `Task`:

```
Task<int[]> processDataTask = Task.Run(() => ProcessMyData(data));
// do other work
var result = processDataTask.Result;
```

The output of the computation is accessed through the `Result` property, which blocks the caller method until the task completes. For tasks that don't return a result, you could call the `Wait` method instead. But this isn't recommended. To avoid blocking the caller thread, you can use the `Task` `async`/`await` keywords:

```
Task<int[]> processDataTask = Task.Run(async () => ProcessMyData(data));
// do other work
var result = await processDataTask;
```

The async keyword notifies the compiler that the method runs asynchronously without blocking. By doing so, the calling thread will be released to process other work. Once the task completes, an available worker thread will resume processing the work.

NOTE Methods marked as `async` can return either `void`, `Task`, or `Task<T>`, but it's recommended that you limit the use of the voided signature. This should only be supplied at the top-level entry point of the program and in UI event handlers. A better approach is to use `Task<Unit>`, introduced in the previous chapter.

Here's the previous code example converted to read a file stream asynchronously using the TAP way (the code to note is in bold):

```
async void ReadFileNoBlocking(string filePath, Action<byte[]> process)
{
    using (var fileStream = new FileStream(filePath, FileMode.Open,
                            FileAccess.Read, FileShare.Read, 0x1000,
                            FileOptions.Asynchronous))
```

```
    {
        byte[] buffer = new byte[fileStream.Length];
        int bytesRead = await fileStream.ReadAsync(buffer, 0, buffer.Length);
        await Task.Run(async () => process(buffer));
    }
}
```

The method `ReadFileNoBlocking` is marked `async`, the contextual keyword used to define an asynchronous function and to enable the use of the `await` keyword within a method. The purpose of the `await` construct is to inform the C# compiler to translate the code into a *continuation* of a task that won't block the current context thread, freeing the thread to do other work.

> **NOTE** The `async`/`await` functionality in C# is based on registering a callback in the form of a continuation, which will be triggered when the task in context completes. It's easy to implement code in a fluent and declarative style. The `async`/`await` is syntactic sugar for a continuation monad, which is implemented as a monadic bind operator using the function `ContinuesWith`. This approach plays well with method chaining because each method returns a task that exposes the `ContinuesWith` method. But it requires working with the tasks directly to get the result and hand it off to the next method. Furthermore, if you have a large number of tasks to chain together, you're forced to drill through the results to get to the value you care about. Instead, what you need is a more generalized approach that can be used across methods and at an arbitrary level within the chain, which is what the `async`/`await` programming model offers.

Under the hood, the continuation is implemented using the `ContinuesWith` function from the `Task` object, which is triggered when the asynchronous operation has completed. The advantage of having the compiler build the continuation is to preserve the program structure and the asynchronous method calls, which then are executed without the need for callbacks or nested lambda expressions.

This asynchronous code has clear semantics organized in a sequential flow. In general, when a method marked as `async` is invoked, the execution flow runs synchronously until it reaches an `await`-able task, denoted with the `await` keyword, that hasn't yet completed. When the execution flow reaches the `await` keyword, it suspends the calling method and yields control back to its caller until the awaited task is complete; in this way, the execution thread isn't blocked. When the operation completes, its result is unwrapped and bound into the content variable, and then the flow continues with the remaining work.

An interesting aspect of TAP is that the execution thread captures the synchronization context and serves back to the thread that continues the flow, allowing direct UI updates without extra work.

8.4.1 *Anonymous asynchronous lambdas*

You may have noticed a curious occurrence in the previous code—an anonymous function was marked `async`:

```
await Task.Run(async () => process(buffer));
```

As you can see, in addition to ordinary named methods, anonymous methods can also be marked `async`. Here's an alternative syntax to make an asynchronous anonymous lambda:

```
Func<string, Task<byte[]>> downloadSiteIcone = async domain =>
{
    var response = await new
        HttpClient().GetAsync($"http://{domain}/favicon.ico");
    return await response.Content.ReadAsByteArrayAsync();
}
```

This is also called an *asynchronous lambda*,[2] which is like any other lambda expression, only with the `async` modifier at the beginning to allow the use of the `await` keyword in its body. Asynchronous lambdas are useful when you want to pass a potentially long-running delegate into a method. If the method accepts a `Func<Task>`, you can feed it an async lambda and get the benefits of asynchrony. Like any other lambda expression, it supports closure to capture variables and the asynchronous operation start, only when the delegate is invoked.

This feature provides an easy means for expressing asynchronous operations on the fly. Inside these asynchronous functions, the `await` expressions can wait for running tasks. This causes the rest of the asynchronous execution to be transparently enlisted as a continuation of the awaited task. In anonymous asynchronous lambdas, the same rules apply as in ordinary asynchronous methods. You can use them to keep code concise and to capture closures.

8.4.2 *Task<T> is a monadic container*

In the previous chapter, you saw that the `Task<T>` type can be thought of as a special wrapper, eventually delivering a value of type `T` if it succeeds. The `Task<T>` type is a monadic data structure, which means, among other things, that it can easily be composed with others. It's not a surprise that the same concept also applies to the `Task<T>` type used in TAP.

> #### The monadic container
> Here's a refresh of the concept of monads introduced earlier in the book. In the context of `Task`, you can imagine a monad acting as a container. A monadic container is a powerful compositional tool used in functional programming to specify a way to chain operations together and to avoid dangerous and unwanted behaviors. Monads essentially mean you're working with *boxed*, or *closed over*, values, like the `Task` and `Lazy` types, which are unpacked only at moment they're needed. For example, monads let you take a value and apply a series of transformations to it in an independent manner that encapsulates side effects. The type signature of a monadic function calls out potential side effects, providing a representation of both the result of the computation and the actual side effects that occurred as a result.

---

[2] Methods or lambdas with the `async` modifier are called asynchronous functions.

With this in mind, you can easily define the monadic operators `Bind` and `Return`. In particular, the `Bind` operator uses the continuation-passing approach of the underlying asynchronous operation to generate a flowing and compositional semantic programming style. Here's their definition, including the *functor map* (or *fmap*) operator:

```
static Task<T> Return<T>(T task)=> Task.FromResult(task);

static async Task<R> Bind<T, R>(this Task<T> task, Func<T, Task<R>> cont)
    => await cont(await task.ConfigureAwait(false)).ConfigureAwait(false);

static async Task<R> Map<T, R>(this Task<T> task, Func<T, R> map)
    => map(await task.ConfigureAwait(false));
```

The definitions of the functions `Map` and `Bind` are simple due to the use of the `await` keyword, as compared to the implementation of `Task<T>` for CPU-bound computations in the previous chapter. The `Return` function lifts a `T` into a `Task<T>` container. `ConfigureAwait`[3] in a `Task` extension method removes the current UI context. This is recommended to obtain better performance in cases where the code doesn't need to be updated or doesn't need to interact with the UI. Now these operators can be exploited to compose a series of asynchronous computations as a chain of operations. The following listing downloads and writes asynchronously into the filesystem an icon image from a given domain. The operators `Bind` and `Map` are applied to chain the asynchronous computations (in bold).

> **Listing 8.3   Downloading an image (icon) from the network asynchronously**

Binds the asynchronous operation, unwrapping the result Task; otherwise it would be Task of Task

```
async Task DownloadIconAsync(string domain, string fileDestination)
{
    using (FileStream stream = new FileStream(fileDestination,
                        FileMode.Create, FileAccess.Write,
                        FileShare.Write, 0x1000, FileOptions.Asynchronous))
    await new HttpClient()
        .GetAsync($"http://{domain}/favicon.ico")
        .Bind(async content => await
                    content.Content.ReadAsByteArrayAsync())
        .Map(bytes => Image.FromStream(new MemoryStream(bytes)))
        .Tap(async image =>
                    await SaveImageAsync(fileDestination,
    ImageFormat.Jpeg, image));
```

The Tap function performs the side effect.

Maps the result of the previous operation asynchronously

In this code, the method `DownloadIconAsync` uses an instance of the `HttpClient` object to obtain asynchronously the `HttpResponseMessage` by calling the `GetAsync` method. The purpose of the response message is to read the HTTP content (in this case, the image) as a byte array. The data is read by the `Task.Bind` operator, and then converted into an image using the `Task.Map` operator. The function `Task.Tap` (also

---

[3] For more information, see http://mng.bz/T8US.

known as *k-combinator)* is used to facilitate a pipeline construct to cause a side effect with a given input and return the original value. Here's the implementation of the `Task` `.Tap` function:

```
static async Task<T> Tap<T>(this Task<T> task, Func<T, Task> action)
{
    await action(await task);
    return await task;
}
```

The `Tap` operator is extremely useful to bridge void functions (such as logging or writing a file or an HTML page) in your composition without having to create additional code. It does this by passing itself into a function and returning itself. `Tap` unwraps the underlying elevated type, applies an action to produce a side effect, and then wraps the original value up again and returns it. Here, the side effect is to persist the image into the filesystem. The function `Tap` can be used for other side effects as well.

At this point, these monadic operators can be used to define the LINQ pattern implementing `Select` and `SelectMany`, similar to the `Task` type in the previous chapter, and to enable LINQ compositional semantics:

```
static async Task<R> SelectMany<T, R>(this Task<T> task,
                        Func<T, Task<R>> then) => await Bind(await task);

static async Task<R> SelectMany<T1, T2, R>(this Task<T1> task,
                        Func<T1, Task<T2>> bind, Func<T1, T2, R> project)
    {
        T taskResult = await task;
        return project(taskResult, await bind(taskResult));
    }
static async Task<R> Select<T, R>(this Task<T> task, Func<T, R> project)
        => await Map(task, project);

static async Task<R> Return<R>(R value) => Task.FromResult(value);
```

The `SelectMany` operator is one of the many functions capable of extending the asynchronous LINQ-style semantic. The job of the `Return` function is to lift the value R into a `Task<R>`. The async/await programming model in C# is based on tasks, and as mentioned in the previous chapter, it's close in nature to the monadic concept of the operators `Bind` and `Return`. Consequently, it's possible to define many of the LINQ query operators, which rely on the `SelectMany` operator. The important point is that using patterns such as monads provides the opportunity to create a series of reusable combinators and eases the application of techniques allowing for improved composability and readability of the code using LINQ-style semantic.

NOTE Section 7.15.3 of the C# specification has a list of operators that can be implemented to support all the LINQ comprehension syntax.

Here's the previous `DownloadIconAsync` example refactored using the LINQ expression semantic:

```
async Task DownloadIconAsync(string domain, string fileDestination)
{
    using (FileStream stream = new FileStream(fileDestination,
```

```
                    FileMode.Create, FileAccess.Write, FileShare.Write,
                                    0x1000, FileOptions.Asynchronous))
    await (from response in new HttpClient()
                               .GetAsync($"http://{domain}/favicon.ico")
           from bytes in response.Content.ReadAsByteArrayAsync()
           select Bitmap.FromStream(new MemoryStream(bytes)))
           .Tap(async image => (await image).Save(fileDestination));
}
```

Using the LINQ comprehension version, the from clause extracts the inner value of
the Task from the async operation and binds it to the related value. In this way, the keywords async/await can be omitted because of the underlying implementation.

TAP can be used to parallelize computations in C#, but as you saw, parallelization
is only one aspect of TAP. An even more enticing proposition is writing asynchronous
code that composes easily with the least amount of noise.

8.5   Task-based Asynchronous Programming: a case study

Programs that compute numerous I/O operations that consume a lot of time are good
candidates for demonstrating how asynchronous programming works and the powerful
toolset that TAP provides to a developer. As an example, in this section TAP is examined
in action by implementing a program that downloads from an HTTP server and analyzes
the stock market history of a few companies. The results are rendered in a chart that's
hosted in a Windows Presentation Foundation (WPF) UI application. Next, the symbols
are processed in parallel and program execution is optimized, timing the improvements.

In this scenario, it's logical to perform the operations in parallel asynchronously. Every
time you want to read data from the network using any client application, you should call
non-blocking methods that have the advantage of keeping the UI responsive (figure 8.5).

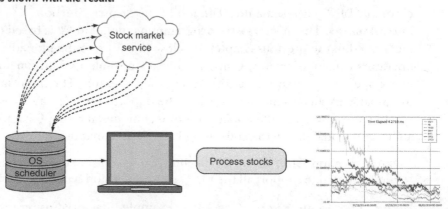

Figure 8.5   Downloading historical stock prices asynchronously in parallel. The number of requests can
exceed the number of available cores, and yet you can maximize parallelism.

Listing 8.4 shows the main part of the program. For the charting control, you'll use the Microsoft `Windows.Forms.DataVisualization` control.[4] Let's examine the asynchronous programming model on .NET in action. First, let's define the data structure `StockData` to hold the daily stock history:

```
struct StockData
{
public StockData(DateTime date, double open,
                 double high, double low, double close)
      {
            Date = date;
            Open = open;
            High = high;
            Low = low;
            Close = close;
      }
public DateTime Date  { get; }
public Double Open     { get; }
public Double High     { get; }
public Double Low      { get; }
public Double Close    { get; }
}
```

Several historical data points exist for each stock, so `StockData` in the shape of value-type struct can increase performance due to memory optimization. The following listing downloads and analyzes the historical stock data asynchronously (the code to note is in bold).

Listing 8.4   **Analyzing the history of stock prices**

Method that parses the string of stock history data and returns an array of StockData

```
async Task<StockData[]> ConvertStockHistory(string stockHistory)
{
      return await Task.Run(() => {
            string[] stockHistoryRows =
                  stockHistory.Split(Environment.NewLine.ToCharArray(),
                              StringSplitOptions.RemoveEmptyEntries);
            return (from row in stockHistoryRows.Skip(1)
                       let cells = row.Split(',')
                       let date = DateTime.Parse(cells[0])
                       let open = double.Parse(cells[1])
                       let high = double.Parse(cells[2])
                       let low = double.Parse(cells[3])
                       let close = double.Parse(cells[4])
                       select new StockData(date, open, high, low, close))
                                                      .ToArray();
      });
}

async Task<string> DownloadStockHistory(string symbol)
{
    string url =
```

Uses an asynchronous parser of the CSV stock history

---

[4] For more information, see http://mng.bz/Jvo1.

Web request for a given endpoint to retrieve the stock history; in this case, the financial Google API

Web request to asynchronously get the HTTP response

```
        $"http://www.google.com/finance/historical?q={symbol}&output=csv";
    var request = WebRequest.Create(url);
    using (var response = await request.GetResponseAsync()
                                 .ConfigureAwait(false))
    using (var reader = new StreamReader(response.GetResponseStream()))
        return await reader.ReadToEndAsync().ConfigureAwait(false);
}
```

Creates a stream reader using the HTTP response to read the content asynchronously; all the CSV text is read in once

```
async Task<Tuple<string, StockData[]>> ProcessStockHistory(string symbol)
{
    string stockHistory = await DownloadStockHistoryAsync(symbol);
    StockData[] stockData = await ConvertStockHistory(stockHistory);
    return Tuple.Create(symbol, stockData);
}
```

A new tuple instance carries information for each stock history analyzed to the chart.

The method ProcessStockHistory asynchronously executes the operation to download and to process the stock history.

```
async Task AnalyzeStockHistory(string[] stockSymbols)
{
    var sw = Stopwatch.StartNew();

    IEnumerable<Task<Tuple<string, StockData[]>>> stockHistoryTasks =
        stockSymbols.Select(stock => ProcessStockHistory(stock));

    var stockHistories = new List<Tuple<string, StockData[]>>();
    foreach (var stockTask in stockHistoryTasks)
        stockHistories.Add(await stockTask);

    ShowChart(stockHistories, sw.ElapsedMilliseconds);
}
```

A lazy collection of asynchronous operations processes the historical data.

Asynchronously processes the operations, one at a time

Shows the chart

The code starts creating a web request to obtain an HTTP response from the server so you can retrieve the underlying `ResponseStream` to download the data. The code uses the instance methods `GetReponseAsync()` and `ReadToEndAsync()` to perform the I/O operations, which can take a long time. Therefore, they're running asynchronously using the TAP pattern. Next, the code instantiates a `StreamReader` to read the data in a *comma-separated values* (CSV) format. The CSV data is then parsed in an understandable structure, the object `StockData`, using a LINQ expression and the function `ConvertStockHistory`. This function performs the data transformation using `Task.Run`,[5] which runs the supplied lambda on the `ThreadPool`.

The function `ProcessStockHistory` downloads and converts the stock history asynchronously, then returns a `Tuple` object. Specifically, this return type is `Task-<Tuple<string, StockData[]>>`. Interestingly, in this method, when the tuple is instantiated at the end of the method, there's no presence of any `Task`. This behavior is

---

[5] Microsoft's recommendation is to use a `Task` method that runs in a GUI with a computational time of more than 50 ms.

possible because the method is marked with the `async` keyword, and the compiler wraps the result automatically into a `Task` type to match the signature. In TAP, by denoting a method as `async`, all wrapping and unwrapping required to turn the result into a task (and vice versa) are handled by the compiler. The resulting data is sent to the method `ShowChart` to display the stock history and the elapsed time. (The implementation of `ShowChart` is online in the source code companion to this book.)

The rest of the code is self-explanatory. The time to execute this program—downloading, processing, and rendering the stock historical data for seven companies—is 4.272 seconds. Figure 8.6 shows the results of the stock price variations for Microsoft (MSFT), EMC, Yahoo (YHOO), eBay (EBAY), Intel (INTC), and Oracle (ORCL).

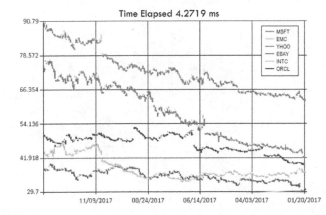

Figure 8.6   Chart of the stock price variations over time

As you can see, TAP returns tasks, allowing a natural compositional semantic for other methods with the same return type of `Task`. Let's review what's happening throughout the process. You used the Google service in this example to download and analyze the stock market history (listing 8.4). This is a high-level architecture of a scalable service with similar behavior, as shown in figure 8.7.

Here's the flow of how the Stock Market service processes the requests:

1 The user sends several requests asynchronously in parallel to download stock history prices. The UI remains responsive.

2 The thread pool schedules the work. Because the operations are I/O-bound, the number of asynchronous requests that can run in parallel could exceed the available number of local cores.

3 The Stock Market service receives the HTTP requests, and the work is dispatched to the internal program, which notifies the thread-pool scheduler to asynchronously handle the incoming requests to query the database.

4 Because the code is asynchronous, the thread-pool scheduler can schedule the work by optimizing local hardware resources. In this way, the number of threads required to run the program is kept to a minimum, the system remains responsive, memory consumption is low, and the server is scalable.

5 The database queries are processed asynchronously without keeping threads blocked.

6 When the database completes the work, the result is sent back to the caller. At this point, the thread-pool scheduler is notified, and a thread is assigned to continue the rest of the work.

7 The responses are sent back to the Stock Market service caller as they complete.

8 The user starts receiving the responses back from the Stock Market service.

9 The UI is notified, and a thread is assigned to continue the rest of the work without blocking.

10 The data received is parsed, and the chart is rendered.

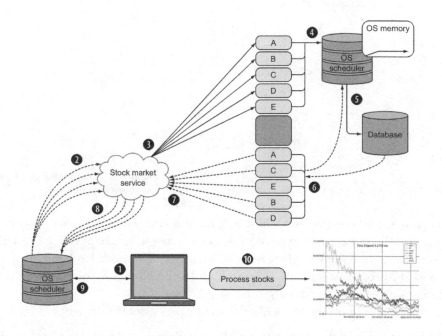

Figure 8.7   Asynchronous programming model for downloading data in parallel from the network

Using the asynchronous approach means all the operations run in parallel, but the overall response time is still correlated to the time of the slowest worker. Conversely, the response time for the synchronous approach increases with each added worker.

8.5.1   *Asynchronous cancellation*

When executing an asynchronous operation, it's useful to terminate execution prematurely before it completes on demand. This works well for long-running, non-blocking operations, where making them cancellable is the appropriate practice to avoid tasks that could hang. You'll want to cancel the operation of downloading the historical stock prices, for example, if the download exceeds a certain period of time.

Starting with version 4.0, the .NET Framework introduced an extensive and convenient approach to cooperative support for canceling operations running in a different thread. This mechanism is an easy and useful tool for controlling task execution flow. The concept of cooperative cancellation allows the request to stop a submitted operation without enforcing the code (figure 8.8). Aborting execution requires code that supports cancellation. It's recommended that you design a program that supports cancellation as much as possible.

These are the .NET types for canceling a `Task` or async operation:

- `CancellationTokenSource` is responsible for creating a cancellation token and sending cancellation requests to all copies of that token.
- `CancellationToken` is a structure utilized to monitor the state of the current token.

Cancellation is tracked and triggered using the cancellation model in the .NET Framework `System.Threading.CancellationToken`.

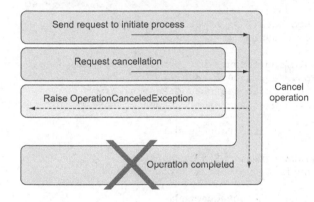

Figure 8.8 **After a request to start a process, a cancellation request is submitted that stops the rest of the execution, which returns to the caller in the form of** `OperationCanceledException`.

NOTE The cancellation is treated as a special exception of type `Operation-CanceledException`, which is convention for the calling code to be notified that the cancellation was observed.

CANCELLATION SUPPORT IN THE TAP MODEL

TAP supports cancellation natively; in fact, every method that returns a task provides at least one overload with a cancellation token as a parameter. In this case, you can pass a cancellation token when creating the task, then the asynchronous operation checks the status of the token, and it cancels the computation if the request is triggered.

To cancel the download of the historical stock prices, you should pass an instance of `CancellationToken` as an argument in the `Task` method and then call the `Cancel` method. The following listing shows this technique (in bold).

Listing 8.5 Canceling an asynchronous task

```
CancellationTokenSource cts = new CancellationTokenSource();

async Task<string> DownloadStockHistory(string symbol,
                                        CancellationToken token)
```

Passes the CancellationToken in the method to cancel

Creates a CancellationTokenSource instance

```
{
    string stockUrl =
        $"http://www.google.com/finance/historical?q={symbol}}&output=csv";
    var request = await new HttpClient().GetAsync(stockUrl, token);    ◄─────┐
    return await request.Content.ReadAsStringAsync();
}
                        Triggers the cancellation token        Passes the CancellationToken in
                                                                 the method to cancel
cts.Cancel();   ◄───
```

Certain programming methods don't have intrinsic support for cancellation. In those cases, it's important to apply manual checking. This listing shows how to integrate cancellation support to the previous stock market example where no asynchronous methods exist to terminate operations prematurely.

Listing 8.6   Canceling manual checks in an asynchronous operation

```
List<Task<Tuple<string, StockData[]>>> stockHistoryTasks =
    stockSymbols.Select(async symbol => {
        var url =
         $"http://www.google.com/finance/historical?q={symbol}&output=csv";
        var request = HttpWebRequest.Create(url);
        using (var response = await request.GetResponseAsync())
        using (var reader = new StreamReader(response.GetResponseStream()))
        {
            token.ThrowIfCancellationRequested();

            var csvData = await reader.ReadToEndAsync();
            var prices = await ConvertStockHistory(csvData);

            token.ThrowIfCancellationRequested();
            return Tuple.Create(symbol, prices.ToArray());
        }
    }).ToList();
```

In cases like this, where the `Task` method doesn't provide built-in support for cancellation, the recommended pattern is to add more `CancellationTokens` as parameters of the asynchronous method and to check for cancellation regularly. The option to throw an error with the method `ThrowIfCancellationRequested` is the most convenient to use because the operation would terminate without returning a result.

Interestingly, the `CancellationToken` (in bold) in the following listing supports the registration of a callback, which will be executed right after cancellation is requested. In this listing, a `Task` downloads the content of the Manning website, and it's canceled immediately afterward using a cancellation token.

Listing 8.7   Cancellation token callback

```
CancellationTokenSource tokenSource = new CancellationTokenSource();
CancellationToken token = tokenSource.Token;

Task.Run(async () =>
{
```

```
        var webClient = new WebClient();
        token.Register(() => webClient.CancelAsync());
        var data = await webClient
                    .DownloadDataTaskAsync(http://www.manning.com);
}, token);
```

Registers a callback that cancels the download of the WebClient instance.

```
tokenSource.Cancel();
```

In the code, a callback is registered to stop the underlying asynchronous operation in case the CancellationToken is triggered.

This pattern is useful and opens the possibility of logging the cancellation and firing an event to notify a listener that the operation has been canceled.

COOPERATIVE CANCELLATION SUPPORT

Use of the CancellationTokenSource makes it simple to create a composite token that consists of several other tokens. This pattern is useful if there are multiple reasons to cancel an operation. Reasons could include a click of a button, a notification from the system, or a cancellation propagating from another operation. The Cancellation-Source.CreateLinkedTokenSource method generates a cancellation source that will be canceled when any of the specified tokens is canceled (the code to note is in bold).

Listing 8.8   Cooperative cancellation token

Instances of CancellationToken to combine

```
CancellationTokenSource ctsOne = new CancellationTokenSource();
CancellationTokenSource ctsTwo = new CancellationTokenSource();
CancellationTokenSource ctsComposite = CancellationTokenSource.
    CreateLinkedTokenSource(ctsOne.Token, ctsTwo.Token);

CancellationToken ctsCompositeToken = ctsComposite.Token;
```

Composes the Cancellation-Tokens into one composite

```
Task.Factory.StartNew(async () => {
    var webClient = new WebClient();
    ctsCompositeToken.Register(() => webClient.CancelAsync());

    var data = await webClient
                    .DownloadDataTaskAsync(http://www.manning.com);
}, ctsComposite.Token);
```

Passes the composite cancellation token as a regular one; the task is then canceled by calling the Cancel() method of any of the tokens in the composite one.

In this listing, a linked cancellation source is created based on the two cancellation tokens. Then, the new composite token is employed. It will be canceled if any of the original CancellationTokens are canceled. A cancellation token is basically a thread-safe flag (Boolean value) that notifies its parent that the CancellationTokenSource has been canceled.

8.5.2   *Task-based asynchronous composition with the monadic Bind operator*

As mentioned previously, async `Task<T>` is a monadic type, which means that it's a container where you can apply the monadic operators `Bind` and `Return`. Let's analyze how these functions are useful in the context of writing a program. Listing 8.9 takes advantage of the `Bind` operator to combine a sequence of asynchronous operations as a chain of computations. The `Return` operator lifts a value into the monad (container or elevated type).

> **NOTE**   As a reminder, the `Bind` operator applies to the asynchronous `Task<T>` type, which allows it to pipeline two asynchronous operations, passing the result of the first operation to the second operation when it becomes available.

In general, a `Task` asynchronous function takes an arbitrary argument type of `'T` and returns a computation of type `Task<'R>` (with signature `'T -> Task<'R>`), and it can be composed using the `Bind` operator. This operator says: "When the value `'R` from the function (`g:'T -> Task<'R>`) is evaluated, it passes the result into the function (`f:'R -> Task<'U>`)."

The function `Bind` is shown in figure 8.9 for demonstration purposes because it's already built into the system.

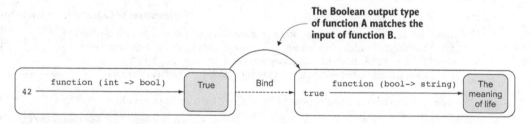

Figure 8.9   The `Bind` operator composes two functions that have the result wrapped into a `Task` type, and where the value returned from the computation of the first `Task` matches the input of the second function.

With this `Bind` function (in bold in the listing), the structure of the stock analysis code can be simplified. The idea is to glue together a series of functions.

Listing 8.9   `Bind` operator in action

```
async Task<Tuple<string, StockData[]>> ProcessStockHistory(string symbol)
{
    return await DownloadStockHistory(symbol)
        .Bind(stockHistory => ConvertStockHistory(stockHistory))
        .Bind(stockData => Task.FromResult(Tuple.Create(symbol,
                                                stockData)));
}       Composes an asynchronous operation
        using continuation-passing style
```

The asynchronous Task computations are composed by invoking the Bind operator on the first async operation and then passing the result to the second async operation, and so forth. The result is an asynchronous function that has as an argument the value returned by the first Task when it completes. It returns a second Task that uses the result of the first as input for its computation.

The code is both declarative and expressive because it fully embraces the functional paradigm. You've now used a monadic operator: specifically, one based on the continuation monad.

8.5.3 *Deferring asynchronous computation enables composition*

In C# TAP, a function that returns a task begins execution immediately. This behavior of eagerly evaluating an asynchronous expression is called a *hot task*, which unfortunately has negative impact in its compositional form. The functional way of handling asynchronous operations is to defer execution until it's needed, which has the benefit of enabling compositionality and provides finer control over the execution aspect.

You have three options for implementing APM:

- *Hot tasks*—The asynchronous method returns a task that represents an already running job that will eventually produce a value. This is the model used in C#.
- *Cold tasks*—The asynchronous method returns a task that requires an explicit start from the caller. This model is often used in the traditional thread-based approach.
- *Task generators*—The asynchronous method returns a task that will eventually generate a value, and that will start when a continuation is provided. This is the preferred way in functional paradigms because it avoids side effects and mutation. (This is the model used in F# to run asynchronous computations.)

How can you evaluate an asynchronous operation on demand using the C# TAP model? You could use a Lazy<T> type as the wrapper for a Task<T> computation (see chapter 2), but a simpler solution is to wrap the asynchronous computation into a Func<T> delegate, which will run the underlying operation only when executed explicitly. In the following code snippet this concept is applied to the stock history example, which defines the onDemand function to lazily evaluate the DownloadStockHistory Task expression:

```
Func<Task<string>> onDemand = async () => await DownloadStockHistory("MSFT");

string stockHistory = await onDemand();
```

From the point of view of the code, to consume the underlying Task of the DownloadStockHistory asynchronous expression, you need to treat and run the onDemand explicitly as a regular Func with the ().

Notice, there's a small glitch in this code. The function onDemand runs the asynchronous expression, which must have a pre-fixed argument (in this case, "MSFT").

How can you pass a different stock symbol to the function? The solution is currying and partial application, FP techniques that allow easier reuse of more abstract functions because you get to specialize. (They are explained in appendix A.)

Currying and partial application

In FP languages, a function is *curried* when it seems to take several parameters but takes only one and returns a function that takes the next parameter, and so on. For example, a function type signature A -> B -> C takes one argument A and returns a function B -> C. Translated into C# code using delegates, this function is defined as Func<A, Func<B, C>>.

This mechanism lets you partially apply a function by calling it with few parameters and creates a new function that applies only to the arguments passed. The same function can have different interpretations according to the number of parameters passed.

Here's the curried version of the onDemand function, which takes a string (symbol) as an argument that is then passed to the inner Task expression and returns a function of type Func<Task<string>>:

```
Func<string, Func<Task<string>>> onDemandDownload = symbol =>
                async () => await DownloadStockHistoryAsync(symbol);
```

Now, this curried function can be partially applied to create *specialized* functions over a given string (in this case, a stock symbol), which will be passed and consumed by the wrapped Task when the onDemand function is executed. Here's the partially applied function to create the specialized onDemandDownloadMSFT:

```
Func<Task<string>> onDemandDownloadMSFT = onDemandDownload("MSFT");

string stockHistoryMSFT = await onDemandDownloadMSFT();
```

The technique of differing asynchronous operations shows that you can build arbitrarily complex logic without executing anything until you decide to fire things off.

8.5.4 *Retry if something goes wrong*

A common concern when working with asynchronous I/O operations, and, in particular, with network requests, is the occurrence of an unexpected factor that jeopardizes the success of the operations. In these situations, you may want to retry an operation if a previous attempt fails. During the HTTP request made by the method Download-StockHistory, for example, there could be issues such as bad internet connections or unavailable remote servers. But these problems could be only a temporary state, and the same operation that fails an attempt once, might succeed if retried a few moments later.

The pattern of having multiple retries is a common practice to recover from temporary problems. In the context of asynchronous operations, this model is achieved by creating a wrapper function, implemented with TAP and returning tasks. This changes the evaluation of an asynchronous expression, as shown in the previous section. Then, if there are a few problems, this function applies the retry logic for a specified number of times with a specified delay between attempts. This listing shows the implementation of the asynchronous `Retry` function as an extension method.

Listing 8.10 `Retry async operation`

If a token isn't passed, then the default (CancellationToken)
sets its value to CancellationToken.None.

Uses a CancellationToken cts to
stop the current execution

```
async Task<T> Retry<T>(Func<Task<T>> task, int retries, TimeSpan delay,
        CancellationToken cts = default(CancellationToken)) =>
   await task().ContinueWith(async innerTask =>       {
      cts.ThrowIfCancellationRequested();
      if (innerTask.Status != TaskStatus.Faulted)
         return innerTask.Result;
      if (retries == 0)
         throw innerTask.Exception ?? throw new Exception();
      await Task.Delay(delay, cts);
      return await Retry(task, retries - 1, delay, cts);
   }).Unwrap();
```

Returns the result if the async
operation is successful

Delays the async
operation if a
failure occurs

Retries the async operation,
decrementing the retry counter

If the function runs over the retries limit,
it throws an exception.

The first argument is the async operation that will be re-executed. This function is specified lazily, wrapping the execution into a `Func<>`, because invoking the operation starts the task immediately. In case of exceptions, the operation `Task<T>` captures error handling via the `Status` and `Exception` properties. It's possible to ascertain if the async operation failed by inspecting these properties. If the operation fails, the `Retry` helper function waits for the specified interval, then retries the same operation, decreasing the number of retries until zero. With this `Retry<T>` helper function in place, the function `DownloadStockHistory` can be refactored to perform the web request operation with the retries logic:

```
async Task<Tuple<string, StockData[]>> ProcessStockHistory(string symbol)
{
    string stockHistory =
         await Retry(() => DownloadStockHistory(symbol), 5,
                                               TimeSpan.FromSeconds(2));
    StockData[] stockData = await ConvertStockHistory(stockHistory);
    return Tuple.Create(symbol, stockData);
}
```

In this case, the retry logic should run for at most five times with a delay of two seconds between attempts. The `Retry<T>` helper function should be typically attached to the end of a workflow.

8.5.5 Handling errors in asynchronous operations

As you recall, the majority of asynchronous operations are I/O-bound; there's a high probability that something will go wrong during their execution. The previous section covered the solution to handle failure by applying retry logic. Another approach is declaring a function combinator that links an async operation to a fallback one. If the first operation fails, then the fallback kicks in. It's important to declare the fallback as a differed evaluated task. The following listing shows the code that defines the `Otherwise` combinator, which takes two tasks and falls back the execution to the second task if the first one completes unsuccessfully.

Listing 8.11   Fallback `Task` combinator

If innerTask fails, then orTask is computed.

otherTask is wrapped into a Func<> to be evaluated only on demand.

```
static Task<T> Otherwise<T>(this Task<T> task,
                                   Func<Task<T>> otherTask)
=> task.ContinueWith(async innerTask => {
   if (innerTask.Status == TaskStatus.Faulted) return await orTask();
   return innerTask.Result;
}).Unwrap();
```

When the task completes, the `Task` type has a concept of whether it finished successfully or failed. This is exposed by the `Status` property, which is equal to `TaskStatus` `.Faulted` when an exception is thrown during the execution of the `Task`. The stock history analysis example requires FP refactoring to apply the `Otherwise` combinator.

Next is the code that combines the retry behavior, the `Otherwise` combinator, and the monadic operators for composing the asynchronous operations.

Listing 8.12   `Otherwise` combinator applied to fallback behavior

Service function that generates endpoints to retrieve the stock history for the given symbol

```
Func<string, string> googleSourceUrl = (symbol) =>
    $"http://www.google.com/finance/historical?q={symbol}&output=csv";

Func<string, string> yahooSourceUrl = (symbol) =>
                $"http://ichart.finance.yahoo.com/table.csv?s={symbol}";

async Task<string> DownloadStockHistory(Func<string, string> sourceStock,
                                                    string symbol)
{
    string stockUrl = sourceStock(symbol);
    var request = WebRequest.Create(stockUrl);
    using (var respone = await request.GetResponseAsync())
    using (var reader = new StreamReader(respone.GetResponseStream()))
        return await reader.ReadToEndAsync;
}

async Task<Tuple<string, StockData[]>> ProcessStockHistory(string symbol)
{
    Func<Func<string, string>, Func<string, Task<string>>> downloadStock =
        service => stock => DownloadStockHistory(service, stock);
```

Generates a stockUrl endpoint using the function sourceStock passed

Curries the function DownloadStockHistory to partially apply the endpoint service function and the stock symbol

Partial application of the DownloadStockHistory function.
downloadStock generates the stock history service.

```
Func<string, Task<string>> googleService =
                        downloadStock(googleSourceUrl);
Func<string, Task<string>> yahooService =
                        downloadStock(yahooSourceUrl);

return await Otherwise(() => googleService(symbol)

    .Retry(()=> yahooService(symbol)), 5, TimeSpan.FromSeconds(2))

    .Bind(data => ConvertStockHistory(data))

    .Map(prices => Tuple.Create(symbol, prices));
}
```

The Retry function applies the Otherwise combinator.

The Otherwise operator runs the googleService operation first; if it fails, then the yahooService operation executes.

Uses a functor Map operator to convert the result

Monadic Bind operator composes the two async Task operations, Retry and ConvertStockHistory

Note that the `ConfigureAwait` Task extension method has been omitted from the code. The application of the `Otherwise` combinator runs the function `Download-StockHistory` for both the primary and the fallback asynchronous operations. The fallback strategy uses the same functionality to download the stock prices, with the web request pointing to a different service endpoint (URL). If the first service isn't available, then the second one is used.

The two endpoints are provided by the functions `googleSourceUrl` and `yahoo-SourceUrl`, which build the URL for the HTTP request. This approach requires a modification of the `DownloadStockHistory` function signature, which now takes the higher-order function `Func<string, string> sourceStock`. This function is partially applied against both the functions `googleSourceUrl` and `yahooSourceUrl`. The result is two new functions, `googleService` and `yahooService`, that are passed as arguments to the `Otherwise` combinator, which ultimately is wrapped into the `Retry` logic. The `Bind` and `Map` operators are then used to compose the operations as a workflow without leaving the async `Task` elevated world. All the operations are guaranteed to be fully asynchronous.

8.5.6 Asynchronous parallel processing of the historical stock market

Because the function `Task` represents operations that take time, it's logical that you'll want to execute them in parallel when possible. One interesting aspect exists in the stock history code example. When the LINQ expression materializes, the asynchronous method `ProcessStockHistory` runs inside the for-each loop by calling one task at a time and awaiting the result. These calls are non-blocking, but the execution flow is sequential; each task waits for the previous one to complete before starting. This isn't efficient.

The following snippet shows the faulty behavior of running asynchronous operations sequentially using a for-each loop:

```
async Task ProcessStockHistory(string[] stockSymbols)
{
    var sw = Stopwatch.StartNew();
```

```
IEnumerable<Task<Tuple<string, StockData[]>>> stockHistoryTasks =
    stockSymbols.Select(stock => ProcessStockHistory(stock));

var stockHistories = new List<Tuple<string, StockData[]>>();

foreach (var stockTask in stockHistoryTasks)
    stockHistories.Add(await stockTask);

ShowChart(stockHistories, sw.ElapsedMilliseconds);
}
```

Suppose this time you want to launch these computations in parallel and then render the chart once all is complete. This design is similar to the Fork/Join pattern. Here, multiple asynchronous executions will be spawned in parallel and wait for all to complete. Then the results will aggregate and continue with further processing. The following listing processes the stocks in parallel correctly.

Listing 8.13   **Running the stock history analysis in parallel**

```
async Task ProcessStockHistory()
{
    var sw = Stopwatch.StartNew();
    string[] stocks = new[] { "MSFT", "FB", "AAPL", "YHOO",
                              "EBAY", "INTC", "GOOG", "ORCL" };

    List<Task<Tuple<string, StockData[]>>> stockHistoryTasks =
        stocks.Select(async stock => await
                          ProcessStockHistory(stock)).ToList();

    Tuple<string, StockData[]>[] stockHistories =
                          await Task.WhenAll(stockHistoryTasks);
    ShowChart(stockHistories, sw.ElapsedMilliseconds);
}
```

Waits asynchronously, without blocking, for all tasks to complete

The List operator guarantees the materialization of the LINQ query, which consequently runs the underlying operations in parallel.

In the listing, stock collection is transformed into a list of tasks using an asynchronous lambda in the Select method of LINQ. It's important to materialize the LINQ expression by calling ToList(), which dispatches the tasks to run in parallel only once. This is possible due to the hot-task property, which means that a task runs immediately after its definition.

TIP   By default, .NET limits open request connections to two at one time; to speed up the process, you must change the value of the connection limit ServicePointManager.DefaultConnectionLimit = stocks.Length.

The method Task.WhenAll (similar to Async.Parallel in F#) is part of the TPL, and its purpose is to combine the results of a set of tasks into a single task array, then wait asynchronously for all to complete:

```
Tuple<string, StockData[]>[] result = await Task.WhenAll(stockHistoryTasks);
```

In this instance, the execution time drops to 0.534 sec from the previous 4.272 sec.

8.5.7 *Asynchronous stock market parallel processing as tasks complete*

An alternative (and better) solution processes each stock history result as it arrives, instead of waiting for the download of all stocks to complete. This is a good pattern for performance improvement. In this case, it also reduces the payload for the UI thread by rendering the data in chunks. Consider the stock market analysis code, where multiple pieces of historical data are downloaded from the web and then used to process an image to render to a UI control. If you wait for all the data to be analyzed before updating the UI, the program is forced to process sequentially on the UI thread. A more performant solution, shown next, is to process and update the chart as concurrently as possible. Technically, this pattern is called *interleaving*. The important code to note is in bold.

Listing 8.14 Stock history analysis processing as each Task completes

```
async Task ProcessStockHistory()                    ToList() materializes the LINQ expression,
{                                                   ensuring the underlying tasks run in parallel.
    var sw = Stopwatch.StartNew();
    string[] stocks = new[] { "MSFT", "FB", "AAPL", "YHOO",
                              "EBAY", "INTC", "GOOG", "ORCL" };

    List<Task<Tuple<string, StockData[]>>> stockHistoryTasks =
             stocks.Select(ProcessStockHistory).ToList();

    while (stockHistoryTasks.Count > 0)             Runs the evaluation in a while loop until
    {                                               there are async Tasks to process

        Task<Tuple<string, StockData[]>> stockHistoryTask =
               await Task.WhenAny(stockHistoryTasks);

        stockHistoryTasks.Remove(stockHistoryTask);
        Tuple<string, StockData[]> stockHistory = await stockHistoryTask;

        ShowChartProgressive(stockHistory);         Removes the completed operation from
    }                                               the list, which is used in the predicate of
}                                                   the while loop

Sends the result from the asynchronous             The Task.WhenAny operator waits asynchronously
operation to be rendered in the chart              for the first operation to complete.
```

The code made two changes from the previous version:

- A `while` loop removes the tasks as they arrive, until the last one.
- `Task.WhenAll` is replaced with `Task.WhenAny`. This method waits asynchronously for the first task that reaches a terminal state and returns its instance.

This implementation doesn't consider either exceptions or cancellations. Alternatively, you could check the status of the task `stockHistoryTask` before further processing to apply conditional logic.

Summary

- You can write asynchronous programs in .NET with Task-based Asynchronous Programming (TAP) in C#, which is the preferred model to use.

- The asynchronous programming model lets you deal effectively with massive concurrent I/O operations by intelligently recycling resources during their idle time and by avoiding the creation of new resources, thereby optimizing memory consumption and enhancing performance.

- The Task<T> type is a monadic data structure, which means, among other things, that it can easily be composed with other tasks in a declarative and effortless way.

- Asynchronous tasks can be performed and composed using monadic operators, which leads to LINQ-style semantics. This has the advantage of providing a clear and fluid declarative programming style.

- Executing relatively long-lasting operations using asynchronous tasks can increase the performance and responsiveness of your application, especially if it relies on one or more remote services.

- The number of asynchronous computations that can run in parallel simultaneously is unrelated to the number of CPUs available, and execution time depends on the period spent waiting for the I/O operations to complete, bound only by the I/O drivers.

- TAP is based on the task type, enriched with the async and await keywords. This asynchronous programming model embraces the functional paradigm in the form of using continuation-passing style (CPS).

- With TAP, you can easily implement efficient patterns, such as downloading parallel multiple resources and processes as soon as they are available, instead of waiting for all resources to download.

Asynchronous functional
programming in F#

This chapter covers

- Making asynchronous computations cooperate

- Implementing asynchronous operations in a functional style

- Extending asynchronous workflow computational expressions

- Taming parallelism with asynchronous operations

- Coordinating cancellation of parallel asynchronous computations

In chapter 8, I introduced asynchronous programming as Tasks executing independently from the main application thread, possibly in a separated environment or across the network on different CPUs. This method leads to parallelism, where applications can perform an inordinately high number of I/O operations on a single-core machine. This is a powerful idea in terms of program execution and data throughput speed, casting away the traditional step-by-step programming approach. Both the F# and C# programming languages provide a slightly different, yet elegant, abstraction for expressing asynchronous computations, making them ideal tools, well suited for modeling real-world problems. In chapter 8, you saw how to use the asynchronous programming model in C#. In this chapter, we look at how to do the same in F#. This chapter helps you understand the performance semantics of the F# asynchronous workflow so you can write efficient and performant programs for processing I/O-bound operations.

I'll discuss the F# approach and analyze it for its unique traits and how they impact code design and explain how to easily implement and compose effective asynchronous operations in a functional style. I'll also teach you how to write non-blocking I/O operations to increase the overall execution, efficiency, and throughput of your applications when running multiple asynchronous operations concurrently, all without worrying about hardware constraints.

You'll see firsthand how to apply functional concepts for writing asynchronous computations. Then you'll evaluate how to use these concepts to handle side effects and interact with the real world without compromising the benefits of the compositional semantics—keeping your code concise, clear, and maintainable. By the end of this chapter, you'll come away with an appreciation of how modern applications must exploit parallelism and harness the power of multicore CPUs to run efficiently and to handle a large number of operations in a functional way.

9.1   Asynchronous functional aspects

An *asynchronous function* is a design idiom where a normal F# function or method returns an asynchronous computation. Modern asynchronous programming models such as the F# asynchronous workflow and C# `async/await` are functional because applying functional programming enables the experienced programmer to write simple and declarative procedural code that runs asynchronously and in parallel.

From the start, F# introduced support for the initiation of an asynchronous programming semantic definition that resembled synchronous code. It's not a coincidence that C#, which has introduced several functional futures in its language, has been inspired by the functional approach of the F# asynchronous workflow to implement the `async/await` asynchronous model, replacing the conventional imperative APM. Moreover, both the C# asynchronous task and the F# asynchronous workflow are monadic containers, which eases factoring out common functionality into generic, reusable components.

9.2   What's the F# asynchronous workflow?

The FP language F# provides full support for asynchronous programming:

- It integrates with the asynchronous programming model provided by .NET.
- It offers an idiomatic functional implementation of APM.
- It supports interoperability with the task-based programming model in C#.

The asynchronous workflow in F# is designed to satisfy the functional paradigm promoting compositionality, simplicity, and expressing non-blocking computations by keeping the sequential structure of code. By definition, the asynchronous workflow is built on computation expressions, a generic component of the F# core language that provides monadic semantics to express a sequence of operations in continuation-passing style (CPS).

A key feature of the asynchronous workflow is combining non-blocking computations with lightweight asynchronous semantics, which resembles a linear control flow.

9.2.1 *The continuation passing style in computation expressions*

Multithreaded code is notoriously resistant to the imperative style of writing. But using CPS, you can embrace the functional paradigm to make your code remarkably concise and easy to write. Let's imagine that you're programming using an old version of .NET Framework that doesn't have the async/await programming model available (see chapter 8). In this case you need to compute a series of Task operations, where the input of each operation depends on the output of the previous one; the code can become complex and convoluted. In the following code example, the code downloads an image from Azure Blob storage and saves the bytes into a file.

For the sake of simplicity, the code that isn't relevant for the example is omitted intentionally; the code to note is in bold. You can find the full implementation in the downloadable source code:

```
let downloadCloudMediaBad destinationPath (imageReference : string) =
    log "Creating connecton..."
    let taskContainer = Task.Run<CloudBlobContainer>(fun () ->
➥ getCloudBlobContainer())
    log "Get blob reference...";
    let container = taskContainer.Result
    let taskBlockBlob = Task.Run<CloudBlob>(fun () ->
➥ container.GetBlobReference(imageReference))
    log "Download data..."
    let blockBlob = taskBlockBlob.Result
    let bytes = Array.zeroCreate<byte> (int blockBlob.Properties.Length)
    let taskData = Task.Run<byte[]>(fun () -> blockBlob.
     DownloadToByteArray(bytes, 0)|>ignore; bytes)
    log "Saving data..."
    let data = taskData.Result
    let taskComplete = Task.Run(fun () ->
➥ File.WriteAllBytes(Path.Combine(destinationPath,imageReference), data))
    taskComplete.Wait()
    log "Complete"
```

Granted, the code is an extreme example that aims to validate the point that using traditional tools (with the same obsolete mindset) to write concurrent code produces verbose and impractical programs. The inexperienced developer can write code in this way more easily, because it's easier to reason sequentially. The result, however, is a program that doesn't scale, and each Task computation calls the instance method

Result, which is a bad practice. In this situation and with a little study, CPS can solve the problem of scalability. First, you define a function used to combine the operations in a pipeline shape:

```
let bind(operation:unit -> 'a, continuation:'a -> unit) =
        Task.Run(fun () -> continuation(operation())) |> ignore
```

The bind function accepts the continuation ('a -> unit) function, which is called when the result of the operation (unit -> 'a) is ready. The main key is that you're not blocking the calling thread, which may then continue executing useful code. When the result is ready, the continuation is called, allowing the computation to continue. You can now use this bind function to rewrite the previous code in a fluent manner:

```
let downloadCloudMediaAsync destinationPath (imageReference : string) =
    bind( (fun () -> log "Creating connecton..."; getCloudBlobContainer()),
        fun connection ->
            bind( (fun () -> log "Get blob reference...";
                connection.GetBlobReference(imageReference)),
                fun blockBlob ->
            bind( (fun () -> log "Download data..."
                let bytes = Array.zeroCreate<byte> (int blockBlob.Properties.
➥ Length)
                blockBlob.DownloadToByteArray(bytes, 0) |> ignore
                bytes), fun bytes ->
            bind( (fun () -> log "Saving data...";
            File.WriteAllBytes(Path.Combine(destinationPath,imageReference),
➥ bytes)), fun () -> log "Complete"))))

["Bugghina01.jpg"; "Bugghina02.jpg"; "Bugghina003.jpg"] |> Seq.iter
    (downloadCloudMediaAsync "Images")
```

Running the code, you'll notice the bind function executes the underlying anonymous lambda in its own thread. Every time the bind function is called, a thread is pulled out from the thread pool, then, when the function completes, the thread is released back to the thread pool.

The F# asynchronous workflow is based on this same concept of CPS, which is useful for modeling calculations that are difficult to capture sequentially.

NOTE It's possible for async functions to hop between any number of threads throughout their lifetime.

Figure 9.1 shows the comparison between incoming requests handled in a synchronous and asynchronous way.

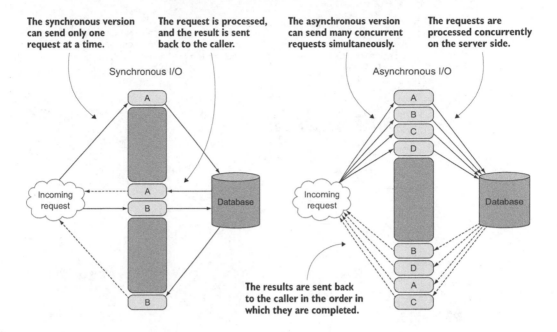

Figure 9.1 Comparison between synchronous (blocking) I/O and asynchronous (non-blocking) I/O operation systems. The synchronous version can send only one request at a time; after the request is processed, the result is sent back to the caller. The asynchronous version can send many concurrent requests simultaneously; after these requests are processed concurrently on the server side, they're sent back to the caller in the order that they complete.

The F# asynchronous workflow also includes cancellation and exception continuations. Before we dig into the asynchronous workflow details, let's look at an example.

9.2.2 *The asynchronous workflow in action: Azure Blob storage parallel operations*

Let's imagine that your boss has decided that the company's digital media assets should be stored in the cloud as well as locally. He asks you to create a simple uploader/downloader tool for that purpose and to synchronize and verify what's new in the cloud. To handle media files as binary data for this scenario, you design a program to download a set of images from the network Azure Blob storage and render these images in a client-side application that's based on WPF. Azure Blob storage (http://mng.bz/X1FB) is a Microsoft cloud service that stores unstructured data in the form of blobs (binary large objects). This service stores any type of data, which makes it a great fit to handle your company's media files as binary data (figure 9.2).

> **NOTE** The code examples in this chapter are in F#, but the same concepts are applicable to C#. The translated versions of these code examples can be found in the downloadable code for this book, available online.

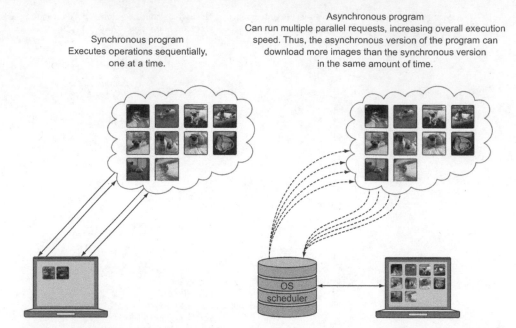

Figure 9.2   The synchronous versus asynchronous programming model. The synchronous program executes each operation sequentially one at a time. The asynchronous version can run multiple requests in parallel, increasing the overall execution speed of the program. As a result, the asynchronous version of the program can download more images in the same period of time as compared to the synchronous version.

As mentioned earlier, to provide visual feedback, the program runs as a client WPF application. This application benefits from a FileSystemWatcher (http://mng.bz/DcRT) that's listening for file-created events to pick up file changes in the local folder. When the images are downloaded and saved in this local folder, FileSystemWatcher triggers an event and synchronizes the updates of a local file collection with the path of the image, which is successively displayed in a WPF UI controller. (The code implementation of the client WPF UI application isn't reviewed here because it's irrelevant to the main topic of this chapter.)

Let's compare the synchronous and asynchronous programs from figure 9.2. The synchronous version of the program executes each step sequentially and iterates, with a conventional for loop, the collection of images to download from the Azure Blob storage. This design is straightforward but doesn't scale. Alternatively, the asynchronous version of the program is capable of processing multiple requests in parallel, which increases the number of images downloaded in the same period of time.

Let's analyze the asynchronous version of the program in more depth. In figure 9.3, the program starts by sending a request to the Azure Blob storage to open the cloud blob container connection. When the connection is opened, the handle of the blob media stream is retrieved to begin downloading the image. The data is read from the stream, and, ultimately, persisted to a local filesystem. Then it repeats this operation for the next image through to the last.

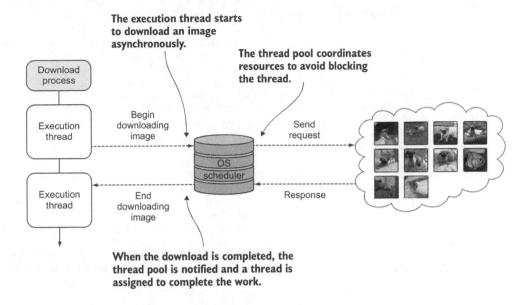

Figure 9.3   Downloading an image asynchronously from the network (Azure Blob storage)

Each download operation takes an average of 0.89 seconds over five runs, for a total time of 89.28 seconds to download 100 images. These values can vary according to the network bandwidth. Obviously, the time to perform multiple synchronous I/O operations sequentially is equal to the sum of the time elapsed for each individual operation, in comparison to the asynchronous approach, which by running in parallel has an overall response time equal to the slowest operation.

NOTE   The Azure Blob storage has an API to download the blob directly into a local file, `DownloadToFile`; but the code intentionally creates a large number of I/O operations to accentuate the problem of running I/O blocking operations synchronously.

The following listing is the asynchronous workflow implementation of the program to download the images asynchronously from Azure Blob storage (the code to note is in bold).

Listing 9.1   Asynchronous workflow implementation to download images

Parses and creates the Azure storage connection

```
let getCloudBlobContainerAsync() : Async<CloudBlobContainer> = async {
    let storageAccount = CloudStorageAccount.Parse(azureConnection)
    let blobClient = storageAccount.CreateCloudBlobClient()
    let container = blobClient.GetContainerReference("media")
    let! _ = container.CreateIfNotExistsAsync()
    return container }
```

Creates the blob client

Retrieves a reference of the media container

Creates the container asynchronously if it doesn't already exist

```
let downloadMediaAsync(blobNameSource:string) (fileNameDestination:string)=
  async {
    let! container = getCloudBlobContainerAsync()
    let blockBlob = container.GetBlockBlobReference(blobNameSource)
    let! (blobStream : Stream) = blockBlob.OpenReadAsync()

    use fileStream = new FileStream(fileNameDestination, FileMode.Create,
  FileAccess.Write, FileShare.None, 0x1000, FileOptions.Asynchronous)
    let buffer = Array.zeroCreate<byte> (int blockBlob.Properties.Length)
    let rec copyStream bytesRead = async {
        match bytesRead with
        | 0 -> fileStream.Close(); blobStream.Close()
        | n -> do! fileStream.AsyncWrite(buffer, 0, n)
               let! bytesRead = blobStream.AsyncRead(buffer, 0, buffer.
  Length)
               return! copyStream bytesRead }
    let! bytesRead = blobStream.AsyncRead(buffer, 0, buffer.Length)
    do! copyStream bytesRead   }
```

Converts a function to async   **Adds computational expression semantics with the !
                                            operator to register continuation of the workflow**

Note that this code looks almost exactly like sequential code. The parts in bold are the only changes necessary to switch the code from synchronous to asynchronous.

The intentions of this code are direct and simple to interpret because of the sequential structure of the code. This code simplification is the result of the pattern-based approach that the F# compiler uses to detect a computation expression, and in the case of an asynchronous workflow, it gives the illusion to the developer that callbacks have disappeared. Without callbacks, the program isn't subject to inversion of control as in APM, which makes F# deliver a clean asynchronous code implementation with a focus on compositionality.

Both the getCloudBlobContainerAsync and downloadMediaAsync functions are wrapped inside an async expression (workflow declaration), which turns the code into a block that can be run asynchronously. The function getCloudBlobContainer-Async creates a reference to the container media. The return type of this asynchronous operation to identify the container is type Task<CloudBlobContainer>, which with the Async<CloudBlobContainer> is handled by the underlying asynchronous workflow expression (explained later in the chapter). The key feature of an asynchronous workflow is to combine non-blocking computations with lightweight asynchronous semantics, which resembles a linear control flow. It simplifies the program structure of traditional callback-based asynchronous programming through syntactic sugar.

The methods that run asynchronously are bound to a different construct that uses the ! (pronounced *bang*) operator, which is the essence of an asynchronous workflow because it notifies the F# compiler to interpret the function in an exclusive way. The body of a let! binding registers the expression as a callback, in context for future evaluation to the rest of the asynchronous workflow, and it extracts the underlying result from Async<'T>.

In the expression

```
let! bytesRead = blobStream.AsyncRead(buffer, 0, buffer.Length)
```

the return type of blobStream.AsyncRead is Async<int>, indicating the number of bytes read from the asynchronous operation, which is extracted into the value bytes-Read. The rec copyStream function recursively and asynchronously copies the blob-Stream into the fileStream. Note the copyStream function is defined inside another async workflow to capture (close over) the stream values that can be accessed to be copied. This code could be rewritten in an imperative style with identical behavior as follows:

```
let! bytesRead = blobStream.AsyncRead(buffer, 0, buffer.Length)
let mutable bytesRead = bytesRead
while bytesRead > 0 do
    do! fileStream.AsyncWrite(buffer, 0, bytesRead)
    let! bytesReadTemp = blobStream.AsyncRead(buffer, 0, buffer.Length)
    bytesRead <- bytesReadTemp
fileStream.Close(); blobStream.Close()
```

The mutation of the variable bytesRead is encapsulated and isolated inside the main function downloadMediaAsync and is thread safe.

Besides let! the other asynchronous workflow constructors are as follows:

- use!—Works like let! for disposable resources that are cleaned up when out of scope
- do!—Binds an asynchronous workflow when the type is Async<unit>
- return—Returns a result from the expression
- return!—Executes the bound asynchronous workflow, returning the value of the expression

The F# asynchronous workflow is based on the polymorphic data type Async<'a> that denotes an arbitrary asynchronous computation, which will materialize in the future, returning a value of type 'a. This concept is similar to the C# TAP model. The main difference is that the F# Async<'a> type isn't hot, which means that it requires an explicit command to start the operation.

When the asynchronous workflow reaches the start primitive, a callback is scheduled in the system, and the execution thread is released. Then, when the asynchronous operation completes the evaluation, the underlying mechanisms will notify the workflow, passing the result to the next step in the code flow.

The real magic is that the asynchronous workflow will complete at a later time, but you don't have to worry about waiting for the result because it will be passed as an argument in the continuation function when completed. The compiler takes care of all of this, organically converting the Bind member calls into the continuation constructs. This mechanism uses CPS for writing, implicitly, a structured callback-based program inside its body expression, which allows a linear style of coding over a sequence of operations.

The asynchronous execution model is all about continuations, where the evaluation of the asynchronous expression preserves the capability of having a function registered as a callback (figure 9.4).

```
bind(fun() ->log "Creating connection...";
               getCloudBlobContainer()), fun connection ->
      bind(fun() ->log "Get blob reference...";
                    connection.GetBlobReference(imageReference)), fun blockBlob ->


                 async {
                     log "Creating connection...";
                     let! connection = getCloudBlobContainerAsync()
                     log "Get blob reference...";
                     let blockBlob = connection.GetBlobReference(imageReference)
                     ...
```

Figure 9.4   A comparison of the `Bind` function with the computation expression version.

The benefits of using an asynchronous workflow are as follows:

- Code that looks sequential but behaves asynchronously
- Simple code that's easy to reason about (because it looks like sequential code), which simplifies updates and modification
- Asynchronous compositional semantics
- Built-in cancellation support
- Simple error handling
- Easy to parallelize

9.3   *Asynchronous computation expressions*

Computation expressions are an F# feature that define a polymorphic construct used to customize the specification and behavior of the code, and lead you toward a compositional programming style. The MSDN online documentation provides an excellent definition:

> *Computation expressions in F# provide a convenient syntax for writing computations that can be sequenced and combined using control flow constructs and bindings. They can be used to provide a convenient syntax for monads, a functional programming feature that can be used to manage data, control, and side effects in functional programs.*[1]

Computation expressions are a helpful mechanism for writing computations that execute a controlled series of expressions as an evaluation of feed-into steps. The first step serves as input to the second step, and that output serves as input for the third step, and so forth through the execution chain—unless an exception occurs, in which case the evaluation terminates prematurely, skipping the remaining steps.

---

[1]   For more information, see http://mng.bz/n1uZ.

Think of a computation expression as an extension of the programming language because it lets you customize a specialized computation to reduce redundant code and apply heavy lifting behind the scenes to reduce complexity. You can use a computation expression to inject extra code during each step of the computation to perform operations such as automatic logging, validation, control of state, and so on.

The F# asynchronous programming model, asynchronous workflow, relies on computation expressions, which are also used to define other implementations, such as sequence and query expressions. The F# asynchronous workflow pattern is syntactic sugar, interpreted by the compiler in a computation expression. In an asynchronous workflow, the compiler must be instructed to interpret the workflow expression as an asynchronous computation. The notification is semantically passed by wrapping the expression in an asynchronous block, which is written using curly braces and the `async` identifier right at the beginning of the block, like so: `async { expression }`

When the F# compiler interprets a computation as an asynchronous workflow, it divides the whole expression into separate parts between the asynchronous calls. This transformation, referred to as *desugaring*, is based on the constituent primitives by the computation builder in context (in this case, the asynchronous workflow).

F# supports computation expressions through a special type called `builder`, associated with the conventional monadic syntax. As you remember, the two primary monadic operators to define a computation builder are `Bind` and `Return`.

In the case of an asynchronous workflow, the generic monadic type is replaced and defined with the specialized type `Async`:

```
async.Bind: Async<'T> → ('T → Async<'R>) → Async<'R>
```

```
async.Return: 'T → Async<'T>
```

Wraps a generic type 'T into an elevated type Async<'T>

The asynchronous operation Async<'T> is passed as the first argument, and a continuation ('T → Async<'R>) is passed as the second.

The asynchronous workflow hides nonstandard operations in the form of computation builder primitives and reconstructs the rest of the computation in continuation. Nonstandard operations are bound in the body expression of the builder constructs with the `!` operator. It's not a coincidence that the computation expression definition, through the `Bind` and `Return` operators, is identical to the monadic definition, which shares the same monadic operators. You can think of a computation expression as a continuation monad pattern.

9.3.1 Difference between computation expressions and monads

You can also think of a computation expression as a general monadic syntax for F#, which is closely related to monads. The main difference between computation expressions and monads is found in their origin. Monads strictly represent mathematical abstractions, whereas the F# computation expression is a language feature that provides a toolset to a program with computation that can—or not—have a monadic structure.

F# doesn't support type classes, so it isn't possible to write a computation expression that's polymorphic over the type of computation. In F# you can select a computation expression with the most specialized behavior and convenient syntax (an example is coming).

Type classes

A type class is a construct that provides specific polymorphism, which is achieved by applying constraint definitions to type variables. Type classes are akin to interfaces that define a behavior, but they're more powerful. The compiler provides specialized behavior and syntax over the type inferred through these constraints. In .NET, you can think of a type class as an interface that defines a behavior, which the compiler can detect, and then provides an ad hoc implementation based on its type definition. Ultimately, a type can be made an instance of a typeclass if it supports that behavior.

The code written using the computation expression pattern is ultimately translated into an expression that uses the underlying primitives implemented by the computation builder in context. This concept will be clearer with an example.

Listing 9.2 shows the desugared version of the function `downloadMediaAsync`, where the compiler translates the computation expression into a chain of method calls. This unwrapped code shows how the behavior of each single asynchronous part is encapsulated in the related primitive member of the computation builder. The keyword `async` tells the F# compiler to instantiate the `AsyncBuilder`, which implements the essential asynchronous workflow members `Bind`, `Return`, `Using`, `Combine`, and so on. The listing shows how the compiler translates the computation expression into a chain of method calls of the code from listing 9.1. (The code to note is in bold.)

Listing 9.2   Desugared `DownloadMediaAsync` computation expression

Delays execution of the function until an explicit request

```
let downloadMediaAsync(blobName:string) (fileNameDestination:string) =
  async.Delay(fun() ->
    async.Bind(getCloudBlobContainerAsync(), fun container ->
      let blockBlob = container.GetBlockBlobReference(blobName)
      async.Using(blockBlob.OpenReadAsync(), fun (blobStream:Stream) ->

        let sizeBlob = int blockBlob.Properties.Length
        async.Bind(blobStream.AsyncRead(sizeBlob), fun bytes ->
          use fileStream = new FileStream(fileNameDestination,
FileMode.Create, FileAccess.Write, FileShare.None, bufferSize,
FileOptions.Asynchronous)
          async.Bind(fileStream.AsyncWrite(bytes, 0, bytes.Length), fun () ->
                     fileStream.Close()
                     blobStream.Close()
                     async.Return())))))
```

The Bind operator is the desugared version of the let! operator.

The Using operator translates to the use! operator.

Returns the operator that completes the computation expression

In the code, the compiler transforms the `let!` binding construct into a call to the `Bind` operation, which unwraps the value from the computation type and executes the rest of the computation converted to a continuation. The `Using` operation handles computation where the resulting value type represents a resource that can be disposed. The first member in the chain, `Delay`, wraps the expression as a whole to manage the execution, which can run later on demand.

Each step of the computation follows the same pattern: the computation builder member, like `Bind` or `Using`, starts the operation and provides the continuation that runs when the operation completes, so you don't wait for the result.

9.3.2 *AsyncRetry: building your own computation expression*

As mentioned, a computation expression is a pattern-based interpretation (like LINQ/ PLINQ), which means that the compiler can infer from the implementation of the members `Bind` and `Return` that the type construct is a monadic expression. By following a few simple specifications, you can build your own computation expression, or even extend an existing one, to deliver to an expression the special connotation and behavior you want.

Computation expressions can contain numerous standard language constructs, as listed in table 9.1; but the majority of these member definitions are optional and can be used according to your implementation needs. The mandatory and basic members to represent a valid computation expression for the compiler are `Bind` and `Return`.

Table 9.1. Computation expression operators

Member	Description
Bind : M<'a> * ('a → M<'b>) → M<'b>	Transformed `let!` and `do!` within computation expressions.
Return : 'a → M<'a>	Transformed `return` within computation expressions.
Delay : (unit → M<'a>) → M<'a>	Used to ensure side effects within a computation expression are performed when expected.
Yield : 'a → M<'a>	Transformed `yield` within computation expressions.
For : seq<'a> * ('a → M<'b>) → M<'b>	Transformed `for ... do ...` within computation expressions. M<'b> can optionally be M<unit>.
While : (unit → bool) * M<'a> → M<'a>	Transformed `while-do` block within computation expressions. M<'b> can optionally be M<unit>.
Using : 'a * ('a → M<'b>) → M<'b> when 'a :> IDisposable	Transformed `use` bindings within computation expressions.
Combine : M<'a> → M<'a> → M<'a>	Transformed sequencing within computation expressions. The first M<'a> can optionally be M<unit>.
Zero : unit → M<'a>	Transformed empty `else` branches of `if/then` within computation expressions.
TryWith : M<'a> → M<'a> → M<'a>	Transformed empty `try/with` bindings within computation expressions.
TryFinally : M<'a> → M<'a> → M<'a>	Transformed `try/finally` bindings within computation expressions.

Let's build a computation expression that can be used with the example in listing 9.2. The first step of the function, `downloadMediaCompAsync`, connects asynchronously to the Azure Blob service, but what happens if the connection drops? An error is thrown and the computation stops. You could check whether the client is online before trying to connect; but it's a general rule of thumb when working with network operations that you retry the connection a few times before aborting.

In the following listing, you're building a computation expression that runs an asynchronous operation successfully a few times, with a delay in milliseconds between each retry before the operation stops (the code to note is in bold).

Listing 9.3   `AsyncRetryBuilder` computation expression

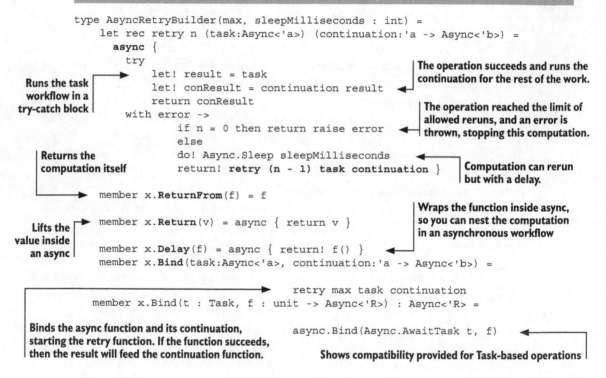

```
type AsyncRetryBuilder(max, sleepMilliseconds : int) =
    let rec retry n (task:Async<'a>) (continuation:'a -> Async<'b>) =
      async {
          try
              let! result = task
              let! conResult = continuation result
              return conResult
          with error ->
              if n = 0 then return raise error
              else
                  do! Async.Sleep sleepMilliseconds
                  return! retry (n - 1) task continuation }
      member x.ReturnFrom(f) = f

      member x.Return(v) = async { return v }

      member x.Delay(f) = async { return! f() }
      member x.Bind(task:Async<'a>, continuation:'a -> Async<'b>) =
                                     retry max task continuation
      member x.Bind(t : Task, f : unit -> Async<'R>) : Async<'R> =
                                     async.Bind(Async.AwaitTask t, f)
```

Runs the task workflow in a try-catch block

The operation succeeds and runs the continuation for the rest of the work.

The operation reached the limit of allowed reruns, and an error is thrown, stopping this computation.

Returns the computation itself

Computation can rerun but with a delay.

Wraps the function inside async, so you can nest the computation in an asynchronous workflow

Lifts the value inside an async

Binds the async function and its continuation, starting the retry function. If the function succeeds, then the result will feed the continuation function.

Shows compatibility provided for Task-based operations

The `AsyncRetryBuilder` is a computation builder used to identify the value to construct the computation. The following code shows how to use the computation builder (the code to note is highlighted in bold).

Listing 9.4 Using `AsyncRetryBuilder` to identify construct value

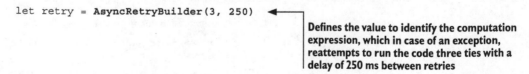

```
let retry = AsyncRetryBuilder(3, 250)
```

Defines the value to identify the computation expression, which in case of an exception, reattempts to run the code three ties with a delay of 250 ms between retries

```
let downloadMediaCompAsync(blobNameSource:string)
                          (fileNameDestination:string) =
async {
        let! container = retry {          ◄─────────── The retry computation expression can
            return! getCloudBlobContainerAsync() }      be nested inside an async workflow.
```

```
... Rest of the code as before
```

The `AsyncRetryBuilder` instance retry re-attempts to run the code in case of an exception three times, with a delay of 250 ms between retries. Now, the `AsyncRetry-Builder` computation expression can be used in combination with the asynchronous workflow, to run and retry asynchronously (in case of failure), the `downloadMedia-CompAsync` operation. It's common to create a global value identifier for a computation expression that can be reused in different parts of your program. For example, the asynchronous workflow and sequence expression can be accessed anywhere in the code without creating a new value.

9.3.3 *Extending the asynchronous workflow*

Besides creating custom computation expressions, the F# compiler lets you extend existing ones. The asynchronous workflow is a perfect example of a computation expression that can be enhanced. In listing 9.4, the connection to the Azure Blob container is established through the asynchronous operation `getCloudBlobContainer-Async`, the implementation of which is shown here:

```
let getCloudBlobContainerAsync() : Async<CloudBlobContainer> = async {
    let storageAccount = CloudStorageAccount.Parse(azureConnection)
    let blobClient = storageAccount.CreateCloudBlobClient()
    let container = blobClient.GetContainerReference("media")
    let! _ = container.CreateIfNotExistsAsync()
    return container }
```

Inside the body of the `getCloudBlobContainerAsync` function, the `CreateIfNotEx-istsAsync` operation returns a `Task` type, which isn't friendly to use in the context of asynchronous workflow. Fortunately, the F# async provides the `Async.AwaitTask`[2] operator, which allows a `Task` operation to be awaited and treated as an F# async computation. A vast number of asynchronous operations in .NET have return types of `Task` or the generic version `Task<'T>`. These operations, designed to work primarily with C#, aren't compatible with the F# out-of-the-box asynchronous computation expressions.

What's the solution? Extend the computation expression. Listing 9.5 generalizes the F# asynchronous workflow model so that it can be used not only in async operations, but also with the `Task` and `Observable` types. The async computation expression needs type-constructs that can create observables and tasks, as opposed to only asynchronous workflows. It's possible to await all kinds of events produced by `Event` or `IObservable` streams and tasks from `Task` operations. These extensions for the computation expression, as you can see, abstract the use of the `Async.AwaitTask` operator (the related commands are in bold).

---

[2] The `Async.AwaitTask` creates computations that wait on the provided task and returns its result.

Listing 9.5   Extending the asynchronous workflow to support `Task<'a>`

```
type Microsoft.FSharp.Control.AsyncBuilder with
    member x.Bind(t:Task<'T>, f:'T -> Async<'R>) : Async<'R> =
        async.Bind(Async.AwaitTask t, f)

    member x.Bind(t:Task, f:unit -> Async<'R>) : Async<'R> =
        async.Bind(Async.AwaitTask t, f)

    member x.Bind (m:'a IObservable, f:'a -> 'b Async) =
        async.Bind(Async.AwaitObservable m, f)

    member x.ReturnFrom(computation:Task<'T>) =
        x.ReturnFrom(Async.AwaitTask computation)
```

Extends the Async Bind operator to perform against other elevated types

The `AsyncBuilder` lets you inject functions to extend the manipulation on other wrapper types, such as `Task` and `Observable`, whereas the `Bind` function in the extension lets you fetch the inner value contained in the `Observable` (or `IEvent`) using the `let!` and `do!` operators. This technique removes the need for adjunctive functions like `Async.AwaitEvent` and `Async.AwaitTask`.

In the first line of code, the compiler is notified to target the `AsyncBuilder`, which manages the asynchronous computation expression transformation. The compiler, after this extension, can determine which `Bind` operation to use, according to the expression signature registered through the `let!` binding. Now you can use the asynchronous operation of type `Task` and `Observable` in an asynchronous workflow.

9.3.4   *Mapping asynchronous operation: the Async.map functor*

Let's continue extending the capabilities of the F# asynchronous workflow. The F# asynchronous workflow provides a rich set of operators; but currently, there's no built-in support for an `Async.map` function (also known as a *functor*) having type signature

```
('a -> 'b) -> Async<'a> -> Async<'b>
```

A functor is a pattern of mapping over structure, which is achieved by providing implementation support for a two-parameter function called `map` (better known as `fmap`). For example, the `Select` operator in LINQ/PLINQ is a functor for the `IEnumerable` elevated type. Mainly, functors are used in C# to implement LINQ-style fluent APIs that are used also for types (or contexts) other than collections.

We discussed the functor type in chapter 7, where you learned how to implement a functor (in bold) for the `Task` elevated type:

```
Task<T> fmap<T, R>(this Task<T> input, Func<T, R> map) =>
                        input.ContinueWith(t => f(t.Result));
```

This function has a signature `('T -> 'R) -> Task<'T> -> Task<R>`, so it takes a map function `'T -> 'R` as a first input (which means it goes from a value type `T` to a value type `R`, in C# code `Func<T, R>`), and then upgrades type `Task<'T>` as a second input and returns a `Task<'R>`. Applying this pattern to the F# asynchronous workflow, the signature of the `Async.map` function is

```
('a -> 'b) -> Async<'a> -> Async<'b>
```

The first argument is a function `'a -> 'b`, the second is an `Async<'a>`, and the output is an `Async<'b>`. Here's the implementation of `Async.map`:

```
module Async =
    let inline map (func:'a -> 'b) (operation:Async<'a>) = async {
        let! result = operation
        return func result }
```

`let! result = operation` runs the asynchronous operation and unwraps the `Async<'a>` type, returning the `'a` type. Then, we can pass the value `'a` to the function `func:'a -> 'b` that converts `'a` to `'b`. Ultimately, once the value `'b` is computed, the return operator wraps the result `'b` into the `Async<>` type.

The inline keyword

The `inline` keyword in F# is used to define a function that's integrated into the calling code by amending the function body directly to the caller code. The most valuable application of the `inline` keyword is inlining higher-order functions to the call site where their function arguments are also inlined to produce a single fully optimized piece of code. F# can also `inline` between compiled assemblies because `inline` is conveyed via .NET metadata.

The `map` function applies an operation to the objects inside the `Async` container,[3] returning a container of the same shape. The `Async.map` function is interpreted as a two-argument function where a value is wrapped in the F# `Async` context, and a function is applied to it. The F# `Async` type is added to both its input and output.

The main purpose of the `Async.map` function is to operate (project) the result of an `Async` computation without leaving the context. Back to the Azure Blob storage example, you can use the `Async.map` function to download and transform an image as follows (the code to note is in bold):

```
let downloadBitmapAsync(blobNameSource:string) = async {
    let! token = Async.CancellationToken
    let! container = getCloudBlobContainerAsync()
    let blockBlob = container.GetBlockBlobReference(blobNameSource)
    use! (blobStream : Stream) = blockBlob.OpenReadAsync()
    return Bitmap.FromStream(blobStream) }

let transformImage (blobNameSource:string) =
    downloadBitmapAsync(blobNameSource)
    |> Async.map ImageHelpers.setGrayscale
    |> Async.map ImageHelpers.createThumbnail
```

The `Async.map` function composes the async operations of downloading the image `blobNameSource` from the Azure Table storage with the transformation functions `setGrayscale` and `createThumbnail`.

---

[3] Polymorphic types can be thought of as containers for values of another type.

> **NOTE** I defined these `ImageHelpers` functions in chapter 7, so they're omitted here intentionally. Please refer to the online source code for the full implementation.

In the snippet, the advantages of using the `Async.map` function are composability and continued encapsulation.

9.3.5   *Parallelize asynchronous workflows: Async.Parallel*

Let's return to the example of downloading 100 images from Azure Blob storage using the F# asynchronous workflow. In section 9.2 you built the function `download-MediaAsync` that downloads one cloud blob image using the asynchronous workflow. It's time to connect the dots and run the code. But instead of iterating through the list of images one operation at a time, the F# asynchronous workflow provides an elegant alternative: `Async.Parallel`.

The idea is to compose all the asynchronous computations and execute them all at once. Parallel composition of asynchronous computations is efficient because of the scalability properties of the .NET thread pool and the controlled, overlapped execution of operations such as web requests by modern operating systems.

Using the F# `Async.Parallel` function, it's possible to download hundreds of images in parallel (the code to note is in bold).

Listing 9.10   `Async.Parallel` downloading all images in parallel

```
let retry = RetryAsyncBuilder(3, 250)          ◄── Defines a Retry computation expression

let downloadMediaCompAsync (container:CloudBlobContainer)
    (blobMedia:IListBlobItem) = retry {        ◄── Runs the asynchronous
                                                    operations using a run
                                                    and retry approach
    let blobName = blobMedia.Uri.Segments.[blobMedia.Uri.Segments.Length-1]
    let blockBlob = container.GetBlockBlobReference(blobName)
    let! (blobStream : Stream) = blockBlob.OpenReadAsync()
    return Bitmap.FromStream(blobStream)
}
let transformAndSaveImage (container:CloudBlobContainer)
                    (blobMedia:IListBlobItem) =
    downloadMediaCompAsync container blobMedia
    |> Async.map ImageHelpers.setGrayscale
    |> Async.map ImageHelpers.createThumbnail
    |> Async.tap (fun image ->
            let mediaName =

            blobMedia.Uri.Segments.[blobMedia.Uri.Segments.Length - 1]
            image.Save(mediaName))

let downloadMediaCompAsyncParallel() = retry {

    let! container = getCloudBlobContainerAsync()
    let computations =
        container.ListBlobs()
```

Returns an image from the operation →

The map functions are extracted in an independent function and applied in the Async.Parallel pipeline.

The tap function applies side effects to its inputs and the result is ignored.

Runs the asynchronous operations using a run and retry approach

Shares CloudBlobContainer argument among parallel non-blocking computations without contention because it's read-only

Gets the list of images to download ┘

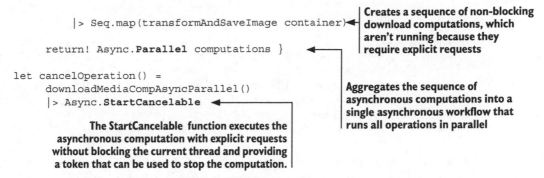

```
                |> Seq.map(transformAndSaveImage container)
        return! Async.Parallel computations }

let cancelOperation() =
    downloadMediaCompAsyncParallel()
    |> Async.StartCancelable
```

Creates a sequence of non-blocking download computations, which aren't running because they require explicit requests

Aggregates the sequence of asynchronous computations into a single asynchronous workflow that runs all operations in parallel

The StartCancelable function executes the asynchronous computation with explicit requests without blocking the current thread and providing a token that can be used to stop the computation.

The `Async.Parallel` function takes an arbitrary collection of asynchronous operations and returns a single asynchronous workflow that will run all the computations in parallel, waiting for all of them to complete. The `Async.Parallel` function coordinates the work with the thread pool scheduler to maximize resource employment using a Fork/Join pattern, resulting in a performance boost.

The library function `Async.Parallel` takes a list of asynchronous computations and creates a single asynchronous computation that starts the individual computations in parallel and waits for their completion to be processed as a whole. When all operations complete, the function returns the results aggregated in a single array. Now you can iterate over the array to retrieve the results for further processing.

Notice the minimal code change and syntax required to convert a computation that executes one operation at a time into one that runs in parallel. Additionally, this conversion is achieved without the need to coordinate synchronization and memory locks.

The `Async.tap` operator applies a function asynchronously to a value passed as input, ignores the result and then returns the original value. The `Tap` operator is introduced in listing 8.3 Here is its implementation using the F# `Async` workflow (in bold):

```
let inline tap (fn:'a -> 'b) (x:Async<'a>) =
        (Async.map fn x) |> Async.Ignore |> Async.Start; x
```

You can find this and other useful `Async` functions in the source code of the book in the FunctionalConcurrencyLib library.

The execution time to download the images in parallel using F# asynchronous workflow in combination with `Async.Parallel` is 10.958 seconds. The result is ~5 seconds faster than APM, which makes it ~8× faster than the original synchronous implementation. The major gains here include code structure, readability, maintainability, and compositionality.

Using an asynchronous workflow, you gained a simple asynchronous semantic to run a non-blocking computation, which provides clear code to understand, maintain, and update. Moreover, thanks to the `Async.Parallel` function, multiple asynchronous computations can easily be spawned in parallel with minimum code changes to dramatically improve performance.

The Async type is not hot

The distinct functional aspect of the asynchronous workflow is its execution time. In F#, when an asynchronous function is called, the `Async<'a>` return type represents a computation that will materialize only with an explicit request. This feature lets you model and compose multiple asynchronous functions that can be executed conditionally on demand. This is the opposite behavior of the C# TAP asynchronous operations (`async/await`), which start the execution immediately.

Ultimately, the implementation of the `Async.StartCancelable` type extension starts an asynchronous workflow, without blocking the thread caller, using a new `Cancellation-Token`, and returns `IDisposable` that cancels the workflow when disposed. You haven't used `Async.Start` because it doesn't provide a continuation-passing semantic, which is useful in many cases to apply the operation to the result of the computation. In the example, you print a message when the computation completes; but the result type is accessible for further processing.

Here's the implementation of the more sophisticated `Async.StartCancelable` operator compared to `Async.Start` (in bold):

```
type Microsoft.FSharp.Control.Async with
    static member StartCancelable(op:Async<'a>) (tap:'a -> unit)(?onCancel)=
        let ct = new System.Threading.CancellationTokenSource()
        let onCancel = defaultArg onCancel ignore
        Async.StartWithContinuations(op, tap, ignore, onCancel, ct.Token)
        { new IDisposable with
            member x.Dispose() = ct.Cancel() }
```

The underlying implementation of the `Async.StartCancelable` function uses the `Async.StartWithContinuations` operator, which provides built-in support for cancellation behavior. When the asynchronous operation `op:Async<'a>` is passed (as the first argument completes), the result is passed as a continuation into the second argument function `tap:'a -> unit`. The optional parameter `onCancel` represents the function that's triggered; in this case, the main operation `op:Async<'a>` is canceled. The result of `Async.StartCancelable` is an anonymous object created dynamically based on the `IDisposable` interface, which will cancel the operation if the `Dispose` method is called.

F# Async API

To create or use the async workflows to program, there's a list of functions that the `Async` module in F# exposes. These are used to trigger other functions providing a variety of ways to create the async workflow. This can be either a background thread or a .NET Framework `Task` object, or running the computation in the current thread itself.

The previously utilized F# Async operators `Async.StartWithContinuations`, `Async.Ignore`, and `Async.Start` may require a bit more explanation.

ASYNC.STARTWITHCONTINUATIONS

`Async.StartWithContinuations` executes an asynchronous workflow starting immediately on the current OS thread, and after its completion passes respectively the result, exception, and cancel (`OperationCancelledException`) to one of specified functions. If the thread that initiates the execution has its own `SynchronizationContext` associated with it, then final continuations will use this `SynchronizationContext` for posting results. This function is a good candidate for updating GUIs. It accepts as arguments three functions to invoke when the asynchronous computation completes successfully, or raises an exception, or is canceled.

Its signature is `Async<'T> ->('T -> unit)*(exn -> unit)*(OperationCanceled-Exception -> unit) -> unit`. `Async.StartWithContinuations` doesn't support a return value because the result of the computation is handled internally by the function targeting the successful output.

Listing 9.7 `Async.StartWithContinuations`

```
let computation() = async {                          The asynchronous computation
    use client = new  WebClient()                       returns a long string.
    let! manningSite =
        client.AsyncDownloadString(Uri("http://www.manning.com"))
    return manningSite
}
                                                     Starts the asynchronous computation
Async.StartWithContinuations(computation(),          immediately using the current OS thread

    (fun site-> printfn "Size %d" site.Length),      The computation completes
                                                     successfully and the continuation
    (fun exn->printfn"exception-%s"<|exn.ToString()),   is invoked, printing the size
                                                     of the downloaded website.
    (fun exn->printfn"cancell-%s"<|exn.ToString())))
```

The operation throws an exception; the exception continuation will execute, printing the exception details.

The operation is canceled, and the cancellation continuation is invoked, printing information regarding the cancellation.

ASYNC.IGNORE

The `Async.Ignore` operator takes a computation and returns a workflow that executes source computation, ignores its result, and returns `unit`. Its signature is `Async.Ignore`: `Async<'T> -> Async<unit>`.

These are two possible approaches that use `Async.Ignore`:

```
Async.Start(Async.Ignore computationWithResult())
```

```
let asyncIgnore = Async.Ignore >> Async.Start
```

The second option creates a function `asyncIgnore`, using function composition to combine the `Async.Ignore` and `Async.Start` operators. The next listing shows the complete example, where the result of the asynchronous operation is ignored using the `asyncIgnore` function (in bold).

Listing 9.8 `Async.Ignore`

```
let computation() = async {
    use client = new  WebClient()
    let! manningSite =
        client.AsyncDownloadString(Uri("http://www.manning.com"))
    printfn "Size %d" manningSite.Length
    return manningSite
}
Async.Ignore (computation())
```

return manningSite ◄────── **This asynchronous computation returns a long string.**

Async.Ignore (computation()) ◄────── **The computation runs asynchronously and the result is discharged (ignored).**

If you need to evaluate the result of an asynchronous operations without blocking, in a pure CPS style, the operator `Async.StartWithContinuations` offers a better approach.

ASYNC.START

The `Async.Start` function in listing 9.9 doesn't support a return value; in fact, its asynchronous computation is type `Async<unit>`. The operator `Async.Start` executes computations asynchronously so the computation process should itself define ways for communication and returning the final result. This function queues an asynchronous workflow for execution in the thread pool and returns control immediately to the caller without waiting to complete. Because of this, the operation can be completed on another thread.

Its signature is `Async.Start: Async<unit> -> unit`. As optional arguments, this function takes a `cancellationToken`.

Listing 9.9 `Async.Start`

```
let computationUnit() = async {
    do! Async.Sleep 1000
    use client = new WebClient()
    let! manningSite =
        client.AsyncDownloadString(Uri("http://www.manning.com"))
    printfn "Size %d" manningSite.Length
    }
Async.Start(computationUnit())
```

let computationUnit() = async { ◄────── **Creates an asynchronous computation to download a website, with a one-second delay to simulate heavy computation**

printfn "Size %d" manningSite.Length ◄────── **Prints the website's size from inside the body of the expression**

Async.Start(computationUnit()) ──► **Runs the computation without blocking the caller thread**

Because `Async.Start` doesn't support a return value, the size of the website is printed inside the expression, where the value is accessible. What if the computation does return a value, and you cannot modify the asynchronous workflow? It's possible to discharge the result from an asynchronous computation using the `Async.Ignore` function before starting the operation.

9.3.6   *Asynchronous workflow cancellation support*

When executing an asynchronous operation, it's useful to terminate execution prematurely, before it completes, on demand. This works well for long-running, non-blocking operations, where making them cancelable is the appropriate practice to avoid tasks that can hang. For example, you may want to cancel the operation of downloading 100 images from Azure Blob storage if the download exceeds a certain period of time. The F# asynchronous workflow supports cancellation natively as an automatic mechanism, and when a workflow is canceled, it also cancels all the child computations.

Most of the time you'll want to coordinate cancellation tokens and maintain control over them. In these cases, you can supply your own tokens, but in many other cases, you can achieve similar results with less code by using the built-in F# asynchronous module default token. When the asynchronous operation begins, this underlying system passes a provided `CancellationToken`, or assigns an arbitrary one if not provided, to the workflow, and it keeps track of whether a cancellation request is received. The computation builder, `AsyncBuilder`, checks the status of the cancellation token during each binding construct (`let!`, `do!`, `return!`, `use!`). If the token is marked "canceled" the workflow terminates.

This is a sophisticated mechanism that eases your work when you don't need to do anything complex to support cancellation. Moreover, the F# asynchronous workflow supports an implicit generation and propagation of cancellation tokens through its execution, and any nested asynchronous operations are included automatically in the cancellation hierarchy during asynchronous computations.

F# supports cancellation in different forms. The first is through the function `Async.StartWithContinuations`, which observes the default token and cancels the workflow when the token is set as canceled. When the cancellation token triggers, the function to handle the cancellation token is called in place of the success one. The other options include passing a cancellation token manually or relying on the default `Async.DefaultCancellationToken` to trigger `Async.CancellationToken` (in bold in listing 9.10).

Listing 9.10 shows how to introduce support for cancellation in the previous `Async.Parallel` image download (listing 9.6). In this example, the cancellation token is passed manually, because in the automatic version using the `Async.DefaultCancellationToken`, there's no code change, only the function to cancel the last asynchronous operation.

Listing 9.10 Canceling an asynchronous computation

```
let tokenSource = new CancellationTokenSource()

let container = getCloudBlobContainer()
let parallelComp() =
    container.ListBlobs()
    |> Seq.map(fun blob -> downloadMediaCompAsync container blob)
    |> Async.Parallel

Async.Start(parallelComp() |> Async.Ignore, tokenSource.Token)

tokenSource.Cancel()
```

Instance of CancellationTokenSource used to generate a CancellationToken

A cancellation token is generated and passed into the asynchronous computation to stop the execution on demand.

You created an instance of a `CancellationTokenSource` that passes a cancellation token to the asynchronous computation, starting the operation with the `Async.Start` function and passing `CancellationToken` as the second argument. Then you cancel the operation, which terminates all nested operations.

In listing 9.11, `Async.TryCancelled` appends a function to an asynchronous workflow. It's this function that will be invoked when the cancellation token is marked. This is an alternative way to inject extra code to run in case of cancellation. The following listing shows how to use the `Async.TryCancelled` function, which also has the advantage of returning a value, providing compositionality. (The code to note is in bold.)

Listing 9.11   Canceling an asynchronous computation with notification

```
let onCancelled = fun (cnl:OperationCanceledException) ->
         printfn "Operation cancelled!"

let tokenSource = new CancellationTokenSource()

let tryCancel = Async.TryCancelled(parallelComp(), onCancelled)
Async.Start(tryCancel, tokenSource.Token)
```

Function that's triggered to handle the OperationCanceledException exception in case an operation is canceled

The parallelComp function is wrapped into the Async.TryCancelled operator to handle the custom behaviors triggered if the operation is canceled.

`TryCancelled` is an asynchronous workflow that can be combined with other computations. Its execution begins on demand with an explicit request, using a starting function such as `Async.Start` or `Async.RunSynchronously`.

ASYNC.RUNSYNCHRONOUSLY

The `Async.RunSynchronously` function blocks the current thread during the workflow execution and continues with the current thread when the workflow completes. This approach is ideal to use in an F# interactive session for testing and in console applications, because it waits for the asynchronous computation to complete. It's not the recommended way to run an asynchronous computation in a GUI program, however, because it will block the UI.

Its signature is `Async<'T> -> 'T`. As optional arguments, this function takes a timeout value and a `cancellationToken`. The following listing shows the simplest way to execute an asynchronous workflow (in bold).

Listing 9.12   `Async.RunSynchronously`

```
let computation() = async {
   do! Async.Sleep 1000
   use client = new  WebClient()
   return! client.AsyncDownloadString(Uri("www.manning.com"))
           }
let manningSite = Async.RunSynchronously(computation())
printfn "Size %d" manningSite.Length
```

Creates an asynchronous computation to download a website

Adds a one-second delay to simulate heavy computation

Downloads a website asynchronously

Prints the size of the downloaded website

Runs the computation

9.3.7 *Taming parallel asynchronous operations*

The `Async.Parallel` programing model is a great feature for enabling I/O parallelism based on the Fork/Join pattern. Fork/Join allows you to execute a series of computation, such that execution branches off in parallel at designated points in the code, to merge at a subsequent point resuming the execution.

But because `Async.Parallel` relies on the thread pool, the maximum degree of parallelism is guaranteed, and, consequently, performance increases. Also, cases exist where starting a large number of asynchronous workflows can negatively impact performance. Specifically, an asynchronous workflow is executed in a semi-preemptive manner, where after many operations (more than 10,000 in a 4 GB RAM computer) begin execution, asynchronous workflows are enqueued, and even if they aren't blocking or waiting for a long-running operation, another workflow is dequeued for execution. This is an edge case that can damage the parallel performance, because the memory consumption of the program is proportional to the number of ready-to-run workflows, which can be much larger than the number of CPU cores.

Another case to pay attention to is when asynchronous operations that can run in parallel are constraints by external factors. For example, running a console application that performs web requests, the default maximum number of concurrent HTTP connections allowed by a `ServicePoint`[4] object is two. In the particular example of Azure Blob storage, you link the `Async.Parallel` to execute multiple long-running operations in parallel, but ultimately, without changing the base configuration, there will be only a limited two parallel web requests. For maximizing the performance of your code, it's recommended you tame the parallelism of the program by throttling the number of concurrent computations.

The following code listing shows the implementation of two functions `Parallel-WithThrottle` and `ParallelWithCatchThrottle`, which can be used to refine the number of running concurrent asynchronous operations.

Listing 9.13 `ParallelWithThrottle` **and** `ParallelWithCatchThrottle`

```
type Result<'a> = Result<'a, exn>                    ◄——  Defines the Result<'a> alias

module Result =
    let ofChoice value =                             ◄——  Helper function to map between
        match value with                                   the Choice and Result DU types
        | Choice1Of2 value -> Ok value
        | Choice2Of2 e -> Error e
                                                           The selector function applies a projection
                                                           to the result of the async computation.
module Async =
    let parallelWithCatchThrottle (selector:Result<'a> -> 'b)   ◄——

                    (throttle:int)                   ◄——  The max number of
                                                           concurrent async operations

            (computations:seq<Async<'a>>) = async {   ◄——

                    Lists async computations to execute in parallel
```

---

[4] Used to get or set the maximum number of concurrent connections allowed.

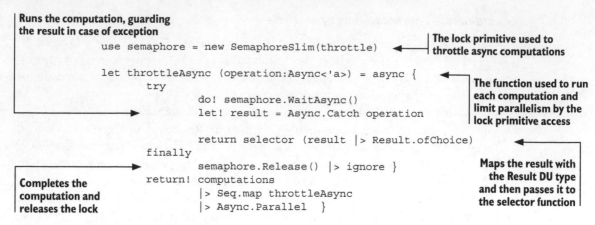

Runs the computation, guarding the result in case of exception

The lock primitive used to throttle async computations

The function used to run each computation and limit parallelism by the lock primitive access

Completes the computation and releases the lock

Maps the result with the Result DU type and then passes it to the selector function

```fsharp
use semaphore = new SemaphoreSlim(throttle)

let throttleAsync (operation:Async<'a>) = async {
    try
        do! semaphore.WaitAsync()
        let! result = Async.Catch operation

        return selector (result |> Result.ofChoice)
    finally
        semaphore.Release() |> ignore }
return! computations
        |> Seq.map throttleAsync
        |> Async.Parallel  }
```

```fsharp
let parallelWithThrottle throttle computations =
    parallelWithCatchThrottle id throttle computations
```

The function `parallelWithCatchThrottle` creates an asynchronous computation that executes all the given asynchronous operations, initially queuing each as work items and using a Fork/Join pattern. The parallelism is throttled, so that the most throttle computations run at one time.

In listing 9.13, the function `Async.Catch` is exploited to protect a parallel asynchronous computation from failure. The function `parallelWithCatchThrottle` doesn't throw exceptions, but instead returns an array of F# `Result` types.

The second function, `parallelWithThrottle`, is a variant of the former function that uses `id` in place of the `selector` argument. The `id` function in F# is called an *identity function*, which is a shortcut for an operation that returns itself: `(fun x -> x)`. In the example, `id` is used to bypass the `selector` and return the result of the operation without applying any transformation.

The release of F# 4.1 introduced the `Result<'TSuccess, 'TError>` type, a convenient DU that supports consuming code that could generate an error without having to implement exception handling. The `Result` DU is typically used to represent and preserve an error that can occur during execution.

The first line of code in the previous listing defined a `Result<'a>` type alias over the `Result<'a, exn>`, which assumes that the second case is always an exception (exn). This `Result<'a>` type alias aims to simplify the pattern matching over the `result`:

```fsharp
let! result = Async.Catch operation
```

You can handle exceptions in F# asynchronous operations in different ways. The most idiomatic is to use `Async.Catch` as a wrapper that safeguards a computation by intercepting all the exceptions within the source computation. `Async.Catch` takes a more functional approach because, instead of having a function as an argument to handle an error, it returns a discriminated union of `Choice<'a, exn>`, where `'a` is the result type of the asynchronous workflow, and exn is the exception thrown. The underlying values of the result `Choice<'a, exn>` can be extracted with pattern matching. I cover error handling in functional programming in chapter 10.

NOTE The nondeterministic behavior of asynchronous parallel computations means you don't know which asynchronous computation will fail first. But the asynchronous combinator `Async.Parallel` reports the first failure between all the computations, and it cancels the other jobs by invoking the cancellation token for the group of tasks.

`Choice<'T, exn>` is a DU[5] with two union cases:

- `Choice1Of2 of 'T` contains the result for successful workflow completion.
- `Choice2Of2 of exn` represents the workflow failure and contains the thrown exception.

Handling exceptions with this functional design lets you construct the asynchronous code in a compositional and natural pipeline structure.

NOTE The `Async.Catch` function preserves information about the error, making it easier to diagnose the problem. Using `Choice<_,_>` lets you use the type system to enforce the processing paths for both results and errors.

`Choice<'T, 'U>` is a DU built into the F# core, which is helpful; but in this case, you can create a better representation of the asynchronous computation result by replacing the DU `Choice` with the meaningful DU `Result<'a>`.[6] (The code to note is in bold.)

Listing 9.14 `ParallelWithThrottle` with Azure Table Storage downloads

```
let maxConcurrentOperations = 100              ◄──────── Sets the limit of max concurrent operations

ServicePointManager.DefaultConnectionLimit <- maxConcurrentOperations   ◄──
                                                          Sets the DefaultConnectionLimit,
let downloadMediaCompAsyncParallelThrottle() = async {    which is two by default
    let! container = getCloudBlobContainerAsync()
    let computations =
        container.ListBlobs()
        |> Seq.map(fun blobMedia -> transformAndSaveImage container blobMedia)

    return! Async.parallelWithThrottle          ◄──────── Executes the async operations,
            maxConcurrentOperations computations }         taming the parallelism
```

Creates a list of async operations → (points to `container.ListBlobs()` line)

The code sets the limit of the concurrent request `maxConcurrentOperations` to 100 using `ServicePointManager.DefaultConnectionLimit`. The same value is passed as an argument to `parallelWithThrottle` to throttle the concurrent requests. `maxConcurrentOperations` is an arbitrary number that can be large, but I recommend that you test and measure the execution time and memory consumption of your program to detect which value has the best performance impact.

---

[5] For more information, see http://mng.bz/03fl.

[6] Introduced in chapter 4.

Summary

- With asynchronous programming, you can download multiple images in parallel, removing hardware dependencies and releasing unbounded computational power.
- The FP language F# provides full support for asynchronous programming integrating within the asynchronous programming model provided by .NET. It also offers an idiomatic functional implementation of the APM called asynchronous workflow, which can interop the task-based programming model in C#.
- The F# asynchronous workflow is based on the Async<'a> type, which defines a computation that will complete sometime in the future. This provides great compositionality properties because it doesn't start immediately. Asynchronous computation requires an explicit request to start.
- The time to perform multiple synchronous I/O operations sequentially is equal to the sum of the time elapsed for each individual operation, in comparison to the asynchronous approach, which runs in parallel, so the overall response time is equal to the slowest operation.
- Using a continuation passing style, which embraces the functional paradigm, your code becomes remarkably concise and easy to write as multithreaded code.
- The F# computation expression, specifically in the form of an asynchronous workflow, performs and chains a series of computations asynchronously without blocking the execution of other work.
- Computation expressions can be extended to operate with different elevated types without the need to leave the current context, or you can create your own to extend the compiler's capabilities.
- It's possible to build tailored asynchronous combinators to handle special cases.

Functional combinators for fluent concurrent programming

10

This chapter covers

- Handling exceptions in a functional style
- Using built-in `Task` combinators
- Implementing custom asynchronous combinators and conditional operators
- Running parallel asynchronous heterogeneous computations

In the previous two chapters, you learned how to apply asynchronous programming to develop scalable and performant systems. You applied functional techniques to compose, control, and optimize the execution of multiple tasks in parallel. This chapter further raises the level of abstraction for expressing asynchronous computations in a functional style.

We'll start by looking at how to manage exceptions in a functional style, with a focus on asynchronous operations. Next, we'll explore *functional combinators*, a useful programming tool for building a set of utility functions that allow you to create complex functions by composing smaller and more concise operators. These combinators and techniques make your code more maintainable and performant, improving your ability to write concurrent computations and handle side effects. Toward the end of this chapter, we'll go through how to interop between C# and F# by calling and passing asynchronous functions from one to the other.

Of all the chapters in this book, this one is the most complex, because it covers FP theory where the lexicon might appear as jargon initially. With great effort, comes great reward . . . .

The concepts explained in this chapter will provide exceptional tools for building sophisticated concurrent programs simply and easily. It's not necessary for the average programmer to know exactly how the .NET garbage collector (GC) works, because it operates in the background. But the developer who understands the operational details of the GC can maximize a program's memory use and performance.

Throughout this chapter, we revisit the examples from chapter 9, with slightly more complex variations. The code examples are in C# or F#, using the programming language that best resonates with the idea in context. But all the concepts apply to both programming languages, and in most cases you'll find the alternate code example in the source code.

This chapter can help you to understand the compositional semantics of functional error handling and functional combinators so you can write efficient programs for processing concurrent (and parallel) asynchronous operations safely, with minimum effort and high-yield performance.

By the end of this chapter, you'll see how to use built-in asynchronous combinators and how to design and implement efficient custom combinators that perfectly meet your applications' requirements. You can raise the level of abstraction in complex and slow-running parts of the code to effortlessly simplify the design, control flow, and reduce the execution time.

10.1 The execution flow isn't always on the happy path: error handling

Many unexpected issues can arise in software development. Enterprise applications, in general, are distributed and depend on a number of external systems, which can lead to a multitude of problems. Examples of these problems are:

- Losing network connectivity during a web request
- Applications that fail to communicate with the server
- Data that becomes inadvertently `null` while processing
- Thrown exceptions

As developers, our goal is to write robust code that accounts for these issues. But addressing potential issues can itself create complexity. In real-world applications, the execution flow isn't always on the "happy path" where the default behavior is error-free (figure 10.1). To prevent exceptions and to ease the debugging process, you must deal with validation logic, value checking, logging, and convoluted code. In general, computer programmers tend to overuse and even abuse exceptions. For example, in code it's common for an exception to be thrown; and, absent the handler in that context, the caller of this piece of code is forced to handle that exception several levels up the call stack.

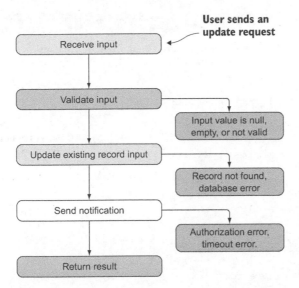

Figure 10.1   The user sends an update request, which can easily stray from the happy path. In general, you write code thinking that nothing can go wrong. But producing quality code must account for exceptions or possible issues such as validation, failure, or errors that prevent the code from running correctly.

In asynchronous programming, error handling is important to guarantee the safe execution of your application. It's assumed that an asynchronous operation will complete, but what if something goes wrong and the operation never terminates? Functional and imperative paradigms approach error handling with different styles:

- The imperative programming approach to handling errors is based on side effects. Imperative languages use the introduction of `try-catch` blocks and `throw` statements to generate side effects. These side effects disrupt the normal program flow, which can be hard to reason about. When using the traditional imperative programming style, the most common approach to handling an error is to guard the method from raising an error and return a `null` value if the payload is empty. This concept of error processing is widely used, but handling errors this way within the imperative languages isn't a good fit because it introduces more opportunities for bugs.

- The FP approach focuses on minimizing and controlling side effects, so error handling is generally done while avoiding mutation of state and without throwing exceptions. If an operation fails, for example, it should return a structural representation of the output that includes the notification of success or failure.

10.1.1   The problem of error handling in imperative programming

In the .NET Framework, it's easy to capture and react to errors in an asynchronous operation. One way is to wrap all the code that belongs to the same asynchronous computation into a `try-catch` block.

To illustrate the error-handling problem and how it can be addressed in a functional style, let's revisit the example of downloading images from Azure Blob storage (covered in chapter 9). Listing 10.1 shows how it makes the method `DownloadImageAsync` safe from exceptions that could be raised during its execution (in bold).

Listing 10.1 `DownloadImageAsync` **with traditional imperative error handling**

```
static async Task<Image> DownloadImageAsync(string blobReference)
{
    try
    {
        var container = await Helpers.GetCloudBlobContainerAsync().
ConfigureAwait(false);
        CloudBlockBlob blockBlob = container.
GetBlockBlobReference(blobReference);
        using (var memStream = new MemoryStream())
        {
            await blockBlob.DownloadToStreamAsync(memStream).
ConfigureAwait(false);
            return Bitmap.FromStream(memStream);
        }
    }
    catch (StorageException ex)
    {
        Log.Error("Azure Storage error", ex);
        throw;
    }
    catch (Exception ex)
    {
        Log.Error("Some general error", ex);
        throw;
    }
}

async RunDownloadImageAsync()
{
    try
    {
        var image = await DownloadImageAsync("Bugghina0001.jpg");
        ProcessImage(image);
    }
    catch (Exception ex)
    {
        HanldlingError(ex);
        throw;
    }
}
```

Observes operations that could raise an exception

Somewhere in the upper the call stack

Handles and re-throws the error to bubble up the exception to the call stack

It seems easy and straightforward: first `DownloadImageAsync` is called by the caller `RunDownloadImageAsync`, and the image returned is processed. This code example already assumes that something could go wrong and wraps the core execution into a `try-catch` block. Banking on the happy path—that's the path in which everything goes right—is a luxury that a programmer cannot afford for building robust applications.

As you can see, when you start accounting for potential failures, input errors, and logging routine, the method starts turning into lengthy boilerplate code. If you remove the error-handling lines of code, there are only 9 lines of meaningful core functionality, compared with 21 of boilerplate orchestration dedicated to error and log handling alone.

A nonlinear program flow like this can quickly become messy because it's hard to trace all existing connections between `throw` and `catch` statements. Furthermore, with exceptions it's unclear exactly where the errors are being caught. It's possible to wrap up the validation routine with a `try-catch` statement right when it's called, or the `try-catch` block can be inserted a couple levels higher. It becomes difficult to know if the error is thrown intentionally.

In listing 10.1, the body of the method `DownloadImageAsync` is wrapped inside a `try-catch` block to safeguard the program in case an exception occurs. But in this case, there's no error handling applied; the exception is rethrown and a log with the error details is applied. The purpose of the `try-catch` block is to prevent an exception by surrounding a piece of code that could be unsafe; but if an exception is thrown, the runtime creates a stack trace of all function calls leading up to the instruction that generated the error.

`DownloadImageAsync` is executed, but what kind of precaution should be used to ensure that potential errors are handled? Should the caller be wrapped up into a `try-catch` block, too, as a precaution?

```
Image image = await DownloadImageAsync("Bugghina001.jpg");
```

In general, the function caller is responsible for protecting the code by checking state of the objects for validity before use. What would happen if the check of state is missing? Easy answer: more problems and bugs appear.

In addition, the complexity of the program increases when the same `Download-ImageAsync` appears in multiple places throughout the code, because each caller could require different error handling, leading to leaks and domain models with unnecessary complexity.

10.2 *Error combinators: Retry, Otherwise, and Task.Catch in C#*

In chapter 8, we defined two extension methods for the `Task` type, `Retry` and `Otherwise` (fallback), for asynchronous `Task` operations that apply logic in case of an exception. Fortunately, because asynchronous operations have external factors that make them vulnerable to exceptions, the .NET `Task` type has built-in error handling via the `Status` and `Exception` properties, as shown here (`Retry` and `Otherwise` are in bold for reference).

Listing 10.2 Refreshing the `Otherwise` **and** `Retry` **functions**

```
static async Task<T> Otherwise<T>(this Task<T> task,
    Func<Task<T>> orTask) =>                                  ◄── Provides a fallback function
        task.ContinueWith(async innerTask => {                    if something goes wrong
            if (innerTask.Status == TaskStatus.Faulted)
    return await orTask();
            return await Task.FromResult<T>(innerTask.Result);
        }).Unwrap();

static async Task<T> Retry<T>(Func<Task<T>> task, int retries, TimeSpan
    delay, CancellationToken cts = default(CancellationToken))        ◄──
        => await task().ContinueWith(async innerTask =>
        {
            cts.ThrowIfCancellationRequested();          Retries the given function a certain
                                                         number of times, with a given delay
                                                                     between attempts
```

```
        if (innerTask.Status != TaskStatus.Faulted)
            return innerTask.Result;
        if (retries == 0)
            throw innerTask.Exception ?? throw new Exception();
        await Task.Delay(delay, cts);
        return await Retry(task, retries - 1, delay, cts);
    }).Unwrap();
```

It's good practice to use the functions `Retry` and `Otherwise` to manage errors in your code. For example, you can rewrite the call of the method `DownloadImageAsync` using the helper functions:

```
Image image = await AsyncEx.Retry(async () =>
    await DownloadImageAsync("Bugghina001.jpg")
    .Otherwise(async () =>
    await DownloadImageAsync("Bugghina002.jpg")),
                    5, TimeSpan.FromSeconds(2));
```

By applying the functions `Retry` and `Otherwise` in the previous code, the function `DownloadImageAsync` changes behavior and becomes safer to run. If something goes wrong when `DownloadImageAsync` is retrieving the image `Bugghina001`, its operation fallback is to download an alternative image. The `Retry` logic, which includes the `Otherwise` (fallback) behavior, is repeated up to five times with a delay of two seconds between each operation, until it's successful (figure 10.2).

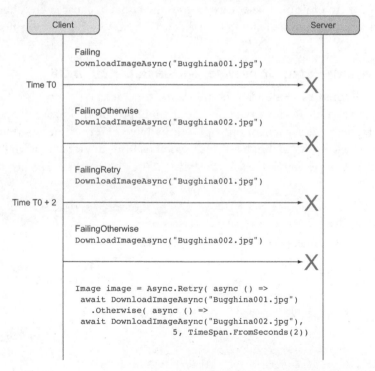

Figure 10.2   The client sends two requests to the server to apply the strategies of `Otherwise` (fallback) and `Retry` in case of failure. These requests (`DownloadImageAsync`) are safe to run because they both apply the `Retry` and `Otherwise` strategies to handle problems that may occur.

Additionally, you can define a further extension method such as the `Task.Catch` function, tailored specifically to handle exceptions generated during asynchronous operations.

Listing 10.3 `Task.Catch` function

```
static Task<T> Catch<T, TError>(this Task<T> task,
    Func<TError, T> onError) where TError : Exception
{
    var tcs = new TaskCompletionSource<T>();
    task.ContinueWith(innerTask =>
    {
        if (innerTask.IsFaulted && innerTask?.Exception?.InnerException
    is TError)
            tcs.SetResult(onError((TError)innerTask.Exception.
    InnerException));
        else if (innerTask.IsCanceled)
            tcs.SetCanceled();
        else if (innerTask.IsFaulted)
            tcs.SetException(innerTask?.Exception?.InnerException ??
    throw new InvalidOperationException());
        else
            tcs.SetResult(innerTask.Result);
    });
    return tcs.Task;
}
```

> An instance of **TaskCompletionSource** returns a **Task** type to keep consistency in the async model.

> Sets the Result or Exception of the **TaskCompletionSource** based on the output of the Task

The function `Task.Catch` has the advantage of expressing specific exception cases as type constructors. The following snippet shows an example of handling `Storage-Exception` in the Azure Blob storage context (in bold):

```
static Task<Image> CatchStorageException(this Task<Image> task) =>
    task.Catch<Image, StorageException>(ex => Log($"Azure Blob
    Storage Error {ex.Message}"));
```

The `CatchStorageException` extension method can be applied as shown in this code snippet:

```
Image image = await DownloadImageAsync("Bugghina001.jpg")
    .CatchStorageException();
```

Yes, this design could violate the principle of nonlocality, because the code used to recover from the exception is different from the originating function call. In addition, there's no support from the compiler to notify the developer that the caller of the `DownloadImageAsync` method is enforcing error handling, because its return type is a regular `Task` primitive type, which doesn't require and convey validation. In this last case, when the error handling is omitted or forgotten, an exception could potentially arise, causing unanticipated side effects that might impact the entire system (beyond the function call), leading to disastrous consequences, such as crashing the application. As you can see, exceptions ruin the ability to reason about the code. Furthermore, the structured mechanism of throwing and catching exceptions in imperative programming has drawbacks that are against functional design principles. As one example, functions that throw exceptions can't be composed or chained the way other functional artifacts can.

Generally, code is read more often than written, so it makes sense that best practices are aimed at simplifying understanding and reasoning about the code. The simpler the code, the fewer bugs it contains, and the easier it is to maintain the software overall. The use of exceptions for program flow control hides the programmer's intention, which is why it's considered a bad practice. Thankfully, you can avoid complex and cluttered code relatively easily.

The solution is to explicitly return values indicating success or failure of an operation instead of throwing exceptions. This brings clarity to potentially error-prone code parts. In the following sections, I show two possible approaches that embrace the functional paradigm to ease the error-handling semantic structure.

10.2.1   *Error handling in FP: exceptions for flow control*

Let's revisit the `DownloadImageAsync` method, but this time handling the error in a functional style. First, look at the code example, followed by the details in the following listing. The new method `DownloadOptionImage` catches the exception in a `try-catch` block as in the previous version of the code, but here the result is the `Option` type (in bold).

Listing 10.4   `Option` type for error handling in a functional style

```
async Task<Option<Image>> DownloadOptionImage(string blobReference)    ◄─────┐
{                                                                             │
    try                                    The output of the function is a composite
    {                                              Task wrapping an Option type.
        var container = await Helpers.GetCloudBlobContainerAsync().
➥ConfigureAwait(false);
        CloudBlockBlob blockBlob = container.
➥GetBlockBlobReference(blobReference);
        using (var memStream = new MemoryStream())
        {
            await
➥ blockBlob.DownloadToStreamAsync(memStream).ConfigureAwait(false);
            return Option.Some(Bitmap.FromStream(memStream));    ◄──────┐
        }                                                               │
    }                                            The result Option type is either a Some
    catch (Exception)                            value for a successful operation or None
    {                                                   (nothing) in case of error.
        return Option.None;    ◄─────────────────────
    }
}
```

The `Option` type notifies the function caller that the operation `DownloadOptionImage` has a particular output, which must be specifically managed. In fact, the `Option` type can have as a result either `Some` or `None`. Consequently, the caller of the function `DownloadOptionImage` is forced to check the result for a value. If it contains the value, then this is a success, but if it doesn't, then it's a failure. This validation requires the programmer to write code to handle both possible outcomes. Use of this design makes the code predictable, avoids side effects, and permits `DownloadOptionImage` to be composable.

CONTROLLING SIDE EFFECTS WITH THE OPTION TYPE

In FP, the notion of `null` values doesn't exist. Functional languages such as Haskell, Scala, and F# resolve this problem by wrapping the `nullable` values in an `Option` type. In F#, the `Option` type is the solution to the null-pointer exception; it's a two-state discriminated union (DU), which is used to wrap a value (`Some`), or no value (`None`). Consider it a box that might contain something or could be empty. Conceptually, you can think the `Option` type as something that's either present or absent. The symbolic definition for `Option` type is

```
type Option<'T> =
| Some of value:T
| None
```

The `Some` case means that data is stored in the associated inner value `T`. The `None` case means there's no data. `Option<Image>`, for example, may or may not contain an image. Figure 10.3 shows the comparison between a nullable primitive type and the equivalent `Option` type.

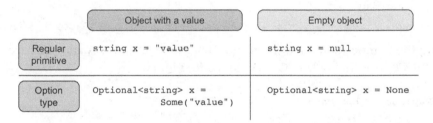

Figure 10.3 This illustrates the comparison between regular `nullable` primitives (first row) and `Option` types (second row). The main difference is that the regular primitive type can be either a valid or invalid (`null`) value without informing the caller, whereas the `Option` type wraps a primitive type suggesting to the caller to check if the underlying value is valid.

An instance of the `Option` type is created by calling either `Some(value)`, which represents a positive response, or `None`, which is the equivalent of returning an empty value. With F#, you don't need to define the `Option` type yourself. It's part of the standard F# library, and there is a rich set of helper functions that go with it.

C# has the `Nullable<T>` type, which is limited to value types. The initial solution is to create a generic `struct` that wraps a value. Using a value type (`struct`) is important for reducing the memory allocation and is ideal for avoiding `null` reference exceptions by assigning a `null` value to an `Option` type itself.

To make the `Option` type reusable, we use a generic C# `struct Option<T>`, which wraps any arbitrary type that may or may not contain a value. The basic structure of `Option<T>` has a property value of type `T` and a flag `HasValue` that indicates whether the value is set.

The implementation of the `Option` type in C# is straightforward, and isn't illustrated here. You can check the source code of this book if you're interested in understanding the C# `Option` type implementation. The higher level of abstraction achieved using the `Option<T>` type allows the implementation of higher-order functions (HOFs), such as `Match` and `Map`, which simplifies the compositional structure of the code, and in this case, with the function `Match`, allows pattern matching and a deconstructive semantic:

```
R Match<R>(Func<R> none, Func<T, R> some) => hasValue ? some(value) : none();
```

The `Match` function belongs to the `Option` type instance, which offers a convenient construct by eliminating unnecessary casts and improving code readability.

10.2.2 *Handling errors with Task<Option<T>> in C#*

In listing 10.4, I illustrated how the `Option` type protects the code from bugs, making the program safer from `null`-pointer exceptions, and suggested that the compiler helps to avoid accidental mistakes. Unlike `null` values, an `Option` type forces the developer to write logic to check if a value is present, thereby mitigating many of the problems of `null` and `error` values.

Back to the Azure Blob storage example, with the `Option` type and the `Match` HOF in place, you can execute the `DownloadOptionImage` function, whose return type is a `Task<Option<Image>>` :

```
Option<Image> imageOpt = await DownloadOptionImage ("Bugghina001.jpg");
```

By using the compositional nature of the `Task` and `Option` types and their extended HOFs, the FP style (in bold) looks like this code snippet:

```
DownloadOptionImage ("Bugghina001.jpg")
     .Map(opt => opt.Match(
                    some: image => image.Save("ImageFolder\Bugghina.jpg"),
                    none: () => Log("There was a problem downloading
➥ the image")));
```

This final code is fluent and expressive, and, more importantly, it reduces bugs because the compiler forces the caller to cover both possible outcomes: success and failure.

10.2.3 *The F# AsyncOption type: combining Async and Option*

The same approach of handling exceptions using the `Task<Option<T>>` type is applicable to F#. The same technique can be exploited in the F# asynchronous workflow for a more idiomatic approach.

The improvement that F# achieves, as compared to C#, is support for *type aliases*, also called *type abbreviations*. A type alias is used to avoid writing a signature repeatedly, simplifying the code experience. Here's the type alias for `Async<Option<'T>>`:

```
type AsyncOption<'T> = Async<Option<'T>>
```

You can use this `AsyncOption<'T>` definition directly in the code in place of `Async-<Option<'T>>` for the same behavior. Another purpose of the type alias is to provide a degree of decoupling between the use of a type and the implementation of a type. This listing shows the equivalent F# implementation of the `DownloadOptionImage` previously implemented in C#.

> **Listing 10.5   F# implementation of the `AsyncOption` type alias in action**

The try-with block safely   **The return type is explicitly set to**
manages potential errors.   **AsyncOption<Image>; this can be omitted.**

```
let downloadOptionImage(blobReference:string) : AsyncOption<Image> =
    async {
        try
            let! container = Helpers.getCloudBlobContainerAsync()
            let blockBlob = container.GetBlockBlobReference(blobReference)
            use memStream = new MemoryStream()
            do! blockBlob.DownloadToStreamAsync(memStream)
            return Some(Bitmap.FromStream(memStream))
        with
        | _ -> return None
    }
```
Constructs the Option type
with a Some value (Image)

```
downloadOptionImage "Bugghina001.jpg"
|> Async.map(fun imageOpt ->
```
Applies the HOF Async.map that accesses and
projects against underlying Option value

```
    match imageOpt with
    | Some(image) -> do! image.SaveAsync("ImageFolder\Bugghina.jpg")
    | None -> log "There was a problem downloading the image")
```

The image SaveAsync extension method implementation   **Pattern matches the Option type to deconstruct**
can be found in the downloadable source code.   **and access the wrapped Image value**

The function `downloadOptionImage` asynchronously downloads an image from Azure Blob storage. The `Async.map` function, with signature `('a -> 'b) -> Async<'a> -> Async<'b>`, wraps the output of the function and allows access to the underlying value. In this case, the generic type `'a` is an `Option<Image>`.

> **NOTE** One important point shown in listing 10.5 is that the linear implementation of asynchronous code allows exception handling in the same way as synchronous code. This mechanism, which is based on the `try-with` block, ensures that the occurring exceptions bubble up through the non-blocking calls and are ultimately handled by the exception handler code. This mechanism is guaranteed to run correctly despite the presence of multiple threads that run in parallel during its execution.

Conveniently, the functions that belong to the F# `Async` module can be applied to the alias `AsyncOption`, because it's an `Async` type that wraps an `Option`. The function inside the `Async.map` operator extracts the `Option` value, which is pattern matched to select the behavior to run according to whether it has the value `Some` or `None`.

10.2.4 *Idiomatic F# functional asynchronous error handling*

At this point, the F# downloadOptionImage function is safely downloading an image, ensuring that it will catch the exception if a problem occurs without jeopardizing the application's stability. But the presence of the try-with block, equivalent to try-catch in C#, should be avoided when possible, because it encourages an impure (with side effects) programming style. In the context of asynchronous computation, the F# Async module provides an idiomatic and functional approach by using the Async.Catch function as a wrapper that protects a computation.

> **NOTE** I introduced Async.Catch in chapter 9. It takes a more functional approach because, instead of having a function as an argument to handle an error, it returns a discriminated union of Choice<'a, exn>, where 'a is the result type of the asynchronous workflow, and exn is the exception thrown.

You can use Async.Catch to safely run and map asynchronous operations into a Choice<'a, exn> type. To reduce the amount of boilerplate required, and generally simplify your code, you can create a helper function that wraps an Async<'T> and returns an AsyncOption<'T> by using the Async.Catch operator. The following code snippet shows the implementation. The helper function ofChoice is supplementary to the F# Option module, whose purpose it is to map and convert a Choice type into an Option type:

```
module Option =
    let ofChoice choice =
        match choice with
        | Choice1Of2 value -> Some value
        | Choice2Of2 _    -> None

module AsyncOption =
        let handler (operation:Async<'a>) : AsyncOption<'a> = async {
            let! result = Async.Catch operation
            return (Option.ofChoice result)
        }
```

Async.Catch is used for exception handling to convert Async<'T> to Async<Choice<'T, exn>>. This Choice is then converted to an Option<'T> using a simple conversion ofChoice function. The AsyncOption handler function can safely run and map asynchronous Async<'T> operations into an AsyncOption type.

Listing 10.6 shows the downloadOptionImage implementation without the need to protect the code with the try-with block. The function AsyncOption.handler is managing the output, regardless of whether it succeeds or fails. In this case, if an error arises, Async.Catch will capture and transform it into an Option type through the Option.ofChoice function (in bold).

Listing 10.6   AsyncOption type alias in action

```
let downloadAsyncImage(blobReference:string) : Async<Image> = async {
        let! container = Helpers.getCloudBlobContainerAsync()
        let blockBlob = container.GetBlockBlobReference(blobReference)
        use memStream = new MemoryStream()
```

```
        do! blockBlob.DownloadToStreamAsync(memStream)
        return Bitmap.FromStream(memStream)
    }

downloadAsyncImage "Bugghina001.jpg"
|> AsyncOption.handler

|> Async.map(fun imageOpt ->

    match imageOpt with
    | Some(image) -> image.Save("ImageFolder\Bugghina.jpg")
    | None -> log "There was a problem downloading the image")
|> Async.Start
```

Executes an asynchronous operation, capturing the exception automatically

Maps the result of the computation to access the underlying imageOpt value

Deconstructs the Option type with pattern matching to handle the different cases

The function AsyncOption.handler is a reusable and composable operator that can be applied to any asynchronous operation.

10.2.5 *Preserving the exception semantic with the Result type*

In section 10.2.2, you saw how the functional paradigm uses the Option type to handle errors and control side effects. In the context of error handling, Option acts as a container, a box where side effects fade and dissolve without creating unwanted behaviors in your program. In FP, the notion of boxing dangerous code, which could throw errors, isn't limited to the Option type.

In this section, you'll preserve the error semantic to use the Result type, which allows different behaviors to dispatch and branch in your program based upon the type of error. Let's say that as part of the implementation of an application, you want to ease the debugging experience or to communicate to the caller of a function the exception details if something goes wrong. In this case, the Option type approach doesn't fit the goal, because it delivers None (nothing) as far as information about what went wrong. While it's unambiguous what a Some result means, None doesn't convey any information other than the obvious. By discarding the exception, it's impossible to diagnose what could have gone wrong.

Going back to our example of downloading an image from Azure Blob storage, if something goes wrong during the retrieval of the data, there are diverse errors generated from different cases, such as the loss of network connectivity and file/image not found. In any event, you need to know the error details to correctly apply a strategy to recover from an exception.

In this listing, the DownloadOptionImage method from the previous example retrieves an image from the Azure Blob storage. The Option type (in bold) is exploited to handle the output in a safer manner, managing the event of errors.

Listing 10.7   Option type, which doesn't preserve error details

```
async Task<Option<Image>> DownloadOptionImage(string blobReference)
    {
        try
        {
            CloudStorageAccount storageAccount =
➥ CloudStorageAccount.Parse("<Azure Connection>");
```

```
                  CloudBlobClient blobClient =
⇒ storageAccount.CreateCloudBlobClient();
                  CloudBlobContainer container =
⇒ blobClient.GetContainerReference("Media");
                  await container.CreateIfNotExistsAsync();

                  CloudBlockBlob blockBlob = container.
⇒ GetBlockBlobReference(blobReference);
                  using (var memStream = new MemoryStream())
                  {
                      await blockBlob.DownloadToStreamAsync(memStream).
⇒ ConfigureAwait(false);
                      return Some(Bitmap.FromStream(memStream));
                  }
              }
              catch (StorageException)
              {
                  return None;
              }
              catch (Exception)
              {
                  return None;
              }
          }
```

Regardless of the exception type raised, the
Option type returns None in both cases.

Regardless of the exception type raised, either a StorageException or a generic Exception, the limitation with the code implementation is that the caller of the method DownloadOptionImage doesn't have any information regarding the exception, so a tailored recover strategy cannot be chosen.

Is there a better way? How can the method provide details of a potential error and avoid side effects? The solution is to use the polymorphic Result<'TSuccess, 'TError> type in place of the Option<'T> type.

Result<'TSuccess, 'TError> can be used to handle errors in a functional style plus carry the cause of the potential failure. Figure 10.4 compares a nullable primitive, the equivalent Option type, and the Result type.

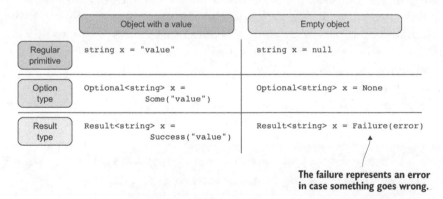

The failure represents an error
in case something goes wrong.

Figure 10.4   Comparing a regular nullable primitive (top row), the Option type (second row), and the Result type (bottom row). The Result Failure is generally used to wrap an error if something goes wrong.

In certain programming languages, such as Haskell, the Result structure is called Either, which represents a logical separation between two values that would never occur at the same time. For example, Result<int, string> models two cases and can have either value int or string.

The Result<'TSuccess, 'TError> structure can also be used to guard your code against unpredictable errors, which makes the code more type safe and side effect free by eliminating the exception early on instead of propagating it.

The F# Result type

The Result type, introduced in chapter 9, is an F# convenient DU that supports consuming code that could generate an error without having to implement exception handling.

Starting with F# 4.1, the Result type is defined as part of the standard F# library. If you're using earlier versions of F#, you can easily define it and its helper functions in a few lines:

```
Type Result<'TSuccess,'TFailure> =
    | Success of 'TSuccess
    | Failure of 'TFailure
```

It's possible, with minimum effort, to interop between the F# core library and C# to share the same F# Result type structure to avoid code repetition. You can find the F# extension methods that facilitate the interoperability of the Result type in C# in the source code.

In listing 10.8, the C# example of the Result type implementation is tailored to be polymorphic in only one type constructor, while forcing the Exception type as an alternative value to handle errors. Consequently, the type system is forced to acknowledge error cases and makes the error-handling logic more explicit and predictable. Certain implementation details are omitted in this listing for brevity but provided in full as part of the downloadable source code.

Listing 10.8 Generic Result<T> type in C#

```
struct Result<T>
{
    public T Ok { get; }
    public Exception Error { get; }          ──┐  Properties to expose the
    public bool IsFailed { get => Error != null; }  values for either the
    public bool IsOk => !IsFailed;              successful or failure
                                                operations

    public Result(T ok)      ◄──────┐
    {                               │
        Ok = ok;                    │
        Error = default(Exception); │
    }                               │
    public Result(Exception error) ◄┘
    {
        Error = error;                Constructors pass the value of the successful
        Ok = default(T);              operation or an exception, in case of failure.
    }
}
```

```
public R Match<R>(Func<T, R> okMap, Func<Exception, R> failureMap)
    => IsOk ? okMap(Ok) : failureMap(Error);

public void Match(Action<T> okAction, Action<Exception> errorAction)
    { if (IsOk) okAction(Ok); else errorAction(Error);}

public static implicit operator Result<T>(T ok) =>
    new Result<T>(ok);
public static implicit operator Result<T>(Exception error) =>
    new Result<T>(error);

public static implicit operator Result<T>(Result.Ok<T> ok) =>
    new Result<T>(ok.Value);
public static implicit operator Result<T>(Result.Failure error) =>
    new Result<T>(error.Error);
}
```

Implicit operators automatically convert any primitive type into a Result.

This convenient Match function deconstructs the Result type and applies dispatching behavioral logic.

The interesting part of this code is in the final lines where the implicit operators simplify the conversion to `Result` during the assignment of primitives. This auto-construct to `Result` type should be used by any function that potentially returns an error.

Here, for example, is a simple synchronous function that loads the bytes of a given file. If the file doesn't exist, then a `FileNotFoundException` exception is returned:

```
static Result<byte[]> ReadFile(string path)
{
    if (File.Exists(path))
        return File.ReadAllBytes(path);
    else
        return new FileNotFoundException(path);
}
```

As you can see, the output of the function `ReadFile` is a `Result<byte[]>`, which wraps either the successful outcome of the function that returns a byte array, or the failure case that returns a `FileNotFoundException` exception. Both return types, `Ok` and `Failure`, are implicitly converted without a type definition.

> **NOTE** The purpose of the `Result` class is similar to the `Option` type discussed earlier. The `Result` type allows you to reason about the code without looking into the implementation details. This is achieved by providing a choice type with two cases, an `Ok` case to return the value when the function succeeds, and a `Failure Error` case to return the value when the function failed.

10.3   *Taming exceptions in asynchronous operations*

The polymorphic `Result` class in C# is a reusable component that's recommended for taming side effects in the case of functions that could generate exceptions. To indicate that a function can fail, the output is wrapped with a `Result` type. The following listing shows the previous `DownloadOptionImage` function refactored to follow the `Result` type model (in bold). The new function is named `DownloadResultImage`.

Listing 10.9 `DownloadResultImage`: **handling errors and preserving semantics**

```
async Task<Result<Image>> DownloadResultImage(string blobReference)
{
    try
    {
        CloudStorageAccount storageAccount =
➥ CloudStorageAccount.Parse("<Azure Connection>");
        CloudBlobClient blobClient =
➥ storageAccount.CreateCloudBlobClient();
        CloudBlobContainer container =
➥ blobClient.GetContainerReference("Media");
        await container.CreateIfNotExistsAsync();

        CloudBlockBlob blockBlob = container.
➥GetBlockBlobReference(blobReference);
        using (var memStream = new MemoryStream())
        {
            await blockBlob.DownloadToStreamAsync(memStream).
➥ConfigureAwait(false);
            return Image.FromStream(memStream);           ◄─────┐
        }                                                        │
    }                                                            │
    catch (StorageException exn)                                 │
    {                                                            │
        return exn;                              ◄───────────────┤
    }                                                            │
    catch (Exception exn)                                        │
    {                                                            │
        return exn;                              ◄───────────────┘
    }
}
```

The Result type implicit operators allow automatic wrapping of the primitive types into a Result, which is also wrapped into a Task.

It's important that the `Result` type provides the caller of the `DownloadResultImage` function the information necessary to handle each possible outcome in a tailored manner, including different error cases. In this example, because `DownloadResultImage` is calling a remote service, it also has the `Task` effect (for asynchronous operations) as well as the `Result` effect. In the Azure storage example (from listing 10.9), when the current state of an image is retrieved, that operation will hit the online media storage. It's recommended to make it asynchronous, as I've mentioned, so the `Result` type should be wrapped in a `Task`. The `Task` and `Result` effects are generally combined in FP to implement asynchronous operations with error handling.

Before diving into how to use the `Result` and `Task` types in combination, let's define a few helper functions to simplify the code. The static class `ResultExtensions` defines a series of useful HOFs for the `Result` type, such as `bind` and `map`, which are applicable for a convenient fluent semantic to encode common error-handling flows. For brevity purpose, in the following listing only the helper functions that treat the `Task` and `Result` types are shown (in bold). The other overloads are omitted, with the full implementation available in the code samples.

> **Listing 10.10**   `Task<Result<T>>` **helper functions for compositional semantics**

```
static class ResultExtensions
{
    public static async Task<Result<T>> TryCatch<T>(Func<Task<T>> func)
    {
        try
        {
            return await func();
        }
        catch (Exception ex)
        {
            return ex;
        }
    }

static async Task<Result<R>> SelectMany<T, R>(this Task<Result<T>>
➥ resultTask, Func<T, Task<Result<R>>> func)
{
    Result<T> result = await resultTask.ConfigureAwait(false);
    if (result.IsFailed)
        return result.Error;
    return await func(result.Ok);
}

static async Task<Result<R>> Select<T, R>(this Task<Result<T>> resultTask,
➥ Func<T, Task<R>> func)
{
    Result<T> result = await resultTask.ConfigureAwait(false);
    if (result.IsFailed)
        return result.Error;
    return await func(result.Ok).ConfigureAwait(false);
}
static async Task<Result<R>> Match<T, R>(this Task<Result<T>> resultTask,
➥ Func<T, Task<R>> actionOk, Func<Exception, Task<R>> actionError)
{
    Result<T> result = await resultTask.ConfigureAwait(false);
    if (result.IsFailed)
        return await actionError(result.Error);
    return await actionOk(result.Ok);
}
}
```

The `TryCatch` function wraps a given operation into a `try-catch` block to safeguard the code from any exceptions if a problem arises. This function is useful for lifting and combining any `Task` computation into a `Result` type. In the following code snippet, the function `ToByteArrayAsync` asynchronously converts a given image into a byte array:

```
Task<Result<byte[]>> ToByteArrayAsync(Image image)
{
    return TryCatch(async () =>
```

```
    {
        using (var memStream = new MemoryStream())
        {
            await image.SaveImageAsync(memStream, image.RawFormat);
            return memStream.ToArray();
        }
    });
}
```

The underlying `TryCatch` function ensures that regardless of the behavior in the operation, a `Result` type is returned which wraps either a successful (`Ok` byte array) or a failure (`Error` exception).

The extension methods `Select` and `SelectMany`, part of the `ResultExtensions` class, are generally known in functional programming as, respectively, `Bind` (or `flatMap`) and `Map`. But in the context of .NET and specifically in C#, the names `Select` and `SelectMany` are the recommended terms because they follow the LINQ convention, which notifies the compiler that treats these functions as LINQ expressions to ease their composition semantic structure. Now, with the higher-order operators from the `ResultExtensions` class, it's easy to fluently chain a series of actions that operate on the underlying `Result` value without leaving the context.

The following listing shows how the caller of `DownloadResultImage` can handle the execution flow in the case of success or failure as well as chaining the sequence of operations (the code to note is in bold).

Listing 10.11 Composing `Task<Result<T>>` operations in functional style

> **Uses HOFs to effortlessly combine the functions, returning the composite type `Task<Result<T>>`**

```
async Task<Result<byte[]>> ProcessImage(string nameImage, string
        destinationImage){
    return await DownloadResultImages(nameImage)
            .Map(async image => await ToThumbnail(image))
            .Bind(async image => await ToByteArrayAsync(image))
            .Tap(async bytes =>
                    await File.WriteAllBytesAsync(destinationImage,
➥ bytes));
```

The WriteAllBytesAsync extension method implementation can be found in the downloadable source code.

As you can see from the `ProcessImage` function signature, providing documentation that a function might have error effects is one of the advantages of using the `Result` type. `ProcessImage` first downloads a given image from the Azure Blob storage, then converts it into a thumbnail format using the `Bind` operator, which checks the previous `Result` instance, and if it's successful, executes the delegate passed in. Otherwise, the `Bind` operator returns the previous result. The `Map` operator also verifies the previous `Result` value and acts accordingly by extracting the byte array from the image.

The chain continues until one of the operations fails. If failure occurs, then the other operations are skipped.

NOTE   The `Bind` function operates over lifted values, in this case a `Task<Result <Image>>`. In contrast, the `Map` function performs against an unwrapped type.

Ultimately, the result byte array is saved in the destination path (`destinationImage`) specified, or a log is executed if an error occurred. Rather than handling failure individually on each call, you should add the failure handling at the end of the computation chain. This way, the failure-handling logic is at a predictable place in the code, making it easier to read and maintain.

You should understand that if any of these operations fails, the rest of the tasks are bypassed and none executed until the first function that handles the error (figure 10.5). In this example, the error is handled by the function `Match` (with the lambda `action- Error`). It's important to perform compensation logic in case the call to a function isn't successful.

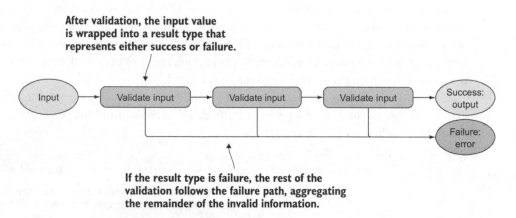

Figure 10.5   The `Result` type handles the operations in a way that, if during each step there is a failure, the rest of the tasks are bypassed and not executed until the first function that handles the error. In this figure, if any of the validations throws an error, the rest of computation is skipped until the `Failure` handler (the `Error` circle).

Because it's both hard and inconvenient to extract the inner value of a `Result` type, use the composition mechanisms of functional error handling. These mechanisms force the caller to always handle both the success and the failure cases. Using this design of the `Result` type, the program flow is declarative and easy to follow. Exposing your intent is crucial if you want to increase readability of your code. Introducing the `Result` class (and the composite type `Task<Result<T>>`) helps to show, without side effects, if the method can fail or isn't signaling something is wrong with your system. Furthermore, the type system becomes a helpful assistant for building software by specifying how you should handle both successful and failure outcomes.

The `Result` type provides a conditional flow in a high-level functional style, where you pick a strategy for dealing with the error and register that strategy as a handler. When the lower-level code hits the error, it can then pick a handler without unwinding the call stack. This gives you more options. You can choose to cope with the problem and continue.

10.3.1 *Modeling error handling in F# with Async and Result*

The previous section discussed the concept of Task and Result types combined for providing safe and declarative error handling in a functional style. In addition to the TPL, the asynchronous workflow computation expression in F# offers a more idiomatic functional approach. This section covers the recipe for taming exceptions by showing how to combine the F# Async type with the Result structure.

Before looking in depth at the F# error-handling model for asynchronous operations, we should define the type structure necessary. First, to fit into the context of error handling (specifically), as explained in chapter 9, you should define a Result<'a> type alias over Result<'a, exn>, which assumes that the second case is always an exception (exn). This alias Result<'a> simplifies pattern matching and deconstruction over the Result<'a, exn> type:

```
Result<'TSuccess> = Result<'TSuccess, exn>
```

Second, the type construct Async has to wrap this Result<'a> structure to define a new type that's used in concurrent operations to signal when an operation is completed. You need to treat Async<'a> and Result<'a> as a single type, which can be done easily using an alias types that acts as a combinatorial structure:

```
type AsyncResult<'a> = Async<Result<'a>>
```

The AsyncResult<'a> type carries the value of an asynchronous computation, with either a success or failure outcome. In the case of an exception, the error information is preserved. Conceptually, AsyncResult is a separate type.

Now, taking inspiration from the AsyncOption type in section 10.2.2, define a helper function AsyncResult.handler to run a computation lifting the output into a Result type. For this purpose, the F# Async.Catch function denotes a perfect fit. The following listing shows a custom alternative representation of Async.Catch, called AsyncResult.handler.

> **Listing 10.12** `AsyncResult` **handler to catch and wrap asynchronous computations**

```
module Result =
    let ofChoice value =
        match value with        ◄——  Maps the function from the Choice DU, which
        | Choice1Of2 value -> Ok value     is the returned type of the Async.Catch
        | Choice2Of2 e -> Error e          operator, to the Result type DU cases. This
                                           map function was defined in chapter 9.

module AsyncResult =
    let handler (operation:Async<'a>) : AsyncResult<'a> = async {
        let! result = Async.Catch operation   ◄——┐

        return (Result.ofChoice result) }        Runs the asynchronous operation
        ▲                                         using the Async.Catch operator to
    The output of the function is                 safeguard against possible error
    mapped in favor of the Result type.
```

The F# AsyncResult.handler is a powerful operator that dispatches the execution flow in case of error. In a nutshell, the AsyncResult.handler runs the Async.Catch function in the background for error handling and uses the ofChoice function to map the product of the computation (Choice<Choice1Of2, Choice2Of2> Discriminated Union) to the Result<'a> DU cases, which then branch the result of the computation respectively to the OK or Error union. (ofChoice was introduced in chapter 9.)

10.3.2 Extending the F# AsyncResult type with monadic bind operators

Before we go further, let's define the monadic helper functions to deal with the Async-Result type.

Listing 10.13   HOF extending the AsyncResult type

```
module AsyncResult =
    let retn (value:'a) : AsyncResult<'a> =
      value |> Ok |> async.Return
```
← Lifts an arbitrary given value into the AsyncResult type

```
    let map (selector : 'a -> Async<'b>) (asyncResult : AsyncResult<'a>)
      : AsyncResult<'b> =
        async {
            let! result = asyncResult
            match result with
            | Ok x -> return! selector x |> handler
            | Error err -> return (Error err)    }
```
← Maps an AsyncResult type running the underlying asynchronous operation asyncResult and applies the given selector function to the result

```
    let bind (selector : 'a -> AsyncResult<'b>) (asyncResult
      : AsyncResult<'a>) = async {
            let! result = asyncResult
            match result with
            | Ok x -> return! selector x
            | Error err -> return Error err    }
```
← Binds a monadic operator that performs a given function over the AsyncResult elevated type

```
    let bimap success failure operation = async {
        let! result = operation
        match result with
        | Ok v -> return! success v |> handler
        | Error x -> return! failure x |> handler }
```
← Executes either the success or failure function against the AsyncResult type operation by branching the result of the computation respectively to the OK or Error union

Uses the AsyncResult.handler function to handle either the success or failure of the async operation

The map and bind higher-order operators are the general functions used for composition. These implementations are straightforward:

- The retn function lifts an arbitrary value 'a into an AsyncResult<'a> elevated type.
- The let! syntax in the map operator extracts the content from the Async (runs it and awaits the result), which is the Result<'a> type. Then, the selector function is applied on a Result value contained in the Ok case using the AsyncResult. handler function, because the outcome of the computation can be success or failure. Ultimately, the result is returned wrapped in the AsyncResult type.
- The function bind uses continuation passing style (CPS) to pass a function that will run a successful computation to further process the result. The continuation function selector crosses the two types Async and Result and has the signature 'a -> AsyncResult<'b>.

- If the inner `Result` is successful, then the continuation function `selector` is evaluated with the result. The `return!` syntax means that the return value is already lifted.
- If the inner `Result` is a failure, then the failure of the async operation is lifted.
- The return syntax in `map`, `retn`, and `bind` lifts the `Result` value to an `Async` type.
- The `return!` syntax in `bind` means that the value is already lifted and not to call `return` on it.
- The `bimap` function aims to execute the asynchronous operation `AsyncResult` and then branches the execution flow to one of the continuation functions, either `success` or `failure`, according to the result.

Alternatively, to make the code more succinct, you can use the built-in function `Result.map` to turn a value into a function that works on a `Result` type. Then, if you pass the output to `Async.map`, the resulting function works on an asynchronous value. Using this compositional programming style, for example, the `AsyncResult` map function can be rewritten as follows:

```
module AsyncResult =
    let map (selector : 'a -> 'b) (asyncResult : AsyncResult<'a>) =
        asyncResult |> Async.map (Result.map selector)
```

This programming style is a personal choice, so you should consider the tradeoff between succinct code and its readability.

THE F# ASYNCRESULT HIGHER-ORDER FUNCTIONS IN ACTION

Let's see how to perform the `AsyncResult` type and its HOFs `bind`, `map`, and `return`. Let's convert the C# code in listing 10.7 that downloads an image from Azure Blob storage into an idiomatic F# way to handle errors in an asynchronous operation context.

We stay with the Azure Blob storage example to simplify the understanding of the two approaches with a direct comparison by converting a function that you're already familiar with (figure 10.6).

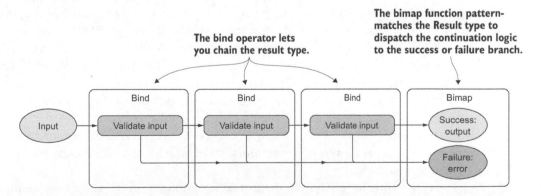

Figure 10.6   The validation logic can be composed fluently with minimum effort, by applying the higher-order operators `bind` and `bimap`. Furthermore, at the end of the pipeline, the `bimap` function pattern-matches the `Result` type to dispatch the continuation logic to either the `success` or `failure` branch in a convenient and declarative style.

This listing shows the processImage function implemented using the F# AsyncResult type with its higher-order compositional operators (in bold).

Listing 10.14   Using AsyncResult HOFs for fluent composition

```
let processImage(blobReference:string) (destinationImage:string)
    : AsyncResult<unit> =
        async {
            let storageAccount = CloudStorageAccount.Parse("< Azure
    Connection >")
            let blobClient = storageAccount.CreateCloudBlobClient()
            let container = blobClient.GetContainerReference("Media")
            let! _ = container.CreateIfNotExistsAsync()
            let blockBlob = container.GetBlockBlobReference(blobReference)
            use memStream = new MemoryStream()
            do! blockBlob.DownloadToStreamAsync(memStream)
            return Bitmap.FromStream(memStream) }
        |> AsyncResult.handler
        |> AsyncResult.bind(fun image -> toThumbnail(image))
        |> AsyncResult.map(fun image -> toByteArrayAsync(image))
        |> AsyncResult.bimap
                (fun bytes -> FileEx.
    WriteAllBytesAsync(destinationImage, bytes))
                (fun ex -> logger.Error(ex) |> AsyncResult.retn)
```

AsyncResult.retn lifts the logger function into the AsyncResult elevated type to match the output signature.

The AsyncResult higher-order operator can be composed in a fluent style.

The behavior of processImage is similar to the related C# method processImage from listing 10.7; the only difference is the result definition AsyncResult type. Semantically, due to the intrinsic F# (|>) pipe operator, the AsyncResult functions handler, bind, map, and bimap are chained in a fluent style, which is the nearest equivalent to the concept of fluent interfaces (or method chaining) used in the C# version of the code.

RAISING THE ABSTRACTION OF THE F# ASYNCRESULT WITH COMPUTATION EXPRESSION

Imagine that you want to further abstract the syntax from code listing 10.12 so you can write AsyncResult computations in a way that can be sequenced and combined using control flow constructs. In chapter 9, you built custom F# *computational expressions* (CEs) to retry asynchronous operations in case of errors. CEs in F# are a safe way of managing the complexity and mutation of state. They provide a convenient syntax to manage data, control, and side effects in functional programs.

In the context of asynchronous operations wrapped into an AsyncResult type, you can use CEs to handle errors elegantly to focus on the happy path. With the Async-Result monadic operators bind and return in place, implementing the related computation expression requires minimal effort to achieve a convenient and fluid programming semantic.

Here, the code listing defines the monadic operators (in bold) for the computation builder that combines the Result and Async types:

```
Type AsyncResultBuilder () =
    Member x.Return m = AsyncResult.retn m
```

```
    member x.Bind (m, f:'a -> AsyncResult<'b>) = AsyncResult.bind f m
    member x.Bind (m:Task<'a>, f:'a -> AsyncResult<'b>) =
            AsyncResult.bind f (m |> Async.AwaitTask |> AsyncResult.handler)
    Ember x.ReturnFrom m = m

Let asyncResult = AsyncResultBuilder()
```

You can add more members to the `AsyncResultBuilder` CE if you need support for more advanced syntax; this is the minimal implementation required for the example. The only line of code that requires a clarification is the `Bind` with `Task<'a>` type:

```
member x.Bind (m:Task<'a>, f) =
            AsyncResult.bind f (m |> Async.AwaitTask
   |> AsyncResult.handler)
```

In this case, as explained in section 9.3.3, the F# CE lets you inject functions to extend the manipulation to other wrapper types, in this case `Task`, whereas the `Bind` function in the extension lets you fetch the inner value contained in the elevated type using the `let!` and `do!` operators. This technique removes the need for adjunctive functions such as `Async.AwaitTask`. The downloadable source code of this book contains a more complete implementation of the `AsyncResultBuilder` CE, but the extra CE implementation details aren't relevant or part of this book's scope.

A simple CE deals with asynchronous calls that return a `Result` type and can be useful for performing computations that may fail and then chain the results together. Let's transform, once again, the `processImage` function, but this time the computation is running inside the `AsyncResultBuilder` CEs, as shown in bold in this listing.

Listing 10.15 Using `AsyncResultBuilder`

```
let processImage (blobReference:string) (destinationImage:string)
   : AsyncResult<unit> =
    asyncResult {
        let storageAccount = CloudStorageAccount.Parse("<Azure Connection>")
        let blobClient = storageAccount.CreateCloudBlobClient()
        let container = blobClient.GetContainerReference("Media")
        let! _ = container.CreateIfNotExistsAsync()
        let blockBlob = container.GetBlockBlobReference(blobReference)
        use memStream = new MemoryStream()
        do! blockBlob.DownloadToStreamAsync(memStream)
        let image = Bitmap.FromStream(memStream)
        let! thumbnail = toThumbnail(image)
        return! toByteArrayAsyncResult thumbnail
    }
    |> AsyncResult.bimap (fun bytes ->
   FileEx.WriteAllBytesAsync(destinationImage, bytes))
                        (fun ex -> logger.Error(ex) |> async.Return.retn)
```

Wraps the code block into an asyncResult to make the bind operator run in the context of the AsyncResultBuilder CEs

Now, all you need do is wrap the operations inside an `asyncResult` CE block. The compiler can recognize the monadic (CE) pattern and treats the computations in a special way. When the `let!` bind operator is detected, the compiler automatically translates the `AsyncResult.Return` and `AsyncResult.Bind` operations of a CE in context.

10.4   *Abstracting operations with functional combinators*

Let's say you need to download and analyze the history of a stock ticker symbol, or you decide you need to analyze the history of more than one stock to compare and contrast the best ones to buy. It's a given that downloading data from the internet is an I/O-bound operation that should be executed asynchronously. But suppose you want to build a more sophisticated program, where downloading the stock data depends on other asynchronous operations (figure 10.7). Here are several examples:

- If either the NASDAQ or the NYSE index is positive
- If the last six months of the stock has a positive trend
- If the volume of the stock compiles any number of positive criteria to buy

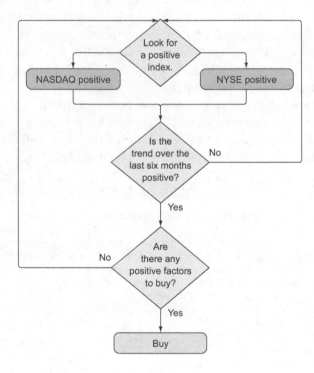

Figure 10.7   This diagram represents a sequential decision tree for buying stock. Each step likely involves an I/O operation to asynchronously interrogate an external service. You must be thoughtful in your approach to maintain this sequential flow, while performing the whole decision tree asynchronously.

What about running the flow in figure 10.7 for each stock symbol that you're interested in? How would you combine the conditional logic of these operations while keeping the asynchronous semantic to parallelize the execution? How would you design the program?

The solution is *functional asynchronous combinators*. The following sections cover the characteristics of functional combinators, with the focus on asynchronous combinators. We'll cover how to use the built-in support in the .NET Framework and how to build and tailor your own asynchronous combinators to maximize the performance of your program using a fluid and declarative functional programming style.

10.5 Functional combinators in a nutshell

The imperative paradigm uses procedural control mechanisms such as `if-else` statements and `for/while` loops to drive a program's flow. This is contrary to the FP style. As you leave the imperative world behind, you'll learn to find alternatives to fill in that gap. A good solution is to use function combinators that orchestrate the flow of the program. FP mechanisms make it easy to combine two or more solutions from smaller problems into a single abstraction that solves a larger problem.

Abstraction is a pillar of FP, which allows you to develop an application without worrying about the implementation details, allowing you to focus on the more important high-level semantics of the program. Essentially, abstraction captures the core of what a function or a whole program does, making it easier to get things done.

In FP, a *combinator* refers to either a function with no free variables (https://wiki .haskell.org/Pointfree) or a pattern for composing and combining any types. This second definition is the central topic of this section.

From a practical viewpoint, *functional combinators* are programming constructs that allow you to merge and link primitive artifacts, such as other functions (or other combinators), and behave as pieces of control logic together, working to generate more-advanced behaviors. In addition, functional combinators encourage modularity, which supports the objective to abstract functions into components that can be understood and reused independently, with codified meaning derived from rules governing their composition. You were introduced to this concept previously with the definition of asynchronous functions (combinators) such as `Otherwise` and `Retry` for the C# Task-based Asynchronous Programming (TAP) model and the F# `AsyncResult.handler`.

In the context of concurrent programming, the main reason to use combinators is to implement a program that can handle side effects without compromising a declarative and compositional semantic. This is possible because combinators abstract away from the developer implementation details that might handle side effects underneath, with the purpose of offering functions that compose effortlessly. Specifically, this section covers combinators that compose asynchronous operations.

If the side effects are limited to the scope of a single function, then the behavior calling that function is idempotent. *Idempotent* means the operation can be applied multiple times without changing the result beyond the initial application—the effect doesn't change. It's possible to chain these idempotent functions to produce complex behaviors where the side effects are isolated and controlled.

10.5.1 The TPL built-in asynchronous combinators

The F# asynchronous workflow and the .NET TPL provide a set of built-in combinators, such as `Task.Run`, `Async.StartWithContinuation`, `Task.WhenAll`, and `Task.WhenAny`. These can be easily extended for implementing useful combinators to compose and build more sophisticated task-based patterns. For example, both the `Task.WhenAll` and the F# `Async.Parallel` operators are used to asynchronously wait on multiple asynchronous operations; the underlying results of those operations are grouped to continue. This continuation is the key that provides opportunities for composing the flow of a program in more complex structures, such as implementing the Fork/Join and Divide and Conquer patterns.

Let's start with a simple case in C# to understand the benefits of combinators. Imagine you must run three asynchronous operations and calculate the sum of their output, awaiting each in turn. Note that each operation takes one second to compute:

```
async Task<int> A() { await Task.Delay(1000); return 1; }
async Task<int> B() { await Task.Delay(1000); return 3; }
async Task<int> C() { await Task.Delay(1000); return 5; }

int a = await A();
int b = await B();
int c = await C();

int result = a + b + c;
```

The result (9) is computed in three seconds, one second for each operation. But what if you want to run those three methods in parallel? To run more than one background task, there are methods available to help you coordinate them. The simplest solution to run multiple tasks concurrently is to start them consecutively and collect references to them. The TPL `Task.WhenAll` operator accepts a `params` array of tasks, and returns a task that is signaled when all the others are complete. You can eliminate the intermediate variables from that last example to make the code less verbose:

```
var results = (await Task.WhenAll(A(), B(), C())).Sum();
```

The results come back in an array, and then the `Sum()` LINQ operator is applied. With this change, the result is computed in only one second. Now the task can completely represent an asynchronous operation and provide synchronous and asynchronous capabilities for joining with the operation, retrieving its results, and so on. This lets you build useful libraries of combinators that compose tasks to build larger patterns.

10.5.2 Exploiting the Task.WhenAny combinator for redundancy and interleaving

A benefit of using tasks is that they enable powerful composition. Once you have a single type capable of representing any arbitrary asynchronous operation, you can write combinators over the type that allow you to combine/compose asynchronous operations in myriad ways.

For example, the TPL `Task.WhenAny` operator allows you to develop parallel programs where one task of multiple asynchronous operations must be completed before the main thread can continue processing. This behavior of asynchronously waiting for the first operation to complete over a given set of tasks, before notifying the main thread for further processing, facilitates the design of sophisticated combinators. Redundancy, interleaving, and throttling are examples of properties that are derived from these combinators.

REDUNDANCY   Executes an asynchronous operation multiple times and selects the one that completes first.

INTERLEAVING   Launches multiple operations but processes them in the order they complete. This was discussed in section 8.5.7.

Consider the case where you want to buy an airplane ticket as soon as possible. You have a few airline web services to contact, but depending on web traffic, each service can have a different response time. In this case, you can use the Task.WhenAny operator to contact multiple web services to produce a single result, selected from the one that completes the fastest.

Listing 10.16   Redundancy with `Task.WhenAny`

Uses CancellationToken to cancel the operations still running after the first one completes

The conceptual asynchronous function that fetches the price of a flight from a given carrier

```
var cts = new CancellationTokenSource();

Func<string, string, string, CancellationToken, Task<string>>
    GetBestFlightAsync = async (from, to, carrier, token) => {
        string url = $"flight provider{carrier}";
        using(var client = new HttpClient()) {
        HttpResponseMessage response = await client.GetAsync(url, token);
        return await response.Content.ReadAsStringAsync();
    }};
```

Lists asynchronous operations to execute in parallel

```
var recommendationFlights = new List<Task<string>>()
{
    GetBestFlightAsync("WAS", "SF", "United", cts.Token),
    GetBestFlightAsync("WAS", "SF", "Delta", cts.Token),
    GetBestFlightAsync("WAS", "SF", "AirFrance", cts.Token),

};
```

Waits for the first operation to complete with the Task.WhenAny operator

Retrieves the result in a try-catch block to accommodate potential exceptions. Even if a first task completes successfully, subsequent tasks may fail.

```
Task<string> recommendationFlight = await Task.
    WhenAny(recommendationFlights);
while (recommendationFlights.Count > 0)
{
    try
    {
        var recommendedFlight = await recommendationFlight;
        cts.Cancel();
        BuyFlightTicket("WAS", "SF", recommendedFlight);
        break;
    }
    catch (WebException)
    {
        recommendationFlights.Remove(recommendationFlight);
    }
}
```

If the operation is successful, the other computations still running are canceled.

In the code, Task.WhenAny returns the task that completed first. It's important to know if the operation completes successfully, because if there's an error you want to discharge the result and wait for the next computation to complete. The code must handle exceptions using a try-catch, where the computation that failed is removed from the list of asynchronous recommended operations. When a first task completes successfully, you want to be sure to cancel the others still running.

10.5.3   *Exploiting the Task.WhenAll combinator for asynchronous for-each*

The Task.WhenAll operator waits asynchronously on multiple asynchronous computations that are represented as tasks. Consider that you want to send an email message to all your contacts. To speed up the process, you want to send the email to all recipients in parallel without waiting for each separate message to complete before sending the next. In such a scenario, it would be convenient to process the list of emails in a for-each loop. How would you maintain the asynchronous semantic of the operation, while sending the emails in parallel? The solution is to implement a ForEachAsync operator based on the Task.WhenAll method.

Listing 10.17   Asynchronous for-each loop with Task.WhenAll

```
static Task ForEachAsync<T>(this IEnumerable<T> source,
    int maxDegreeOfParallelism, Func<T, Task> body)
{
    return Task.WhenAll(
        from partition in Partitioner.Create(source).
      GetPartitions(maxDegreeOfParallelism)
        select Task.Run(async () =>
            {
                using (partition)
                while (partition.MoveNext())
                await body(partition.Current);
        }));
}
```

For each partition of the enumerable, the operator ForEachAsync runs a function that returns a Task to represent the completion of processing that group of elements. Once the work starts asynchronously, you can achieve concurrency and parallelism, invoking the body for each element and waiting on them all at the end, rather than waiting for each in turn.

The Partitioner created limits the number of operations that can run in parallel to avoid making more tasks than necessary. This maximum degree of parallelism value is managed by partitioning the input data set into maxDegreeOfParallelism number of chunks and scheduling a separate task to begin execution for each partition. The ForEachAsync batches work to create fewer tasks than total work items. This can provide significantly better overall performance, especially if the loop body has a small amount of work per item.

NOTE   This last example is similar in nature to `Parallel.ForEach`, the primary difference being that `Parallel.ForEach` is a synchronous method and uses synchronous delegates.

Now you can use the `ForEachAsync` operator to send multiple emails asynchronously.

Listing 10.18   Using the asynchronous `for-each` loop

```
async Task SendEmailsAsync(List<string> emails)
{
    SmtpClient client = new SmtpClient();
    Func<string, Task> sendEmailAsync = async emailTo =>
    {
        MailMessage message = new MailMessage("me@me.com", emailTo);
        await client.SendMailAsync(message);
    };

    await emails.ForEachAsync(Environment.ProcessorCount, sendEmailAsync);
}
```

These are a few simple examples that show how to use the built-in TPL combinators `Task.WhenAll` and `Task.WhenAny`. In section 10.6, you'll focus on constructing custom combinators and composing existing ones in which both F# and C# principles apply. You'll see that there's an infinite number of combinators. We'll look at several of the most common ones that are used to implement an asynchronous logical flow in a program: `ifAsync`, `AND` (async), and `OR` (async).

Before jumping into building asynchronous combinators, let's review the functional patterns that have been discussed so far. This refresher will lead to a new functional pattern, which is used to compose heterogeneous concurrent functions. Don't worry if you aren't familiar with this term; you will be shortly.

10.5.4 *Mathematical pattern review: what you've seen so far*

In the previous chapters, I introduced the concepts of monoids, monads, and functors, which come from a branch of mathematics called *category theory*. Additionally, I discussed their important relationship to functional programming and functional concurrency.

Category theory lexicon

Category theory is a branch of mathematics that defines any collection of objects that can relate to each other via morphisms in sensible ways, such as composition and associativity. *Morphisms* is a buzzword that defines something that can mutate; think of applying a `map` (or `select`) function from one mathematical structure to another. Essentially, category theory consists of objects and arrows that are connected to each other, providing the basis of the composition. Category theory is a powerful idea generated from a need to organize mathematical concepts based on shared structure. Many useful concepts fall under the category theory umbrella, but you don't need to have a mathematical background to understand them and use their powerful properties, which for the majority are all about creating opportunities for composition.

In programming, these mathematical patterns are adopted to control the execution of side effects and to maintain functional purity. These patterns are interesting because of their properties of abstraction and compositionality. Abstraction favors composability, and together they're the pillars of functional and concurrent programming. The following sections rehash the definition of these mathematical concepts.

MONOIDS FOR DATA PARALLELISM

A monoid, as explained earlier, is a binary associative operation with an identity; it provides a way to mash values of the same type together. The associative property allows you to run a computation in parallel effortlessly by providing the ability to divide a problem into chunks so it can be computed independently. Then, when each block of computation completes, the result is recomposed. A variety of interesting parallel operations turn out to be both associative and commutative, expressed using monoids: `Map-Reduce` and `Aggregation` in various forms such as `sum`, `variance`, `average`, `concatenation`, and more. The .NET PLINQ, for example, uses monoidal operations that are both associative and commutative to parallelize work correctly.

The following code example, based on content from chapter 4, shows how to use PLINQ for parallelizing the `sum` of the power of an array segment. The data set is partitioned in subarrays that are accumulated separately on their own threads using the accumulator initialized to the seed. Ultimately, all accumulators will be combined using the final reduce function (the `AsParallel` function is in bold):

```
var random = new Random();
var size = 1024 * Environment.ProcessorCount;
int[] array = Enumerable.Range(0, size).Select(_ =>
   random.Next(0, size)).ToArray();

long parallelSumOfSquares = array.AsParallel()
    .Aggregate(
      seed: 0,                                              Seed for each partition
      updateAccumulatorFunc: (partition, value) =>
   partition + (int)Math.Pow(value, 2),
      combineAccumulatorsFunc: (partitions, partition) =>
   partitions + partition,
      resultSelector: result => result);
```

Despite the unpredictable order of the computation compared to the sequential version of the code, the result is deterministic because of the associativity and commutativity properties of the + operator.

FUNCTORS TO MAP ELEVATED TYPES

The functor is a pattern of mapping over elevated structures, which is archived and provides support for a two-parameter function called `Map` (also known as `fmap`). The type signature of the `Map` function takes as a first argument the function `(T -> R)`, which in C# is translated into `Func<T, R>`. When given an input type `T`, it applies a transformation and returns a type `R`. A functor elevates functions with only one input.

The LINQ/PLINQ `Select` operator can be considered a functor for the `IEnumerable` elevated type. Mainly, functors are used in C# to implement LINQ-style fluent APIs that are used for types other than collections. In chapter 7, you implemented a functor for the `Task` elevated type (the `Map` function is in bold):

```
static Task<R> Map<T, R>(this Task<T> input, Func<T, R> map) =>
                        input.ContinueWith(t => map(t.Result));
```

The function `Map` takes a function map (`T -> R`) and a functor (wrapped context) `Task<T>` and returns a new functor `Task<R>` containing the result of applying the function to the value and closing it once more.

The following code, from chapter 8, downloads an icon image from a given website and converts it into a bitmap. The operator `Map` is applied to chain the asynchronous computations (the code to note is in bold).

```
Bitmap icon = await new HttpClient()
                .GetAsync($"http://{domain}/favicon.ico")
                .Bind(async content => await
                    content.Content.ReadAsByteArrayAsync())
                .Map(bytes =>
                    Bitmap.FromStream(new MemoryStream(bytes)));
```

This function has a signature (`T -> R`) `-> Task<T> -> Task<R>`, which means that it takes a map function `T -> R` as the first input that goes from a value type `T` to a value type `R`, and then upgrades the type `Task<T>` as a second input and returns the `Task<R>`.

A functor is nothing more than a data structure that you can use to map functions with the purpose of lifting values into a wrapper (elevated type), modifying them, and then putting them back into a wrapper. The reason for having `fmap` return the same elevated type is to continue chaining operations. Essentially, functors create a context or an abstraction that allows you to securely manipulate and apply operations to values without changing any original values.

MONADS TO COMPOSE WITHOUT SIDE EFFECTS

Monads are a powerful compositional tool used in functional programming to avoid dangerous and unwanted behaviors (side effects). They allow you to take a value and apply a series of transformations in an independent manner encapsulating side effects. The type signature of monadic function calls out potential side effects, providing a representation of both the result of the computation and the actual side effects that occurred as a result. A monadic computation is represented by generic type `M<'a>` where the type parameter specifies the type of value (or values) produced as the result of monadic computation (internally, the type may be a `Task` or `List`, for example). When writing code using monadic computations, you don't use the underlying type directly. Instead you use two operations that every monadic computation must provide: `Bind` and `Return`.

These operations define the behavior of the monad and have the following type signatures (for certain monads of type `M<'a>` that could be replaced with `Task<'a>`):

```
Bind: ('a -> M<'b>) -> M<'a> -> M<'b>
Return: 'a -> M<'a>
```

The `Bind` operator takes an instance of an elevated type, extracts the underlying value from it, and runs the function over that value, returning a new elevated value:

```
Task<R> Bind<R, T>(this Task<T> task, Func<T, Task<R>> continuation)
```

You can see in this implementation that the `SelectMany` operator is built into the LINQ/PLINQ library.

`Return` is an operator that lifts (wraps) any type into a different elevated context (monad type, like `Task`), usually converting a non-monadic value into a monadic value. For example, `Task.FromResult` produces a `Task<T>` from any given type `T` (in bold):

```
Task<T> Return<T>(T value) => Task.FromResult(value);
```

These monadic operators are essential to LINQ/PLINQ and generate the opportunity for many other operators. For example, the previous code that downloads and converts an icon from a given website into a bitmap format can be rewritten using the monadic operators (in bold) in the following manner:

```
Bitmap icon = await (from content in new HttpClient().GetAsync($"http://
    {domain}/favicon.ico")
                    from bytes in content.Content.ReadAsByteArrayAsync())
                    select Bitmap.FromStream(new MemoryStream(bytes)));
```

The monad pattern is an amazingly versatile pattern for doing function composition with amplifying types while maintaining the ability to apply functions to instances of the underlying types. Monads also provide techniques for removing repetitive and awkward code and can allow you to significantly simplify many programming problems.

What is the importance of laws?

As you've seen, each of the mathematical patterns mentioned must satisfy specific laws to expose their property, but why? The reason is, laws help you to reason about your program, providing information for the expected behavior of the type in context. Specifically, a concurrent program must be deterministic; therefore, a deterministic and predictable way to reason about the code helps to prove its correctness. If an operation is applied to combine two monoids, then you can assume, due to the monoid laws, that the computation is associative, and the result type is also a monoid. To write concurrent combinators, it's important to trust the laws that are derived from the abstract interface, such as monads and functors.

10.6 *The ultimate parallel composition applicative functor*

At this point, I've discussed how a functor (`fmap`) can be used to upgrade functions with one argument to work with elevated types. You've also learned how the monadic `Bind` and `Return` operators are used to compose elevated types in a controlled and fluent manner. But there's more! Let's assume that you have a function from the *normal world*: for example, a method that processes an image to create a `Thumbnail` over a given `Bitmap` object. How would you apply such functionality to values from the *elevated world* `Task<Bitmap>`?

> **NOTE** *Normal world*, in this case, refers to a function that performs over a normal primitive, such as a bitmap. In contrast, a function from the *elevated world* would operate against an elevated type: for example, a bitmap elevated to `Task<Bitmap>`.

Here's the function ToThumbnail to process a given image (the code to note is in bold):

```
Image ToThumbnail (Image bitmap, int maxPixels)
{
    var scaling = (bitmap.Width > bitmap.Height)
                    ? maxPixels / Convert.ToDouble(bitmap.Width)
                    : maxPixels / Convert.ToDouble(bitmap.Height);
    var width = Convert.ToInt32(Convert.ToDouble(bitmap.Width) * scaling);
    var heiht = Convert.ToInt32(Convert.ToDouble(bitmap.Height) * scaling);
    return new Bitmap(bitmap.GetThumbnailImage(width, height, null,
    IntPtr.Zero));
}
```

Although you can obtain a substantial number of different compositional shapes using core functions such as map and bind, there's the limitation that these functions take only a single argument as an input. How can you integrate multiple-argument functions in your workflows, given that map and bind both take as input a unary function? The solution is *applicative functors*.

Let's start with a problem to understand the reasons why you should apply the Applicative Functor pattern (technique). The functor has the map operator to upgrade functions with one and only one argument.

It's common that functions that map to elevated types usually take more than one argument, such as the previous ToThumbnail method that takes an image as the first argument and the maximum size in pixels for the image transformation as the second argument. The problem with such functions is that they aren't easy to elevate in other contexts. If you load an image, for simplicity using the Azure Blob storage function DownloadImageAsync as earlier, and later you want to apply the ToThumbnail function transformation, then the functor map cannot be used because the type signature doesn't match. ToThumbnail (in bold in the following listing) takes two arguments, while the map function takes a single argument function as input.

Listing 10.19 Compositional limitation of the Task functor map

```
Task<R> map<T, R>(this Task<T> task, Func<T, R> map) =>
                                    task.ContinueWith(t => map(t.Result));

static async Task<Image> DownloadImageAsync(string blobReference)
{
    var container = await Helpers.GetCloudBlobContainerAsync().
    ConfigureAwait(false);
    CloudBlockBlob blockBlob = container.
    GetBlockBlobReference(blobReference);
    using (var memStream = new MemoryStream())
    {
        await blockBlob.DownloadToStreamAsync(memStream).
    ConfigureAwait(false);
        return Bitmap.FromStream(memStream);
    }
}
static async Bitmap CreateThumbnail(string blobReference, int maxPixels)
```

```
{
    Image thumbnail =
            await DownloadImageAsync("Bugghina001.jpg")
                .map(ToThumbnail);                    ◄─────┐ Compilation error
    return thumbnail;
}
```

The problem with this code is that it doesn't compile when you're trying to apply ToThumbnail to the Task map extension method map(ToThumbnail). The compiler throws an exception due to the signature mismatch.

How can you apply a function to several contexts at once? How can a function that takes more than one argument be upgraded? This is where applicative functors come into play to apply a multi-parameter function over an elevated type. The following listing exploits applicative functors to compose the ToThumbnail and DownloadImageAsync functions, matching the type signature and maintaining the asynchronous semantic (in bold).

Listing 10.20   Better composition of the asynchronous operation

```
Static Func<T1, Func<T2, TR>> Curry<T1, T2, TR>(this Func<T1, T2, TR> func) =>
➥ p1 => p2 => func(p1, p2);

static async Task<Image> CreateThumbnail(string blobReference, int maxPixels)
{
    Func<Image, Func<int, Image>> ToThumbnailCurried =
➥ Curry<Image, int, Image>(ToThumbnail);           ◄─────────────┤ Curries the function

    Image thumbnail = await TaskEx.Pure(ToThumbnailCurried)
                        .Apply(DownloadImageAsync(blobReference))
                        .Apply(TaskEx.Pure(maxPixels));

    return thumbnail;                                 Uses an applicative function to chain the
}                                                     computations without exiting the Task context
```

Lifts the function ToThumbnailCurried
to the Task elevated type

Let's explore this listing for clarity. The Curry function is part of a helper static class, which is used to facilitate FP in C#. In this case, the curried version of the method ToThumbnail is a function that takes an image as input, and returns a function that takes an integer (int) as input for the maximum size in pixels allowed, and as output an Image type: Func<Image, Func<int, Image>> ToThumbnailCurried. Then, this unary function is wrapped in the container Task type, and overloads so greater arities can be defined by currying that function.

In practice, the function that takes more than one argument, in this case ToThumbnail, is curried and lifted into the Task type using the Task Pure extension method. Then, the resulting Task<Func<Image, Func<int, Image>>> is passed over the applicative functor Apply, which injects its output, Task<Image>, into the next function applied over DownloadImageAsync.

Ultimately, the last applicative functor operator `Apply` handles the transient parameter `maxPixels` elevated using the `Pure` extension method. From the perspective of the functor `map` operator, the curried function `ToThumbnailCurried` is partially applied and is exercised against an `image` argument and then wrapped into the task. Therefore, conceptually, the signature is

```
Task<ToThumbnailCurried(Image)>
```

The function `ToThumbnailCurried` takes an `image` as input and then returns the partially applied function in the form of a `Func<int, Image>` delegate, whose signature definition correctly matches the input of the applicative functor: `Task<Func<int, Image>>`.

The `Apply` function can be viewed as a partial application for elevated functions, whose next value is provided for every call in the form of an elevated (boxed) value. In this way, you can turn every argument of a function into a boxed value.

Currying and partial application

Currying is the technique of transforming a function with multiple arguments into a series of functions with only one argument, which always returns a value. The F# programming language performs currying automatically. In C# you need to enable it manually or rather by using a defined helper function, as in the example. This is the reason why function signatures in FP are represented with multiple -> symbols, which is basically the symbol for a function. Look at a signature such as: `string -> int -> Image`.

The function has two arguments, `string` and `int`, and it returns `Image`. But the correct way to read the function signature is a function that has only one argument: `string`. It will return a new function with signature `int -> Image`.

In C#, the lack of support for the currying technique and partial application may make the applicative functor seem inconvenient. But after practice you'll break through the initial barrier and see the real power and flexibility of the applicative functor technique.

Partial application refers to a function of many arguments that doesn't have to be applied to all its inputs at once. You can imagine that applying it to the first argument doesn't yield a value but rather a function on $n - 1$ arguments. In this spirit, you could bind a multi-parameter function to a single `Task` and get an asynchronous operation of $n - 1$ arguments. Then you are left with the problem of applying a task of a function to a task of an argument, and that's exactly what the applicative pattern solves.

More details about currying can be found in appendix A.

The Applicative Functor pattern aims to lift and apply a function over an elevated context, and then apply a computation (transformation) to a specific elevated type. Because both the value and the function are applied in the same elevated context, they can be smashed together.

Let's analyze the functions `Pure` and `Apply`. An applicative functor is a pattern implemented by two operations, defined here, where `AF` represents any elevated type (in bold):

```
Pure  : T -> AF<R>
Apply : AF<T -> R> -> AF<T> -> F<R>
```

Intuitively, the `Pure` operator lifts a value into an elevated domain, and it's equivalent to the `Return` monadic operator. The name `Pure` is a convention for an applicative functor definition. But in the case of applicative functions, this operator elevates a function. The `Apply` operator is a two-parameter function, both part of the same elevated domain.

From the code example in the section "Functors to map elevated types," you can see that an applicative functor is any container (elevated type) that offers a way to transform a normal function into one that operates on contained values.

> **NOTE** An applicative functor is a construct to provide the midpoint between functor's `map` and monad's `bind`. Applicative functors can work with elevated functions, because the values are wrapped in a context, the same as functors, but in this case the wrapped value is a function. This is useful if you want to apply a function that's inside a functor to a value inside a functor.

Applicative functors are useful when sequencing a set of actions in parallel without the need for any intermediate results. In fact, if the tasks are independent, then their execution can be composed and parallelized using an applicative. An example is running a set of concurrent actions that read and transform parts of a data structure in order, then combine their results, shown in figure 10.8.

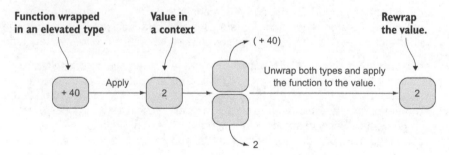

Figure 10.8   The `Apply` operator implements the function wrapped inside an elevated type to a value in the context. The process triggers the unwrapping of both values; then, because the first value is a function, it's applied automatically to the second value. Finally, the output is wrapped back inside the context of the elevated type.

In the context of the `Task` elevated type, it takes a value `Task<T>` and a wrapped function `Task<(T -> R)>` (translated in C# as `Task<Func<T, R>>`) and then returns a new value Task<R> generated by applying the underlying function to the value of Task<T>:

```
static Task<R> Apply<T, R>(this Task<Func<T, R>> liftedFn, Task<T> task) {
    var tcs = new TaskCompletionSource<R>();
    liftedFn.ContinueWith(innerLiftTask =>
            task.ContinueWith(innerTask =>
                tcs.SetResult(innerLiftTask.Result(innerTask.Result))
        ));
            return tcs.Task;
}
```

Here's a variant of the Apply operator defined for async Task in the TAP world, which can be implemented rather than in terms of async/await:

```
static async Task<R> Apply<T, R> (this Task<Func<T, R>> f, Task<T> arg)
                => (await f. ConfigureAwait(false))
                   (await arg.ConfigureAwait(false));
```

Both Apply functions have the same behavior despite their different implementations. The first input value of Apply is a function wrapped into a Task: Task<Func<T, R>>. This signature could look strange initially, but remember that in FP, functions are treated as values and can be passed around in the same way as strings or integers.

Now, extending the Apply operator to a signature that accepts more inputs becomes effortless. This function is an example:

```
static Task<Func<b, c>> Apply<a, b, c>(this Task<Func<a, b, c>> liftedFn,
➡ Task<a> input) =>
```

Apply(liftedFn.**map**(**Curry**), input);

Notice that this implementation is clever, because it applies the Curry function to Task<Func<a, b, c>> liftedFn using the functor map, and then applies it over the elevated input value using the Apply operator with smaller arity as previously defined. With this technique, you continue to expand the Apply operator to take as an input a function lifted with any number of parameters.

> **NOTE** The Apply operator has the argument order inverted compared to the standard signature because it's implemented as a static method to ease its use.

It turns out that functor and applicative functor work well together to facilitate composition, including the composition of expressions running in parallel. When passing a function with more than one argument to the functor map, the result type matches the input of the Apply function.

You can use an alternative way to implement an applicative functor in terms of using the monadic operators bind and return. But this approach prevents the code from running in parallel, because the execution of an operation would depend on the outcome of the previous one.

With the applicative functor in place, it's effortless to compose a series of computations with no limit on the number of arguments each expression takes. Let's imagine that you need to blend two images to create a third new image, which is the overlap of the given images into a frame having a specific size. This listing shows you how (the Apply function is in bold).

Listing 10.21   Parallelizing the chain of computation with applicative functors

```
static Image BlendImages(Image imageOne, Image imageTwo, Size size)
{
    var bitmap = new Bitmap(size.Width, size.Height);
    using (var graphic = Graphics.FromImage(bitmap)) {
        graphic.InterpolationMode = InterpolationMode.HighQualityBicubic;
        graphic.DrawImage(imageOne,
                new Rectangle(0, 0, size.Width, size.Height),
                new Rectangle(0, 0, imageOne.Width, imageTwo.Height),
                GraphicsUnit.Pixel);
        graphic.DrawImage(imageTwo,
                new Rectangle(0, 0, size.Width, size.Height),
                new Rectangle(0, 0, imageTwo.Width, imageTwo.Height),
                GraphicsUnit.Pixel);
        graphic.Save();
    }
    return bitmap;
}
async Task<Image> BlendImagesFromBlobStorageAsync(string blobReferenceOne,
➥  string blobReferenceTwo, Size size)
{
        Func<Image, Func<Image, Func<Size, Image>>> BlendImagesCurried =
                            Curry<Image, Image, Size, Image>(BlendImages);
        Task<Image> imageBlended =
                TaskEx.Pure(BlendImagesCurried)
                    .Apply(DownloadImageAsync(blobReferenceOne))
                    .Apply(DownloadImageAsync(blobReferenceTwo))
                    .Apply(TaskEx.Pure(size));
            return await imageBlended;
}
```

When you call Apply the first time, with the DownloadImageAsync(blobReferenceOne) task, it immediately returns a new Task without waiting for the DownloadImageAsync task to complete; consequently, the program immediately goes on to create the second DownloadImageAsync(blobReferenceTwo). As a result, both tasks run in parallel.

The code assumes that all the functions have the same input and output; but this is not a constraint. As long as the output type of an expression matches the input of the next expression, then the computation is still enforced and valid. Notice that in listing 10.21, each call starts independently, so they run in parallel and the total execution time for BlendImagesFromBlobStorageAsync to complete is determined by the longest time required of the Apply calls to complete.

> **Apply vs. bind**
>
> The differential behavior between the `bind` and `Apply` operators is denoted by their function signature. In the context of an async workflow, for example, the first `Async` type in the `bind` operator is executed and awaiting completion to start the second async operation. The `bind` operator should be used when the execution of an async operation depends on the returned value of another async operation.
>
> The `Apply` operator has provided both async operations as an argument in the signature. It should be used when the async operations can be started independently.
>
> These concepts are valid for other elevated types such as the `Task` type.

This example enforces the compositional aspect of concurrent functions. Alternatively, you could implement custom methods that blend the images directly, but in the larger scheme this approach enables the flexibility to combine more sophisticated behaviors.

10.6.1 Extending the F# async workflow with applicative functor operators

Continuing your introduction to applicative functors, in this section you'll practice the same task concepts to extend the F# asynchronous workflow. Note that F# supports the TPL because it is part of the .NET ecosystem, and the applicative functors are based on the `Task` type applied.

The following listing implements the two applicative functor operators `pure` and `apply`, which are purposely defined inside the `Async` module to extend this type. Note that because `pure` is a future reserved keyword in F#, the compiler will give a warning.

Listing 10.22   F# async applicative functor

```
module Async =
    let pure value = async.Return value          ◄─────┤ Lifts value to an Async

    let apply funAsync opAsync = async {                     Starts the two
       let! funAsyncChild = Async.StartChild funAsync   ◄─── asyncs in parallel
       let! opAsyncChild = Async.StartChild opAsync

       let! funAsyncRes = funAsyncChild
       let! opAsyncRes = opAsyncChild          ◄─────┤ Waits for the results
       return funAsyncRes opAsyncRes
    }
```

The `apply` function executes the two parameters, `funAsync` and `opAsync`, in parallel using the Fork/Join pattern, and then it returns the result of applying the output of the first function against the other.

Notice that the implementation of the `apply` operator runs in parallel because each asynchronous function starts the evaluation using the `Async.StartChild` operator.

The Async.StartChild operator

The `Async.StartChild` operator takes a computation that starts within an asynchronous workflow, and returns a token (of type `Async<'T>`) that can be used to wait until the operation completes. Its signature is as follows:

```
Async.StartChild : Async<'T> * ?int -> Async<Async<'T>>
```

This mechanism allows multiple asynchronous computations to be executed simultaneously. If a parent computation requests the result and the child computation isn't finished, then the parent computation is suspended until the child completes.

Let's see the capabilities that these functions provide in place. The same applicative functor concepts introduced in C# apply here; but the compositional semantic style provided in F# is nicer. Using the F# pipe (|>) operator to pass the intermediate result of a function on to the next one produces a more readable code.

The following listing implements the same chain of functions using the applicative functor in F# for blending asynchronously two images, as shown in C# in listing 10.21. In this case, the function blendImagesFromBlobStorage in F# returns an Async type rather than a Task (in bold).

Listing 10.23   Parallel chain of operations with an F# async applicative functor

```
let blendImages (imageOne:Image) (imageTwo:Image) (size:Size) : Image =
    let bitmap = new Bitmap(size.Width, size.Height)
    use graphic = Graphics.FromImage(bitmap)
    graphic.InterpolationMode <- InterpolationMode.HighQualityBicubic
    graphic.DrawImage(imageOne,
                        new Rectangle(0, 0, size.Width, size.Height),
                        new Rectangle(0, 0, imageOne.Width, imageTwo.
Height),
                        GraphicsUnit.Pixel)
    graphic.DrawImage(imageTwo,
                    new Rectangle(0, 0, size.Width, size.Height),
                        new Rectangle(0, 0, imageTwo.Width, imageTwo.
Height),
                        GraphicsUnit.Pixel)
    graphic.Save() |> ignore
    bitmap :> Image

let blendImagesFromBlobStorage (blobReferenceOne:string)
    (blobReferenceTwo:string) (size:Size) =
    Async.apply(
        Async.apply(
            Async.apply(
                Async.``pure`` blendImages)
                (downloadOptionImage(blobReferenceOne)))
                (downloadOptionImage(blobReferenceTwo)))
                (Async.``pure`` size)
```

The function `blendImages` is lifted to the `Task` world (elevated type) using the `Async`
`.pure` function. The resulting function, which has the signature `Async<Image ->`
`Image -> Size -> Image>`, is applied over the output of the functions `download-`
`OptionImage(blobReferenceOne)` and `downloadOptionImage(blobReferenceTwo)`.
The lifted value `size` runs in parallel.

As mentioned earlier, functions in F# are curried by default; the extra boilerplate
required in C# isn't necessary. Even if F# doesn't support applicative functors as a
built-in feature, it's easy to implement the `apply` operator and exercise its compositional benefits. But this code isn't particularly elegant, because the `apply` function operators are nested rather than chained. A better way is to create a custom infix operator.

10.6.2 *Applicative functor semantics in F# with infix operators*

A more declarative and convenient approach in F# to write functional composition is
to use custom infix operators. Unfortunately, this feature isn't supported in C#. The
support for custom infix operators means that you can define operators to achieve
the desired level of precedence when operating over the arguments passed. An infix
operator in F# is an operator that's expressed using a mathematical notation called
infix notation. For example, the multiply operator takes two numbers that are then multiplied by each other. In this case, using infix notation, the multiplication operator is
written between the two numbers it operates on. Operators are basically two-argument
functions, but in this case, instead of writing a function `multiply x y`, an infix operator
is positioned between the two arguments: `x Multiply y`.

You're already familiar with a few infix operators in F#: the `|>` pipe operator and `>>`
composition operators. But according to section 3.7 of the F# language specification,
you can define your own operators. Here, an infix operator (in bold) is defined for
both asynchronous functions `apply` and `map`:

```
let (<*>) = Async.apply
let (<!>) = Async.map
```

> **NOTE** The `<!>` operator is the infix version of `Async.map`, while the `<*>` opera-
> tor is the infix version of `Async.apply`. These infix operators are generally used
> in other programming languages such as Haskell, so they've become the stan-
> dard. The `<!>` operator is defined as `<$>` in other programming languages; but
> in F# the `<$>` operator is reserved for future use, so `<!>` is used.

Using these operators, you can rewrite the previous code in a more concise manner:

```
let blendImagesFromBlobStorage (blobReferenceOne:string)
   (blobReferenceTwo:string) (size:Size) =
      blendImages
      <!> downloadOptionImage(blobReferenceOne)
      <*> downloadOptionImage(blobReferenceOne)
      <*> Async.``pure`` size
```

In general, I recommend that you not overuse or abuse the utilization of infix operators, but instead find the right balance. You can see how, in the case of functors and
applicative functors, the infix operator is a welcome feature.

10.6.3 *Exploiting heterogeneous parallel computation with applicative functors*

Applicative functors lead to a powerful technique that allows you to write heterogeneous parallel computations. *Heterogeneous* means an object is composed of a series of parts of different kinds (versus *homogenous*, of a similar kind). In the context of parallel programming, it means executing multiple operations together, even if the result type between each operation is different.

For example, with the current implementation, both the F# `Async.Parallel` and the TPL `Task.WhenAll` take as an argument a sequence of asynchronous computations having the same result type. This technique is based on the combination of applicative functors and the concept of lifting, which aims to elevate any type into a different context. This idea is applicable to values and functions; in this specific case, the target is functions with an arbitrary cardinality of different argument types. To enable this feature to run heterogeneous parallel computation, the applicative functor `apply` operator is combined with the technique of lifting a function. This combination is then used to construct a series of helpful functions generally called `Lift2`, `Lift3`, and so forth. The `Lift` and `Lift1` operators aren't defined because they're functor `map` functions.

The following listing shows the implementation of the `Lift2` and `Lift3` functions in C#, which represents a transparent solution to performing parallel `Async` returning heterogeneous types. Those functions will be used next.

Listing 10.24   C# asynchronous lift functions

The lift functions apply a given function to the outputs of a set of Tasks.

```
static Task<R> Lift2<T1, T2, R>(Func<T1, T2, R > selector, Task<T1> item1,
    Task<T2> item2)
{
        Func<T1, Func<T2, R>> curry = x => y => selector(x, y);
        var lifted1 = Pure(curry);
        var lifted2 = Apply(lifted1, item1);
        return Apply(lifted2, item2);
}

static Task<R> Lift3<T1, T2, T3, R>(Func<T1, T2, T3, R> selector,
    Task<T1> item1, Task<T2> item2, Task<T3> item3)
{
        Func<T1, Func<T2, Func<T3, R>>> curry = x => y => z =>
                                            selector(x, y, z);
        var lifted1 = Pure(curry);
        var lifted2 = Apply(lifted1, item1);
        var lifted3 = Apply(lifted2, item2);
        return Apply(lifted3, item3);
}
```

Curries the function to partially apply

The lift functions apply a given function to the outputs of a set of Tasks.

Elevates the partially applied function

The Apply operator exercises the lifting.

Elevates the partially applied function

The implementation of the Lift2 and Lift3 functions is based on applicative functors that curry and elevate the function selector, enabling its applicability to the elevated argument types.

The same concepts to implement the Lift2 and Lift3 functions affect the F# design. But due to the intrinsic functional feature of the programming language, and the conciseness provided by infix operators, the implementation of the lift functions (in bold) in F# is concise:

```
let lift2 (func:'a -> 'b -> 'c) (asyncA:Async<'a>) (asyncB:Async<'b>) =
    func <!> asyncA <*> asyncB

let lift3 (func:'a -> 'b -> 'c -> 'd) (asyncA:Async<'a>)
     (asyncB:Async<'b>) (asyncC:Async<'c>) =
    func <!> asyncA <*> asyncB <*> asyncC
```

Due to the F# type inference system, the input values are wrapped into an Async type, and the compiler can interpret that the infix operators <*> and <!> are the functor and applicative functor in the context of the Async elevated type. Also, note that it's convention in F# to start the module-level functions with a lowercase initial letter.

10.6.4 *Composing and executing heterogeneous parallel computations*

What can you do with these functions in place? Let's analyze an example that exploits these operators.

Imagine you're tasked to write a simple program to validate the decision to buy stock options based on a condition set by analyzing market trends and the history of the stocks. The program should be divided into three operations:

1. Check the total amount available for purchase based on the bank account available balance and the current price of the stock:
   a. Fetch the bank account balance.
   b. Fetch the stock price from the stock market.
2. Validate if a given stock symbol is recommended to buy:
   a. Analyze the market indexes.
   b. Analyze the historical trend of the given stock.
3. Given a stock ticker symbol, decide to buy or not buy a certain number of stock options based upon the money available calculated in step 1.

The next listing shows the asynchronous functions to implement the program, which ideally should be combined (in bold). Certain code implementation details are omitted because they're irrelevant for this example.

Listing 10.25 Asynchronous operations to compose and run in parallel

```
let calcTransactionAmount amount (price:float) =          Calculates the transaction
    let readyToInvest = amount * 0.75                     amount including arbitrary fees
    let cnt = Math.Floor(readyToInvest / price)
    if (cnt < 1e-5) && (price < amount)
    then 1 else int(cnt)

let rnd = Random()
```

```
let mutable bankAccount = 500.0 + float(rnd.Next(1000))
let getAmountOfMoney() = async {
    return bankAccount
}
```

Simulates an asynchronous web service request to
the bank account that returns a random value

```
let getCurrentPrice symbol = async {
        let! (_,data) = processStockHistory symbol
        return data.[0].open'
}
```

processStockHistory (see chapter 8) downloads and parses
the historical trend of a given stock ticker symbol.

```
let getStockIndex index =  async {
        let url = sprintf "http://download.finance.yahoo.com/d/quotes.
csv?s=%s&f=snl1" index
        let req = WebRequest.Create(url)
        let! resp = req.AsyncGetResponse()
        use reader = new StreamReader(resp.GetResponseStream())
        return! reader.ReadToEndAsync()
    }
    |> Async.map (fun (row:string) ->
        let items = row.Split(',')
        Double.Parse(items.[items.Length-1]))
    |> AsyncResult.handler
```

**Retrieves the
last price of the
stock**

Downloads and retrieves asynchronously the price of a
given stock ticker symbol from the stock market

Maps the data of the stock ticker
by retrieving the closing price.
The output is an AsyncResult
type because the operation could
throw an exception.

```
let analyzeHistoricalTrend symbol = asyncResult {
        let! data = getStockHistory symbol (365/2)
        let trend = data.[data.Length-1] - data.[0]
        return trend
    }
```

Analyzes the historical trend of a
given stock ticker symbol. The
operation runs asynchronously in an
asyncResult computation expression
to handle potential errors.

```
let withdraw amount = async {
    return
        if amount > bankAccount
        then Error(InvalidOperationException("Not enough money"))
        else
            bankAccount <- bankAccount - amount
            Ok(true)
    }
```

**Retrieves the current withdraw available asynchronously.
Otherwise, an Error is returned if the bank account does not
contain sufficient funds to proceed with the trade operation.**

Each operation runs asynchronously to evaluate the result of a different type. Respectively, the function calcTransactionAmount returns a hypothetical cost for the trade(buy) transaction, the function analyzeHistoricalTrend returns the value of the stock historical analysis that's used to evaluate if the stock option is a recommended buy, the function getStockIndex returns the current value of the stock price, and the function getCurrentPrice returns the last stock price.

How would you compose and run these computations in parallel using a Fork/Join pattern, for example, when the result type isn't the same? A simple solution should be spawning an independent task for each function, then waiting for all tasks to complete to pass the results into a final function that aggregates the results and continues the work. It would be much nicer to glue all these functions together using a more generic combinator, which promotes reusability and, of course, better compositionality with a set of polymorphic tools.

The following listing applies the technique to run heterogeneous computations in parallel using the `lift2` function in F# to evaluate how many stock options are recommended to buy after running a few simple diagnostics asynchronously (in bold).

> **Listing 10.26 Running heterogeneous asynchronous operations**

Lifts the heterogeneous function to apply the calcTransactionAmount operation against the output of the getAmountOfMoney and getCurrentPrice functions

```
let howMuchToBuy stockId : AsyncResult<int> =
    Async.lift2 (calcTransactionAmount)
        (getAmountOfMoney())
        (getCurrentPrice stockId)
    |> AsyncResult.handler
```

The output is run through the AsyncResult.handler validator.

Runs the analysis of a given stock ticker symbol, returning the recommendation to proceed with the buy

```
let analyze stockId =
    howMuchToBuy stockId
    |> Async.StartCancelable(function
        | Ok (total) -> printfn "I recommend to buy %d unit" total
        | Error (e) -> printfn "I do not recommend to buy now")
```

Starts the computation using the Async.StartCancelable operator. The continuation function pattern matches the input Result to dispatch the rest of the computation according to whether it's successful (Ok) or a failure (Error).

`howMuchToBuy` is a two-parameter function with an `AsyncResult<float>` type as output. The result type definition is from the output of the underlying function `calcTransactionAmount`, in which the `AsyncResult<float>` indicates either the success of the operation with the amount of stock to buy, or not to buy. The first argument of `stockId` is an arbitrary stock ticker symbol to analyze. The `howMuchToBuy` function uses the `lift2` operator and waits without blocking the two underlying async expressions (`getAmountOfMoney` and `getCurrentPrice`) to complete each computation. The `analyze` function executes `howMuchToBuy` to collect and output the recommended result. In this case, the execution is performed asynchronously using the `Async.StartCancelable` function defined in section 9.3.5.

One of the many benefits of using applicative, functor, monads, and combinator is their reproducibility and common patterns (regardless of the technology used). This makes it easy to understand and create a vocabulary that can be used to communicate to the developers and express the intention of the code.

10.6.5 *Controlling flow with conditional asynchronous combinators*

In general, it's common to implement combinators by gluing other combinators together. Once you have a set of operators that can represent any arbitrary asynchronous operation, you can easily design new combinators over the type that allow you to combine and compose asynchronous operations in myriad different and sophisticated ways.

There are limitless possibilities and opportunities to customize asynchronous combinators to respond to your needs. You could implement an asynchronous combinator that emulates an `if-else` statement equivalent to the imperative conditional logic, but how?

The solution is found in the functional patterns:

- Monoids can be used to create the Or combinator.
- Applicative functors can be used to create the And combinator.
- Monads chain asynchronous operations and glue combinatory.

In this section, you're going to define a few conditional asynchronous combinators and consume them to understand what capabilities are offered and the limited effort required. In fact, by using the combinators introduced so far, it's a matter of composing them to achieve different behaviors. Furthermore, in the case of F# infix operators, it's easy to use the feature to elevate and operate functions inline, avoiding the need for intermediate functions. For example, you've defined functions such as lift2 and lift3 by which it's possible to apply heterogeneous parallel computation.

You can abstract away the combination notion into conditional operators such as IF, AND, and OR. The following listing shows a few combinators that apply to the F# asynchronous workflow. Semantically, they're concise and easy to compose due to the functional property of this programming language. But the same concepts can be ported into C# effortlessly, or perhaps by using the interoperability option (the code to note is in bold).

> **Listing 10.27   Async-workflow conditional combinators**

```
module AsyncCombinators =
    let inline ifAsync (predicate:Async<bool>) (funcA:Async<'a>)
        (funcB:Async<'a>) =
            async.Bind(predicate, fun p -> if p then funcA else funcB)

    let inline iffAsync (predicate:Async<'a -> bool>) (context:Async<'a>) =
        async {
            let! p = predicate <*> context
            return if p then Some context else None }

    let inline notAsync (predicate:Async<bool>) =
                            async.Bind(predicate, not >> async.Return)

    let inline AND (funcA:Async<bool>) (funcB:Async<bool>) =
        ifAsync funcA funcB (async.Return false)

    let inline OR (funcA:Async<bool>) (funcB:Async<bool>) =
        ifAsync funcA (async.Return true) funcB

    let (<&&>)(funcA:Async<bool>) (funcB:Async<bool>) = AND funcA funcB
    let (<||>)(funcA:Async<bool>) (funcB:Async<bool>) = OR funcA funcB
```

The ifAsync combinator will take an asynchronous predicate and two arbitrary asynchronous operations as arguments, where only one of those computations will run according to the outcome of the predicate. This is a useful pattern to branch the logic of your asynchronous program without leaving the asynchronous context.

The iffAsync combinator takes a HOF condition that verifies the given context. If the condition holds true, then it asynchronously returns the context; otherwise it returns None asynchronously. The combinators from the previous code may be applied in any combination before execution starts, and they act as syntactic sugar, by which the code looks the same as in the sequential case.

Inline functions

The `inline` keyword inlines the body of a function at its call sites. In this way, functions marked `inline` will be inserted verbatim whenever the function is called at compile time, improving the performance of the code execution. Note that inlining is a compiler process that trades code size for speed, whereby method calls to small or simple methods are replaced by the method's body.

Let's analyze in more detail these logical asynchronous combinators for a better understanding of how they work. This knowledge is key to building your own custom combinators.

THE AND LOGICAL ASYNCHRONOUS COMBINATOR

The asynchronous `AND` combinator returns the result after both functions `funcA` and `funcB` complete. This behavior is similar to `Task.WhenAll`, but it runs the first expression and waits for the result, then calls the second one and combines the results. If the evaluation is canceled, or fails, or returns the wrong result, then the other function will not run, applying a short-circuit logic.

Conceptually, the `Task.WhenAll` operator previously described is a good fit to perform logical `AND` over multiple asynchronous operations. This operator takes a pair of iterators to a container of tasks or a variable number of tasks, and returns a single `Task` that fires when all the arguments are ready.

The `AND` operator can be combined into chains as long as they all return the same type. Of course, it can be generalized and extended using applicative functors. Unless the functions have side effects, the result is deterministic and independent of order, so they can run parallel.

THE OR LOGICAL ASYNCHRONOUS COMBINATOR

The asynchronous `OR` combinator works like the addition operator with monoid structure, which means that the operations must be associative. The `OR` combinator starts two asynchronous operations in parallel, waiting for the first one to complete. The same properties of the `AND` combinators apply here. The `OR` combinator can be combined into chains; but the result cannot be deterministic unless both function evaluations return the same type, and both are canceled.

The combinator that acts like a logical `OR` of two asynchronous operations can be implemented using the `Task.WhenAny` operator, which starts the computations in parallel and picks the one that finishes first. This is also the basis of speculative computation, where you pitch several algorithms against each other.

The same approach for building `Async` combinators can be applied to the `Async-Result` type, which provides a more powerful way to define generic operations where the output depends on the success of the underlying operations. In other words,

AsyncResult acts as two state flags, which can represent either a failure or a successful operation, where the latter provides the final value. Here are a few examples of Async-Result combinators (in bold).

Listing 10.28   `AsyncResult` conditional combinators

```
module AsyncResultCombinators =
    let inline AND (funcA:AsyncResult<'a>) (funcB:AsyncResult<'a>)
    : AsyncResult<_> =
        asyncResult {
                let! a = funcA
                let! b = funcB
                return (a, b)
        }

    let inline OR (funcA:AsyncResult<'a>) (funcB:AsyncResult<'a>)
    : AsyncResult<'a> =
        asyncResult {
            return! funcA
            return! funcB
        }

    let (<&&>) (funcA:AsyncResult<'a>) (funcB:AsyncResult<'a>) =
        AND funcA funcB
    let (<||>) (funcA:AsyncResult<'a>) (funcB:AsyncResult<'a>) =
        OR funcA funcB

    let (<|||>) (funcA:AsyncResult<bool>) (funcB:AsyncResult<bool>) =
        asyncResult {
            let! rA = funcA
            match rA with
            | true -> return! funcB
            | false -> return false
        }

    let (<&&&>) (funcA:AsyncResult<bool>) (funcB:AsyncResult<bool>) =
        asyncResult {
            let! (rA, rB) = funcA <&&> funcB
            return rA && rB
        }
```

The AsyncResult combinators, compared to the Async combinators, expose the logical asynchronous operators AND and OR that perform conditional dispatch over generic types instead of bool types. Here's the comparison between the AND operators implemented for Async and AsyncResult:

```
    let inline AND (funcA:Async<bool>) (funcB:Async<bool>) =
        ifAsync funcA funcB (async.Return false)

    let inline AND (funcA:AsyncResult<'a>) (funcB:AsyncResult<'a>)
    : AsyncResult<_> =
        asyncResult {
                let! a = funcA
                let! b = funcB
                return (a, b)
        }
```

The AsyncResult AND uses the Result discriminated union to treat the Success case as the true value, which is carried over to the output of the underlying function.

Tips to implement custom asynchronous combinators

Use this general strategy to create custom combinators:

1 Describe the problem purely in terms of concurrency.
2 Simplify the description until it's reduced to a name.
3 Consider alternative paths for simplification.
4 Write and test (or import) the concurrency construct.

10.6.6 Asynchronous combinators in action

In listing 10.26, the stock ticker symbol was analyzed and a recommendation decided asynchronously to buy a given stock. Now you need to add the conditional check if-else, which behaves asynchronously using the ifAsync combinator: if the stock option is recommended to buy, then proceed with the transaction; otherwise it returns an error message. The code to note is in bold.

Listing 10.29   AsyncResult conditional combinators

Applies the logical async OR operator to evaluate the given functions. This function represents a predicate that says whether or not you should buy based on the current market.

```
let gt (value:'a) (ar:AsyncResult<'a>) = asyncResult {
    let! result = ar
    return result > value
}
```
Checks if a given value is greater than the result of an asynchronous operation returning an AsyncResult type. The generic type 'a must be comparable.

```
let doInvest stockId =
    let shouldIBuy =
        ((getStockIndex "^IXIC" |> gt 6200.0)
         <|||>
         (getStockIndex "^NYA" |> gt 11700.0 ))
        <&&&> ((analyzeHistoricalTrend stockId) |> gt 10.0)
        |> AsyncResult.defaultValue false
```
Exploits the async infix OR operator

Applies the logical async infix AND operator to evaluate the given functions

```
    let buy amount = async {
        let! price = getCurrentPrice stockId
        let! result = withdraw (price*float(amount))
        return result |> Result.bimap (fun x -> if x then amount else 0)
                                      (fun _ -> 0)
    }
```
Checks the current bank balance returning the amount of stocks that can be purchased

Verifies if the transaction is successful and then either returns Async<int>, wrapping the amount value if the transaction is successful, or returns Async<int> zero

Helper function that returns the default value of a given type, lifting the output into the AsyncResult type. This function is used in case of error during the calculation process.

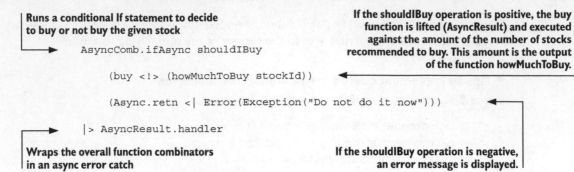

Runs a conditional If statement to decide to buy or not buy the given stock

If the shouldIBuy operation is positive, the buy function is lifted (AsyncResult) and executed against the amount of the number of stocks recommended to buy. This amount is the output of the function howMuchToBuy.

```
AsyncComb.ifAsync shouldIBuy

    (buy <!> (howMuchToBuy stockId))

    (Async.retn <| Error(Exception("Do not do it now")))

|> AsyncResult.handler
```

Wraps the overall function combinators in an async error catch

If the shouldIBuy operation is negative, an error message is displayed.

In this code example, the doInvest function analyzes a given stock symbol, its historical trend, and the current stock market to recommend a trading transaction. This function doInvest combines asynchronous functions that operate as a whole to determine the recommendation. The function shouldIBuy applies the asynchronous OR logical operator to check if either the ^IXIC or ^NYA index is greater than a given threshold. The result is used as base value to evaluate if the current stock market is good for buying operations.

If the result of the shouldIBuy function is successful (true), the asynchronous AND logical operator proceeds, executing the analyzeHistoricalTrend function, which returns the historical trend analysis of the given stock. Next, the buy function verifies that the bank account balance is sufficient to buy the desired stock options; otherwise it returns an alternative value or zero if the balance is too low.

Ultimately, these functions are combined. The ifAsync combinator runs should-IBuy asynchronously. According to its output, the code branches to either proceed with a buy transaction or return an error message. The purpose of the map infix operator (<!>) is to lift the function buy into the AsyncResult elevated type, which is then executed against the number of stocks recommended to purchase calculated by the function howMuchToBuy.

NOTE   The functions in listing 10.29 run as a unit of work, but each step is executed asynchronously, on demand.

Summary

- Exposing your intent is crucial if you want to increase the readability of your code. Introducing the Result class helps to show if the method is a failure or success, removes unnecessary boilerplate code, and results in a clean design.
- The Result type gives you an explicit, functional way to handle errors without introducing side effects (unlike throwing/catching exceptions), which leads to expressive and readable code implementations.
- When you consider the execution semantics of your code, Result and Option fill a similar goal, accounting for anything other than the happy path when code executes. Result is the best type to use when you want to represent and preserve

an error that can occur during execution. `Option` is better for when you wish to represent the existence or absence of a value, or when you want consumers to account for an error, but you don't care about preserving that error.

- FP unmasks patterns to ease composition of asynchronous operations through the support of mathematical patterns. For example, applicative functors, which are amplified functors, can combine functions with multiple arguments directly over elevated types.

- Asynchronous combinators can be used to control the asynchronous execution flow of a program. This control of execution includes conditional logic. It's effortless to compose a few asynchronous combinators to construct more sophisticated ones, such as the asynchronous versions of the `AND` and `OR` operators.

- F# has support for infix operators, which can be customized to produce a convenient set of operators. These operators simplify the programming style to easily construct a very sophisticated chain of operations in a non-standard manner.

- Applicatives and functors can be combined to lift conventional functions, whose execution against elevated types can be performed without leaving the context. This technique allows you to run in parallel a set of heterogeneous functions, whose outputs can be evaluated as a whole.

- Using core functional functions, such as `Bind`, `Return`, `Map`, and `Apply`, makes it straightforward to define rich code behavior that composes, run in parallel, and performs applications in an elevated world that mimics conditional logic, such as `if-else`.

Applying reactive programming everywhere with agents

This chapter covers

- Using the message-passing concurrent model
- Handling millions of messages per second
- Using the agent programming model
- Parallelizing a workflow and coordinating agents

Web applications play an important role in our lives, from large social networks and media streaming to online banking systems and collaborative online gaming. Certain websites now handle as much traffic as the entire internet did less than a decade ago. Facebook and Twitter, two of the most popular websites, have billions of users each. To ensure that these applications thrive, concurrent connections, scalability, and distributed systems are essential. Traditional architectures from years past cannot operate under this high volume of requests.

High-performance computing is becoming a necessity. The message-passing concurrent programming model is the answer to this demand, as evidenced by the increasing support for the message-passing model in mainstream languages such as Java, C#, and C++.

The number of concurrent online connections will certainly continue to grow. The trend is shifting to physical devices that are interconnected, generating sophisticated and massive networks constantly operating and exchanging messages. It's predicted that the *Internet of Things* (IoT) will expand to an installed base of 75 billion units by 2025 (http://mng.bz/wiwP).

> ## What is the Internet of Things?
>
> The Internet of Things (IoT), as its name implies, is a giant network of things (refrigerators, washing machines, and more) connected to the internet. Basically, anything with an on/off switch that can be connected to the internet can be part of the IoT. One analyst firm estimates that by 2020 there will be 26 billion connected devices (www.forbes.com/companies/gartner/). Other estimates put this number at more than 100 billion. That's a lot of data transfer. One challenge of the IoT is to convey the data in real time, with no slowing or bottlenecks, and to continually improve response time. Another challenge is security: all those things connected to the internet are open to hacking.

The continual evolution of devices connected online is inspiring a revolution in how developers design the next generation of applications. The new applications will have to be non-blocking, fast, and capable of reacting to high volumes of system notifications. Events will control the execution of reactive applications. You'll need a highly available and resource-efficient application able to adapt to this rapid evolution and respond to an infinitely increasing volume of internet requests. The event-driven and asynchronous paradigms are the primary architectural requirements for developing such applications. In this context, you'll need asynchronous programming processed in parallel.

This chapter is about developing responsive and reactive systems, starting with the exceptional message-passing programming model, a general-purpose concurrent one with particularly wide applicability. The message-passing programming model has several commonalities with the microservices architecture (http://microservices.io/).

You'll use the agent-based concurrent programming style, which relies on message passing as a vehicle to communicate between small units of computations called *agents*. Each agent may own an internal state, with single-threaded access to guarantee thread safety without the need of any lock (or other any other synchronization primitive). Because agents are easy to understand, programming with them is an effective tool for building scalable and responsive applications that ease the implementation of advanced asynchronous logic.

By the end of this chapter, you'll know how to use asynchronous message-passing semantics in your applications to simplify and improve responsiveness and performance in your application. (If you are shaky on asynchronicity, review chapters 8 and 9.)

Before we plunge into the technical aspects of the message-passing architecture and the agent model, let's look at the reactive system, with an emphasis on the properties that make an application valuable in the reactive paradigm.

11.1   *What's reactive programming, and how is it useful?*

Reactive programming is a set of design principles used in asynchronous programming to create cohesive systems that respond to commands and requests in a timely manner. It is a way of thinking about systems' architecture and design in a distributed environment where implementation techniques, tooling, and design patterns are components of a larger whole—a system. Here, an application is divided into multiple distinct steps, each of which can be executed in an asynchronous and non-blocking fashion. Execution threads that compete for shared resources are free to perform other useful work while the resource is occupied, instead of idling and wasting computational power.

In 2013, reactive programming became an established paradigm with a formalized set of rules under the umbrella of the Reactive Manifesto (www.reactivemanifesto.org/), which describes the number of constituent parts that determine a reactive system. The Reactive Manifesto outlines patterns for implementing robust, resilient, and responsive systems. The reason behind the Reactive Manifesto is the recent changes to application requirements (table 11.1).

Table 11.1   Comparison between the requirements for past and present applications

Past requirements for applications	Present requirements for applications
Single processors	Multicore processors
Expensive RAM	Cheap RAM
Expensive disk memory	Cheap disk memory
Slow networks	Fast networks
Low volume of concurrent requests	High volume of concurrent requests
Small data	Big data
Latency measured in seconds	Latency measured in milliseconds

In the past, you might have had only a few services running on your applications, with ample response time, and time available for systems to be offline for maintenance. Today, applications are deployed over thousands of services, and each can run on multiple cores. Additionally, users expect response times in milliseconds, as opposed to seconds, and anything less than 100% uptime is unacceptable. The Reactive Manifesto seeks to solve these problems by asking developers to create systems that have four properties. They must be responsive (react to users), resilient (react to failure), message-driven (react to events), and scalable (react to load). Figure 11.1 illustrates these properties and how they relate to each other.

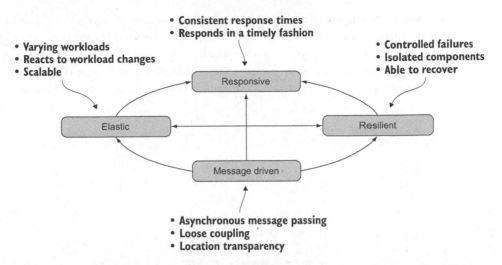

Figure 11.1 According to the Reactive Manifesto, for a system to be called reactive, it must have four properties: it must be responsive (must react to users), resilient (react to failure), message-driven (react to events), and scalable (react to load).

A system built using the manifesto's requirements will:

- Have a consistent response time regardless of the workload undertaken.
- Respond in a timely fashion, regardless of the volume of requests coming in. This ensures that the user isn't spending significant amounts of time idly waiting for operations to complete, thereby providing a positive user experience.

This responsiveness is possible because reactive programming optimizes the use of the computing resources on multicore hardware, leading to better performance. Asynchronicity is one of the key elements of reactive programming. Chapters 8 and 9 cover the APM and how it plays an important role in building scalable systems. In chapter 14, you'll build a complete server-side application that fully embraces this paradigm.

A message-driven architecture is the foundation of reactive applications. *Message-driven* means that reactive systems are built on the premise of asynchronous message passing; furthermore, with a message-driven architecture, components can be loosely coupled. The primary benefit of reactive programming is that it removes the need for explicit coordination between active components in a system, simplifying the approach to asynchronous computation.

11.2 *The asynchronous message-passing programming model*

In a typical synchronous application, you sequentially perform an operation with a request/response model of communication, using a procedure call to retrieve data or modify a state. This pattern is limited due to a blocking programming style and design that cannot be scaled or performed out of sequence.

A message-passing-based architecture is a form of asynchronous communication where data is queued, to be processed at a later stage, if necessary. In the context of reactive programming, the message-passing architecture uses an asynchronous semantic to communicate between the individual parts of the system. As a result, it can handle millions of messages per second, producing an incredible boost to performance (figure 11.2).

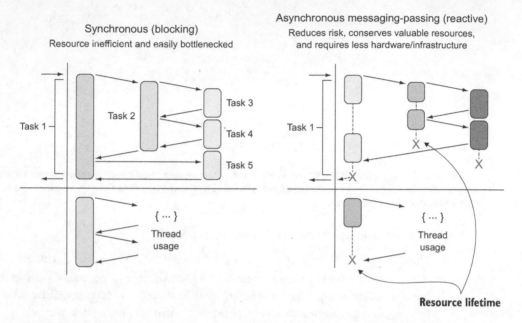

Figure 11.2   The synchronous (blocking) communication is resource inefficient and easily bottlenecked. The asynchronous message-passing (reactive) approach reduces blocking risks, conserves valuable resources, and requires less hardware/infrastructure.

NOTE   The message-passing model has become increasingly popular and has been implemented into many new programming languages, often as a first-class language concept. In many other programming languages, it's available using third-party libraries that build on top of conventional multithreading.

The idea of message-passing concurrency is based on lightweight units of computation (or processes) that have exclusive ownership of state. The state, by design, is protected and unshared, which means it can be either mutable or immutable without running into any pitfalls due to a multithreaded environment (see chapter 1). In a message-passing architecture, two entities run in separate threads: the sender of a message and a receiver of the message. The benefit of this programming model is that all issues of memory sharing and concurrent access are hidden inside the communication channel. Neither entity involved in the communication needs to apply any low-level synchronization strategies, such as locking. The message-passing architecture (message-passing concurrent model) doesn't communicate by sharing memory, but instead communicates by sending messages.

Asynchronous message passing decouples communication between entities and allows senders to send messages without waiting for their receivers. No synchronization is necessary between senders and receivers for message exchange, and both entities can run independently. Keep in mind that the sender cannot know when a message is received and handled by the recipient.

The message-passing concurrent model can at first appear more complicated than sequential or even parallel systems, as you'll see in the comparison in figure 11.3 (the squares represent objects, and arrows represent a method call or a message).

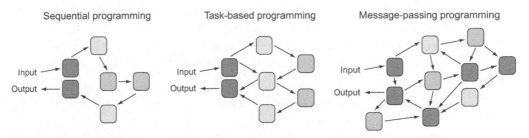

Figure 11.3   Comparison between task-based, sequential, and agent-based programming. Each block represents a unit of computation.

In figure 11.3, each block represents a unit of work:

- Sequential programming is the simplest with a single input and produces a single output using a single control flow, where the blocks are connected directly in a linear fashion, each task dependent on the completion of the previous task.
- Task-based programming is similar to the sequential programming model, but it may MapReduce or Fork/Join the control flow.
- Message-passing programming may control the execution flow because the blocks are interconnected with other blocks in a continuous and direct manner. Ultimately, each block sends messages directly to other blocks, non-linearly. This design can seem complex and difficult to understand at first. But because blocks are encapsulated into active objects, each message is passed independent of other messages, with no blocking or lag time. With the message-passing concurrent model, you can have multiple building blocks, each with an independent input and output, which can be connected. Each block runs in isolation, and once isolation is achieved, it's possible to deploy the computation into different tasks.

We'll spend the rest of chapter on agents as the main tool for building message-passing concurrent models.

11.2.1   *Relation with message passing and immutability*

By this point, it should be clear that immutability ensures increased degrees of concurrency. (Remember, an immutable object is an object whose state cannot be modified after it's created.) Immutability is a foundational tool for building concurrent, reliable, and predictable programs. But it isn't the only tool that matters. Natural isolation is also critically important, perhaps more so, because it's easier to achieve in programming languages that don't support immutability intrinsically. It turns out that agents enforce coarse-grained isolation through message passing.

11.2.2   *Natural isolation*

Natural isolation is a critically important concept for writing lockless concurrent code. In a multithreaded program, isolation solves the problem of shared state by giving each thread a copied portion of data to perform local computation. With isolation, there's no race condition, because each task processes an independent copy of its own data.

> **Isolation for building resilient systems**
>
> *Isolation* is an aspect of building resilient systems. For example, in the event that a single component fails, the rest of the system is seemingly immune to this failure. Message passing is a tremendous help in simplifying the building process for correct concurrent systems enabled due to the isolation approach, also called the *share-nothing approach*.

The natural isolation or share-nothing approach is less complex to achieve than immutability, but both options represent orthogonal approaches and should be used in conjunction for reducing runtime overheads and avoiding race condition and deadlocks.

11.3   *What is an agent?*

An *agent* is a single-thread unit of computation used to design concurrent applications based on message passing in isolation (share-nothing approach). These agents are lightweight constructs that contain a queue and can receive and process messages. In this case, lightweight means that agents have a small memory footprint as compared to spawning new threads, so you can easily spin up 100,000 agents in a computer without a hitch.

Think of an agent as a process that has exclusive ownership of some mutable state, which can never be accessed from outside of the agent. Although agents run concurrently with each other, *within* a single agent everything is sequential. The isolation of the agent's internal state is a key concept of this model, because it is completely inaccessible from the outside world, making it thread safe. Indeed, if state is isolated, mutation can happen freely.

An agent's basic functionality is to do the following:

- Maintain a private state that can be accessed safely in a multithreaded environment
- React to messages differently in different states

- Notify other agents
- Expose events to subscribers
- Send a reply to the sender of a message

One of the most important features of agent programming is that messages are sent asynchronously, and the sender doesn't initiate a block. When a message is sent to an agent, it is placed in a mailbox. The agent processes one message at a time sequentially in the order in which it was added to the mailbox, moving on to the next message only when it has finished processing the current message. While an agent processes a message, the other incoming messages aren't lost, but are buffered into the internal isolated mailbox. Consequently, multiple agents can run in parallel effortlessly, which means that the performance of a well-written agent-based application scales with the number of cores or processors.

An agent isn't an actor

On the surface, there are similarities between agents and actors, which sometimes cause people to use these terms interchangeably. But the main difference is that agents are *in* a process, while actors may be running *on* another process. In fact, the reference to an agent is a pointer to a specific instance, whereas an actor reference is determined through location transparency. *Location transparency* is the use of names to identify network resources, rather than their actual location, which means that the actor may be running in the same process, or on another process, or possibly on a remote machine.

Agent-based concurrency is inspired by the actor model, but its construction is much simpler. Actor systems have built-in sophisticated tools for distribution support, which include supervision to manage exceptions and potentially self-heal the system, routing to customize the work distribution, and more.

Several libraries and tool kits, such as Akka.net (http://getakka.net/), Proto.Actor (http://proto.actor/), and Microsoft Orleans (https://dotnet.github.io/orleans/), implement the actor model for the .NET ecosystem . It's no surprise that Microsoft Azure Service-Fabric (https://azure.microsoft.com/en-us/services/service-fabric), used to build distributed, scalable, and fault-tolerant microservices in the cloud, is based on the actor model. For more information about the actor model in .NET, I recommend Anthony Brown's *Reactive Applications with Akka.Net* (Manning, 2017).

The tools and features provided by the actor libraries can be implemented and replicated easily for agents. You can find several libraries that overcome missing functionalities such as supervision and routing (http://mbrace.io/ and http://akka.net).

11.3.1 The components of an agent

Figure 11.4 shows the fundamental component parts of an agent:

- *Mailbox*—An internal queue to buffer incoming messages implemented as asynchronous, race-free, and non-blocking.

- *Behavior*—The internal function applied sequentially to each incoming message. The behavior is single-threaded.
- *State*—Agents can have an internal state that's isolated and never shared, so they never need to compete for locks to be accessed.
- *Message*—Agents can communicate only through messages, which are sent asynchronously and are buffered in a mailbox.

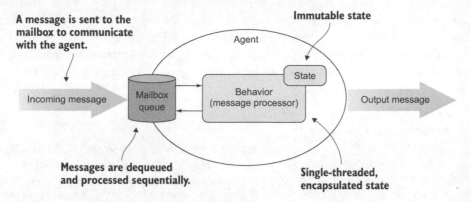

Figure 11.4   An agent consists of a mailbox that queues the income messages, a state, and a behavior that runs in a loop, which processes one message at a time. The behavior is the functionality applied to the messages.

11.3.2 What an agent can do

The agent programming model provides great support for concurrency and has an extensive range of applicability. Agents are used in data collection and mining, reducing application bottlenecks by buffering requests, real-time analysis with bounded and unbounded reactive streaming, general-purpose number crunching, machine learning, simulation, Master/Worker pattern, Compute Grid, MapReduce, gaming, and audio and video processing, to mention a few.

11.3.3 The share-nothing approach for lock-free concurrent programming

The share-nothing architecture refers to message-passing programming, where each agent is independent and there's no single point of contention across the system. This architecture model is great for building concurrent and safe systems. If you don't share anything, then there's no opportunity for race conditions. Isolated message-passing blocks (agents) are a powerful and efficient technique to implement scalable programming algorithms, including scalable request servers and scalable distributed-programming algorithms. The simplicity and intuitive behavior of the agent as a building block allows for designing and implementing elegant, highly efficient asynchronous and parallel applications that don't share state. In general, agents perform calculations in reaction to the messages they receive, and they can send messages to other agents in a fire-and-forget manner or collect the responses, called *replies* (figure 11.5).

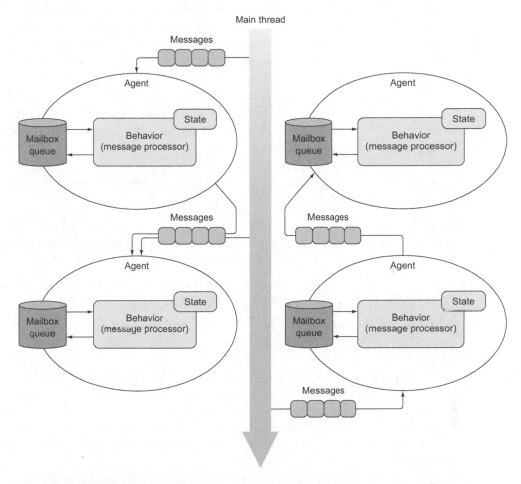

Figure 11.5 Agents communicate with each other through a message-passing semantic, creating an interconnected system of units of computation that run concurrently. Each agent has an isolated state and independent behavior.

11.3.4 How is agent-based programming functional?

Certain aspects of agent-based programming aren't functional. Although agents (and actors) were developed in the context of functional languages, their purpose is to generate side effects, which is against the tenets of FP. An agent often performs a side effect, or sends a message to another agent, which will, in turn, perform a new side effect.

Less important, but worth mentioning, is that FP in general separates logic from data. But agents contain data and the logic for the processing function. Additionally, sending a message to an agent doesn't force any constraint on the return type. An agent behavior, which is the operation applied to each message, can either return a result or not return any result. In the latter scenario, the design of a message sent in a fire-and-forget fashion encourages program agents in a unidirectional flow pattern, which means that the messages flow forward from one agent to the next. This unidirectional message flow between agents can preserve their compositional semantic aspect, achieved by linking a given set of agents. The result is a pipeline of agents that represents the steps of operations to process the messages, each executed independently and potentially in parallel.

The primary reason that the agent model is functional is that agents can *send behavior to the state instead of sending state to the behavior.* In the agent model, the sender, besides sending messages, can provide the function which implements an action to process the incoming messages. Agents are an in-memory slot where you can put in data structure, such as a bucket (container). In addition to providing data storage, agents allow you to send messages in the shape of a function, which is then applied atomically to the internal bucket.

> **NOTE** *Atomically* refers to a set of operations (atomic operations) that, when they start, must complete before any interrupt in a single step, such that other parallel threads can only ever see either the old or new state.

The function can be composed from other functions and then sent to the agent as a message. The advantage is the ability to update and change behavior at runtime using functions and function-composition fitting with the functional paradigm.

11.3.5 *Agent is object-oriented*

It's interesting to note that Alan Kay's (https://en.wikipedia.org/wiki/Alan_Kay) original vision for objects in Smalltalk is much closer to the agent model than it is to the objects found in most programming languages (the basic concept of "messaging," for example). Kay believed that state changes should be encapsulated and not done in an unconstrained way. His idea of passing messages between objects is intuitive and helps to clarify the boundaries between objects.

Clearly, message passing resembles OOP, and you can lean on the OOP-style message passing, which is only calling a method. Here, an agent is like an object in an object-oriented program, because it encapsulates state and communicates with other agents by exchanging messages.

11.4 *The F# agent: MailboxProcessor*

The support for the APM in F# doesn't stop with asynchronous workflows (introduced in chapter 9). Additional support is provided inherently by the F# programming language, including `MailboxProcessor`, a primitive type that behaves as a lightweight in-memory message-passing agent (see figure 11.6).

`MailboxProcessor` works completely asynchronously, and provides a simple concurrent programming model that can deliver fast and reliable concurrent programs.

I could write an entire book about `MailboxProcessor`, its multipurpose uses, and the flexibility that it provides for building a wide range of diverse applications. The benefits of using it include having a dedicated and isolated message queue combined with an asynchronous handler, which is used to throttle the message processing to automatically and transparently optimize the usage of the computer's resources.

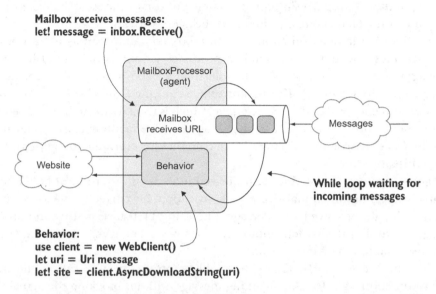

Figure 11.6 `MailboxProcessor` (agent) waits asynchronously for incoming messages in the `while` loop. The messages are strings representing the URL, which are applied to the internal behavior to download the related website.

The following listing shows a simple code example using a `MailboxProcessor`, which receives an arbitrary URL to print the length of the website.

Listing 11.1 Simple `MailboxProcessor` **with a** `while` **loop**

```
type Agent<'T> = MailboxProcessor<'T>

let webClientAgent =
  Agent<string>.Start(fun inbox -> async {
    while true do
      let! message = inbox.Receive()
      use client = new WebClient()
      let uri = Uri message
      let! site = client.AsyncDownloadString(uri)
      printfn "Size of %s is %d" uri.Host site.Length
  })

agent.Post "http://www.google.com"
agent.Post "http://www.microsoft.com"
```

The method MailboxProcessor.Start returns a running agent.

Waits asynchronously to receive a message

Uses the asynchronous workflow to download the data

Sends a message to the MailboxProcessor in a fire-and-forget fashion

Let's look at how to construct an agent in F#. First, there must be a name of the instance. In this case `webClientAgent` is the address of the mailbox processor. This is how you'll post a message to be processed. The `MailboxProcessor` is generally initialized with the `MailboxProcessor.Start` shortcut method, though you can create an instance by invoking the constructor directly, and then run the agent using the instance method `Start`. To simplify the name and use of the `MailboxProcessor`, you establish it as the alias agent and then start the agent with `Agent.Start`.

Next, there's a lambda function with an inbox containing an asynchronous workflow. Each message sent to the mailbox processor is sent asynchronously. The body of the agent functions as a message handler that accepts a mailbox (inbox:Mailbox-Processor) as an argument. This mailbox has a running logical thread that controls a dedicated and encapsulated message queue, which is thread safe, to use and coordinate the communication with other threads, or agents. The mailbox runs asynchronously, using the F# asynchronous workflow. It can contain long-running operations that don't block a thread.

In general, messages need to be processed in order, so there must be a loop. This example uses a non-functional `while-true` style loop. It's perfectly fine to use this or to use a functional, recursive loop. The agent in listing 11.1 starts getting and processing messages by calling the asynchronous function `agent.Receive()` using the `let!` construct inside an imperative `while` loop.

Inside the loop is the heart of the mailbox processor. The call of the mailbox `Receive` function waits for the incoming message without blocking the actual thread, and resumes once a message is received. The use of the `let!` operator ensures that the computation is started immediately.

Then the first message available is removed from the mailbox queue and is bound to the message identifier. At this point, the agent reacts by processing the message, which in this example downloads and prints the size of a given website address. If the mailbox queue is empty and there are no messages to process, then the agent frees the thread back to the thread pool scheduler. That means no threads are idle while `Receive` waits for incoming messages, which are sent to the `MailboxProcessor` in a fire-and-forget fashion using the `agent.Post` method.

11.4.1 *The mailbox asynchronous recursive loop*

In the previous example, the agent mailbox waits for messages asynchronously using an imperative `while` loop. Let's modify the imperative loop so it uses a functional recursion to avoid mutation and possibly so it holds local state.

The following listing is the same version of the agent that counts its messages (shown in listing 11.1), but this time it uses a recursive asynchronous function that maintains a state.

Listing 11.2   Simple `MailboxProcessor` with a recursive function

```
let agent = Agent<string>.Start(fun inbox ->
    let rec loop count = async {
        let! message = inbox.Receive()
```

◄—— **Uses an asynchronous recursive function that maintains a state in an immutable manner**

```
        use client = new WebClient()
        let uri = Uri message
        let! site = client.AsyncDownloadString(uri)
        printfn "Size of %s is %d - total messages %d" uri.Host
➥ site.Length (count + 1)
        return! loop (count + 1) }
    loop 0)
  agent.Post "http://www.google.com"
  agent.Post "http://www.microsoft.com"
```

> **The recursive function is a tail call, asynchronously passing an updated state.**

This functional approach is a little more advanced, but it greatly reduces the amount of explicit mutation in your code and is often more general. In fact, as you'll see shortly, you can use the same strategy to maintain and safely reuse the state for caching.

Pay close attention to the line of code for the `return! loop (n + 1)`, where the function uses asynchronous workflows recursively to execute the loop, passing the increased value of the count. The call using `return!` is tail-recursive, which means that the compiler translates the recursion more efficiently to avoid stack overflow exceptions. See chapter 3 for more details about recursive function support (also in C#).

A MailboxProcessor's most important functions

A `MailboxProcessor`'s most important functions are as follows:

- `Start`—This function defines the async callback that forms the message looping.
- `Receive`—This is the `async` function to receive messages from the internal queue.
- `Post`—This function sends a message to the `MailboxProcessor` in a fire-and-forget manner.

11.5 Avoiding database bottlenecks with F# MailboxProcessor

The core feature of most applications is database access, which is frequently the real source of bottlenecks in code. A simple database performance tuning can speed up applications significantly and keep the server responsive.

How do you guarantee consistently high-throughput database access? To better facilitate database access, the operation should be asynchronous, because of the I/O nature of database access. Asynchronicity ensures that the server can handle multiple requests in parallel. You may wonder about the number of parallel requests that a database server can handle before performance degrades (figure 11.7 shows performance degradation at a high level). No exact answer exists. It depends on many different factors: for example, the size of the database connection pool.

A critical element of the bottleneck problem is controlling and throttling the incoming requests to maximize the application's performance. `MailboxProcessor` provides a solution by buffering the incoming messages and taming possible overflow of requests (see figure 11.8). Using `MailboxProcessor` as a mechanism to throttle the database operations provides a granular control for optimizing the database connection-pool use. For example, the program could add or remove agents to execute the database operations in a precise grade of parallelism.

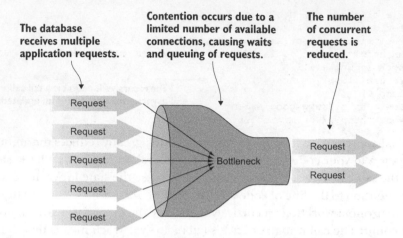

Figure 11.7   A large number of concurrent requests to access the database are reduced due to the limited size of the connection pool.

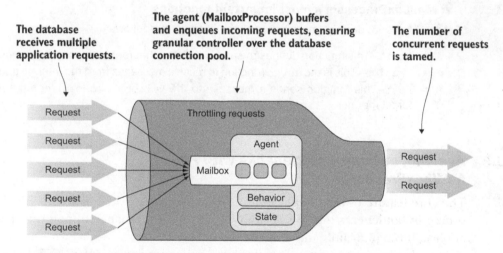

Figure 11.8   The agent (`MailboxProcessor`) controls the incoming requests to optimize the database connection-pool use.

Listing 11.3 shows a fully asynchronous function in F#. This function queries a given database and encapsulates the query in a `MailboxProcessor` body. Encapsulating an operation as behavior of an agent assures only one database request at a time is processed.

TIP   One obvious solution to handling a higher number of requests is to set the database's connection pool size to the maximum, but this isn't a good practice. Often, your application isn't the only client connected to the database, and if your application takes up all the connections, then the database server can't perform as expected.

To access the database, use the traditional .NET Access-Data-Object (ADO). Alternatively, you could use Microsoft Entity Framework or any other data access you choose. I don't cover how to access the Entity Framework data access component in this book. For more detail, refer to the MSDN online documentation at http://mng.bz/4sdU.

> **Listing 11.3   Using `MailboxProcessor` to manage database calls**

Uses a Person record type

Uses a single-case DU for defining the MailboxProcessor message

```
type Person  =
    { id:int; firstName:string; lastName:string; age:int }

type SqlMessage =
    | Command of id:int * AsyncReplyChannel<Person option>

let agentSql connectionString =
    fun (inbox: MailboxProcessor<SqlMessage>) ->
        let rec loop() = async {
            let! Command(id, reply) = inbox.Receive()
                use conn = new SqlConnection(connectionString)
                use cmd = new SqlCommand("Select FirstName, LastName, Age
    from db.People where id = @id")
                cmd.Connection <- conn
                cmd.CommandType <- CommandType.Text
                cmd.Parameters.Add("@id", SqlDbType.Int).Value <- id
                if conn.State <> ConnectionState.Open then
                    do! conn.OpenAsync()
                use! reader = cmd.ExecuteReaderAsync(
    CommandBehavior.SingleResult ||| CommandBehavior.CloseConnection)
                let! canRead = (reader:SqlDataReader).ReadAsync()
                if canRead then
                    let person =
                        {   id = reader.GetInt32(0)
                            firstName = reader.GetString(1)
                            lastName = reader.GetString(2)
                            age = reader.GetInt32(3)  }
                    reply.Reply(Some person)
                else reply.Reply(None)
                return! loop() }
        loop()

type AgentSql(connectionString:string) =
    let agentSql = new MailboxProcessor<SqlMessage>
                                    (agentSql connectionString)

    member this.ExecuteAsync (id:int) =
        agentSql.PostAndAsyncReply(fun ch -> Command(id, ch))

    member this.ExecuteTask (id:int) =
        agentSql.PostAndAsyncReply(fun ch -> Command(id, ch))
        |> Async.StartAsTask
```

Deconstructs pattern-matching against the message received to access the underlying values

Opens the SQL connection asynchronously using the do! asynchronous workflow operator

Asynchronously creates an SQL reader instance

If the SQL command can run, it replies to the caller with the Some result of the operation.

If the SQL command can't run, it replies to the caller with a None result.

Exposes an API to interact with encapsulated MailboxProcessor

Initially, the `Person` data structure is defined as a record type, which can be consumed easily as an immutable class by any .NET programming language. The function `agentSql` defines the body of a `MailboxProcessor`, whose behavior receives messages and performs database queries asynchronously. You make your application more robust by using an `Option` type for the `Person` value, which would otherwise be `null`. Doing so helps prevent `null` reference exceptions.

The type `AgentSql` encapsulates the `MailboxProcessor`, which originated from running the function `agentSql`. The access of the underlying agent is exposed through the methods `ExecuteAsync` and `ExecuteTask`.

The purpose of the `ExecuteTask` method is to encourage interoperability with C#. You can compile the `AgentSql` type into an F# library and distribute it as a reusable component. If you want to use the component from C#, then you should also provide methods that return a type `Task` or `Task<T>` for the F# functions that run an asynchronous workflow object (`Async<'T>`). How to interop between F# `Async` and .NET `Task` types is covered in appendix C.

11.5.1 *The MailboxProcessor message type: discriminated unions*

The type `SqlMessage Command` is a single-case DU used to send a message to the `Mailbox-Processor` with a well-defined type, which can be pattern-matched:

```
type SqlMessage =
    | Command of id:int * AsyncReplyChannel<Person option>
```

A common F# practice is to use a DU to define the different types of messages that a `MailboxProcessor` can receive and pattern match them to deconstruct and obtain the underlying data structure (for more on F#, see appendix B). Pattern matching over DUs gives a succinct way to process messages. A common pattern is to call `inbox.Receive()` or `inbox.TryReceive()` and follow that call with a match on the message contents.

Performance tip for an F# single-case DU

Using single-case DU types (as in listing 11.3) to wrap primitive values is an effective design. But because union cases are compiled into classes, expect a performance drop. This performance drop is the trade-off for allocating, and later for collecting, the class by the GC. A better solution (available since F# 4.1) is to decorate the DUs with the `Struct` attribute, allowing the compiler to treat these types as values, avoiding the extra heap allocation and GC pressure.

Using strongly typed messages makes it possible for the `MailboxProcessor` behavior to distinguish between different types of messages and to supply different handling codes associated with each type of message.

11.5.2 MailboxProcessor two-way communication

In listing 11.3, the underlying `MailboxProcessor` returns (replies) to the caller the result of the database query in the shape of a `Person` option type. This communication uses the `AsyncReplyChannel<'T>` type, which defines the mechanism used to reply to the channel parameter established during message initialization (figure 11.9).

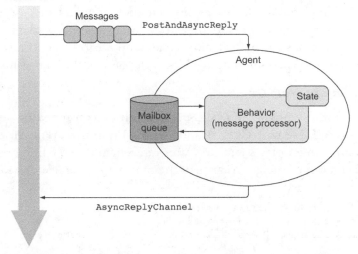

Figure 11.9 The agent two-way communication generates an `AsyncReplyChannel`, which is used by the agent as a callback to notify the caller when the computation is completed, generally supplying a result.

The code that can wait asynchronously for a response uses the `AsyncReplyChannel`. Once the computation is complete, use the `Reply` function to return the results from the mailbox:

```
type SqlMessage =
    | Command of id:int * AsyncReplyChannel<Person option>

    member this.ExecuteAsync (id:int) =
        agentSql.PostAndAsyncReply(fun ch -> Command(id, ch))
```

The `PostAndAsyncReply` method initializes the channel for the `Reply` logic, which hands off the reply channel to the agent as part of the message using an anonymous lambda (function). At this point, the workflow is suspended (without blocking) until the operation completes and a `Reply`, carrying the result, is sent back to the caller by the agent through the channel:

```
reply.Reply(Some person)
```

As good practice, you should embed the `AsyncReplyChannel` handler inside the message itself, as shown in the DU `SqlMessage.Command of id:int * AsyncReplyChannel<Person option>`, because the reply of the sent message can be easily enforced by the compiler.

You might be thinking: Why would you use a `MailboxProcessor` to handle multiple requests if only one message at a time can be processed? Are the incoming messages lost if the `MailboxProcessor` is busy?

Sending messages to a `MailboxProcessor` is always non-blocking; but from the agent's perspective, receiving them is a blocking operation. Even if you're posting multiple messages to the agent, none of the messages will get lost, because they're buffered and inserted into the mailbox queue.

It's also possible to implement selective receive semantics to target and *scan* (http://mng.bz/1lJr) for exact message types, and, depending on the agent behavior, the handler can wait for a specific message in the mailbox and temporarily defer others. This is a technique used to implement a finite-state machine with pause-and-resume capabilities.

11.5.3 *Consuming the AgentSQL from C#*

At this point, you want to employ the `AgentSql` so it can be consumed by other languages. The exposed APIs are both C# `Task` and F# asynchronous workflow friendly.

Using C#, it's simple to employ `AgentSql`. After referencing the F# library containing the `AgentSql`, you can create an instance of the object and then call the `Execute-Task` method:

```
AgentSql agentSql = new AgentSql("<< ConnectionString Here >>");
Person person = await agentSql.ExecuteTask(42);
Console.WriteLine($"Fullname {person.FirstName} {person.LastName}");
```

`ExecuteTask` reruns a `Task<Person>`, so you can use the C# async/await model to extract the underlying value when the operation completes as a continuation.

You can use a similar approach in F#, an approach that supports the task-based programming model, although due to the intrinsic and superior support for the async workflow, I recommend that you use the `ExecuteAsync` method. In this case, you can either call the method inside an async computation expression, or call it by using the `Async.StartWithContinuations` function. With this function, a continuation handler can continue the work when the `AgentSql` replies with the result (see chapter 9). The following listing is an example using both F# approaches (the code to note is in bold).

Listing 11.4   Interacting asynchronously with `AgentSql`

```
let token = CancellationToken()                              ◀── Stops the MailboxProcessor
                                                                 with a cancellation token
let agentSql = AgentSql("< Connection String Here >")
let printPersonName id = async {
    let! (Some person) = agentSql.ExecuteAsync id           ◀──── Sends the message and waits
        printfn "Fullname %s %s" person.firstName person.lastName      asynchronously for the response
}                                                                      from the MailboxProcessor

Async.Start(printPersonName 42, token)

Starts the computation asynchronously
```

```
Async.StartWithContinuations(agentSql.ExecuteAsync 42,
    (fun (Some person) ->
        printfn "Fullname %s %s" person.firstName person.lastName),
    (fun exn -> printfn "Error: %s" exn.Message),
    (fun cnl -> printfn "Operation cancelled"), token)
```

Functions are triggered respectively if the operation completes successfully, completes with an error, or is canceled

Starts the computation, asynchronously managing how the operation completes

The `Async.StartWithContinuations` function specifies the code to run when the job completes as a continuation. `Async.StartWithContinuations` accepts three different continuation functions that are triggered with the output of the operation:

- The code to run when the operation completes successfully, and a result is available.
- The code to run when an exception occurs.
- The code to run when an operation is canceled. The cancellation token is passed as an optional argument when you start the job.

See chapter 9 or the MSDN documentation online for more information (http://mng .bz/teA8). `Async.StartWithContinuations` isn't complicated, and it provides a convenient control over dispatching behaviors in the case of success, error, or cancellation. These functions passed are referred to as *continuation functions*. Continuation functions can be specified as a lambda expression in the arguments to `Async.StartWith-Continuations`. Specifying code to run as a simple lambda expression is extremely powerful.

11.5.4 *Parallelizing the workflow with group coordination of agents*

The main reason to have an agent process the messages to access a database is to control the throughput and to properly optimize the use of the connection pool. How can you achieve this fine control of parallelism? How can a system perform multiple requests in parallel without encountering a decrease in performance? `Mailbox-Processor` is a primitive type that's flexible for building reusable components by encapsulating behavior and then exposing general or tailored interfaces that fit your program needs.

Listing 11.5 shows a reusable component, `parallelWorker` (in bold), that spawns a set of agents from a given count (`workers`). Here, each agent implements the same behavior and processes the incoming requests in a round-robin fashion. *Round-robin* is an algorithm that, in this case, is employed by the agent mailbox queue to process the incoming messages as first-come first-served, in circular order, handling all processes without particular priority.

Listing 11.5   Parallel `MailboxProcessor` workers

```
type MailboxProcessor<'a> with
    static member public parallelWorker (workers:int)
        (behavior:MailboxProcessor<'a> -> Async<unit>)
```

Behavior to construct the underlying agent children

The workers value defines the agents that run in parallel.

If the cancellation token or error handler isn't passed, a default is created.

```
                    (?errorHandler:exn -> unit) (?cts:CancellationToken) =
let cts = defaultArg cts (CancellationToken())
let errorHandler = defaultArg errorHandler ignore
let agent = new MailboxProcessor<'a>((fun inbox ->
    let agents = Array.init workers (fun _ ->
            let child = MailboxProcessor.Start(behavior, cts)
            child.Error.Subscribe(errorHandler)
            child)
    cts.Register(fun () -> agents |> Array.iter(
                    fun a -> (a :> IDisposable).Dispose()))
    let rec loop i = async {
        let! msg = inbox.Receive()
        agents.[i].Post(msg)
        return! loop((i+1) % workers)
    }
        loop 0), cts)
    agent.Start()
```

Initializes the agent children

Sends the message to the agents in a round-robin fashion using a loop

Registers the cancellation token function, which stops and disposes of all the agents

The error handler is subscribed for each agent.

The main agent (`agentCoordinator`) initializes a collection of sub-agents to coordinate the work and to provide access to the agent's children through itself. When the parent agent receives a message sent to the `parallelWorker` MailboxProcessor, the parent agent dispatches the message to the next available agent child (figure 11.10).

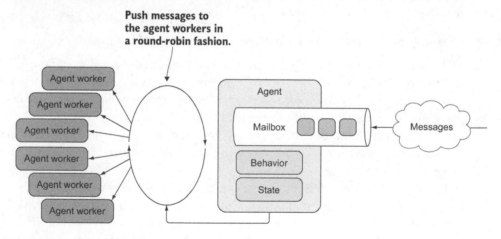

Push messages to the agent workers in a round-robin fashion.

Figure 11.10   The parallel worker agent receives the messages that are sent to the children's agents in a round-robin fashion to compute the work in parallel.

The `parallelWorker` function uses a feature called *type extensions* (http://mng.bz/Z5q9) to attach a behavior to the MailboxProcessor type. The type extension is similar to an extension method. With this type extension, you can call the `parallelWorker` function using dot notation; as a result, the `parallelWorker` function can be used and called by any other .NET programming language, keeping its implementation hidden.

The arguments of this function are as follows:

- `workers`—The number of parallel agents to initialize.
- `behavior`—The function to identically implement the underlying agents.
- `errorHandler`—The function that each child agent subscribes to, to handle eventual errors. This is an optional argument and can be omitted. In this case, an ignore function is passed.
- `cts`—A cancellation token used to stop and dispose of all the children's agents. If a cancellation token isn't passed as an argument, a default is initialized and passed into the agent constructor.

11.5.5　*How to handle errors with F# MailboxProcessor*

Internally, the `parallelWorker` function creates an instance of the `MailboxProcessor` agent, which is the parent coordinator of the agent's array (children), equaling in number the value of the `workers` argument:

```
let agents = Array.init workers (fun _ ->
                let child = MailboxProcessor.Start(behavior, cts)
                child.Error.Subscribe(errorHandler)
                    child)
```

During the initialization phase, each agent child subscribes to its error event using the function `errorHandler`. In the case of an exception thrown from the body of a `MailboxProcessor`, the error event triggers and applies the function subscribed.

Detecting and notifying the system in case of errors is essential in agent-based programming because it applies logic to react accordingly. The `MailboxProcessor` has built-in functionality for detecting and forwarding errors.

When an uncaught error occurs in a `MailboxProcessor` agent, the agent raises the error event:

```
let child = MailboxProcessor.Start(behavior, cts)
child.Error.Subscribe(errorHandler)
```

To manage the error, you can register a callback function to the event handler. It's common practice to forward the errors to a supervising agent. For example, here a simple supervisor agent displays the error received:

```
let supervisor = Agent<System.Exception>.Start(fun inbox ->
    async { while true do
                let! err = inbox.Receive()
                printfn "an error occurred in an agent: %A" err })
```

You can define the error handler function that's passed as an argument to initialize all the agent children:

```
let handler = fun error -> supervisor.Post error

let agents = Array.init workers (fun _ ->
                let child = MailboxProcessor.Start(behavior, cts)
                child.Error.Subscribe(errorHandler)
                child)
```

In critical application components, such as server-side requests represented as agents, you should plan to use the `MailboxProcessor` to handle errors gracefully and restart the application appropriately.

To facilitate error handling by notifying a supervisor agent, it's convenient to define a helper function:

```
module Agent =
    let withSupervisor (supervisor: Agent<exn>) (agent: Agent<_>) =
        agent.Error.Subscribe(fun error -> supervisor.Post error); agent
```

`withSupervisor` abstracts the registration for error handling in a reusable component. Using this helper function, you can rewrite the previous portion of code that registers error handling for the `parallelWorker`, as shown here:

```
let supervisor = Agent<System.Exception>.Start(fun inbox -> async {
                    while true do
                        let! error = inbox.Receive()
                        errorHandler error })
let agent = new MailboxProcessor<'a>((fun inbox ->
let agents = Array.init workers (fun _ ->
                    MailboxProcessor.Start(behavior)
                    |> withSupervisor supervisor)
```

The `parallelWorker` encapsulates the agent supervisor, which uses the `errorHandler` function as constructor behavior to handle the error messages from the children's agent.

11.5.6 Stopping MailboxProcessor agents—CancellationToken

To instantiate the children's agent, use the `MailboxProcessor` constructor that takes a function parameter as a behavior of the agent, and takes as a second argument a `CancellationToken` object. `CancellationToken` registers a function to dispose and stop all the agents running. This function is executed when `CancellationToken` is canceled:

```
cts.Register(fun () ->
        agents |> Array.iter(fun a -> (a :> IDisposable).Dispose()))
```

Each child in the `MailboxProcessor` part of the `parallelWorker` agent, when running, is represented by an asynchronous operation associated with a given `Cancellation-Token`. Cancellation tokens are convenient when there are multiple agents that depend on each other, and you want to cancel all of them at once, similar to our example.

A further implementation is to encapsulate the `MailboxProcessor` agent into a disposable:

```
type AgentDisposable<'T>(f:MailboxProcessor<'T> -> Async<unit>,
                         ?cancelToken:CancellationTokenSource) =
    let cancelToken = defaultArg cancelToken (new CancellationTokenSource())
    let agent = MailboxProcessor.Start(f, cancelToken.Token)

    member x.Agent = agent
    interface IDisposable with
        member x.Dispose() = (agent :> IDisposable).Dispose()
                             cancelToken.Cancel())
```

In this way, the `AgentDisposable` facilitates the cancellation and the memory deallocation (`Dispose`) of the underlying `MailboxProcessor` by calling the `Dispose` method from the `IDisposable` interface.

Using the `AgentDisposable`, you can rewrite the previous portion of code that registers the cancellation of the children's agent for `parallelWorker`:

```
let agents = Array.init workers (fun _ ->
                    new AgentDisposable<'a>(behavior, cancelToken)
                    |> withSupervisor supervisor)

thisletCancelToken.Register(fun () ->
        agents |> Array.iter(fun agent -> agent.Dispose()))
```

When the cancellation token `thisletCancelToken` is triggered, the `Dispose` method of all the children's agents is called, causing them to stop. You can find the full implementation of the refactored `parallelWorker` in this book's source code.

11.5.7 Distributing the work with MailboxProcessor

The rest of the code is self-explanatory. When a message is posted to the `parallelWorker`, the parent agent picks it up and forwards it to the first agent in line. The parent agent uses a recursive loop to maintain the state of the last agent served by index. During each iteration, the index is increased to deliver the following available message to the next agent:

```
let rec loop i = async {
        let! msg = inbox.Receive()
        agents.[i].Post(msg)
        return! loop((i+1) % workers) }
```

You can use the `parallelWorker` component in a wide range of cases. For the previous `AgentSql` code example, you applied the `parallelWorker` extension to reach the original goal of having control (management) over the number of parallel requests that can access the database server to optimize connection-pool consumption.

Listing 11.6 Using `parallelWorker` to parallelize database reads

Sets an arbitrary value for the maximum database connections opened concurrently

Retrieves the connection string from the configuration

```
let connectionString =
    ConfigurationManager.ConnectionStrings.["DbConnection"].ConnectionString

let maxOpenConnection = 10

let agentParallelRequests =
    MailboxProcessor<SqlMessage>.parallelWorker(maxOpenConnection,
                                            agentSql connectionString)

let fetchPeopleAsync (ids:int list) =
    let asyncOperation =
```

Creates an instance of parallelWorker with an agent for connection

Uses a bulk operation to retrieve a range of IDs from the database

```
        ids
        |> Seq.map (fun id -> agentParallelRequests.PostAndAsyncReply(
                                         fun ch -> Command(id, ch)))
        |> Async.Parallel
Async.StartWithContinuations(asyncOperation,
        (fun people -> people |> Array.choose id
                     |> Array.iter(fun person ->
        printfn "Fullname %s %s" person.firstName person.lastName)),
          (fun exn -> printfn "Error: %s" exn.Message),
          (fun cnl -> printfn "Operation cancelled"))
```

In this example the maximum number of open connections is arbitrary, but in a real case, this value varies. In this code, you first create the MailboxProcessor agent-ParallelRequests, which runs in parallel with the maxOpenConnection number of agents. The function fetchPeopleAsync is the final piece to glue together all the parts. The argument passed into this function is a list of people IDs to fetch from the database. Internally, the function applies the agentParallelRequests agent for each of the IDs to generate a collection of asynchronous operations that will run in parallel using the Async.Parallel function.

> **NOTE** To access a database in an asynchronous and parallel fashion, it's best to control and prioritize the read/write operation. Databases work best with a single writer at a time. In the previous example, all the operations are read, so the problem doesn't exist. In chapter 13, as part of the real-world recipes, there's a version of MailboxProcessor parallelWorker that prioritizes one write and multiple reads in parallel.

In the example, the people IDs are retrieved in parallel; a more efficient way is to create an SqlCommand that fetches the data in one database round trip. But the purpose of the example still stands. The level of parallelism is controlled by the number of agents. This is an effective technique. In this book's source code, you can find a complete and enhanced production-ready parallelWorker component that you can reuse in your daily work.

11.5.8   *Caching operations with an agent*

In the previous section, you used the F# MailboxProcessor to implement a performant and asynchronous database access agent, which could control the throughput of parallel operations. To take this a step further to improve the response time (speed) for the incoming requests, you can reduce the actual number of database queries. This is possible with the introduction of a database cache in your program. There's no reason why a single query should be executed more than once per request if the result won't change. By applying smart caching strategies in database access, you can unlock a significant increase in performance. Let's implement an agent-based reusable cache component, which then can be linked to the agentParallelRequests agent.

The cache agent's objective is to isolate and store the state of the application while handling the messages to read or update this state. This listing shows the implementation of the `MailboxProcessor CacheAgent`.

Listing 11.7 Cache agent using the `MailboxProcessor`

```
type CacheMessage<'Key> =
    | GetOrSet of 'Key * AsyncReplyChannel<obj>          Uses a DU to define the message type
    | UpdateFactory of Func<'Key,obj>                    that the MailboxProcessor handles
    | Clear
                                                         The constructor takes a factory
                                                         function for changing the
type Cache<'Key when 'Key : comparison>                  agent's behavior at runtime.
    (factory : Func<'Key, obj>,  ?timeToLive : int) =
    let timeToLive = defaultArg timeToLive 1000
    let expiry = TimeSpan.FromMilliseconds (float timeToLive)
                                                                 Sets the time-to-live
                                                                 timeout for the
    let cacheAgent = Agent.Start(fun inbox ->                    cache invalidation
        let cache = Dictionary<'Key, (obj * DateTime)>(
        HashIdentity.Structural)
                    let rec loop (factory:Func<'Key, obj>) = async {
  Uses an internal lookup         let! msg = inbox.TryReceive timeToLive
  state for caching               match msg with
                                  | Some (GetOrSet (key, channel)) ->
                                    match cache.TryGetValue(key) with
                                    | true, (v,dt) when DateTime.Now - dt < expiry ->
                                        channel.Reply v
  Tries to get a value from the       return! loop factory
  cache; if it can't get the value, | _ ->
  it creates a new one using the        let value = factory.Invoke(key)
  factory function. Then it sends       channel.Reply value
  the value to the caller.              cache.Add(key, (value, DateTime.Now))
                                        return! loop factory
                                  | Some(UpdateFactory newFactory) ->
                                    return! loop (newFactory)         Updates the
                                  | Some(Clear) ->                    factory function
                                    cache.Clear()
                                    return! loop factory         Waits asynchronously for a message
                                  | None ->                      until the timeout expires. If the timeout
                                    cache                        expired, the cache runs a cleanup.
                                    |> Seq.filter(function KeyValue(k,(_, dt)) ->
                                                            DateTime.Now - dt > expiry)
                                    |> Seq.iter(function KeyValue(k, _) ->
                                                          cache.Remove(k) |> ignore)
                                  return! loop factory }
                  loop factory )
        member this.TryGet<'a>(key : 'Key) = async {
            let! item = cacheAgent.PostAndAsyncReply(
                            fun channel -> GetOrSet(key, channel))
```

When the value is retrieved from the cache agent, it validates the types and returns Some if successful; otherwise it returns None.

```
match item with
| :? 'a as v -> return Some v
| _ -> return None  }
```

Exposes member for friendly compatibility with C#

```
member this.GetOrSetTask (key : 'Key) =
    cacheAgent.PostAndAsyncReply(fun channel -> GetOrSet(key, channel))
    |> Async.StartAsTask
```

```
member this.UpdateFactory(factory:Func<'Key, obj>) =
    cacheAgent.Post(UpdateFactory(factory))
```

Updates the factory function

In this example, the first type, CacheMessage, is the definition of the message that is sent to the MailboxProcessor in the form DUs. This DU determines the valid messages to send to the cache agent.

> **NOTE** At this point in the book, DUs are not a new topic, but it's worth mentioning that they are a mighty tool in combination with the MailboxProcessor, because they allow each defined type to contain a different signature. Consequently, they provide the ability to specify related groups of types and message contracts that are used to select and to branch into different reactions of the agent.

The core of the CacheAgent implementation is to initialize and immediately start a MailboxProcessor that constantly watches for incoming messages.

The constructs of F# make it easy to use lexical scoping to achieve isolation within asynchronous agents. This agent code uses the standard and mutable .NET dictionary collection to maintain the state originated from the different messages sent to an agent:

```
let cache = Dictionary<'Key, (obj * DateTime)>()
```

The internal dictionary is lexically private to the asynchronous agent, and no ability to read/write to the dictionary is made available other than to the agent. The mutable state in the dictionary is isolated. The agent function is defined as a recursive function loop that takes a single parameter factory, as shown here:

```
Agent.Start(fun inbox ->
    let rec loop (factory:Func<'Key, obj>) = async { ... }
```

The factory function represents the initialization policy to create and add an item when it isn't found by the cacheAgent in the local state cache. This factory function is continuously passed into the recursive function loop for state management, which allows you to swap the initialization procedure at runtime. In the case of caching the AgentSql requests, if the database or the system goes offline, then the response strategy can change. This is easily achieved by sending a message to the agent.

The agent receives the message semantic of the MailboxProcessor, which has a timeout to specify the expiration time. This is particularly useful for caching components to provoke a data invalidation, and then a data refresh:

```
let! msg = inbox.TryReceive timeToLive
```

The `TryReceive` of the inbox function returns a message option type, which can be either `Some`, when a message is received before the time `timeToLive` elapses, or `None` when no message is received during the `timeToLive` time:

```
| None ->
  cache
  |> Seq.filter(function KeyValue(k,(_, dt)) -> DateTime.Now - dt > expiry)
  |> Seq.iter(function KeyValue(k, _) -> cache.Remove(k) |> ignore)
```

In this case, when the timeout expires, the agent auto-refreshes the cached data by automatically invalidating (removing) all the cache items that expired. But if a message is received, the agent uses pattern matching to determine the message type so that the appropriate processing can be done. Here's the range of capabilities for incoming messages:

- `GetOrSet`—In this case, the agent searches the cache dictionary for an entry that contains the specified key. If the agent finds the key and the invalidation time isn't expired, then it returns the associated value. Otherwise, if the agent doesn't find the key or the invalidation time is expired, then it applies the factory function to generate a new value, which is stored into the local cache in combination with the timestamp of its creation. The timestamp is used by the agent to verify the expiration time. Finally, the agent returns the result to the sender of the message:

```
| Some (GetOrSet (key, channel)) ->
            match cache.TryGetValue(key) with
            | true, (v,dt) when DateTime.Now - dt < expiry ->
                channel.Reply v
                return! loop factory
            | _ ->
                let value = factory.Invoke(key)
                channel.Reply value
                cache.Add(key, (value, DateTime.Now))
                return! loop factory
```

- `UpdateFactory`—This message type, as already explained, allows the handler to swap the runtime initialization policy for the cache item:

```
| Some(UpdateFactory newFactory) ->
            return! loop (newFactory)
```

- `Clear`—This message type clears the cache to reload all items.

Ultimately, here's the code that links the previous parallel `AgentSql` `agentParallel-Requests` to the `CacheAgent`:

```
let connectionString =
    ConfigurationManager.ConnectionStrings.["DbConnection"].ConnectionString

let agentParallelRequests =
    MailboxProcessor<SqlMessage>.parallelWorker(8, agentSql connectionString)

let cacheAgentSql =
    let ttl = 60000
```

```
CacheAgent<int>(fun id ->
    agentParallelRequests.PostAndAsyncReply(fun ch -> Command(id, ch)), ttl)

let person = cacheAgentSql.TryGet<Person> 42
```

When the cacheAgentSql agent receives the request, it checks whether the value 42 exists in the cache and if it's expired. Otherwise, it interrogates the underlying parallel-Worker to return the expected item and save it into the cache to speed up future requests (see figure 11.11).

Each incoming request is processed asynchronously in the CacheAgent loop. If a value associated with the request (key) exists in the internal cache, it's sent back to the caller. This ensures that the operation to compute the value isn't repeated. If the value isn't in the cache, the operation computes the value, adds it to the cache, and then sends the value back to the caller.

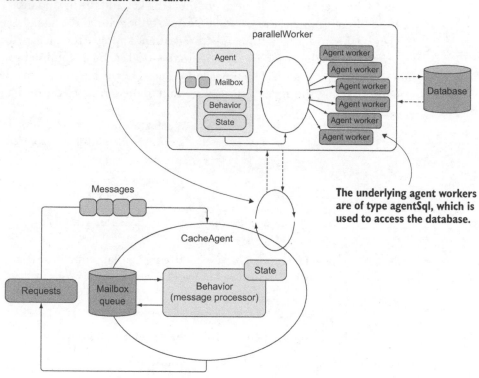

The underlying agent workers are of type agentSql, which is used to access the database.

Figure 11.11   The CacheAgent maintains a local cache composed of key/value pairs, which associate an input (from a request) to a value. When a request arrives, the CacheAgent verifies the existence of the input/key and then either returns the value (if the input/key already exists in the local cache) without running any computation, or it calculates the value to send to the caller. In the latter case, the value is also persisted in the local cache to avoid repeated computation for the same inputs.

11.5.9 *Reporting results from a MailboxProcessor*

Sometimes, the `MailboxProcessor` needs to report a state change to the system, where a subscribed component is to handle the state change. For example, for the `Cache-Agent` example to be more complete, you could extend it to include such features as notification when data changes or when there's a cache removal.

But how does a `MailboxProcessor` report notifications to the outside system? This is accomplished by using events (listing 11.8). You've already seen how the `Mailbox-Processor` reports when an internal error occurs by triggering a notification to all of its subscribers. You can apply the same design to report any other arbitrary events from the agent. Using the previous `CacheAgent`, let's implement an event reporting that can be used to notify when data invalidation occurs. For the example, you'll modify the agent for an auto-refresh that can be used to notify when data has changed (the code to note is in bold).

NOTE This notification pattern isn't recommended in situations where the `CacheAgent` handles many items, because, depending on the factory function and the data to reload, the auto-refresh process could take more time to complete.

> **Listing 11.8   Cache with event notification for refreshed items**

Uses an event to report a cache item refreshed, which indicates a change of state

Triggers the event using the specified synchronization context, or directly if no synchronization context is specified

```fsharp
type Cache<'Key when 'Key : comparison>
        (factory : Func<'Key, obj>,  ?timeToLive : int,
         ?synchContext:SynchronizationContext) =
    let timeToLive = defaultArg timeToLive 1000
    let expiry = TimeSpan.FromMilliseconds (float timeToLive)

    let cacheItemRefreshed = Event<('Key * 'obj)[]>()

    let reportBatch items =
        match synchContext with
        | None -> cacheItemRefreshed.Trigger(items)
        | Some ctx ->
          ctx.Post((fun _ -> cacheItemRefreshed.Trigger(items)),null)

    let cacheAgent = Agent.Start(fun inbox ->
        let cache = Dictionary<'Key, (obj *
    DateTime)>(HashIdentity.Structural)
        let rec loop (factory:Func<'Key, obj>) = async {
            let! msg = inbox.TryReceive timeToLive
            match msg with
            | Some (GetOrSet (key, channel)) ->
                match cache.TryGetValue(key) with
                | true, (v,dt) when DateTime.Now - dt < expiry ->
                    channel.Reply v
                    return! loop factory
                | _ ->
```

No synchronization context exists so it triggers as in the first case.

Uses the Post method of the context to trigger the event

```
            let value = factory.Invoke(key)
            channel.Reply value
            reportBatch ([| (key, value) |])
            cache.Add(key, (value, DateTime.Now))
            return! loop factory
      | Some(UpdateFactory newFactory) ->
        return! loop (newFactory)
      | Some(Clear) ->
        cache.Clear()
        return! loop factory
      | None ->
        cache
        |> Seq.choose(function KeyValue(k,(_, dt)) ->
              if DateTime.Now - dt > expiry then
                  let value, dt = factory.Invoke(k), DateTime.Now
                  cache.[k] <- (value,dt)
                  Some (k, value)
              else None)
        |> Seq.toArray
        |> reportBatch
      }
    loop factory )
  member this.TryGet<'a>(key : 'Key) = async {
    let! item = cacheAgent.PostAndAsyncReply(
              fun channel -> GetOrSet(key, channel))
    match item with
    | :? 'a as v -> return Some v
    | _ -> return None  }
  member this.DataRefreshed = cacheItemRefreshed.Publish
  member this.Clear() = cacheAgent.Post(Clear)
```

> **Triggers the event for the refreshed items** (annotation pointing to `reportBatch ([| (key, value) |])`)

> **Uses an event to report a cache item refreshed, which indicates a change of state** (annotation pointing to `member this.DataRefreshed = cacheItemRefreshed.Publish`)

In this code, the event `cacheItemRefreshed` channel dispatches the changes of state. By default, F# events execute the handlers on the same thread on which they're triggered. In this case, it uses the agent's current thread. But depending on which thread originated the `MailboxProcessor`, the current thread can be either from the `thread-Pool` or coming from the UI thread, specifically from `SynchronizationContext`, a class from `System.Threading` that captures the current synchronization context. The latter might be useful when the notification is triggered in response to an event that targets to update the UI. This is the reason the agent constructor, in the example, has the new parameter `synchContext`, which is an option type that provides a convenient mechanism to control where the event is triggered.

NOTE The optional parameters in F# are written using the question mark (?) prefix syntax, `?synchContext`, which passes the types as option values.

The `Some ctx` command means that the `SynchronizationContext` isn't null, and `ctx` is an arbitrary name given to access its value. When the synchronization context is `Some ctx`, the reporting mechanism uses the `Post` method to notify the state changes on the thread selected by the synchronization context. The method signature of the synchronization context `ctx.Post` takes a delegate and an argument used by the delegate.

Although the second argument isn't required, `null` is used as replacement. The function `reportBatch` triggers the event `cacheItemRefreshed`:

```
this.DataRefreshed.Add(printAgent.Post)
```

In the example, the change-of-state notification handler posts a message to a `Mailbox-Processor` to print a report in a thread-safe manner. But you could use the same idea in more complex scenarios, such as for updating a web page automatically with the most recent data using `SignalR`.

11.5.10 Using the thread pool to report events from MailboxProcessor

In most cases, to avoid unnecessary overhead, it is preferable to trigger an event using the current thread. Still, there may be circumstances where a different threading model could be better: for example, if triggering an event could block for a time or throw an exception that could kill the current process. A valid option is to trigger the event operating the thread pool to run the notification in a separate thread. The `reportBatch` function can be refactored using the F# asynchronous workflow and the `Async.Start` operator:

```
let reportBatch batch =
    async { batchEvent.Trigger(batch) } |> Async.Start
```

Be aware with this implementation, the code running on a thread pool cannot access UI elements.

11.6 F# MailboxProcessor: 10,000 agents for a game of life

`MailboxProcessor`, combined with asynchronous workflows, is a lightweight unit of computation (primitives), compared to threads. Agents can be spawned and destroyed with minimal overhead. You can distribute the work to various `MailboxProcessors`, similar to how you might use threads, without having to incur the overhead associated with spinning up a new thread. For this reason, it's completely feasible to create applications that consist of hundreds of thousands of agents running in parallel with minimum impact to the computer resources.

> **NOTE** In a 32-bit OS machine, you can create a little more than 1,300 threads before an out-of-memory exception is thrown. This limitation doesn't apply to `MailboxProcessor`, which is backed up by the thread pool and isn't directly mapped to a thread.

In this section, we use `MailboxProcessor` from multiple instances by implementing the Game of Life (https://en.wikipedia.org/wiki/Game_of_Life). As described on Wikipedia, Life, as it is simply known, is a cellular automaton. It is a zero-player game, which means that once the game starts with a random initial configuration, it runs without any other input. This game consists of a collection of cells that run on a grid, each cell following a few mathematical rules. Cells can live, die, or multiply. Every cell interacts with its eight neighbors (the adjacent cells). A new state of the grid needs to be continually calculated to move the cells around to respect these rules.

These are the Game of Life rules:

- Each cell with one or no neighbors dies, as if by solitude.
- Each cell with four or more neighbors dies, as if by overpopulation.
- Each cell with two or three neighbors survives.
- Each cell with three neighbors becomes populated.

Depending on the initial conditions, the cells form patterns throughout the course of the game. The rules are applied repeatedly to create further generations until the cells reach a stable state (figure 11.12).

AgentCell connects and communicates with the surrounding neighbor cells to verify their state as dead or alive. The survival of the AgentCell is affected by these surrounding cells.

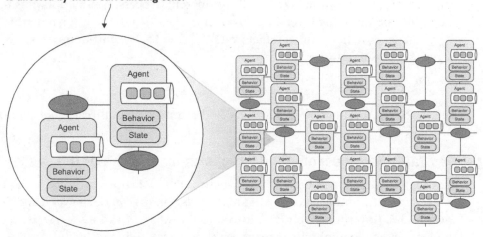

Figure 11.12   When the Game of Life is set up, each cell (in the code example there are 100,000 cells) is constructed using an `AgentCell MailboxProcessor`. Each agent can be dead, a black circle, or alive depending the state of its neighbors.

Listing 11.9 is the implementation of the Game of Life cell, `AgentCell`, which is based on the F# `MailboxProcessor`. Each agent cell communicates with the adjacent cells through asynchronous message passing, producing a fully parallelized Game of Life. For conciseness, and because they're irrelevant for the main point of the example, I omitted a few parts of the code. You can find the full implementation in this book's source code.

Listing 11.9   Game of Life with `MailboxProcessor` as cells

```
type CellMessage =
    | NeighborState of cell:AgentCell * isalive:bool
    | State of cellstate:AgentCell
    | Neighbors of cells:AgentCell list
    | ResetCell              ◀──── Uses a DU that defines the
and State =                        message for the agent cell
    {   neighbors:AgentCell list
        wasAlive:bool
```

```
        isAlive:bool }                                    Record type used to keep track of the
    static member createDefault isAlive =                 state for each cell agent
        { neighbors=[]; isAlive=isAlive; wasAlive=false; }

and AgentCell(location, alive, updateAgent:Agent<_>) as this =
    let neighborStates = Dictionary<AgentCell, bool>()
    let AgentCell =
        Agent<CellMessage>.Start(fun inbox ->          Internal state of each agent, to
            let rec loop state = async {               keep track of the state of each
                let! msg = inbox.Receive()             cell agent's neighbors
                match msg with
                | ResetCell ->                            Notifies all the cell's
                    state.neighbors                       neighbors of its current state
                    |> Seq.iter(fun cell -> cell.Send(State(this)))
                    neighborStates.Clear()
                    return! loop { state with wasAlive=state.isAlive }
                | Neighbors(neighbors) ->
                    return! loop { state with neighbors=neighbors }
                | State(c) ->
                    c.Send(NeighborState(this, state.wasAlive))
                    return! loop state                       Recursively maintains
                | NeighborState(cell, alive) ->              a local state
                    neighborStates.[cell] <- alive
                    if neighborStates.Count = 8 then
                        let aliveState =
                            let numberOfneighborAlive =
                                neighborStates
                                |> Seq.filter(fun (KeyValue(_,v)) -> v)
                                |> Seq.length
                            match numberOfneighborAlive with
                            | a when a > 3 || a < 2 -> false
                            | 3 -> true
                            | _ -> state.isAlive
                        updateAgent.Post(Update(aliveState, location))
                        return! loop { state with isAlive = aliveState }
                    else return! loop state }
            loop (State.createDefault alive ))
```

- **Uses an algorithm that updates the current cell state according to the state of the neighbors**
- **Runs the rules of the Game of Life**
- **Updates the agent that refreshes the UI**

```
    member this.Send(msg) = AgentCell.Post msg
```

AgentCell represents a cell in the grid of the Game of Life. The main concept is that each agent communicates with the neighbor cells about its (the agent's) current state using asynchronous message passing. This pattern creates a chain of interconnected parallel communications that involves all the cells, which send their updated state to the updateAgent MailboxProcessor. At this point, the updateAgent refreshes the graphic in the UI.

Listing 11.10 `updateAgent` that refreshes the WPF UI in real time

The updateAgent constructor takes the captures that the SynchronizationContext used to update the WPF controller using the correct thread.

```
    let updateAgent grid (ctx: SynchronizationContext) =
        let gridProduct = grid.Width * grid.Height
        let pixels = Array.zeroCreate<byte> (gridProduct)
```

Array of pixels used to render the state of the Game of Life. Each pixel represents a cell state.

Shared grid state that represents the state of current generation of cells

```
Agent<UpdateView>.Start(fun inbox ->
    let gridState = Dictionary<Location, bool>(HashIdentity.Structural)
    let rec loop () = async {
        let! msg = inbox.Receive()
        match msg with
        | Update(alive, location, agent) ->
                agentStates.[location] <- alive
            agent.Send(ResetCell)
            if agentStates.Count = gridProduct then
                agentStates.AsParallel().ForAll(fun s ->
                    pixels.[s.Key.x+s.Key.y*grid.Width]
                            <- if s.Value then 128uy else 0uy
                )
                do! Async.SwitchToContext ctx
                image.Source <- createImage pixels
                do! Async.SwitchToThreadPool()
                agentStates.Clear()
            return! loop()
    }
    loop())
```

Lists the Update message that updates the state of the given cell and resets cell state

The pixel of a related cell is updated with the state alive (color) or dead (white).

Updates the UI using the correct thread passed from the constructor

When all cells notify that they're updated, a new image representing the updated grid is generated to refresh the WPF UI application.

updateAgent, as its name suggests, updates the state of each pixel with the correlated cell value received in the Update message. The agent maintains the status of the pixels and uses that status to create a new image when all the cells have sent their new state. Next, updateAgent refreshes the graphical WPF UI with this new image, which represents the current grid of the Game of Life:

```
do! Async.SwitchToContext ctx
image.Source <- createImage pixels
do! Async.SwitchToThreadPool()
```

It's important to note that updateAgent agent uses the current synchronization context to update the WPF controller correctly. The current thread is switched to the UI thread using the Async.SwitchToContext function (discussed in chapter 9).

The final piece of code to run the Game of Life generates a grid that acts as the playground for the cells, and then a timer notifies the cells to update themselves (listing 11.11). In this example, the grid is a square of 100 cells per side, for a total of 10,000 cells (MailboxProcessors) that run in parallel with a refresh timer of 50 ms, as shown in figure 11.13. There are 10,000 MailboxProcessors communicating with each other and updating the UI 20 times every second (the code to note is in bold).

Listing 11.11   Creating the Game of Life grid and starting the timer to refresh

Indicates the size of each side of the grid

Defines the grid using a record type with the accessible properties Width and Height

```
let run(ctx:SynchronizationContext) =
    let size = 100
    let grid = { Width= size; Height=size}
    let updateAgent = updateAgent grid ctx
```

```
let cells = seq { for x = 0 to grid.Width - 1 do
                    for y = 0 to grid.Height - 1 do
                      let agent = AgentCell({x=x;y=y},
                          alive=getRandomBool(),
                          updateAgent=updateAgent)
                yield (x,y), agent  } |> dict
let neighbours (x', y') =
    seq {
      for x = x' - 1 to x' + 1 do
        for y = y' - 1 to y' + 1 do
          if x <> x' || y <> y' then
            yield cells.[(x + grid.Width) % grid.Width,
                         (y + grid.Height) % grid.Height]
    } |> Seq.toList

cells.AsParallel().ForAll(fun pair ->
    let cell = pair.Value
    let neighbours = neighbours pair.Key
    cell.Send(Neighbors(neighbours))
    cell.Send(ResetCell)
)
```

Generates a 100 x 100 grid, creating one MailboaxProcessor per cell (for a total of 10,000 agents)

Notifies all the cells in parallel about their neighbors and resets their state

The notifications to all the `cells` (agents) are sent in parallel using PLINQ. The `cells` are an F# sequence that's treated as a .NET `IEnumerable`, which allows an effortless integration of LINQ/PLINQ.

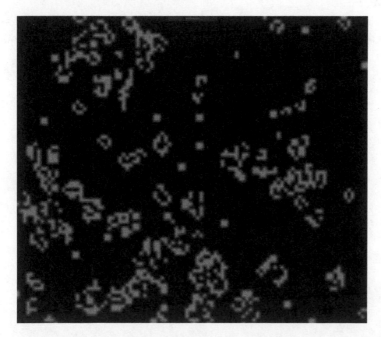

Figure 11.13   Game of Life. The GUI is a WPF application.

When the code runs, the program generates 10,000 F# `MailboxProcessors` in less than 1 ms with a memory consumption, specific for the agents, of less than 25 MB. Impressive!

Summary

- The agent programming model intrinsically promotes immutability and isolation for writing concurrent systems, so even complex systems are easier to reason about because the agents are encapsulated into active objects.
- The Reactive Manifesto defines the properties to implement a reactive system, which is flexible, loosely coupled, and scalable.
- Natural isolation is important for writing lockless concurrent code. In a multi-threaded program, isolation solves the problem of shared state by giving each thread a copied portion of data to perform local computation. When using isolation, there's no race condition.
- By being asynchronous, agents are lightweight, because they don't block threads while waiting for a message. As a result, you can use hundreds of thousands of agents in a single application without any impact on the memory footprint.
- The F# `MailboxProcessor` allows two-way communication: the agent can use an asynchronous channel to return (reply) to the caller the result of a computation.
- The agent programming model F# `MailboxProcessor` is a great tool for solving application bottleneck issues, such as multiple concurrent database accesses. In fact, you can use agents to speed up applications significantly and keep the server responsive.
- Other .NET programming languages can consume the F# `MailboxProcessor` by exposing the methods using the friendly TPL task-based programming model.

12

Parallel workflow and agent programming with TPL Dataflow

This chapter covers

- Using TPL Dataflow blocks

- Constructing a highly concurrent workflow

- Implementing a sophisticated Producer/ Consumer pattern

- Integrating Reactive Extensions with TPL Dataflow

Today's global market requires that businesses and industries be agile enough to respond to a constant flow of changing data. These workflows are frequently large, and sometimes infinite or unknown in size. Often, the data requires complex processing, leading to high throughput demands and potentially immense computational loads. To cope with these requirements, the key is to use parallelism to exploit system resources and multiple cores.

But today's .NET Framework's concurrent programming models weren't designed with dataflow in mind. When designing a reactive application, it's fundamental to build and treat the system components as units of work. These units react to messages, which are propagated by other components in the chain of processing. These reactive models emphasize a push-based model for applications to work, rather than a pull-based model (see chapter 6). This push-based strategy ensures that the individual components are easy to test and link, and, most importantly, easy to understand.

This new focus on push-based constructions is changing how programmers design applications. A single task can quickly grow complex, and even simple-looking requirements can lead to complicated code.

In this chapter, you'll learn how the .NET Task Parallel Library Dataflow (TPL Dataflow, or TDF) helps you to tackle the complexity of developing modern systems with an API that builds on TAP. TDF fully supports asynchronous processing, in combination with a powerful compositionality semantic and a better configuration mechanism than the TPL. TDF eases concurrent processing and implements tailored asynchronous parallel workflow and batch queuing. Furthermore, it facilitates the implementation of sophisticated patterns based on combining multiple components that talk to each other by passing messages.

12.1 *The power of TPL Dataflow*

Let's say you're building a sophisticated Producer/Consumer pattern that must support multiple producers and/or multiple consumers in parallel, or perhaps it has to support workflows that can scale the different steps of the process independently. One solution is to exploit Microsoft TPL Dataflow. With the release of .NET 4.5, Microsoft introduced TPL Dataflow as part of the tool set for writing concurrent applications. TDF is designed with the higher-level constructs necessary to tackle easy parallel problems while providing a simple-to-use, powerful framework for building asynchronous data-processing pipelines. TDF isn't distributed as part of the .NET 4.5 Framework, so to access its API and classes, you need to import the official Microsoft NuGet Package (install-Package Microsoft.Tpl.DataFlow).

TDF offers a rich array of components (also called *blocks*) for composing dataflow and pipeline infrastructures based on the in-process message-passing semantic (see figure 12.1). This dataflow model promotes actor-based programming by providing in-process message passing for coarse-grained dataflow and pipelining tasks.

TDF uses the task scheduler (TaskScheduler, http://mng.bz/4N8F) of the TPL to efficiently manage the underlying threads and to support the TAP model (async/await) for optimized resource utilization. TDF increases the robustness of highly concurrent applications and obtains better performance for parallelizing CPU and I/O intensive operations, which have high throughput and low latency.

> **NOTE** TPL Dataflow enables effective techniques for running *embarrassingly parallel problems*, explained in chapter 3, meaning there are many independent computations that can be executed in parallel in an evident way.

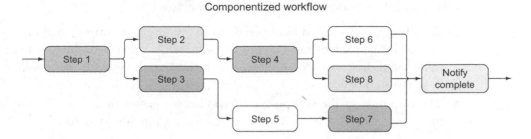

Figure 12.1   Workflow composed by multiple steps. Each operation can be treated as an independent computation.

The concept behind the TPL Dataflow library is to ease the creation of multiple patterns, such as with batch-processing pipelines, parallel stream processing, data buffering, or joining and processing batch data from one or more sources. Each of these patterns can be used as a standalone, or may be composed with other patterns, enabling developers to easily express complex dataflow.

12.2   Designed to compose: TPL Dataflow blocks

Imagine you're implementing a complex workflow process composed of many different steps, such as a stock analysis pipeline. It's ideal to split the computation in blocks, developing each block independently and then gluing them together. Making these blocks reusable and interchangeable enhances their convenience. This composable design would simplify the application of complex and convoluted systems.

Compositionality is the main strength of TPL Dataflow, because its set of independent containers, known as blocks, is designed to be combined. These blocks can be a chain of different tasks to construct a parallel workflow, and are easily swapped, reordered, reused, or even removed. TDF emphasizes a component's architectural approach to ease the restructure of the design. These dataflow components are useful when you have multiple operations that must communicate with one another asynchronously or when you want to process data as it becomes available, as shown in figure 12.2.

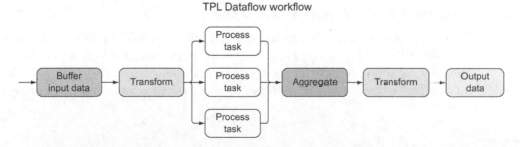

Figure 12.2   TDF embraces the concepts of reusable components. In this figure, each step of the workflow acts as reusable components. TDF brings a few core primitives that allow you to express computations based on Dataflow graphs.

Here's a high-level view of how TDF blocks operate:

1 Each block receives and buffers data from one or more sources, including other blocks, in the form of messages. When a message is received, the block reacts by applying its behavior to the input, which then can be transformed and/or used to perform side effects.

2 The output from the component (*block*) is then passed to the next linked block, and to the next one, if any, and so on, creating a pipeline structure.

NOTE The term *reactive programming* has been used for a long time to describe dataflow because the reaction is generated from receiving a piece of data.

TDF excels at providing a set of configurable properties by which it's possible, with small changes, to control the level of parallelism, manage the buffer size of the mailbox, and process data and dispatch the outputs.

There are three main types of dataflow blocks:

- *Source*—Operates as producer of data. It can also be read from.
- *Target*—Acts as a consumer, which receives the data and can be written to.
- *Propagator*—Acts as both a Source and a Target block.

For each of these dataflow blocks, TDF provides a set of subblocks, each with a different purpose. It's impossible to cover all the blocks in one chapter. In the following sections we focus on the most common and versatile ones to adopt in general pipeline composition applications.

TIP TPL Dataflow's most commonly used blocks are the standard `Buffer-Block`, `ActionBlock`, and `TransformBlock`. Each is based on a delegate, which can be in the form of anonymous function that defines the work to compute. I recommend that you keep these anonymous methods short, simple to follow, and easier to maintain.

For more information about the Dataflow library, see the online MSDN documentation (http://mng.bz/GDbF).

12.2.1 *Using BufferBlock<TInput> as a FIFO buffer*

TDF `BufferBlock<T>` acts as an unbounded buffer for data that's stored in a first in, first out (FIFO) order (figure 12.3). In general, `BufferBlock` is a great tool for enabling and implementing asynchronous Producer/Consumer patterns, where the internal message queue can be written to by multiple sources, or read from multiple targets.

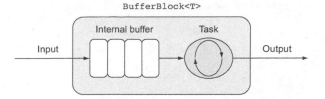

Figure 12.3 The TDF `BufferBlock` has an internal buffer where messages are queued, waiting to be processed by the task. The input and output are the same types, and this block doesn't apply any transformation on the data.

Here is a simple Producer/Consumer using the TDF `BufferBlock`.

Listing 12.1 Producer/Consumer based on the TDF `BufferBlock`

```
BufferBlock<int> buffer = new BufferBlock<int>();          ◀── Hands off through a bounded
                                                                 BufferBlock<T>
async Task Producer(IEnumerable<int> values)
{                                                      Sends a message to the BufferBlock
        foreach (var value in values)
            buffer.Post(value);              ◀──
        buffer.Complete();          ◀──
}                                          Notifies the BufferBlock that there are no
async Task Consumer(Action<int> process)   more items to process, and completes
{
        while (await buffer.OutputAvailableAsync())    ◀──
            process(await buffer.ReceiveAsync());   ◀──
}                                                      Signals when a new item is
                                    Receives a message  available to be retrieved
async Task Run()                    asynchronously
{
        IEnumerable<int> range = Enumerable.Range(0,100);
        await Task.WhenAll(Producer(range), Consumer(n =>
            Console.WriteLine($"value {n}")));
}
```

The items of the `IEnumerable` values are sent through the `buffer.Post` method to the `BufferBlock` buffer, which retrieves them asynchronously using the `buffer.ReceiveAsync` method. The `OutputAvailableAsync` method knows when the next item is ready to be retrieved and makes the notification. This is important to protect the code from an exception; if the buffer tries to call the `Receive` method after the block completes processing, an error is thrown. This `BufferBlock` block essentially receives and stores data so that it can be dispatched to one or more other target blocks for processing.

12.2.2 *Transforming data with TransformBlock<TInput, TOutput>*

The TDF `TransformBlock<TInput,TOutput>` acts like a mapping function, which applies a projection function to an input value and provides a correlated output (figure 12.4). The transformation function is passed as an argument in the form of a delegate `Func<TInput,TOutput>`, which is generally expressed as a lambda expression. This block's default behavior is to process one message at a time, maintaining strict FIFO ordering.

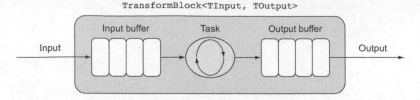

Figure 12.4   The TDF `TransformBlock` has an internal buffer for both the input and output values; this type of block has the same buffer capabilities as `BufferBlock`. The purpose of this block is to apply a transformation function on the data; the `Input` and `Output` are likely different types.

Note that `TransformBlock<TInput,TOutput>` performs as the `BufferBlock<TOutput>`, which buffers both the input and output values. The underlying delegate can run synchronously or asynchronously. The asynchronous version has a type signature `Func<TInput,Task<TOutput>>` whose purpose it is to run the underlying function asynchronously. The block treats the process of that element as completed when the returned `Task` appears terminated. This listing shows how to use the `TransformBlock` type (the code to note is in bold).

Listing 12.2   Downloading images using the TDF `TransformBlock`

Uses a lambda expression to process the urlImage asynchronously

```
var fetchImageFlag = new TransformBlock<string, (string, byte[])>(
    async urlImage => {
        using (var webClient = new WebClient()) {
            byte[] data = await webClient.DownloadDataTaskAsync(urlImage);
            return (urlImage, data);
        }
});
```

Output consists of a tuple with the image URL and the related byte array.

Downloads the flag image and returns the relative byte array

```
List<string> urlFlags = new List<string>{
    "Italy#/media/File:Flag_of_Italy.svg",
    "Spain#/media/File:Flag_of_Spain.svg",
    "United_States#/media/File:Flag_of_the_United_States.svg"
    };

foreach (var urlFlag in urlFlags)
    fetchImageFlag.Post($"https://en.wikipedia.org/wiki/{urlFlag}");
```

In this example, the `TransformBlock<string,(string, byte[])> fetchImageFlag` block fetches the flag image in a tuple string and byte array format. In this case, the output isn't consumed anywhere, so the code isn't too useful. You need another block to process the outcome in a meaningful way.

12.2.3   *Completing the work with ActionBlock<TInput >*

The TDF `ActionBlock` executes a given callback for any item sent to it. You can think of this block logically as a buffer for data combined with a task for processing that data.

`ActionBlock<TInput>` is a target block that calls a delegate when it receives data, similar to a for-each loop (figure 12.5).

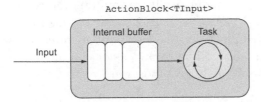

Figure 12.5 The TDF `ActionBlock` **has an internal buffer for input messages that are queued if the task is busy processing another message. This type of block has the same buffer capabilities as** `BufferBlock`**. The purpose of this block is to apply an action that completes the workflow without output that likely produces side effects. In general, because** `ActionBlock` **doesn't have an output, it cannot compose to a following block, so it's used to terminate the workflow.**

`ActionBlock<TInput>` is usually the last step in a TDF pipeline; in fact, it doesn't produce any output. This design prevents `ActionBlock` from being combined with further blocks, unless it posts or sends the data to another block, making it the perfect candidate to terminate the workflow process. For this reason, `ActionBlock` is likely to produce side effects as a final step to complete the pipeline processing.

The following code shows the `TransformBlock` from the previous listing pushing its outputs to the `ActionBlock` to persist the flag images in the local filesystem (in bold).

Listing 12.3 Persisting data using the TDF `ActionBlock`

Uses a lambda expression to process data asynchronously

Deconstructs the tuple to access underlying items

```
var saveData = new ActionBlock<(string, byte[])>(async data => {
    (string urlImage, byte[] image) = data;
    string filePath = urlImage.Substring(urlImage.IndexOf("File:") + 5);
    await File.WriteAllBytesAsync(filePath, image);
});
```

Writes the data to the local filesystem asynchronously

```
fetchImageFlag.LinkTo(saveData);
```

Links the output from the TransformBlock fetchImageFlag to the saveData ActionBlock

The argument passed into the constructor during the instantiation of the `Action-Block` block can be either a delegate `Action<TInput>` or `Func<TInput,Task>`. The latter performs the internal action (behavior) asynchronously for each message input (received). Note that the `ActionBlock` has an internal buffer for the incoming data to be processed, which works exactly like the `BufferBlock`.

It's important to remember that the `ActionBlock saveData` is linked to the previous `TransformBlock fetchImageFlag` using the `LinkTo` extension method. In this way, the output produced by the `TransformBlock` is pushed to the `ActionBlock` as soon as available.

12.2.4 Linking dataflow blocks

TDF blocks can be linked with the help of the `LinkTo` extension method. Linking dataflow blocks is a powerful technique for automatically transmitting the result of each computation between the connected blocks in a message-passing manner. The key component for building sophisticated pipelines in a declarative manner is to use connecting blocks. If we look at the signature of the `LinkTo` extension method from the conceptual point of view, it looks like a function composition:

```
LinkTo: (a -> b) -> (b -> c)
```

12.3 Implementing a sophisticated Producer/Consumer with TDF

The TDF programming model can be seen as a sophisticated Producer/Consumer pattern, because the blocks encourage a pipeline model of programming, with producers sending messages to decoupled consumers. These messages are passed asynchronously, maximizing throughput. This design provides the benefits of not blocking the producers, because the TDF blocks (queue) act as a buffer, eliminating waiting time. The synchronization access between producer and consumers may sound like an abstract problem, but it's a common task in concurrent programming. You can view it as a design pattern for synchronizing two components.

12.3.1 A multiple Producer/single Consumer pattern: TPL Dataflow

The Producer/Consumer pattern is one of the most widely used patterns in parallel programming. Developers use it to isolate work to be executed from the processing of that work. In a typical Producer/Consumer pattern, at least two separated threads run concurrently: one produces and pushes the data to process into a queue, and the other verifies the presence of the new incoming piece of data and processes it. The queue that holds the tasks is shared among these threads, which requires care for accessing tasks safely. TDF is a great tool for implementing this pattern, because it has intrinsic support for multiple readers and multiple writers concurrently, and it encourages a pipeline pattern of programming with producers sending messages to decoupled consumers (figure 12.6).

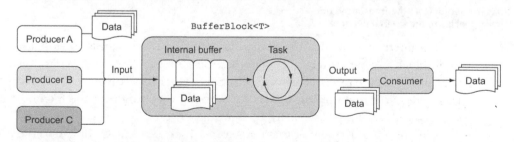

Figure 12.6   Multiple-producers/one-consumer pattern using the TDF `BufferBlock`, which can manage and throttle the pressure of multiple producers

In the case of a multiple-Producer/single-Consumer pattern, it's important to enforce a restriction between the number of items generated and the number of items consumed. This constraint aims to balance the work between the producers when the consumer cannot handle the load. This technique is called *throttling*. Throttling protects the program from running out of memory if the producers are faster than the consumer. Fortunately, TDF has built-in support for throttling, which is achieved by setting the maximum size of the buffer through the property BoundedCapacity, part of the DataFlowBlockOptions. In listing 12.4, this property ensures that there will never be more than 10 items in the BufferBlock queue. Also, in combination with enforcing the limit of the buffer size, it's important to use the function SendAsync, which waits without blocking for the buffer to have available space to place a new item.

Listing 12.4 Asynchronous Producer/Consumer using TDF

Sends the message to the buffer block asynchronously. The SendAsync method helps throttle the messages sent.

Sets the BoundedCapacity to manage and throttle the pressure from multiple producers

```
BufferBlock<int> buffer = new BufferBlock<int>(
     new DataFlowBlockOptions { BoundedCapacity = 10 });

async Task Produce(IEnumerable<int> values)
{
     foreach (var value in values)
          await buffer.SendAsync(value);;
}

async Task MultipleProducers(params IEnumerable<int>[] producers)
{
     await Task.WhenAll(
          from values in producers select Produce(values).ToArray())
               .ContinueWith(_ => buffer.Complete());
}

async Task Consumer(Action<int> process)
{
     while (await buffer.OutputAvailableAsync())
          process(await buffer.ReceiveAsync());
}

async Task Run() {
     IEnumerable<int> range = Enumerable.Range(0, 100);

     await Task.WhenAll(MultipleProducers(range, range, range),
          Consumer(n => Console.WriteLine($"value {n} - ThreadId
          {Thread.CurrentThread.ManagedThreadId}")));
}
```

Runs multiple producers in parallel, waiting for all to terminate before notifying the buffer block to complete

When all producers terminate, the buffer block is notified as complete.

Safeguards the buffer block from receiving a message only if there are any items available in the queue

By default, TDF blocks have the value DataFlowBlockOptions.Unbounded set to -1, which means that the queue is unbounded (unlimited) to the number of messages. But you can reset this value to a specific capacity that limits the number of messages the block may be queuing. When the queue reaches maximum capacity, any additional incoming messages will be postponed for later processing, making the producer wait before further work. Likely, making the producer slow down (or wait) isn't a problem because the messages are sent asynchronously.

12.3.2 A single Producer/multiple Consumer pattern

The TDF BufferBlock intrinsically supports a single Producer/multiple Consumer pattern. This is handy if the producer performs faster than the multiple consumers, such as when they're running intensive operations.

Fortunately, this pattern is running on a multicore machine, so it can use multiple cores to spin up multiple processing blocks (consumers), each of which can handle the producers concurrently.

Achieving the multiple-consumer behavior is a matter of configuration. To do so, set the MaxDegreeOfParallelism property to the number of parallel consumers to run. Here's listing 12.4 modified to apply a max-degree-of-parallelism set to the number of available logical processors:

```
BufferBlock<int> buffer = new BufferBlock<int>(new DataFlowBlockOptions {
                BoundedCapacity = 10,
                MaxDegreeOfParallelism = Environment.ProcessorCount });
```

NOTE *Logical cores* are the number of physical cores times the number of threads that can run on each core. An 8-core processor that runs two threads per core has 16 logical processors.

By default, the TDF block setting processes only one message at a time, while buffering the other incoming messages until the previous one completes. Each block is independent of others, so one block can process one item while another block processes a different item. But when constructing the block, you can change this behavior by setting the MaxDegreeOfParallelism property in the DataFlowBlockOptions to a value greater than 1. You can use TDF to speed up the computations by specifying the number of messages that can be processed in parallel. The internals of the class handle the rest, including the ordering of the data sequence.

12.4 Enabling an agent model in C# using TPL Dataflow

TDF blocks are designed to be stateless by default, which is perfectly fine for most scenarios. But there are situations in an application when it's important to maintain a state: for example, a global counter, a centralized in-memory cache, or a shared database context for transactional operations.

In such situations, there's a high probability that the shared state is also the subject of mutation, because of continually tracking certain values. The problem has always been the difficulty of handling asynchronous computations combined with mutable state. As previously mentioned, the mutation of shared state becomes dangerous in a multithreaded environment by leading you into a tar pit of concurrent issues (http://curtclifton .net/papers/MoseleyMarks06a.pdf). Luckily, TDF encapsulates the state inside the blocks, while the channels between blocks are the only dependencies. By design, this permits isolated mutation in a safe manner.

As demonstrated in chapter 11, the F# MailboxProcessor can solve these problems because it embraces the agent model philosophy, which can maintain an internal state by safeguarding its access to be concurrent safe (only one thread at a time can access the agent). Ultimately, the F# MailboxProcessor can expose a set of APIs to the C# code that can consume it effortlessly. Alternatively, you can reach the same performance using TDF to implement an agent object in C#, and then that agent object can act as the F# MailboxProcessor.

The implementation of StatefulDataFlowAgent relies on the instance of actionBlock to receive, buffer, and process incoming messages with an unbounded limit (figure 12.7). Note that the max degree of parallelism is set to the default value 1 as designed, embracing the single-threaded nature of the agent model. The state of the agent is initialized in the constructor and is maintained through a polymorphic and mutable value TState, which is reassigned as each message is processed. (Remember that the agent model only allows access by one thread at a time, ensuring that the messages are processed sequentially to eliminate any concurrent problems.) It's good practice to use an immutable state, regardless of the safety provided by the agent implementation.

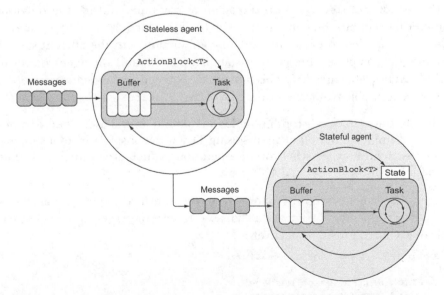

Figure 12.7 The stateful and stateless agents implemented using the TDF `ActionBlock`. The stateful agent has an internal isolated arbitrary value to maintain in memory a state that can change.

The next listing shows the implementation of the StatefulDataFlowAgent class, which defines a stateful and generic agent that encapsulates the TDF AgentBlock to process and store type values (in bold).

Listing 12.5   Stateful agent in C# using TDF

```
class StatefulDataFlowAgent<TState, TMessage> : IAgent<TMessage>
{
    private TState state;
    private readonly ActionBlock<TMessage> actionBlock;

    public StatefulDataFlowAgent(                          Uses an asynchronous function to
        TState initialState,                               define the behavior of the agent
        Func<TState, TMessage, Task<TState>> action,
        CancellationTokenSource cts = null)
    {
        state = initialState;
        var options = new ExecutionDataFlowBlockOptions {
            CancellationToken = cts != null ?
            cts.Token : CancellationToken.None
        };
        actionBlock = new ActionBlock<TMessage>(
                async msg => state = await action(state, msg), options);
    }
    public Task Send(TMessage message) => actionBlock.SendAsync(message);
    public void Post(TMessage message) => actionBlock.Post(message);
}
```

If a cancellation token isn't provided in the constructor, a new token is provided.

Constructs the internal ActionBlock that acts as an encapsulated agent

The CancellationToken can stop the agent at any time, and it's the only optional parameter passed into the constructor. The function Func<TState,TMessage, Task-<TState>> is applied to each message, in combination with the current state. When the operation completes, the current state is updated, and the agent moves to process the next available message. This function is expecting an asynchronous operation, which is recognizable from the return type of Task<TState>.

> **NOTE**   In the source code for this book, you can find several useful helper functions and implementation of agents using TDF with constructors that support either asynchronous or synchronous operations, which are omitted in listing 12.5 for brevity.

The agent implements the inheritances from the interface IAgent<TMessage>, which defines the two members Post and Send, used to pass messages to the agent synchronously or asynchronously, respectively:

```
public interface IAgent<TMessage>
{
    Task Send(TMessage message);
    void Post(TMessage message);
}
```

Use the helper factory function Start, as in the F# MailboxProcessor, to initialize a new agent, represented by the implemented interface IAgent<TMessage> :

```
IAgent<TMessage> Start<TState, TMessage>(TState initialState,
➥ Func<TState, TMessage, Task<TState>> action,
➥ CancellationTokenSource cts = null) =>
    new StatefulDataFlowAgent<TState, TMessage>(initialState, action, cts);
```

Because the interaction with the agent is only through sending (Post or Send) a message, the primary purpose of the IAgent<TMessage> interface is to avoid exposing the type parameter for the state, which is an implementation detail of the agent.

In listing 12.6, agentStateful is an instance of the StatefulDataFlowAgent agent, which receives a message containing the web address where it should download its content asynchronously. Then, the result of the operation is cached into the local state, Immutable-Dictionary<string, string>, to avoid repeating identical operations. For example, the Google website is mentioned twice in the urls collections, but it's downloaded only once. Ultimately, the content of each website is persisted in the local filesystem for the sake of the example. Notice that, apart from any side effects that occur when downloading and persisting the data, the implementation is side effect free. The changes in state are captured by always passing the state as an argument to the action function (or Loop function).

Listing 12.6 Agent based on TDF in action

```
List<string> urls = new List<string> {
                @"http://www.google.com",            Uses an asynchronous anonymous
                @"http://www.microsoft.com",         function to construct the agent. This
                @"http://www.bing.com",              function performs the current state
                @"http://www.google.com"             and input message received.
            };
var agentStateful = Agent.Start(ImmutableDictionary<string,string>.Empty,
    async (ImmutableDictionary<string,string> state, string url) => {
        if (!state.TryGetValue(url, out string content))
            using (var webClient = new WebClient()){
                content = await webClient.DownloadStringTaskAsync(url);
                await File.WriteAllTextAsync(createFileNameFromUrl(url), content);
                return state.Add(url, content);
        }
    return state;                      The function, which acts as the behavior
    });                               of the agent, returns the updated state
urls.ForEach(url => agentStateful.Post(url));    to keep track of any changes available to
                                                  the next message processing.
```

12.4.1 Agent fold-over state and messages: Aggregate

The current state of an agent is the result of reducing all the messages it has received so far using the initial state as an accumulator value, and then processing the function as a reducer. You can imagine this agent as a fold (aggregator) in time over the stream of messages received. Interestingly, the StatefulDataFlowAgent constructor shares a signature and behavior similar to the LINQ extension method Enumerable.Aggregate. For demonstration purposes, the following code swaps the agent construct from the previous implementation with its counterpart, the LINQ Aggregate operator:

```
urls.Aggregate(ImmutableDictionary<string,string>.Empty,
            async (state, url) => {
```

```
            if (!state.TryGetValue(url, out string content))
               using (var webClient = new WebClient())
               {
                     content = await webClient.DownloadStringTaskAsync(url);
                     await File.WriteAllTextAsync(createFileNamFromUrl(url),
content);
                     return state.Add(url, content);
               }
        return state;
});
```

As you can see, the core logic hasn't changed. Using the `StatefulDataFlowAgent` con-structor, which operates over message passing instead of in a collection, you imple-mented an asynchronous reducer similar to the LINQ `Aggregate` operator.

12.4.2 *Agent interaction: a parallel word counter*

According to the *actor* definition from Carl Hewitt,[1] one of the minds behind the actor model: "One actor is no actor. They come in systems." This means that actors come in systems and communicate with each other. The same rule applies to agents. Let's look at an example of using agents that interact with each other to group-count the number of times a word is present in a set of text files (figure 12.8).

Let's start with a simple stateless agent that takes a string message and prints it. You can use this agent to log the state of an application that maintains the order of the messages:

```
IAgent<string> printer = Agent.Start((string msg) =>
        WriteLine($"{msg} on thread {Thread.CurrentThread.
    ManagedThreadId}"));
```

The output also includes the current thread ID to verify the multiple threads used. This listing shows the implementation of the agent system for the group-count of words.

Listing 12.7   Word counter pipeline using agents

The agent posts a log to the printer agent.

The reader agent asynchronously reads all the text lines from a given file.

```
IAgent<string> reader = Agent.Start(async (string filePath) => {
    await printer.Send("reader received message");

    var lines = await File.ReadAllLinesAsync(filePath);

    lines.ForEach(async line => await parser.Send(line));
});
```

Sends all the lines of a given text file to the parser agent.
ForEach is an extension method in the source code.

```
char[] punctuation = Enumerable.Range(0, 256).Select(c => (char)c)
        .Where(c => Char.IsWhiteSpace(c) || Char.IsPunctuation(c)).ToArray();

IAgent<string> parser = Agent.Start(async (string line) => {
    await printer.Send("parser received message");
    foreach (var word in line.Split(punctuation))
       await counter.Send(word.ToUpper());
});
```

The parser agent splits the text into single words and sends them to the counter agent.

---

[1] For more information on Carl Eddie Hewitt, see https://en.wikipedia.org/wiki/Carl_Hewitt.

```
IReplyAgent<string, (string, int)> counter =
    Agent.Start(ImmutableDictionary<string, int>.Empty,
        (state, word) => {
            printer.Post("counter received message");
            int count;
            if (state.TryGetValue(word, out count))
                return state.Add(word, count++);
            else return state.Add(word, 1);
        }, (state, word) => (state, (word, state[word]))));

foreach (var filePath in Directory.EnumerateFiles(@"myFolder", "*.txt"))
    reader.Post(filePath);

var wordCount_This = await counter.Ask("this");
var wordCount_Wind = await counter.Ask("wind");
```

The agent posts a log to the printer agent.

The counter agent allows two-way communication, so you can send an ask message to receive a result back (reply) asynchronously

The counter agent checks if the word exists in the local state, and increments a counter or creates a new entry accordingly.

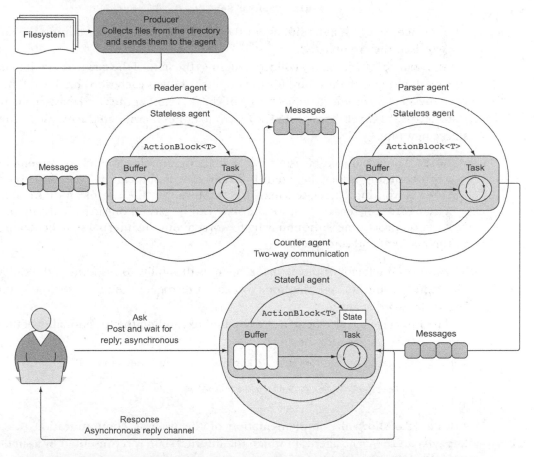

Figure 12.8. Simple interaction between agents by exchanging messages. The agent programming model promotes the single responsibility principle to write code. Note the counter agent provides a two-way communication, so the user can ask (interrogate) the agent, sending a message at any given time and receiving a reply in the form of a channel, which acts as asynchronous callback. When the operation completes, the callback provides the result.

The system is composed of three agents that communicate with each other to form a chain of operations:

- The reader agent
- The parser agent
- The counter agent

The word-counting process starts with a for-each loop to send the file paths of a given folder to the first reader agent. This agent reads the text from a file, and then sends each line of the text to the parser agent:

```
var lines = await File.ReadAllLinesAsync(filePath);
lines.ForEach(async line => await parser.Send(line));
```

The parser agent splits the text message into single words, and then passes each of those words to the last counter agent:

```
lines.Split(punctuation).ForEach(async word =>
                await counter.Send(word.ToUpper()));
```

The counter agent is a stateful agent that does the work of maintaining the count of the words as they're updated.

An ImmutableDictionary collection defines the state of the counter agent that stores the words along with the count for the number of times each word has been found. For each message received, the counter agent checks whether the word exists in an internal state ImmutableDictionary<string, int> to either increment the existing counter or start a new one.

> **NOTE** The advantage of using the agent programming model to implement word counting is that the agent is thread safe, and it can be shared between threads working on related texts freely. Moreover, the use of an immutable ImmutableDictionary to store the state can be passed outside the agent and carry on processing without having to worry about the internal state becoming inconsistent and corrupted.

The interesting factor of the counter agent is the ability to respond to the caller asynchronously using the Ask method. You can interrogate the agent for the count of a particular word at any time.

The interface IReplyAgent is the result of expanding the functionality of the previous interface IAgent with the Ask method:

```
interface IReplyAgent<TMessage, TReply> : IAgent<TMessage>
{
        Task<TReply> Ask(TMessage message);
}
```

Listing 12.8 shows the implementation of the two-way communication Stateful-ReplyDataFlowAgent agent, in which the internal state is represented by a single polymorphic mutable variable.

This agent has two different behaviors:

- One to handle the Send a message method.
- One to handle the Ask method. The Ask method sends a message and then waits asynchronously for a response.

These behaviors are passed in the form of generic Func delegates into the agent's constructor. The first function (Func<TState, TMessage, Task<TState>>) processes each message in combination with the current state and updates it accordingly. This logic is identical to the agent StatefulDataFlowAgent.

Conversely, the second function (Func<TState, TMessage, Task<(TState, TReply)>>) handles the incoming messages, computes the agent's new state, and ultimately replies to the sender. The output type of this function is a tuple, which contains the state of the agent, including a handle (callback) that acts as response (reply). The tuple is wrapped into a Task type to be awaited without blocking, as with any asynchronous function.

When creating the message Ask to interrogate the agent, the sender passes an instance of TaskCompletionSource<TReply> into the payload of the message, and a reference is returned by the Ask function to the caller. This object, TaskCompletion-Source, is fundamental for providing a channel to communicate asynchronously back to the sender through a callback, and the callback is notified from the agent when the result of the computation is ready. This model effectively generates two-way communication.

Listing 12.8   Stateless agent in C# using TDF

The IReplyAgent interface defines the Ask method to ensure that the agent enables two-way communication.

The ActionBlock message type is a tuple, where a TaskCompletionSource option is passed into the payload to supply a channel for communicating back to the caller asynchronously.

```
class StatefulReplyDataFlowAgent<TState, TMessage, TReply> :
                                    IReplyAgent<TMessage, TReply>
{
    private TState state;
    private readonly ActionBlock<(TMessage,
            Option<TaskCompletionSource<TReply>>)> actionBlock;

    public StatefulReplyDataFlowAgent(TState initialState,
        Func<TState, TMessage, Task<TState>> projection,
        Func<TState, TMessage, Task<(TState, TReply)>> ask,
        CancellationTokenSource cts = null)
    {
        state = initialState;
        var options = new ExecutionDataFlowBlockOptions {
        CancellationToken = cts?.Token ?? CancellationToken.None };

        actionBlock = new ActionBlock<(TMessage,
                    Option<TaskCompletionSource<TReply>>)>(
            async message => {
```

The agent construct takes two functions to respectively define the fire-and-forget and two-way communications.

If the TaskCompletionSource is None, then the projection function is applied.

```
(TMessage msg, Option<TaskCompletionSource<TReply>> replyOpt) = message;
  await replyOpt.Match(
        None: async () => state = await projection(state, msg),
        Some: async reply => {
           (TState newState, TReply replyresult) = await ask(state, msg);
              state = newState;
           reply.SetResult(replyresult);
           });
     }, options);
  }
```

If the TaskCompletionSource is Some, then the Ask function is applied to reply to the caller.

```
  public Task<TReply> Ask(TMessage message)
  {
     var tcs = new TaskCompletionSource<TReply>();
     actionBlock.Post((message, Option.Some(tcs)));
     return tcs.Task;
  }

  public Task Send(TMessage message) =>
     actionBlock.SendAsync((message, Option.None));
}
```

The Match extension method of the Option type is used to branch behavior over the TaskCompletionSource option.

The Ask member creates a TaskCompletionSource used as channel to communicate back to the caller when the operation run by the agent is completed.

> **NOTE** TDF makes no guarantee of built-in isolation, and consequently, an immutable state could be shared across the process function and be mutated outside the scope of the agent, resulting in unwanted behavior. Diligence in restricting and controlling access to the shared mutable state is highly recommended.

To enable StatefulReplyDataFlowAgent to handle both types of communications, one-way Send and two-way Ask, the message is constructed by including a TaskCompletion-Source option type. In this way, the agent infers if a message is either from the Post method, with None TaskCompletionSource, or from the Ask method, with Some Task-CompletionSource. The Match extension method of the Option type, Match<T, R>(None : Action<T>, Some(item) : Func<T,R>(item)), is used to branch out to the corresponding behavior of the agent.

12.5 A parallel workflow to compress and encrypt a large stream

In this section, you'll build a complete asynchronous and parallelized workflow combined with the agent programming model to demonstrate the power of the TDF library. This example uses a combination of TDF blocks and the StatefulDataFlowAgent agent linked to work as a parallel pipeline. The purpose of this example is to analyze and architect a real case application. It then evaluates the challenges encountered during the development of the program, and examines how TDF can be introduced in the design to solve these challenges.

TDF processes the blocks that compose a workflow at different rates and in parallel. More importantly, it efficiently spreads the work out across multiple CPU cores to maximize the speed of computation and overall scalability. This is particularly useful when you need to process a large stream of bytes that could generate hundreds, or even thousands, of chunks of data.

12.5.1 Context: the problem of processing a large stream of data

Let's say that you need to compress a large file to make it easier to persist or transmit over the network, or that a file's content must be encrypted to protect that information. Often, both compression and encryption must be applied. These operations can take a long time to complete if the full file is processed all at once. Furthermore, it's challenging to move a file, or stream data, across the network, and the complexity increases with the size of the file, due to external factors, such as latency and unpredictable bandwidth. In addition, if the file is transferred in one transaction, and something goes wrong, then the operation tries to resend the entire file, which can be time- and resource-consuming. In the following sections, you'll tackle this problem step by step.

In .NET, it isn't easy to compress a file larger than 4 GB, due to the framework limitation on the size of data to compress. Due to the maximum addressable size for a 32-bit pointer, if you create an array over 4 GB, an OutOfMemoryArray exception is thrown. Starting with .NET 4.5 and for 64-bit platforms, the option gcAllowVeryLargeObjects (http://mng.bz/x0c4) is available to enable arrays greater than 4 GB. This option allows 64-bit applications to have a multidimensional array with size UInt32.MaxValue (4,294,967,295) elements. Technically, you can apply the standard GZip compression that's used to compress streams of bytes to data larger than 4 GB; but the GZip distribution doesn't support this by default. The related .NET GZipStream class inheritably has a 4 GB limitation.

How can you compress and encrypt a large file without being constrained by the 4 GB limit imposed by the framework classes? A practical solution involves using a chunking routine to chop the stream of data. Chopping the stream of data makes it easier to compress and/or encrypt each block individually and ultimately write the block content to an output stream. The chunking technique splits the data, generally into chunks of the same size, applies the appropriate transformation to each chunk (compression before encryption), glues the chunks together in the correct order, and compresses the data. It's vital to guarantee the correct order of the chunks upon reassembly at the end of the workflow. Due to the intensive I/O asynchronous operations, the packages might not arrive in the correct sequence, especially if the data is transferred across the network. You must verify the order during reassembly (figure 12.9).

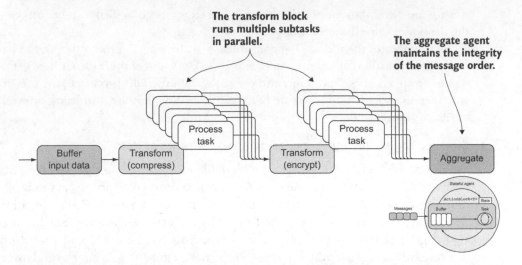

Figure 12.9 **The transform blocks process the messages in parallel. The result is sent to the next block when the operation completes. The aggregate agent's purpose is to maintain the integrity of the order of the messages, similar to the AsOrdered PLINQ extension method.**

The opportunity for parallelism fits naturally in this design, because the chunks of the data can be processed independently.

Encryption and compression: order matters

It might seem that because the compression and encryption operations are independent of one another, it makes no difference in which order they're applied to a file. This isn't true. *The order in which the operations of compression and encryption are applied is vital.*

Encryption has the effect of turning input data into high-entropy data,[2] which is a measure of the unpredictability of information content. Therefore, the encrypted data appears like a random array of bytes, which makes finding common patterns less probable. Conversely, compression algorithms work best when there are several similar patterns in the data, which can be expressed with fewer bytes.

When data must be both compressed and encrypted, you achieve the best results by first compressing and then encrypting the data. In this way, the compression algorithm can find similar patterns to shrink, and consequently the encryption algorithm produces the chunks of data having almost the same size. Furthermore, if the order of the operations is compression then encryption, not only should the output be a smaller file, but the encryption will most likely take less time because it'll operate on less data.

Listing 12.9 shows the full implementation of the parallel compression–encryption workflow. Note that in the source code, you can find the reverse workflow to decrypt

---

2   Information entropy is defined as the average amount of information produced by a stochastic source of data. See https://en.wikipedia.org/wiki/Entropy_(information_theory).

and decompress the data, as well as use asynchronous helper functions for compressing and encrypting bytes array.

The function CompressAndEncrypt takes as an argument the source and destination streams to process, the chunkSize argument defines the size in which the data is split (the default is 1 MB if no value is provided), and CancellationTokenSource stops the dataflow execution at any point. If no CancellationTokenSource is provided, a new token is defined and propagated through the dataflow operations.

The core of the function consists of three TDF building blocks, in combination with a stateful agent that completes the workflow. The inputBuffer is a BufferBlock type that, as the name implies, buffers the incoming chunks of bytes read from the source stream, and holds these items to pass them to the next blocks in the flow, which is the linked TransformBlock compressor (the code to note is in bold).

Listing 12.9 Parallel stream compression and encryption using TDF

A new cancellation token is provided if none is supplied in the constructor.

Sets the BoundedCapacity value to throttle the messages and reduce memory consumption by limiting the number of MemoryStreams created at the same time

```
async Task CompressAndEncrypt(
    Stream streamSource, Stream streamDestination,
    long chunkSize = 1048576, CancellationTokenSource cts = null)
{
    cts = cts ?? new CancellationTokenSource();

    var compressorOptions = new ExecutionDataflowBlockOptions {
    MaxDegreeOfParallelism = Environment.ProcessorCount,
    BoundedCapacity = 20,
    CancellationToken = cts.Token
    };

    var inputBuffer = new BufferBlock<CompressingDetails>(
            new DataflowBlockOptions {
                CancellationToken = cts.Token, BoundedCapacity = 20 });
```

Asynchronously compresses the data (the method is provided in the source code of the book)

```
    var compressor = new TransformBlock<CompressingDetails,
        CompressedDetails>(async details => {
            var compressedData = await IOUtils.Compress(details.Bytes);
            return details.ToCompressedDetails(compressedData);
    }, compressorOptions);
```

Combines the data and metadata into a byte array pattern that will be deconstructed and parsed during the revert operation decrypt–decompress

```
    var encryptor = new TransformBlock<CompressedDetails, EncryptDetails>(
        async details => {
            byte[] data = IOUtils.CombineByteArrays(details.CompressedDataSize,
    details.ChunkSize, details.Bytes);
            var encryptedData = await IOUtils.Encrypt(data);
            return details.ToEncryptDetails(encryptedData);
```

Asynchronously encrypts the data (the method is provided in the source code of the book)

Converts the current data structure into the message shape to send to the next block

```
        }, compressorOptions);
```

The behavior of the asOrderedAgent Agent keeps track of the order of the messages received to maintain the order (persist the data).

```
    var asOrderedAgent = Agent.Start((new Dictionary<int, EncryptDetails>(),0),
     async((Dictionary<int,EncryptDetails>,int)state,EncryptDetails msg)=>{
        Dictionary<int, EncryptDetails> details, int lastIndexProc) = state;
        details.Add(msg.Sequence, msg);
        while (details.ContainsKey(lastIndexProc+1)) {
            msg = details[lastIndexProc + 1];
            await streamDestination.WriteAsync(msg.EncryptedDataSize, 0,
                                        msg.EncryptedDataSize.Length);
            await streamDestination.WriteAsync(msg.Bytes, 0,
                                        msg.Bytes.Length);
            lastIndexProc = msg.Sequence;
            details.Remove(lastIndexProc);
        }
        return (details, lastIndexProc);
    }, cts);
```

Persists the data asynchronously; the file stream could be replaced with a network stream to send the data across the wire.

The chunk of data that is processed is removed from the local state, keeping track of the items to perform.

The ActionBlock reader sends the chunk of data wrapped into a details data structure to the asOrdered agent.

```
    var writer = new ActionBlock<EncryptDetails>(async details => await
                        asOrderedAgent.Send(details), compressorOptions);

    var linkOptions = new DataflowLinkOptions { PropagateCompletion = true };
    inputBuffer.LinkTo(compressor, linkOptions);
    compressor.LinkTo(encryptor, linkOptions);
    encryptor.LinkTo(writer, linkOptions);
```

Links the dataflow blocks to compose the workflow

```
    long sourceLength = streamSource.Length;
    byte[] size = BitConverter.GetBytes(sourceLength);
    await streamDestination.WriteAsync(size, 0, size.Length);
```

The total size of the file stream is persisted as the first chunk of data; in this way, the decompression algorithm knows how to retrieve the information and how long to run.

Determines the chunk size to partition data

```
    chunkSize = Math.Min(chunkSize, sourceLength);
    int indexSequence = 0;
    while (sourceLength > 0) {
        byte[] data = new byte[chunkSize];
        int readCount = await streamSource.ReadAsync(data, 0, data.Length);
        byte[] bytes = new byte[readCount];
        Buffer.BlockCopy(data, 0, bytes, 0, readCount);
        var compressingDetails = new CompressingDetails {
                Bytes = bytes,
                ChunkSize = BitConverter.GetBytes(readCount),
                Sequence = ++indexSequence
            };
    await inputBuffer.SendAsync(compressingDetails);
    sourceLength -= readCount;
    if (sourceLength < chunkSize)
        chunkSize = sourceLength;
    if (sourceLength == 0)
        inputBuffer.Complete();
    }
```

Reads the source stream into chunks until the end of the stream

Sends the chunk of data read from the source stream to the inputBuffer

Checks the current source stream position after each read operation to decide when to complete the operation

Notifies the input buffer when the source stream reaches the end

```
await inputBuffer.Completion.ContinueWith(task => compressor.Complete());
await compressor.Completion.ContinueWith(task => encryptor.Complete());
await encryptor.Completion.ContinueWith(task => writer.Complete());
await writer.Completion;
await streamDestination.FlushAsync();
    }
```

The bytes read from the stream are sent to the buffer block by using the SendAsync method:

```
var compressingDetails = new CompressingDetails {
        Bytes = bytes,
        ChunkSize = BitConverter.GetBytes(chunkSize),
        Sequence = ++indexSequence
    };
await buffer.SendAsync(compressingDetails);
```

Each chunk of bytes read from the stream source is wrapped into the data structure's CompressingDetails, which contains the additional information of byte-array size. The monotonic value is later used in the sequence of chunks generated to preserve the order. A *monotonic value* is a function between ordered sets that preserves or reverses the given value, and the value always either decreases or increases. The order of the block is important both for a correct compression–encryption operation and for correct decryption and decompression into the original shape.

In general, if the purpose of the block is purely to forward item operations from one block to several others, then you don't need the BufferBlock. But in the case of reading a large or continuous stream of data, this block is useful for taming the backpressure generated from the massive amount of data partitioned to the process by setting an appropriate BoundedCapacity. In this example, the BoundedCapacity is restricted to a capacity of 20 items. When there are 20 items in this block, it will stop accepting new items until one of the existing items passes to the next block. Because the dataflow source of data originated from asynchronous I/O operations, there's a risk of potentially large amounts of data to process. It's recommended that you limit internal buffering to throttle the data by setting the BoundedCapacity property in the options defined when constructing the BufferBlock.

The next two block types are compression transformation and encryption transformation. During the first phase (compression), the TransformBlock applies the compression to the chunk of bytes and enriches the message received Compressing-Details with the relative data information, which includes the compressed byte array and its size. This information persists as part of the output stream accessible during the decompression.

The second phase (encryption) enciphers the chunk of compressed byte array and creates a sequence of bytes resulting from the composition of three arrays: Compressed-DataSize, ChunkSize, and data array. This structure instructs the decompression and decryption algorithms to target the right portion of bytes to revert from the stream.

> **NOTE** Keep in mind that when there are multiple TDF blocks, certain TDF tasks may be idle while the others are executing, so you have to tune the block's execution option to avoid potential starvation. Details regarding this optimization are explained in the coming section.

12.5.2 *Ensuring the order integrity of a stream of messages*

The TDF documentation guarantees that `TransformBlock` will propagate the messages in the same order in which they arrived. Internally, `TransformBlock` uses a reordering buffer to fix any out-of-order issues that might arise from processing multiple messages concurrently. Unfortunately, due to the high number of asynchronous and intensive I/O operations running in parallel, keeping the integrity of the message order doesn't apply to this case. This is why you implemented the additional sequential ordering preservation using monotonically values.

If you decide to *send* or *stream* the data over the network, then the guarantee of delivering the packages in the correct sequence is lost, due to variables such as the unpredictable bandwidth and unreliable network connection. To safeguard the order integrity when processing chunks of data, your final step in the workflow is the stateful `asOrderedAgent` agent. This agent behaves as a *multiplexer* by reassembling the items and persists them in the local filesystem, maintaining the correct sequence. The order value of the sequence is kept in a property of the `EncryptDetails` data structure, which is received by the agent as a message.

The multiplexer pattern

The multiplexer is a pattern generally used in combination with a Producer/Consumer design. It allows its consumer, which in the previous example is the last stage of the pipeline, to receive the chunks of data in the correct sequential order. The chunks of data don't need to be sorted or reordered. Instead, the fact that each producer (TDF block) queue is locally ordered allows the multiplexer to look for the next value (message) in the sequence. The multiplexer waits for a message from a producer dataflow block. When a chunk of data arrives, the multiplexer looks to see if the chunk's sequence number is the next in the expected sequence. If it is, the multiplexer persists the data to the local filesystem. If the chunk of data isn't the one expected next in the sequence, the multiplexer holds the value in an internal buffer and repeats the analysis operation for the next message received. This algorithm allows the multiplexer to put together the inputs from the incoming producer message in a way that ensures sequential order without sorting the values.

The accuracy for the whole computation requires preservation of the order of the source sequence and the partitions to ensure that the order is consistent at merge time.

> **NOTE** In the case of sending the chunks of data over the network, the same strategy of persisting the data in the local filesystem is applicable by having the agent working as a receiver on the other side of the wire.

The state of this agent is preserved using a tuple. The first item of the tuple is a collection `Dictionary<int, EncryptDetails>`, where the key represents the sequence value of the original order by which the data was sent. The second item, `lastIndex-Proc`, is the index of the last item processed, which prevents reprocessing the same chunks of data more than once. The body of `asOrderedAgent` runs the `while` loop that uses this value `lastIndexProc` and makes sure that the processing of the chunks of data starts from the last item unprocessed. The loop continues to iterate until the order of the items is continued; otherwise it breaks out from the loop and waits for the next message, which might complete the missing gap in the sequence.

The `asOrderedAgent` agent is plugged into the workflow through the TDF `Action-Block` writer, which sends it to the `EncryptDetails` data structure for the final work.

GZipStream vs. DeflateStream: how to choose

The .NET Framework provides a few option classes for compressing a stream of bytes. Listing 12.9 used `System.IO.Compression.GZipStream` for the compression module; but the alternative `System.IO.Compression.DeflateStream` presents a valid option. Starting with .NET Framework 4.5, the `DeflateStream` compression stream uses the zlib library, which results in a better compression algorithm and, in most cases, smaller compressed data as compared to earlier versions. The `DeflateStream` compression algorithm optimization maintains back-compatibility with data compressed with the earlier version. One reason to choose the `GZipStream` class is that it adds a cyclic redundancy check (CRC) to the compressed data to determine if it has been corrupted. Please refer to the MSDN online documentation (http://mng.bz/h082) for further details about these streams.

12.5.3 Linking, propagating, and completing

The TDF blocks in the compress-encrypt workflow are linked using the `LinkTo` extension method, which by default propagates only data (messages). But if the workflow is linear, as in this example, it's good practice to share information among the blocks through an automatic notification, such as when the work is terminated or eventual errors accrue. This behavior is achieved by constructing the `LinkTo` method with the `DataFlowLinkOptions` optional argument and the `PropagateCompletion` property set to true. Here's the code from the previous example with this option built in:

```
var linkOptions = new DataFlowLinkOptions { PropagateCompletion = true };

inputBuffer.LinkTo(compressor, linkOptions);
compressor.LinkTo(encryptor, linkOptions);
encryptor.LinkTo(writer, linkOptions);
```

The `PropagateCompletion` optional property informs the dataflow block to automatically propagate its results and exceptions to the next stage when it completes. This is accomplished by calling the Complete method when the buffer block triggers the complete notification upon reaching the end of the stream:

```
if (sourceLength < chunkSize)
    chunkSize = sourceLength;
if (sourceLength == 0)
    buffer.Complete();
```

Then all the dataflow blocks are announced in a cascade as a chain that the process has completed:

```
await inputBuffer.Completion.ContinueWith(task => compressor.Complete());
await compressor.Completion.ContinueWith(task => encryptor.Complete());
await encryptor.Completion.ContinueWith(task => writer.Complete());
await writer.Completion;
```

Ultimately, you can run the code as follows:

```
using (var streamSource = new FileStream(sourceFile, FileMode.OpenOrCreate,
                    FileAccess.Read, FileShare.None, useAsync: true))
using (var streamDestination = new FileStream(destinationFile,
        FileMode.Create, FileAccess.Write, FileShare.None, useAsync: true))
    await CompressAndEncrypt(streamSource, streamDestination)
```

Table 12.1 shows the benchmarks for compressing and encrypting different file sizes, including the inverted operation of decrypting and decompressing. The benchmark result is the average of each operation run three times.

Table 12.1   Benchmarks for compressing and encrypting different file sizes

File size in GB	Degree of parallelism	Compress-encrypt time in seconds	Decrypt-decompress time in seconds
3	1	524.56	398.52
3	4	123.64	88.25
3	8	69.20	45.93
12	1	2249.12	1417.07
12	4	524.60	341.94
12	8	287.81	163.72

12.5.4 *Rules for building a TDF workflow*

Here are few good rules and practices for successfully implementing TDF in your workflow:

- *Do one thing, and do it well.* This is a principal of modern OOP, the *single responsibility principle* (https://en.wikipedia.org/wiki/Single_responsibility_principle). The idea is that your block should perform only one action and should have only one reason to change.

- *Design for composition.* In the OOP world, this is known as the *open closed principle* (https://en.wikipedia.org/wiki/Open/closed_principle), where the dataflow building blocks are designed to be open for extension but closed to modification.
- *DRY.* This principle (don't repeat yourself) encourages you to write reusable code and reusable dataflow building block components.

Performance tip: recycling MemoryStreams

The .NET programming languages rely on a mark-and-sweep GC that can negatively impact the performance of a program that generates a large number of memory allocations due to GC pressure. This is a performance penalty that the code (such as in listing 12.9) pays when creating a `System.IO.MemoryStream` instance for each compress and encrypt operation, including its underlying byte array.

The quantity of `MemoryStream` instances increases with the number of chunks of data to process, which can be hundreds in a large stream/file. As that byte array grows, the `MemoryStream` resizes it by allocating a new and larger array, and then copying the original bytes into it. This is inefficient, not only because it creates new objects and throws the old ones away, but also because it has to do the legwork of copying the content each time it resizes.

One way to alleviate the memory pressure that can be caused by the frequent creation and destruction of large objects is to tell the .NET GC to compact the large object heap (LOH) using this setting:

```
GCSettings.LargeObjectHeapCompactionMode =
GCLargeObjectHeapCompactionMode.CompactOnce
```

This solution, while it may reduce the memory footprint of your application, does nothing to solve the initial problem of allocating all that memory in the first place. A better solution is to create an object pool, also known as pooled buffers, to pre-allocate an arbitrary number of `MemoryStreams` that can be reused (a generic and reusable object pool is available in chapter 13).

Microsoft has released a new object, called `RecyclableMemoryStream`, which abstracts away the implementation of an object pool optimized for `MemoryStream`, and minimizes the number of large object heap allocations and memory fragmentation. The discussion of `RecyclableMemoryStream` is out of the scope of this book. For more information, refer to the MSDN online documentation.

12.5.5 Meshing Reactive Extensions (Rx) and TDF

TDF and Rx (discussed in chapter 6) have important similarities, despite having independent characteristics and strengths, and these libraries complement each other, making them easy to integrate. TDF is closer to an agent-based programming model, focused on providing building blocks for message passing, which simplifies the implementation of parallel CPU- and I/O-intensive applications with high throughput and low latency, while also providing developers explicit control over how data is buffered.

Rx is keener to the functional paradigm, providing a vast set of operators that predominantly focused on coordination and composition of event streams with a LINQ-based API.

TDF has built-in support for integrating with Rx, which allows it to expose the source dataflow blocks as both observables and observers. The `AsObservable` extension method transforms TDF blocks into an observable sequence, which allows the output of the dataflow chain to flow efficiently into an arbitrary set of Reactive fluent extension methods for further processing. Specifically, the `AsObservable` extension method constructs an `IObservable<T>` for an `ISourceBlock<T>`.

> **NOTE**   TDF can also act as an observer. The `AsObserver` extension method creates an `IObserver<T>` for an `ITargetBlock<T>`, where the `OnNext` calls for the observer result in the data being sent to the target. The `OnError` calls result in the exception faulting the target, and the `OnCompleted` calls will result in `Complete` being called on the target.

Let's see the integration of Rx and TDF in action. In listing 12.9, the last block of the parallel compress-encrypt stream dataflow is the stateful `asOrderedAgent`. The particularity of this component is the presence of an internal state that keeps track of the messages received and their order. As mentioned, the construct signature of a stateful agent is similar to the LINQ `Aggregate` operator, which in terms of Rx can be replaced with the RX `Observable.Scan` operator. This operator is covered in chapter 6.

The following listing shows the integration between Rx and TDF by replacing the `asOrderedAgent` agent from the last block of the parallel compress-encrypt stream workflow.

Listing 12.10   Integrating Reactive Extensions with TDF

```
inputBuffer.LinkTo(compressor, linkOptions);
compressor.LinkTo(encryptor, linkOptions);          Enables Rx integration with TDF

encryptor.AsObservable()
         .Scan((new Dictionary<int, EncryptDetails>(), 0),
 (state, msg) => Observable.FromAsync(async() => {
 (Dictionary<int,EncryptDetails> details, int lastIndexProc) = state;
 details.Add(msg.Sequence, msg);
 while (details.ContainsKey(lastIndexProc + 1)) {      Runs the Rx Scan
    msg = details[lastIndexProc + 1];                  operation asynchronously
    await streamDestination.WriteAsync(msg.EncryptedDataSize, 0,
                                      msg.EncryptedDataSize.Length);
    await streamDestination.WriteAsync(msg.Bytes, 0, msg.Bytes.Length);
    lastIndexProc = msg.Sequence;
    details.Remove(lastIndexProc);
    }
 return (details, lastIndexProc);                Rx subscribes to TaskPoolScheduler
}) .SingleAsync().Wait())
.SubscribeOn(TaskPoolScheduler.Default).Subscribe();
```

As you can see, you swapped the asOrderedAgent with the Rx Observable.Scan operator without changing the internal functionality. TDF blocks and Rx observable streams can be completed successfully or with errors, and the AsObservable method will translate the block completion (or fault) into the completion of the observable stream. But if the block faults with an exception, that exception will be wrapped in an Aggregate-Exception when it is passed to the observable stream. This is similar to how linked blocks propagate their faults.

Summary

- A system written using TPL Dataflow benefits from a multicore system because all the blocks that compose a workflow can run in parallel.
- TDF enables effective techniques for running embarrassingly parallel problems, where many independent computations can be executed in parallel in an evident way.
- TDF has built-in support for throttling and asynchrony, improving both I/O-bound and CPU-bound operations. In particular, it provides the ability to build responsive client applications while still getting the benefits of massively parallel processing.
- TDF can be used to parallelize the workflow to compress and encrypt a large stream of data by processing blocks at different rates.
- The combination and integration of Rx and TDF simplifies the implementation of parallel CPU- and I/O-intensive applications, while also providing developers explicit control over how data is buffered.

Part 3

Modern patterns of concurrent programming applied

This third and final part of the book allows you to put into practice all the functional concurrent programming techniques you've learned thus far. These chapters will become your go-to reference for questions and answers about concurrency.

Chapter 13 covers recipes to solve both common and complex problems you may encounter in concurrent applications using the functional paradigm. Chapter 14 walks you through the full implementation of a scalable and highly performant stock market server application, which includes iOS and WPF versions for the client side.

Functional paradigm principles learned in the book will be applied in the design and architecture decisions, as well as to code development, to achieve a highly performant and scalable solution. You'll see in this section the positive side effects that come from applying functional principles to reduce bugs and increase maintainability.

Recipes and design patterns for successful concurrent programming

This chapter covers

- Twelve code recipes that answer common problems in parallel programming

The 12 recipes presented in this chapter have broad applications. You can use the core ideas as a reference when you're facing a similar problem and require a quick answer. The material demonstrates how the functional concurrent abstractions covered throughout this book make it possible to solve complex problems by developing sophisticated and rich functions with relatively few lines of code. I've kept the implementations of the recipes as simple as possible, so you'll need to deal from time to time with cancellations and exception handling.

This chapter shows you how to put together everything you've learned so far to combine concurrent programming models using the functional programming abstraction as a glue to write efficient and performant programs. By the end of this chapter, you'll have at your disposal a set of useful and reusable tools for solving common concurrent coding problems.

Each recipe is built in either C# or F#; for the majority of the code implementation, you can find both versions in the downloadable code online. Also, keep in mind that F# and C# are .NET programming languages with interoperability support to interact with each other. You can easily use a C# program in F# and vice versa.

13.1   *Recycling objects to reduce memory consumption*

In this section you'll implement a reusable asynchronous object pool. This should be used in cases where the recycling of objects benefits the reduction of memory consumption. Minimizing the number of GC generations allows your program to enjoy better performance speed. Figure 13.1, repeated from chapter 12, shows how to apply concurrent Producer/Consumer patterns, from listing 12.9, to compress and encrypt a large file in parallel.

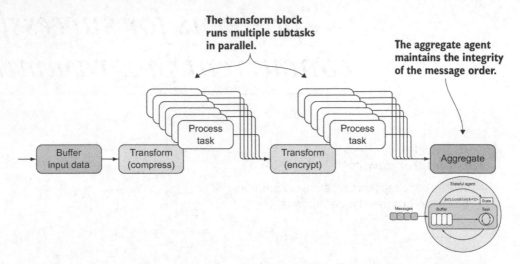

Figure 13.1. The `Transform` blocks process the messages in parallel. The result is sent to the next block when the operation completes. The Aggregate agent's purpose is to maintain the integrity of order of the messages, similar to the `AsOrdered` PLINQ extension method.

The function `CompressAndEncrypt`, from listing 12.9, partitions a large file in a set of byte-array chunks, which has the negative effect of producing a large volume of GC generations due to high memory consumption. Each memory chunk is created, processed, and collected by the GC when the memory pressure reaches the trigger point for demanding for more resources.

This high volume operation of creating and destroying byte array causes many GC generations, which negatively impact the overall performance of the application. In fact, the program allocates a considerable number of memory buffers (byte arrays) for its full execution in a multithreaded fashion, meaning that multiple threads can simultaneously allocate the same amount of memory. Consider that each buffer is 4,096 bytes of memory, and 25 threads are running simultaneously; in this case, about 102,400 bytes are being simultaneously allocated in the heap. Additionally, when each thread completes its execution, many buffers are out of scope, pressuring the GC to start a generation. This is bad for performance, because the application is under heavy memory management.

13.1.1 Solution: asynchronously recycling a pool of objects

To optimize the performance of a concurrent application with intense memory consumption, recycle the objects that otherwise are subject to be garbage collected by the system. In the parallel compress and encrypt stream example, you want to reuse the same byte buffers (byte arrays) generated instead of creating new ones. This is possible using `ObjectPool`, a class designed to provide a cached pool of objects that recycles the items that aren't being used. This reuse of objects avoids expensive acquisition and release of resources, minimizing the potential memory allocation. Specifically, in the highly concurrent example, you need a thread-safe and non-blocking (task-based) concurrent object pool (figure 13.2).

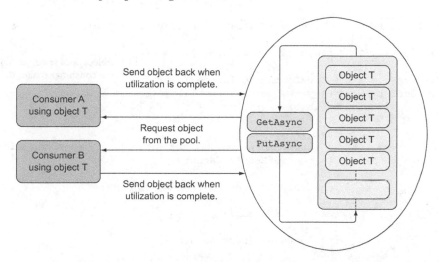

Figure 13.2 An object pool can asynchronously handle multiple concurrent requests for reusable objects from multiple consumers. The consumer then sends the object back to the object pool when it's done with the work. Internally, object pool generates a queue of objects using a given factory delegate. These objects are then recycled to reduce memory consumption and the cost of new instantiation.

In listing 13.1 the implementation of `ObjectPoolAsync` is based on a TDF that uses the `BufferBlock` as a building block. The `ObjectPoolAsync` pre-initializes a set of objects for an application to use and reuse when needed. Furthermore, TDF is intrinsically thread safe while providing an asynchronous, non-blocking semantic.

Listing 13.1 Asynchronous object pool implementation using TDF

```
public class ObjectPoolAsync<T> :IDisposable
{
    private readonly BufferBlock<T> buffer;
    private readonly Func<T> factory;
    private readonly int msecTimeout;
```

During the initialization of the object pool, the buffer is filled with instances of type T to have objects available from the start.

When the consumer is done, the object type T is sent back to the object pool to be recycled.

```
public ObjectPoolAsync(int initialCount, Func<T> factory,
  CancellationToken cts, int msecTimeout = 0)
    {
        this.msecTimeout = msecTimeout;
        buffer = new BufferBlock<T>(
            new DataflowBlockOptions { CancellationToken = cts });
        this.factory = () => factory();

        for (int i = 0; i < initialCount; i++)
            buffer.Post(this.factory());
    }

public Task<bool> PutAsync(T item) => buffer.SendAsync(item);

public Task<T> GetAsync(int timeout = 0)
    {
        var tcs = new TaskCompletionSource<T>();
        buffer.ReceiveAsync(TimeSpan.FromMilliseconds(msecTimeout))
            .ContinueWith(task =>
            {
                if (task.IsFaulted)
                    if (task.Exception.InnerException is TimeoutException)
                        tcs.SetResult(factory());
                    else
                        tcs.SetException(task.Exception);
                else if (task.IsCanceled)
                    tcs.SetCanceled();
                else
                    tcs.SetResult(task.Result);
            });
        return tcs.Task;
    }
public void Dispose() => buffer.Complete();

}
```

Uses BufferBlock to asynchronously coordinate the underlying set of types T

Uses a factory delegate to generate a new instance of type T

The object pool sends an object type T when a consumer makes the request.

ObjectPoolAsync accepts as arguments an initial number of objects to create and a factory delegate constructor. ObjectPoolAsync exposes two functions to orchestrate the object's recycle:

- PutAsync—An item can be Put into the pool asynchronously.
- GetAsync—An item can be taken from the pool asynchronously.

In the downloadable source code, you can find the full solution of the CompressAnd-Encrypt program updated to use ObjectPoolAsync. Figure 13.3 is a graphical comparison of the GC generations for different file sizes between the original version of the program and the new one that exploits ObjectPoolAsync.

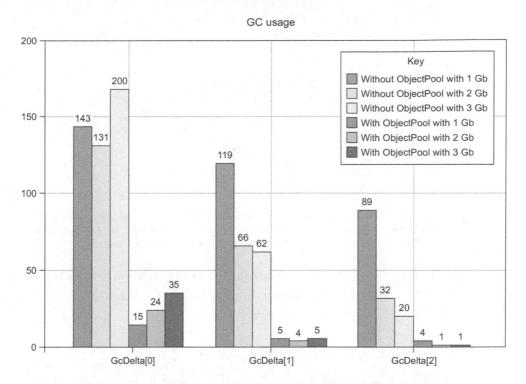

Figure 13.3 Comparison of chapter 12's `CompressAndEncrypt` **program, which processes different large files (1 GB, 2 GB, and 3 GB), implemented with and without** `AsyncObjectPool`**. The implementation using the object pool has a low number of GC generations compared to the original one. Minimizing GC generation results in better performance.**

The results displayed in the chart demonstrate how the `CompressAndEncrypt` program implemented using `ObjectPoolAsync` dramatically reduces the GC generations, speeding up overall application performance. In an eight-core machine, the new version of `CompressAndEncrypt` is about 8% faster.

13.2 Custom parallel Fork/Join operator

In this section you implement a reusable extension method to parallelize Fork/Join operations. Let's say you detected a piece of code in your program that would benefit from being executed in parallel using a Divide and Conquer pattern to speed up performance. You decide to refactor the code to use a concurrent Fork/Join pattern (figure 13.4). And the more you check the program, the more similar patterns arise.

> **NOTE** As you may recall from section 4.2, Fork/Join, like Divide and Conquer, breaks the work into small tasks until each small task is simple enough that it can be solved without further breakups, and then it coordinates the parallel workers.

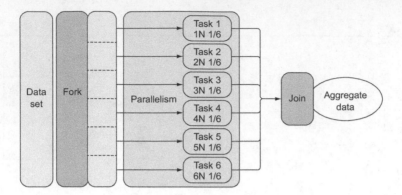

Figure 13.4   The Fork/Join pattern splits a task into subtasks that can be executed independently in parallel. When the operations complete, the subtasks are joined again. It isn't a coincidence that this pattern is often used to achieve data parallelism. In fact, there are clearly similarities.

Unfortunately, in .NET, there's no built-in support for parallel Fork/Join extension methods to be reused on demand. But you can create this and more to have a reusable and flexible operator that does the following:

- Splits the data
- Applies the Fork/Join pattern in parallel
- Optionally allows you to configure the degree of parallelism
- Merges the results using a reducer function

The .NET operator `Task.WhenAll` and the F# `Async.Parallel` can compose a set of given tasks in parallel; but these operators don't provide an aggregate (or reduce) functionality to join the results. Moreover, they lack configurability when you want to control the degree of parallelism. To get your desired operator, you need a tailored solution.

13.2.1   Solution: composing a pipeline of steps forming the Fork/Join pattern

With TDF, you can compose different building blocks together as a pipeline. You can use the pipeline to define the steps of a Fork/Join pattern (figure 13.5), where the Fork step runs a set of tasks in parallel, then the following step joins the results, and the final step applies a reducer block for the ultimate output. For the later step of the workflow that aggregates the results, you need an object that maintains the state of the previous steps. In this case, you use the agent-based block built in chapter 12 using TDF.

The Fork/Join pattern is implemented as an extension method over a generic `IEnu-merable` to be accessed conveniently in a fluent style from the code, as shown in listing 13.2 (the code to note is in bold).

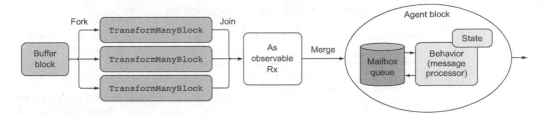

Figure 13.5 Fork/Join pattern implemented using TDF, where each step of the computation is defined using a different dataflow block

Listing 13.2   Parallel `ForkJoin` using TDF

The functions map and aggregate return a Task type to ensure concurrent behavior.

The partitionLevel is set to a default value of 8 and the boundCapacity to 20; these are arbitrary values that can, and should, be updated according to your needs.

```
public static async Task<R> ForkJoin<T1, T2, R>(
    this IEnumerable<T1> source,
        Func<T1, Task<IEnumerable<T2>>> map,
    Func<R, T2, Task<R>> aggregate,
    R initialState, CancellationTokenSource cts = null,
    int partitionLevel = 8, int boundCapacity = 20)
{
    cts = cts ?? new CancellationTokenSource();
    var blockOptions = new ExecutionDataflowBlockOptions {
        MaxDegreeOfParallelism = partitionLevel,
        BoundedCapacity = boundCapacity,
        CancellationToken = cts.Token
    };

    var inputBuffer = new BufferBlock<T1>(
            new DataflowBlockOptions {
                CancellationToken = cts.Token,
                BoundedCapacity = boundCapacity
            });

    var mapperBlock = new TransformManyBlock<T1, T2>
    (map, blockOptions);
    var reducerAgent = Agent.Start(initialState, aggregate, cts);
    var linkOptions = new DataflowLinkOptions{PropagateCompletion=true};
    inputBuffer.LinkTo(mapperBlock, linkOptions);

    IDisposable disposable = mapperBlock.AsObservable()
        .Subscribe(async item => await reducerAgent.Send(item));

    foreach (var item in source)
        await inputBuffer.SendAsync(item);
    inputBuffer.Complete();
```

Instances of the building blocks that are shaping the Fork/Join pipeline

Packages up the properties of the execution details to configure the inputBuffer BufferBlock

Connects the building blocks to form and link the steps to run the Fork/Join pattern

The TransformManyBlock is transformed into an Observable, which is used to push the outputs as a message to the reducerAgent.

Starts the Fork/Join process by pushing the items of the input collection into the first step of the pipeline

```
        var tcs = new TaskCompletionSource<R>();

        await inputBuffer.Completion.ContinueWith(task =>
                                    mapperBlock.Complete());
        await mapperBlock.Completion.ContinueWith(task => {
            var agent = reducerAgent as StatefulDataflowAgent<R, T2>;
            disposable.Dispose();
            tcs.SetResult(agent.State);
        });
        return await tcs.Task;
    }
```

When the mapperBlock is completed, the continuation Task sets the reducerAgent as a result for the tcs Task passed to the caller as output.

The ForkJoin extension method accepts as an argument the IEnumerable source to process a mapping function, to transform its items, as well as an aggregate (reducer) function to merge all the results coming from the mapping computation. The argument initialState is the seed required by the aggregate function for the initial state value. But if the result type T2 can be combined (because the monoidal laws are satisfied), you could modify the method to use a reducer function with zero initial state, as explained in listing 5.10.

The underlying dataflow blocks are linked to form a pipeline. Interestingly, mapperBlock is converted into an Observable using the AsObservable extension method, which is then subscribed to send messages to the reducerAgent when an output is materialized. The values partitionLevel and boundCapacity are used respectively to set the degree of parallelism and the bound capacity.

Here is a simple example of how to exploit the ForkJoin operator:

```
Task<long> sum = Enumerable.Range(1, 100000)
        .ForkJoin<int, long, long>(
                        async x => new[] { (long)x * x },
                        async (state, x) => state + x, 0L);
```

The previous code sums the squares of all number from 1 to 100,000 using the Fork/Join pattern.

13.3   *Parallelizing tasks with dependencies: designing code to optimize performance*

Let's imagine you need to write a tool that can execute a series of asynchronous tasks—each with a different set of dependencies that influence the order of the operations. You can address this with sequential and imperative execution; but if you want to maximize performance, sequential operations won't do. Instead, you must build the tasks to run in parallel. Many concurrent problems can be considered a static collection of atomic operations with dependencies between their inputs and outputs. On completion of the operation, the output is used as input to other dependent operations. To optimize performance, these tasks need to be scheduled based on the dependency, and the algorithm must be optimized to run the dependent tasks in serial as necessary and in parallel as much as possible.

You want a reusable component that runs a series of tasks in parallel, ensuring that all the dependencies that could influence the order of the operations are respected. How do you create a programming model that exposes the underlying parallelism of a collection of operations that are executed efficiently, either in parallel or serially depending on the dependencies with other operations?

13.3.1 Solution: implementing a dependencies graph of tasks

The solution is called a directed acyclic graph (DAG), which aims to form a graph by breaking down operations into a series of atomic tasks with defined dependencies. The acyclic nature of the graph is important because it removes the possibility of deadlocks between tasks, provided the tasks are truly atomic. When specifying the graph, it's important to understand all dependencies between tasks, especially hidden dependencies that may result in deadlocks or race conditions. Figure 13.6 is a typical example of a data structure in the shape of a graph, which can be used to represent scheduling constraints between the operations of the graph. A graph is an extremely powerful data structure in computer science that gives rise to strong algorithms.

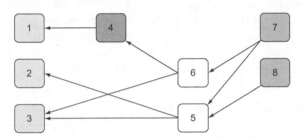

Figure 13.6   A graph is a collection of vertices connected by edges. In this representation of a DAG, node 1 has dependencies on nodes 4 and 5, node 2 depends on node 5, node 3 has dependencies on nodes 5 and 6, and so on.

You can apply the DAG structure as a strategy to run tasks in parallel while respecting the order of the dependencies for increasing performance. You can define this graph structure using the F# `MailboxProcessor`, which keeps an internal state for the tasks registered to be performed in the shape of edge dependencies.

Validating a directed acyclic graph

When working with any graph data structure, like a DAG, you need to deal with the problem of registering the edges correctly. In figure 13.6, what if node 2 with dependencies to nodes 7 and 8 is registered, but node 8 doesn't exist? It could also happen that some edges depend on each other, which would lead to a directed cycle. In the case of a directed cycle, it's critical to run tasks in parallel; otherwise certain tasks could wait forever on another to complete, in a deadlock.

The solution is called *topological sort*, which means that you can order all the vertices of the graph in such a way that all its directed edges target from a vertex earlier in the order to a vertex later in that order. For example, if task A must complete before task B, and task B must complete before task C which must complete before task A, then there's a cycle reference, and the system will notify you of the mistake by throwing an exception. If a precedence constraint has a direct cycle, then there's no solution. This kind of checking is called *directed cycle detection*. If a directed graph has satisfied these rules, it's considered a DAG, which is primed to run several tasks that have dependencies in parallel.

You can find the complete version of listing 13.4, which includes the DAG validation, in the source code online.

The following example uses the F# `MailboxProcessor` as a perfect candidate to implement a DAG to run in parallel operations with dependencies. First, let's define the discriminated union used to manage the tasks and run their dependencies.

Listing 13.3   Message type and data structure to coordinate task execution

```
type TaskMessage =
    | AddTask of int * TaskInfo
    | QueueTask of TaskInfo
    | ExecuteTasks
and TaskInfo =
    { Context : System.Threading.ExecutionContext
      Edges : int array; Id : int; Task : Func<Task>
      EdgesLeft : int option; Start : DateTimeOffset option
      End : DateTimeOffset option }
```

> Commands are sent to the ParallelTasksDAG underlying dagAgent agent, which is responsible for the task's execution coordination.

> Wraps the details of each task to run

The `TaskMessage` type represents the message cases sent to the underlying agent of the `ParallelTasksDAG`, implemented in listing 13.4. These messages are used for task coordination and dependency synchronization. The `TaskInfo` type contains and tracks the details of the registered tasks during the execution of the DAG, including the dependency edges. The execution context (http://mng.bz/2F9o) is captured to access information during the delayed execution, such as the current user, any state associated with the logical thread of execution, code-access security information, and so forth. The start and end for the execution time are published when the event fires.

Listing 13.4   DAG F# agent to parallelize the execution of operations

> Event that shows an instance of onTaskCompletedEvent, utilized to notify when a task completes

> Agent internal state to track the tasks and their dependencies. The collections are mutable because the state changes during the execution of the ParallelTasksDAG, and because they inherited thread safety from being inside an agent.

```
type ParallelTasksDAG() =
    let onTaskCompleted = new Event<TaskInfo>()

    let dagAgent = new MailboxProcessor<TaskMessage>(fun inbox ->
        let rec loop (tasks : Dictionary<int, TaskInfo>)
                     (edges : Dictionary<int, int list>) = async {
        let! msg = inbox.Receive()
        match msg with
        | ExecuteTasks ->
            let fromTo = new Dictionary<int, int list>()
            let ops = new Dictionary<int, TaskInfo>()
            for KeyValue(key, value) in tasks do
                let operation =
                    { value with EdgesLeft = Some(value.Edges.Length) }
                for from in operation.Edges do
                  let exists, lstDependencies = fromTo.TryGetValue(from)
                  if not <| exists then
                    fromTo.Add(from, [ operation.Id ])
                  else fromTo.[from] <- (operation.Id :: lstDependencies)
                  ops.Add(key, operation)
            ops |> Seq.iter (fun kv ->
```

> Waits asynchronously for a message

> Message case that starts execution of ParallelTasksDAG

> Collection that maps a monotonically increased index with a task to run

> The process iterates through the task list, analyzing the dependencies among the other tasks to create a topological structure representing the order of the task execution.

Message case to queue up a task, run it, and ultimately, remove it from the agent state as an active dependency when it completes

```
                      match kv.Value.EdgesLeft with
                      | Some(n) when n = 0 -> inbox.Post(QueueTask(kv.Value))
                      | _ -> ())
                    return! loop ops fromTo
              | QueueTask(op) ->
                    Async.Start <| async {
                      let start = DateTimeOffset.Now
                      match op.Context with
                      | null -> op.Task.Invoke() |> Async.AwaitATsk
                      | ctx -> ExecutionContext.Run(ctx.CreateCopy(),
                              (fun op -> let opCtx = (op :?> TaskInfo)
                                          opCtx.Task.Invoke().ConfigureAwait(false)),
    ➥       taskInfo)
                      let end' = DateTimeOffset.Now
                      onTaskCompleted.Trigger  { op with Start = Some(start)
                                                        End = Some(end') }
                      let exists, deps = edges.TryGetValue(op.Id)
                      if exists && deps.Length > 0 then
                        let depOps = getDependentOperation deps tasks []
                        edges.Remove(op.Id)  |> ignore
                        depOps |> Seq.iter (fun nestedOp ->
                                        inbox.Post(QueueTask(nestedOp))) }
                    return! loop tasks edges
              | AddTask(id, op) -> tasks.Add(id, op)
                                      return! loop tasks edges }
            loop (new Dictionary<int, TaskInfo>(HashIdentity.Structural))
                 (new Dictionary<int, int list>(HashIdentity.Structural)))

        [<CLIEventAttribute>]
        member this.OnTaskCompleted = onTaskCompleted.Publish
        member this.ExecuteTasks() = dagAgent.Post ExecuteTasks
        member this.AddTask(id, task, [<ParamArray>] edges : int array) =
          let data = { Context = ExecutionContext.Capture()
                       Edges = edges; Id = id; Task = task
                       NumRemainingEdges = None; Start = None; End = None }
          dagAgent.Post(AddTask(id, data))
```

If the ExecutionContext captured is null, then runs the task function in the current context.

Runs the task using the ExecutionContext captured

Triggers and publishes the onTaskCompleted event to notify that a task is completed. The event contains the task information.

Message case that adds a task to be executed according to its dependencies, if any

Starts the execution of the tasks registered

Adds a task, its dependencies, and the current ExecutionContext for the DAG execution.

The purpose of the function AddTask is to register a task including arbitrary dependency edges. This function accepts a unique ID, a function task that must be executed, and a set of edges that represent the IDs of other registered tasks, all of which must be completed before the current task can be executed. If the array is empty, it means there are no dependencies. The MailboxProcessor named dagAgent keeps the registered tasks in a current state tasks, which is a map (tasks : Dictionary<int, TaskInfo>) between the ID of each task and its details. The agent also keeps the state of the edge dependencies for each task ID (edges : Dictionary<int, int list>). The Dictionary collections are mutable because the state changes during the execution of the ParallelTasksDAG, and because they inherited thread safety from being inside an agent. When the agent receives the notification to start the execution, part of the process involves verifying that all the edge dependencies are registered and that there are no cycles within the graph. This verification step is available in the full implementation of the `ParallelTasksDAG` in the downloadable source code. The following code is an example in C# that references and consumes the F# library to run the `ParallelTasks-DAG`. The tasks registered mirror the dependencies from figure 13.6:

```
Func<int, int, Func<Task>> action = (id, delay) => async () => {
    Console.WriteLine($"Starting operation{id} in Thread Id
{Thread.CurrentThread.ManagedThreadId} . . . ");
    await Task.Delay(delay);
};

var dagAsync = new DAG.ParallelTasksDAG();
dagAsync.OnTaskCompleted.Subscribe(op =>
    Console.WriteLine($"Operation {op.Id} completed in Thread Id        {
      Thread.CurrentThread.ManagedThreadId}"));

dagAsync.AddTask(1, action(1, 600), 4, 5);
dagAsync.AddTask(2, action(2, 200), 5);
dagAsync.AddTask(3, action(3, 800), 6, 5);
dagAsync.AddTask(4, action(4, 500), 6);
dagAsync.AddTask(5, action(5, 450), 7, 8);
dagAsync.AddTask(6, action(6, 100), 7);
dagAsync.AddTask(7, action(7, 900));
dagAsync.AddTask(8, action(8, 700));
dagAsync.ExecuteTasks();
```

The helper function's `action` purpose is to print when a task starts, indicating the current thread `Id` as a reference to prove the multithreaded functionality. The event `OnTaskCompleted` is registered to notify when each task completes printing in the console the task ID and the current thread `Id`. Here's the output when the method `ExecuteTasks` is called:

```
Starting operation 8 in Thread Id 23...
Starting operation 7 in Thread Id 24...
Operation 8 Completed in Thread Id 23
Operation 7 Completed in Thread Id 24
Starting operation 5 in Thread Id 23...
Starting operation 6 in Thread Id 25...
Operation 6 Completed in Thread Id 25
Starting operation 4 in Thread Id 24...
Operation 5 Completed in Thread Id 23
Starting operation 2 in Thread Id 27...
Starting operation 3 in Thread Id 30...
Operation 4 Completed in Thread Id 24
Starting operation 1 in Thread Id 28...
Operation 2 Completed in Thread Id 27
Operation 1 Completed in Thread Id 28
Operation 3 Completed in Thread Id 30
```

As you can see, the tasks run in parallel with a different thread of execution (different thread ID), and the dependency order is preserved.

13.4 Gate for coordinating concurrent I/O operations sharing resources: one write, multiple reads

Imagine you're implementing a server application where there are many concurrent client requests coming in. These concurrent requests came into the server application because of the need to access shared data. Occasionally, a request that needs to modify the shared data would come in, requiring the data to be synchronized.

When a new client request arrives, the thread pool dispatches a thread to handle the request and to start the processing. Imagine if at this point the request wants to update data in the server in a thread-safe manner. You must face the problem of how to coordinate the read and write operations so that they access the resources concurrently without blocking. In this case, blocking means to coordinate the access of a shared resource. In doing so, the write operation locks the other operations to take ownership of the resource until its operation is complete.

A possible solution is to use primitive lock, such as `ReaderWriterLockSlim` (http://mng.bz/FY0J), which also manages access to a resource, allowing multiple threads.

But in this book you learned that you should avoid using primitive locks when possible. Locks prevent the code from running in parallel, and in many cases, overwhelm the thread pool by forcing it to create a new thread for each request. The other threads are blocked from acquiring access to the same resources. Another downside is that locks could be held for an extremely long time, causing the threads that have been awakened from the thread pool to process the read requests, to be immediately put to sleep waiting for the writer thread to complete its task. Additionally, this design doesn't scale.

Finally, the read and write operations should be handled differently to allow multiple reads to happen simultaneously, because these operations don't change the data. This should be balanced by ensuring write operations are only processed one at a time, while blocking the reads from retrieving stale data.

You need a custom coordinator that can synchronize the read and write operations asynchronously without blocking. This coordinator should execute the writes one at a time in sequential order without blocking any threads and leave the reads to run in parallel.

13.4.1 Solution: applying multiple read/write operations to shared thread-safe resources

`ReaderWriterAgent` offers reader-writer asynchronous semantics without blocking any threads and maintains a FIFO order of operations. It reduces resource consumption and improves the performance of the application. In fact, `ReaderWriterAgent` can perform an extraordinary amount of work using only a few threads. Regardless of the number of operations being made against the `ReaderWriterAgent`, only a few resources are required.

In the examples that follow, you want to send multiple read and write operations to a shared database. These operations are processed giving higher priority to reader threads than writers, as shown in figure 13.7. The same concepts can be applied to any other resources, such as a filesystem.

NOTE In general, `ReaderWriterAgent` is a better fit for programs that concurrently access resources asynchronously using I/O operations.

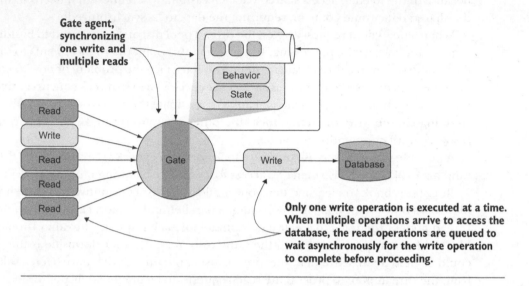

Gate agent, synchronizing one write and multiple reads

Only one write operation is executed at a time. When multiple operations arrive to access the database, the read operations are queued to wait asynchronously for the write operation to complete before proceeding.

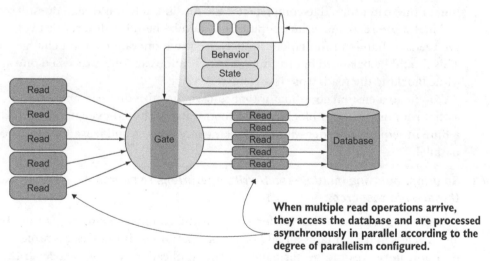

When multiple read operations arrive, they access the database and are processed asynchronously in parallel according to the degree of parallelism configured.

Figure 13.7 `ReaderWriterAgent` acts as a gate agent to asynchronously synchronize the access to share resources. In the top image, only one write operation at a time is executed, while the read operations are queued up to wait asynchronously for the write operation to complete before proceeding. In the bottom image, multiple read operations are processed asynchronously in parallel according to the degree of parallelism configured.

Listing 13.5 is the implementation of `ReaderWriterAgent` using the F# `MailboxProcessor`. The reason for choosing the F# `MailboxProcessor` is for simplicity in defining state machines, which are convenient to implement a reader-writer asynchronous coordinator. First, you need to define the message types to represent the operations by which the `ReaderWriterAgent` coordinates and synchronizes the read and write operations.

Listing 13.5   Message types used by the `ReaderWriterAgent` coordinator

```
type ReaderWriterMsg <'r,'w> =
    | Command of ReadWriteMessages<'r,'w>
    | CommandCompleted
and ReaderWriterGateState =
    | SendWrite
    | SendRead of count:int
    | Idle
and ReadWriteMessages<'r,'w> =
    | Read of r:'r
    | Write of w:'w
```

Uses a DU about the command cases to send to queue up the read/write operations

Uses message types to change the state and coordinate the operations in the internal queue of the **ReaderWriterAgent**

The `ReaderWriterMsg` message type denotes the command to either read or write to the database or to notify that the operation is completed. `ReaderWriterGateState` is a DU used to queue up the read/write operations to the `ReaderWriterAgent`. Ultimately, the `ReadWriteMessages` DU identifies the cases for the read/write operations queued in the internal `ReaderWriterAgent`.

This listing shows the implementation of the `ReaderWriterAgent` type.

Listing 13.6   `ReaderWriterAgent` coordinates asynchronous operations

If the optional arguments aren't passed into the constructor, they're initialized with the default value.

```
type ReaderWriterAgent<'r,'w>(workers:int,
behavior: MailboxProcessor<ReadWriteMessages<'r,'w>> ->
  Async<unit>,?errorHandler, ?cts:CancellationTokenSource) =

    let cts = defaultArg cts (new CancellationTokenSource())
    let errorHandler = defaultArg errorHandler ignore
    let supervisor = MailboxProcessor<Exception>.Start(fun inbox -> async {
            while true do
                let! error = inbox.Receive(); errorHandler error })

    let agent = MailboxProcessor<ReaderWriterMsg<'r,'w>>.Start(fun inbox ->
        let agents = Array.init workers (fun _ ->
            (new AgentDisposable<ReadWriteMsg<'r,'w>>(behavior, cts))
                .withSupervisor supervisor)
```

The supervisor agent handles exceptions. A while-true loop is used to wait asynchronously for incoming messages.

Each newly created agent registers the error handler to notify the supervisor agent.

The constructor takes the number of workers to configure the degree of parallelism, the behavior of the agent that accesses the database for the read/write operations, and the optional arguments to handle errors and to cancel the underlying agent to stop the still-active operations.

Creates a collection of agents with given behavior passed to parallelize the read/write operations to the database. Access is synchronized.

```
            cts.Token.Register(fun () ->
             agents |> Array.iter(fun agent -> (agent:>IDisposable).Dispose()))

          let writeQueue = Queue<_>()
          let readQueue = Queue<_>()
          let rec loop i state = async {
              let! msg = inbox.Receive()
              let next = (i+1) % workers
              match msg with
              | Command(Read(req)) ->
                match state with
                | Idle -> agents.[i].Agent.Post(Read(req))
                       return! loop next (SendRead 1)
                | SendRead(n) when writeQueue.Count = 0 ->
                   agents.[i].Agent.Post(Read(req))
                   return! loop next (SendRead(n+1))
                | _ -> readQueue.Enqueue(req)
                     return! loop i state
              | Command(Write(req)) ->
                match state with
                | Idle -> agents.[i].Agent.Post(Write(req))
                        return! loop next SendWrite
                | SendRead(_) | SendWrite -> writeQueue.Enqueue(req)
                                      return! loop i state
              | CommandCompleted ->
                match state with
                | Idle -> failwith "Operation no possible"
                | SendRead(n) when n > 1 -> return! loop i (SendRead(n-1))
                | SendWrite | SendRead(_) ->
                   if writeQueue.Count > 0 then
                      let req = writeQueue.Dequeue()
                      agents.[i].Agent.Post(Write(req))
                      return! loop next SendWrite
                   elif readQueue.Count > 0 then
                      readQueue |> Seq.iteri (fun j req ->
                         agents.[(i+j)%workers].Agent.Post(Read(req)))
                      let count = readQueue.Count
                      readQueue.Clear()
                      return! loop ((i+ count)%workers) (SendRead count)
                   else return! loop i Idle }
          loop 0 Idle), cts.Token)

     let postAndAsyncReply cmd createRequest =
         agent.PostAndAsyncReply(fun ch ->
                      createRequest(AsyncReplyChannelWithAck(ch, fun () ->
       agent.Post(CommandCompleted))) |> cmd |> ReaderWriterMsg.Command

       member this.Read(readRequest) = postAndAsyncReply Read  readRequest
       member thisWrite(writeRequest) = postAndAsyncReply Write writeRequest
```

Registers the cancellation strategy to stop the underlying agent workers

Uses internal queues to manage the access and execution of the read/write operations

The Command Read case, based on the current agent state, can queue up a new read operation, start an Read operation when the writeQueue is empty, or stay idle.

The Command Write case, based on the current agent state, can either stay idle or queue up a Write operation.

CommandCompleted notifies when an operation completes to update the current state of the read/write queues.

This function establishes asynchronous bidirectional communication between the agent and the caller to send the command and wait, without blocking, for the response.

The implementation of the underlying F# `MailboxProcessor`, in the `ReaderWriter-Agent` type, is a multi-state machine that coordinates exclusive writes and reads access to shared resources. The `ReaderWriterAgent` creates sub-agents that access the resources based on the `ReadWriteMsg` message type received. When the agent coordinator receives a `Read` command, its current state is checked using pattern matching to apply exclusive access logic:

- If the state is `Idle`, the `Read` command is sent to the agent children to be processed. If there are no active writes, then the state of the main agent is changed to `SendRead`.
- If the state is `SendRead`, the `Read` operation is sent to the agent's children to be performed only if there are no active writes.
- In all other cases, the `Read` operation is placed in the local `Read` queue for later processing.

In the case of a `Write` command sent to the agent coordinator, the message is pattern matched and processed according to its current state:

- If the state is `Idle`, the `Write` command is sent to the sub-agent inboxes to be processed. The state of the main agent is then changed to `SendWrite`.
- In all other cases, the `Write` operation is placed in the local `Write` queue for later processing.

Figure 13.8 shows the `ReaderWriterAgent` multi-state machine.

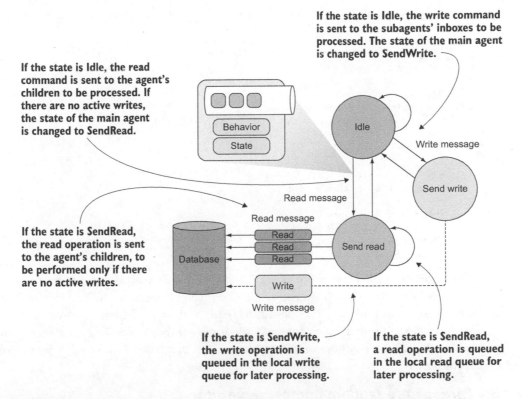

Figure 13.8 The `ReaderWriterAgent` works as a state machine, where each state aims to asynchronously synchronize the access to share resources (in this case, a database).

The following code snippet is a simple example that uses ReaderWriterAgent. For simplicity, instead of concurrently accessing a database, you're accessing a local mutable dictionary in a thread-safe and non-blocking manner:

```
type Person = { id:int; firstName:string; lastName:string; age:int }

let myDB = Dictionary<int, Person>()

let agentSql connectionString =
    fun (inbox: MailboxProcessor<_>) ->
        let rec loop() = async {
            let! msg = inbox.Receive()
            match msg with
            | Read(Get(id, reply)) ->
                match myDB.TryGetValue(id) with
                | true, res -> reply.Reply(Some res)
                | _ -> reply.Reply(None)
            | Write(Add(person, reply)) ->
                let id = myDB.Count
                myDB.Add(id, {person with id = id})
                reply.Reply(Some id)
            return! loop() }
        loop()

let agent = ReaderWriterAgent(maxOpenConnection, agentSql connectionString)

let write person = async {
    let! id = agent.Write(fun ch -> Add(person, ch))
    do! Async.Sleep(100)
}

let read personId = async {
    let! resp = agent.Read(fun ch -> Get(personId, ch))
    do! Async.Sleep(100)
}

[ for person in people do
    yield write  person
    yield read person.Id
    yield write  person
    yield read person.Id
    yield read person.Id ]
    |> Async.Parallel
```

The code example creates the agentSql object, whose purpose it is to emulate a database accessing the local resource myDB. The instance agent of the ReaderWriterAgent type coordinates the parallel operations reads and writes, which accesses concurrently and in a thread-safe manner the myDB dictionary without blocking. In a real-world scenario, the mutable collection myDB represents a database, a file, or any sort of shared resource.

13.5   *Thread-safe random number generator*

Often, when dealing with multithreaded code, you need to generate random numbers for an operation in the program. For example, suppose you're writing a web server application that needs to randomly send back an audio clip when a user sends a request. For performance reasons, the set of audio clips is loaded in the memory of the server, which is concurrently receiving a large number of requests. For each request, an audio clip must be randomly selected and sent back to the user to be played.

In most cases, the System.Random class is a fast-enough solution for producing random number values. But an effective application of a Random instance that is accessed in parallel becomes a challenging problem to solve in a high-performance style. When an instance of the Random class is used by multiple threads, its internal state can be compromised, and it will potentially always return zero.

> **NOTE** The System.Random class may not be random in the crypto-graphical sense. If you care about the quality of the random numbers, you should be using RNGCryptoServiceProvider, which generates cryptographically strong random numbers.

13.5.1 Solution: using the ThreadLocal object

ThreadLocal<T> ensures that each thread receives its own instance of a Random class, guaranteeing completely thread-safe access even in a multithreaded program. The following listing shows the implementation of the thread-safe random number generator using the ThreadLocal<T> class, which provides a strongly typed and locally scoped type to create object instances that are kept separate for each thread.

Listing 13.7 Thread-safe random number generator

```
public class ThreadSafeRandom : Random          Creates a thread-safe random number
{                                               generator using the ThreadLocal<T> class
    private ThreadLocal<Random> random =
      new ThreadLocal<Random>(() => new Random(MakeRandomSeed()));

    public override int Next() => random.Value.Next();

    public override int Next(int maxValue) =>
                               random.Value.Next(maxValue);

    public override int Next(int minValue, int maxValue) =>
                          random.Value.Next(minValue, maxValue);

    public override double NextDouble() => random.Value.NextDouble();

    public override void NextBytes(byte[] buffer) =>
                               random.Value.NextBytes(buffer);

    static int MakeRandomSeed() =>
                  Guid.NewGuid().ToString().GetHashCode();
}
```

Exposes the Random class methods

Creates a seed that doesn't depend on the system clock. A unique value is created with each invocation.

ThreadSafeRandom represents a thread-safe pseudo random number generator. This class is a subclass of Random and overrides the methods Next, NextDouble, and

NextBytes. The MakeRandomSeed method provides a unique value for each instance of the underlying Random class, which does not depend on the system clock.

The constructor for ThreadLocal<T> accepts a Func<T> delegate to create a thread-local instance of the Random class. The ThreadLocal<T>.Value is used to access the underlying value. Here you access the ThreadSafeRandom instance from a parallel loop to simulate a concurrent environment.

In this example, the parallel loop calls ThreadSafeRandom concurrently to obtain a random number for accessing the clips array:

```
var safeRandom = new ThreadSafeRandom();

string[] clips = new string[] { "1.mp3", "2.mp3", "3.mp3", "4.mp3"};

Parallel.For(0, 1000, (i) =>
{
    var clipIndex = safeRandom.Next(4);
    var clip = clips[clipIndex];

    Console.WriteLine($"clip to play {clip} - Thread Id
                        {Thread.CurrentThread.ManagedThreadId}");
});
```

Here's the result, in print or on the console:

```
clip to play 2.mp3 - Thread Id 11
clip to play 2.mp3 - Thread Id 8
clip to play 1.mp3 - Thread Id 20
clip to play 2.mp3 - Thread Id 20
clip to play 4.mp3 - Thread Id 13
clip to play 1.mp3 - Thread Id 8
clip to play 4.mp3 - Thread Id 11
clip to play 3.mp3 - Thread Id 11
clip to play 2.mp3 - Thread Id 20
clip to play 3.mp3 - Thread Id 13
```

> **NOTE** A single instance of ThreadLocal<T> allocates a few hundred bytes, so it's important to consider how many of these active instances are necessary at any time. If the program requires many parallel operations, it's recommended to work on a local copy to avoid accessing thread-local storage as much as possible.

13.6   *Polymorphic event aggregator*

In this section, assume that you need a tool to work in a program that requires raising several events of different types in the system, and then has a publish and subscribe system that can access these events.

13.6.1   *Solution: implementing a polymorphic publisher-subscriber pattern*

Figure 13.9 illustrates how to manage events of different types. Listing 13.8 shows the EventAggregator implementation using Rx (in bold).

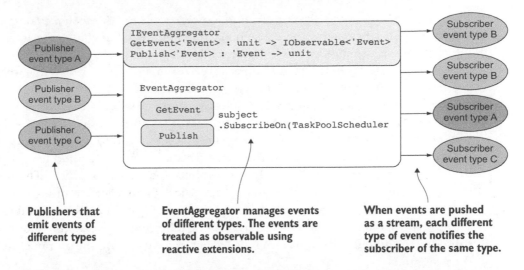

Figure 13.9 The `EventAggregator` manages events of different types. When the events are published, the `EventAggregator` matches and notifies the subscriber and events of the same type.

Listing 13.8 `EventAggregator` using Rx

Interfaces to define the contract for the EventAggregator, which also implements the IDisposable interface to ensure the cleanup of the resource subject

Instance of the Subject type (Rx) that coordinates event registration and notification

```
type IEventAggregator =
    inherit IDisposable
    abstract GetEvent<'Event> : unit -> IObservable<'Event>
    abstract Publish<'Event> : eventToPublish:'Event -> unit

type internal EventAggregator() =
    let disposedErrorMessage = "The EventAggregator is already disposed."

    let subject = new Subject<obj>()
```

Retrieves the event as IObservable based on the type

```
    interface IEventAggregator with
        member this.GetEvent<'Event>(): IObservable<'Event> =
            if (subject.IsDisposed) then failwith disposedErrorMessage

            subject.OfType<'Event>().AsObservable<'Event>()
                .SubscribeOn(TaskPoolScheduler.Default)
```

Subscribes Observable in the TaskPool scheduler to enforce concurrent behavior

```
        member this.Publish(eventToPublish: 'Event): unit =
            if (subject.IsDisposed) then failwith disposedErrorMessage

            subject.OnNext(eventToPublish)

        member this.Dispose(): unit = subject.Dispose()
```

Publishes event notifications to all subscribers of the event type

```
    static member Create() = new EventAggregator():>IEventAggregator
```

The interface IEventAggregator helps to loosely couple the EventAggregator implementation. This means that the consuming code won't need to change (as long as the interface doesn't change), even if the inner workings of the class change. Notice that IEventAggregator inherits from IDisposable to clean up any resources that were allocated when an instance of EventAggregator was created.

The methods GetEvent and Publish encapsulate an instance of the Rx Subject type, which behaves as a hub for events. GetEvent exposes IObservable from the subject instance to allow a simple way to handle event subscriptions. By default, the Rx Subject type is single threaded, so you use the SubscribeOn extension method to ensure that EventAggregator runs concurrently and exploits TaskPoolScheduler. The method Publish notifies all the subscribers to the EventAggregator concurrently.

The static member Create generates an instance of EventAggregator and exposes only the single interface IEventAggregator. The following code example shows how to subscribe to and publish events using the EventAggregator, and the output of running the program:

```
let evtAggregator = EventAggregator.Create()

type IncrementEvent = { Value: int }
type ResetEvent = { ResetTime: DateTime }

evtAggregator
    .GetEvent<ResetEvent>()
    .ObserveOn(Scheduler.CurrentThread)
    .Subscribe(fun evt -> printfn "Counter Reset at: %A - Thread Id %d"
        evt.ResetTime Thread.CurrentThread.ManagedThreadId)


evtAggregator
    .GetEvent<IncrementEvent>()
    .ObserveOn(Scheduler.CurrentThread)
    .Subscribe(fun evt ->  printfn "Counter Incremented. Value: %d - Thread
        Id %d" evt.Value Thread.CurrentThread.ManagedThreadId)

for i in [0..10] do
    evtAggregator.Publish({ Value = i })
evtAggregator.Publish({ ResetTime = DateTime(2015, 10, 21) })
```

Here's the output:

```
Counter Incremented. Value: 0 - Thread Id 1
Counter Incremented. Value: 1 - Thread Id 1
Counter Incremented. Value: 2 - Thread Id 1
Counter Incremented. Value: 3 - Thread Id 1
Counter Incremented. Value: 4 - Thread Id 1
Counter Incremented. Value: 5 - Thread Id 1
Counter Incremented. Value: 6 - Thread Id 1
Counter Incremented. Value: 7 - Thread Id 1
Counter Incremented. Value: 8 - Thread Id 1
Counter Incremented. Value: 9 - Thread Id 1
Counter Incremented. Value: 10 - Thread Id 1
Counter Reset at: 10/21/2015 00:00:00 AM - Thread Id 1
```

The interesting idea of the `EventAggregator` is how it handles events of different types. In the example, the `EventAggregator` instance registers two different event types (`IncrementEvent` and `ResetEvent`), and the `Subscribe` function sends the notification by targeting only the subscribers for a specific event type.

13.7 Custom Rx scheduler to control the degree of parallelism

Let's imagine you need to implement a system for querying large volumes of event streams asynchronously, and it requires a level of concurrency control. A valid solution for composing asynchronous and event-based programs is Rx, which is based on observables to generate sequence data concurrently. But as discussed in chapter 6, Rx isn't multithreaded by default. To enable a concurrency model, it's necessary to configure Rx to use a scheduler that supports multithreading by invoking the `SubscribeOn` extension. For example, Rx provides a few scheduler options including the `TaskPool` and `ThreadPool` types, which schedule all the actions to take place potentially using a different thread.

But there's a problem, because both schedulers start with one thread by default and then have a time delay of about 500 ms before they'll increase the number of threads required on demand. This behavior can have performance-critical consequences.

For example, consider a computer with four cores where there are eight actions scheduled. The Rx thread pool, by default, starts with one thread. If each action takes 2.000 ms, then three actions are queued up waiting for 500 ms before the Rx scheduler thread pool's size is increased. Consequently, instead of executing four actions in parallel right away, which would take 4 seconds in total for all eight actions, the work isn't completed for 5.5 sec, because three of the tasks are idle in the queue for 500 ms. Fortunately, the cost of expanding the thread pool is only a one-time penalty. In this case, you need a custom Rx scheduler that supports concurrency with fine control over the level of parallelism. It should initialize the internal thread pool at startup time rather than when needed to avoid the cost during critical time computation.

If you enable concurrency in Rx using one of the available schedulers, there's no option to configure the max degree of parallelism. This is a limitation, because in certain circumstances you only want few threads to be concurrently processing the event stream.

13.7.1 Solution: implementing a scheduler with multiple concurrent agents

The Rx `SubscribeOn` extension method requires passing as an argument an object that implements the `IScheduler` interface. The interface defines the methods responsible for scheduling the action to be performed, either as soon as possible or at a point in the future. You can build a custom scheduler for Rx that supports the concurrency model with the option of configuring a degree of parallelism, shown in figure 13.10.

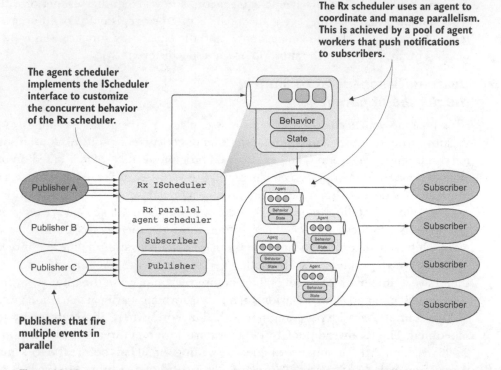

The agent scheduler implements the IScheduler interface to customize the concurrent behavior of the Rx scheduler.

The Rx scheduler uses an agent to coordinate and manage parallelism. This is achieved by a pool of agent workers that push notifications to subscribers.

Publishers that fire multiple events in parallel

Figure 13.10 `ParallelAgentScheduler` **is a custom scheduler that aims to tailor the concurrent behavior of the Rx. The Rx scheduler uses an agent to coordinate and manage the parallelism. This is achieved by a pool of agent workers that push notifications to subscribers.**

The following listing shows the implementation of the `ParallelAgentScheduler` scheduler for Rx, which uses the agent `parallelWorker` (shown in listing 11.5) to manage the degree of parallelism (the code to note is in bold).

Listing 13.9   Rx custom scheduler for managing the degree of parallelism

Uses a message type to schedule a job. The message response is an IDisposable wrapped in a reply channel. The IDisposable object is used to cancel/unsubscribe the notification.

The schedulerAgent function creates an instance of a MailboxProcessor that prioritizes and coordinates the request of jobs to run.

```
type ScheduleMsg = ScheduleRequest * AsyncReplyChannel<IDisposable>

let schedulerAgent (inbox:MailboxProcessor<ScheduleMsg>) =
    let rec execute (queue:IPriorityQueue<ScheduleRequest>) =  async {
        match queue |> PriorityQueue.tryPop with
        | None -> return! idle queue -1
        | Some(req, tail) ->
            let timeout =
                int <| (req.Due - DateTimeOffset.Now).TotalMilliseconds
            if timeout > 0 && (not req.IsCanceled)
            then return! idle queue timeout
            else
                if not req.IsCanceled then req.Action.Invoke()
```

When the agent is in execution and it receives a job request, the agent tries to pop a job to run from the internal priority-queue. If there are no jobs to execute, the agent switches to an idle state.

```
                              return! execute tail   }
        and idle (queue:IPriorityQueue<_>) timeout = async {
            let! msg = inbox.TryReceive(timeout)
            let queue =
                match msg with
                | None -> queue
                | Some(request, replyChannel)->
                        replyChannel.Reply(Disposable.Create(fun () ->
                                            request.IsCanceled <- true))
                    queue |> PriorityQueue.insert request
            return! execute queue }
        idle (PriorityQueue.empty(false)) -1

    type ParallelAgentScheduler(workers:int) =
        let agent = MailboxProcessor<ScheduleMsg>
                        .parallelWorker(workers, schedulerAgent)

        interface IScheduler with
            member this.Schedule(state:'a, due:DateTimeOffset,
      action:ScheduledAction<'a>) =
                    agent.PostAndReply(fun repl ->
                        let action () = action.Invoke(this :> IScheduler, state)
                        let req = ScheduleRequest(due, Func<_>(action))
                        req, repl)

            member this.Now = DateTimeOffset.Now
            member this.Schedule(state:'a, action) =
                let scheduler = this :> IScheduler
                let due = scheduler.Now
                scheduler.Schedule(state, due, action)
            member this.Schedule(state:'a, due:TimeSpan,
                                          action:ScheduledAction<'a>) =
                let scheduler = this :> IScheduler
                let due = scheduler.Now.Add(due)
                scheduler.Schedule(state, due, action)
```

Callout annotations:
- **When the agent is in an idle state, and a job request arrives, the job is pushed to the local queue and scheduled for execution.**
- **Returns a disposable object used to cancel the scheduled action**
- **Creates an instance of the agent parallelWorker (from chapter 11), creating a collection of sub-agent workers passing the schedulerAgent behavior**
- **Implements the IScheduler that defines a Reactive Extensions scheduler**
- **Posts and schedules a job request to the instance of the parallelWorker, which dispatches the jobs to run in parallel through its internal agent workers**

`ParallelAgentScheduler` introduces a level of concurrency to schedule and perform the tasks pushed in a distributed pool of running agents (F# `MailboxProcessor`). Note that all actions sent to `ParallelAgentScheduler` can potentially run out of order. `ParallelAgentScheduler` can be used as an Rx scheduler by injecting a new instance into the `SubscribeOn` extension method. The following code snippet is a simple example to use this custom scheduler:

```
    let scheduler = ParallelAgentScheduler(4)

    Observable.Interval(TimeSpan.FromSeconds(0.4))
        .SubscribeOn(scheduler)
        .Subscribe(fun _ ->
            printfn "ThreadId: %A " Thread.CurrentThread.ManagedThreadId)
```

The instance scheduler of the `ParallelAgentScheduler` object is set to have four concurrent agents running and ready to react when a new notification is pushed. In the example, the observable operator `Interval` sends a notification every 0.4 seconds, which is handled concurrently by the underlying agents of the `parallelWorker`. The benefits of using this custom `ParallelAgentScheduler` scheduler is that there's no downtime and delay in creating new threads, and it provides fine control over the degree of parallelism. There are times, for example, when you'll want to limit the level of parallelism for analyzing an event stream, such as when events waiting to be processed are buffered in the internal queue of the underlying agents and consequently not lost.

13.8   *Concurrent reactive scalable client/server*

The challenge: You need to create a server that listens asynchronously on a given port for incoming requests from multiple TCP clients. Additionally, you want the server to be

- Reactive
- Able to manage a large number of concurrent connections
- Scalable
- Responsive
- Event driven

These requirements ensure that you can use functional high-order operations to compose the event stream operations over the TCP socket connections in a declarative and non-blocking way.

Next, the client requests need to be processed concurrently by the server, with resulting responses sent back to the client. The Transmission Control Protocol (TCP) server connection can be either secured or unsecured. TCP is the most-used protocol on the internet today, used to provide accurate delivery that preserves the order of data packets from one endpoint to another. TCP can detect when packets are wrong or missing, and it manages the action necessary for resending them. Connectivity is ultra-important in applications, and the .NET Framework provides a variety of different ways to help you support that need.

You also need a long-running client program that uses TCP sockets to connect to the server. After the connection is established, both the client and server endpoints can send and receive bytes asynchronously and sometimes close the connection properly and reopen it at a later time.

The client program that attempts to connect to the TCP server is asynchronous, non-blocking, and capable of maintaining the application's responsiveness, even under pressure (from sustaining a large number of data transfers). For this example, the client/server socket-based application continually transfers volumes of packets at a high rate of speed as soon as the connection is established. The data is transmitted from the server to the client streaming in chunks, where each chunk represents the historical stocks prices on a particular date. This stream of data is generated by reading and parsing the comma-separated values (CSV) files in the solution. When the client receives the data, it begins to update a chart in real time.

This scenario is applicable to any operations that use reactive programming based on streams. Examples you may encounter are remote binary listeners, socket programming, and any other unpredictable event-oriented application, such as when a video needs to be streamed across the network.

13.8.1 Solution: combining Rx and asynchronous programming

To build the client/server program shown in listing 13.10, the CLR `TcpListener` and `TcpClient` classes provide a convenient model for creating a socket server with a few code lines. Used in combination with TAP and Rx, they increase the level of scalability and reliability of the program. But to work in the reactive style, the traditional application design must change.

Specifically, to achieve the requirements of a high-performing TCP client/server program, you need to implement the TCP sockets in an asynchronous style. For this reason, consider using a combination of Rx and TAP. Reactive programming, in particular, fits this scenario because it can deal with source events from any stream regardless of its type (network, file, memory, and so on). Here's the Rx definition from Microsoft:

> *The Reactive Extensions (Rx) is a library for composing asynchronous and event-based programs using observable sequences and LINQ-style query operators, and parameterize the concurrency in the asynchronous data streams using Schedulers.*

To implement the server in a scalable way, the instance of the `TcpListener` class listens for incoming connections. When a connection is established, it's routed, as a `TcpClient`, from the listener handler to manage the `NetworkStream`. This stream is then used for reading and writing bytes for data-sharing between client and server. Figure 13.11 shows the connection logic of the server program.

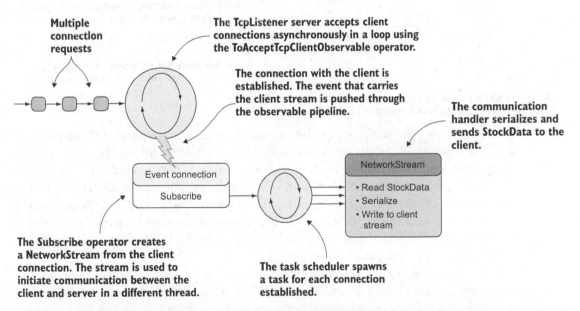

Figure 13.11 The `TcpListener` server accepts client connections asynchronously in a loop. When a connection is established, the event that carries the client stream is pushed through the `Observable` pipeline to be processed. Next, the connection handlers start reading the stock ticker symbol histories, serialize, and write the data to the client `NetworkStream`.

Listing 13.10   Reactive `TcpListener` server program

```
static void ConnectServer(int port, string sslName = null)
{
    var cts = new CancellationTokenSource();
    string[] stockFiles = new string[] { "aapl.csv", "amzn.csv", "fb.csv",
    "goog.csv", "msft.csv" };

    var formatter = new BinaryFormatter();

    TcpListener.Create(port)
        .ToAcceptTcpClientObservable()
        .ObserveOn(TaskPoolScheduler.Default)
        .Subscribe(client =>  {
        using (var stream = GetServerStream(client, sslName))
        {



                stockFiles
               .ObservableStreams(StockData.Parse)
               .Subscribe(async stock => {
                  var data = Serialize(formatter, stock);
                  await stream.WriteAsync(data, 0, data.Length, cts.Token);
               });
        }
    },
    error => Console.WriteLine("Error: " + error.Message),
    () => Console.WriteLine("OnCompleted"),
    cts.Token);
}
```

Collects stock ticker files (csv) — points to the `string[] stockFiles` line.

.NET Binary Formatter used for convenience. The formatter type can be replaced with any other serializer. — points to the `var formatter` line.

Subscribes the event flow from the ToAcceptTcpClientObservable to run on the current TaskPoll scheduler to ensure concurrent behavior — points to the `.ObserveOn` line.

Creates the Network stream to start the communication and data transfer. If the sslName value is provided, the Network stream returned uses a secure SSL base socket — points to the `using (var stream = GetServerStream...` line.

Converts a TcpListener into an observable sequence on a given port — points to the `TcpListener.Create(port)` block.

Subscribes the event notification from ObservableStreams to serialize the StockData received into a byte array and then to write the data into the Network stream — points to the `.Subscribe(async stock...` block.

Implements the Observer methods OnError and OnCompleted — points to the `error =>` / `() =>` lines.

Returns an observable that pushes and parses the stock histories from each file into a collection of StockData type — points to the `stockFiles` / `.ObservableStreams` block.

In the example, the server shows the implementation of a reactive TCP listener that acts as an observable of the stock ticker. The natural approach for a listener is to subscribe to an endpoint and receive clients as they connect. This is achieved by the extension method `ToAcceptTcpClientObservable`, which produces an observable of the `IObservable<TcpClient>`. The `ConnectServer` method uses the `TcpListener.Create` construct to generate a `TcpListener` using a given port number on which the server is listening asynchronously, and an optional name of the Secure Sockets Layer (SSL) to establish a secure or regular connection.

The custom observable extension method `ToAcceptTcpClientObservable` uses the given `TcpListener` instance to provide mid-level network services across an underlying socket object. When a remote client becomes available and a connection is established, a `TcpClient` object is created to handle the new communication, which is then sent into a different long-running thread with the use of a `Task` object.

Next, to guarantee the concurrent behavior of the socket handler, the scheduler is configured using the `ObserveOn` operator to subscribe and move the work to another scheduler, `TaskPoolScheduler`. In this way, the `ToAcceptTcpClientObservable` operator can orchestrate a large number of `TcpClients` concurrently as a sequence.

Then, the internals of the observable `ToAcceptTcpClientObservable` fetch the `TcpClient` reference from the task, and create the network stream used as a channel to send the packets of data generated by the `ObservableStreams` custom observable operator. The `GetServerStream` method retrieves either a secure or regular stream according to the value that `nameSsl` passed. This method determines whether the `nameSsl` value for an SSL connection has been set and, if so, creates an `SslStream` using `TcpClient.GetStream` and the configured server name to get the server certificate.

Alternatively, if SSL isn't used, `GetServerStream` gets the `NetworkStream` from the client using the `TcpClient.GetStream` method. You can find the `GetServerStream` method in the source code. When the `ObservableStreams` materialize, the event stream that's generated flows into the `Subscribe` operator. The operator then asynchronously serializes the incoming data into chunks of byte arrays that are sent across the network through the client stream. For simplicity, the serializer is the .NET binary formatter, but you can replace it with one that better fits your needs.

The data is sent across the network in the form of byte arrays, because it's the only reusable data message type that can contain any shape of object. This listing shows an implementation of the core observable operator `ToAcceptTcpClientObservable` used by the underlying `TcpListener` to listen for remote connections and react accordingly.

Listing 13.11   Asynchronous and reactive `ToAcceptTcpClientObservable`

Starts listening with a given client's buffer backlog

Creates the Observable operator that captures a cancellation token from the context

```
static IObservable<TcpClient> ToAcceptTcpClientObservable(this TcpListener
    listener, int backlog = 5)
{
    listener.Start(backlog);

    return Observable.Create<TcpClient>(async (observer, token) =>
    {
        try
        {
            while (!token.IsCancellationRequested)
            {
                var client = await listener.AcceptTcpClientAsync();
                Task.Factory.StartNew(_ => observer.OnNext(client), token,
                    TaskCreationOptions.LongRunning);
            }
            observer.OnCompleted();
        }
        catch (OperationCanceledException)
        {
            observer.OnCompleted();
        }
        catch (Exception error)
        {
            observer.OnError(error);
        }
        finally
        {
```

The while loop continues to iterate until the cancellation token requests a cancellation.

Accepts new clients from the listener, asynchronously

Routes the client connections to the observer into an asynchronous task to let multiple clients connect together

Implements the Observer methods OnCompleted and OnError to respectively handle the cases of cancellation and exception

```
            listener.Stop();
        }
        return Disposable.Create(() =>          ◄──  │ Creates a cleanup function that runs
        {                                             │ when the observable is disposed
            listener.Stop();
            listener.Server.Dispose();
        });
    });
}
```

`ToAcceptTcpClientObservable` takes an instance of `TcpListener`, which starts listening asynchronously for new incoming connection requests in a `while` loop, until the operation is canceled using a cancellation token. When a client successfully connects, a `TcpClient` reference flows out as a message within a sequence. This message executes into an asynchronous `Task` to service the client/server interaction, letting multiple clients connect concurrently to the same listener. Once a connection is accepted, another `Task` starts repeating the procedure of listening for new connection request.

Ultimately, when the observable is disposed, or the cancellation token requests a cancellation, the function passed into the `Disposable.Create` operator is triggered to stop and close the underlying server listener.

NOTE In general, use the `Disposable.Create` method to write an action to clean up resources and to stop useless messages flowing to an observer that has been disposed.

The data transferred is generated through the `ObservableStreams` extension method, which reads and parses a set of CSV files to extract the historical stocks prices. This data is then pushed to the clients, connected through the `NetworkStream`.

This shows the implementation of `ObservableStreams`.

Listing 13.12   Custom `Observable` stream reader and parser

The ObservableStreams custom observable extension method takes as an argument a list of file paths to process, and a lambda function for the file content transformation.

An instance of FileLinesStream is created for each file and used to generate an observable. This observable reads each line of the file and applies the map function for the transformation.

```
static IObservable<StockData> ObservableStreams
    (this IEnumerable<string> filePaths,
 ➡ Func<string, string, StockData> map, int delay = 50)
{
    return filePaths
      .Select(key =>
          new FileLinesStream<StockData>(key, row => map(key, row)))    ◄──
      .Select(fsStock => {
          var startData = new DateTime(2001, 1, 1);
          return Observable.Interval(TimeSpan.FromMilliseconds(delay))
                .Zip(fsStock.ObserveLines(), (tick, stock) => {          ◄──
                    stock.Date = startData + TimeSpan.FromDays(tick);
                    return stock;
                });
        }
```

The Interval operator is used to apply a delay between notifications. The value can be zero to disable the delays.

The Zip operator combines an element from each sequence in turn. In this case, one sequence is generated from the Interval operator, which ensures that a delay is applied for each notification.

```
        )
        .Aggregate((o1, o2) => o1.Merge(o2));
}
```

The Aggregate operator merges (reduces) all the observables into one.

`ObservableStreams` generates a series of observables of `StockData` type, one for each of the `filePaths` passed. The class `FileLinesStream`, whose implementation is omitted for simplicity, opens the `FileStream` of a given file path. It then reads the content text from the stream as an observable and applies a projection to transform each line of text read into a `StockData` type. Ultimately it pushes the results out as an observable.

The most interesting part of the code is the application of the two `Observable` operators `Interval` and `Zip`, which are used together to apply an arbitrary delay, if specified, between messages. The `Zip` operator combines an element from each sequence in turn, which means that each `StockData` entry is paired with an element, produced every interval time. In this case, the combination of a `StockData` with the interval time ensures a delay for each notification.

Ultimately, the combination of the `Aggregate` and `Merge` operators is used to merge the observables generated from each file:

```
.Aggregate((o1, o2) => o1.Merge(o2));
```

Next, to complete the client/server program, you implement the reactive client class, shown in figure 13.12. Listing 13.13 shows the implementation of the client side.

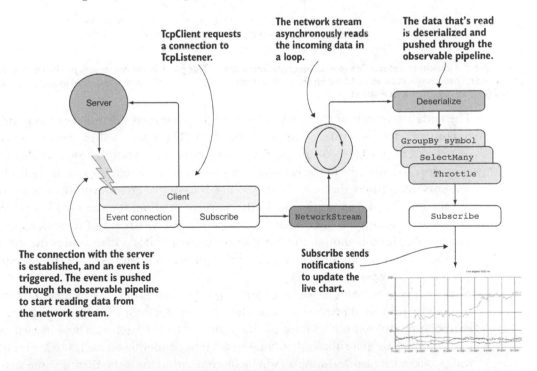

Figure 13.12 `TcpClient` requests a connection to the `TcpListener` server. When the connection is established, it triggers an event that carries the client stream, which is pushed through the observable pipeline. Next, a `NetworkStream` is created to start reading the data asynchronously in a loop from the server. The data read is next deserialized and analyzed through the observable pipeline to ultimately update the live chart.

Listing 13.13   Reactive `TcpClient` program

Creates an observable over an instance of the TcpClient object to initiate and notify when the connection to the server is established

Delivers continuous chunks of bytes from the underlying stream until it can be read or a cancellation is requested. The byte array flows through the observable pipeline in an asynchronous way.

```
var endpoint = new IPEndPoint(IPAddress.Parse("127.0.0.1"), 8080);
var cts = new CancellationTokenSource();
var formatter = new BinaryFormatter();

endpoint.ToConnectClientObservable()
    .Subscribe(client => {
        GetClientStream(client, sslName)

        .ReadObservable(0x1000, cts.Token)
        .Select(rawData => Deserialize<StockData>(formatter, rawData))
        .GroupBy(item => item.Symbol)

        .SelectMany(group =>
                    group.Throttle(TimeSpan.FromMilliseconds(20))
            .ObserveOn(TaskPoolScheduler.Default))

        .ObserveOn(ctx)
        .Subscribe(stock =>
            UpdateChart(chart, stock, sw.ElapsedMilliseconds) );
    },
    error => Console.WriteLine("Error: " + error.Message),
    () => Console.WriteLine("OnCompleted"),
    cts.Token);
```

Creates a stream from the network streams used for the communication between the server and client

Groups the incoming data by the stock symbol, creating an observable for each stock ticker symbol

The last step of the observable pipeline subscribes the notification to update a live chart.

Throttles the incoming notification to avoid overwhelming the consumer. Throttling can be done based on the data stream itself (rather than just a timespan).

This partition of the stream by the stock symbol starts a new thread for each partition.

The code starts with an `IPEndPoint` instance, which targets the remote server endpoint to connect. The observable operator `ToConnectClientObservable` creates an instance of a `TcpClient` object to initiate the connection. Now, you can use the `Observable` operators to subscribe to the remote client connection. When the connection with the server is established, the `TcpClient` instance is passed as an observable to begin receiving the stream of data to process. In this implementation, the remote `NetworkStream` is accessed calling the `GetClientStream` method. The stream of data flows into the observable pipeline though the `ReadObservable` operator, which routes the incoming messages from the underlying `TcpClient` sequence into another observable sequence of type `ArraySegment` bytes.

As part of the stream-processing code, after the chunks of `rawData` received from the server are converted into `StockData`, the `GroupBy` operator filters the stock tickers by symbol into multiple observables. At this point, each observable can have its own unique operations. Grouping allows throttling to act independently on each stock symbol, and only stocks with identical symbols will be filtered within the given throttle time span.

A common problem with writing reactive code is when the events come in too quickly. A fast-moving stream of events can overwhelm your program's processing. In listing 13.13, because you have a bunch of UI updates, using the throttling operator can help deal with a massive flood of stream data without overwhelming the live updates. The operator after the throttling, `ObserveOn(TaskPoolScheduler.Default)`, starts a new thread for each partition originated by the `GroupBy`. The `Subscribe` method ultimately updates the live chart with the stock values. Here's the implementation of the `ToConnectClientObservable` operator.

Listing 13.14 Custom Observable `ToConnectClientObservable` operator

Creates an observable, passing the cancellation token from the current context

Starts waiting asynchronously for a connection to the server to be established

```
static IObservable<TcpClient> ToConnectClientObservable(this IPEndPoint
    endpoint)
{
    return Observable.Create<TcpClient>(async (observer, token) => {
        var client = new TcpClient();
        try
        {
            await client.ConnectAsync(endpoint.Address, endpoint.Port);

            token.ThrowIfCancellationRequested();

            observer.OnNext(client);
        }
        catch (Exception error)
        {
            observer.OnError(error);
        }
        return Disposable.Create(() => client.Dispose());
    });
}
```

Checks if a cancellation has been sent to stop observing the connection

The connection is established, and the notification is pushed to the observers.

When the observable is disposed, TcpClient and its connection are closed.

`ToConnectClientObservable` creates an instance of `TcpClient` from the given `IPEndPoint` endpoint, and then it tries to connect asynchronously to the remote server. When the connection is established successfully, the `TcpClient` client reference is pushed out through the observer.

The last phase of the code to program is the `ReadObservable` observable operator, which is built to asynchronously and continuously read chunks of data from a stream. In this program, the stream is the `NetworkStream` produced as result of the connection between the server and client.

Listing 13.15 Observable stream reader

```
public static IObservable<ArraySegment<byte>> ReadObservable(this Stream
    stream, int bufferSize, CancellationToken token =
    default(CancellationToken))
{
    var buffer = new byte[bufferSize];
    var asyncRead = Observable.FromAsync<int>(async ct => {
        await stream.ReadAsync(buffer, 0, sizeof(int), ct);
```

Converts an asynchronous operation to an observable

Reads the size of the chunk of data (buffer) from the stream to configure the read length, and reads the buffer with the given size

Continues reading in a while loop until there is data to be read

Reads the size of the chunk of data (buffer) from the stream to configure the read length, and reads the buffer with the given size

```
            var size = BitConverter.ToInt32(buffer, 0);
            await stream.ReadAsync(buffer, 0, size, ct);
            return size});
    return Observable.While(
        () => !token.IsCancellationRequested && stream.CanRead,
        Observable.Defer(() =>
                !token.IsCancellationRequested && stream.CanRead
                ? asyncRead
                : Observable.Empty<int>())
            .Catch((Func<Exception, IObservable<int>>)(ex =>
Observable.Empty<int>()))
            .TakeWhile(returnBuffer => returnBuffer > 0)
            .Select(readBytes =>
new ArraySegment<byte>(buffer, 0, readBytes)))
        .Finally(stream.Dispose);
}
```

Handles the case of an error silently, passing an empty result

Iteratively invokes the observable factory, which starts from the current stream position. The Defer observable operator starts the process only when a subscriber exists.

When a chunk of data is read, an instance of ArraySegment is created to wrap the buffer, which is then pushed to the observers.

One important note to consider when implementing this ReadObservable is that the stream must be read in chunks to be reactive. That's why the ReadObservable operator takes a buffer size as an argument to define the size of the chunks.

The purpose of the ReadObservable operator is to read a stream in chunks to facilitate working with data that's larger than the memory available, or that could be infinite with an unknown size, like streaming from the network. In addition, it promotes the compositional nature of Rx for applying multiple transformations to the stream itself, because reading chunks at a time allows data transformations while the stream is still in motion. At this point, you have an extension method that iterates on the bytes from a stream.

In the code, the FromAsync extension method allows you to convert a Task<T>, in this case stream.ReadAsync, into an IObservable<T> to treat the data as a flow of events and to enable programming with Rx. Underneath, Observable.FromAsync creates an observable that only starts the operation independently every time it's subscribed to.

Then, the underlying stream is read as an Observable while loop until data is available or the operation is canceled. The Observable Defer operator waits until an observer subscribes to it, and then starts pushing the data as a stream. Next, during each iteration, a chunk of data is read from the stream. This data is then pushed into a buffer that takes the form of an ArraySegment<byte>, which slices the payload in the right length. ReadObservable returns an IObservable of ArraySegment<byte>, which is an efficient way to manage the byte arrays in a pool. The buffer size may be larger than the payload of bytes received, for example, so the use of ArraySegment<byte> holds the byte array and payload length.

In conclusion, when receiving and processing data, the .NET Rx allows shorter and cleaner code than traditional solutions. Furthermore, the complexity of building a

TCP-based reactive client/server program is heavily reduced in comparison to a traditional model. In fact, you don't have to deal with low-level `TcpClient` and `TcpListener` objects, and the flow of bytes is handled through a high-level abstraction offered by observable operators.

13.9 Reusable custom high-performing parallel filter-map operator

You have a collection of data, and you need to perform the same operation on each element of the data to satisfy a given condition. This operation is CPU-bound and may take time. You decide to create a custom and reusable high-performant operator to filter and map the elements of a given collection. The combination of filtering and transforming the elements of a collection is a common operation for analyzing data structures. It's possible to achieve a solution using LINQ or PLINQ in parallel with the `Where` and `Select` operators; but a more optimal performance solution is available. As you saw in section 5.2.1, for each call and repeated use of high-order operators such as map (`Select`), filter (`Where`), and other similar functions of the PLINQ query (and LINQ), as shown in figure 13.13, intermediate sequences are generated that unnecessarily increase memory allocation. This is due to the intrinsic functional nature of LINQ and PLINQ, where collections are transformed instead of mutated. In the case of transforming large sequences, the penalty paid to the GC to free up memory becomes increasingly higher, with negative consequences to the performance of the program.

`[numbers].Where(IsPrime).Select(ToPow)`

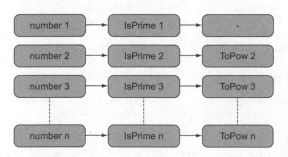

Figure 13.13 In this diagram, each number (first column) is first filtered by `IsPrime` (second column) to verify if it's a prime number. Then, the prime numbers are passed into the `ToPow` function (third column). For example, the first value, number 1, is not a prime number, so the `ToPow` function isn't running.

In this example, you want to derive the sum of all the prime numbers in 100 million digits.

13.9.1 Solution: combining filter and map parallel operations

The implementation of a custom and parallel filter and map operator with top performance requires attention to minimize (or eliminate) unnecessary temporary data allocation, as shown in figure 13.14. This technique of reducing data allocation during data manipulation to increase the performance of the program is known as *deforestation*.

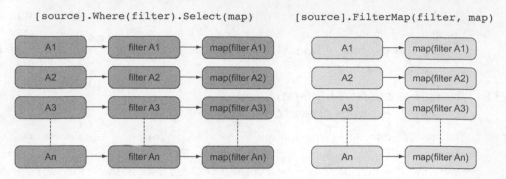

Figure 13.14 The left graph shows the operations `Where` and `Select` over a given source, done in separate steps, which introduces extra memory allocation and consequentially more GC generations. The right graph shows that applying the `Where` and `Select` (filter and map) operations together in a single step avoids extra allocation and reduces GC generations, increasing the speed of the program.

The next listing shows the code of the `ParallelFilterMap` function, which uses the `Parallel.ForEach` loop to eliminate intermediate data allocations by processing only one array, instead of creating one temporary collection for each operator.

Listing 13.16 `ParallelFilterMap` operator

The extension method takes the lambda functions to filter (predicate) and map (transform) the input values from the source.

Creates an instance of the Atom object (defined in chapter 3) to apply compare-and-swap update operations over the underlying ImmutableList in a thread-safe manner

```
static TOutput[] ParallelFilterMap<TInput, TOutput>(this IList<TInput>
   input, Func<TInput, Boolean> predicate,
                 Func<TInput, TOutput> transform,
                 ParallelOptions parallelOptions = null)
{
    parallelOptions = parallelOptions ?? new ParallelOptions();

    var atomResult = new Atom<ImmutableList<List<TOutput>>>
                             (ImmutableList<List<TOutput>>.Empty);

    Parallel.ForEach(Partitioner.Create(0, input.Count),
        parallelOptions,
        () => new List<TOutput>(),
      delegate (Tuple<int, int> range, ParallelLoopState state,
            List<TOutput> localList)
        {
            for (int j = range.Item1; j < range.Item2; j++)
            {
                var item = input[j];
                if (predicate(item))
                    localList.Add(transform(item));
            }
            return localList;
```

Applies the filter and map functions for each item of the current portioned set of data

Each thread uses a Local-Thread instance of List<TOutput> for isolated and thread-safe operations.

Each iteration runs an independent thread (task) from the thread pool that performs the filter and map operations over a partitioned set from the input source.

```
        }, localList => atomResult.Swap(r => r.Add(localList)));
    return atomResult.Value.SelectMany(id => id).ToArray();
}
```

**When each iteration completes, the shared atomResult
Atom object updates the underlying ImmutableList.**

**Ultimately, the result is
flattened into an array.**

The parallel ForEach loop applies the predicate and map functions for each element of the input collection. In general, if the body of the parallel loop performs only a small amount of work, better performance results come from partitioning the iterations into larger units of work. The reason for this is the overhead when processing a loop, which involves the cost of managing worker threads and the cost of invoking a delegate method. Consequently, it's good practice to partition the parallel iteration space by a certain constant using the Partitioner.Create constructor. Then each body invokes the filter and map functions for a certain range of elements, amortizing invocations of the loop body delegate.

NOTE Due to parallelism, the order in which the values will be processed doesn't guarantee the result will be in the same order.

For each iteration of the ForEach loop, there's an anonymous delegate invocation that causes a penalty in terms of memory allocation and, consequently, performance. One invocation occurs for the filter function, a second invocation occurs for the map function, and ultimately an invocation happens for the delegate passed into the parallel loop. The solution is to tailor the parallel loop specific to the filter and map operations to avoid extra invocations of the body delegate.

The parallel ForEach operator forks off a set of threads, each of which calculates an intermediate result by performing the filter and map functions over its own partition of data and placing the value into its dedicated slot in the intermediate array.

Each thread (task) governed by the parallel loop captures an isolated instance of a local List<TOutput> through the concept of local values. Local values are variables that exist locally within a parallel loop. The body of the loop can access the value directly, without having to worry about synchronization.

NOTE The reason to use local and isolated instance of List<TOutput> is to avoid *excessive contention*, which happens when too many threads try to access a single shared resource simultaneously, leading to bad performance.

Each partition will compute its own intermediate value that will then combine into a single final value.

When the loop completes, and it's ready to aggregate each of its local results, it does so with the localFinally delegate. But the delegate requires synchronization access to the variable that holds the final result. An instance of the ImmutableList collection is used to overcome this limitation to merge the final results in a thread-safe manner.

NOTE Write operations (such as adding an item) in immutable collections return a new immutable instance instead of changing the existing instance. This isn't as wasteful as it first sounds because immutable collections share their memory.

Note the `ImmutableList` is encapsulated in an `Atom` object, from chapter 3. The `Atom` object uses a compare-and-swap (CAS) strategy to apply thread-safe writes and updates of objects without the need of locks and other forms of primitive synchronization. In this example, the `Atom` class holds a reference to the immutable list and updates it automatically.

The following code snippet tests the parallel sum of only the prime numbers from 100 million digits:

```
bool IsPrime(int n)
{
    if (n == 1) return false;
    if (n == 2) return true;
    var boundary = (int) Math.Floor(Math.Sqrt(n));
    for (int i = 2; i <= boundary; ++i)
        if (n % i == 0) return false;
    return true;
}

BigInteger ToPow(int n) => (BigInteger) Math.BigMul(n, n);
var nums = Enumerable.Range(0, 100000000).ToList();

BigInteger SeqOperation() =>
            nums.Where(IsPrime).Select(ToPow).Aggregate(BigInteger.Add);

BigInteger ParallelLinqOperation() =>
  nums.AsParallel().Where(IsPrime).Select(ToPow).Aggregate(BigInteger.Add);

BigInteger ParallelFilterMapInline() =>
        nums.ParallelFilterMap(IsPrime, ToPow).Aggregate(BigInteger.Add);
```

Figure 13.15 compares the sequential code (as baseline), the PLINQ version, and the custom `ParallelFilterMap` operator. The figure shows the result of the benchmark code running the sum of the prime numbers for the 100 million digits. The benchmark was performed in a quad-core machine with 6 GB of RAM. The sequential code takes an average of 196.482 seconds to run and is used as baseline. The PLINQ version of the code is faster and runs in 74.926 seconds, almost three times faster, which is expected in a quad-core computer. The custom `ParallelFilterMap` operator is the fastest, at approximately 52.566 seconds.

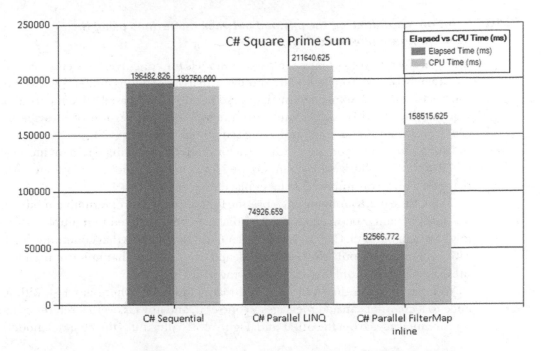

Figure 13.15 Benchmark chart comparing the Sequential and Parallel LINQ versions of the code with the custom `ParallelFilterMap` operator. In a quad-core machine, the custom `ParallelFilterMap` operator is approximately 80% faster than the sequential version of the code, and 30% faster than the PLINQ version.

13.10 *Non-blocking synchronous message-passing model*

Let's imagine you need to build a scalable program capable of handling a large number of operations without blocking any threads. You need a program that loads, processes, and saves a large number of images, for example. These operations are handled with few threads in a collaborative way, which optimizes the resources without blocking any threads and without jeopardizing the performance of the program.

Similar to the Producer/Consumer pattern, there are two flows of data. One flow is the input, where the processing starts, followed by intermediate steps to transform the data, followed by the output with the final result of the operations. These processes, the producer and the consumer, share a common fixed-size buffer used as a queue. The queue is buffered to increase the overall speed and increase throughput to allow for multiple consumers and producers. In fact, when the queue is safe to use by multiple consumers and producers, then it's easy to change the level of concurrency for different parts of the pipeline at runtime. The producer, however, could write into the queue when it isn't full, or conversely, it can block when the queue is full. On the other side, the consumer could read from the queue when it is not empty, but it will block in other cases when the queue is empty. You want to implement a producer and consumer pattern based on message passing to avoid thread blocking and maximize the application's scalability.

13.10.1 Solution: coordinating the payload between operations using the agent programming model

There are two flavors of message passing models for concurrent systems: synchronous and asynchronous. You're already familiar with asynchronous models such as the agent (and actor) model, explained in chapters 11 and 12, and based on asynchronous message passing. In this recipe, you'll use the synchronous version of message passing, which is also known as communicating sequential processes (CSP).

CSP has much in common with the actor model, both being based on message passing. But CSP emphasizes the channels used for communication, rather than the entities between which communication takes place.

This CSP synchronous message passing for concurrent programming models is used for data exchange between channels, which can be scheduled to multiple threads and might run in parallel. Channels are similar to thread workers that communicate directly with each other by publishing messages, and where other channels can then listen for these messages without the sender knowing who's listening.

You can imagine the channel as a thread-safe queue, where any task with a reference to a channel can add messages to one end, and any task with a reference to it can remove messages from the other end. Figure 13.16 illustrates the channel model.

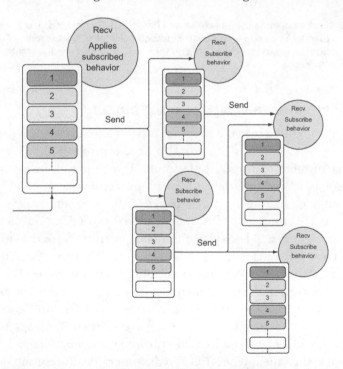

Figure 13.16 The channel receives (`Recv`) a message, and applies the subscribed behavior. The channels communicate by sending (`Send`) messages, often creating an interconnected system that's similar to the actor model. Each channel contains a local queue of messages used to synchronize the communication with other channels without blocking.

A channel doesn't need to know about what channel will process the message later in the pipeline. It only has to know what channel to forward the messages to. On the other side, listeners on channels can subscribe and unsubscribe without affecting any channels sending the messages. This design promotes loose coupling between channels.

The primary strength of CSP is its flexibility, where channels are first-class and can be independently created, written to, read from, and passed between tasks. The following listing shows the implementation of the channel in F#, which uses `Mailbox-Processor` for the underlying message synchronization due to the close similarity with the agent-programming model. The same concepts apply to C#. You can find the full implementation in C# using TDF in the downloadable source code.

Listing 13.17 `ChannelAgent` for CSP implementation using `MailboxProcessor`

Uses a DU to define the message type to send to the ChannelAgent in order to coordinate the channel operations

Uses internal queues to keep track of the read and write operations of the channel

```
type internal ChannelMsg<'a> =
    | Recv of ('a -> unit) * AsyncReplyChannel<unit>
    | Send of 'a * (unit -> unit) * AsyncReplyChannel<unit>

type [<Sealed>] ChannelAgent<'a>() =
    let agent = MailboxProcessor<ChannelMsg<'a>>.Start(fun inbox ->
        let readers = Queue<'a -> unit>()
        let writers = Queue<'a * (unit -> unit)>()

        let rec loop() = async {
            let! msg = inbox.Receive()
            match msg with
            | Recv(ok , reply) ->
                if writers.Count = 0 then
                    readers.Enqueue ok
                    reply.Reply( () )
                else
                    let (value, cont) = writers.Dequeue()
                    TaskPool.Spawn cont
                    reply.Reply( (ok value) )
                return! loop()
            | Send(x, ok, reply) ->
                if readers.Count = 0 then
                    writers.Enqueue(x, ok)
                    reply.Reply( () )
                else
                    let cont = readers.Dequeue()
                    TaskPool.Spawn ok
                    reply.Reply( (cont x) )
                return! loop() }
        loop())

    member this.Recv(ok: 'a -> unit)  =
        agent.PostAndAsyncReply(fun ch -> Recv(ok, ch)) |> Async.Ignore

    member this.Send(value: 'a, ok:unit -> unit)  =
        agent.PostAndAsyncReply(fun ch -> Send(value, ok, ch)) |> Async.
    Ignore
```

When a Recv message is received, if the current writer queue is empty, then the read function is queued up, waiting for a writer function to balance the work.

When a Recv message is received and there is at least one writer function available in the queue, a task is spawned to run the read function.

When a Send message is received, if the current reader queue is empty, then the write function is queued up, waiting for a reader function to balance the work.

When a Send message is received, if the current reader queue is empty, then the write function is queued up, waiting for a reader function to balance the work.

When a Send message is received and there's at least one reader function available in the queue, a task is spawned to run the write function.

```
member this.Recv() =
    Async.FromContinuations(fun (ok, _,_) ->
        agent.PostAndAsyncReply(fun ch -> Recv(ok, ch))
        |> Async.RunSynchronously)

member this.Send (value:'a) =
    Async.FromContinuations(fun (ok, _,_) ->
        agent.PostAndAsyncReply(fun ch -> Send(value, ok, ch))
        |> Async.RunSynchronously )

let run (action:Async<_>) = action |> Async.Ignore |> Async.Start

let rec subscribe (chan:ChannelAgent<_>) (handler:'a -> unit) =
    chan.Recv(fun value -> handler value
                           subscribe chan handler) |> run
```

This helper function registers a handler applied to the next available message in the channel. The function recursively and asynchronously (without blocking) waits for messages from the channel (without blocking).

Runs an asynchronous operation in a separate thread, discharging the result

The ChannelMsg DU represents the message type that ChannelAgent handles. When a message arrives, the Recv case is used to execute a behavior applied to the payload passed. The Send case is used to communicate a message to the channel.

The underlying MailboxProcessor contains two generic queues, one for each operation, Recv or Send. As you can see, when a message is either received or sent, the behavior of the agent, in the function loop(), checks the count of available messages to load balance and synchronize the communication without blocking any threads. ChannelAgent accepts continuation functions with its Recv and Send operations. If a match is available, the continuation is invoked immediately; otherwise, it's queued for later. Keep in mind that a synchronous channel eventually gives a result, so the call is logically blocking. But when using F# async workflows, no actual threads are blocked while waiting.

The last two functions in the code help run a channel operation (usually Send), while the subscribe function is used to register and apply a handler to the messages received. This function runs recursively and asynchronously waiting for messages from the channel.

The TaskPool.Spawn function assumes a function with signature (unit -> unit) -> unit that forks the computation on a current thread scheduler. This listing shows the implementation of TaskPool, which uses the concepts covered in chapter 7.

Listing 13.18   Dedicated TaskPool agent (MailboxProcessor)

The constructor of TaskPool takes the number of workers to set the degree of parallelism.

Uses a record type to wrap the current ExecutionContext captured when the operation cont is added to the TaskPool

```
type private Context = {cont:unit -> unit; context:ExecutionContext}

type TaskPool private (numWorkers) =
```

A Context type is processed using the
captured ExecutionContext when
received by one of the worker agents.

```
let worker (inbox: MailboxProcessor<Context>) =        ◄───  Sets the behavior of
    let rec loop() = async {                                  each worker agent
        let! ctx = inbox.Receive()
        let ec = ctx.context.CreateCopy()
        ExecutionContext.Run(ec, (fun _ -> ctx.cont()), null)
        return! loop() }
    loop()
let agent = MailboxProcessor<Context>.parallelWorker(numWorkers,
    worker)   ◄─────────────────────  Creates an instance of the F# MailboxProcessor
                                       parallelWorker to concurrently run multiple
static let self = TaskPool(2)          operations limited by the degree of parallelism

member private this.Add (continutaion:unit -> unit) =
    let ctx = { cont = continutaion;
                context = ExecutionContext.Capture() }  ◄────────────┐
    agent.Post(ctx)
static member Spawn (continuation:unit -> unit) =
    self.Add continuation
```

Adds a continuation action to the TaskPool. The current   **When a continuation task is sent to the underlying**
ExecutionContext is captured and sent to the   **agent, the current Execution context is captured and**
parallelWorker agent in the form of a Context record type.   **passed as part of the message payload.**

The Context record type is used to capture the ExecutionContext at the moment when the continuation function cont was passed to the pool. TaskPool initializes the MailboxProcessor parallelWorker type to handle multiple concurrent consumers and producers (refer to chapter 11 for the implementation and details of the parallelWorker agent).

The purpose of TaskPool is to control how many tasks to schedule and to dedicate to run the continuation function in a tight loop. In this example, it runs only one task, but you can have any number.

Add enqueues the given continuation function, which will be executed when a thread on a channel offers communication and another thread offers matching communication. Until such compensation between channels is achieved, the thread will wait asynchronously.

In this code snippet, the ChannelAgent implements a CSP pipeline, which loads an image, transforms it, and then saves the newly created image into the local MyPicture folder:

```
let rec subscribe (chan:ChannelAgent<_>) (handler:'a -> unit) =
    chan.Recv(fun value -> handler value
                           subscribe chan handler) |> run

let chanLoadImage = ChannelAgent<string>()
let chanApply3DEffect = ChannelAgent<ImageInfo>()
let chanSaveImage = ChannelAgent<ImageInfo>()

subscribe chanLoadImage (fun image ->
    let bitmap = new Bitmap(image)
```

```
    let imageInfo = { Path = Environment.GetFolderPath(Environment.
     SpecialFolder.MyPictures)
                      Name = Path.GetFileName(image)
                      Image = bitmap }
    chanApply3DEffect.Send imageInfo |> run)

subscribe chanApply3DEffect (fun imageInfo ->
    let bitmap = convertImageTo3D imageInfo.Image
    let imageInfo = { imageInfo with Image = bitmap }
    chanSaveImage.Send imageInfo |> run)

subscribe chanSaveImage (fun imageInfo ->
    printfn "Saving image %s" imageInfo.Name
    let destination = Path.Combine(imageInfo.Path, imageInfo.Name)
    imageInfo.Image.Save(destination))

let loadImages() =
    let images = Directory.GetFiles(@".\Images")
    for image in images do
        chanLoadImage.Send image |> run

loadImages()
```

As you can see, implementing a CSP-based pipeline is simple. After you define the
channels chanLoadImage, chanApply3DEffect, and chanSaveImage, you have to register the behaviors using the subscribe function. When a message is available to be
processed, the behavior is applied.

13.11 Coordinating concurrent jobs using the agent programming model

The concepts of parallelism and asynchronicity were covered extensively earlier in this
book. Chapter 9 shows how powerful and convenient the Async.Parallel operator is
for running a large number of asynchronous operations in parallel. Often, however,
you may need to map across a sequence of asynchronous operations and run functions
on the elements in parallel. In this case, a feasible solution can be implemented:

```
    let inline asyncFor(operations: #seq<'a> Async, map:'a -> 'b) =
        Async.map (Seq.map map) operations
```

Now, how would you limit and tame the degree of parallelism to process the elements
to balance resource consumption? This issue comes up surprisingly often when a
program is doing CPU-heavy operations, and there's no reason to run more threads
than the number of processors on the machine. When there are too many concurrent
threads running, contention and context-switching make the program enormously
inefficient, even for a few hundred tasks. This is a problem of throttling. How can you
throttle asynchronous and CPU-bound computations awaiting results without blocking? The challenge becomes even more difficult because these asynchronous operations are spawned at runtime, which makes the total number of asynchronous jobs to
run unknown.

13.11.1 Solution: implementing an agent that runs jobs with a configured degree of parallelism

The solution is using an agent model to implement a job coordinator that lets you throttle the degree of parallelism by limiting the number of tasks that are processed in parallel, as shown in figure 13.17. In this case, the agent's only mission is to gate the number of concurrent tasks and send back the result of each operation without blocking. In addition, the agent should conveniently expose an observable channel where you can register to receive notifications when a new result is computed.

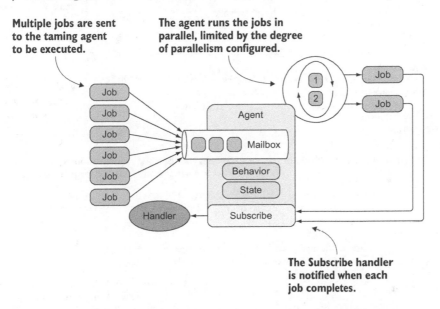

Figure 13.17 The `TamingAgent` runs the jobs in parallel, limited by the degree of parallelism configured. When an operation completes, the `Subscribe` operator notifies the registered handlers with the output of the job.

Let's define the agent that can tame the concurrent operations. The agent must receive a message, but must also send back to the caller, or subscriber, a response for the result computed.

In the following listing, the implementation of the `TamingAgent` runs asynchronous operations, efficiently throttling the degree of parallelism. When the number of concurrent operations exceeds this degree, they're queued and processed later.

Listing 13.19 TamingAgent

```
type JobRequest<'T, 'R> =
    | Ask of 'T * AsyncReplyChannel<'R>
    | Completed
    | Quit

type TamingAgent<'T, 'R>(limit, operation:'T -> Async<'R>) =
```

Uses a DU representing the message to send to the TamingAgent to start a new job and notify when it completes

An event object is used to notify the subscriber when a job completes.

Helper functions dispose of and stop the TamingAgent.

```
let jobCompleted = new Event<'R>()

let tamingAgent = Agent<JobRequest<'T, 'R>>.Start(fun agent ->
    let dispose() = (agent :> IDisposable).Dispose()
    let rec running jobCount = async {
        let! msg = agent.Receive()
        match msg with
        | Quit -> dispose()
        | Completed -> return! running (jobCount - 1)
        | Ask(job, reply) ->
            do!
                async { try
                    let! result = operation job
                    jobCompleted.Trigger result
                    reply.Reply(result)
                finally agent.Post(Completed) }
```

Represents a state when the agent is working

Decrements the count of work items when a job completes

Starts the job item and continues in a running state

Runs the job asynchronously to obtain the result

When the job completes, the event jobCompleted is triggered to notify the subscribers.

Sends the result of the job completed back to the caller

When the job completes, the inbox sends itself a notification to decrease the job count

Represents the idle state when the agent is blocked because the limit of concurrent jobs is reached

Queues the specified asynchronous workflow for processing in a separate thread to guarantee concurrent behavior

```
                |> Async.StartChild |> Async.Ignore
            if jobCount <= limit - 1 then return! running (jobCount + 1)
            else return! idle () }
    and idle () =
        agent.Scan(function
            | Completed -> Some(running (limit - 1))
            | _ -> None)
    running 0)
```

Uses the Scan function to wait for completion of work and change the agent state

Provides support to subscribe the jobCompleted event as Observable

Starts in a running state with zero job items

Queues an operation and waits asynchronously for a response

```
member this.Ask(value) = tamingAgent
                            .PostAndAsyncReply(fun ch -> Ask(value, ch))
member this.Stop() = tamingAgent.Post(Quit)
member x.Subscribe(action) = jobCompleted.Publish |>
    Observable.subscribe(action)
```

The `JobRequest` DU represents the message type for the agent `tamingAgent`. This message has a `Job` case, which handles the value to send to compute and a reply channel with the result. The `Completed` case is used by an agent to notify when a computation is terminated and the next job available can be processed. Ultimately, the `Quit` case (message) is sent to stop the agent when needed.

The `TamingAgent` constructor takes two arguments: the concurrent execution limit and the asynchronous operation for each job. The body of the `TamingAgent` type relies on two mutually recursive functions to track the number of concurrently running operations. When the agent starts with zero operations, or the number of running jobs doesn't pass the limit of the degree of parallelism imposed, the function running will wait for a new incoming message to process. Conversely, when the jobs running reach the enforced limit, the execution flow of the agent switches the function to idle. It uses the Scan operator to wait for a type of message to discharge the others.

The Scan operator is used in the F# MailboxProcessor (agent) to process only a subset and targeted type of messages. The Scan operator takes a lambda function that returns an Option type. The messages you want to be found during the scanning process should return Some, and the messages you want to ignore for now should return None.

The operation signature passed into the constructor is 'T -> Async<'R>, which resembles the Async.map function. This function is applied to each job that's sent to the agent through the method member Ask, which takes a value type that is passed to the agent to initiate, or queue, a new job. When the computation completes, the subscribers of the underlying event jobCompleted are notified with the new result, which is also replied back asynchronously to the caller that sent the message across the channel AsyncReplyChannel.

As mentioned, the purpose of the event jobCompleted is to notify the subscribers that have registered a callback function through the method member Subscribe, which uses the Observable module for convenience and flexibility.

Here's how the TamingAgent is used to transform a set of images. This example is similar to the CPS Channel one, allowing you to compare code between different approaches.

Listing 13.20   TamingAgent in action for image transformation

```fsharp
let loadImage = (fun (imagePath:string) -> async {
    let bitmap = new Bitmap(imagePath)
    return { Path = Environment.GetFolderPath(Environment.SpecialFolder.
     MyPictures)
             Name = Path.GetFileName(imagePath)
             Image = bitmap } })
```
Loads an image from the given file path, returning a record type with the image and its information loaded

```fsharp
let apply3D = (fun (imageInfo:ImageInfo) -> async {
    let bitmap = convertImageTo3D imageInfo.Image
    return { imageInfo with Image = bitmap } })
```
Functions to apply a 3D effect to the image

```fsharp
let saveImage = (fun (imageInfo:ImageInfo) -> async {
    printfn "Saving image %s" imageInfo.Name
    let destination = Path.Combine(imageInfo.Path, imageInfo.Name)
    imageInfo.Image.Save(destination)
    return imageInfo.Name})
```
Saves the image to the local MyPicture folder

Composes the previously defined asynchronous functions using the monadic return and bind async operators

```fsharp
let loadandApply3dImage (imagePath:string) =
    Async.retn imagePath >>= loadImage >>= apply3D >>= saveImage
```

```fsharp
let loadandApply3dImageAgent = TamingAgent<string, string>(2,
    loadandApply3dImage)
```
Creates an instance of the TamingAgent capable of running two jobs concurrently, applying the composed function loadandApply3dImage for each job

**Subscribes a handler to run when a
job-completed notification arrives**

```
loadandApply3dImageAgent.Subscribe(fun imageName -> printfn "Saved image %s
 from subscriber" imageName)

let transformImages() =
    let images = Directory.GetFiles(@".\Images")
    for image in images do
        loadandApply3dImageAgent.Ask(image)
        |> run (fun imageName ->
                    printfn "Saved image %s - from reply back" imageName)
```

**Starts the process by reading the
image files and pushing a new job
to the loadandApply3dImageAgent
TamingAgent instance**

The three asynchronous functions, loadImage, apply3D, and saveImage, are composed together, forming the function loadandApply3dImage using the F# async bind infix operator >>= defined in chapter 9. As a refresher, here's the implementation:

```
let bind (operation:'a -> Async<'b>) (xAsync:Async<'a>) = async {
    let! x = xAsync
    return! operation x }

let (>>=) (item:Async<'a>) (operation:'a -> Async<'b>) =
                                        bind operation item
```

Then, the loadandApply3dImageAgent instance of the TamingAgent is defined by passing the argument limit into the constructor. This sets the degree of parallelism of the agent and the argument function loadandApply3dImage, which represents the behavior for the job computations. The Subscribe function registers a callback that runs when each job completes. In this example, it displays the name of the image of the completed job.

NOTE The image paths are sent sequentially. The TamingAgent is thread safe, so multiple threads can send messages simultaneously without any problem.

The loadImages() function reads the image paths from the directory Images, and in a for-each loop sends the values to the loadandApply3dImageAgent TamingAgent. The run function uses CPS to execute a callback when the result is computed and replied back.

13.12 *Composing monadic functions*

You have functions that take a simple type and return an elevated type like Task or Async, and you need to compose those functions. You might think you need to get the first result and next apply it to the second function, and then repeat for all the functions. This process can be rather cumbersome. This is a case for employing the concept of function composition. As a reminder, you can create a new function from two smaller ones. It usually works, as long as the functions have matching output and input types.

This rule doesn't apply for monadic functions, because they don't have matching input/output types. For example, monadic Async and Task functions cannot be composed because Task<T> isn't the same as T.

Here's the signature for the monadic `Bind` operator:

```
Bind : (T -> Async<R>) -> Async<T> -> Async<R>
Bind : (T -> Task<R>) -> Task <T> -> Task <R>
```

The `Bind` operator can pass elevated values into functions that handle the wrapped underlying value. How can you compose monadic functions effortlessly?

13.12.1 Solution: combining asynchronous operations using the Kleisli composition operator

The composition between monadic functions is named *Kleisli composition*, and in FP it's usually represented with the infix operator `>=>` that can be constructed using the monadic `Bind` operator. The `Kleisli` operator essentially provides a composition construct over monadic functions, which instead of composing regular functions like a `->` b and b `->` c, is used to compose over a `->` M b and b `->` M c, where M is an elevated type.

The signature of the `Kleisli` composition operator for elevated types, such as the `Async` and `Task` types, is

```
Kleisli (>=>) : ('T -> Async<TR>) -> (TR -> Async<R>) -> T -> Async<R>
Kleisli (>=>) : ('T -> Task<TR>) -> (TR -> Task <R>) -> T -> Task <R>
```

With this operator, two monadic functions can compose directly as follows:

```
(T -> Task<TR>) >=> (TR -> Task<R>)
(T -> Async<TR>) >=> (TR -> Async<R>)
```

The result is a new monadic function:

```
T -> Task<R>
T -> Async<R>
```

The next code snippet shows the implementation of the `Kleisli` operator in C#, which uses the monadic `Bind` operator underneath. The operator `Bind` (or `SelectMany`) for the `Task` type was introduced in chapter 7:

```
static Func<T, Task<U>> Kleisli<T, R, U>(Func<T, Task<R>> task1,
  Func<R, Task<U>> task2) => async value => await task1(value).Bind(task2);
```

The equivalent function in F# can also be defined using the conventional `kleisli` infix operator `>=>`, in this case applied to the `Async` type:

```
let kleisli (f:'a -> Async<'b>) (g:'b -> Async<'c>) (x:'a) = (f x) >>= g
let (>=>) (f:'a -> Async<'b>) (g:'b -> Async<'c>) (x:'a) = (f x) >>= g
```

The `Async` bind and `infix` operator `>>=` was introduced in chapter 9. Here's the implementation as a reminder:

```
let bind (operation:'a -> Async<'b>) (xAsync:Async<'a>) = async {
        let! x = xAsync
        return! operation x }

let (>>=) (item:Async<'a>) (operation:'a -> Async<'b>) = bind operation item
```

Let's see where and how the `Kleisli` operator can help. Consider the case of multiple asynchronous operations that you want to compose effortlessly. These functions have the following signature:

```
operationOne   : ('a -> Async<'b>)
operationTwo   : ('b -> Async<'c>)
operationThree : ('c -> Async<'d>)
```

Conceptually, the composed function would look like:

```
('a -> Async<'b>) -> ('b -> Async<'c>) -> ('c -> Async<'d>)
```

At a high level, you can think of this composition over monadic functions as a pipeline, where the result of the first function is piped into the next one and so on until the last step. In general, when you think of piping, you can think of two approaches: applicative (`<*>`) and monadic (`>>=`). Because you need the result of the previous call in your next call, the monadic style (`>>=`) is the better choice.

For this example, you use the `TamingAgent` from the previous recipe. The `TamingAgent` has the method member `Ask`, whose signature matches the scenario, where it takes a generic argument `'T` and returns an `Async<'R>` type. At this point, you use the `Kleisli` operator to compose a set of `TamingAgent` types to form a pipeline of agents, as shown in figure 13.18. The result of each agent is computed independently and passed as input, in the form of a message, to the next agent until the last node of the chain performs the final side effect. The technique of linking and composing agents can lead to robust designs and concurrent systems. When an agent returns (replies back) a result to the caller, it can be composed into a pipeline of agents.

Figure 13.18   The pipeline processing pattern is useful when you want to process data in multiple steps. The idea behind the pattern is that inputs are sent to the first agent in the pipeline. The main benefit of the pipeline processing pattern is that it provides a simple way to balance the tradeoff between overly sequential processing (which may reduce performance) and overly parallel processing (which may have a large overhead).

This listing shows the `TamingAgent` composition in action. The example is a rework of listing 13.20, which reuses the same function for loading, transforming, and saving an image.

Listing 13.21   `TamingAgent` with the `Kleisli` operator

```
let pipe limit operation job : Async<_> =        ◄─────
    let agent = TamingAgent(limit, operation)
    agent.Ask(job)

let loadImageAgent = pipe 2 loadImage
let apply3DEffectAgent = pipe 2 apply3D
let saveImageAgent = pipe 2 saveImage
```

Creates an instance of the TamingAgent type and exposes its asynchronous Ask method, which ensures a reply back to the caller through the AsyncReplyChannel when the job completes

Creates an instance of the TamingAgent agent pipe for each function about image processing

> **Combines the asynchronous operations generated from the pipe function using the Kleisli operator**

```
let pipeline =
        loadImageAgent >=> apply3DEffectAgent >=> saveImageAgent
```

```
let transformImages() =
    let images = Directory.GetFiles(@".\Images")
    for image in images do
        pipeline image
        |> run (fun imageName -> printfn "Saved image %s" imageName)
```

> **Starts the process by reading the image files and pushing a new job to the pipeline**

In this example, the program uses the `TamingAgent` to transform an image, different than listing 13.20. In earlier recipes, the three functions that load, transform, and save, in that order, an image to the local filesystem are composed together to form a new function. This function is handled and applied to all the incoming messages by a single instance of `TamingAgent` type. In this application (listing 13.21), an instance of `TamingAgent` is created for each function to run, and then the agents are composed through the underlying method `Ask` to form a pipeline. The `Ask` asynchronous function ensures a reply to the caller through the `AsyncReplyChannel` when the job completes. The composition of the agents is eased by the `Kleisli` operator.

The purpose of the `pipe` function is to help create an instance of the `TamingAgent` and expose the function `Ask`, whose signature `'a -> Async<'b>` resembles the monadic `Bind` operator used for the composition with other agents.

After the definition of the three agents, `loadImageAgent`, `apply3DEffectAgent`, and `saveImageAgent`, using the `pipe` helper function, it becomes simple to create a pipeline by composing these agents using the `Kleisli` operator.

Summary

- You should use a concurrent object pool to recycle instances of the same objects without blocking to optimize the performance of a program. The number of GC generations can be dramatically reduced by using a pool of objects, which improves the speed of a program's execution.

- You can parallelize a set of dependent tasks with a constrained order of execution. This process is useful because it maximizes parallelism as much as possible among the execution of multiple tasks, regardless of dependency.

- Multiple threads can coordinate the access of shared resources for reader-writer types of operations without blocking, maintaining a FIFO ordering. This coordination allows the read operations to run simultaneously, while asynchronously (non-blocking) waiting for eventual write operations. This pattern increases the performance of an application due to introduction of parallelism and the reduced consumption of resources.

- An event aggregator acts similar to the mediator design pattern, where all events go through a central aggregator and can be consumed from anywhere in the application. Rx allows you to implement an event aggregator that supports multi-threading to handle multiple events concurrently.

- You can implement a custom Rx scheduler using the `IScheduler` interface, to allow the taming of incoming events with a fine control over the degree of parallelism. Furthermore, by explicitly setting the level of parallelism, the Rx scheduler internal thread pool isn't penalized with downtime for expanding the size of threads when required.
- Even without built-in support for the CSP programming model in .NET, you can use either the F# `MailboxProcessor` or TDF to coordinate and balance the payload between asynchronous operations in a non-blocking synchronous message-passing style.

Building a scalable mobile app with concurrent functional programming

This chapter covers

- Designing scalable, performant applications

- Using the CQRS pattern with WebSocket notifications

- Decoupling an ASP.NET Web API controller using Rx

- Implementing a message bus

Leading up to this chapter, you learned about and mastered concurrent functional techniques and patterns for building highly performant and scalable applications. This chapter is the culmination and practical application of those techniques, where you use your knowledge of TPL tasks, asynchronous workflow, message-passing programming, and reactive programming with reactive extensions to develop a fully concurrent application.

The application you're building in this chapter is based on a mobile interface that communicates with a Web API endpoint for real-time monitoring of the stock market. It includes the ability to send commands to buy and sell stocks and to maintain those orders using a long-running asynchronous operation on the server side. This operation reactively applies the trade actions when the stocks reach the desired price point.

Discussion points include architecture choice and explanation of how the functional paradigm fits well in both the server and client sides of a system when designing a scalable and responsive application. By the end of this chapter, you'll know how to design optimal concurrent functional patterns and how to choose the most effective concurrent programming model.

14.1 *Functional programming on the server in the real world*

A server-side application must be designed to handle multiple requests concurrently. In general, conventional web applications can be thought of as embarrassingly parallel, because requests are entirely isolated and easy to execute independently. The more powerful the server running the application, the higher the number of requests it can handle.

The program logic of modern, large-scale web applications is inherently concurrent. Additionally, highly interactive modern web and real-time applications, such as multiplayer browser games, collaborative platforms, and mobile services are a huge challenge in terms of concurrency programming. These applications use instant notifications and asynchronous messaging as building blocks to coordinate the different operations and communicate between different concurrent requests that likely run in parallel. In these cases, it's no longer possible to write a simple application with a single sequential control flow; instead, you must plan for the synchronization of independent components in a holistic manner. You might ask, why should you use FP when building a server-side application?

In September 2013, Twitter published the paper "Your Server as a Function" (Marius Eriksen, https://monkey.org/~marius/funsrv.pdf). Its purpose was to validate the architecture and programming model that Twitter adopted for building server-side software on a large scale, where systems exhibit a high degree of concurrency and environmental variability. The following is a quote from the paper:

> *We present three abstractions around which we structure our server software at Twitter. They adhere to the style of functional programming—emphasizing immutability, the composition of first-class functions, and the isolation of side effects—and combine to present a large gain in flexibility, simplicity, ease of reasoning, and robustness.*

The support provided for concurrent FP in .NET is key to making it a great tool for server-side programming. Support exists for running operations asynchronously in a declarative and compositional semantic style; additionally, you can use agents to develop thread-safe components. You can combine these core technologies for declarative processing of events and for efficient parallelism with the TPL.

Functional programming facilitates the implementation of a stateless server (figure 14.1), which is an important asset for building scalability when architecting large web applications required to handle a huge number of request concurrently, such as social networks or e-commerce sites. A program is stateless when the operations (such as functions, methods, and procedures) aren't sensitive to the state of the computation. Consequently, all the data used in an operation is passed as *inputs* to the operation, and all the data used by the operations invoked is passed back as *outputs*. A stateless design never stores application or user data for later computational needs. The stateless design eases concurrency, because it's easy for each stage of the application to run on a different thread. The stateless design is the key that makes the design able to scale out perfectly according to Amdahl's Law.

In practice, a stateless program can be effortlessly parallelized and distributed among computers and processes to scale out performance. You don't need to know where the computation runs, because no part of the program will modify any data structures, which avoids data races. Also, the computation can run in different processes or different computers without being constrained to perform in a specific environment.

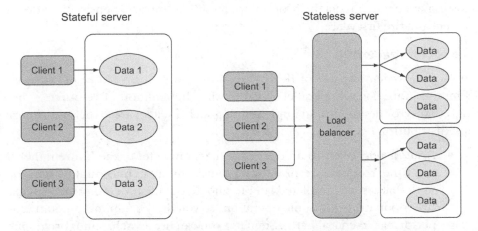

Figure 14.1   Server with state (stateful) compared to a server without state (stateless). The stateful server must keep the state between requests, which limits the scalability of the system, requiring more resources to run. The stateless server can auto-scale because there's no sharing of state. Before stateless servers, there can be a load balancer that distributes the incoming requests, which can be routed to any machine without worrying about hitting a particular server.

Using FP techniques, you can build sophisticated, fully asynchronous and adaptive systems that auto-scale using the same level of abstractions, with the same semantics, across all dimensions of scale, from CPU cores to data centers.

14.2   *How to design a successful performant application*

When processing hundreds of thousands of requests simultaneously per second in a large-scale setting, you need a high degree of concurrency and efficiency in handling I/O and synchronization to ensure maximum throughput and CPU use in server software. Efficiency, safety, and robustness are paramount goals that have traditionally conflicted with code modularity, reusability, and flexibility. The functional paradigm emphasizes a declarative programming style, which forces asynchronous programs to be structured as a set of components whose data dependencies are witnessed by the various asynchronous combinators.

NOTE   As discussed in chapter 8, asynchronous I/O operations should run in parallel, because their scalability can outnumber the processors available by an order of magnitude. Furthermore, to correctly achieve such unbounded resource capability, the asynchronous operations have to be written in a functional style, to not manipulate state in memory, and instead deal with immutable values.

When implementing a program, you should bake performance goals into the design up front. Performance is an aspect of software design that cannot be an afterthought; it must be included as an explicit goal from the start. It's not *impossible* to redesign an existing application from the ground up, but it's far more expensive than designing it correctly in the first place.

14.2.1   *The secret sauce: ACD*

You want a system capable of flexing to an increase (or decrease) of requests with a commensurate boost in parallel speedup with the addition of resources. The secret ingredients for designing and implementing such a system are asynchronicity, caching, and distribution (ACD):

- *Asynchronicity* refers to an operation that completes in the future rather than in real time. You can interpret asynchronicity as an architectural design—queuing work that can be completed later to smooth out the processing load, for example. It's important to decouple operations so you do the minimal amount of work in performance-critical paths. Similarly, you can use asynchronous programming to schedule requests for nightly processes.
- *Caching* aims to avoid repeating work. For example, caching saves the results of earlier work that can be used again later, without repeating the work performed to get those results. Usually, caching is applied in front of time-consuming operations that are frequently repeated and whose output doesn't change often.
- *Distribution* aims to partition requests across multiple systems to scale out processing. It's easier to implement distribution in a stateless system: the less state the server holds, the easier it is to distribute work.

NOTE   When designing a performant, scalable, and resilient web application, it's important to consider the points made in "Fallacies of Distributed Computing" (www.rgoarchitects.com/Files/fallacies.pdf). Arnon Rotem-Gal-Oz, the author, refers to the assumption that distributed systems work in a secure, reliable, homogeneous network that has zero latency, infinite bandwidth, and zero transport cost, and in which the topology doesn't change.

ACD is a main ingredient for writing scalable and responsive applications that can maintain high throughput under a heavy workload. That's a task that's becoming increasingly vital.

14.2.2 *A different asynchronous pattern: queuing work for later execution*

At this point, you should have a clear idea of what asynchronous programming means. Asynchronicity, as you recall, means you dispatch a job that will complete in the *future*. This can be achieved using two patterns. The first is based on continuation passing style (CPS), or callbacks, discussed in chapters 8 and 9. The second is based on asynchronous message passing, covered in chapters 11 and 12. As mentioned in the previous section, asynchronicity can also be the result (behavior) of a design in an application.

The pattern in figure 14.2 implements asynchronous systems at a design level, aiming to smooth the workload of the program by sending the operations, or requests to do work, to a service that queues tasks to be completed in the future. The service can be in a remote hardware device, a remote server in a cloud service, or a different process in a local machine. In the latter case, the execution thread sends the request in a fire-and-forget fashion, which releases it for further work at a later time. An example of a task that uses this design is scheduling a message to be sent to a mailing list.

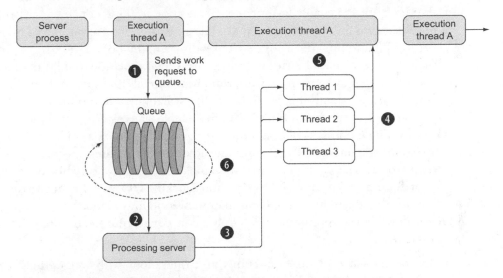

Figure 14.2   The work is passed to a queue, and the remote worker picks up the message and performs the requested action later in the future.

When the operation completes, it can send a notification to the origin (sender) of the request with details of the outcome. Figure 14.2 shows six steps:

1 The execution thread sends the job or request to the service, which queues it. The task is picked up and stored to be performed in the future.

2 At some point, the service grabs the task from the queue and dispatches the work to be processed. The processing server is responsible for scheduling a thread to run the operation.

3 The scheduled thread runs the operation, likely using a different thread per task.

4 Optimally, when the work is completed, the service notifies the origin (sender) that the work is completed.

5 While the request is processed in the background, the execution thread is free to perform other work.

6 If something goes wrong, the task is rescheduled (re-queued) for later execution.

Initially, online companies invested in more powerful hardware to accommodate the increased volume of requests. This approach proved to be a pricey option, considering the associated costs. In recent years, Twitter, Facebook, StackOverflow.com, and other companies have proven that it's possible to have a quick, responsive system with fewer machines through the use of good software design and patterns such as ACD.

14.3 *Choosing the right concurrent programming model*

Increasing the performance of a program using concurrency and parallelism has been at the center of discussion and research for many years. The result of this research has been the emergence of several concurrency programming models, each with its own strengths and weaknesses. The common theme is a shared ambition to perform and offer characteristics to enable faster code. In addition to these concurrency programming models, companies have developed tools to assist such programming: Microsoft created the TPL and Intel incorporated Threading Building Blocks (TBB) to produce high-quality and efficient libraries to help professional developers build parallel programs. There are many concurrency programming models that vary in their task interaction mechanisms, task granularities, flexibility, scalability, and modularity.

After years of experience in building high-scalable systems, I'm convinced that the right programing model is a combination of programming models tailored to each part of your system. You might consider using the actor model for message-passing systems, and PLINQ for data parallelism computation in each of your nodes, while downloading data for pre-computation analysis by using non-blocking I/O asynchronous processing. The key is finding the right tool or combination of tools for the job.

The following list represents my choice for concurrent technology based on common cases:

- In the presence of pure functions and operations with well-defined control dependencies, where the data can be partitioned or operate in a recursive style, consider using TPL to establish a dynamic task parallel computation in the form of either the Fork/Join or Divide and Conquer pattern.
- If a parallel computation requires preserving the order of the operations, or the algorithm depends on logical flow, then consider using a DAG with either the TPL task primitive or the agent model (see chapter 13).
- In the case of a sequential loop, where each iteration is independent and there are no dependencies among the steps, the TPL Parallel Loop can speed up performance by computing the data in simultaneous operations running in separate tasks.
- In the case of processing data in the form of a combination operator, for example by filtering and aggregating the input elements, Parallel LINQ (PLINQ) is likely a good solution to speed up computation. Consider a parallel reducer (also called a fold or aggregate), such as the parallel `Aggregator` function, for merging the results and using the Map-Reduce pattern.

- If the application is designed to perform a sequence of operations as a workflow, and if the order of execution for a set of tasks is relevant and must be respected, then use either the Pipeline or Producer/Consumer pattern; these are great solutions for parallelizing the operations effortlessly. You can easily implement these patterns using either the TPL Dataflow or F# `MailboxProcessor`.

Keep in mind when building deterministic parallel programs that you can build them from the bottom up by composing deterministic parallel patterns of computation and data access. It's recommended that parallel patterns should provide control over the granularity of their execution, expanding and contracting the parallelism based on the resources available.

In this section, you'll build an application that simulates an online stock market service (figure 14.3). This service periodically updates stock prices and pushes the updates to all connected clients in real time. This high-performance application can handle huge numbers of simultaneous connections inside a web server.

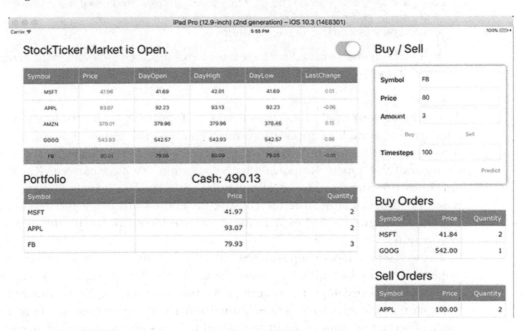

Figure 14.3 UI of the mobile (Apple iPad) stock market example. The panel on the left side provides stock price updates in real time. The panel on the right is used to manage the portfolio and set trade orders for buying and selling stocks.

The client is a mobile application, an iOS app for iPhone built using Xamarin and Xamarin.Forms. In the mobile client, the values change in real time in response to notifications from the server. Users of the application can manage their own portfolio by setting orders to buy and/or sell a specific stock when it reaches a predetermined price. In addition to the mobile application, a WPF version of the client program is provided in the downloadable source code.

NOTE   To run the mobile project, install Xamarin (www.xamarin.com). Reference the online documentation for further instructions.

Xamarin and Xamarin.Forms

Xamarin is a framework that developers can use to rapidly create cross-platform user interfaces. It provides an abstraction for the user interface that will be rendered using native controls on iOS, Android, Windows, or Windows Phone. This means that applications can share a large portion of their user interface code and still retain the native look and feel of the target platform.

Xamarin.Forms is a cross-platform, natively backed UI toolkit abstraction that developers can use to easily create user interfaces that can be shared across Android, iOS, Windows, and Windows Phone. The user interfaces are rendered using the native controls of the target platform, making it possible for Xamarin.Forms applications to retain the appropriate look and feel for each platform.

Both Xamarin and Xamarin.Forms are huge topics that aren't relevant in the context of this book. For more information, see www.xamarin.com/forms.

As you build your application, you'll take a closer look at how to apply functional concurrency to such an application. You'll combine this knowledge with concurrent functional techniques and patterns presented in previous chapters. You'll use the Command and Query Responsibility Segregation (CQRS) pattern, Rx, and asynchronous programming to handle parallel requests. You'll include event sourcing based on functional persistence (that is, an event store using the agent-programming model), and more. I explain these patterns later with the pertinent part of the application.

The web server application is an ASP.NET Web API that uses Rx to push the messages originated by the incoming requests from the controller to other components of the application. These components are implemented using agents (F# `MailboxProcessor`) that spawn a new agent for each established and active user connection. In this way, the application can be maintained in an isolated state per user, and provide an easy opportunity for scalability.

The mobile application is built in C#, which is, in general, a good choice for client-side development in combination with the TAP model and Rx. Instead of C#, for the web-server code you'll use F#; but you can find the C# version of the program in the source code of this book. The primary reason for choosing F# for the server-side code is immutability as a default construct, which fits perfectly in the stateless architecture used in the stock market example. Also, the built-in support for the agent programming model with the F# `MailboxProcessor` can encapsulate and maintain state effortlessly in a thread-safe manner. Furthermore, as you'll see shortly, F# represents a less-verbose solution compared to C# for implementing the CQRS pattern, making the code explicit and capturing what happens in a function without hidden side effects.

The application uses ASP.NET SignalR to provide server broadcast functionality for real-time updates. *Server broadcast* refers to a communication initiated by the server and then sent to clients.

14.3.1 Real-time communication with SignalR

Microsoft's SignalR library provides an abstraction over some of the transports that are required to push server-side content to the connected clients as it happens in real time. This means that servers and their clients can push data back and forth in real time, establishing a bidirectional communication channel. SignalR takes advantage of several transports, automatically selecting the best available transport given the client and server.

The connection starts as HTTP and is then promoted to a WebSocket connection if available. WebSocket is the ideal transport for SignalR since it makes the most efficient use of server memory, has the lowest latency, and has the greatest number of underlying features. If these requirements aren't met, SignalR falls back, attempting to use other transports to make its connections, such as Ajax long polling. SignalR will always try to use the most efficient transport and will keep falling back until it selects the best one that's compatible with the context. This decision is made automatically during an initial stage in the communication between the client and the server, known as *negotiation*.

14.4 Real-time trading: stock market high-level architecture

Before diving into the code implementation of the stock market application, let's review the high-level architecture of the application so you have a good handle on what you're developing. The architecture is based on the CQRS pattern, which enforces the separation between domain layers and the use of models for reading and writing.

> **NOTE** The code used to implement the server side of the application in this chapter is in F#, but you can find the full C# version in the online downloadable source code. The same principles explained in the following sections apply to both C# and F#.

The key tenet of CQRS is to separate *commands*, which are operations that cause state change (side effects in the system), from *query* requests that provide data for read-only activities without changing the state of any object, as shown in figure 14.4. The CQRS patterns are also based on the *separation of concerns*, which is important in all aspects of software development and for solutions built on message-based architectures.

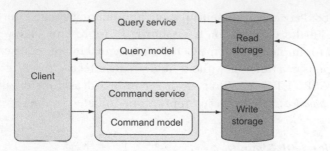

Figure 14.4   The CQRS pattern enforces the separation between domain layers and the use of models for reading and writing. To maximize the performance of the read operations, the application can benefit from a separate data storage optimized specifically for queries. Often, such storage might be a NoSQL database. The synchronization between the read/write storage instances is performed asynchronously in the background mode, and can take some time. Such data storages are considered to be eventually consistent.

The benefits of using the CQRS pattern include adding the ability to manage more business complexity while making your system easier to scale down, the ability to write optimized queries, and simplifying the introduction of the caching mechanism by wrapping the read portion of the API. Employing CQRS in the case of systems with a massive disparity between the workload of writes and reads allows you to drastically scale the read portion. Figure 14.5 shows the diagram of the stock market web-server application based on the CQRS pattern.

You can think about this functional architecture as a dataflow architecture. Inside the application, data flows through various stages. In each step, the data is filtered, enriched, transformed, buffered, broadcast, persisted, or processed any number of ways. The steps of the flow shown in figure 14.5 are as follows:

1 The user sends a request to the server. The request is shaped as a command to set a trading order to buy or sell a given stock. The ASP.NET Web API controller implements the IObservable interface to expose the Subscribe method, which registers observers that listen to the incoming request. This design transforms the controller in a message publisher, which sends the command to the subscribers. In this example, there's only one subscriber, an agent (MailboxProcessor) that acts as a message bus. But there could be any number of subscribers, for example for logging and performance metrics.

2 The incoming requests into the Web API actions are validated and transformed into a system command, which is wrapped into an envelope that enriches it with metadata such as a timestamp and a unique ID. This unique ID, which usually is represented by the SignalR connection ID, is used later to store the events aggregated by a unique identifier that's user-specific, which simplifies the targeting and execution of potential queries and replaying event histories.

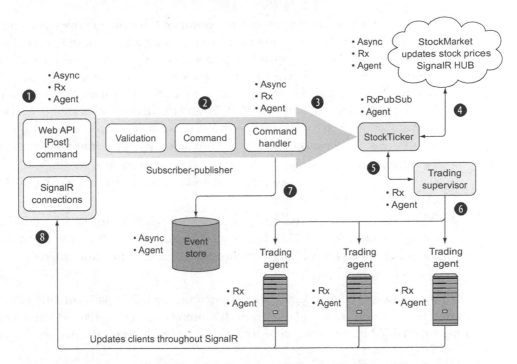

Figure 14.5 A representative model of the stock market web-server application, which is based on the CQRS pattern. The commands (`Writes`) are pushed across the application pipeline to perform the trading operations in a different channel than the queries (`Reads`). In this design, the queries (`Reads`) are performed automatically by the system in the form of server notifications, which are broadcast to the clients through SignalR connections. Imagine SignalR as the channel that allows the client to receive the notifications generated from the server. In the callouts it's specified as the technologies used to implement the specified component.

3   The command is passed into a command handler, which pushes the message to subscribers through a message bus. The subscriber of the command handler is the `StockTicker`, an object implemented using an agent to maintain the state, as the name implies, of the stock market tickers.

4   The `StockTicker` and `StockMarket` types have established a bidirectional communication, which is used to notify about stock price updates. In this case, Rx is used to randomly and constantly update the stock prices that are sent to the `StockMarket` and then flow to the `StockTicker`. The SignalR hub then broadcasts the updates to all the active client connections.

5   The `StockTicker` sends the notification to the `TradingCoordinator` object, which is an agent that maintains a list of active users. When a user registers with the application, the `TradingCoordinator` receives a notification and spawns a new agent if the user is new. The application server creates a new agent instance for each incoming request that represents a new client connection. The `TradingCoordinator` object implements the `IObservable` interface, which is used to establish a reactive publisher-subscriber with Rx to send the messages to the registered observers, the `TradingAgents`.

6   The `TradingCoordinator` receives the commands for trading operations, and dispatches them to the associated agent (user), verifying the unique client connection identifier. The `TradingAgent` type is an agent that implements the `IObserver` interface, which is registered to receive the notification from the `IObservable` `TradingCoordinator`. There's a `TradingAgent` for each user, and the main purpose is to maintain the state of a portfolio and the trading orders to buy and sell the stocks. This object is continuously receiving stock market updates to verify whether any of the orders in its state satisfy the criteria to trigger the trading operation.

7   The application implements event sourcing to store the trading events. The events are per group—by user and ordered by timestamp. Potentially, the history of each user can be replayed.

8   When a trade is triggered, the `TradingAgent` notifies the client's mobile application through SignalR. The application's objective is to have the client sending the trade orders and waiting asynchronously for a notification when each operation is completed.

The application diagram in figure 14.5 is based on the CQRS pattern, with a clear separation between the reads and the writes. It's interesting to note that real-time notifications are enabled for the query side (reads), so the user doesn't need to send a request to retrieve updates.

The envelope

In general, it's good practice to wrap messages in envelopes, because they can carry extra information about the message, which is convenient for implementing a message-passing system. Usually, the most important pieces of extra information are a unique ID and a timestamp when the message was created. The message IDs are important because they enable detection of replays and can make your system idempotent.

Going back to the CQRS pattern diagram from figure 14.4, which is repeated in figure 4.6, you can see that there are two separate storages: one for the read and one for the write. Designing storage separation in this way, using the CQRS pattern, is recommended to maximize performance of the read operations. In the case of two detached storages, the write side must update the read side. This synchronization is performed asynchronously in the background mode and can take time, so the read data storage is considered to be eventually consistent.

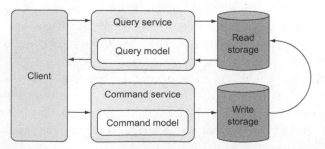

Figure 14.6   The CQRS pattern

Eventual consistency and the consistency, availability, and partition (CAP) theorem

The CAP theorem argues that persisting state in distributed systems is difficult to implement correctly. This theorem says that there are three distinct and desirable properties for distributed systems with an inherent correlation, but any real system can have at most two of these properties for any shared data:

- *Consistency* is a property that describes a consistent view of data on all nodes of the distributed system, where the system assures that write operations have an atomic characteristic and the updates are disseminated simultaneously to all nodes, yielding the same results.
- *Availability* is the demand property, where the system will eventually answer every request in reasonable time, even in the case of failures.
- *Partition* tolerance describes the fact that the system is resilient to message losses between nodes. A partition is an arbitrary split between nodes of a system, resulting in complete message loss between nodes.

Eventual consistency is a consistency model used in distributed computing to achieve high availability, guaranteeing that eventually all accesses to that item will return the last updated value. In the stock market application, however, the eventual consistency is automatically handled by the system. The users will receive the updates and latest values through real-time notifications when the data changes. This is possible due to the SignalR bidirectional communication between the server and the clients, which is a convenient mechanism because users don't have to ask for updates, the server will provide updates automatically.

14.5 *Essential elements for the stock market application*

You haven't yet learned several essential elements for the stock market application because it's assumed you've already encountered the topics. I'll briefly review these items and include where you can continue your study as needed.

The first essential element is F#. If you have a shallow background in F#, see appendix B for information and summaries that you might find useful.

The server-side application is based on the ASP.NET Web API, which requires knowledge of that technology. For the client side, the mobile application uses Xamarin and Xamarin.Forms with the *Model-View-ViewModel* (MVVM) pattern for data binding; but you don't need to have any particular knowledge of these frameworks.

The MVVM pattern

The MVVM pattern can be used on all XAML platforms. Its intent is to provide a clean separation of concerns between the UI controls and their logic. There are three core components in the MVVM pattern: the *Model* (business rule, data access, model classes), the *View* (UI Extensible Application Markup Language, or XAML), and the *ViewModel* (agent or middle man between View and Model). Each serves a distinct and separate role. The ViewModel acts as an interface between Model and View. It provides data binding between View and Model data as well as handling all UI actions by using commands. The View binds its control value to properties on a ViewModel, which, in turn, exposes data contained in Model objects.

Throughout the rest of this chapter, you're going to use the following:

- Reactive Extensions for .NET
- Task Parallel Library
- F# `MailboxProcessor`
- Asynchronous workflows

The same concepts applied in the following code examples are relevant for all the .NET programming languages.

14.6   *Let's code the stock market trading application*

This section covers the code examples to implement the real-time mobile stock market application with trading capabilities, as shown in figure 14.7. The parts of the program that aren't relevant or strictly important with the objective of the chapter are intentionally omitted. But you can find the full functional implementation in the downloadable source code.

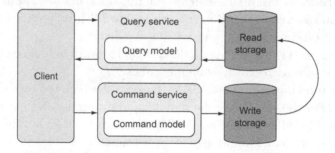

Figure 14.7   The architecture diagram of the stock market web-server application. This is a high-level diagram compared to figure 14.5, which aims to clarify the components of the application. Note that each component, other than `Validation` and `Command`, is implemented using a combination of Rx, the `IObservable` and `IObserver` interfaces, and the agent-programming model.

Let's start with the server Web API controller, where the client mobile application sends the requests to perform the trading operations.

NOTE The source code companion for the book has also a WPF implementation of the client-side application.

Note that the controller represents the write domain of the CQRS pattern; in fact, the actions are HTTP POST only, as shown here (the code to note is in bold).

Listing 14.1 Web API trading controller

```
[<RoutePrefix("api/trading")>]
type TradingController() =
    inherit ApiController()

    let subject = new Subject<CommandWrapper>()

    let publish connectionId cmd =
        match cmd with
        | Result.Ok(cmd) ->

            CommandWrapper.Create connectionId cmd
            subject.OnNext
        | Result.Error(e) -> subject.OnError(exn (e))
        cmd

    let toResponse (request : HttpRequestMessage) result =
        match result with
        | Ok(_) -> request.CreateResponse(HttpStatusCode.OK)
        | _ -> request.CreateResponse(HttpStatusCode.BadRequest)


    [<Route("sell"); HttpPost>]
    member this.PostSell([<FromBody>] tr : TradingRequest) = async {
        let connectionId = tr.ConnectionID

        return
            { Symbol = tr.Symbol.ToUpper()
              Quantity = tr.Quantity
              Price = tr.Price
              Trading = TradingType.Sell }
            |> tradingdValidation

            |> publish connectionId

            |> toResponse this.Request

    } |> Async.StartAsTask

    interface IObservable<CommandWrapper> with
        member this.Subscribe observer = subject.Subscribe observer

    override this.Dispose disposing =
        if disposing then subject.Dispose()
        base.Dispose disposing
```

The controller uses a Subject instance to behave as an observable to publish commands to the observer registered.

Validates the command using the Result type

Publishes the command using Rx

Creates a wrapper around a given command to enrich the type with metadata

Uses a helper function for the controller actions to deliver an HTTP response

Shows the current connection ID from SignalR context

Validates using a function composition

Publishes the command using Rx

Starts the actions as a Task to make the action run asynchronously

The controller uses a Subject instance to behave as an observable to publish commands to the registered observer.

Disposes the Subject; important to free up the resources

The Web API controller `TradingController` exposes the sell (`PostSell`) and the buy (`PostBuy`) actions. Both these actions have an identical code implementation with different purposes. Only one is presented in the listing, to avoid repetition.

Each action control is built around two core functions, validate and publish. `tradingdValidation` is responsible for validating messages per-connection because they're received from the client. `publish` is responsible for publishing the messages to the control subscribers for core processing.

The `PostSell` action validates the incoming request through the `tradingValidation` function, which returns either `Result.Ok` or `Result.Error` according to the validity of its input. Then, the output from the validation function is wrapped into a command object using the `CommandWrapper.Create` function and published to the subscribed observers `subject.OnNext`.

The `TradingController` uses an instance of the `Subject` type, from the Rx library, to act as an observable by implementing the `IObservable` interface. In this way, this controller is loosely coupled and behaves as a Publisher/Subscriber pattern, sending the commands to the observers that are registered. The registration of this controller as an `Observable` is plugged into the Web API framework using a class that implements the `IHttpControllerActivator`, as shown here (the code to note is in bold).

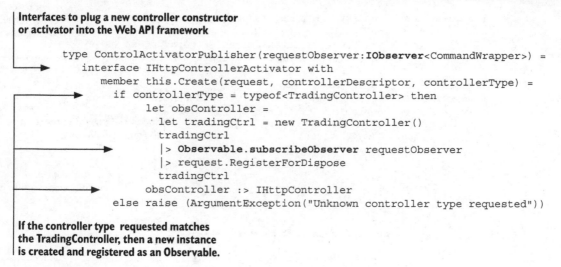

Listing 14.2   Registering a Web API controller as `Observable`

Interfaces to plug a new controller constructor
or activator into the Web API framework

```
type ControlActivatorPublisher(requestObserver:IObserver<CommandWrapper>) =
    interface IHttpControllerActivator with
        member this.Create(request, controllerDescriptor, controllerType) =
            if controllerType = typeof<TradingController> then
                let obsController =
                    let tradingCtrl = new TradingController()
                    tradingCtrl
                    |> Observable.subscribeObserver requestObserver
                    |> request.RegisterForDispose
                    tradingCtrl
                obsController :> IHttpController
            else raise (ArgumentException("Unknown controller type requested"))
```

If the controller type requested matches
the TradingController, then a new instance
is created and registered as an Observable.

The `ControlActivatorPublisher` type implements the interface `IHttpController-Activator`, which injects a custom controller activator into the Web API framework. In this case, when a request matches the type of the `TradingController`, the `ControlActivatorPublisher` transforms the controller in an `Observable` publisher, and then it registers the controller to the command dispatcher. The `tradingRequestObserver` observer, passed into the `CompositionRoot` constructor, is used as subscription for the `TradingController` controller, which can now dispatch messages from the actions to the subscribers in a reactive and decoupled manner.

Ultimately, the sub-value of the subscribed observer requestObserver represents the subscription and must be registered for disposal together with the TradingController instance tradingCtrl, using the request.RegisterForDispose method.

This listing shows the next step, the subscriber of the TradingController observable controller.

Listing 14.3 Configuring the SignalR hub and agent message bus

```
type Startup() =                                              Instance of an
    let agent = new Agent<CommandWrapper>(fun inbox ->        agent that acts as
        let rec loop () = async {                             message bus to
            let! (cmd:CommandWrapper) = inbox.Receive()       send commands
            do! cmd |> AsyncHandle
            return! loop() }
        loop())
    do agent.Start()
```

The agent asynchronously handles the
commands received, publishing them through
the AsyncHandle command handler.

```
                                                              Replaces the default
    member this.Configuration(builder : IAppBuilder) =        IHttpControllerActivator
        let config =                                          built in the Web API
            let config = new HttpConfiguration()              framework with the custom
            config.MapHttpAttributeRoutes()                   ControlActivatorPublisher

            config.Services.Replace(typeof<IHttpControllerActivator>,
                ControlActivatorPublisher(Observer.Create(fun x ->
                                                     agent.Post(x))))
```

The root subscriber passed into the
ControlActivatorPublisher constructor
is an observer that sends messages
asynchronously to the agent instance.

```
                                                              Enables the SignalR
                                                              hubs in the application
            let configSignalR =
                new HubConfiguration(EnableDetailedErrors = true)
```

```
    Owin.CorsExtensions.UseCors(builder, Cors.CorsOptions.AllowAll)
    builder.MapSignalR(configSignalR) |> ignore
    builder.UseWebApi(config) |> ignore
```

The Startup function is executed when the web application begins to apply the configuration settings. This is where the CompositionRoot class (defined in listing 14.2) belongs, to replace the default IHttpControllerActivator with its new instance. The subscriber type passed into the ControlActivatorPublisher constructor is an observer, which posts the messages that arrive from the TradingController actions to the MailboxProcessor agent instance. The TradingController publisher sends the messages through the OnNext method of the observer interface to all the subscribers, in this case the agent, which only depends on the IObserver implementation, and therefore reduces the dependencies.

The MailboxProcessor Post method, agent.Post, publishes the wrapped message into a Command type using Rx. Note that the controller itself implements the IObservable interface, so it can be imagined as a message endpoint, command wrapper, and publisher.

The subscriber `MailboxProcessor` agent asynchronously handles the incoming messages like a message bus, but at a smaller and more focused level (figure 14.8). A message bus provides a number of advantages, ranging from scalability to a naturally decoupled system to multiplatform interoperability. Message-based architectures that use a message bus focus on common message contracts and message passing. The rest of the configuration method enables the SignalR hubs in the application throughout the `IAppBuilder` provided.

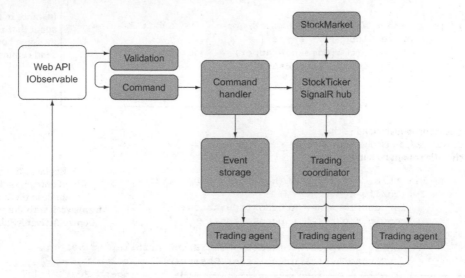

Figure 14.8   The command and command-handler are implemented in listing 14.4.

This listing shows the implementation of the `AsyncHandle` function, which handles the agent messages in the form of CQRS commands.

Listing 14.4   Command handler with async retry logic

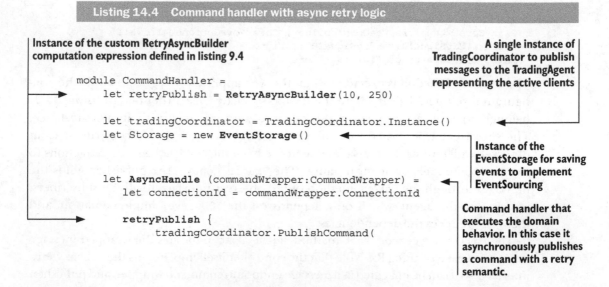

Instance of the custom RetryAsyncBuilder computation expression defined in listing 9.4

A single instance of TradingCoordinator to publish messages to the TradingAgent representing the active clients

```
module CommandHandler =
    let retryPublish = RetryAsyncBuilder(10, 250)

    let tradingCoordinator = TradingCoordinator.Instance()
    let Storage = new EventStorage()


    let AsyncHandle (commandWrapper:CommandWrapper) =
        let connectionId = commandWrapper.ConnectionId

        retryPublish {
            tradingCoordinator.PublishCommand(
```

Instance of the EventStorage for saving events to implement EventSourcing

Command handler that executes the domain behavior. In this case it asynchronously publishes a command with a retry semantic.

Publishes the command and the user-specified ID to the stock market. The ID is defined by the SignalR connection unique identifier.

```
                              PublishCommand(connectionId, commandWrapper))
```

```
let event =                          Uses a pattern match to transform
    let cmd = commandWrapper.Command      the command into an event type
    match cmd with
    | BuyStockCommand(connId,trading) ->
            StocksBuyedEvent(commandWrapper.Id, trading)
    | SellStockCommand(connId, trading) ->
            StocksSoldEvent(commandWrapper.Id, trading)

let eventDescriptor = Event.Create (commandWrapper.Id, event)
Storage.SaveEvent (Guid(connectionId)) eventDescriptor
}
```

Persists the event into the event storage

The `retryPublish` is an instance of the custom `RetryAsyncBuilder` computation expression defined in listing 9.4. This computation expression aims to run operations asynchronously, and it retries the computation, with an applied delay, in case something goes wrong. `AsyncHandle` is a command handler responsible for executing the Command behaviors on the domain. The commands are represented as trading operations to either buy or sell stocks. In general, commands are directives to perform an action to the domain (behaviors).

The purpose of `AsyncHandle` is to publish the commands received from the `TradingCoordinator` instance, the next step of the application pipeline, in a message-passing style. The command is the message received by the `MailboxProcessor` agent, defined during the application `Startup` (listing 14.3).

This message-driven programming model leads to an event-driven type of architecture, where the message-driven system recipients await the arrival of messages and react to them, otherwise lying dormant. In an event-driven system notification, the listeners are attached to the sources of events and are invoked when the event is emitted.

Event-driven architecture

Event-driven architecture (EDA) is an application design style that builds on the fundamental aspects of event notifications to facilitate immediate information dissemination and reactive business process execution. In an application based on EDA, information is propagated in real time throughout a highly distributed environment, enabling the different components of the application that receive a notification to proactively respond to business activities. EDA promotes low latency and a highly reactive system. The difference between event-driven and message-driven systems is that event-driven systems focus on addressable event sources, whereas a message-driven system concentrates on addressable recipients.

The `AsyncHandle` handler is also responsible for transforming each command received into an `Event` type, which is then persisted in the event storage (figure 14.9). The event storage is part of the event sourcing strategy implementation to store the current state of the application in listing 14.5.

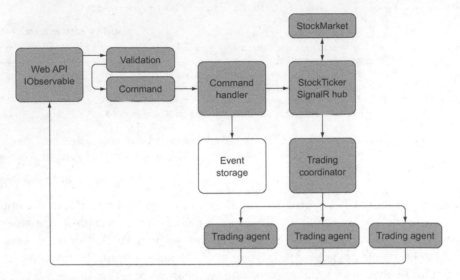

Figure 14.9   The event storage is implemented in listing 14.5.

Listing 14.5   `EventBus` implementation using an agent

```
module EventBus =
    let public EventPublisher = new Event<Event>()          ◄── Event broker for event-
                                                                based communication
                                                                based on the Publisher/
                                                                Subscriber pattern

    let public Subscribe (eventHandle: Events.Event -> unit) =
        EventPublisher.Publish |> Observable.subscribe(eventHandle)  ◄──

    let public Notify (event:Event) = EventPublisher.Trigger event   ◄──
```

Uses event storage message types to save events or get the history

```
module EventStorage =
    type EventStorageMessage =
    | SaveEvent of id:Guid * event:EventDescriptor
    | GetEventsHistory of Guid * AsyncReplyChannel<Event list option>

    type EventStorage() =        ◄── In-memory implementation of the event storage
                                     using a MailboxProcessor for thread safety

        let eventstorage = MailboxProcessor.Start(fun inbox ->
            let rec loop (history:Dictionary<Guid, EventDescription list>) =
              async {       ◄──              State of the MailboxProcessor
                                             to implement an in-memory
                let! msg = inbox.Receive()   event storage
                match msg with
                | SaveEvent(id, event) ->
```

Saves the event using the user connection SignalR unique ID as a key. if an entry with the same key already exists, the event is appended.

```
                        EventBus.Notify event.EventData
                        match history.TryGetValue(id) with
```

Event broker for event-based communication based on Publisher/Subscriber pattern

```
                  | true, events -> history.[id] <- (event :: events)
                  | false, _ -> history.Add(id, [event])
                | GetEventsHistory(id, reply) ->
                    match history.TryGetValue(id) with
                    | true, events ->
                        events |> List.map (fun i -> i.EventData) |> Some
                          |> reply.Reply
                    | false, _ -> reply.Reply(None)
                return! loop history    }
```

Retrieves the event history →

State of the MailboxProcessor to implement an in-memory event storage

```
            loop (Dictionary<Guid, EventDescriptor list>()))
```

Saves the event using the user connection SignalR unique ID as key; if an entry with the same key already exists, the event is appended

```
        member this.SaveEvent(id:Guid) (event:EventDescriptor) =
              eventstorage.Post(SaveEvent(id, event))
```

```
        member this.GetEventsHistory(id:Guid) =
            eventstorage.PostAndReply(fun rep -> GetEventsHistory(id,rep))
              |> Option.map(List.iter)
```

Retrieves the event history

Reorders the event history

The EventBus type is a simple implementation of a Publisher/Subscriber pattern over events. Internally, the Subscribe function uses Rx to register any given event, which is notified when the EventPublisher is triggered through the Notify function. The EventBus type is a convenient way to signal different parts of the application when a notification is emitted by a component upon reaching a given state.

Events are the result of an action that has already happened, which is likely the output of executing a command. The EventStorage type is an in-memory storage for supporting the concept of event sourcing, which is basically the idea of persisting a sequence of state-changing events of the application, rather than storing the current state of an entity. In this way, the application is capable of reconstructing, at any given time, an entity's current state by replaying the events. Because saving an event is a single operation, it's inherently atomic.

The EventStorage implementation is based on the F# agent MailboxProcessor, which guarantees thread safety for accessing the underlying event data-structure history Dictionary<Guid, EventDescriptor list>. The EventStorageMessage DU defines two operations to run against the event storage:

- SaveEvent adds an EventDescriptor to the internal state of the event storage agent by the given unique ID. If the ID exists, then the event is appended.
- GetEventsHistory retrieves the event history in ordered sequence by time within the given unique ID. In general, the event history is replayed using a given function action, as in listing 14.5.

The implementation uses an agent because it's a convenient way to abstract away the basics of an event store. With that in place, you can easily create different types of event stores by changing only the two `SaveEvent` and `GetEventsHistory` functions.

Let's look at the `StockMarket` object shown in figure 14.10. Listing 14.6 shows the core implementation of the application, the `StockMarket` object.

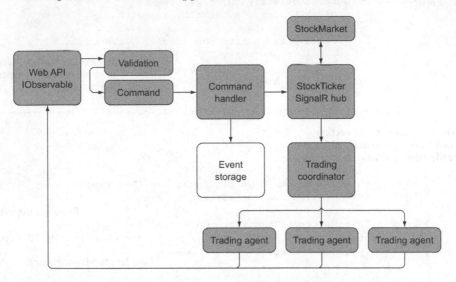

Figure 14.10   The `StockMarket` **object is implemented in listing 14.6.**

Listing 14.6   `StockMarket` type to coordinate the user connections

```
type StockMarket (initStocks : Stock array) =            This instance simulates the stock
    let subject = new Subject<Trading>()                 market, updating the stocks.

Instance of the Rx Subject that implements a
Publisher/Subscriber pattern

        static let instanceStockMarket =
            Lazy.Create(fun () -> StockMarket(Stock.InitialStocks()))

        let stockMarketAgent =                           Uses two states of the agent to change the
                                                         Market between the Open or Close state

        Agent<StockTickerMessage>.Start(fun inbox ->
            let rec marketIsOpen (stocks : Stock array)
                (stockTicker : IDisposable) = async {

State of the
MailboxProcessor to keep        let! msg = inbox.Receive()      Uses pattern matching to dispatch
the updated stock values        match msg with                  the messages to the relative behavior
                                | GetMarketState(c, reply) ->
                                    reply.Reply(MarketState.Open)
                                    return! marketIsOpen stocks stockTicker
                                | GetAllStocks(c, reply) ->
                                    reply.Reply(stocks |> Seq.toList)
```

Updates the stock values, sending notifications to the subscribers

Uses parallel iteration using PSeq to dispatch stock updates as fast as possible

```
                    return! marketIsOpen stocks stockTicker
        | UpdateStockPrices ->
            stocks
            |> PSeq.iter(fun stock ->
                let isStockChanged = updateStocks stock stocks
                isStockChanged
                |> Option.iter(fun _ ->
                    subject.OnNext(Trading.UpdateStock(stock))))
            return! marketIsOpen stocks stockTicker
        | CloseMarket(c) ->
            stockTicker.Dispose()
            return! marketIsClosed stocks
        | _ -> return! marketIsOpen stocks stockTicker }
    and marketIsClosed (stocks : Stock array) = async {
        let! msg = inbox.Receive()
        match msg with
        | GetMarketState(c, reply) ->
            reply.Reply(MarketState.Closed)
            return! marketIsClosed stocks
        | GetAllStocks(c,reply) ->
            reply.Reply((stocks |> Seq.toList))
            return! marketIsClosed stocks
        | OpenMarket(c) ->
            return! marketIsOpen stocks (startStockTicker inbox)
        | _ -> return! marketIsClosed stocks }
    marketIsClosed (initStocks))

member this.GetAllStocks(connId) =
    stockMarketAgent.PostAndReply(fun ch -> GetAllStocks(connId, ch))

member this.GetMarketState(connId) =
    stockMarketAgent.PostAndReply(fun ch -> GetMarketState(connId, ch))

member this.OpenMarket(connId) =
    stockMarketAgent.Post(OpenMarket(connId))

member this.CloseMarket(connId) =
    stockMarketAgent.Post(CloseMarket(connId))

member this.AsObservable() = subject.AsObservable().
  SubscribeOn(TaskPoolScheduler.Default)

static member Instance() = instanceStockMarket.Value
```

Uses two states of the agent to change the market between the open and closed states

Uses pattern matching to dispatch the messages to the relative behavior

Exposes the StockMarket type as an observable to subscribe the underlying changes

The StockMarket type is responsible for simulating the stock market in the application. It uses operations such as OpenMarket and CloseMarket to either start or stop broadcasting notifications of stock updates, and GetAllStocks retrieves stock tickers to monitor and manage for users. The StockMarket type implementation is based on the agent model using the MailboxProcessor to take advantage of the intrinsic thread safety and convenient concurrent asynchronous message-passing semantic that's at the core of building highly performant and reactive (event-driven) systems.

The StockTicker price updates are simulated by sending high-rate random requests to the stockMarketAgent MailboxProcessor using UpdateStockPrices, which then notifies all active client subscribers.

The AsObservable member exposes the StockMarket type as a stream of events throughout the IObservable interface. In this way, the type StockMarket can notify the IObserver subscribed to the IObservable interface of the stock updates, which are generated when the message UpdateStock is received.

The function that updates the stock uses a Rx timer to push random values for each of the stock tickers registered, increasing or decreasing the prices with a small percentage, as shown here.

Listing 14.7   Function to update the stock ticker prices every given interval

```
let startStockTicker (stockAgent : Agent<StockTickerMessage>) =
    Observable.Interval(TimeSpan.FromMilliseconds 50.0)
    |> Observable.subscribe(fun _ -> stockAgent.Post UpdateStockPrices)
```

startStockTicker is a fake service provider that tells StockTicker every 50 ms that it's time to update the prices.

> **NOTE** Sending messages to an F# MailboxProcessor agent (or TPL Dataflow block) is unlikely to be a bottleneck in your system, because the MailboxProcessor can handle 30 million messages per second on a machine with a 3.3 GHz core.

The TradingCoordinator (figure 14.11) type's purpose is to manage the underlying SignalR active connections and TradingAgent subscribers, which act as observers, through the MailboxProcessor coordinatorAgent. Listing 14.8 shows the implementation.

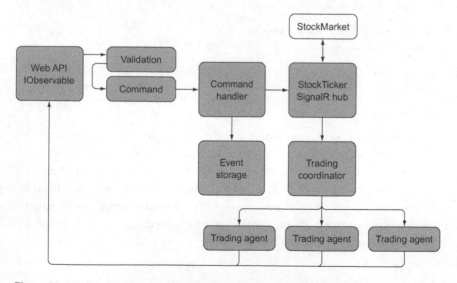

Figure 14.11   The trading coordinator is implemented in listing 14.8.

Listing 14.8 `TradingCoordinator` **agent to handle active trading children agent**

Uses a discriminated union to define the
message type for the TradingCoordinator

```
type CoordinatorMessage =
    | Subscribe of  id : string * initialAmount : float *
       caller:IHubCallerConnectionContext<IStockTickerHubClient>
    | Unsubscribe of   id : string
    | PublishCommand of connId : string * CommandWrapper
```

```
type TradingCoordinator() =
```

Uses an agent-based type, which is the core for the
subscription of the sub-registered observer agents
and for the coordination of their execution operation

Reactive Publisher/Subscriber
defined in listing 6.6

```
    //Listing 6.6 Reactive Publisher Subscriber in C#
    let subject = new RxPubSub<Trading>()
    static let tradingCoordinator =
              Lazy.Create(fun () -> new TradingCoordinator())
```

Uses a singleton instance of
the type TradingCoordinator

```
    let coordinatorAgent =
        Agent<CoordinatorMessage>.Start(fun inbox ->
            let rec loop (agents : Map<string,
  (IObserver<Trading> * IDisposable)>) = async {
                let! msg = inbox.Receive()
                match msg with
                | Subscribe(id, amount, caller) ->
                    let observer = TradingAgent(id, amount, caller)
                    let dispObsrever = subject.Subscribe(observer)
                    observer.Agent
                    |> reportErrorsTo id supervisor |> startAgent
                    caller.Client(id).SetInitialAsset(amount)
                    return! loop (Map.add id (observer :>
          IObserver<Trading>, dispObsrever) agents)
                | Unsubscribe(id) ->
                    match Map.tryFind id agents with
                    | Some(_, disposable) ->
                        disposable.Dispose()
                        return! loop (Map.remove id agents)
                    | None -> return! loop agents
                | PublishCommand(id, command) ->
                    match command.Command with
                    | TradingCommand.BuyStockCommand(id, trading) ->
                        match Map.tryFind id agents with
                        | Some(a, _) ->
                          let tradingInfo = { Quantity=trading.Quantity;
                                              Price=trading.Price;
                                              TradingType = TradingType.Buy}
                            a.OnNext(Trading.Buy(trading.Symbol, tradingInfo))
                            return! loop agents
                        | None -> return! loop agents
                    | TradingCommand.SellStockCommand(id, trading) ->
                        match Map.tryFind id agents with
                        | Some(a, _) ->
```

Subscribes a new
TradingAgent that
will be notified
when a stock price
is updated

Uses an instance of
the TradingAgent that
acts as an observer to
receive notifications
in a reactive style

Applies supervision logic to the
newly created TradingAgents
defined in chapter 11

Notifies the
client of its
successful
registration
using SignalR

Unsubscribes an existing
TradingAgent from a
given unique ID and
closes the channel to
receive notifications.
The unsubscription is
performed by disposing
the observer.

Publishes the
commands using
reactive Publisher/
Subscriber to set
the orders to Buy
or Sell a stock

```
                      let tradingInfo = { Quantity=trading.Quantity;
                                          Price=trading.Price;
                                          TradingType = TradingType.Sell}
                      a.OnNext(Trading.Sell(trading.Symbol, tradingInfo))
                      return! loop agents
                    | None -> return! loop agents }
              loop (Map.empty))
```

> **Subscribes a new TradingAgent that will be notified when a stock price is updated**

```
    member this.Subscribe(id : string, initialAmount : float,
➥      caller:IHubCallerConnectionContext<IStockTickerHubClient>) =
        coordinatorAgent.Post(Subscribe(id, initialAmount, caller))
```

```
    member this.Unsubscribe(id : string) =
                    coordinatorAgent.Post(Unsubscribe(id))
```

```
    member this.PublishCommand(command) =
                    coordinatorAgent.Post(command)
```

> **The TradingCoordinator is exposed as an observable through an instance of the Reactive Publisher/Subscriber RxPubSub type.**

```
    member this.AddPublisher(observable : IObservable<Trading>) =
                    subject.AddPublisher(observable)
```

> **Uses a member that is allowed to add publishers to trigger the notification for the RxPubSub**

> **Uses a singleton instance of the type TradingCoordinator**

```
    static member Instance() = tradingCoordinator.Value
```

```
    interface IDisposable with
        member x.Dispose() =  subject.Dispose()
```

> **Disposes the underlying RxPubSub subject type (important)**

The CoordinatorMessage discriminated union defines the messages for the coordinatorAgent. These message types are used for coordinating the operations for the underlying TradingAgents subscribed for update notifications.

You can think of the coordinatorAgent as an agent that's responsible for maintaining the active clients. It either subscribes or unsubscribes them according to whether they're connecting to the application or disconnecting from it, and then it dispatches operational commands to the active ones. In this case, the SignalR hub notifies the TradingCoordinator when a new connection is established or an existing one is dropped so it can register or unregister the client accordingly.

The application uses the agent model to generate a new agent for each incoming request. For parallelizing request operations, the TradingCoordinator agent spawns new agents and assigns work via messages. This enables parallel I/O-bound operations as well as parallel computations. The TradingCoordinator exposes the IObservable interface through an instance of the RxPubSub type, which is defined in listing 6.6. RxPubSub is used here to implement a high-performant reactive Publisher/Subscriber, where the TradingAgent observers can register to receive potential notifications when a stock ticker price is updated. In other words, the TradingCoordinator is an Observable that the TradingAgent observer can subscribe to, implementing a reactive Publisher/Subscriber pattern to receive notifications.

The method member `AddPublisher` registers any type that implements the `IObservable` interface, which is responsible for updating all the `TradingAgents` subscribed. In this implementation, the `IObservable` type registered as `Publisher` in the `TradingCoordinator` is the `StockMarket` type.

The `StockMarket` member methods `Subscribe` and `Unsubscribe` are used to register or unregister client connections received from the `StockTicker` SignalR hub. The requests to subscribe or unsubscribe are passed directly to the underlying `coordinatorAgent` observable type.

The subscription operation triggered by the `Subscribe` message checks if a `TradingAgent` (figure 14.12) type exists in the local observer state, verifying the connection unique ID. If the `TradingAgent` doesn't exist, then a new instance is created, and it's subscribed to the subject instance by implementing the `IObserver` interface. Then, the supervision strategy `reportErrorsTo` (to report and handle errors) is applied to the newly created `TradingAgent` observer. This supervision strategy was discussed in section 11.5.5.

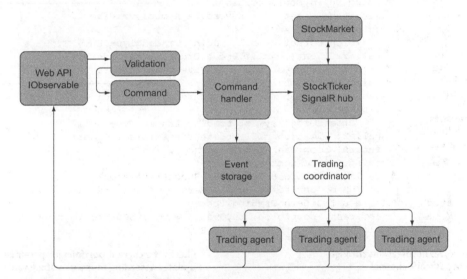

Figure 14.12 The `TradingAgent` represents an agent-based portfolio for each user connected to the system. This agent keeps the user portfolio up to date and coordinates the operations of buying and selling a stock. The `TradingAgent` is implemented in listing 14.9.

Note that the `TradingAgent` construct takes a reference to the underlying SignalR channel, which is used to enable direct communication to the client, in this case a mobile device for real-time notifications. The trading operations `Buy` and `Sell` are dispatched to the related `TradingAgent`, which is identified using the unique ID from the local observer's state. The dispatch operation is performed using the `OnNext` semantic of the `Observer` type. As mentioned, the `TradingCoordinator`'s responsibility is to coordinate the operations of the `TradingAgent`, whose implementation is shown in listing 14.9.

Listing 14.9   `TradingAgent` that represents an active user

The constructor accepts a reference of the SignalR connection to enable real-time notifications.

```
type TradingAgent(connId : string, initialAmount : float, caller :
    IHubCallerConnectionContext<IStockTickerHubClient>) =
      let agent = new Agent<Trading>(fun inbox ->
         let rec loop cash (portfolio : Portfolio)
            (buyOrders : Treads) (sellOrders : Treads) = async {
           let! msg = inbox.Receive()
           match msg with
```

The TradingAgent maintains local in-memory state of the client portfolio and the trading orders in process.

Uses a special message to implement the observer method to complete (terminate) the notifications and handle errors

```
           | Kill(reply) -> reply.Reply()
           | Error(exn) -> raise exn
           | Trading.Buy(symbol, trading) ->
              let items = setOrder buyOrders symbol trading
              let buyOrders =
                 createOrder symbol trading TradingType.Buy
              caller.Client(connId).UpdateOrderBuy(buyOrders)
              return! loop cash portfolio items sellOrders
           | Trading.Sell(symbol, trading) ->
              let items = setOrder sellOrders symbol trading
              let sellOrder =
                 createOrder symbol trading TradingType.Sell
              caller.Client(connId).UpdateOrderSell(sellOrder)
              return! loop cash portfolio buyOrders items
           | Trading.UpdateStock(stock) ->
              caller.Client(connId).UpdateStockPrice stock
              let cash, portfolio, sellOrders = updatePortfolio cash
    stock portfolio sellOrders TradingType.Sell
              let cash, portfolio, buyOrders = updatePortfolio cash
    stock portfolio buyOrders TradingType.Buy
```

Shows the trade order messages

Updates the value of the stock, which notifies the client and updates the portfolio if the new value satisfies any of the trading orders in progress

The client receives notifications through the underlying SignalR channel.

Checks the current portfolio for potential updates according to the new stock value

```
              let asset = getUpdatedAsset portfolio sellOrders
    buyOrders cash
              caller.Client(connId).UpdateAsset(asset)
              return! loop cash portfolio buyOrders sellOrders  }
         loop initialAmount (Portfolio(HashIdentity.Structural))
         (Treads(HashIdentity.Structural)) (Treads(HashIdentity.Structural)))

      member this.Agent = agent

      interface IObserver<Trading> with
         member this.OnNext(msg) = agent.Post(msg:Trading)
         member this.OnError(exn) = agent.Post(Error exn)
         member this.OnCompleted() = agent.PostAndReply(Kill)
```

The TradingAgent implements the IObserver interface to act as subscribers for the observable TradingCoordinator type

Uses a special message to implement the observer method to complete (terminate) the notifications and handle errors

The TradingAgent type is an agent-based object that implements the IObserver inter-face to allow sending messages to the underlying agent using a reactive semantic. Fur-thermore, because the TradingAgent type is an Observer, it can be subscribed to the TradingCoordinator, and consequently receives notifications automatically in the form of message passing. This is a convenient design to decouple parts of the applica-tion that can communicate by flowing messages in a reactive and independent man-ner. The TradingAgent represents a single active client, which means that there's an instance of this agent for each user connected. As mentioned in chapter 11, having thousands of running agents (MailboxProcessors) doesn't penalize the system.

The local state of the TradingAgent maintains and manages the current client portfolio, including the trading orders for buying and selling stocks. When either a TradingMessage.Buy or TradingMessage.Sell message is received, the TradingAgent validates the trade request, adds the operation to the local state, and then sends a notifi-cation to the client, which updates the local state of the transaction and the related UI.

The TradingMessage.UpdateStock message is the most critical. The TradingAgent could potentially receive a high volume of messages, whose purpose it is to update the Portfolios with a new stock price. More importantly, because the price of a stock could be changed in the update, the functionality triggered with the UpdateStock message checks if any of the existing (in-progress) trading operations, buyOrders and sellOrders, are satisfied with the new value. If any of the trades in progress are performed, the portfolio is updated accordingly, and the client receives a notification for each update.

As mentioned, the TradingAgent entity keeps the channel reference of the connec-tion to the client for communicating eventual updates, which is established during the OnConnected event in the SignalR hub (figure 14.13 and listing 14.10).

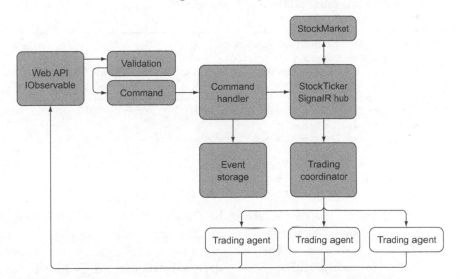

Figure 14.13   The StockTicker SignalR hub is implemented in listing 14.10.

Listing 14.10   StockTicker SignalR hub

Uses the SignalR attribute to define the hub name
that is referenced from the client to be accessed

The StockTickerHub implements the strongly
typed Hub< IStockTickerHubClient> class to
enable SignalR communications.

```
[<HubName("stockTicker")>]
type StockTickerHub() as this =
    inherit Hub<IStockTickerHubClient>()
```

Uses a single instance of the StockMarket and
TradingCoordinator types, which is agent-based and can
be used as a singleton instance in a thread-safe manner

```
let stockMarket : StockMarket = StockMarket.Instance()
let tradingCoordinator : TradingCoordinator = TradingCoordinator.
 Instance()
```

For each
connection
event raised, an
agent is either
subscribed or
unsubscribed
accordingly.

Uses SignalR base events to manage
new and dropped connections

```
override x.OnConnected() =
    let connId = x.Context.ConnectionId
    stockMarket.Subscribe(connId, 1000., this.Clients)
    base.OnConnected()

override x.OnDisconnected(stopCalled) =
    let connId = x.Context.ConnectionId
    stockMarket.Unsubscribe(connId)
    base.OnDisconnected(stopCalled)
```

Methods that manage
the stock market events

```
member x.GetAllStocks() =
    let connId = x.Context.ConnectionId
    let stocks = stockMarket.GetAllStocks(connId)
    for stock in stocks do
        this.Clients.Caller.SetStock stock

member x.OpenMarket() =
    let connId = x.Context.ConnectionId
    stockMarket.OpenMarket(connId)
    this.Clients.All.SetMarketState(MarketState.Open.ToString())

member x.CloseMarket() =
    let connId = x.Context.ConnectionId
    stockMarket.CloseMarket(connId)
    this.Clients.All.SetMarketState(MarketState.Closed.ToString())

member x.GetMarketState() =
    let connId = x.Context.ConnectionId
    stockMarket.GetMarketState(connId).ToString()
```

The StockTickerHub class derives from the SignalR Hub class, which is designed to handle the connections, bidirectional interaction, and calls from clients. A SignalR Hub class instance is created for each operation on the hub, such as connections and calls from the client to the server. If you instead put state in the SignalR Hub class, then you'd lose it because the hub instances are transient. This is the reason you're using the TradingAgents to manage the mechanism that keeps stock data, updates prices, and broadcasts price updates.

The Singleton pattern is a common option to keep alive an instance object inside a SignalR hub. In this case, you're creating a singleton instance of the StockMarket type; and because its implementation is agent-based, there are no thread-race issues and performance penalties, as explained in section 3.1.

The SignalR base methods OnConnected and OnDisconnected are raised each time a new connection is established or dropped, and a TradingAgent instance is either created and registered or unregistered and destroyed accordingly.

The other methods handle the stock market operations, such as opening and closing the market. For each of those operations, the underlying SignalR channel notifies the active clients immediately, as shown in the following listing.

Listing 14.11   Client StockTicker interface to receive notifications using SignalR

```
interface IStockTickerHub
{
    Task Init(string serverUrl, IStockTickerHubClient client);
    string ConnectionId { get; }
    Task GetAllStocks();
    Task<string> GetMarketState();
    Task OpenMarket();
    Task CloseMarket();
}
```

The IStockTickerHub interface is used in the client side to define the methods in the SignalR Hub class that clients can call. To expose a method on the hub that you want to be callable from the client, declare a public method. Note that the methods defined in the interface can be long running, so they return a Task (or Task<T>) type designed to run asynchronously to avoid blocking the connection when the WebSocket transport is used. When a method returns a Task object, SignalR waits for the task to complete, and then it sends the unwrapped result back to the client.

You're using a Portable Class Library (PCL) to share the same functionality among different platforms. The purpose of the IStockTickerHub interface is to establish an ad hoc platform-specific contract for the SignalR hub implementation. In this way, each platform has to satisfy a precise definition of this interface, injected at runtime using the DependencyService class provider (http://mng.bz/vFc3):

```
IStockTickerHub stockTickerHub = DependencyService.Get<IStockTickerHub>();
```

After having defined the IStockTickerHub contract to establish the way that the client and server communicate, listing 14.12 shows the implementation of the mobile application, in particular of the ViewModel class, which represents the core functionality. Several of the properties have been removed from the original source code, because repetitive logic could distract from the main objective of the example.

Listing 14.12   Client-side mobile application using Xamarine.Forms

```
public class MainPageViewModel : ModelObject, IStockTickerHubClient
{
    public MainPageViewModel(Page page)          Uses observable collections to notify the
    {                                            auto-updates for the ViewModel properties

        Stocks = new ObservableCollection<StockModelObject>();
        Portfolio = new ObservableCollection<Models.OrderRecord>();
        BuyOrders = new ObservableCollection<Models.OrderRecord>();
        SellOrders = new ObservableCollection<Models.OrderRecord>();

        SendBuyRequestCommand =
                new Command(async () => await SendBuyRequest());
        SendSellRequestCommand =
                new Command(async () => await SendSellRequest());
```

Uses asynchronous commands to send
the trading orders to buy or sell

Initializes the stockTickerHub to establish a connection
to the server. During the initialization and client-server
connection, the UI is updated accordingly.

```
        stockTickerHub = DependencyService.Get<IStockTickerHub>();
        hostPage = page;

        var hostBase = "http://localhost:8735/";
        stockTickerHub
            .Init(hostBase, this)
            .ContinueWith(async x =>
            {
                var state = await stockTickerHub.GetMarketState();
                isMarketOpen = state == "Open";
                OnPropertyChanged(nameof(IsMarketOpen));
                OnPropertyChanged(nameof(MarketStatusMessage));

                await stockTickerHub.GetAllStocks();
            }, TaskScheduler.FromCurrentSynchronizationContext());
```

The stockTickerHub
initialization is
performed in the
UI synchronization
context to freely
update the UI
controls.

```
        client = new HttpClient();                  Initializes the HttpClient
        client.BaseAddress = new Uri(hostBase);      used to send requests
        client.DefaultRequestHeaders.Accept.Clear();  to the Web Server API
        client.DefaultRequestHeaders.Accept.Add(
            new MediaTypeWithQualityHeaderValue("application/json"));
    }
    private IStockTickerHub stockTickerHub;
    private HttpClient client;
    private Page hostPage;

    public Command SendBuyRequestCommand { get; }
    public Command SendSellRequestCommand { get; }

    private double price;                    Property in the ViewModel used for data
    public double Price                      binding with the UI. Only one property
    {                                        is shown for demonstration purposes; other
        get => price; set                    properties follow the same structure.
        {
            if (price == value)
```

```
                    return;
            price = value;
            OnPropertyChanged();                          Uses a function to send
        }                                                 requests to the Web Server API
    }
    private async Task SendTradingRequest(string url)  ◄──────────────┐
    {                                                                  │
        if (await Validate()) {                                        │
        var request = new                                             │
➟ TradingRequest(stockTickerHub.ConnectionId, Symbol, Price, Amount); │
        var response = await client.PostAsJsonAsync(url, request);    │
        response.EnsureSuccessStatusCode();                           │
        }                                                             │
    }                                                                 │
    private async Task SendBuyRequest() =>                            │
            await SendTradingRequest("/api/trading/buy");  ◄──────────┤
    private async Task SendSellRequest() =>                           │
            await SendTradingRequest("/api/trading/sell");  ◄─────────┘

    public ObservableCollection<Models.OrderRecord> Portfolio { get; }
    public ObservableCollection<Models.OrderRecord> BuyOrders { get; }
    public ObservableCollection<Models.OrderRecord> SellOrders { get; }
    public ObservableCollection<StockModelObject> Stocks { get; }
```

Uses observable collections to notify the auto-updates for the ViewModel properties

Uses functions triggered by the SignalR channel when sending notifications from the web server application to the client. These functions update the UI.

```
    public void UpdateOrderBuy(Models.OrderRecord value) =>
                                        BuyOrders.Add(value);   ◄─────┐
    public void UpdateOrderSell(Models.OrderRecord value) =>          │
                                        SellOrders.Add(value);  ◄─────┘
}
```

The class `MainPageViewModel` is the `ViewModel` component of the mobile client application, which is based on the MVVM pattern (http://mng.bz/qfbR) to enable communication and data binding between the UI (View) and the ViewModel. In this way, the UI and the presentation logic have separate responsibilities, providing a clear separation of concerns in the application.

Note that the class `MainPageViewModel` implements the interface `IStockTickerHubClient`, which permits the notifications from the SignalR channel after the connection is established. The interface `IStockTickerHubClient` is defined in the StockTicker.Core project, and it represents the contract for the client that the server relies on. This code snippet shows the implementation of this interface:

```
type IStockTickerHubClient =
    abstract SetMarketState : string -> unit
    abstract UpdateStockPrice : Stock -> unit
    abstract SetStock : Stock -> unit
    abstract UpdateOrderBuy : OrderRecord -> unit
    abstract UpdateOrderSell : OrderRecord -> unit
    abstract UpdateAsset : Asset -> unit
    abstract SetInitialAsset : float -> unit
```

These notifications will flow in the application automatically from the server side into the mobile application, updating the UI control in real time. In listing 14.12, the observable collections defined at the top of the class are used to communicate in a bidirectional manner with the UI. When one of these collections is updated, the changes are propagated to the bind UI controllers to reflect the state (http://mng.bz/nvma).

The `Command` of the ViewModel is used to define a user operation, which is data bound to a button, to send the request asynchronously to the web server to perform a trade for the stock defined in the UI.[1] The request is executed, launching the `SendTradingRequest` method that's used to buy or sell a stock according to the API endpoint targeted.

The SignalR connection is established through the initialization of the `stockTickerHub` interface, and an instance is created by calling the `DependencyService.Get<IStockTickerHub>` method. After the creation of the `stockTickerHub` instance, the application initialization is performed by calling the `Init` method, which calls the remote server for locally loading the stocks with the method `stockTickerHub.GetAllStocks` and the current state of the market with the method `stockTickerHub.GetMarketState` to update the UI.

The application initialization is performed asynchronously using the `FromCurrentSynchronizationContext TaskScheduler`, which provides functionality for propagating updates to the UI controllers from the main UI thread without the need to apply any thread-marshal operation.

Ultimately, the application receives the notifications from the SignalR channel, which is connected to the stock market server, through the invocation of the methods defined in the `IStockTickerHubClient` interface. These methods are `UpdateOrderBuy`, `UpdatePortofolio`, and `UpdateOrderSell`, which are responsible updating the UI controllers by changing the relative observable collections.

14.6.1 *Benchmark to measure the scalability of the stock ticker application*

The stock ticker application was deployed on Microsoft Azure Cloud with a medium configuration (two cores and 3.5 GB of RAM), and stress-tested using an online tool to simulate 5,000 concurrent connections, each generating hundreds of HTTP requests. This test aimed to verify the web server performance under excessive loads to ensure that critical information and services are available at speeds that end users expect. The result was green, validating that web server application can sustain many concurrent active users and cope with excessive loads of HTTP requests.

---

[1] "Stephen Cleary, Async Programming: Patterns for Asynchronous MVVM Applications: Data Binding," https://msdn.microsoft.com/magazine/dn605875.

Summary

- Conventional web applications can be thought of as embarrassingly parallel because requests are entirely isolated and easy to execute independently. The more powerful the server running the application, the more requests it can handle.
- You can effortlessly parallelize and distribute a stateless program among computers and processes to scale out performance. There's no need to maintain any state where the computation runs, because no part of the program will modify any data structures, avoiding data races.
- Asynchronicity, caching, and distribution (ACD) are the secret ingredients when designing and implementing a system capable of flexing to an increase (or decrease) of requests with a commensurate parallel speedup with the addition of resources.
- You can use Rx to decouple an ASP.NET Web API and push the messages originated by the incoming requests from the controller to other components of the subscriber application. These components could be implemented using the agent programming model, which spawns a new agent for each established and active user connection. In this way, the application can be maintained in an isolated state per user, and provide an easy opportunity for scalability.
- The support provided for concurrent FP in .NET is key to making it a great tool for server-side programming. Support exists for running operations asynchronously in a declarative and compositional semantic style; additionally, agents can be used to develop thread-safe components. These core technologies can be combined for declarative processing of events and for efficient parallelism with TPL.
- Event-driven architecture (EDA) is an application design style that builds on the fundamental aspects of event notifications to facilitate immediate information dissemination and reactive business process execution. In an EDA, information is propagated in real time throughout a highly distributed environment, enabling the different components of the application that receive a notification to proactively respond to business activities. EDA promotes low latency and a highly reactive system. The difference between event-driven and message-driven systems is that event-driven systems focus on addressable event sources; message-driven systems concentrate on addressable recipients.

appendix a
Functional programming

It's anecdotal to say that learning FP makes you a better programmer. It's true that FP provides an alternative, often simpler, way of thinking about problems. Moreover, many techniques from FP can be successfully applied to other languages. No matter what language you work in, programming in a functional style provides benefits.

FP is more a mindset than a particular set of tools or languages. Getting familiar with different programming paradigms is what makes you a better programmer, and a multiparadigm programmer is more powerful than a polyglot programmer. Therefore . . .

With the technical background having been sorted out in the chapters of this book, this appendix doesn't cover the aspects of FP applied to concurrency, such as immutability, referential transparency, side-effect-free functions, and lazy evaluations. Rather, it covers general information about what FP means and the reasons why you should care about it.

What is functional programming?

FP means different things to different people. It's a program paradigm that treats a computation as an evaluation of an expression. A *paradigm* in science describes distinct concepts or thought patterns.

FP involves using state and mutable data to solve domain problems, and it's based on lambda calculus. Consequently, functions are *first-class values*.

First-class values

A first-class value in a programming language is an entity that supports all the operations available to other entities. These operations typically include being passed as a parameter, returned from a function, or assigned to a variable.

FP is a programming style that reasons in terms of evaluation of expressions versus the execution of a statement. The term *expression* comes from mathematics; an expression is always returning a result (value) without mutating the program state. A *statement* doesn't return anything and can change the program state:

- *Execution of statements* refers to a program expressed as a sequence of commands or statements. Commands specify how to achieve an end result by creating objects and manipulating them.
- *Evaluation of expressions* refers to how a program specifies object properties that you want to get as result. You don't specify the steps necessary to construct the object, and you can't accidentally use the object before it's created.

The benefits of functional programming

Here's a list of the benefits of FP:

- *Composability and modularity*—With the introduction of pure functions, you can compose functions and create higher-level abstractions from simple functions. Using modules, the program can be organized in a better way. Composability is the most powerful tool to defeat complexity; it lets you define and build solutions for complex problems.
- *Expressiveness*—You can express complex ideas in a succinct and declarative format, improving the clarity of the intention and ability to reason about your program and reducing code complexity.
- *Reliability and testing*—Functions exist without side effects; a function only evaluates and returns a value that depends on its arguments. Therefore, you can examine a function by focusing solely on its arguments, which allows for better testing to easily validate the correctness of your code.
- *Easier concurrency*—Concurrency encourages referential transparency and immutability, which are the primary keys for writing correct, lock-free concurrent applications to run effectively on multiple cores.
- *Lazy evaluation*—You can retrieve the result of the function on demand. Suppose you have a big data stream to analyze. Thanks to LINQ, you can use deferred execution and lazy evaluation to process your data analysis on demand (only when needed).
- *Productivity*—This is an enormous benefit: you can write fewer lines of code while achieving the same implementation as other paradigms. Productivity reduces the time it takes to develop programs, which can translate to a larger profit margin.

- *Correctness*—You can write less code, naturally reducing the possible number of bugs.
- *Maintainability*—This benefit results from the other benefits, such as the code being composable, modular, expressive, and correct.

Learning to program functionally leads to more modular, expression-oriented, conceptually simple code. The combinations of these FP assets let you understand what your code is doing, regardless of how many threads it's executing.

The tenets of functional programming

There are four main tenets to FP that lead to a composable and declarative programming style:

- Higher-order functions (HOFs) as first-class values
- Immutability
- Pure functions, also known as side-effect-free functions
- Declarative programming style

The clash of program paradigms: from imperative to object-oriented to functional programming

> *Object-oriented programming makes code understandable by encapsulating moving parts.*
> *Functional programming makes code understandable by minimizing moving parts.*
>
> —*Michael Feathers, author of* Working with Legacy Code, *via Twitter*

This section describes three programming paradigms:

- *Imperative programming* describes computations in terms of statements that change the program's state and define the sequence of commands to perform. Therefore, an imperative paradigm is a style that computes a series of statements to mutate a state.
- *Functional programming* builds the structures and elements of a program by treating computations as the evaluation of expressions; therefore, FP promotes immutability and avoids state.
- *Object-oriented programming* (OOP) organizes objects rather than actions, and its data structures contain data rather than logic. The main programming paradigms can be distinguished between imperative and functional. OOP is orthogonal to imperative and functional programming, in the sense that it can be combined with both. You don't have to prefer one paradigm over another, but you can write software with an OOP style using functional or imperative concepts.

OOP has been around for almost two decades, and its design principles were used by languages such as Java, C#, and VB.Net. OOP has had great success because of its ability to represent and model the user domain, raising the level of abstraction. The primary idea behind the introduction of OOP languages was code reusability, but this idea is often corrupted by modifications and customizations required for specific scenarios and ad hoc objects. OOP programs developed with low coupling and good code reusability felt like a complex maze, with many secret and convoluted passages reducing code readability.

To mitigate this hard-to-achieve code reusability, developers started to create design patterns to address OOP's cumbersome nature. Design patterns encouraged developers to tailor software around the patterns, making the code base more complex, difficult to understand, and, in certain cases, maintainable but still far from reusable. In OOP, design patterns are useful when defining solutions to recurring design problems, but they can be considered a defect of abstraction in the language itself.

In FP, design patterns have a different meaning; in fact, most of the OOP-specific design patterns are unnecessary in functional languages because of the higher level of abstraction and HOFs used as building blocks. The higher level of abstraction and reduced workload around the low-level details in FP style has the advantage of producing shorter programs. When the program is small, it's easier to understand, improve, and verify. FP has fantastic support for code reuse and for reducing repetitive code, which is the most effective way to write code that's less prone to error.

Higher-order functions for increasing abstraction

The principle of an HOF means that functions can be passed as arguments to other functions, and functions can return different functions within their return values. .NET has the concept of generic delegates, such as `Action<T>` and `Func<T, TResult>`, which can be used as HOFs to pass functions as parameters with lambda support. Here's an example of using the generic delegate `Func<T, R>` in C#:

```
Func<int, double> fCos = n => Math.Cos( (double)n );
double x = fCos(5);
IEnumerable<double> values = Enumerable.Range(1, 10).Select(fCos);
```

The equivalent code can be represented in F# with function semantics, without the need to use the `Func<T, TResult>` delegate explicitly:

```
let fCos = fun n -> Math.Cos( double n )
let x = fCos 5
let values = [1..10] |> List.map fCos
```

HOFs are at the core of harnessing the power of FP. HOFs have the following benefits:

- Composition and modularity
- Code reusability
- Ability to create highly dynamic and adaptable systems

Functions in FP are considered first-class values, meaning that functions can be named by variables, can be assigned to variables, and can appear anywhere that any other language constructs can appear. If you're coming from a straight OOP experience, this concept allows you to use functions in a non-canonical way, such as applying relatively generic operations to standard data structures. HOFs let you focus on results, not steps. This is a fundamental and powerful shift in approaching functional languages. Different functional techniques allow you to achieve functional composition:

- Composition
- Currying
- Partially applied functions or partial applications

The power of using delegates leads to express functionality that targets not only methods that do one thing, but also behavioral engines that you can enhance, reuse, and extend. This kind of programming style, which is at the root of the functional paradigm, has the benefit of reducing the amount of code refactoring: instead of having several specialized and rigid methods, the program can be expressed by fewer but much more general and reusable methods that can be amplified to handle multiple and different scenarios.

HOFs and lambda expressions for code reusability

One of the many useful reasons for using lambda expressions is to refactor the code, reducing redundancy. It's good practice in memory-managed languages such as C# to dispose of resources deterministically when possible. Consider the following example:

```
string text;
using (var stream = new StreamReader(path))
{
    text = stream.ReadToEnd();
}
```

In this code, the StreamReader resource is disposed with the using keyword. This is a well-known pattern, but limitations do exist. The pattern isn't reusable because the disposable variable is declared inside the using scope, making it impossible to reuse after it's disposed, and it generates exceptions if it calls the disposed objects. Refactoring the code in a classic OOP style is no trivial task. It's possible to use a template method pattern, but this solution also introduces more complexity with the need for a new base class and implementation for each derived class. A better and more elegant solution is to use a lambda expression (anonymous delegate). Here's the code to implement the static helper method and its use:

```
R Using<T,R>(this T item, Func<T, R> func) where T : IDisposable {
    using (item)
            return func(item);
}

string text = new StreamReader(path).Using(stream => stream.ReadToEnd());
```

This code implements a flexible and reusable pattern for cleaning up disposable resources. Here the only constraint is that the generic type T must be a type that implements IDisposable.

Lambda expressions and anonymous functions

The term *lambda* or *lambda expression* most often refers to anonymous functions. The intention behind a lambda expression is to express computations based on a function, using variable binding and substitution. In simpler terms, a lambda expression is an unnamed method written in place of a delegate instance that introduces the notion of *anonymous functions.*

Lambda expressions raise the level of abstraction to simplify the programming experience. Functional languages such as F# are based on lambda calculus, which is used to express computations on function abstractions; therefore, a lambda expression is part of the FP language. In C#, however, the main motivation for introducing lambdas is to facilitate streaming abstractions that enable stream-based declarative APIs. Such abstraction presents an accessible and natural path to multicore parallelism, making lambda expressions a valuable tool in the domain of current computing.

Lambda calculus vs. lambda expressions

Lambda calculus (also known as λ-calculus) is a formal system in mathematical logic and computer science for expressing computations using variable binding and substitution using functions as its only *data structure*. Lambda calculus behaves as a small programming language that expresses and evaluates any computable function. For example, .NET LINQ is based on lambda calculus.

A *lambda expression* defines a special anonymous method. Anonymous methods are delegate instances with no actual method declaration name. The terms *lambda* and *lambda expression* most often refer to anonymous functions.

A *lambda method* is syntactic sugar and a more compact syntax for embedding an anonymous method in code:

```
Func<int, int> f1 = delegate(int i) { return i + 1; };   ◀── Anonymous method
Func<int, int> f2 = i => i+1;              ◀──┤ Lambda expression
```

To create a lambda expression, you specify input parameters (if any) on the left side of the lambda operator => (pronounced "goes to"), and you put the expression or statement block on the right side. For example, the lambda expression (x, y) => x + y specifies two parameters x and y and returns the sum of these values.

Each lambda expression has three parts:

- (x, y) —A set of parameters.
- =>—The goes to operator (=>) that separates an argument list from the result expression.
- x + y—A set of statements that perform an action or return a value. In this example, the lambda expression returns the sum of x and y.

Here's how you implement three lambda expressions with the same behavior:

```
Func<int, int, int> add = delegate(int x, int x){ return x + y; };
Func<int, int, int> add = (int x, int y) => { return x + y; };
Func<int, int, int> add = (x, y) => x + y
```

The part `Func<int, int, int>` defines a function that takes two integers and returns a new integer.

In F#, the strong type system can bind a name or label to a function without an explicit declaration. F# functions are primitive values, similar to integers and strings. It's possible to translate the previous function into the equivalent F# syntax as follows:

```
let add = (fun x y -> x + y)
let add = (+)
```

In F#, the *plus* (+) operator is a function that has the same signature as *add*, which takes two numbers and returns the sum as a result.

Lambda expressions are a simple and effective solution to assign and execute a block of inline code, especially in an instance when the block of code serves one specific purpose and you don't need to define it as a method. There are numerous advantages for introducing lambda expressions into your code. Here is a short list:

- You don't need explicit parameterization of types; the compiler can figure out the parameter types.
- Succinct inline coding (the functions exist within the line) avoids disruptions caused when developers must look elsewhere in the code to find functionality.
- Captured variables limit the exposure of class-level variables.
- Lambda expressions make the code flow readable and understandable.

Currying

The term *currying* originates from Haskell Curry, a mathematician who was an important influence on the development of FP. *Currying* is a technique that lets you modularize functions and reuse code. The basic idea is to transform the evaluation of a function that takes multiple parameters into the evaluation of a sequence of functions, each with a single parameter. Functional languages are closely related to mathematical concepts, where functions can have only one parameter. F# follows this concept because functions with multiple parameters are declared as a series of new functions, each with only one parameter.

In practice, the other .NET languages have functions with more than one argument; and from the OOP perspective, if you don't pass into a function all the arguments expected, the compiler throws an exception. Conversely, in FP it's extremely easy to write a curried function that returns any function you give it. But as previously mentioned, lambda expressions provide a great syntax for creating anonymous delegates, thereby making it easy to implement a curried function. Moreover, it's possible to implement currying in any programming language that supports closure—an interesting concept because this technique simplifies lambda expressions, including only single-parameter functions.

The currying technique makes it possible to treat all functions with one or any number of arguments as if they take only one argument, independent of the number of arguments needed to execute. This creates a chain of functions where each consumes a single parameter.

At the end of this chain of functions, all parameters are available at once, which allows the original function to execute. Moreover, currying allows you to create specialized groups of functions generated from fixing the arguments of a base function. For instance, when you curry a function of two arguments and apply it to the first argument, then the functionality is limited by one dimension. This isn't a limitation but a powerful technique, because then you can apply the new function to the second argument to compute a particular value.

In mathematic notation, an important difference exists between these two functions:

```
Add(x, y, z)
Add x y z
```

The difference is that the first function takes a single argument of type `tuple` (composed by the three items x, y, and z), and the second function takes the input item x and returns a function that takes the input item y, which returns a function that takes item z and then returns the result of the final computation. In simpler words, the equivalent function can be rewritten as

```
(((Add x) y) z)
```

It's important to mention that function applications are left associative, taking one argument at a time. The previous function `Add` is an application against x, and the result is then applied to y. The result of this application `((Add x) y)` is then applied to z. Because each of these transitional steps yields a function, it's perfectly acceptable to define a function as

```
Plus2 = Add 2
```

This function is equivalent to `Add x`. In this case, you can expect the function `Plus2` to take two input arguments, and it always passes 2 as a fixed parameter. For clarity, it's possible to rewrite the previous function as follows:

```
Plus2 x = Add 2 x
```

The process of yielding intermediate functions (each taking one input argument) is called *currying*. Let's see currying in action. Consider the following simple C# function that uses a lambda expression:

```
Func<int,int,int> add = (x,y) => x + y;
Func<int,Func<int,int>> curriedAdd = x => y => x + y;
```

This code defines the function `Func<int, int, int>` add, which takes two integers as arguments and returns an integer as a result. When this function is called, the compiler requires both arguments x and y. But the curried version of the function add, `curried-Add`, results in a delegate with the special signature `Func<int,Fun< int, int>>`.

In general, any delegate of type `Func<A,B,R>` can be transformed into a delegate of type `Func<A, Func<B,R>>`. This curried function takes only one argument and returns a function that takes the original function as an argument and then returns a value of type A. The curried function `curriedAdd` can be used to create powerful specialized functions. For example, you can define an `increment` function by adding the value 1:

```
Func<int,int> increment = curriedAdd(1)
```

Now, you can use this function to define other functions that perform several forms of addition:

```
int a = curriedAdd(30)
int b = increment(41)

Func<int, int> add30 = curriedAdd(30)
int c = add30(12)
```

One benefit of currying a function is that the creation of specialized functions is easier to reuse; but the real power is that curried functions introduce a useful concept called *partially applied functions*, which is covered in the next section. Additional benefits of the currying technique are function parameter reduction and easy-to-reuse abstract functions.

AUTOMATIC CURRYING IN C#

It's possible to automate and raise the level of abstraction of the currying technique in C# with the help of extension methods. In this example, the purpose of the curry extension method is to introduce syntactic sugar to hide the currying implementation:

```
static Func<A, Func<B, R>> Curry<A, B, R>(this Func<A, B, R> function)
{
    return a => b => function(a, b);
}
```

This is the previous code refactored using the helper extension method:

```
Func<int,int,int> add = (x,y) => x + y;
Func<int,Func<int,int>> curriedAdd = add.Curry();
```

This syntax looks more succinct. It's important to notice that the compiler can infer the types used in all the functions and, for this, it's most helpful. In fact, even though `Curry` is a generic function, it's not required to pass generic parameters explicitly. Using this currying technique lets you use a different syntax that's more conducive to building a library of complex composite functions from simple functions. The source code, which you can download as part of the resources for this book, has a library that contains a full implementation of helper methods, including an extension method for automatic currying.

UN-CURRYING

As easily as applying the curry technique to a function, you can un-curry a function by using higher-order functions to revert the curried function. Un-currying is, obviously, the opposite transformation to currying. Think of un-currying as a technique to undo currying by applying a generic un-curry function.

   In the following example, the curried function with signature Func<A, Func<B, R>> will be converted back to a multi-argument function:

```
public static Func<A, B, R> Uncurry<A, B, R>(Func<A, Func<B, R>> function)
                                      => (x, y) => function(x)(y);
```

The primary purpose of un-currying a function is to bring the signature of a curried function back into a more OOP style.

CURRYING IN F#

In F#, function declarations are curried by default. But even though this is done automatically by the compiler for you, it's helpful to understand how F# handles curried functions.

   The following example shows two F# functions that multiply two values. If you're not familiar with F#, these functions may seem equivalent or at least similar, but they aren't:

```
let multiplyOne (x,y) = x * y
let multiplyTwo x y = x * y

let resultOne = multiplyOne(7, 8)
let resultTwo = multiplyTwo 7 8
let values = (7,8)
let resultThree = multiplyOne values
```

Besides the syntax, no apparent difference exists between these functions, but they behave differently. The first function has only one parameter, which is a tuple with the required values, but the second function has two distinct parameters x and y.

   The difference becomes clear when you look into the signatures of these functions' declarations:

```
val multiplyOne : (int * int) -> int
val multiplyTwo : int -> int -> int
```

Now it's obvious that these functions are different. The first function takes a tuple as an input argument and returns an integer. The second function takes an integer as its first input and returns a function that takes an integer as input and then returns an integer. This second function, which takes two arguments, is transformed automatically by the compiler into a chain of functions, each with one input argument.

   This example shows the equivalent curried functions, which is how the compiler interprets it for you:

```
let multiplyOne x y = x * y
let multiplyTwo = fn x -> fun y -> x * y

let resultOne = multiplyOne 7 8
let resultTwo = multiplyTwo 7 8
let resultThree =
    let tempMultiplyBy7 = multiplyOne 7
    tempMultiplyBy7 8
```

In F#, the implementation of these functions is equivalent because, as previously mentioned, they're curried by default. The main purpose of currying is to optimize a function for easily applying partial application.

Partially applied functions

The *partially applied function* (or partial function application) is a technique of fixing multiple arguments to a function and producing another function of smaller arity (the *arity* of a function is the number of its arguments). In this way, a partial function provides a function with fewer arguments than expected, which produces a specialized function for the given values. Partially applied functions, in addition to function composition, make functional modularization possible.

More simply, a partial function application is a process of binding values to parameters, which means that partially applied functions are functions that reduce the number of function arguments by using fixed (default) values. If you have a function with N arguments, it's possible to create a function with N-1 arguments that calls the original function with a fixed argument. Because partial application depends on currying, the two techniques occur together. The difference between partial application and currying is that partial application binds more than one parameter to a value, so to evaluate the rest of the function you need to apply the remaining arguments.

In general, partial application transforms a generic function into a new and specialized function. Let's take the C# curried function:

```
Func<int,int,int> add = (x,y) => x + y;
```

How can you create a new function with a single argument?

This is the case where partial function application becomes useful, because you can partially apply a function against an HOF with a default value for the first argument to the original function. Here's the extension method that can be used to partially apply a function:

```
static Func<B, R> Partial<A, B, R>(this Func<A, B, R> function, A argument)
                      => argument2 => function(argument, argument2);
```

And here's an example to exercise this technique:

```
Func<int, int, int> max = Math.Max;
Func<int, int> max5 = max.Partial(5);

int a = max5(8);
int b = max5(2);
int c = max5(12);
```

Math.Max(int,int) is an example of a function that can be extended with partially applied functions. Introducing a partially applied function in this case, the default argument 5 is fixed, and it creates a new specialized function max5 that evaluates the maximum value between two numbers with a default of 5. Thanks to partial application, you created a new and more specific function out of an existing one.

From an OOP perspective, think of partial function applications as a way to override functions. It's also possible to use this technique to extend on-the-fly functionality of a third-party library that isn't extensible.

As mentioned, in F# functions are curried by default, which leads to an easier way to create partial functions than in C#. Partial function applications have many benefits, including the following:

- They allow functions to be composed without hesitation.
- They alleviate the need to pass a separate set of parameters, by avoiding building unnecessary classes that contain override versions of same method with a different number of inputs.
- They enable the developer to write highly general functions by parameterizing their behavior.

The practical benefit of using partial function applications is that functions constructed by supplying only a portion of the argument are good for code reusability, functional extensibility, and composition. Moreover, partially applied functions simplify the use of HOFs in your programming style. Partial function application can also be deferred for performance improvement, which was introduced in section 2.6.

Power of partial function application and currying in C#

Let's consider a more complete example of partial function application and currying that can cover a real-use scenario. Retry in listing A.1 is an extension method for a delegate Func<T> for any function that takes no parameters and returns a value of type T. The purpose of this method is to execute the incoming function in a try-catch block, and if an exception is thrown while executing, the function will retry the operation up to a maximum of three times.

Listing A.1   Retry extension method in C#

```
public static T Retry<T>(this Func<T> function)          ◄──  Applies a static method to a
{                                                              general Func<T> delegate
    int retry = 0;              ◄──┤ Sets the counter
        T result = default(T);      ◄──  Sets the result to a default value of T
        bool success = false;
    do{
        try {                                          ◄──  Increases count if an error occurs
                result = function();
                success = true;       ◄───────┐
        }                                      │      Executes the function. If successful, then
        catch {                                │      the while loop stops and the result returns;
                retry++;      ◄────────────────┤      otherwise, a new iteration computes.
        }
    } while (!success && retry < 3);      ◄──┘
    return result;
}                                              Iterates three times or until success
```

Let's say that this method tries to read text from a file. In the following code, the method ReadText accepts a file path as input and returns the text from a file. To execute the functionality with the attached Retry behavior to fall back on and recover in case of issues, you can use a closure, as shown here:

```
static string ReadText(string filePath) => File.ReadAllText(filePath);

string filePath = "TextFile.txt";
Func<string> readText = () => ReadText(filePath);

string text = readText.Retry();
```

You can use a lambda expression to capture the local variable `filePath` and pass it into the method `ReadText`. This process lets you create a `Func<string>` that matches the signature of the `Retry` extension method, which can be attached. If the file is blocked or owned by another process, an error is thrown, and the `Retry` functionality kicks in as expected. If the first call fails, the method will retry a second time and a third time. Finally, it returns the default value of `T`.

This works, but you might wonder what happens if you want to retry a function that needs a string parameter. The solution is to partially apply the function. The following code implements a function that takes a string as a parameter, which is the file path to read the text from, and then it passes that parameter to the `ReadText` method. The `Retry` behavior only works with functions that take no parameters, so the code doesn't compile:

```
Func<string, string> readText = (path) => ReadText(path);

string text = readText.Retry();
string text = readText(filePath).Retry();
```

The behavior of `Retry` doesn't work with this version of `readText`. One possible solution is to write another version of the `Retry` method that takes an additional generic-type parameter that specifies the type of the parameter you need to pass once invoked. This isn't ideal, because you have to figure out how to share this new `Retry` logic across all the methods using it, each with different arguments or implementations.

A better option is to use and combine currying and partial function application. In the following listing, the helper methods `Curry` and `Partial` are defined as extension methods.

Listing A.2   `Retry` helper extensions in C#

```
static class RetryExtensions
{
    public static Func<R> Partial<T, R>(this Func<T, R> function, T arg){
            return () => function(arg);
    }

    public static Func<T, Func<R>> Curry<T, R>(this Func<T, R> function){
        return arg => () => function(arg);
    }
}

Func<string, string> readText = (path) => ReadText(path);

string text = readText.Partial("TextFile.txt").Retry();
```

```
Func<string, Func<string>> curriedReadText = readText.Curry();
string text = curriedReadText("TextFile.txt").Retry();
```

This approach lets you inject the file path and use the `Retry` function smoothly. This is possible because both helper functions, `Partial` and `Curry`, adapt the function `readText` into a function that doesn't need a parameter, ultimately matching the signature of `Retry`.

appendix B
F# overview

This appendix explores the basic syntax of F#, which is an established general-purpose functional first language with object-oriented programming (OOP) support. In fact, F# embraces the .NET common language infrastructure (CLI) object model, which allows the declaration of interfaces, classes, and abstract classes. Furthermore, F# is a statically and strongly typed language, which means that the compiler can detect the data type of variables and functions at compile time. F#'s syntax is different from C-style languages, such as C#, because curly braces aren't used to delimit blocks of code. Moreover, whitespace rather than commas and indentation is important to separate arguments and delimit the scope of a function body. In addition, F# is a cross-platform programming language that can run inside and outside the .NET ecosystem.

The let binding

In F#, `let` is one of the most important keywords that binds an identifier to a value, which means giving a name to value (or, bind a value to a name). It's defined as `let <identifier> = <value>`.

The `let` bindings are immutable by default. Here are a few code examples:

```
let myInt = 42
let myFloat = 3.14
let myString = "hello functional programming"
let myFunction = fun number -> number * number
```

As you can see from the last line, you can name a function by binding the identifier `myFunction` to the lambda expression `fun number -> number * number`.

The `fun` keyword is used to define a lambda expression (anonymous function) in the syntax as `fun args -> body`. Interestingly, you don't need to define types in code because, due to its strong built-in type-inference system, the F# compiler can understand them natively. For example, in the previous code, the compiler inferred that the argument of the `myFunction` function is a number due to the multiplication (`*`) operator.

Understanding function signatures in F#

In F#, as in most of the functional languages, function signatures are defined with an arrow notation that reads from left to right. Functions are expressions that always have an output, so the last right arrow will always point to the return type. For example, when you see `typeA -> typeB`, you can interpret it as a function that takes an input value of `typeA` and produces a value of `typeB`. The same principle is applicable to functions that take more than two arguments. When the signature of a function is `typeA -> typeB -> typeC`, you read the arrows from left to right, which creates two functions. The first function is `typeA -> (typeB -> typeC)`, which takes an input of `typeA` and produces the function `typeB -> typeC`.

Here's the signature for the `add` function:

```
val add : x:int -> y:int -> int
```

This takes one argument `x:int` and returns as a result a function that takes `y:int` as input and returns an `int` as a result. The arrow notation is intrinsically connected to currying and anonymous functions.

Creating mutable types: mutable and ref

One of the main concepts in FP is immutability. F# is a functional-first programming language; but explicitly using the `immutable` keywords lets you create mutable types that behave like variables, as in this example:

```
let mutable myNumber = 42
```

Now it's possible to change the value of `myNumber` with the goes-to (`<-`) operator:

```
myNumber <- 51
```

Another option when defining a mutable type is to use a *reference cell* that defines a storage location that lets you create mutable values with reference semantics. The `ref` operator declares a new reference cell that encapsulates a value, which can then be changed using the `:=` operator and accessed using the `!` (bang) operator:

```
let myRefVar = ref 42
myRefVar := 53
printfn "%d" !myRefVar
```

The first line declares the reference cell `myRefVar` with the value 42, and the second line changes its value to 53. In the last line of code, the underlying value is accessed and printed.

Mutable variables and reference cells can be used in almost the same situations; but the mutable types are preferred, unless the compiler doesn't allow it and a reference cell can be used instead. In expressions that generate a closure where a mutable state is required, for example, the compiler will report that a mutable variable cannot be used. In this case, a reference cell overcomes the problem.

Functions as first-class types

In F#, functions are first-order data types; they can be declared using the `let` keyword and used in exactly the same way as any other variable:

```
let square x = x * x
let plusOne x = x + 1
let isEven x = x % 2 = 0
```

Functions always return a value, despite not having an explicit `return` keyword. The value of the last statement executed in the function is the return value.

Composition: pipe and composition operators

The pipe (`|>`) and the composition (`>>`) operators are used to chain functions and arguments to improve code readability. These operators let you establish *pipelines* of functions in a flexible manner. The definition of these operators is simple:

```
let inline (|>) x f = f x
let inline (>>) f g x = g(f x)
```

The following example shows how to take advantage of these operators to build a functional pipeline:

```
let squarePlusOne x =  x |> square |> plusOne
let plusOneIsEven = plusOne >> isEven
```

In the last line of code, the composition (`>>`) operator lets you eliminate the explicit need for an input parameter definition. The F# compiler understands that the function `plusOneIsEven` is expecting an integer as input. The kind of function that doesn't need parameter definitions is called a *point-free function*.

The main differences between the pipe (`|>`) and composition (`>>`) operators are their signature and use. The pipeline operator takes functions and arguments, while composition combines functions.

Delegates

In .NET, a *delegate* is a pointer to a function; it's a variable that holds the reference to a method that shares the same common signature. In F#, function values are used in place of delegates; but F# provides support for delegates to interop with the .NET APIs. This is the syntax in F# to define a delegate:

```
type delegate-typename = delegate of typeA -> typeB
```

The following code shows the syntax for creating a delegate with a signature that represents an addition operation:

```
type MyDelegate = delegate of (int * int) -> int
let add (a, b) = a + b
let addDelegate = MyDelegate(add)
let result = addDelegate.Invoke(33, 9)
```

In the example, the F# function `add` is passed directly as arguments to the delegate constructor `MyDelegate`. Delegates can be attached to F# function values and to static or instance methods. The `Invoke` method on the delegate type `addDelegate` calls the underlying function `add`.

Comments

Three kinds of comments are used in F#: block comments are placed between the symbols (`*` and `*`), line comments start with the symbols `//` and continue until the end of the line, and XML doc comments come after the symbols `///` that let you use XML tags to generate code documentation based on the compiler-generated file. Here's how these look:

```
(* This is block comment *)
// Single line comments use a double forward slash
/// This comment can be used to generate documentation.
```

Open statements

You use the `open` keyword to open a namespace or module, similar to statements in C#. This code opens the `System` namespace: `open System`.

Basic data types

Table B.1 shows the list of F# *primitive types*.

Table B.1 Basic data types

F# type	.NET type	Size in bytes	Range	Example
sbyte	System.SByte	1	-128 to 127	42y
byte	System.Byte	1	0 to 255	42uy
int16	System.Int16	2	-32,768 to 32,767	42s
uint16	System.UInt16	2	0 to 65,535	42us
int / int32	System.Int32	4	-2,147,483,648 to 2,147,483,647	42
uint32	System.UInt32	4	0 to 4,294,967,295	42u
int64	System.Int64	8	-9,223,372,036,854,775,808 to 9,223,372,036,854,775,807	42L
uint64	System.UInt64	8	0 to 18,446,744,073,709,551,615	42UL
float32	System.Single	4	±1.5e-45 to ±3.4e38	42.0F
float	System.Double	8	±5.0e-324 to ±1.7e308	42.0
decimal	System.Decimal	16	±1.0e-28 to ±7.9e28	42.0M
char	System.Char	2	U+0000 to U+ffff	'x'
string	System.String	20 + (2 * size of string)	0 to about 2 billion characters	"Hello World"
bool	System.Boolean	1	Only two possible values: true or false	true

Special string definition

In F#, the string type is an alias for the System.String type; but in addition to the conventional .NET semantic, you have a special triple-quoted way to declare strings. This special string definition lets you declare a string without the need of escaping special characters as in the verbatim case. The following example defines the same string the standard way and the F# triple-quoted way to escape special characters:

```
let verbatimHtml = @"<input type="submit" value="Submit">"
let tripleHTML = """<input type="submit" value="Submit">"""
```

Tuple

A *tuple* is a group of unnamed and ordered values, which can be of different types. Tuples are useful for creating ad hoc data structures and are a convenient way for a function to return multiple values. A tuple is defined as a comma-separated collection of values. Here's how to construct tuples:

```
let tuple = (1, "Hello")
let tripleTuple = ("one", "two", "three")
```

A tuple can also be deconstructed. Here the tuple values 1 and "Hello" are bound, respectively, to the identifiers a and b, and the function swap switches the order of two values in a given tuple (a, b):

```
let (a, b) = tuple
let swap (a, b) = (b, a)
```

Tuples are normally objects, but they can also be defined as value type structs, as shown here:

```
let tupleStruct = struct (1, "Hello")
```

Note that the F# type inference can automatically generalize the function to have a generic type, which means that tuples work with any type. It's possible to access and obtain the first and second elements of the tuple using the fst and snd functions:

```
let one = fst tuple
let hello = snd tuple
```

Record types

A *record type* is similar to a tuple, except the fields are named and defined as a semicolon-separated list. While tuples provide one method of storing potentially heterogeneous data in a single container, it can become difficult to interpret the purpose of the elements when more than a few exist. In this case, a record type helps to interpret the purpose of data by labeling their definition with a name. A record type is explicitly defined using the type keyword, and it's compiled down to an immutable, public, and sealed .NET class. Furthermore, the compiler automatically generates the structural equality and comparison functionality, as well as providing a default constructor that populates all the fields contained in the record.

> **NOTE**   If the record is marked with the CLIMutable attribute, it will include a default, no-argument constructor for use in other .NET languages.

This example shows how to define and instantiate a new record type:

```
type Person = { FirstName : string; LastName : string; Age : int }
let fred = { FirstName = "Fred"; LastName = "Flintstone"; Age = 42 }
```

Records can be extended with properties and methods:

```
type Person with
    member this.FullName = sprintf "%s %s" this.FirstName this.LastName
```

Records are immutable types, which means that instances of records cannot be modified. But you can conveniently clone records by using the `with` clone semantic:

```
let olderFred = { fred with Age = fred.Age + 1 }
```

A record type can also be represented as a structure using the `[<Struct>]` attribute. This is helpful in situations where performance is critical and overrides the flexibility of reference types:

```
[<Struct>]
type Person = { FirstName : string; LastName : string; Age : int }
```

Discriminated unions

Discriminated unions (DUs) are a type that represents a set of values that can be one of several well-defined cases, each possibly with different values and types. DUs can be thought of in the object-oriented paradigm as a set of classes that are inherited from the same base class. In general, DUs are the tool used for building complicated data structures, to model domains, and to represent recursive structures like a `Tree` data type.

The following code shows the suit and the rank of a playing card:

```
type Suit = Hearts | Clubs | Diamonds | Spades

type Rank =
        | Value of int
        | Ace
        | King
        | Queen
        | Jack
      static member GetAllRanks() =
          [ yield Ace
            for i in 2 .. 10 do yield Value i
            yield Jack
            yield Queen
            yield King ]
```

As you can see, DUs can be extended with properties and methods. The list representing all the cards in the deck can be computed as follows:

```
    let fullDeck =
      [ for suit in [ Hearts; Diamonds; Clubs; Spades] do
            for rank in Rank.GetAllRanks() do
                yield { Suit=suit; Rank=rank } ]
```

Additionally, DUs can also be represented as structures with the `[<Struct>]` attribute.

Pattern matching

Pattern matching is a language construct that empowers the compiler to interpret the definition of a data type and apply a series of conditions against it. In this way, the compiler forces you to write pattern-matching constructs by covering all possible cases to match the given value. This is known as *exhaustive* pattern matching. Pattern-matching constructs are used for control flow. They're conceptually similar to a series of if/then or case/switch statements but are much more powerful. They let you decompose data structures into their underlying components during each match and then perform certain computations on these values. In all programming languages, *control flow* refers to the decisions made in code that affect the order in which statements are executed in an application.

In general, most common patterns involve algebraic data types, such as discriminated unions, record types, and collections. The following code example has two implementations of the Fizz-Buzz (https://en.wikipedia.org/wiki/Fizz_buzz) game. The first pattern-matching construct has a set of conditions to test the evaluation of the function divisibleBy. If either condition is true or false, the second implementation uses the when clause, called *guard*, to specify and integrate additional tests that must succeed to match the pattern:

```
let fizzBuzz n =
    let divisibleBy m = n % m = 0
    match divisibleBy 3,divisibleBy 5 with
    | true, false -> "Fizz"
    | false, true -> "Buzz"
    | true, true -> "FizzBuzz"
    | false, false -> sprintf "%d" n

let fizzBuzz n =
    match n with
    | _ when (n % 15) = 0 -> "FizzBuzz"
    | _ when (n % 3) = 0 -> "Fizz"
    | _ when (n % 5) = 0 -> "Buzz"
    | _ -> sprintf "%d" n

[1..20] |> List.iter fizzBuzz
```

When a pattern-matching construct is evaluated, the expression is passed into the match <expression>, which is tested against each pattern until the first positive match. Then the corresponding body is evaluated. The _ (underscore) character is known as a *wildcard*, which is one way to always have a positive match. Often, this pattern is used as final clause for a general catch to apply to a common behavior.

Active patterns

Active patterns are constructs that extend the capabilities of pattern matching, allowing for partition and deconstruction of a given data structure, thus guaranteeing the flexibility to transform and extract underlying values by making the code more readable and making the results of the decomposition available for further pattern matching.

Additionally, active patterns let you wrap arbitrary values in a DU data structure for easy pattern matching. It's possible to wrap objects with an active pattern, so that you can use those objects in pattern matching as easily as any other union type.

Sometimes active patterns do not generate a value; in this case, they're called *partial active patterns* and result in a type that is an option type. To define a partial active pattern, you use the underscore wildcard character (_) at the end of the list of patterns inside the banana clips (| |) created with the combination of parentheses and pipe characters. Here's how a typical partial active pattern looks:

```
let (|DivisibleBy|_|) divideBy n =
    if n % divideBy = 0 then Some DivisibleBy else None
```

In this partial active pattern, if the value n is divisible by the value divideBy, then the return type is Some(), which indicates that the active pattern succeeds. Otherwise, the None return type indicates that the pattern failed and moved to the next match expression. Partial active patterns are used to partition and match only part of the *input* space. The following code illustrates how to pattern match against a partial active pattern:

```
let fizzBuzz n =
    match n with
    | DivisibleBy 3 & DivisibleBy 5 -> "FizzBuzz"
    | DivisibleBy 3 -> "Fizz"
    | DivisibleBy 5 -> "Buzz"
    | _ -> sprintf "%d" n

[1..20] |> List.iter fizzBuzz
```

This function uses the partial active pattern (|DivisibleBy|_|) to test the input value n. If it's divisible by a value 3 and 5, the first case succeeds. If it's divisible by only 3, then the second cause succeeds, and so forth. Note that the & operator lets you run more than one pattern on the same argument.

Another type of active pattern is the *parameterized active pattern*, which is similar to the partial active pattern, but takes one or more additional arguments as input.

More interesting is the *multicase active pattern*, which partitions the entire input space into different data structures in the shape of a DU. Here's the FizzBuzz example, implemented using multicase active patterns:

```
let (|Fizz|Buzz|FizzBuzz|Val|) n =
    match n % 3, n % 5 with
    | 0, 0 -> FizzBuzz
    | 0, _ -> Fizz
    | _, 0 -> Buzz
    | _ -> Val n
```

Because active patterns convert data from one type to another, they're great for data transformation and validation. Active patterns come in four related varieties: single case, partial case, multicase, and partial parameterized. For more details about active patterns, see the MSDN documentation (http://mng.bz/Itmw) and Isaac Abraham's *Get Programming with F#* (Manning, 2018).

Collections

F# supports the standard .NET collections like arrays and sequences (IEnumerable). In addition, it offers a set of immutable functional collections: lists, sets, and maps.

Arrays

Arrays are zero-based, mutable collections with a fixed-size number of elements of the same type. They support fast, random access of elements because they are compiled as a contiguous block of memory. Here are the different ways to create, filter, and project an array:

```
let emptyArray= Array.empty
let emptyArray = [| |]
let arrayOfFiveElements = [| 1; 2; 3; 4; 5 |]
let arrayFromTwoToTen= [| 2..10 |]
let appendTwoArrays = emptyArray |> Array.append arrayFromTwoToTen
let evenNumbers = arrayFromTwoToTen |> Array.filter(fun n -> n % 2 = 0)
let squareNumbers = evenNumbers |> Array.map(fun n -> n * n)
```

The elements of an array can be accessed and updated by using the dot operator (.) and brackets [ ]:

```
let arr = Array.init 10 (fun i -> i * i)
arr.[1] <- 42
arr.[7] <- 91
```

Arrays can also be created in various other syntaxes, using the functions from the Array module:

```
let arrOfBytes = Array.create 42 0uy
let arrOfSquare = Array.init 42 (fun i -> i * i)
let arrOfIntegers = Array.zeroCreate<int> 42
```

Sequences (seq)

Sequences are a series of elements of the same type. Different from the List type, sequences are lazily evaluated, which means that elements can be computed on demand (only when they are needed). This provides better performance than a list in cases where not all the elements are needed. Here's a different way to create, filter, and project a sequence:

```
let emptySeq = Seq.empty
let seqFromTwoToFive = seq { yield 2; yield 3; yield 4; yield 5 }
let seqOfFiveElements = seq { 1 .. 5 }
let concatenateTwoSeqs = emptySeq |> Seq.append seqOfFiveElements
let oddNumbers = seqFromTwoToFive |> Seq.filter(fun n -> n % 2 <> 0)
let doubleNumbers = oddNumbers |> Seq.map(fun n -> n + n)
```

Sequences can use the yield keyword to lazily return a value that becomes part of the sequence.

Lists

In F#, the `List` collection is an immutable, singly linked list of elements of the same type. In general, lists are a good choice for enumeration, but aren't recommended for random access and concatenation when performance is critical. Lists are defined using the [...] syntax. Here are a few examples to create, filter, and map a list:

```
let emptyList = List.empty
let emptyList = [ ]
let listOfFiveElements = [ 1; 2; 3; 4; 5 ]
let listFromTwoToTen = [ 2..10 ]
let appendOneToEmptyList = 1::emptyList
let concatenateTwoLists = listOfFiveElements @ listFromTwoToTen
let evenNumbers = listOfFiveElements |> List.filter(fun n -> n % 2 = 0)
let squareNumbers = evenNumbers |> List.map(fun n -> n * n)
```

Lists use brackets ([ ]) and the semicolon (;) delimiters to append multiple items to the list, the symbol :: to append one item, and the at-sign operator (@) to concatenate two given lists.

Sets

A *set* is a collection based on binary trees, where the elements are of the same type. With sets, the order of insertion is not preserved, and duplicates aren't allowed. A set is immutable, and every operation to update its elements creates a new set. Here are a few different ways to create a set:

```
let emptySet = Set.empty<int>
let setWithOneItem = emptySet.Add 8
let setFromList = [ 1..10 ] |> Set.ofList
```

Maps

A *map* is an immutable, key-value pair of a collection of elements with the same type. This collection associates values with a key, and it behaves like the `Set` type, which doesn't allow duplicates or respect the order of insertion. The following example shows how to instantiate a map in different ways:

```
let emptyMap = Map.empty<int, string>
let mapWithOneItem = emptyMap.Add(42, "the answer to the meaning of life")
let mapFromList = [ (1, "Hello"), (2, "World") ] |> Map.ofSeq
```

Loops

F# supports loop constructs to iterate over enumerable collections like lists, arrays, sequences, maps, and so forth. The `while...do` expression performs iterative execution while a specified condition is true:

```
let mutable a = 10
while (a < 20) do
   printfn "value of a: %d" a
   a <- a + 1
```

The for...to expression iterates in a loop over a set of values of a loop variable:

```
for i = 1 to 10 do
  printf "%d " i
```

The for...in expression iterates in a loop over each element in a collection of values:

```
for i in [1..10] do
  printfn "%d" i
```

Classes and inheritance

As previously mentioned, F# supports OOP constructs like other .NET programming languages. In fact, it's possible to define class objects to model real-world domains. The type keyword used in F# to declare a class can expose properties, methods, and fields. The following code shows the definition of the subclass Student that's inherited from the class Person:

```
type Person(firstName, lastName, age) =
    member this.FirstName = firstName
    member this.LastName = lastName
    member this.Age = age

    member this.UpdateAge(n:int) =
        Person(firstName, lastName, age + n)

    override this.ToString() =
        sprintf "%s %s" firstName lastName

type Student(firstName, lastName, age, grade) =
    inherit Person(firstName, lastName, age)

    member this.Grade = grade
```

The properties FirstName, LastName, and Age are exposed as fields; the method UpdateAge returns a new Person object with the modified Age. It's possible to change the default behavior of methods inherited from the base class using the override keyword. In the example, the ToString base method is overridden to return the full name.

The object Student is a subclass defined using the inherit keyword, and inherits its members from the base class Person, in addition to adding its own member Grade.

Abstract classes and inheritance

An *abstract class* is an object that provides a template to define classes. Usually it exposes one or more incomplete implementations of methods or properties and requires you to create subclasses to fill in these implementations. But it's possible to define a default behavior, which can be overridden. In the following example, the abstract class Shape defines the Rectangle and Circle classes:

```
[<AbstractClass>]
type Shape(weight :float, height :float) =
    member this.Weight = weight
    member this.Height = height
```

```
    abstract member Area : unit -> float
    default this.Area() = weight * height

type Rectangle(weight :float, height :float) =
    inherit Shape(weight, height)

type Circle(radius :float) =
    inherit Shape(radius, radius)
    override this.Area() = radius * radius * Math.PI
```

The `AbstractClass` attribute notifies the compiler that the class has abstract members. The `Rectangle` class uses the default implementation of the method `Area`, and the `Circle` class overrides it with a custom behavior.

Interfaces

An *interface* represents a contract for defining the implementation details of a class. But in an interface declaration, the members aren't implemented. An interface provides an abstract way to refer to the public members and functions that it exposes. In F#, to define an interface, the members are declared using the `abstract` keyword, followed by their type signature:

```
type IPerson =
    abstract FirstName : string
    abstract LastName : string
    abstract FullName : unit -> string
```

The interface methods implemented by a class are accessed through the interface definition, rather than through the instance of the class. Thus, to call an interface method, a cast operation is applied against the class using the `:>` (upcast) operator:

```
type Person(firstName : string, lastName : string) =
    interface IPerson with
        member this.FirstName = firstName
        member this.LastName = lastName
        member this.FullName() = sprintf "%s %s" firstName lastName

let fred = Person("Fred", "Flintstone")

(fred :> IPerson).FullName()
```

Object expressions

Interfaces represent a useful implementation of code that can be shared between other parts of a program. But it might require cumbersome work to define an ad hoc interface implemented through the creation of new classes. A solution is to use an *object expression*, which lets you implement interfaces on the fly by using anonymous classes. Here's an example to create a new object that implements the `IDisposable` interface to apply a color to the console and then revert to the original:

```
let print color =
    let current = Console.ForegroundColor
    Console.ForegroundColor <- color
```

```
{   new IDisposable with
        member x.Dispose() =
            Console.ForegroundColor <- current
}

using(print ConsoleColor.Red) (fun _ -> printf "Hello in red!!")
using(print ConsoleColor.Blue) (fun _ -> printf "Hello in blue!!")
```

Casting

The conversion of a primitive value into an object type is called *boxing*, which is applied using the function box. This function upcasts any type to the .NET System.Object type, which in F# is abbreviated by the name obj.

The *upcast* function applies an "up" conversion for classes and interface hierarchies, which goes from a class up to the inherited one. The syntax is expr :> type. The success of the conversion is checked at compile time.

The *downcast* function is used to apply a conversion that goes "down" a class or interface hierarchy: for example, from an interface to an implemented class. The syntax is expr :?> type, where the question mark inside the operator suggests that the operation may fail with an InvalidCastException. It's safe to compare and test the type before applying the downcast. This is possible using the type test operator :?, which is equivalent to the is operator in C#. The *match expression* returns true if the value matches a given type; otherwise, it returns false:

```
let testPersonType (o:obj) =
    match o with
    | o :? IPerson -> printfn "this object is an IPerson"
    | _ -> printfn "this is not an IPerson"
```

Units of measure

Units of measure (UoM) are a unique feature of F#'s type system and provide the ability to define a context and to annotate statically typed unit metadata to numeric literals. This is a convenient way to manipulate numbers that represent a specific unit of measure, such as meters, seconds, pounds, and so forth. The F# type system checks that a UoM is used correctly in the first place, eliminating runtime errors. For example, the F# compiler will throw an error if a float<m/sec> is used where it expects a float<mil>. Furthermore, it's possible to associate specific functions to a defined UoM that performs work on units rather than on numeric literals. Here, the code shows how to define the meter (m) and second (sec) UoM and then executes an operation to calculate speed:

```
[<Measure>]
type m

[<Measure>]
type sec

let distance = 25.0<m>
let time = 10.0<sec>
let speed = distance / time
```

Event module API reference

The *event module* provides functions for managing event streams. Table B.1 lists the API references from the online MSDN documentation (http://mng.bz/a0hG).

Table B.2 API references

Function	Description

add :
 	
      ('T -> unit) ->
          Event<'Del,'T> ->
          unit
	Runs the function each time the event is triggered.

choose :
 	
      ('T -> 'U option) ->
          IEvent<'Del,'T> ->
          IEvent<'U>
	Returns a new event that fires on a selection of messages from the original event. The selection function takes an original message to an optional new message.

filter :
 	
      ('T -> bool) ->
          IEvent<'Del,'T> ->
          IEvent<'T>
	Returns a new event that listens to the original event and triggers the resulting event only when the argument to the event passes the given function.

map :
 	
      ('T -> 'U) ->
          IEvent<'Del, 'T> ->
          IEvent<'U>
	Returns a new event that passes values transformed by the given function.

merge :
 	
    IEvent<'Del1,'T> ->
          IEvent<'Del2,'T> ->
          IEvent<'T>
	Fires the output event when either of the input events fire.

pairwise :
 	
    IEvent<'Del,'T> ->
          IEvent<'T * 'T>
	Returns a new event that triggers on the second and subsequent triggerings of the input event. The *N*th triggering of the input event passes the arguments from the *N* − 1th and *N*th triggerings as a pair. The argument passed to the *N* − 1th triggering is held in hidden internal state until the *N*th triggering occurs.

partition :
 	
      ('T -> bool) ->
          IEvent<'Del,'T>
          -> IEvent<'T> *
          IEvent<'T>
	Returns a pair of events that listen to the original event. When the original event triggers, either the first or second event of the pair is triggered accordingly with the result of the predicate.

Table B.2 API references *(continued)*

Function	Description

scan :
 	
    ('U -> 'T -> 'U) -> 'U ->
        IEvent<'Del,'T> ->
        IEvent<'U>
	Returns a new event consisting of the results of applying the given accumulating function to successive values triggered on the input event. An item of internal state records the current value of the state parameter. The internal state is not locked during the execution of the accumulation function, so care should be taken that the input IEvent isn't triggered by multiple threads simultaneously.

split :
 	
    ('T -> Choice<'U1,'U2>)
        -> IEvent<'Del,'T>
        -> IEvent<'U1> *
        IEvent<'U2>
	Returns a new event that listens to the original event and triggers the first resulting event if the application of the function to the event arguments returned a Choice1Of2, and the second event if it returns a Choice2Of2.

Learn more

For more information about learning F#, I recommend Isaac Abraham's *Get Programming with F#: A Guide for .NET Developers* (Manning, 2018, www.manning.com/books/get-programming-with-f-sharp).

appendix C
Interoperability between an F# asynchronous workflow and .NET Task

Despite the similarities between the asynchronous programming models exposed by C# and F# programming languages, their interoperability isn't a trivial accomplishment. F# programs tend to use more asynchronous computation expressions than .NET Task. Both types are similar, but they do have semantic differences, as shown in chapters 7 and 8. For example, tasks start immediately after their creation, while F# Async must be explicitly started.

How can you interop between F# asynchronous computation expressions and .NET Task? It's possible to use F# functions such as Async.StartAsTask<T> and Async.AwaitTask<T> to interop with a C# library that returns or awaits a Task type.

Conversely, there are no equivalent methods for converting an F# Async to a Task type. It would be helpful to use the built-in F# Async.Parallel computation in C#. In this listing, repeated from chapter 9, the F# downloadMediaAsyncParallel function downloads asynchronously in parallel images from Azure Blob storage.

Listing C.1   Async parallel function to download images from Azure Blob storage

```
let downloadMediaAsyncParallel containerName = async {
    let storageAccount = CloudStorageAccount.Parse(azureConnection)
    let blobClient = storageAccount.CreateCloudBlobClient()
    let container = blobClient.GetContainerReference(containerName)
    let computations =
        container.ListBlobs()
        |> Seq.map(fun blobMedia -> async {
    let blobName = blobMedia.Uri.Segments.
                        [blobMedia.Uri.Segments.Length - 1]
    let blockBlob = container.GetBlockBlobReference(blobName)
    use stream = new MemoryStream()
```

513

```
do! blockBlob.DownloadToStreamAsync(stream)
let image = System.Drawing.Bitmap.FromStream(stream)
return image })
return! Async.Parallel computations }
```
◄—— **Runs the sequence of F# async computations in parallel**

The return type from downloadMediaAsyncParallel is an Async<Image[]>. As mentioned, an F# Async type is in general difficult to interop with and acts as a task (async/await) from the C# code. In the following code snippet, the C# code runs the F# downloadMediaAsyncParallel function as a Task using the Async.Parallel operator:

```
var cts = new CancellationToken();
var images = await downloadMediaAsyncParallel("MyMedia").AsTask(cts);
```

The code interoperability becomes effortless with the help of the AsTask extensions method. The interoperability solution is to implement a utilities F# module that exposes a set of extension methods that can be consumed by other .NET languages.

Listing C.2 Helper extension methods to interop Task and an async workflow

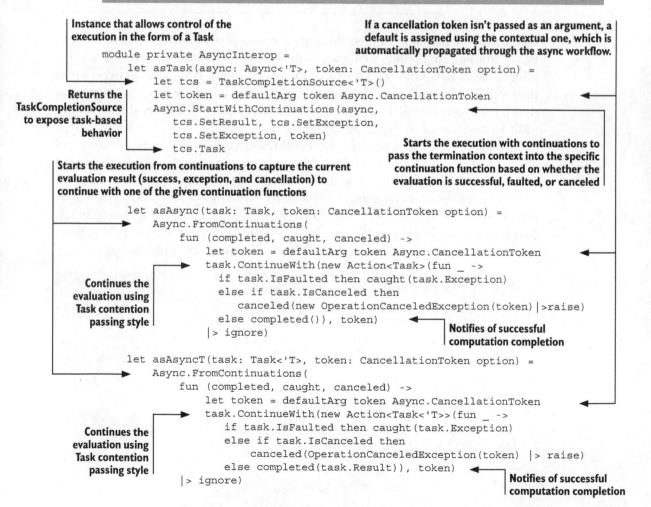

Instance that allows control of the execution in the form of a Task

If a cancellation token isn't passed as an argument, a default is assigned using the contextual one, which is automatically propagated through the async workflow.

```
module private AsyncInterop =
    let asTask(async: Async<'T>, token: CancellationToken option) =
        let tcs = TaskCompletionSource<'T>()
        let token = defaultArg token Async.CancellationToken
        Async.StartWithContinuations(async,
            tcs.SetResult, tcs.SetException,
            tcs.SetException, token)
        tcs.Task
```

Returns the TaskCompletionSource to expose task-based behavior

Starts the execution with continuations to pass the termination context into the specific continuation function based on whether the evaluation is successful, faulted, or canceled

Starts the execution from continuations to capture the current evaluation result (success, exception, and cancellation) to continue with one of the given continuation functions

```
    let asAsync(task: Task, token: CancellationToken option) =
        Async.FromContinuations(
            fun (completed, caught, canceled) ->
                let token = defaultArg token Async.CancellationToken
                task.ContinueWith(new Action<Task>(fun _ ->
                    if task.IsFaulted then caught(task.Exception)
                    else if task.IsCanceled then
                        canceled(new OperationCanceledException(token)|>raise)
                    else completed()), token)
                |> ignore)
```

Continues the evaluation using Task contention passing style

Notifies of successful computation completion

```
    let asAsyncT(task: Task<'T>, token: CancellationToken option) =
        Async.FromContinuations(
            fun (completed, caught, canceled) ->
                let token = defaultArg token Async.CancellationToken
                task.ContinueWith(new Action<Task<'T>>(fun _ ->
                    if task.IsFaulted then caught(task.Exception)
                    else if task.IsCanceled then
                        canceled(OperationCanceledException(token) |> raise)
                    else completed(task.Result)), token)
                |> ignore)
```

Continues the evaluation using Task contention passing style

Notifies of successful computation completion

```
[<Extension>]
type AsyncInteropExtensions =
  [<Extension>]
  static member AsAsync (task: Task<'T>) = AsyncInterop.asAsyncT
➡ (task, None)                         ◄───────────

  [<Extension>]
  static member AsAsync (task: Task<'T>, token: CancellationToken) =
      AsyncInterop.asAsyncT (task, Some token)   ◄───────

  [<Extension>]
  static member AsTask (async: Async<'T>) = AsyncInterop.asTask
➡ (async, None)                         ◄───────────

  [<Extension>]
  static member AsTask (async: Async<'T>, token: CancellationToken) =
      AsyncInterop.asTask (async, Some token)   ◄───────
```

Exposes the helper functions through the extension method to be consumed by other .NET programming languages

The AsyncInterop module is private, but the core functions that allow interoperability between the F# Async and the C# Task are exposed through the AsyncInteropExtensions type. The attribute Extension upgrades the methods as an extension, making it accessible by other .NET programming languages.

The asTask method converts an F# Async type to a Task, starting the asynchronous operation with the Async.StartWithContinuations function. Internally, this function uses the TaskCompletionSource to return an instance of a Task, which maintains the state of the operation. When the operation completes, the returned state can be a cancellation, an exception, or the actual result if successful.

> **NOTE** These extension methods are built into F# to allow access to the async workflow, but the module is compiled into a library that can be referenced and consumed in C#. Even if this code is in F#, it targets the C# language.

The function asAsync aims to convert a Task into an F# Async type. This function uses Async.FromContinuations to create an asynchronous computation, which provides the callback that will execute one of the given continuations for success, exception, or cancellation.

All these functions take as a second argument an optional CancellationToken, which can be used to stop the current operation. If no token is provided, then the DefaultCancellationToken in the context will be assigned by default.

These functions provide interoperability between the Task-based Asynchronous Pattern (TAP) of .NET TPL and the F# asynchronous programming model.

index

E